Quick Reference

 Get ConnectED

connectED.mcgraw-hill.com

The icons found throughout *Math Connects* provide you with the opportunity to connect the print textbook with online interactive learning.

Investigate ▶

Animations present an animation of a math concept or graphic novel.

Vocabulary presents visual representations of math concepts.

Math Songs reinforce math concepts through songs.

Multilingual eGlossary presents key vocabulary in 13 languages.

Learn ▶

Personal Tutor presents a teacher explaining step-by-step solutions to problems.

Virtual Manipulatives provide digital ways to explore concepts.

Audio recordings provide an opportunity to build oral and listening fluency.

Foldables provide a unique way to enhance students' study skills.

Practice ▶

Self-Check Practice allows students to assess their knowledge of foundational skills.

eGames allow students to practice math concepts using interactive games.

Worksheets provide additional practice and reteach opportunities.

Online Assessment checks understanding of concepts and terms.

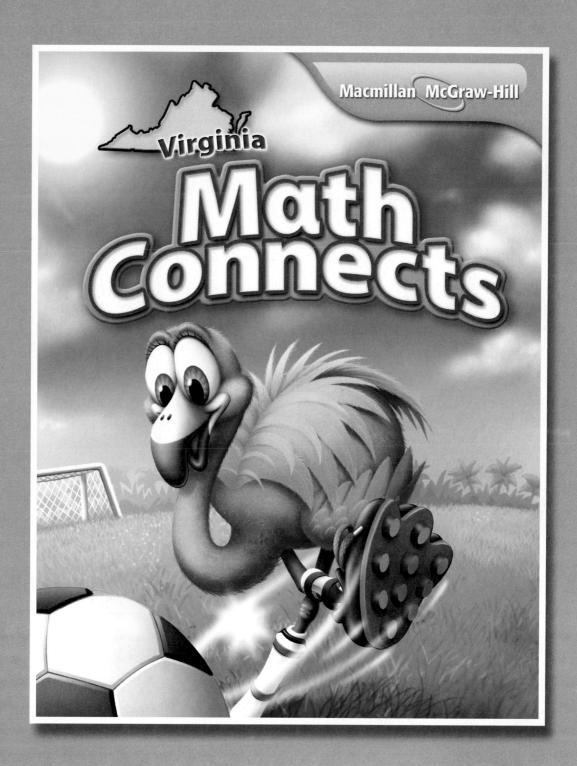

Macmillan McGraw-Hill

Virginia

Math Connects

Authors

Carter • Cuevas • Day • Malloy • Altieri • Balka
Gonsalves • Grace • Krulik • Molix-Bailey • Moseley • Mowry
Myren • Price • Reynosa • Santa Cruz • Silbey • Vielhaber

Macmillan/McGraw-Hill

The *McGraw-Hill* Companies

Macmillan/McGraw-Hill

Copyright © 2012 by the McGraw-Hill Companies, Inc. All rights reserved. Except as permitted under the United States Copyright Act, no part of this publication may be reproduced or distributed in any form or by any means, or stored in a database or retrieval system, without prior permission of the publisher.

Send all inquiries to:
Macmillan/McGraw-Hill
8787 Orion Place
Columbus, OH 43240-4027

ISBN: 978-0-02-103220-4
MHID: 0-02-103220-3

Math Connects, Grade 3

Printed in the United States of America

3 4 5 6 7 8 9 10 11 12   RJE   20 19 18 17 16 15 14 13 12 11

Contents in Brief

Master the Virginia SOLs

Start Smart A review of concepts from Grade 2

CHAPTER

1 Numbers Through Ten Thousands

2 Add and Subtract to Solve Problems

3 Model Multiplication and Division Problems

4 Solve Multiplication and Division Problems

5 Solve More Multiplication and Division Problems

6 Collect and Analyze Data

7 Geometric Figures and Spatial Reasoning

8 Use Patterns and Algebraic Thinking

9 Fractions

10 Mixed Numbers

11 Measurement

12 More Measurement

13 Multiply by a One-Digit Number

End-of-Year Option

Problem-Solving Projects

 I Want to Go THERE

 Basket-Golf

 Crazy Cooks

 I Have Always Wanted a Llama

Online Guide

Get ConnectED

connectED.mcgraw-hill.com

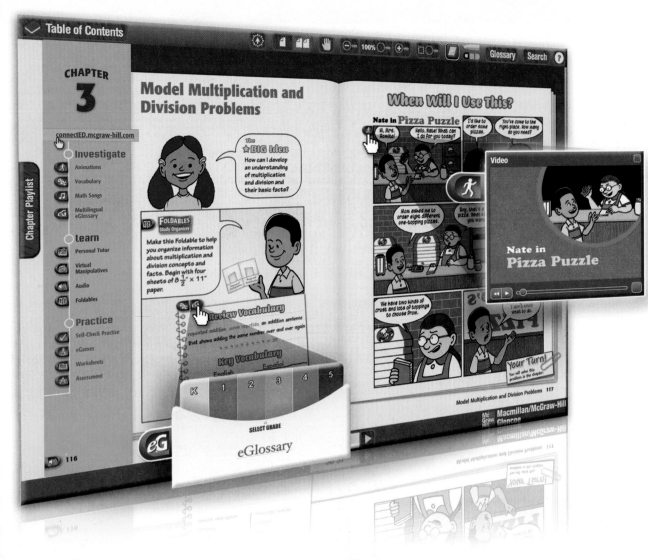

"It's easy to do my assignments online and quick to find everything I need."

Investigate ▷

Animations present an animation of a math concept or graphic novel.

Vocabulary presents visual representations of math concepts.

Math Songs reinforce math concepts through songs.

Multilingual eGlossary presents key vocabulary in 13 languages.

The icons found throughout Math Connects provide you with the opportunity to connect the print textbook with online interactive learning.

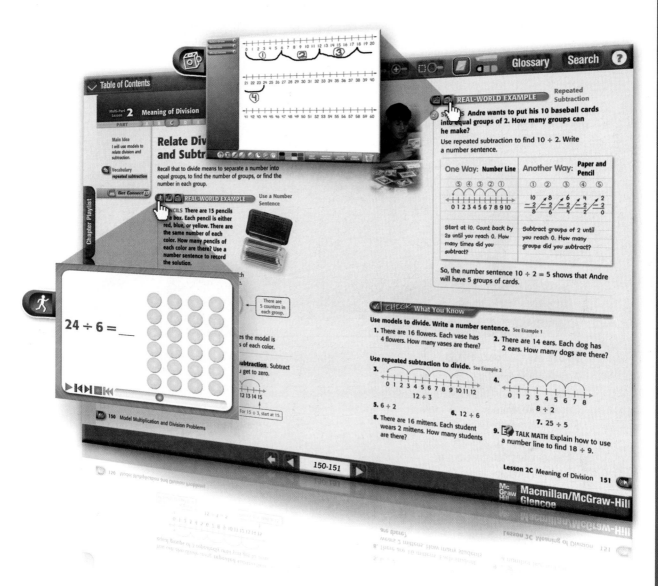

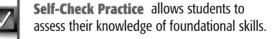

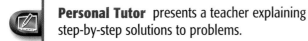

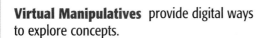

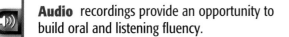

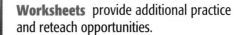

○ Learn ▷

Personal Tutor presents a teacher explaining step-by-step solutions to problems.

Virtual Manipulatives provide digital ways to explore concepts.

Audio recordings provide an opportunity to build oral and listening fluency.

Foldables provide a unique way to enhance students' study skills.

○ Practice ▷

Self-Check Practice allows students to assess their knowledge of foundational skills.

eGames allow students to practice math concepts using interactive games.

Worksheets provide additional practice and reteach opportunities.

Online Assessment checks understanding of concepts and terms.

Authors

Our lead authors ensure that the Macmillan/McGraw-Hill and Glencoe/McGraw-Hill mathematics programs are truly vertically aligned by beginning with the end in mind—success in Algebra 1 and beyond. By "backmapping" the content from the high school programs, all of our mathematics programs are well articulated in their scope and sequence.

Lead Authors

John A. Carter, Ph.D.
Assistant Principal for Teaching and Learning
Adlai E. Stevenson High School
Lincolnshire, Illinois
Areas of Expertise: Using technology and
  manipulatives to visualize concepts;
  Mathematics Achievement of
  English-Language Learners

Gilbert J. Cuevas, Ph.D.
Professor of Mathematics Education
Texas State University–San Marcos
San Marcos, Texas
Areas of Expertise: Applying concepts and
  skills in mathematically rich contexts;
  Mathematical Representations

Roger Day, Ph.D., NBCT
Mathematics Department Chairperson
Pontiac Township High School
Pontiac, Illinois
Areas of Expertise: Understanding and applying
  probability and statistics; Mathematics Teacher
  Education

Carol E. Malloy, Ph.D.
Associate Professor
University of North Carolina at Chapel Hill
Chapel Hill, North Carolina
Areas of Expertise: Representations and critical
  thinking; Student Success in Algebra 1

 **Get ConnectED** **Meet the Authors.**

Program Authors

Mary Behr Altieri
Putnam/Northern
  Westchester BOCES
Yorktown Heights, New York

Don S. Balka
Professor Emeritus
Saint Mary's College
Notre Dame, Indiana

Philip D. Gonsalves
Mathematics Coordinator
Alameda County Office of
  Education and California
  State University East Bay
Hayward, California

Ellen C. Grace
Consultant
Albuquerque, New Mexico

Stephen Krulik
Professor Emeritus
Mathematics Education
Temple University
Cherry Hill, New Jersey

Rhonda J. Molix-Bailey
Mathematics Consultant
Mathematics by Design
Desoto, Texas

Lois Gorden Moseley
Staff Developer
NUMBERS: Mathematics
  Professional Development
Houston, Texas

Brian Mowry
Independent Math Educational
  Consultant/Part-time Pre-K
  Instructional Specialist
Austin Independent
  School District
Austin, Texas

Christina L. Myren
Consultant Teacher
Conejo Valley Unified
  School District
Thousand Oaks, California

Jack Price, Ed. D.
Professor Emeritus
California State
  Polytechnic University
Pomona, California

Mary Esther Reynosa
Instructional Specialist for
  Elementary Mathematics
Northside Independent
  School District
San Antonio, Texas

Rafaela M. Santa Cruz
SDSU/CGU Doctoral Program in
  Education
San Diego State University
San Diego, California

Robyn Silbey
Math Content Coach
Montgomery County
  Public Schools
Gaithersburg, Maryland

Kathleen Vielhaber
Mathematics Consultant
St. Louis, Missouri

Contributing Author

Dinah Zike FOLDABLES
Educational Consultant
Dinah-Might Activities, Inc.
San Antonio, Texas

Lead Consultant

Viken Hovsepian
Professor of Mathematics
Rio Hondo College
Whittier, California

Consultants and Reviewers

T hese professionals were instrumental in providing valuable input and suggestions for improving the effectiveness of the mathematics instruction.

Consultants

Mathematical Content
Grayson H. Wheatley, Ph.D.
Emeritus Professor
Florida State University
Tallahassee, Florida

Differentiated Instruction
Jennifer Taylor-Cox, Ph.D.
Educational Consultant
Innovative Instruction: Connecting Research
  and Practice in Education
Severna Park, Maryland

Reading in the Content Areas
Sue Z. Beers
President/Consultant
Tools for Learning, Inc.
Jewell, Iowa

Reading and Vocabulary
Donald R. Bear, Ph.D.
Macmillan/McGraw-Hill *Treasures* Author
Director, E.L. Cord Foundation Center
  for Learning and Literacy
Professor of Educational Specialties
College of Education
University of Nevada, Reno
Reno, Nevada

Graphic Novels
Douglas Fisher, Ph.D.
Macmillan/McGraw-Hill *Treasures* Author
Associate Professor in the
  College of Education
Department of Teacher Education
San Diego State University
San Diego, California

Family Involvement
Paul Giganti, Jr.
Children's Author
Director, Math Festival Program
California Math Council
Albany, California

Literature
David M. Schwartz
Children's Author, Speaker, Storyteller
Oakland, California

English Learners
Kathryn Heinze
Graduate School of Education
Hamline University
St. Paul, Minnesota

Gladis Kersaint, Ph.D.
Associate Professor of
  Mathematics Education, K-12
University of South Florida
Tampa, Florida

Cognitively Guided Instruction
Susan B. Empson, Ph.D.
Associate Professor of Mathematics
  and Science Education
University of Texas at Austin
Austin, Texas

Virginia Advisory Board

Elizabeth Beckner
Elementary Mathematics Coach
Instructional Division Center
Chesterfield, VA

Rebecca Bienvenue
Secondary Mathematics Coach
Instructional Division Center
Chesterfield, VA

Linda W. Bowden
K-12 Math Coordinator
Roanoke County Public Schools
Roanoke, VA

Lisa Douglass
5th Grade Teacher
Lee Hill Elementary
Fredericksburg, VA

Nancy H. Hicks
Director of Curriculum, Instruction,
and School Improvement
Brunswick County Public Schools
Lawrenceville, VA

Joe Hill
Director of Math and Technology
Rockingham County Public Schools
Harrisonburg, VA

Carolyn E. Holmes
Curriculum Leader
Hampton City Schools
Hampton, VA

Kathryn Munson
Elementary Mathematics Coach
Instruction Division Center
Chesterfield, VA

Sara O'Donnell
5th Grade Teacher
Park Avenue Elementary
Danville, VA

Tina Weiner
Retired
Consultant
UVA Adjunct Faculty
Roanoke, VA

Contents

Start Smart

You may want to use these optional lessons to refresh key prerequisite skills taught in previous grades.

1 The Four-Step Plan **4**

2 Patterns **6**

3 Geometric Figures **8**

Contents

Get Connect ED

connectED.mcgraw-hill.com

Investigate ▷

Learn ▷

Practice ▷

Every chapter and every lesson has a wealth of interactive learning opportunities.

CHAPTER 1 Numbers Through Ten Thousands

Are You Ready for the Chapter? **12**

Multi-Part Lesson 1 **Identify Place Value**

  A Explore Place Value **13**
  B Place Value Through Thousands **16**
  C Place Value Through Ten Thousands...................... **20**

Multi-Part Lesson 2 **Compare and Order Numbers**

  A **Problem-Solving Skill:** Four-Step Plan **24**
  B Compare Numbers.. **26**
  C Order Numbers **30**

Mid-Chapter Check **33**
Problem-Solving in Geography: The Mighty Mississippi **34**

Multi-Part Lesson 3 **Round Numbers**

  A Round to the Nearest Ten and Hundred **36**
    Game Time: Round Numbers **39**
  B Round to the Nearest Thousand. **40**
  C **Problem-Solving Investigation:** Four-Step Plan **44**

Multi-Part Lesson 4 **Coins and Bills**

  A Value of Coins and Bills.................................. **46**
  B Determine Change....................................... **50**

Chapter Study Guide and Review **54**
Practice Chapter Test. **59**
Test Practice **60**

xi

CHAPTER 2 Add and Subtract to Solve Problems

Are You Ready for the Chapter? 64

Multi-Part Lesson 1 Add to Solve Problems

A Algebra: Addition Properties 65
B Estimate Sums 68
C Explore Add Three-Digit Numbers. 72
D Three-Digit Addition. 74
E **Problem-Solving Skill:** Estimate or Exact Answers 78
F Add Four-Digit Numbers 80
 Game Time: How Low Can You Go?. 84

Mid-Chapter Check 85

Multi-Part Lesson 2 Subtract to Solve Problems

A Estimate Differences 86
B Explore Subtract Three-Digit Numbers with Regrouping 90
C Subtract Three-Digit Numbers with Regrouping. 92
D Subtract Four-Digit Numbers 96

Problem-Solving in Music: The Sounds of the Symphony 100
E Subtract Across Zeros. 102
F **Problem-Solving Investigation:** Choose a Strategy 106

Chapter Study Guide and Review. 108
Practice Chapter Test. 113
Test Practice. 114

CHAPTER 3
Model Multiplication and Division Problems

Are You Ready for the Chapter?.....................................**118**

Multi-Part Lesson 1 **Meaning of Multiplication**

- **A** **Explore** Model Multiplication................................**119**
- **B** Multiplication as Repeated Addition **121**
- **C** **Explore** Multiplication with Arrays.........................**124**
- **D** Arrays and Multiplication..................................**126**
- **E** Use Multiplication to Compare.............................**130**
- **F** Use Multiplication to Find Combinations **134**
- **G** **Problem-Solving Strategy:** Make a Table..................**138**

Problem-Solving in Science: Lots of Arms and Legs...................**140**

Game Time: Row and Columns........................**142**

Mid-Chapter Check **143**

Multi-Part Lesson 2 **Meaning of Division**

- **A** **Explore** Model Division **144**
- **B** Division as Equal Sharing **146**
- **C** Relate Division and Subtraction **150**
- **D** **Explore** Relate Division and Multiplication **154**
- **E** Inverse Operations...**156**
- **F** **Problem-Solving Investigation:** Choose a Strategy **160**

Chapter Study Guide and Review....................................**162**

Practice Chapter Test...**167**

Test Practice **168**

CHAPTER 4 Solve Multiplication and Division Problems

Are You Ready for the Chapter? 172

Multi-Part Lesson 1 Multiplication and Division Facts for 2 and 3

A Multiply by 2..173
B Divide by 2 176
C **Explore** Find a Missing Factor 180
D Multiply by 3..182
E Divide by 3 186
F **Problem-Solving Strategy:** Work Backward................190
G **Extend** Model Multiplication 192
Mid-Chapter Check 193

Multi-Part Lesson 2 Multiplication and Division Facts for 5 and 10

A Multiply by 5..194
   Game Time: Factor Power 197
B Divide by 5 198
C Multiply by 10...202
D Divide by 10 206
   Facts Practice 209
Problem-Solving in Social Studies: Communities Within Communities ...210

Multi-Part Lesson 3 Multiply and Divide with 0 and 1

A **Problem-Solving Investigation:** Choose a Strategy 212
B Multiply by 0 and 1 214
C Divide with 0 and 1 216
   Facts Practice 218
Chapter Study Guide and Review 219
Practice Chapter Test...223
Test Practice 224

Investigate ▷

Learn ▷

Practice ▷

Every chapter and every lesson has a wealth of interactive learning opportunities.

CHAPTER 5
Solve More Multiplication and Division Problems

Are You Ready for the Chapter? **228**

Multi-Part Lesson 1 **Multiplication and Division Facts for 4**

A **Explore** Double a Known Fact **229**
B Multiply by 4 .... **231**
C Divide by 4 .... **234**
D **Problem-Solving Skill:** Extra or Missing Information **238**

Multi-Part Lesson 2 **Multiplication and Division Facts for 6 and 7**

A Multiply by 6 .... **240**
B Multiply by 7 .... **244**
  Facts Practice **247**
C Divide by 6 and 7 .... **248**
D **Extend** Model Division **251**
Mid-Chapter Check **253**

Multi-Part Lesson 3 **Multiplication and Division Facts for 8 and 9**

A Multiply by 8 .... **254**
B Multiply by 9 .... **258**
  Facts Practice **261**
C Divide by 8 and 9 .... **262**
  Game Time: Number Cubes **265**
D **Problem-Solving Investigation:** Choose a Strategy **266**

Multi-Part Lesson 4 **Multiplication and Division Facts for 11 and 12**

A Multiply by 11 and 12 .... **268**
B Divide by 11 and 12 .... **272**
Problem-Solving in Art: Not Just a Blanket **276**
Chapter Study Guide and Review **278**
Practice Chapter Test **281**
Test Practice **282**

CHAPTER 6 Collect and Analyze Data

Are You Ready for the Chapter? **286**

Multi-Part Lesson 1 Collect Data

A Explore Collect Data **287**
B Construct Frequency Tables **289**
C **Problem-Solving Strategy:** Make a List **292**

Multi-Part Lesson 2 Graphs with Pictures

A Explore Picture Graphs and Pictographs. **294**
B Construct and Analyze Picture Graphs and Pictographs **296**
Mid-Chapter Check **300**
Game Time: Catch Me If You Can! **301**

Multi-Part Lesson 3 Bar Graphs

A Explore Bar Graphs. **302**
B Construct and Analyze Bar Graphs. **304**
Problem-Solving in Science: Eggs!. **308**

Multi-Part Lesson 4 Line Plots

A Construct and Analyze Line Plots **310**
B **Problem-Solving Investigation:** Choose a Strategy **314**

Multi-Part Lesson 5 Probability

A Identify Probability. **316**
B Make Predictions **320**
Chapter Study Guide and Review. **324**
Practice Chapter Test. **329**
Test Practice **330**

Contents

connectED.mcgraw-hill.com

Investigate ▷

Learn ▷

Practice ▷

Every chapter and every lesson has a wealth of interactive learning opportunities.

CHAPTER 7
Geometric Figures and Spatial Reasoning

Are You Ready for the Chapter? **334**

Multi-Part Lesson 1 Geometric Figures

A   Lines, Line Segments, and Rays **335**
B   Explore Angles **338**
C   Two-Dimensional Figures: Polygons **340**
D   Quadrilaterals **344**
E   **Problem-Solving Strategy:** Guess, Check, and Revise **348**
F   Three-Dimensional Figures **350**
Mid-Chapter Check **355**

Multi-Part Lesson 2 Spatial Reasoning

A   Explore Congruent Figures **356**
B   Congruency **358**
C   Explore Lines of Symmetry **360**
D   Draw Lines of Symmetry **362**
E   Extend Symmetry **366**
     Game Time: Art is Shaping Up **367**
Problem-Solving in Art: Gardens Under Glass **368**
F   **Problem-Solving Investigation:** Choose a Strategy **370**
Chapter Study Guide and Review **372**
Practice Chapter Test **377**
Test Practice **378**

CHAPTER 8 Use Patterns and Algebraic Thinking

Are You Ready for the Chapter? **382**

Multi-Part Lesson 1 Patterns

A Geometric Patterns **383**
B Number Patterns **386**
C **Problem-Solving Strategy:** Look for a Pattern. **390**
D **Explore** Represent Patterns **392**
E Patterns in Graphs **394**
    Game Time: Pick a Pattern. **398**
Mid-Chapter Check **399**

Multi-Part Lesson 2 Number Sentences

A **Explore** Model Expressions **400**
B Write Expressions. **402**
C Write Number Sentences **406**
D Expressions and Equations **410**

Multi-Part Lesson 3 Functions Tables

A Make a Table to Find a Rule **414**
B Make a Function Table $(+, -)$ **418**
C **Problem-Solving Investigation:** Choose a Strategy **422**
D Make a Function Table $(\times, \div)$ **424**
Problem-Solving in Science: A Visit to the Supermarket **428**
Chapter Study Guide and Review. **430**
Practice Chapter Test. **435**
Test Practice **436**

Get Connect**ED**

connectED.mcgraw-hill.com

Investigate ▷

Learn ▷

Practice ▷

Every chapter and every lesson has a wealth of interactive learning opportunities.

CHAPTER 9 Fractions

Are You Ready for the Chapter?. 440

Multi-Part Lesson 1 Understand Fractions

A Explore Model Fractions. 441
B Part of a Whole. 443
C Part of a Set 446
D **Problem-Solving Strategy:** Draw a Picture 450

Multi-Part Lesson 2 Compare and Order Fractions

A Explore Compare Fractions 452
B Compare Fractions. 454
C Order Fractions. 458
Mid-Chapter Check 461

Multi-Part Lesson 3 Equivalent Fractions

A **Problem-Solving Investigation:** Choose a Strategy 462
B Explore Equivalent Fractions 464
C Equivalent Fractions. 466
D Extend Equivalent Fractions. 469
Problem Solving in Science: The Buzz on Insects 470

Multi-Part Lesson 4 Add and Subtract Fractions

A Explore Add Like Fractions. 472
B Add Like Fractions 474
C Explore Subtract Like Fractions 478
D Subtract Like Fractions. 480
Game Time: Fraction Concentration 484
Chapter Study Guide and Review 485
Practice Chapter Test. 489
Test Practice 490

CHAPTER 10 Mixed Numbers

Are You Ready for the Chapter?.................................**494**

Multi-Part Lesson 1 Understand Mixed Numbers

A Explore Mixed Numbers...............................**495**
B Mixed Numbers......................................**497**
C **Problem-Solving Strategy:** Make a Model................**502**
Problem-Solving in Social Studies: Red, White, and Blueberries........**504**
Game Time: Mixed Number Match....................**506**
Mid-Chapter Check..**507**

Multi-Part Lesson 2 Compare and Order Mixed Numbers

A Compare and Order Mixed Numbers.......................**508**
B **Problem-Solving Investigation:** Choose a Strategy.........**512**
C Explore Find Equivalent Mixed Numbers....................**514**
D Equivalent Mixed Numbers..............................**516**
Chapter Study Guide and Review.....................................**520**
Practice Chapter Test...**523**
Test Practice **524**

Get ConnectED

connectED.mcgraw-hill.com

Investigate ▷

Learn ▷

Practice ▷

Every chapter and every lesson has a wealth of interactive learning opportunities.

CHAPTER 11 Measurement

Are You Ready for the Chapter?...................................**528**

Multi-Part Lesson 1 **Measure Length**

- **A** Explore Length to the Nearest Inch and Half Inch...........**529**
- **B** Length to the Nearest Half Inch **532**
  Game Time: Hit the Target.........................**535**
- **C** Customary Units of Length **536**
- **D** **Problem-Solving Strategy:** Solve a Simpler Problem........**540**
- **E** Explore Centimeter...................................**542**
- **F** Metric Units of Length **544**

Problem Solving in Science: The Life and Lengths of Leap Frogs **548**

Mid-Chapter Check **550**

Multi-Part Lesson 2 **Perimeter**

- **A** Explore Finding Perimeter **551**
- **B** Perimeter **552**
- **C** **Problem-Solving Investigation:** Choose a Strategy **556**

Multi-Part Lesson 3 **Area**

- **A** Explore Measure Area....................................**558**
- **B** Measure Area **560**

Chapter Study Guide and Review...................................**563**

Practice Chapter Test....................................**567**

Test Practice....................................**568**

CHAPTER
12 More Measurement

Are You Ready for the Chapter? 572

Multi-Part Lesson 1 | **Measure Capacity**

A Explore Capacity 573
B Customary Units of Capacity 575
C **Problem-Solving Strategy:** Guess, Check, and Revise 578
D Metric Units of Capacity 580
　Game Time: Capacity Guess 583

Multi-Part Lesson 2 | **Measure Weight and Mass**

A Customary Units of Weight 584
Problem-Solving in Science: Lengths, Heights, and Weights Oh My! 588
B Metric Units of Mass 590
Mid-Chapter Check 594

Multi-Part Lesson 3 | **Measure Time and Temperature**

A Time to the Minute 595
B **Problem-Solving Investigation:** Choose a Strategy 598
C Elapsed Time 600
D Calendars and Time Lines 604
E Fahrenheit and Celsius 608
Chapter Study Guide and Review 610
Practice Chapter Test 615
Test Practice 616

Contents

CHAPTER 13 Multiply By a One-Digit Number

Are You Ready for the Chapter?.....................620

Multi-Part Lesson 1   Multiples of 10, 100, and 1,000

A Multiples of 10, 100, and 1,000.....................**621**
B Estimate Products.....................**624**
Problem Solving in Art: Stamp Collecting.....................**628**

Multi-Part Lesson 2   Multiply without Regrouping

A **Problem-Solving Strategy:** Use Logical Reasoning.....................**630**
B Multiply by a One-Digit Number.....................**632**
Mid-Chapter Check **635**

Multi-Part Lesson 3   Multiply with Regrouping

A Explore Multiply with Regrouping **636**
B Multiply Two-Digit Numbers.....................**638**
C **Problem-Solving Investigation:** Choose a Strategy **642**
D Multiply Greater Numbers.....................**644**
    Game Time: High and Low **648**
Chapter Study Guide and Review **649**
Practice Chapter Test.....................**653**
Test Practice **654**

Get ConnectED

connectED.mcgraw-hill.com

Investigate ▷

Learn ▷

Practice ▷

Every chapter and every lesson has a wealth of interactive learning opportunities.

End-of-Year Projects

You may want to use these Problem-Solving Projects to finish the school year.

Problem-Solving Projects

PROJECT 1   I Want to Go THERE **658**

PROJECT 2   Basket-Golf **660**

PROJECT 3   Crazy Cooks **662**

PROJECT 4   I Have Always Wanted a Llama **664**

connectED.mcgraw-hill.com

Investigate ▷

Learn ▷

Practice ▷

Every chapter and every lesson has a wealth of interactive learning opportunities.

Student Handbook

Extra Practice **EP2**

Facts Practice **EP46**

Reference

    Photo Credits **R1**

    English-Spanish Glossary **R3**

    Index **R29**

Start Smart

connectED.mcgraw-hill.com

Investigate

 Animations

 Vocabulary

 Math Songs

 Multilingual eGlossary

Learn

 Personal Tutor

 Virtual Manipulatives

 Audio

 Foldables

Practice

 Self-Check Practice

 eGames

 Worksheets

 Assessment

The Four-Step Plan.................... 4

Patterns................................ 6

Geometric Figures.................... 8

Here are some characters you are going to meet throughout the book.

Alyssa

"My friends and I like to ride our bikes. Sometimes we ride to the park to play baseball."

Carlos

"I love animals! I have two dogs and a hamster. Monkeys are my favorite wild animals."

Eva

"My mom says I should be an engineer when I grow up because I like to build things."

Jacob

"I like to visit my grandma. She helped me take the training wheels off my bike when I was little."

Jamie

"I like to play basketball. I am the captain of our team."

Kendra

"I like to go hiking. I taught my friend, Morgan, how to skip rocks."

Kim

"Friends are the best! I like to skateboard with my best friend, Jacob."

Luke

"I enjoy playing sports, especially baseball. I play shortstop."

Morgan

"I enjoy hanging out with my family. We spend most of our free time at the swimming pool."

Nate

"Cooking is so much fun. My favorite foods to make are pizza and spaghetti with meatballs."

Let's Get Started!
We're going to review a little before we begin Chapter 1.

The Four-Step Plan

Math, Math, Everywhere! ▶
A four-square court can measure as little as 16 feet or as much as 24 feet on each side.

Reinforcement of 2.21 The student will solve problems by completing numerical sentences involving the basic facts for addition and subtraction. The student will create story problems, using the numerical sentences. Also addresses 2.8.

REAL-WORLD EXAMPLE ▸ Bar Diagram

1 **RECESS Mrs. Landeg's third grade class had a four-square tournament during recess. Four students played on each court. If there were 5 courts, how many students played at the same time?**

Understand

- A total of 4 students played on each court.
- There were **5 courts.**

Plan

Use a bar diagram to find how many students played at the same time.

← - - - - - - - - - - - - - ? students in all - - - - - - - - - - - - - →				
4 students	4 students	4 students	4 students	4 students
⊢– Court 1 –⊣	⊢– Court 2 –⊣	⊢– Court 3 –⊣	⊢– Court 4 –⊣	⊢– Court 5 –⊣

Solve

Use a bar diagram to s

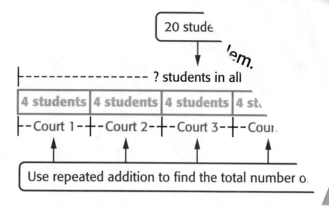

$4 + 4 + 4 + 4 + 4 = \textbf{20 students}$

So, 20 students played four-square at the same time.

Check

- Does your answer make sense?
- If not, solve the problem another way.

Practice and Problem Solving

Use the four-step plan and a bar diagram to solve each problem.

See Example 1

1. Rob, Nina, and Megan each have 5 stickers. How many stickers do they have in all?

```
┝-------- ? stickers in all --------┥
│ 5 stickers │ 5 stickers │ 5 stickers │
┝--- Rob --+--- Nina --+- Megan --┥
```

2. Yoko bought 2 tickets for the musical. Each ticket cost $7. How much did she spend altogether?

```
┝--- ? $ spent altogether ---┥
│     $7     │     $7     │
┝-- Ticket 1 --+-- Ticket 2 --┥
```

3. **WRITE MATH** Write a real-world problem about a game you like to play during recess. Then ask a classmate to solve.

Patterns

...ng Savings ▶
. a weekly
.ce?

Reinforcement of 2.4 The student will **a)** count forward by twos, fives, and tens to 100, starting at various multiples of 2, 5, or 10. **Reinforcement of 2.20** The student will identify, create, and extend a wide variety of patterns.

REAL-WORLD EXAMPLE Skip Counting

1. **MONEY** Kevin is saving his allowance. He gets $5 a week. How much money will he have after 6 weeks?

Each week Kevin has $5 more than the week before.

The pattern shows that 5 is added to the number that came before.

Kevin's Savings	
Week	**Total Saved**
1	$5
2	$10
3	$15
4	$20
5	$25
6	▪

You can add 5 or count by 5s.

$5, $10, $15, $20, $25, $30

So, Kevin will have $30 after 6 weeks.

Identify a pattern. See Example 1

1. 13, 16, 19, 22, 25

2. 92, 86, 80, 74, 68

3. 74, 78, 82, 86, 90

4. 61, 66, 71, 76, 81

Identify a pattern. Find the missing number. See Example 1

5. 12, 16, 20, 24, ■

6. 50, ■, 40, 35, 30

7. 25, 28, 31, ■, 37

8. 41, 49, ■, 65, 73

9. 88, 68, 48, 28, ■

10. 32, 37, 42, ■, 52

11. A crab has 10 legs. What is the total number of legs for 5 crabs?

Crab Legs	
Number of Crabs	**Total Legs**
1	10
2	20
3	30
4	40
5	■

12. Justin made bows to put on his 6 kites. He put 4 bows on each kite. How many bows did Justin make?

13. Emma bought a lock for her locker at the gym. She sees a pattern in the numbers on the lock. If the pattern continues, what would be the next number?

14. Lyn plans to walk 3 miles every week. How many total miles will Lyn have walked in week 5?

Lyn's Walking Chart	
Weeks	**Total Miles**
1	3
2	6
3	9
4	12
5	■

15. This week, Kimi is going to pack her lunch for school every other day starting Monday. Is she going to pack her lunch on Thursday? Explain.

16. **WRITE MATH** Buses arrive at the bus stop at 7:00, 7:30, 8:00, and 8:30. Tell what time the next bus will arrive if the pattern continues. Describe the pattern.

Geometric Figures

 Reinforcement of 2.16 The student will identify, describe, compare, and contrast plane and solid geometric figures (circle/sphere, square/cube, and rectangle/rectangular prism).

A three-dimensional figure is a solid figure that has length, width, and height.

REAL-WORLD EXAMPLE　**Three-Dimensional Figures**

1 **FRUIT** Sonia noticed that her blueberries and sandwich are three-dimensional figures. What three-dimensional figures are the blueberries and sandwich?

A blueberry's shape is a sphere.

A sandwich's shape is a rectangular prism.

 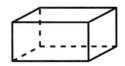

A two-dimensional figure is a plane figure that has length and width.

 **EXAMPLE** Two-Dimensional Figures

2 **Identify and describe the figures below.**

This figure is a square.
A square has 4 sides.

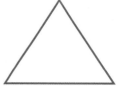

This figure is a triangle.
A triangle has 3 sides.

So, a square and a triangle are examples of two-dimensional figures.

Practice and Problem Solving

Identify each three-dimensional figure. See Example 1

1.

cylinder or cube

2.

cone or rectangular prism

3.

pyramid or cone

4.
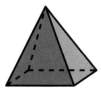
sphere or pyramid

5.
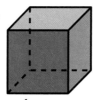
cube or cone

6.

cube or sphere

Copy and complete the table. See Example 2

	7. ▭	8. ⬡	9. ◯	10. ⬠
Figure				
Name				
Sides				

11. **WRITE MATH** How is a square different from a cube? How are they alike?

Numbers Through Ten Thousands

connectED.mcgraw-hill.com

Investigate

 Animations

 Vocabulary

 Math Songs

 Multilingual eGlossary

Learn

 Personal Tutor

 Virtual Manipulatives

 Audio

 Foldables

Practice

 Self-Check Practice

 eGames

 Worksheets

 Assessment

The ☆BIG Idea

How can I solve problems using numbers through ten thousands?

 FOLDABLES Study Organizer

Make this Foldable to help you organize information about place value. Start with three sheets of $8\frac{1}{2}'' \times 11''$ paper.

Numbers Through Ten Thousands

Place Value
Four-Step Plan
Compare and Order
Round Numbers
Coins and Bills

Review Vocabulary

cents(¢) centavo(¢) a value of coins less than $1.00

37¢

Key Vocabulary

English	Español
place value	valor de posición
is greater than (>)	es mayor que >
is less than (<)	es menor que <
is equal to (=)	es igual a (=)
round	redondear

When Will I Use This?

Are You Ready for the Chapter?

You have two options for checking Prerequisite Skills for this chapter.

Text Option Take the Quick Check below.

QUICK Check

Write each number.

1.

Ones		
hundreds	tens	ones
	1	4

2.

Ones		
hundreds	tens	ones
	3	3

3.

Ones		
hundreds	tens	ones
1	1	0

4. 1 ten 5 ones

5. 1 hundred 2 ones

6. twenty-four

7. one hundred thirty-eight

Write the number of tens and ones in each number.

8. 12   **9.** 26   **10.** 31   **11.** 85

12. Manuel and his family went to the circus. They spent a total of $65. Tell how many tens and ones are in 65.

Compare. Use >, <, or =.

13. 70 ● 61   **14.** 98 ● 99   **15.** 155 ● 55

Round to the nearest ten.

16. 72   **17.** 19   **18.** 59   **19.** 85

20. Deidra has three game cards each with a value of 10 and two cards each with a value of 1. Raul has three cards each with a value of 1 and two cards each with a value of 10. Whose cards have the lesser value?

 Online Option Take the Online Readiness Quiz.

Explore Place Value

Main Idea

I will use models to explore place value through thousands.

Materials

base-ten blocks

rubber band

Get ConnectED

3.1 The student will **a)** read and write six-digit numerals and identify the place value and value of each digit.

A **digit** is any symbol used to write whole numbers. The numbers 0, 1, 2, 3, 4, 5, 6, 7, 8, and 9 are all digits. The **place value** of a digit tells what value it has in a number. Base-ten blocks can be used to explore place value.

ACTIVITY

1. Use base-ten blocks to model 142 in two ways.

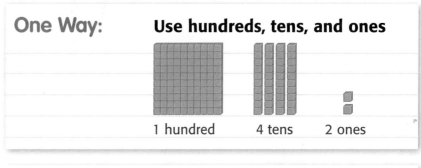

One Way: **Use hundreds, tens, and ones**

1 hundred 4 tens 2 ones

Another Way: **Use tens and ones**

14 tens 2 ones

2 Use base-ten blocks to model 1,025 in two ways.

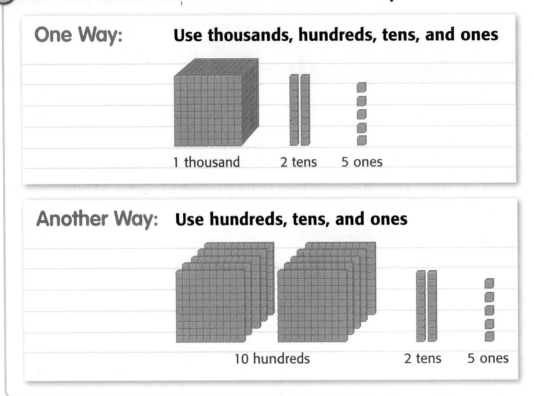

One Way: Use thousands, hundreds, tens, and ones

1 thousand   2 tens   5 ones

Another Way: Use hundreds, tens, and ones

10 hundreds   2 tens   5 ones

Think About It

1. Why can you use different combinations of thousands, hundreds, tens, and ones to model the same number?

Practice and Apply It

Use base-ten blocks to model each number in two ways.

2. 135   **3.** 304   **4.** 1,283   **5.** 1,890

Write each number modeled.

6.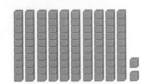

7.

8. WRITE MATH Explain how base-ten blocks are helpful in understanding numbers.

3 **Use base-ten blocks to model 10,000.**

Step 1 **Show 1,000.**
Put 10 hundreds together to form a thousand
base-ten block. Wrap with a rubber band.

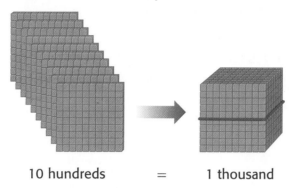

10 hundreds   =   1 thousand

Step 2 **Show 10,000.**
Since 1 thousands base-ten block = 1,000

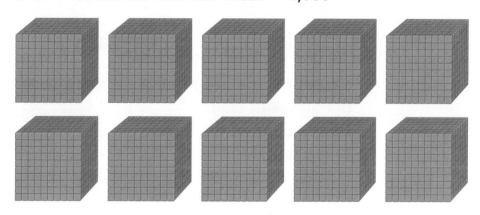

10 thousands base-ten blocks = 10,000

Think About It

9. How many hundreds base-ten blocks would you use to
model 10,000?

10. How many tens are in 1,000? 10,000?

11. Describe another way to model 10,000 using base-ten blocks.

12. **WRITE MATH** What number pattern do you see as you
move from the ones place to the ten thousands place of
a number?

Place Value Through Thousands

The number 1,813 has four **digits**. A digit is any symbol used to write whole numbers. The **place value** of a digit tells what value it has in a number.

1 thousand   8 hundreds   1 ten   3 ones

A place-value chart can help you understand place value.

 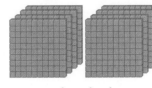   **REAL-WORLD EXAMPLE**   Identify Place Value

1 **SYMBOLS** **The height of the Statue of Liberty from the top of the base to the top of the torch is 1,813 inches. Identify the place of the underlined digit in 1,813. Then write the value of the digit.**

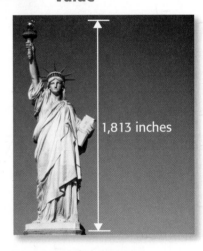

1,813 inches

Thousands			Ones		
hundreds	tens	ones	hundreds	tens	ones
		1	8	1	3

1 thousand   8 hundreds   1 ten   3 ones
The value   The value   The value   The value
is 1,000.   is 800.   is 10.   is 3.

The underlined digit, 1, is in the thousands place. Its value is 1,000.

2 STATUES If ten people climb the stairs to the top of the Statue of Liberty and back down, they will have walked 7,080 steps. Identify the place of the underlined digit in 7,080. Then write its value.

The place-value chart shows 7,080.

Thousands			Ones		
hundreds	tens	ones	hundreds	tens	ones
		7	0	8	0

A comma is placed between the thousands and hundreds place.

The underlined digit, 0, is in the hundreds place. Its value is zero. There are no hundreds. When 0 is used in a number, it is sometimes called a place holder.

Remember

In 7,080, there are two place holders, the zero in the hundreds place and the zero in the ones place.

Numbers can be written in different ways. **Standard form** shows only the digits. **Expanded form** shows the sum of the value of the digits. **Word form** uses words.

3 TRAVEL It is 1,215 miles from Mobile, Alabama, to the Statue of Liberty in New York City. Write 1,215 three ways.

The place-value chart shows 1,215.

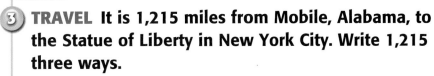

Thousands			Ones		
hundreds	tens	ones	hundreds	tens	ones
		1	2	1	5

Standard Form: 1,215

Expanded Form: 1,000 + 200 + 10 + 5

Word Form: one thousand, two hundred fifteen

Write the place of the underlined digit. Then write the value of the digit. See Examples 1 and 2

1. <u>8</u>70

2. <u>2</u>,312

3. 7,5<u>0</u>9

Write each number in standard form. See Example 3

4. 800 + 50 + 6

5. one thousand, six hundred four

Write each number in expanded form and word form. See Example 3

6. 375

7. 5,230

8. 9,909

9. Lindsey uses each digit 3, 8, 0, and 1 once. Find the greatest whole number she can make.

10.  **TALK MATH** How do you tell the place value of each digit when given a number?

Practice and Problem Solving

EXTRA *PRACTICE*
Begins on page EP2.

Write the place of the underlined digit. Then write the value of the digit. See Examples 1 and 2

11. <u>5</u>01

12. 5,77<u>2</u>

13. 1,0<u>2</u>0

14. 4,81<u>0</u>

15. <u>3</u>,176

16. 8<u>0</u>4

Write each number in standard form. See Example 3

17. 4,000 + 600 + 70 + 8

18. 3,000 + 20 + 1

19. seven thousand, six hundred forty-one

20. eight thousand, seven hundred sixty

Write each number in expanded form and word form. See Example 3

21. 4,332

22. 1,324

23. 6,219

24. 6,503

25. 8,150

26. 1,001

27. A motorcycle costs $3,124. What is the value of each digit?

28. Write all of the three-digit numbers that have 3 in the tens place and 5 in the ones place.

29. CHALLENGE Carlos is thinking of a four-digit number. The thousands digit is double the ones digit. The sum of these two digits is 9. What is the number? Explain your work.

30. FIND THE ERROR Alyssa is writing 2,013 in word form. Find and correct her mistake.

two hundred thirteen

31. **WRITE MATH** Explain why a zero needs to be used when writing the number four thousand, sixty-eight in standard form.

Test Practice

32. The model represents the number of days the South Pole does not have sun each year.

 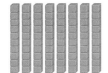

Choose the standard form of this number. (Lesson 1B)

A. 1,802   **C.** 281

B. 1,082   **D.** 182

33. Martin earned 7,283 points while playing a video game. Choose the correct word form of this number. (Lesson 1B)

F. seven thousand, eight hundred twenty-three

G. seven thousand, two hundred eighty-three

H. seven thousand, two hundred thirty-eight

J. 7,000 + 200 + 80 + 3

34. Marcus has 1,270 baseball cards. What is the value of the digit 2? (Lesson 1B)

A. 2   **C.** 200

B. 20   **D.** 2,000

35. Most people have more than 14 hundred dreams a year. What number is 14 hundreds? (Lesson 1A)

F. 140   **H.** 1,400

G. 1,040   **J.** 14,000

Main Idea

I will read, write, and identify place value of whole numbers through ten thousands.

 **Vocabulary**

period

 *Get Connect*ED

3.1 The student will
a) read and write six-digit numerals and identify the place value and value of each digit.

Place Value Through Ten Thousands

A place-value chart can be used to help read large numbers. A group of 3 digits is called a **period**. Commas separate the periods. When reading a number, say the name of the period at each comma.

🏃 ✏️ 📷 **REAL-WORLD EXAMPLES** Place Value

① **TRAVEL** There are 14,858 airports in the United States. This is more than any other country. Identify the place of the underlined digit in 1̱4,858. Then write its value.

The place-value chart shows 14,858.

Thousands			Ones		
hundreds	tens	ones	hundreds	tens	ones
	1	4	8	5	8

The underlined digit, 1, is in the ten thousands place. So, its value is 10,000.

② **Write 14,858 in three ways.**

Standard Form: 14,858

Expanded Form: 10,000 + 4,000 + 800 + 50 + 8

Word Form: fourteen thousand, eight hundred fifty-eight

3 **BIRDS** Miss Denison's students are learning about how far some birds travel as the seasons change.

Bird Migration	
Arctic Tern	35,406 km
Red Knot	32,187 km
Lesser Yellowleg	28,968 km

Remember

Place a comma between the thousands and hundreds place.

Write the distance a Red Knot may fly in expanded form.

$32,187 = 30,000 + 2,000 + 100 + 80 + 7$

4 **Write the distance an Arctic Tern may fly in word form.**

thirty-five thousand, four hundred six

✓ **CHECK What You Know**

Write the place of the underlined digit. Then write its value. See Example 1

1. 49,62<u>4</u>   **2.** 26,<u>0</u>21   **3.** <u>5</u>4,610   **4.** 6<u>2</u>,543

Write each number in standard form. See Example 2

5. 30,000 + 3,000 + 300 + 3   **6.** twenty thousand, four hundred ten

Write each number in expanded form and word form. See Examples 2–4

7. 14,751   **8.** 99,001   **9.** 25,252   **10.** 80,911

11. Sasha collected ten thousand, one hundred thirty-two digital photos. Write this number in standard form and expanded form.

12. **TALK MATH** Explain why the number 46,012 is not the same as 40,000 + 6,000 + 100 + 2.

Practice and Problem Solving

EXTRA PRACTICE
Begins on page EP2.

Write the place of each underlined digit. Then write its value. See Example 1

13. 15,3<u>8</u>8
14. 1<u>9</u>,756
15. 3<u>0</u>,654
16. <u>4</u>3,543

17. 57,08<u>1</u>
18. <u>6</u>9,003
19. 70,0<u>0</u>0
20. 86,0<u>6</u>0

Write each number in standard form. See Example 2

21. 20,000 + 4,000 + 200 + 20 + 2
22. 10,000 + 1,000 + 100 + 10 + 1

23. forty thousand, three hundred eighty
24. thirty-two thousand, twenty-five

Write each number in expanded form and word form. See Examples 2–4

25. 12,194
26. 28,451
27. 39,234
28. 51,160

29. 60,371
30. 73,100
31. 81,001
32. 99,027

Data File

The table lists the location and altitude of the world's largest telescopes.

33. Which altitudes have a digit in the ten thousands place?

34. Write the altitude of the Palomar Mountain observatory in word form.

35. Which observatory's altitude has a digit with a value of 700?

Location and Altitude of Largest Telescopes

Location	Altitude (feet)
Mauna Kea, Hawaii	13,527
Mount Fowlkes, Texas	6,796
Palomar Mtn, California	6,232
Mt. Graham, Arizona	10,397

H.O.T. Problems

36. OPEN ENDED Write three different numbers that have 5 in the thousands place.

37. WRITE MATH Explain the difference between standard form and expanded form.

More About Place Value

A place-value chart can help you read and write numbers in the hundred thousands.

REAL-WORLD EXAMPLE   Identify the Value of Digits

1 **SPACE** The distance from earth to the moon is **238,900 miles.**

Write the value of the underlined digit in **2̲38,900.**

Thousands			Ones		
hundreds	tens	ones	hundreds	tens	ones
2	3	8	9	0	0

The underlined digit has a value of 200,000. This is because the 2 is in the hundred thousands place.

Remember, you can write a number three different ways.

EXAMPLE   Read and Write Numbers

2 **Write 238,900 three different ways.**

Standard Form: 238,900

Expanded Form: 200,000 + 30,000 + 8,000 + 900

Word Form: two hundred thirty-eight thousand, nine hundred

Write the place of the underlined digit. Then write the value of the digit.

38. 412,6̲04   **39.** 8̲15,084   **40.** 95̲6,497

Write each number in standard form.

41. 700,000 + 50,000 + 2,000 + 10 + 1   **42.** 60,000 + 800 + 40 + 5

Write each number in expanded form and word form.

43. 243,895   **44.** 485,830   **45.** 649,320

46. 784,132   **47.** 505,050   **48.** 891,074

Problem-Solving Skill: Four-Step Plan

Main Idea I will use the four-step plan to solve problems.

 Dina's family went to a zoo. They learned that a roadrunner is 1 foot tall. An African elephant is 12 feet tall. How much taller is an African elephant than a roadrunner?

Roadrunner

Understand	**What facts do you know?** • The roadrunner is 1 foot tall. • The African elephant is 12 feet tall. **What do you need to find?** • You need to find how much taller an African elephant is than a roadrunner.
Plan	To find out how much taller an African elephant is than a roadrunner, subtract.
Solve	$\begin{array}{r} 12 \\ -\ 1 \\ \hline 11 \end{array}$ ← height of elephant ← height of roadrunner So, the elephant is 11 feet taller than the roadrunner.
Check	Since addition and subtraction are inverse operations, you can use addition to check the subtraction. $\begin{array}{r} 12 \\ -\ 1 \\ \hline 11 \end{array}$ ✕ $\begin{array}{r} 11 \\ +\ 1 \\ \hline 12 \end{array}$ So, the answer is correct.

3.1 The student will **a)** read and write six-digit numerals and identify the place value and value of each digit.

Refer to the problem on the previous page.

1. Explain why you subtract 1 from 12 to find how much taller an elephant is than a roadrunner.

2. Suppose an elephant is 8 feet tall. How much shorter is a roadrunner?

3. Suppose a roadrunner is 3 feet tall. How much taller would an elephant be than the roadrunner?

4. Look back at Exercise 3. Check your answer. How do you know that it is correct? Explain.

PRACTICE

EXTRA PRACTICE
Begins on page EP2.

Solve. Use the four-step plan.

5. Cameron and Mara walked 2 blocks. Then they turned a corner and walked 4 blocks. How many blocks do they need to walk to return to their starting place?

6. Choose four of the game tiles, without adding tiles together of the same place value, to make the greatest 5-digit number possible.

7. Cortez bought a loaf of wheat, a loaf of rye, and a loaf of white bread. Gloria bought a loaf of raisin, a loaf of cinnamon, and a loaf of rye bread. How many different loaves of bread did they buy?

8. Follow the directions to find the correct height of the CN Tower in Toronto, Canada. Start with 781 feet. Add 1 hundred. Add 1 thousand. Subtract 7 tens and add 4 ones.

9. Marjorie modeled a 4-digit number. She modeled 1 thousand, 5 hundreds, 3 ones, and 2 tens. Write Marjorie's number in standard form and expanded form.

10. In 1,000 years from now, what year will it be? What year will it be 100 years from now? 10 years from now?

11. ✎ **WRITE MATH** Explain how the four-step plan helps you solve a problem.

Main Idea

I will compare numbers through ten thousands.

 Vocabulary

is less than (<)

is greater than (>)

is equal to (=)

Get ConnectED

 3.1 The student will **c)** compare two whole numbers between 0 and 9,999, using symbols (>, <, or =) and words (greater than, less than, or equal to).

Compare Numbers

When comparing two numbers, the first number is either less than, greater than, or equal to the second number.

Symbol	Meaning
<	**is less than**
>	**is greater than**
=	**is equal to**

REAL-WORLD EXAMPLE   **Use a Number Line**

① **MEASUREMENT The Tyee family is planning a road trip to the Grand Canyon. One route is about 840 miles. A second route is about 835 miles. Which route is shorter?**

You can use a number line to compare 835 and 840.

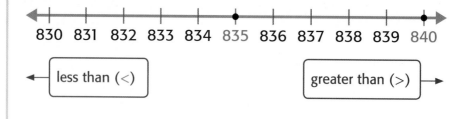

835 **is to the left** of 840   840 **is to the right** of 835

835 **is less than** 840   840 **is greater than** 835

835 < 840   840 > 835

So, the second route is shorter.

② TIME **Which is greater, 19,870 days or 1,400 days?**

You need to compare
19,870 and 1,400.
Line up the numbers.
Then compare.

Thousands			Ones		
hundreds	tens	ones	hundreds	tens	ones
1	9	8	7	0	
	1	4	0	0	

19,870 has 1 ten thousand,
but 1,400 has 0 ten thousands.

1 ten thousand is greater than 0 ten thousands.
So, 19,870 > 1,400.

③ HOCKEY **During his hockey career, Mark Messier scored 1,887 points. Gordie Howe scored 1,850 points during his career. Who scored fewer points during their career?**

Compare 1,887 and 1,850 to see who scored fewer points.

Step 1 Line up the numbers by place value.

Thousands	Hundreds	Tens	Ones
1	8	8	7
1	8	5	0

Step 2 Compare. Start with the greatest place-value position.

Thousands	Hundreds	Tens	Ones
1	8	8	7
1	8	5	0

same

different, 5 tens < 8 tens

Since 5 is less than 8, 1,850 < 1,887.
So, Gordie Howe scored fewer points.

Compare. Use >, <, or =. See Examples 1–3

1. 604 ● 592

2. 188 ● 198

3. 1,000 ● 850

4. 2,644 ● 2,464

5. 1,000 ● 1,000

6. 32,345 ● 32,357

7. The Flips Gymnastics Club has 131 members. The Tumblers have 113 members. Which club has more members? Explain.

8. TALK MATH Why is it not necessary to compare the ones digits in the numbers 4,365 and 4,378?

Practice and Problem Solving

EXTRA PRACTICE
Begins on page EP2.

Compare. Use >, <, or =. See Examples 1–3

9. 555 ● 725

10. 999 ● 999

11. 700 ● 800

12. 931 ● 8,310

13. 1,121 ● 1,112

14. 6,573 ● 7,650

15. 3,039 ● 33,019

16. 998 ● 989

17. 8,008 ● 8,080

18. 32,753 ● 2,735

19. 7,654 ● 7,654

20. 19,999 ● 11,000

Algebra Compare. Use >, <, or =.

21. 65 ● 62 + 3

22. 335 + 4 ● 339

23. 2,209 ● 2,200 + 90

24. The table shows the number of tickets sold for a movie. Which showing sold more tickets?

Revenge of Dinosaurs	
Showing	**Tickets Sold**
5:00 P.M.	235
7:00 P.M.	253

25. Measurement Which day was warmer in the desert, Tuesday or Wednesday? Explain.

Desert Temperature	
Day	**Temperature**
Tuesday	119°F
Wednesday	109°F

26. There are 165 students in the third grade. There are 35 students in each of the five classes in the second grade. Which grade has more students? Explain.

27. Keith's family bought a computer for $1,200. Margareta's family bought a computer for $1,002. Which computer cost less? Explain.

Use the information to solve the problem.

Wet Weekend Fun!

Remember, I am going to the water park this weekend, and want to go to the most popular park.

Morgan, look at this! Slide Island's website says they had 89,868 visitors last year.

Well, my favorite, Wave City, had 79,416 visitors last year.

28. Which water park is Morgan going to visit this weekend? Explain.

H.O.T. Problems

29. OPEN-ENDED Write the greatest and least 4-digit number you can make using the numerals 3, 6, 7, and 9 one time.

30. WHICH ONE DOESN'T BELONG? Identify the number that is less than 4,259.

| 4,295 | 4,260 | 4,300 | 4,209 |

31. **WRITE MATH** Explain the first step in comparing 2,032 and 203. Which number is greater? Explain.

Test Practice

32. Which number will make the number sentence true? (Lesson 2B)

$$1,426 > \blacksquare$$

A. 1,425   **C.** 1,452

B. 1,426   **D.** 1,524

33. Mrs. Phillips' class is having a pizza party. There are 30 students. Each pizza is cut into 10 pieces. If each student gets one piece, how many pizzas are there? (Lesson 2A)

F. 3   **H.** 7

G. 5   **J.** 10

Get Connect**ED**

Main Idea

I will use a number line and place value to order numbers through ten thousands.

Order Numbers

Comparing numbers can help you to order numbers.

REAL-WORLD EXAMPLE

Order Least to Greatest

1 MEASUREMENT
The table shows the length of three whales. Order the lengths from least to greatest.

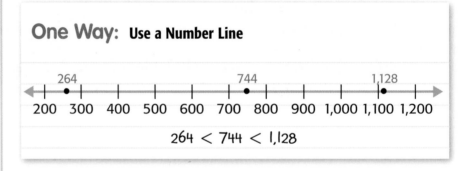

Average Length of Whales

Whale	Length (inches)
Orca Whale	264
Blue Whale	1,128
Humpback Whale	744

One Way: Use a Number Line

264   744   1,128
◄─┼─●─┼──┼──┼──┼──┼──┼──┼──┼──●─┼──►
  200 300 400 500 600 700 800 900 1,000 1,100 1,200

264 < 744 < 1,128

Another Way: Use a Place-Value Chart

Line up the numbers by their place value from the right. Compare from the left.

Thousands			Ones		
hundreds	tens	ones	hundreds	tens	ones
			2	6	4
		1	1	2	8
			7	4	4

1 thousand is the greatest number. →

7 hundreds > 2 hundreds →

The order is 264 inches, 744 inches, and 1,128 inches.

REAL-WORLD EXAMPLE Order Greatest to Least

② **MEASUREMENT** The table shows the distances whales travel to feed in the summertime. This is called migration. Order these distances from greatest to least.

Whale Migration	
Whale	**Distance (miles)**
Humpback Whale	3,500
Gray Whale	12,000
Orca Whale	900

Use the place value chart to line up the numbers by their place value. Compare from the left.

12,000 is the greatest number.

Thousands			Ones		
hundreds	tens	ones	hundreds	tens	ones
		3	5	0	0
	1	2	0	0	0
			9	0	0

3 thousands > no thousands so 3,500 is the next greatest number.

The order is 12,000 miles, 3,500 miles, and 900 miles.

> **Remember**
>
> When you move to the left on a number line, the numbers get smaller.

✓ CHECK What You Know

Order the numbers from least to greatest. See Example 1

1. 39; 32; 68

2. 224; 124; 441

3. 202; 2,202; 220

Order the numbers from greatest to least. See Example 2

4. 231; 136; 178

5. 1,500; 150; 15

6. 99,009; 9,909; 69,999

7. Team A won 19 games, Team B won 40 games, and Team C won 22 games during the season. What place did each team earn for the season?

8. **TALK MATH** Order these numbers from greatest to least: 435; 345; and 3,453. Explain how you can tell which number is greatest.

Order the numbers from least to greatest. See Example 1

9. 303; 30; 3,003

10. 4,404; 4,044; 4,040

11. 39; 78; 123

12. 1,234; 998; 2,134

13. 598; 521; 3,789

14. 22,673; 22,787; 22,900

Order the numbers from greatest to least. See Example 2

15. 60; 600; 6,006

16. 288; 209; 2,899

17. 349; 343; 560

18. 3,587; 875; 2,435

19. 451; 409; 415

20. 999; 81,342; 72,000

21. Carra's dad is shopping for a car. Which car costs the most?

22. Kurt wants to buy a parrot, pony, or dog. Order the animals from the least to the most expensive.

23. Three elementary schools have 2,500 students, 3,002 students, and 2,536 students. Which is the least number of students?

24. In a set of numbers, 59 is the least number and 10,000 is the greatest. Write four ordered numbers that could be between these numbers.

H.O.T. Problems

25. NUMBER SENSE Suppose you are ordering the numbers 1,467; 1,980; and 1,745 from greatest to least. Between which two numbers will 1,567 be placed?

26. WRITE MATH Write a real-world problem in which you need to order numbers from least to greatest.

Mid-Chapter Check

Write the place of each underlined digit. Then write the value of the digit.
(Lesson 1B)

1. 5<u>4</u>9

2. 3,<u>5</u>20

3. **MULTIPLE CHOICE** How is five thousand, three hundred nineteen written in standard form? (Lesson 1B)

 A. 5,193   **C.** 5,319

 B. 5,309   **D.** 5,391

4. **Measurement** A hippopotamus at a zoo weighs 3,525 pounds. Write this number in expanded and word form. (Lesson 1B)

Write the place of each underlined digit. Then write the value of the digit.
(Lesson 1C)

5. <u>1</u>6,846   6. <u>2</u>8,950

Write each number in standard form. (Lesson 1C)

7. twenty-three thousand, seven hundred forty-two

8. 60,000 + 4,000 + 8

9. Mrs. Cassady made tea for her grandchildren. She used 3 tea bags for one pitcher. If she makes 4 pitchers, how many tea bags will she use? (Lesson 2A)

Write each number in expanded form. (Lesson 1C)

10. Jennifer hopes to read 10,240 pages this summer.

11. Forty-five thousand, sixty-seven people attended the concert.

Compare. Use <, >, or =. (Lesson 2B)

12. 80,000 ● 8,008

13. 9,638 ● 10,721

Order the numbers from greatest to least. (Lesson 2C)

14. 278; 476; 285

15. 9,009; 909; 6,999

16. 58,431; 42,646; 58,430

17. **MULTIPLE CHOICE** Hong has saved $37. He spends $19 on clothes. He earns $15 for mowing the neighbor's yard. How much money does Hong have now? (Lesson 2A)

 F. $3   **H.** $34

 G. $33   **J.** $71

18. **WRITE MATH** Explain how the value of the 5 changes in 4,756 if it is moved to the thousands place. (Lesson 1B)

THE MIGHTY MISSISSIPPI

The Mississippi River is part of the largest river system in North America. The river begins in Minnesota and empties into the Gulf of Mexico. The Mississippi River system extends from the Rocky Mountains in the western United States to the Appalachian Mountains in the east.

The Mississippi River is about 2,340 miles long. The shallowest point is 3 feet. The deepest point is 198 feet. It's no wonder that the Mississippi River is called the "Mighty Mississippi."

MAJOR RIVERS OF THE MISSISSIPPI RIVER SYSTEM

River	Length (miles)
Arkansas	1,469
Mississippi	2,340
Missouri	2,540
Ohio	1,310
Red	1,290

Real-World Math

Use the information on the previous page to solve each problem.

1 Which river is the longest?

2 Which river lengths have the same value for the hundreds place? What is that value?

3 Write the length of the Arkansas River in expanded form.

4 The total of the lengths of the Missouri River and Mississippi River is 4,880 miles. How is this number written in words?

5 How does the length of the Red River compare to the lengths of the other 4 rivers? Use >, <, or = for each comparison.

6 Which is the third longest river?

7 Which river has the length of 2,000 + 300 + 40 miles? What is its length in standard form?

8 Write the length of the Ohio River in word form.

9 What is the difference in the depths of the Mississippi from its shallowest point to its deepest point?

10 The Amazon River in South America is 3,920 miles long. Which river is longer, the Amazon or the Missouri?

Main Idea
I will round numbers to the nearest ten and hundred.

 Vocabulary
round

 Get ConnectED

3.1 The student will **b)** round whole numbers, 9,999 or less, to the nearest ten, hundred, and thousand.

Round to the Nearest Ten and Hundred

To **round** is to change the value of a number to one that is easier to work with. You can use a number line to round.

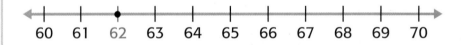 **REAL-WORLD EXAMPLE**

Round to the Nearest Ten

① **TECHNOLOGY** Cassandra used 62 minutes on her family's cell phone plan. About how many minutes did Cassandra use? Round to the nearest ten.

The closest ten *less than* 62 is 60.
The closest ten *greater than* 62 is 70.
Use a number line from 60 to 70.

```
◄──┼───┼───●───┼───┼───┼───┼───┼───┼───┼───┼──►
   60  61  62  63  64  65  66  67  68  69  70
```

62 is closer to 60 than to 70. So, Cassandra used about 60 minutes.

② **TECHNOLOGY** Cassandra's brother, Matao, used 186 minutes. About how many minutes did he use? Round to the nearest ten.

The closest ten *less than* 186 is 180. The closest ten *greater than* 186 is 190. Use a number line from 180 to 190.

```
◄──┼───┼───┼───┼───┼───┼───●───┼───┼───┼───┼──►
  180 181 182 183 184 185 186 187 188 189 190
```

186 is closer to 190 than to 180. Matao used about 190 minutes.

You can also round numbers to the nearest hundred.

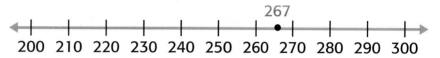

REAL-WORLD EXAMPLES Round to the Nearest Hundred

Vocabulary Link

round

Everyday Use in the form of a circle

Math Use to change the value of a number to one that is easier to work with

③ BOOKS Bruno read a book that was 267 pages long. To the nearest hundred, how many pages did he read?

```
                              267
 ◄──┼──┼──┼──┼──┼──┼──●┼──┼──┼──┼──►
   200 210 220 230 240 250 260 270 280 290 300
```

267 is closer to 300 than to 200. Bruno read about 300 pages.

④ SHELLS Olivia collected shells. To the nearest hundred, how many seashells did she collect?

OLIVIA'S SEASHELL COLLECTION

1,423

```
          1,423
 ◄──┼──────●───────┼───────┼───────┼──►
  1,400    1,425   1,450   1,475   1,500
```

1,423 is closer to 1,400 than to 1,500. Olivia collected about 1,400 shells.

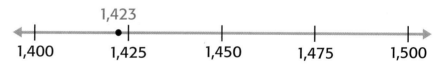

✓ **CHECK What You Know**

Round to the nearest ten. See Examples 1 and 2

1. 58   **2.** 62   **3.** 685   **4.** 552

Round to the nearest hundred. See Examples 3 and 4

5. 449   **6.** 473   **7.** 415   **8.** 1,450

9. Kayla has to read 67 pages for homework tonight. To the nearest ten, how many pages does she need to read?

10. **TALK MATH** What should you do to round the number 5 because it is halfway between two numbers?

Round to the nearest ten. See Examples 1 and 2

11. 77   **12.** 67   **13.** 13   **14.** 21

15. 285   **16.** 195   **17.** 157   **18.** 679

Round to the nearest hundred. See Examples 3 and 4

19. 123   **20.** 244   **21.** 749   **22.** 750

23. 353   **24.** 850   **25.** 1,568   **26.** 4,829

27. Myron has 179 baseball cards. He says he has about 200 cards. Did he round the number of cards to the nearest ten or hundred? Explain.

28. **Measurement** A passenger train traveled 1,687 miles. To the nearest hundred, how many miles did the train travel?

29. In May, Coco collected 528 cans of food for a food drive. She collected 479 cans in June. Rounding to the nearest hundred, did she collect about the same amount each month? Compare using < or >.

30. Mrs. Boggs ran for mayor. She received 1,486 votes. Mrs. Swain received 1,252 votes. What is the number of votes each person got, rounded to the nearest ten? Compare using < or >.

REAL-WORLD PROBLEM SOLVING

Sports Danilo is practicing bowling. The table shows his scores for one week.

31. Round all scores to the nearest hundred. Which days were the scores about 300?

32. To the nearest ten, what was the score on Tuesday?

33. To the nearest ten, which day's score rounds to 250?

BOWLING SCORES

Monday	252
Tuesday	83
Wednesday	164
Thursday	256
Friday	290
Saturday	283
Sunday	173

H.O.T. Problems

34. **OPEN ENDED** I am thinking of a number that when rounded to the nearest hundred is 400. What is the number? Explain.

35. **WRITE MATH** Explain why 238 can be rounded to 240 or 200.

Game Time

Round Numbers
Round to the Nearest Hundred

You will need: pencil and paper

Get Ready!

Players: 2 players

Get Set!

Each player draws the game board.

Go!

⭐ Each player secretly writes a 4-digit number on a piece of paper.

⭐ In the center of the game board, each player writes their 4-digit number rounded to the nearest hundred.

⭐ Player 1 guesses 1 digit that he or she thinks is in the other player's secret number.

⭐ If the digit is correct, Player 2 writes it on the correct line. If it is incorrect, Player 2 fills in one space.

⭐ Player 2 takes his or her turn guessing Player 1's secret number.

⭐ Play continues until the number is guessed or all spaces are filled in.

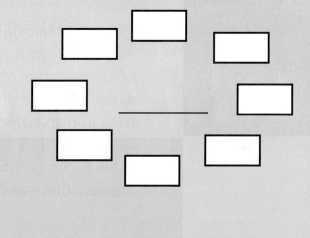

Main Idea

I will round numbers to the nearest thousand.

 Get Connect**ED**

 **3.1** The student will **b)** round whole numbers, 9,999 or less, to the nearest ten, hundred, and thousand.

Round to the Nearest Thousand

Numbers can also be rounded to the nearest thousand.

🏃 📝 **REAL-WORLD EXAMPLES** Use a Number Line

1. **VISITORS Mr. Chou's Arcade keeps a record of the number of visitors it has each week. About how many visitors went to the arcade in week 3? Round this number to the nearest thousand.**

Week	Number of Visitors
1	1,258
2	2,341
3	4,684
4	2,500
5	3,499

4,684

```
+-----------+-----------●-----+
4,000      4,500    5,000
```

4,684 is closer to 5,000 than to 4,000. About 5,000 people visited the arcade in week 3.

2. **About how many visitors went to the arcade in week 2? Round to the nearest thousand.**

The closest thousand *less than* 2,341 is 2,000. The closest thousand *greater than* 2,341 is 3,000.

2,341

```
+---●-------+-----------+
2,000    2,500      3,000
```

2,341 is closer to 2,000 than to 3,000. About 2,000 people visited the arcade in week 2.

You can use rounding rules to round a number.

Key Concept — Rounding Whole Numbers

Step 1 Underline the digit to be rounded.

Step 2 Look at the digit to the right of the place being rounded.

Step 3 If the digit is 4 or less, do not change the underlined digit. If the digit is 5 or greater, add 1 to the underlined digit.

Step 4 Replace all digits after the underlined digit with zeros.

 **REAL-WORLD EXAMPLE** Use Rounding Rules

③ ZOO A zoo has a membership of **47,499 families. To the nearest thousand, about how many families are members?**

Remember
Use rounding rules for rounding in *all* place values.

Step 1 Underline the digit in the place to be rounded. In this case, the 7 is in the thousands place. 47,499

Step 2 Look at the 4, the digit to the right of the underlined digit. 47,499

Step 3 This digit is less than 5, so do not change the underlined digit. 47,499

Step 4 Replace all digits after the underlined digit with zeros. 47,000

Check To the nearest thousand, 47,499 rounds to 47,000. ✔

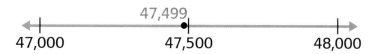

47,499

47,000   47,500   48,000

So, there are about 47,000 families who are members of the zoo.

Round to the nearest thousand. See Examples 1–3

1. 3,922

2. 2,798

3. 7,099

4. 1,499

5. 12,500

6. 43,601

7. There are 1,250 houses in a city. Round the number of houses to the nearest thousand.

8. TALK MATH Explain how you would use the rounding rules to round 5,299 to the nearest thousand.

Practice and Problem Solving

EXTRA PRACTICE
Begins on page EP2.

Round to the nearest thousand. See Examples 1–3

9. 8,611

10. 3,651

11. 1,099

12. 4,243

13. 2,698

14. 1,503

15. 1,257

16. 5,598

17. 5,299

18. 51,500

19. 62,400

20. 33,789

21. The fourth-grade class read a total of 12,389 pages this month. Round the number of pages to the nearest thousand.

22. The attendance at a recent high school football game was 1,989. What is the attendance rounded to the nearest thousand?

23. To the nearest thousand, what will the cost be for the third grade to take a trip to the zoo?

24. Irene's scores on her favorite video game got better each day. What is her score on Wednesday rounded to the nearest thousand?

Third Grade Trip to the Zoo
$1,855

Video Game Scores	
Day	Score
Monday	31,735
Tuesday	42,200
Wednesday	42,585

25. Alton and his friends collected 1,683 stickers. How many stickers is this rounded to the nearest thousand?

26. Measurement Chong rode a train 2,156 miles one way. To the nearest thousand, what is the total number of miles he rode the train both ways?

27. NUMBER SENSE Describe all the four-digit numbers that when rounded to the nearest thousand are 8,000.

28. WHICH ONE DOESN'T BELONG? Identify the number that is not rounded correctly to the nearest thousand. Explain.

| 2,184 → 2,000 | 5,500 → 5,000 | 3,344 → 3,000 | 8,456 → 8,000 |

29. WRITE MATH Round 499 to the nearest hundred. Then round 499 to the nearest ten. Are the two answers the same? Explain.

Test Practice

30. Which number is 549 rounded to the nearest ten? (Lesson 3A)

    A. 500   **C.** 540

    B. 600   **D.** 550

31. Margo rounded the number of beads in her craft set to 4,000. Which number could be the exact number of beads? (Lesson 3B)

    F. 2,989   **H.** 4,576

    G. 3,576   **J.** 5,004

Spiral Review

Round to the nearest ten. (Lesson 3A)

32. 89   **33.** 319   **34.** 5,568   **35.** 8,728

Order the numbers from greatest to least. (Lesson 2C)

36. 1,234; 998; 2,134   **37.** 598; 521; 3,789   **38.** 12,673; 12,787; 12,900

39. Elias purchased the following items. He also bought a book about sports for $8. How much did he spend in all? (Lesson 2A)

Problem-Solving Investigation

Main Idea I will use the four-step plan to solve a problem.

P.S.I. TEAM +

TWYLA: Building Set A has 1,025 pieces, with 24 bonus parts. Set B has 995 pieces and 75 bonus parts. I want to buy the set with more pieces and parts.

YOUR MISSION: Find which set has the greater total.

Understand

There 1,025 pieces and 24 bonus parts in Set A. Set B has 995 pieces and 75 bonus parts. Find the greater total.

Plan

You do not need an exact number. So, you can round to estimate the total.

Solve

Round the numbers in each set to the nearest ten. Then add.

	Set A			Set B	
1,025 →	1,030	pieces	995 →	1,000	pieces
24 →	+ 20	bonus parts	75 →	+ 80	bonus parts
	1,050	total		1,080	total

Set A has about 1,050 pieces. Set B has about 1,080 pieces.

1,050 < 1,080 So, Set B has the greater number of pieces.

Check

Use a number line to check your work.

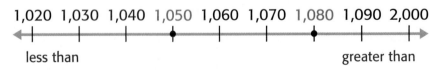

1,020 1,030 1,040 1,050 1,060 1,070 1,080 1,090 2,000

less than   greater than

So, the answer is correct. ✓

3.1 The student will **b)** round whole numbers, 9,999 or less, to the nearest ten, hundred, and thousand.

Mixed Problem Solving

EXTRA PRACTICE
Begins on page EP2.

Use the four-step plan to solve each problem.

1. Measurement Juan exercised 20 minutes yesterday. Today he is going to exercise twice as long. How long does Juan plan to exercise today? Explain.

2. Algebra What is the next figure in the pattern?

3. Sylvia's cards

Meli's cards

How many points do Sylvia and Meli have? Who has the greater number of points? Use < or >.

4. Gabriela buys the following items. She gives the cashier $20. How much change will she receive?

5. Measurement Joshua gets up at 8:30 A.M. He needs to leave for school by 9:00 A.M. How many minutes does he have to get ready?

6. The table shows the number of play tickets four friends sold on Saturday.

Louise	Malcolm
10 + 7	fourteen
Bobby	**Shelly**
20 − 5	19 + 2

Write the number of tickets sold in standard form. Then order the numbers from greatest to least.

7. Look at the table. How many pens do Cesar and Pamela have in all? How many more pens does Carmen have than Pamela?

Name	Pens
Pamela	7
Cesar	9
Carmen	20

8. Mrs. Reinhart read her students one book each day for 2 weeks. There are 5 days in each school week. How many books did she read in all? Explain your reasoning.

9. **WRITE MATH** Explain how the plan step is different than the solve step in the four-step plan.

To assess mastery of SOL 3.1, see your Virginia Assessment Book. **45**

Main Idea

I will find the value of coins and bills.

 Vocabulary

bill

dollar

3.8 The student will determine, by counting, the value of a collection of bills and coins whose total value is $5.00 or less, compare the value of the bills and coins, and make change.

Value of Coins and Bills

In the United States, money includes coins and bills.

REAL-WORLD EXAMPLE   **Find the Value of Coins**

1. **MONEY** Allison used the coins shown to buy a salad. How much money did Allison spend on her salad?

Key Concept   Value of Coins

Penny			1¢ or $0.01
Nickel			5¢ or $0.05
Dime			10¢ or $0.10
Quarter			25¢ or $0.25
Half-Dollar			50¢ or $0.50

Allison used 2 quarters, 1 dime, 1 nickel, and 5 pennies.

Add the value of the coins. Start with the greatest value.

$25 + 25 + 10 + 5 + 1 + 1 + 1 + 1 + 1 = 70$¢

So, Allison spent 70 cents, 70¢, or $0.70.   (¢ is read *cents*)

You can also use the dollar sign ($) to write amounts of money.

one dollar ↔ 100¢ ↔ 100 cents ↔ $1.00

REAL-WORLD EXAMPLE   **Find the Value of Coins**

2) MONEY What is the value of the coins shown?

There are 4 nickels, 2 quarters, 2 pennies, and 4 dimes.

First, put the coins in order from greatest to least in value. Use skip counting to add the values of each coin.

| $0.25 | $0.50 | $0.60 | $0.70 | $0.80 | $0.90 | $0.95 | $1.00 | $1.05 | $1.10 | $1.11 | $1.12 |

So, the value of the coins shown is $1.12.

Another name for paper money is **bill**. The unit is dollar ($).

REAL-WORLD EXAMPLE   **Find the Value of Bills and Coins**

3) MONEY What is the value of the money shown?

The value of each bill is shown in the corners.

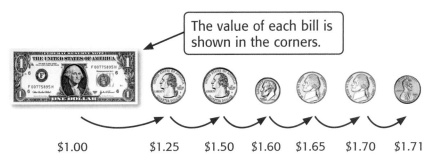

| $1.00 | $1.25 | $1.50 | $1.60 | $1.65 | $1.70 | $1.71 |

$1.00 + $0.25 + $0.25 + $0.10 + $0.05 + $0.05 + $0.01 = $1.71

The value of the money shown is 1 dollar and 71 cents or $1.71.

Remember

Group the coins in order from greatest to least value before you count the money.

Find the value of the coins. See Examples 1 and 2

1.

2.

Find the value of the bills and coins. See Example 3

3.

4.

5. Monique has 95¢. Which coins could she have?

6. TALK MATH Is there more than one way to make 4¢? Explain.

Practice and Problem Solving

EXTRA PRACTICE
Begins on page EP2.

Find the value of the coins. See Examples 1 and 2

7.

8.

9.

Find the value of the bills and coins. See Example 3

10.

11.

12.

13.

14. Garrett has one $1-bill, 5 quarters, and 3 dimes. Does he have enough money to buy a yo-yo for $2.45? Explain.

15. Todd has 3 nickels and 2 dimes. Will he have enough money to buy a snack for $0.25? Explain.

16. Which coins could be used to make $2.00?

17. Tara has 7 coins that equal $1.25. Which coins does she have?

Problems

18. OPEN ENDED Describe three different combinations of coins and bills, less than $5, that add up to the same amount of money.

19. CHALLENGE What is the least number of coins needed to make 99¢? Which coins are used?

20.  **WRITE MATH** Explain why a person might trade a dollar bill for four quarters.

 **Test Practice**

21. What is the value of the coins?
(Lesson 4A)

A. $0.164   **C.** $1.16

B. $0.86   **D.** $1.21

22. What numeral means the same as 30,000 + 4,000 + 200 + 8?
(Lesson 1C)

F. 30,208   **H.** 34,208

G. 30,280   **J.** 34,280

Spiral Review

Round to the nearest ten. (Lesson 3A)

23. 48   **24.** 82   **25.** 692

Order the numbers from greatest to least. (Lesson 2C)

26. 902; 962; 692   **27.** 444; 333; 555   **28.** 41,645; 41,564; 41,465

Write each number in word, standard, and expanded form.
(Lesson 1C)

29. 37,026

30. 80,000 + 1,000 + 600 + 50 + 4

31. thirty two thousand, six hundred one

32. Ricardo said the word form of 6,287 is sixty thousand, two hundred eighty-seven. Is he correct? Explain. (Lesson 1B)

Main Idea

I will determine change.

Get Connect**ED**

3.8 The student will determine, by counting, the value of a collection of bills and coins whose total value is $5.00 or less, compare the value of the bills and coins, and make change.

Determine Change

You can use coins and bills to make change.

 **REAL-WORLD EXAMPLE**   Determine Change

1) **MONEY** Michael and his father are shopping at a toy store. The table shows the cost of toys in a box. Michael buys a yo-yo. He gives the cashier a five-dollar bill. How much change should Michael receive?

Toy Store	
Item	**Cost**
Yo-yo	$0.77
Toy car	$0.95
Jump rope	$1.25
Stuffed animal	$3.45

Step 1   Count up to determine the change.

Start at $0.77 → $0.78 → $0.79 → $0.80 → $0.90 → $1.00
(cost of yo-yo)

→ $2.00 → $3.00 → $4.00 → $5.00
(amount paid)

Step 2   Count the change back.

Start at $1.00 → $2.00 → $3.00 → $4.00
(greatest value)
→ $4.10 → $4.20 → $4.21 → $4.22 → $4.23
(change received)

So, Michael will receive $4.23 in change.

2 **MONEY** Janet buys a stuffed animal for $3.45. She pays with a $5-bill. How much change should she receive?

Count up to find the change.

Step 1   Count the cents.

Start at $3.45 and go to the next whole dollar, $4.00. $3.45 to $4 is 55 cents.

Step 2   Count the dollars.

Start at $4 and count to $5. $4 to $5 is 1 dollar.

So, Janet should receive $1.55 in change.

✓ **CHECK What You Know**

A $5-bill was used to buy each item. Determine the change. Use coins and bills if needed. See Examples 1 and 2

1.  $4.59

2.  $2.65

3.  $3.29

Solve. Write the amount of change that should be received.

4. Keisha buys a yo-yo for 89¢. She pays with 4 quarters.

5. Jorge buys a sandwich for $4.49. He pays with a $5-bill.

6. 🗨️ **TALK MATH** A notebook costs $3.72. Explain how to determine the change if you pay with a $5-bill.

A $5-bill was used to buy each item. Determine the change. Use coins and bills if needed. See Examples 1 and 2

7.

$2.49

8.

$1.97

9.

$3.99

Solve. Write the amount of change that should be received.

10. Sam buys a video for $4.28. He pays with a $5-bill.

11. Kara buys a sticker for $0.78. She pays with a $1-bill.

12. Kendra buys a ring for $1.29. She pays with a $5-bill.

13. Nick buys a baseball for $2.89. He pays with a $5-bill.

14. Lexie buys a new bone for her dog for $3.65. She pays with a $5-bill.

15. Ben buys lunch for $4.09. He pays with a $5-bill.

H.O.T. Problems

16. **NUMBER SENSE** Sally received $2.23 in change when she bought a birthday card. If she paid with a $5-bill, how much did the birthday card cost? Explain.

17. **FIND THE ERROR** Eva determined the amount of change she should receive if she buys a pack of baseball cards for $4.38 with a $5-bill. Find and correct her mistake.

$1.62

18. **WRITE MATH** Sidney bought a box of crayons for $3.83. She paid with a $5-bill. Explain two different ways she can receive her change.

You can compare sets of money by counting the value of the coins and bills in each set. Then determine which set has the greater value by comparing the numbers.

EXAMPLE   **Who has saved more money, Allie or David?**

Allie has $2.25   David has $5.45

Since $2.25 < $5.45, David has saved more money.

Write a number sentence comparing the sets of money.
Use >, <, or =.

19.

20.

21. Paulo received one $5-bill and two $1-bills for his birthday. Anna has three $1-bills and one $5-bill. Does Paulo or Anna have more money?

22. Juanita has three $10-bills, two $5-bills, two quarters, and one nickel. Mike has two $20-bills and five dimes. Bill has five $5-bills. Order the value of the sets of money from greatest to least.

Chapter Study Guide and Review

Be sure the following Key Concepts are noted in your Foldable.

Numbers Through Ten Thousands
Place Value
Four-Step Plan
Compare and Order
Round Numbers
Coins and Bills

Key Concepts

- **Place value** is the value given to a digit by its place in a number. (Lesson 1)

Ones		
hundreds	tens	ones
9	8	3

- To compare numbers use **is less than <**, **is greater than >**, or **is equal to =**. (Lesson 2)

  246 < 250   246 is less than 250.

  1,125 > 189   1,125 is greater than 189.

  4,260 = 4,260   4,260 is equal to 4,260.

- A number line can help you **round** numbers, or make them easier to work with. 3,275 rounded to the nearest thousand is 3,000. (Lesson 3)

3,275

3,000	3,500	4,000

Key Vocabulary

bill

dollar

is equal to (=)

place value

round

standard form

Vocabulary Check

Choose the vocabulary word that completes each sentence.

1. One _____?_____ is the same as 100¢.

2. Another name for paper money is _____?_____.

3. The number 887 _____?_____ eight hundred eighty-seven.

4. When you _____?_____ 87 to the nearest 10, you get 90.

5. The _____?_____ of eight thousand, four hundred fifty-four is 8,454.

6. The value of a digit in a number is its _____?_____.

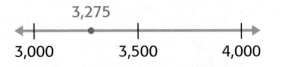

Multi-Part Lesson Review

Lesson 1 — Identify Place Value

Place Value Through Ten Thousands (Lessons 1B and 1C)

Write each number in expanded form and word form.

7. 4,013　　　　　**8.** 6,047

Write each number in standard form.

9. 7,000 + 600 + 20 + 2

10. one thousand, two hundred three

Write the place of the underlined digit. Then write its value.

11. 4<u>6</u>,887　　　　**12.** <u>6</u>3,004

13. Write 60,457 in expanded form and word form.

14. Write forty-seven thousand, nine hundred seventy-one in standard form.

EXAMPLE 1

Write 3,456 in expanded form and word form.

Standard Form: 3,456

Expanded Form: 3,000 + 400 + 50 + 6

Word Form: three thousand, four hundred fifty-six

EXAMPLE 2

Write the place of the underlined digit in <u>2</u>3,456. Then write its value.

Thousands			Ones		
hundreds	tens	ones	hundreds	tens	ones
	2	3	4	5	6

2 is in the ten thousands place. So, its value is 20,000.

Lesson 2 — Compare and Order Numbers

Problem-Solving Skill: The Four-Step Plan (Lesson 2A)

15. Vincent played soccer for 3 seasons. Mitchell has played for 3 years. If there are 2 seasons each year, who has played more seasons? Explain.

16. Bo brought 25 pencils to school the first week. He used 5 the first week and 7 the second week. How many pencils are still unused?

EXAMPLE 3

Estella runs 1 mile one week and then doubles her miles each week after that. In what week will she run 8 miles?

Start with 1. Keep doubling it until you reach 8.

1 mile	Week 1
1 + 1 = 2 miles	Week 2
2 + 2 = 4 miles	Week 3
4 + 4 = 8 miles	Week 4

Estella will run 8 miles in Week 4.

Compare and Order Numbers (Lessons 2B and 2C)

17. A school sold 235 tickets for the third grade play. There were 253 tickets sold for the fourth grade play. For which play were more tickets sold?

Compare. Then order the numbers from greatest to least.

18. 36,201; 35,201; 36,102

19. 89,554; 98,554; 87,554

20. Explain how you know which number is greatest without comparing the value of the digits.
535; 354; 4,435

EXAMPLE 4

Compare then order the numbers from least to greatest.

7,541; 5,300; 6,108

Thousands			Ones		
hundreds	tens	ones	hundreds	tens	ones
		7	5	4	1
		5	3	0	0
		6	1	0	8

5,300 < 6,108 < 7,541

Lesson 3 ## Round Numbers

Round to the Nearest Ten, Hundred, and Thousand (Lessons 3A and 3B)

Round to the nearest ten.

21. 56   **22.** 801

Round to the nearest hundred.

23. 569   **24.** 1,593

Round to the nearest thousand.

25. 4,509   **26.** 39,852

27. Gayla found the receipt below. What is the total amount spent rounded to the nearest thousand?

The Sports Store	
Treadmill	$ 2,500
Weight set	$ 2,000
Volleyball set	$ 150
Total	$ 4,650
CUSTOMER COPY	

EXAMPLE 5

Coty has 236 marbles. Rounded to the nearest hundred, how many marbles does he have?

Round 236 to the nearest hundred.

The closest hundred *less than* 236 is 200. The closest hundred *greater than* 236 is 300.

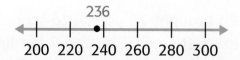

236 is closer to 200 than to 300. So, Coty has about 200 marbles.

Problem-Solving Investigation: Use the Four-Step Plan (Lesson 3C)

Use the four-step plan to solve each problem.

28. Algebra Garrett has twice as many coins as Luke. Luke has 12. How many coins do they have together?

29. For each coupon book Julie sells, she earns 100 points. If she sold 4 books last week and 5 this week, does she have enough points for an 800-point prize? Explain.

30. Measurement Mr. Jonas needs to put a fence around part of his yard for his dog. How many feet of fence will he need?

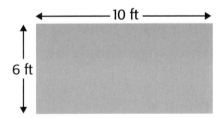

31. Raul says he has 200 knights on horses when he rounds the total to the nearest hundred. How many knights could Raul have? Explain.

32. Star gave each of her 6 friends 5 pieces of paper. She kept the rest. The pack now has 70 pieces of paper left. How many pieces did Star have to begin with?

EXAMPLE 6

Bart lives 30 miles from a water park. Clint lives 25 miles more than Bart from the same water park. How many miles does Clint live from the water park?

Add to find the total.

$$
\begin{array}{rl}
30 & \text{distance Bart lives} \\
+\ 25 & \text{distance farther Clint lives} \\
\hline
55 & \text{total distance Clint lives}
\end{array}
$$

So, Clint lives 55 miles from the water park.

Check by subtracting.

$55 - 25 = 30$ ✓

EXAMPLE 7

Raini wants a bike that costs $65. Raini's father will match any amount of money Raini saved. Raini saved $30. With his father's help, can he buy the bike?

Add to find the total Raini has.

$$
\begin{array}{rl}
\$30 & \text{Raini saved} \\
+\ \$30 & \text{Raini's dad's match} \\
\hline
\$60 & \text{total}
\end{array}
$$

$$
\begin{array}{cc}
\$60 & < & \$65 \\
\text{Raini has} & & \text{Raini needs}
\end{array}
$$

No, Raini cannot buy the bike.

Check

Lesson 4 Coins and Bills

Value of Coins and Bills (Lesson 4A)

Find the value of the bills and coins.

33.

34.

35. Kathy has 8 coins that equal $2. Which coins does she have?

EXAMPLE 8

Catherine used the money shown to buy a journal. How much did she spend?

Add the value of each coin and bill. Start with the greatest value.

$1.00 + $0.25 + $0.25 + $0.25 + $0.25 + $0.10 + $0.10 + $0.05 = $2.25

So, Catherine spent $2.25.

Determine Change (Lesson 4B)

A $5-bill was used to buy each item. Determine the change.

36.  $3.67

37. $4.20

38. Quincy buys a vase for his mom. It costs $3.32. He pays with a $5-bill. How much change will he receive?

39. Monica buys earrings for $4.44. She pays with a $5-bill. What coins could she receive as change?

EXAMPLE 9

Leo bought a piggy bank for $3.69. How much change should he receive from a $5-bill?

Step 1 Count the cents.
Start at $3.69 and go to the next whole dollar, $4.00. $3.69 to $4.00 is 31 cents.

Step 2 Count the dollars.
Start at $4 and count to $5. $4 to $5 is $1.

So, Leo should receive $1.31.

Practice Chapter Test

Tell whether each statement is _true_ or _false._

1. The number 3,578 is written in standard form.

2. Expanded form is a way to write a number in words.

Write the amount of change that should be received.

3. Mel buys a watercolor brush for $0.89. He pays with a $1-bill.

4. Kendra buys a box of jumbo chalk for $2.15. She pays with a $5-bill.

Identify the place of the underlined digit. Then write its value.

5. <u>3</u>,720

6. 5<u>2</u>9

7. Measurement Darlene noticed that the meter on her family's new car showed they have driven two thousand, eight hundred eighteen miles so far. How is that number written in standard form?

Write each number in expanded form and word form.

8. 6,191

9. 19,804

10. MULTIPLE CHOICE How is four thousand, three hundred twenty-one written in standard form?

A. 3,421

C. 4,231

B. 4,021

D. 4,321

11. Find the value of the coins.

Compare. Use >, <, or =.

12. 8,415 ● 8,541

13. 500 + 80 + 9 ● 589

14. Order from least to greatest.
4,804; 4,408; 8,440

15. Order the number of baskets from least to greatest.

Career Baskets	
Player	**Baskets**
Roz	2,308
Marquez	2,803
Amada	2,083

Round each number to the nearest ten, hundred, and thousand.

16. 2,942

17. 9,267

18. MULTIPLE CHOICE Which digit is in the thousands place in the number 92,108?

F. 1

H. 8

G. 2

J. 9

19. WRITE MATH Give an example of when it is appropriate to round numbers.

Test Practice

TEST EXAMPLE

A pet shop sold 1,372 turtles. Which of these equals 1,372?

A. 1 + 3 + 7 + 2

B. 1 + 30 + 70 + 2000

C. 100 + 300 + 70 + 2

D. 1000 + 300 + 70 + 2

TEST-TAKING TIP

You can use a number line to help you compare and order numbers.

Read the Question

You need to find which equals 1,372.

Solve the Question

You can use a place-value chart to find the value of each digit in 1,372.

1,372 = 1000 + 300 + 70 + 2.

So, the answer is D.

Thousands			Ones		
hundreds	tens	ones	hundreds	tens	ones
		1	3	7	2

Read each question. Then fill in the correct answer on the answer sheet provided by your teacher or on a separate sheet of paper.

1. The train traveled 415 miles. Which point represents 415?

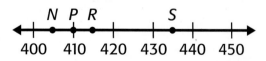

A. N   **C.** R

B. P   **D.** S

2. Which of the following is three hundred forty-two?

F. 234

G. three hundred twenty-four

H. 342

J. 300 + 40 + 20

3. Darcy walked 3,737 steps this morning. What number is 3,737 rounded to the nearest ten?

A. 3,740

B. 3,780

C. 3,800

D. 4,000

---

4. What is this number in standard form?

Thousands			Ones		
hundreds	tens	ones	hundreds	tens	ones
		1	3	4	2

F. 1,432

G. 1,342

H. 1,234

J. 132

---

5. Robert received the change shown below. What is the value of his change?

A. $1.60

B. $1.65

C. $1.70

D. $1.75

---

6. Leonardo has 158 baseball cards in his collection. What is 158 in expanded form?

F. $1 + 5 + 8$

G. $15 + 8$

H. $10 + 50 + 8$

J. $100 + 50 + 8$

---

7. There are 6,624 hours in 276 days. What is 6,624 rounded to the nearest thousand?

A. 7,000

B. 6,620

C. 6,600

D. 6,000

---

8. Tell the value of the digit in the thousands place.

17,523

F. 10,000

G. 7,000

H. 500

J. 20

---

9. Bertram played with 5 toy sailboats in the pool. He gave 2 to a friend. How many sailboats does Bertram have now?

A. 7

B. 5

C. 3

D. 1

NEED EXTRA HELP?									
If You Missed Question . . .	1	2	3	4	5	6	7	8	9
Go to Chapter-Lesson . . .	1-2C	1-1B	1-3A	1-1B	1-4A	1-1B	1-3B	1-1C	1-2A
For help with . . .	SOL 3.1a	SOL 3.1a	SOL 3.1b	SOL 3.1b	SOL 3.8	SOL 3.1a	SOL 3.1b	SOL 3.1a	SOL 3.4

CHAPTER

2

Add and Subtract to Solve Problems

connectED.mcgraw-hill.com

Investigate

 Animations

 Vocabulary

 Math Songs

 Multilingual eGlossary

Learn

 Personal Tutor

 Virtual Manipulatives

 Audio

 Foldables

Practice

 Self-Check Practice

 eGames

 Worksheets

 Assessment

The ☆BIG Idea

How can I develop strategies for multi-digit addition and subtraction problems?

 FOLDABLES
Study Organizer

Make this Foldable to help you organize information about addition and subtraction concepts. Start with one sheet of 11″ × 17″ paper.

Estimate Sums and Differences | Add Three- and Four-Digit Numbers
Subtract Three- and Four-Digit Numbers | Regrouping in Subtraction
Subtract Across Zeros | Estimate or Exact Answers

Review Vocabulary

difference diferencia the answer to a subtraction problem

$$17 - 9 = 8 \longleftarrow \boxed{\text{difference}}$$

Key Vocabulary

English	Español
Commutative Property of Addition	propiedad conmutativa de la adición
Identity Property of Addition	propiedad de identidad de la suma
estimate	estimación
regroup	reagrupar

When Will I Use This?

Carnival Cash!

Your Turn!

You will solve this problem in the chapter.

Add and Subtract to Solve Problems   **63**

You have two options for checking Prerequisite Skills for this chapter.

Text Option Take the Quick Check below.

QUICK Check

Add or subtract. Use the inverse operation if needed.

1. 5
+ 4

2. 6
+ 7

3. 15
− 9

4. 12
− 4

5. 9 + 2

6. 4 + 6

7. 17 − 9

8. 14 − 7

9. Percy swam 8 laps today and 4 laps yesterday. How many laps did he swim in 2 days?

10. Dalila had a package of 36 pens. She gave 14 to her friends. How many pens does she have left?

Find each sum.

11.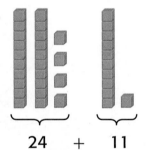

24 + 11

12.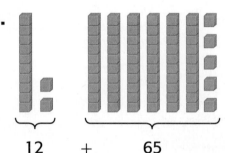

12 + 65

Round to the nearest ten.

13. 72

14. 19

15. 59

16. 89

Round to the nearest hundred.

17. 470

18. 771

19. 301

20. 149

 Online Option Take the Online Readiness Quiz.

Main Idea
I will use addition properties to add whole numbers.

 Vocabulary

Commutative Property of Addition

Identity Property of Addition

Associative Property of Addition

 Get ConnectED

3.4 The student will estimate solutions to and solve single-step and multistep problems involving the sum or difference of two whole numbers, each 9,999 or less, with or without regrouping.
3.2 The student will recognize and use the inverse relationships between addition/subtraction and multiplication/division to complete basic fact sentences. The student will use these relationships to solve problems. Also addresses 3.20a, 3.20b.

Algebra: Addition Properties

In math, properties are rules you can use with numbers.

Sal has 2 pieces of quartz and 3 pieces of granite. Ruby has 3 pieces of quartz and 2 pieces of granite. They both have the same number of rocks.

$$2 + 3 = 3 + 2$$

Key Concept · Addition Properties

Models

Examples $2 + 3 = 5$ $3 + 2 = 5$

Words   **Commutative Property of Addition** The order in which addends are added does not change the sum.

Examples $3 + 0 = 3$ $0 + 3 = 3$

Words   **Identity Property of Addition** The sum of any number and zero is the number.

Examples $(3 + 2) + 4 =$ $3 + (2 + 4) =$

$5 + 4 =$ $3 + 6 =$

9 9

Words   **Associative Property of Addition** The way the addends are grouped does not change the sum.

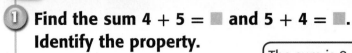

EXAMPLE — Use Properties to Add

1 **Find the sum 4 + 5 = ▇ and 5 + 4 = ▇. Identify the property.**

$$4 + 5 = ▇ \text{ and } 5 + 4 = ▇$$

> The sum is 9. The order in which the numbers are added does not change the sum.

This is the Commutative Property of Addition.

Remember

Parentheses tell you which numbers to add first.

REAL-WORLD EXAMPLE — Use the Associative Property to Add

2 **ANIMALS A zoo has 4 owl chicks, 2 cheetah cubs, and 6 lion cubs. How many baby animals are at the zoo?**

You need to find $4 + 2 + 6$. Rearrange the numbers so they are easier to add.

$$4 + 2 + 6$$
$$= 2 + 4 + 6 \quad \leftarrow \text{Commutative Property of Addition}$$
$$= 2 + (4 + 6) \quad \leftarrow \text{Associative Property of Addition–}$$

> The grouping of the addends does not change the sum.

$$= 2 + 10$$
$$= 12$$

So, there are 12 baby animals.

✓ CHECK What You Know

Find each sum. Identify the property. See Examples 1 and 2

1. $6 + 5 = ▇$
$5 + 6 = ▇$

2. $(5 + 7) + 3 = ▇$
$5 + (7 + 3) = ▇$

3. $0 + 12 = ▇$

4. Algebra Write a number sentence to show how many shells were collected. Which property did you use?

Seashell Collection			
Day	Friday	Saturday	Sunday
Shells	6	7	4

5. 📝 **TALK MATH** Describe how you can use the Commutative and Associative Properties of Addition to add 7, 8, and 3.

Find each sum. Identify the property. See Examples 1 and 2

6. $0 + 9 = $ ▥

7. $9 + 2 = $ ▥
$2 + 9 = $ ▥

8. $(2 + 5) + 8 = $ ▥
$2 + (5 + 8) = $ ▥

9. $2 + 8 = $ ▥
$8 + 2 = $ ▥

10. $100 + 0 = $ ▥

11. $4 + (6 + 3) = $ ▥
$(4 + 6) + 3 = $ ▥

Algebra **Find each missing number. Identify the property.**

12. $6 + $ ▥ $ = 6$

13. $(7 + 9) + 3 = (9 + $ ▥ $) + 3$

14. $9 + $ ▥ $ = 2 + 9$

15. $(8 + 3) + $ ▥ $ = 8 + (3 + 2)$

Find each sum mentally.

16.
$$\begin{array}{r} 1 \\ 7 \\ +9 \\ \hline \end{array}$$

17.
$$\begin{array}{r} 5 \\ 7 \\ +5 \\ \hline \end{array}$$

18.
$$\begin{array}{r} 4 \\ 2 \\ 6 \\ +2 \\ \hline \end{array}$$

19.
$$\begin{array}{r} 2 \\ 1 \\ 9 \\ +3 \\ \hline \end{array}$$

Solve.

20. Necie has 3 dogs. Simona has 5 fish and 6 birds. Peyton has 1 snake. How many pets do the children have?

21. Luis drew the picture below. Write two number sentences that would be examples of the Associative Property of Addition.

22. Mrs. Jackson bought 6 blue, 2 red, and 2 yellow notebooks. There are 7 notebooks left on the store's shelf. How many notebooks were there to begin with?

H.O.T. Problems

23. OPEN ENDED Describe three different ways to find the sum of $7 + 9 + 3$. Which properties of addition did you use? Explain which method was easiest for you.

24. WRITE MATH Is there a Commutative Property of Subtraction? Explain.

Main Idea
I will estimate sums using rounding and compatible numbers.

 Vocabulary
estimate
compatible numbers

 Get ConnectED

3.4 The student will estimate solutions to and solve single-step and multistep problems involving the sum or difference of two whole numbers, each 9,999 or less, with or without regrouping. **3.1** The student will **b)** round whole numbers, 9,999 or less, to the nearest ten, hundred, and thousand.

Estimate Sums

Sometimes you do not need an exact answer.

When the word *about* is used in a problem, you can find an estimate instead. An **estimate** is a number close to the exact number.

When estimating, you can round to the nearest ten, hundred, or thousand.

🏃 🖊 **REAL-WORLD EXAMPLE**   **Rounding to Estimate**

1 **MONEY** The Board Shop sold 342 snowboards and 637 pairs of boots in the last year. *About how many snowboards and pairs of boots did they sell together?*

Estimate 342 + 637. Round, and then add.

One Way:	Hundreds Place	Another Way:	Tens Place
$\begin{array}{r} 342 \\ + 637 \\ \hline \end{array}$ → $\begin{array}{r} 300 \\ + 600 \\ \hline 900 \end{array}$		$\begin{array}{r} 342 \\ + 637 \\ \hline \end{array}$ → $\begin{array}{r} 340 \\ + 640 \\ \hline 980 \end{array}$	
The Board Shop sold about 900 snowboards and pairs of boots.		The Board Shop sold about 980 snowboards and pairs of boots.	

Both estimates are close. Both estimates are reasonable.

REAL-WORLD EXAMPLE — Estimate Greater Sums

2 GAMES A board game has $4,140 in play money. About how much money would there be if two games were put together? Estimate $4,140 + $4,140. Round to the thousands place.

$$\begin{array}{rcl} \$4{,}140 & \longrightarrow & \$4{,}000 \\ +\,\$4{,}140 & \longrightarrow & +\,\$4{,}000 \\ \hline & & \$8{,}000 \end{array}$$

So, the two games have about $8,000 in play money.

You can also use **compatible numbers** to estimate. Compatible numbers are numbers that are easy to add.

EXAMPLES — Use Compatible Numbers

3 Estimate 12 + 39.

Numbers ending in 0 are easy to add.

$12 \longrightarrow 10$
$39 \longrightarrow 40$

$10 + 40 = 50$
So, 12 + 39 is *about* 50.

4 Estimate 73 + 23.

The numbers 25, 50, 75, and 100 are easy to add.

$73 \longrightarrow 75$
$23 \longrightarrow 25$

 $= 100¢$

$75 \quad + \quad 25 \; = 100$

So, 73 + 23 is *about* 100.

CHECK What You Know

Estimate. Round to the indicated place value. See Examples 1 and 2

1. 312 + 27; tens   **2.** 383 + 122; hundreds   **3.** $2,746 + $1,529; thousands

Estimate. Use compatible numbers. See Examples 3 and 4

4. 143 + 560   **5.** 1,910 + 1,947   **6.** 521 + 1,701

7. A movie theater will show 153 movies this week and 245 movies next week. Rounded to the nearest ten, about how many movies will they show in the two weeks?

8. **TALK MATH** Look at the problem in Exercise 7. How could it be rewritten so an exact answer is needed?

Estimate. Round to the indicated place value. See Examples 1 and 2

9. $34 + $23; tens

10. 636 + 27; tens

11. 687 + 231; hundreds

12. 1,624 + 334; hundreds

13. 72,647 + 2,560; thousands

14. $41,236 + $20,425; thousands

Estimate. Use compatible numbers. See Examples 3 and 4

15. 35 + 42

16. 455 + 229

17. 272 + 593

18. 515 + 339

19. 21,629 + 5,364

20. $46,986 + $31,664

21. Rounded to the nearest ten, about how many racers were in the Summer Fun Race?

Summer Fun Race		
Start Time	Group	Entrants
9:00 A.M.	runners	79
10:00 A.M.	race walkers	51

FINISH

22. Rounded to the nearest thousand, what would be a reasonable estimate for attendance at the county fair for the two days?

County Fair Attendance	
Saturday	Sunday
3,621	2,924

23. The largest NBA arena can seat 22,076 people. Two games are sold out. Rounded to the nearest thousand, about how many people will attend the two games?

24. Look at the table below. There are 112 soccer players trying out for Team A. Team B has 74 soccer players trying out. Match the number of boys and girls to each team.

Team A and Team B Players	
Boys	Girls
55	33
41	57

25. Measurement Two walls of a room measure 21 feet each, and the other two measure 26 feet each. Estimate the total length of all four walls to the nearest ten.

26. OPEN ENDED Using the digits 1, 2, 3, 4, 5, and 6 once, write two 3-digit numbers whose estimated sum rounded to the nearest ten, is less than 500.

27. WHICH ONE DOESN'T BELONG? Identify the number that is not correctly rounded to the nearest thousand. Explain.

22,184 → 22,000	15,550 → 15,000	33,344 → 33,000	81,456 → 81,000

28. WRITE MATH Describe a real-world situation in which finding the exact sum would be better than finding an estimate.

Test Practice

29. For the party, Evelina cut 39 celery sticks and made 58 egg rolls. Rounded to the nearest ten, about how many snacks does she have for the party? (Lesson 1B)

A. 60   **C.** 90

B. 70   **D.** 100

30. Mr. Moseley will plant 11 flowers in each of his four window boxes. Rounded to the nearest ten, about how many flowers does he need to buy? (Lesson 1B)

F. 11   **H.** 30

G. 20   **J.** 40

Algebra Copy and complete each number sentence. Identify the property or rule used. (Lesson 1A)

31. $(8 + 4) + 7 = \blacksquare$
$\blacksquare + (4 + 7) = 19$

32. $25 + \blacksquare = 25$

33. $9 + \blacksquare = 16$
$7 + \blacksquare = 16$

34. Measurement Miss Sylvia drove 8 miles from home to the store. Then, she drove another 11 miles to work. At the end of the day, she drove 12 miles home. Use the Associative Property of Addition to find how many miles she drove that day. (Lesson 1A)

Explore Add Three-Digit Numbers

Main Idea

I will use models to explore adding three-digit numbers.

Materials

base-ten blocks

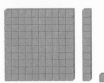

WorkMat 1

Hundreds	Tens	Ones

Get ConnectED

3.4 The student will estimate solutions to and solve single-step and multistep problems involving the sum or difference of two whole numbers, each 9,999 or less, with or without regrouping.

You can use base-ten blocks to model three-digit addition.

ACTIVITY

1. **Find 148 + 153.**

Step 1 **Model 148 and 153.**

Hundreds	Tens	Ones

148

153

Step 2 **Add the ones.**

Hundreds	Tens	Ones

8 ones + 3 ones = 11 ones

Regroup 11 ones as

1 ten and 1 one.

Step 3 **Add the tens.**

Hundreds	Tens	Ones

5 tens + 5 tens = 10 tens

Regroup 10 tens as 1 hundred and 0 tens.

Step 4 **Add the hundreds.**

1 hundred + 1 hundred + 1 hundred = 3 hundreds

So, 148 + 153 = 301.

Think About It

1. Describe the sum of the digits that needed to be regrouped.

2. Why were the ones and the tens regrouped?

3. Does changing the order of the addends make a difference in whether you need to regroup? Explain.

Practice and Apply It

Add. Use base-ten blocks to model, if needed.

4. 259 + 162

5. 138 + 371

6. 362 + 172

7. 541 + 169

8. 261 + 139

9. 285 + 75

10. **WRITE MATH** Write a rule that would explain when to regroup.

Main Idea

I will add three-digit numbers and use estimation to check for reasonableness.

Vocabulary

regroup

3.4 The student will estimate solutions to and solve single-step and multistep problems involving the sum or difference of two whole numbers, each 9,999 or less, with or without regrouping.

Three-Digit Addition

When you add, you sometimes need to regroup. **Regroup** means to rename a number using place value.

REAL-WORLD EXAMPLE   Add with Regrouping

1 **BIRDS** During a backyard bird count, birdwatchers saw 127 wrens and 58 eagles. How many wrens and eagles did the bird watchers see?

Add 127 + 58.

Estimate
$$127 \rightarrow 130$$
$$+\ 58 \rightarrow +\ 60$$
$$\overline{\ 190}$$

Step 1 Add the ones.

$$\begin{array}{r} {\scriptstyle 1} \\ 127 \\ +\ 58 \\ \hline 5 \end{array}$$

7 ones + 8 ones = 15 ones

Regroup 15 ones as 1 ten and 5 ones.

Step 2 Add the tens and hundreds.

$$\begin{array}{r} {\scriptstyle 1} \\ 127 \\ +\ 58 \\ \hline 185 \end{array}$$

1 ten + 2 tens + 5 tens = 8 tens

Bring the 1 hundred down.

Check for Reasonableness

185 is close to the estimate of 190. The answer is reasonable. ✔

So, the birdwatchers saw 185 wrens and eagles.

REAL-WORLD EXAMPLE   Add Money

2 MONEY One box of butterfly nets costs $175. Another costs $225. How much do the nets cost altogether?

Find $175 + $225.

Remember

When adding 3-digit numbers, be sure to align the ones column, tens column, and hundreds column.

Estimate
$$\begin{array}{r} \$175 \rightarrow \$200 \\ + \$225 \rightarrow + \$200 \\ \hline \$400 \end{array}$$

Step 1 Add the ones.

$$\begin{array}{r} 1 \\ \$17\mathbf{5} \\ + \$22\mathbf{5} \\ \hline \mathbf{0} \end{array}$$ 5 ones + 5 ones = 10 ones
Regroup 10 ones as 1 ten and 0 ones.

Step 2 Add the tens.

$$\begin{array}{r} 1\,1 \\ \$1\mathbf{7}5 \\ + \$2\mathbf{2}5 \\ \hline \mathbf{0}0 \end{array}$$ 1 ten + 7 tens + 2 tens = 10 tens
Regroup 10 tens as 1 hundred + 0 tens.

Step 3 Add the hundreds.

$$\begin{array}{r} 1\,1 \\ \$\mathbf{1}75 \\ + \$\mathbf{2}25 \\ \hline \$\mathbf{4}00 \end{array}$$ 1 hundred + 1 hundred + 2 hundreds = 4 hundreds

Check for Reasonableness

$400 is the same as the estimate. The answer is reasonable. ✓

Together, the nets cost $400.

✓ CHECK What You Know

Add. Check for reasonableness. See Examples 1 and 2

1. 164 + 17

2. 156 + 255

3.   468
       + 35

4.   227
        + 26

5. $355
       + $156

6. $272
       + $148

7. Chase has 176 video games. Estaban has 238 games. What is the total number of games the boys have?

8. **TALK MATH** Why is it important to check for reasonableness?

Add. Check for reasonableness. See Examples 1 and 2

9. 759
  + 19

10. 445
  + 26

11. $345
  + $93

12. $427
  + $217

13. 597
  + 51

14. 599
  + 59

15. $298
  + $408

16. $287
  + $453

17. 43 + 217

18. 607 + 27

19. $173 + $591

20. $108 + $589

21. 635 + 285

22. 398 + 355

23. $797 + $185

24. $490 + $288

25. A 10-speed bike is on sale for $199, and a 12-speed racing bike is on sale for $458. How much do the two bikes cost altogether?

26. Measurement Russell's bean stalk grew 24 inches the first month and 27 inches the second month. How tall was Russell's bean stalk after two months?

27. Measurement Use the map at the right. What is the total distance from the entrance of the park to Leonora's house and back to the park again?

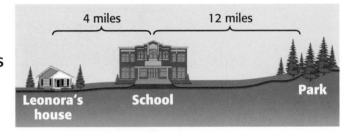

Algebra **Find each missing number. Identify the property.**

28. 240 + 679 = ■ + 240

29. (13 + 24) + 6 = ■ + (24 + 6)

30. 989 + ■ = 989

31. (565 + 6) + 39 = 565 + (■ + 39)

32. Jade wrote this number sentence about three groups of books on a library shelf.

(l26 + 52) + 8l = 259

Blake wrote a different number sentence about the same group of books. What sentence might Blake have written?

33. Find the amount of food each group of animals may eat for two weeks.

Animal Food		
Animal	**Food**	**One Week**
Koalas	eucalyptus leaves	180 pounds
Manatees	head of lettuce	840 heads

34. OPEN ENDED Write an addition problem whose sum is between 450 and 500.

35. CHALLENGE Use the digits 3, 5, and 7 to make two three-digit numbers. Use each digit one time in each number. Write an addition problem that would make the greatest sum possible.

36. **WRITE MATH** Would you ever need to regroup more than one time while finding a sum? Show an example to support your answer.

Test Practice

37. A store sold 346 clocks last year. This year they sold 251 clocks. How many clocks did they sell in the two years?

(Lesson 1D)

A. 697   **C.** 495

B. 597   **D.** 95

38. The Knights track team scored 117 points at a meet. At another meet, they scored 119 points. Rounded to the nearest ten, about how many points did they score at the two meets? (Lesson 1B)

F. 100   **H.** 190

G. 150   **J.** 240

39. Matt has 15 stamps. His sister gives him 5 more stamps. How many stamps will he have after he buys the stamps below?

(Lesson 1A)

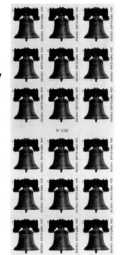

A. 20   **C.** 38

B. 22   **D.** 45

40. Students in the second, third, and fourth grades from Parkville Elementary School are going on a field trip. Rounded to the nearest hundred, about how many students will go? (Lesson 1B)

Grade	Number of Students
Second	192
Third	215
Fourth	189

F. 200   **H.** 600

G. 400   **J.** 800

Problem-**S**olving **S**kill: **Estimate or Exact Answers**

Main Idea I will decide whether an estimate or an exact answer is needed to solve a problem.

To celebrate Arbor Day, a city planted trees one weekend. On Saturday, 1,536 trees were planted. Another 380 trees were planted on Sunday. About how many trees were planted in all?

Understand **What facts do you know?**

- On Saturday, 1,536 trees were planted.

- On Sunday, 380 trees were planted.

What do you need to find?

- Find *about* how many trees were planted in all.

Plan You need to decide whether to estimate or find an exact answer. Since the question asks *about* how many trees were planted, you need to estimate.

Solve

- First, find about how many trees were planted each day. Estimate by rounding to the closest hundred.

$$1,536 \longrightarrow 1,500 \longleftarrow \boxed{\text{Round 1,536 to 1,500.}}$$
$$380 \longrightarrow 400 \longleftarrow \boxed{\text{Round 380 to 400.}}$$

- Then, add.

$$\begin{array}{r} 1,500 \\ + 400 \\ \hline 1,900 \end{array}$$

So, about 1,900 trees were planted in all.

Check If the question asked for an exact answer you would find $1,536 + 380 = 1,916$. The estimate is close to the exact answer. So, the estimate makes sense. ✓

3.4 The student will estimate solutions to and solve single-step and multistep problems involving the sum or difference of two whole numbers, each 9,999 or less, with or without regrouping.

Refer to the problem on the previous page.

1. How do you know when to find an estimate or an exact answer?

2. Describe a situation when an exact answer is needed.

3. Would underestimating ever be a problem? Explain.

4. Explain one reason why only an estimate is needed for the number of trees planted.

PRACTICE

EXTRA PRACTICE
Begins on page EP2.

Tell whether an estimate or an exact answer is needed. Then solve.

5. On career day, the students gave an author stories they wrote. How many stories did they write?

Student Stories	
Second grade	26
Third grade	35

6. **Measurement** Kishi cut two lengths of rope. One was 32 inches long. The other was 49 inches long. Will he have enough rope for a project that needs 47 inches and 29 inches of rope? Explain.

7. A bus can carry 60 students. Can 32 boys and 26 girls ride the bus? Explain.

8. The number 7 septillion has 24 zeros after it. The number 7 octillion has 27 zeros after it. How many zeros is that altogether?

9. **Measurement** Each tablespoon of mix makes one glass of lemonade. Will 96 ounces of water be enough for 15 glasses of lemonade? Explain.

Lemonade Directions	
Water	**Mix**
32 ounces	4 tablespoons
64 ounces	8 tablespoons
96 ounces	12 tablespoons

10. Rosaline walked 33 paces forward. Then she turned right and walked 15 paces. How many paces did she walk altogether?

11. **WRITE MATH** Write two real-world problems. One should involve estimation and the other should involve an exact answer.

Main Idea

I will add four-digit numbers with regrouping.

Get ConnectED

3.4 The student will estimate solutions to and solve single-step and multistep problems involving the sum or difference of two whole numbers, each 9,999 or less, with or without regrouping.

Add Four-Digit Numbers

You can use what you know about adding lesser numbers to add greater numbers.

 REAL-WORLD EXAMPLE

Add with Regrouping

1 **RADIO** In the United States, 869 radio stations play rock music. There are 2,179 news and talk radio stations. How many radio stations play these two formats?

Step 1 Add the ones.

$$
\begin{array}{r}
1 \\
2,179 \\
+\ 869 \\
\hline
8
\end{array}
$$

9 ones + 9 ones = 18 ones
Regroup as 1 ten and 8 ones.

Step 2 Add the tens.

$$
\begin{array}{r}
1\,1 \\
2,179 \\
+\ 869 \\
\hline
48
\end{array}
$$

1 ten + 7 tens + 6 tens = 14 tens
Regroup as 1 hundred and 4 tens.

Step 3 Add the hundreds.

$$
\begin{array}{r}
1\,1\,1 \\
2,179 \\
+\ 869 \\
\hline
048
\end{array}
$$

1 hundred + 1 hundred + 8 hundreds = 10 hundreds
Regroup as 1 thousand and 0 hundreds.

Step 4 Add the thousands.

$$
\begin{array}{r}
1\,1\,1 \\
2,179 \\
+\ 869 \\
\hline
3,048
\end{array}
$$

1 thousand + 2 thousands = 3 thousands

So, 3,048 radio stations play the two formats.

 **REAL-WORLD EXAMPLE**

2) PLANES The world's fastest plane can fly 2,139 miles in 32 minutes. What is the total distance if it flew another 2,314 miles?

Find 2,139 + 2,314.

Estimate
$$2,139 \longrightarrow 2,100$$
$$+ 2,314 \longrightarrow + 2,300$$
$$4,400$$

Remember

To check if your answer makes sense, estimate first. Then compare the answer to the estimate.

One Way: Partial Sums	**Another Way:** Mental Math
2,139 + 2,314 13 Add ones. 40 Add tens. 400 Add hundreds. + 4,000 Add thousands. 4,453	2,139 = 2,000 + 100 + 30 + 9 + 2,314 = 2,000 + 300 + 10 + 4 4,000 + 400 + 40 + 13 400 40 + 13 4,453

Check for Reasonableness

4,453 is close to 4,400. So, the answer is reasonable. ✔

So, the total distance is 4,453 miles.

A bar diagram may help you decide what operation to use.

 **REAL-WORLD EXAMPLE**   Use a Bar Diagram

3) SPORTS Last year $3,295 was spent on a skate park. This year $3,999 was spent. How much money was spent over the two years?

Find $3,295 + $3,999.

Estimate $3,295 + $3,999 ⟶ $3,000 + $4,000 = $7,000

⌐------? $ spent------⌐	
$3,295	**$3,999**
last year	this year

$$\begin{array}{r} 1\ 1\ 1 \\ \$3,295 \\ + \$3,999 \\ \hline \$7,294 \end{array}$$

Check for Reasonableness

$7,294 is close to $7,000. So, the answer is reasonable. ✔

So, $7,294 was spent over the two years.

Find each sum. Use estimation to check for reasonableness.

See Examples 1–3

1. 3,345
   + 654

2. 4,234
   + 500

3. $3,205
   + $1,709

4. 678 + 4,789

5. $3,445 + $6,547

6. $9,299 + $701

7. BAR DIAGRAM Lou's dad's car uses 1,688 gallons of gas a year. His mom's car uses 1,297 gallons. Find the total gallons of gas used.

8.  **TALK MATH** How is finding the sum of 4-digit numbers like finding the sum of 3-digit numbers?

Practice and Problem Solving

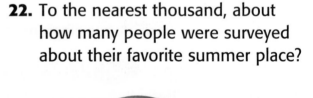

EXTRA PRACTICE
Begins on page EP2.

Find each sum. Use estimation to check for reasonableness.

See Examples 1–3

9. 6,999
   + 543

10. $1,998
   + $300

11. $2,507
   + $2,899

12. $8,285
   + $1,456

13. $2,390
   + $3,490

14. 5,555
   + 3,555

15. 2,865 + 5,522

16. 3,075 + 5,640

17. $1,603 + $3,509

18. $5,788 + $2,550

19. $3,999 + $4,800

20. 1,250 + 1,520

21. Algebra Write a number sentence to represent the total number of minutes each group read this month. Use > or <.

22. To the nearest thousand, about how many people were surveyed about their favorite summer place?

Time Spent Reading	
Group	**Minutes**
A	2,600
B	2,574

Favorite
Summer Place
Beach   2,311
Amusement park 2,962

H.O.T. Problems

23. CHALLENGE Use the digits 0 through 9 to create two 5-digit numbers whose sum is greater than 100,000. Use each digit once.

24.  **WRITE MATH** Explain what it means to check for reasonableness.

More About Adding Greater Numbers . . . .

When you add greater numbers, it may be necessary to regroup more than one time.

REAL-WORLD EXAMPLE Add Greater Numbers

ANIMALS In one year, a zoo fed some of its animals 57,200 bananas and 39,824 night crawlers. Find the total number.

Find 57,200 + 39,824.

Estimate

$$
\begin{array}{r}
57,200 \longrightarrow 57,000 \\
+\ 39,824 \longrightarrow +\ 40,000 \\
\hline
97,000
\end{array}
$$

Step 1 Add the ones, tens, and hundreds.

$$
\begin{array}{r}
1 \\
57,\mathbf{200} \\
+\ 39,\mathbf{824} \\
\hline
024
\end{array}
$$

2 + 8 = 10 hundreds Regroup 10 hundreds as 1 thousand and 0 hundreds.

Step 2 Add the thousands and ten thousands.

$$
\begin{array}{r}
11 \\
\mathbf{57},200 \\
+\ \mathbf{39},824 \\
\hline
97,024
\end{array}
$$

1 + 7 + 9 = 17 thousands Regroup 17 thousands as 7 thousands and 1 ten thousand.

Check for Reasonableness The estimate is 97,000. Since 97,024 is close to the estimate, the answer is reasonable. ✔

So, the total number of bananas and night crawlers was 97,024.

Find each sum. Use estimation to check.

25. 12,962 + 10,845   **26.** 29,380 + 18,253   **27.** 36,458 + 39,784

Data File

The table shows the seating capacities for some events held at an arena.

28. What is the greatest number of people that could attend the circus in two days?

29. To make enough money, the arena must have at least 35,000 people attend an event over two nights. What two different events could give that attendance?

Arena	
Event	**Seating Capacity**
Basketball	17,248
Football	15,924
Circus	15,788
Hockey	15,948
Concert	18,039

Game Time

How Low
Can You Go?

Add Three-Digit Numbers
You will need: spinner

Get Ready!
Players: 2 players

Get Set!
 Divide and label a spinner as shown.

 Make two game sheets.

Go!
 Player 1 spins the spinner and records the digit in any box on his or her game sheet.

 Player 2 spins the spinner and records the digit in any box on his or her game sheet.

 Players repeat taking turns and recording numbers until all boxes are filled.

 Players find the sums of their numbers. The least sum wins.

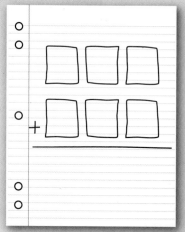

Mid-Chapter Check

Estimate. Round to the indicated place value. (Lesson 1B)

1. 221 + 437; tens

2. 145 + 237; tens

3. 520 + 356; hundreds

4. 6,290 + 2,769; thousands

Add. Check for reasonableness.

(Lesson 1D)

5. 356
     + 622

6. 825
     + 130

7. 720
     + 291

8. 449
     + 289

9. MULTIPLE CHOICE The diagram shows the number of seats in a theater. What is the greatest number of people who can attend a show at one time?

(Lesson 1D)

A. 1,933

B. 1,943

C. 2,033

D. 2,043

Stage

Left Side 914 | Right Side 876

Balcony 253

Tell whether an estimate or an exact answer is needed. Then solve. (Lesson 1E)

10. Cole practices violin for 45 minutes three nights a week. Two other nights he has soccer practice for 25 minutes. About how many minutes does Cole spend practicing each week?

11. Mrs. Barnes bought supplies for the classroom. Estimate the total number of items by rounding to the nearest ten. (Lesson 1B)

235 markers   28 scissors

Find each missing number. Identify the property. (Lesson 1A)

12. 2 + (7 + ▦) = (2 + ▦) + 3

13. ▦ + 4 = 4 + 7

Find each sum. Use estimation to check. (Lesson 1F)

14. 2,267
      +1,037

15. 1,248
      + 7,229

16. MULTIPLE CHOICE The first year Rick owned his car, he drove 9,363 miles. The next year he drove 8,934 miles. How many miles did Rick drive these two years? (Lesson 1F)

F. 27,297 miles   **H.** 18,297 miles

G. 27,307 miles   **J.** 28,307 miles

17. **WRITE MATH** Explain why an addition problem that has 4-digit addends could have a 5-digit sum. (Lesson 1F)

Main Idea

I will estimate differences using rounding and compatible numbers.

Get ConnectED

 3.4 The student will estimate solutions to and solve single-step and multistep problems involving the sum or difference of two whole numbers, each 9,999 or less, with or without regrouping. **3.1** The student will **b)** round whole numbers, 9,999 or less, to the nearest ten, hundred, and thousand.

Estimate Differences

When subtracting, just as in addition, you do not always need an exact answer.

REAL-WORLD EXAMPLE   Round to Tens and Hundreds

1 **MUSEUM** **A museum has 237 works of art on its first floor. The second floor has 349 works of art. *About* how many more works of art are found on the second floor?**

Estimate 349 − 237.
Round, and then subtract.

One Way: **Hundreds Place**	Another Way: **Tens Place**
349 ⟶ 300 − 237 ⟶ − 200 ‾‾‾‾‾ 100	349 ⟶ 350 − 237 ⟶ − 240 ‾‾‾‾‾ 110
There are about 100 more paintings on the second floor.	There are about 110 more paintings on the second floor.

Each estimate is close and reasonable.

Numbers can also be rounded to the nearest thousand.

REAL-WORLD EXAMPLE Round to Thousands

2 **TRAINS** China has more than 3,728 miles of high-speed train tracks. Japan has 1,528 miles of high-speed tracks. About how many more miles of high-speed tracks does China have?

Estimate 3,728 − 1,528.

Step 1 Round each number to the thousands place.

```
                              3,728
←——+———————————+————————•——+→
  3,000       3,500          4,000
```

3,728 rounds to 4,000.

```
                    1,528
←——+———————————•———————————+→
  1,000       1,500        2,000
```

1,528 rounds to 2,000.

Step 2 Subtract.

$$4,000 - 2,000 = 2,000$$

So, China has about 2,000 more miles of tracks.

Compatible numbers are numbers that make it easier to mentally estimate differences.

EXAMPLE Use Compatible Numbers

3 **Estimate 3,728 − 1,528.**

```
  3,728  ⟶     4,000
− 1,528  ⟶   − 1,000
              3,000
```
easy to work with numbers

So, 3,728 − 1,528 can round to 3,000 using compatible numbers.

Remember

There can be more than one reasonable estimate when solving a problem.

✓ CHECK What You Know

Estimate. Round to the given place value. See Examples 1 and 2

1. 488 − 351; tens

2. 1,561 − 305; hundreds

3. 37,215 − 6,972; thousands

Estimate each difference using compatible numbers. See Example 3

4. $7,542 − $3,225

5. 42,811 − 21,510

6. 48,632 − 34,313

7. Belinda is going to buy a car that costs $18,460 new and $15,788 used. Round to the nearest thousand, about how much money would she save if she bought the used car?

8. ⬛ **TALK MATH** To the nearest hundred and to the nearest thousand estimate 1,560 − 829. Compare both estimates to the actual difference. What do you notice?

Practice and Problem Solving

EXTRA *PRACTICE* Begins on page EP2.

Estimate. Round to the given place value. See Examples 1 and 2

9. 986 − 664; tens

10. 550 − 284; hundreds

11. 5,327 − 4,284; thousands

12. 1,836 − 1,648; hundreds

13. 34,281 − 10,829; thousands

14. 27,621 − 8,000; thousands

Estimate each difference using compatible numbers. See Example 3

15. 937 − 338

16. 5,751 − 4,824

17. 5,947 − 3,770

18. 9,584 − 7,341

19. 73,716 − 39,607

20. 78,457 − 52,741

21. Is 400 a reasonable estimate for the difference in attendance on Monday and Wednesday? Explain.

State Fair Attendance	
Monday	13,951
Tuesday	12,475
Wednesday	18,342

22. On Monday, Dylan used a pedometer to record 15,525 steps. On Tuesday, he took 15,806 steps. Rounding to the nearest hundred, about how many more steps did he take on Tuesday?

23. A theater compared weekend ticket sales. Estimate by rounding to the nearest thousand, to find in which month fewer tickets were sold. Explain.

Theater Ticket Sales		
Day	January	February
Saturday	8,924	2,945
Sunday	7,789	1,754

24. Gina's brother is starting college in the fall. Estimate by rounding to the nearest hundred, to find the difference in the total cost between attending College A and College B.

College Costs		
College	Tuition	Other Expenses
College A	$5,491	$10,065
College B	$6,071	$9,075

H.O.T. Problems

25. NUMBER SENSE Fran rounded 4,749 to 4,750. Did she round to the nearest ten, hundred, or thousand? Explain.

26. CHALLENGE Write a subtraction problem in which the estimated difference is 7,000.

27. **WRITE MATH** Explain a situation in which an estimate would be better than an exact number when rounding to estimate the difference.

Test Practice

28. When rounded to the nearest thousand, about how much money will Chun save if he buys the computer on sale? (Lesson 2A)

Giant Computer Sale
$2,895 $950   Sale

A. $1,000   **C.** $3,000

B. $2,000   **D.** $4,000

29. The table shows the attendance at two baseball games.

Day	Attendance
Saturday	4,237
Sunday	3,176

About how many more people attended Saturday's baseball game? (Lesson 2A)

F. 1,000   **H.** 7,413

G. 7,000   **J.** 7,611

Find each sum. Use estimation to check for reasonableness.
(Lesson 1F)

30. 6,532 + 420   **31.** 3,158 + 2,479   **32.** 6,732 + 4,098

33. An auditorium has 448 seats. There are 215 second graders and 231 third graders. Are there enough seats in the auditorium for all the second and third graders? Explain. (Lesson 1E)

34. Last week 1,567 people shopped at a mall. This week 1,809 people shopped. Round to the nearest thousand. About how many people shopped at the mall over the last two weeks? (Lesson 1B)

Find each sum. Identify the property. (Lesson 1A)

35. 8 + (3 + 2) = ▨   **36.** 0 + 5 = ▨   **37.** 2 + 8 = ▨
(8 + 3) + 2 = ▨   8 + 2 = ▨

Explore

Main Idea

I will model subtraction with regrouping.

Materials

base-ten blocks

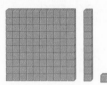

WorkMat 1

Hundreds	Tens	Ones

3.4 The student will estimate solutions to and solve single-step and multistep problems involving the sum or difference of two whole numbers, each 9,999 or less, with or without regrouping.

Subtract Three-Digit Numbers with Regrouping

You can use models to regroup tens and hundreds.

ACTIVITY

Find 244 − 137.

Step 1 Use models.

$$\begin{array}{r} 244 \\ -\ 137 \end{array}$$

Hundreds	Tens	Ones

Step 2 Subtract ones.

$$\begin{array}{r} 3\ 14 \\ 2\cancel{44} \\ -\ 137 \\ \hline 7 \end{array}$$

You cannot take 7 ones from 4 ones.
Regroup 1 ten as 10 ones.
4 ones + 10 ones = 14 ones
Subtract. 14 ones − 7 ones = 7 ones

Hundreds	Tens	Ones

Step 3 Subtract tens.

$$\begin{array}{r} 3\ 14 \\ 2\cancel{44} \\ -\ 137 \\ \hline 07 \end{array}$$

3 tens − 3 tens = 0 tens

Hundreds	Tens	Ones

Step 4 Subtract hundreds.

$$\begin{array}{r} 3\,1\,4 \\ 2\,\cancel{4}\,\cancel{4} \\ -\,1\,3\,7 \\ \hline 1\,0\,7 \end{array}$$

2 hundreds − 1 hundred = 1 hundred

Hundreds	Tens	Ones

So, 244 − 137 = 107.

Step 5 Addition and Subtraction are inverse operations. They *undo* each other. Use addition to check a subtraction problem.

─── same ───

$$\begin{array}{r} 244 \\ -\,137 \\ \hline 107 \end{array} \qquad \begin{array}{r} 107 \\ +\,137 \\ \hline 244 \end{array}$$

The answer is correct. ✔

Think About It

1. In Step 2, why did you regroup 1 ten as 10 ones?

2. What did you notice about the tens in Step 3 when you subtracted them?

Practice and Apply It

Use models to subtract. Use addition to check.

4. 181 − 93

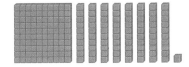

5. 322 − 148

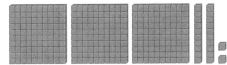

6. 342 − 179

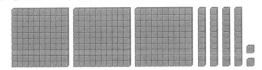

7. 212 − 123

8.
$$\begin{array}{r} 328 \\ -\,19 \\ \hline \end{array}$$

9.
$$\begin{array}{r} 308 \\ -\,125 \\ \hline \end{array}$$

10.
$$\begin{array}{r} 437 \\ -\,243 \\ \hline \end{array}$$

11.
$$\begin{array}{r} 513 \\ -\,155 \\ \hline \end{array}$$

12. **WRITE MATH** Explain when to regroup in subtraction.

Main Idea

I will subtract three-digit numbers with regrouping.

3.4 The student will estimate solutions to and solve single-step and multistep problems involving the sum or difference of two whole numbers, each 9,999 or less, with or without regrouping.

Subtract Three-Digit Numbers with Regrouping

In the Explore Activity, you learned to regroup tens. Regrouping hundreds works the same way.

REAL-WORLD EXAMPLE

Subtract with Regrouping

1 **CRAFTS** Liseta, Will, and Alano each have craft paper. How many more sheets does Will have than Liseta?

Find 265 − 79.

Craft Paper	
Name	**Sheets**
Liseta	79
Will	265
Alano	128

Step 1   Subtract ones.

$$\begin{array}{r} 5\;15 \\ 26\!\!\!/5 \\ -\;79 \\ \hline 6 \end{array}$$

You cannot take 9 ones from 5 ones.
Regroup 1 ten as 10 ones.
5 ones + 10 ones = 15 ones
Subtract. 15 ones − 9 ones = 6 ones

Step 2   Subtract tens.

$$\begin{array}{r} 15 \\ 15\;15 \\ 26\!\!\!/5 \\ -\;79 \\ \hline 86 \end{array}$$

You cannot take 7 tens from 5 tens.
Regroup 1 hundred as 10 tens.
5 tens + 10 tens = 15 tens
Subtract. 15 tens − 7 tens = 8 tens

Step 3   Subtract hundreds.

$$\begin{array}{r} 15 \\ 1\;5\;15 \\ 26\!\!\!/5 \\ -\;79 \\ \hline 186 \end{array}$$

Subtract. 1 hundred − 0 hundreds = 1 hundred

So, Will has 186 more sheets of craft paper than Liseta.

② **AIRPLANE** Denzel wants to buy a remote control airplane for $179. He has $350. How much money will he have left?

Find $350 − $179.

Step 1 Subtract ones.

$$\overset{410}{\$3\cancel{5}\cancel{0}}$$
$$\$179$$
$$\overline{1}$$

You cannot take $9 from $0.

Regroup $50 as $40 + $10.

Subtract. $10 − $9 = $1

Step 2 Subtract tens and hundreds.

$$\overset{14}{\overset{2\cancel{4}10}{\$\cancel{3}\cancel{5}\cancel{0}}}$$
$$-\ \$179$$
$$\overline{\$171}$$

You cannot take $70 from $40.

Regroup $300 as $200 + $100.

Subtract. $140 − $70 = $70

$200 − $100 = $100

Place the dollar sign before the difference.

Check

same

$$\begin{array}{c} \$350 \\ -\ \$179 \\ \hline \$171 \end{array} \qquad \begin{array}{c} \$171 \\ +\ \$179 \\ \hline \$350 \end{array}$$

The answer is correct. ✔

So, Denzel will have $171 left.

✓ CHECK **What You Know**

Subtract. Check your answer. See Examples 1 and 2

1. $764
      − $138

2. 458
      − 121

3. $614
      − $457

4. 391 − 178

5. 567 − 142

6. 317 − 198

7. This year, the third grade raised $342 for a dog shelter. Last year, they raised $279. How much more money did they raise this year than last year?

8. **TALK MATH** What happens to the tens when you have to regroup twice when subtracting three-digit numbers?

Subtract. Check your answer. See Examples 1 and 2

9. $687
        − $353

10. $177
        − $94

11. 233
        − 172

12. 884
        − 63

13. $843
        − $187

14. $769
        − $359

15. 267
        − 178

16. 728
        − 259

17. 492 − 383

18. 614 − 270

19. 856 − 637

20. 531 − 499

21. Greta is saving to buy a camera and tripod from the Electronic Store. Mulan is saving to buy a cell phone. How much more money does Greta need to save than Mulan?

The Electronics Store	
Item	**Cost**
Camera	$189
Tripod	$34
Cell Phone	$175

22. Measurement The Bank of America building in Charlotte is 871 feet tall. The One Liberty Place building in Philadelphia is 945 feet tall. How much taller is the One Liberty Place building?

REAL-WORLD PROBLEM SOLVING

Use the bar graph about students who buy their lunch.

23. How many more 3rd graders than 4th graders are buying their lunch?

24. What is the total number of students buying their lunch?

25. The lunchroom holds 150 students at one time. Name two classes that can eat at the same time. Explain.

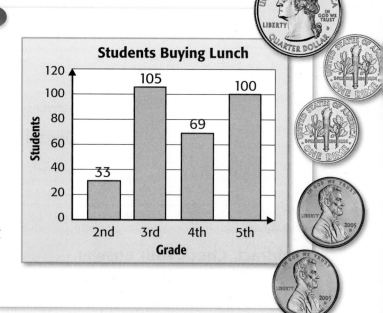

Students Buying Lunch

Algebra Find each missing digit. Use the inverse operation as needed.

26. 61■
        − 417
        ■02

27. ■99
        − 1■9
        750

28. 798
        − ■97
        4■1

29. 989
        − 77■
        ■18

30. NUMBER SENSE When Federico subtracted 308 from 785, he got 477. To check his answer he added 308 and 785. What did he do wrong?

31. **WRITE MATH** Explain how you would check a subtraction problem to see if the answer is correct.

Use the information to solve the problems.

32. If Morgan, Jacob, and Nate put their money together to buy one prize for Jamie, can they afford the basketball hoop? Explain.

33. How much money will they have left after they buy the basketball hoop?

Test Practice

34. Mr. Neal's family will drive 1,008 miles on vacation. They have traveled 641 miles so far. Round to the nearest hundred. About how many more miles will they drive? (Lesson 2A)

   A. 300 miles   **C.** 1,400 miles

   B. 400 miles   **D.** 1,700 miles

35. Ty will hike 281 yards to get to the end of the trail. His friend is 187 yards from the end. What is the difference in the distance the boys have yet to walk? (Lesson 2C)

   F. 94 yards   **H.** 106 yards

   G. 104 yards   **J.** 194 yards

Main Idea

I will subtract four-digit numbers.

 *Get Connect*ED

 3.4 The student will estimate solutions to and solve single-step and multistep problems involving the sum or difference of two whole numbers, each 9,999 or less, with or without regrouping.

Subtract Four-Digit Numbers

Subtracting greater numbers is similar to subtracting smaller numbers.

🏃 ✍ **REAL-WORLD EXAMPLE**   **Use Paper and Pencil**

1 **MEASUREMENT** The table shows the height of four waterfalls. What is the difference in height between Ribbon Falls and Kalambo Falls?

Find 1,612 − 726.

Waterfalls

Name	Height (ft)
Ribbon	1,612
Angel	3,212
Yosemite	2,425
Kalambo	726

Step 1 Subtract ones.

$$
\begin{array}{r}
0\,1\,2 \\
1{,}6\cancel{1}\cancel{2} \\
-\ 726 \\
\hline
6
\end{array}
$$

You cannot take 6 ones from 2 ones.
Regroup 1 ten as 10 ones.
2 ones + 10 ones = 12 ones
12 ones − 6 ones = 6 ones

Step 2 Subtract tens.

$$
\begin{array}{r}
10 \\
5\,\cancel{0}\,12 \\
1{,}\cancel{6}\cancel{1}\cancel{2} \\
-\ 726 \\
\hline
86
\end{array}
$$

You cannot take 2 tens from 0 tens.
Regroup 1 hundred as 10 tens.
0 tens + 10 tens = 10 tens
10 tens − 2 tens = 8 tens

Step 3 Subtract hundreds and thousands.

$$
\begin{array}{r}
15\,10 \\
0\ \cancel{5}\,\cancel{0}\,12 \\
\cancel{1}{,}\cancel{6}\cancel{1}\cancel{2} \\
-\ 726 \\
\hline
886
\end{array}
$$

You cannot take 7 hundreds from 5 hundreds.
Regroup 1 thousand as 10 hundreds.
5 hundreds + 10 hundreds = 15 hundreds
15 hundreds − 7 hundreds = 8 hundreds
0 thousands − 0 thousands = 0 thousands

So, the difference in height is 886 feet.

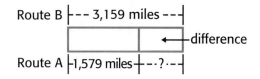 **REAL-WORLD EXAMPLE**   Use a Bar Diagram

2 **BIKING** The bar diagram shows the length of two popular cross-country bike routes. How many more miles is Route B than Route A?

Route B |--- 3,159 miles ---|

| | | ← difference

Route A |-1,579 miles-|--?--|

 **Remember**

Thinking of a related addition fact can help you subtract.

Find 3,159 − 1,579.

Step 1 Subtract ones.

$$\begin{array}{r} 3,15\mathbf{9} \\ -\ 1,57\mathbf{9} \\ \hline 0 \end{array}$$

Step 2 Subtract tens.

$$\begin{array}{r} ^{0\,15} \\ 3,1\cancel{5}9 \\ -\ 1,579 \\ \hline 80 \end{array}$$

Step 3 Subtract hundreds and thousands.

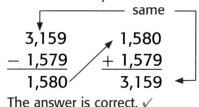

$$\begin{array}{r} ^{10} \\ ^{2}\ \cancel{0}15 \\ \cancel{3},\cancel{1}59 \\ -\ 1,579 \\ \hline 1,580 \end{array}$$

Check Check your answer.

	same
3,159	1,580
− 1,579	+ 1,579
1,580	3,159

The answer is correct. ✓

So, Route B is 1,580 miles longer.

✓ **CHECK** **What You Know**

Subtract. Check your answer. See Examples 1 and 2

1. $7,371
      − $365

2. $3,457
      − $649

3. 2,421
      − 865

4. 7,234
      − 6,487

5. Cell phones were invented in 1983. The TV was invented 56 years before that. What year was the TV invented?

6. **TALK MATH** Explain the steps to find 8,422 − 5,995.

Lesson 2D Subtract to Solve Problems **97**

Subtract. Check your answer. See Examples 1 and 2

7. 1,392
   − 238

8. 3,298
   − 858

9. 3,475
   − 1,267

10. 3,665
   − 1,643

11. $3,421
   − $1,049

12. $5,452
   − $1,187

13. $4,875
   − $3,168

14. $6,182
   − $581

15. 6,340
   − 3,451

16. 5,123
   − 2,736

17. $1,856
   − $969

18. $4,137
   − $1,562

19. Of the 2,159 pre-sold concert tickets, only 1,947 tickets were used. How many tickets were not used?

20. Measurement The distance around a rectangular swimming pool is 300 yards. What are the measurements of the remaining three sides?

21. To earn money for a trip, band members had to sell 1,590 boxes of popcorn. So far they have sold 779 boxes. How many more boxes do they have to sell?

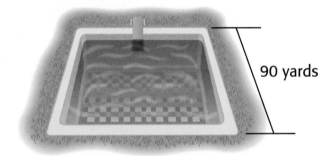

90 yards

Algebra Compare. Use >, <, or =.

22. 1,543 − 984 ● 5,193 − 4,893

23. 2,006 − 781 ● 5,224 − 3,999

24. 8,937 − 3,038 ● 3,598 − 1,084

25. 5,070 − 2,345 ● 8,765 − 1,965

H.O.T. Problems

26. OPEN ENDED Explain the importance of checking your subtraction with addition or estimation.

27. CHALLENGE Write a subtraction problem in which the difference is 1,735.

28. ✍ **WRITE MATH** Explain how subtracting four-digit numbers is like subtracting three-digit numbers.

More About **Subtracting Greater Numbers** . . . .

When subtracting greater numbers, it is important to line up the digits in their correct columns.

REAL-WORLD EXAMPLE Subtract Greater Numbers

SCULPTURE A group of students used 12,212 cans of food to create a sculpture. Another group made a sculpture using 6,403 cans. What is the difference in the number of cans used for the sculptures?

Find $12,212 - 6,403$.

Step 1 Subtract ones and tens.

```
   012
 12,2\12
- 6,403
   09
```

Step 2 Subtract hundreds.

```
 112012
 1 2,2\1\2
- 6,403
   ,809
```

Step 3 Subtract thousands and ten thousands.

```
    11
  0\1 12012
  1\2,2\1\2
 - 6,403
   5,809
```

Check

```
 12,212          5,809
- 6,403        + 6,403
 5,809          12,212
```

The answer is correct. ✓

So, there was a difference of 5,809 cans used.

Subtract. Use addition to check.

| 29. | 12,962 − 10,845 | 30. | 18,327 − 15,709 | 31. | 53,458 − 36,784 |

32. $94,244 - 26,403$ **33.** $63,717 - 41,804$ **34.** $82,956 - 38,919$

35. Measurement Mount Everest has an elevation of 29,035 feet. A climber started at Base Camp and hiked 2,300 feet. How much farther does the climber have before reaching the top of the mountain?

Top (29,035 ft)
X Base Camp (17,600 ft)

The Sounds of the Symphony

The Los Angeles Philharmonic is a popular symphony orchestra. The orchestra has four instrument families—woodwinds, strings, brass, and percussion.

A conductor leads the orchestra because there are over 100 musicians.

The Los Angeles Philharmonic plays at Walt Disney Concert Hall. Ticket prices are based on how close the seats are to the orchestra.

Los Angeles Philharmonic

Instrument Family	Number of Musicians
Percussion	4
Brass	15
Woodwinds	19
Strings	65

Friday Series

Seats	Ticket Price
A	$160
B	$93
C	$67
D	$48

Did You Know?

The oldest flute is over 43,000 years old.

Real-World Math

Use the information on the previous page to solve each problem.

1. How many more woodwind musicians are there than percussion musicians?

2. Thirty-two of the string musicians play the violin. How many string musicians are not violinists?

3. What is the total number of musicians? How many musicians do not play brass instuments?

4. On Saturdays, the cost of a ticket in section D is $53. How much money do you save by going to the orchestra on Friday instead of Saturday?

5. Estimate the difference in the price of a ticket in section B and a ticket for a seat in section D.

6. If you paid for a ticket in section C with a $100-bill, how much change would you get?

7. How many musicians do not play brass or woodwind instruments?

8. Estimate the cost of each ticket to the nearest ten. Would it cost less to buy a ticket in section A and a ticket in section D or a ticket in section B and a ticket in section C?

Main Idea
I will subtract across zeros.

3.4 The student will estimate solutions to and solve single-step and multistep problems involving the sum or difference of two whole numbers, each 9,999 or less, with or without regrouping.

Subtract Across Zeros

Sometimes before you can begin subtracting, you have to regroup more than one time.

REAL-WORLD EXAMPLE Subtract Across Zeros

① **WATERMELONS** A large box of watermelons weighs 300 pounds. A smaller box weighs 134 pounds. What is the difference in the weight of the two boxes?

You need to find $300 - 134$.

Step 1 Regroup.

$$\begin{array}{r} {\scriptstyle 210} \\ {\cancel{3}\cancel{0}0} \\ -134 \\ \hline \end{array}$$

You cannot take 4 ones from 0 ones.
Regroup.
There are no tens to regroup.
Regroup 3 hundreds as 2 hundreds and 10 tens.

Step 2 Regroup.

$$\begin{array}{r} {\scriptstyle 9} \\ {\scriptstyle 2\cancel{10}10} \\ {\cancel{3}\cancel{0}\cancel{0}} \\ -134 \\ \hline \end{array}$$

Regroup 10 tens as 9 tens and 10 ones.

Step 3 Subtract.

$$\begin{array}{r} {\scriptstyle 9} \\ {\scriptstyle 2\cancel{10}10} \\ {\cancel{3}\cancel{0}\cancel{0}} \\ -134 \\ \hline 166 \end{array}$$

Subtract the ones, tens, and hundreds.

Check Use addition to check.

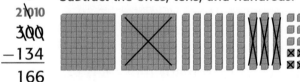
——Same——

$$\begin{array}{r} 300 \\ -134 \\ \hline 166 \end{array} \qquad \begin{array}{r} 166 \\ +134 \\ \hline 300 \end{array}$$

The answer is correct. ✔

So, the difference in weight is 166 pounds.

② **MONEY** A school bought music equipment for $5,004. The drums cost $2,815. How much money was spent on the other music equipment?

Step 1 Subtract ones.

```
    9  9
 4 10 10 14
$ 5, 0 0 4
− $ 2, 8 1 5
          9
```

Regroup 1 thousand as 10 hundreds. Regroup 1 hundred as 10 tens. Regroup 1 ten as 10 ones. 14 − 5 = 9

Step 2 Subtract tens.

```
    9  9
 4 10 10 14
$ 5, 0 0 4
− $ 2, 8 1 5
        8 9
```
9 − 1 = 8

Step 3 Subtract hundreds.

```
    9  9
 4 10 10 14
$ 5, 0 0 4
− $ 2, 8 1 5
      1 8 9
```
9 − 8 = 1

Step 4 Subtract thousands.

```
    9  9
 4 10 10 14
$ 5, 0 0 4
− $ 2, 8 1 5
$ 2, 1 8 9
```
4 − 2 = 2

Check $2,189 + $2,815 = $5,004. The answer is correct. ✔

So, $2,189 was spent on the other music equipment.

✓ CHECK What You Know

Subtract. Use addition to check. See Examples 1 and 2

1. 309
      − 57

2. 608
      − 45

3. $707
      − $535

4. 903
      − 791

5. 2,006
      − 536

6. $8,005
      − $4,423

7. On Saturday, there were 1,000 balloons at a hot air balloon festival. On Sunday, there were 350 balloons. How many more balloons were there on Saturday than on Sunday?

8. **TALK MATH** Explain where you would start regrouping to find the difference in the problem below.
66,000
− 23,475

Subtract. Use addition to check. See Examples 1 and 2

9. 408
    − 36

10. 805
    − 75

11. 604
    − 492

12. $502
    − $130

13. $708 − $222

14. 809 − 566

15. $8,001 − $6,930

16. 9,006 − 7,474

17. 8,007 − 4,836

18. $9,003 − $5,295

19. 30,070 − 14,021

20. Ava guessed that there were 1,007 marbles in a jar. There were actually 972 marbles. How far off was Ava's guess?

21. **Measurement** Dillan hiked one and a half miles, or 7,920 feet. Sato hiked two miles, or 10,560 feet. How many more feet did Sato hike?

For Exercises 22–24, use the art to the right.

22. How much more does the bike cost than the skates?

23. Anton purchased the bike. He gave the clerk one $100-bill, one $50-bill, and one $20-bill. How much change should Anton receive?

24. Suppose Anton decided to purchase the skates also, after he gave the clerk his money. How much more money does Anton need to give the clerk?

$29

$153

H.O.T. Problems

25. **OPEN ENDED** Identify a number that results in a 3-digit number when 35,475 is subtracted from it.

26. **FIND THE ERROR** Eva is solving the subtraction problem shown. Find and correct her mistake.

    5,300
  − 4,547
    1,853

27. **WRITE MATH** Explain how you would regroup to subtract 3,406 from 5,000.

28. The table shows the number of visitors to an amusement park over 2 weeks.

Week	Visitors
Week 1	34,007
Week 2	21,829

About how many more visitors were at the park during Week 1? (Lesson 2A)

A. 12,000   **C.** 13,000

B. 12,912   **D.** 14,000

29. Four of the longest rivers in the world are listed below.

River	Miles
Nile, Africa	4,180
Amazon, Peru	3,912
Mississippi, USA	3,710
Yangtze, China	3,602

How much longer is the Nile River than the Yangtze River? (Lesson 2D)

F. 268 miles   **H.** 578 miles

G. 470 miles   **J.** 1,588 miles

30. Ms. Bennett had two choices for vacation.

BEACH TRIP $3,459

SKI TRIP $1,982

About how much more does the beach vacation cost? (Lesson 2D)

A. $2,000   **C.** $1,000

B. $1,500   **D.** $500

31. Yesterday's attendance at a baseball game was 4,237. Today's attendance was 3,176. What was the attendance for the two days? (Lesson 1F)

F. 7,313

G. 7,403

H. 7,413

J. 7,611

Spiral Review ....

Subtract. Check your answer. (Lesson 2D)

32. 2,354 − 136   **33.** 3,198 − 289   **34.** 4,574 − 1,377

Estimate. Round to the given place value. (Lesson 2A)

35. 832 − 225; tens   **36.** 1,356 − 278; hundreds   **37.** 46,207 − 5,581; thousands

38. Mrs. Vallez bought 2 packages of 127 stickers each. She added these to the 219 stickers she already had. How many stickers does she have now? (Lesson 1D)

Problem-Solving Investigation

Main Idea I will choose the best strategy to solve a problem.

P.S.I. TEAM +

MIRANDA: Last year, our school district collected 3,179 cans of food. This year, one school collected 938 cans, another collected 737 cans, and my school collected 1,006 cans.

YOUR MISSION: Find how many more cans are needed to pass last year's total.

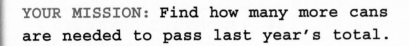

Understand

You know last year's total. You also know the number of cans three schools have collected so far this year. Find how many more cans are needed to pass last year's total.

Plan

Add to find the number of cans collected so far. Then, subtract to find the number still needed.

Solve

Add

```
      2
    938  ⎫
  1 737  ⎬ three schools
+ 1,006  ⎭
  2,681  this year's total,
         so far
```

Subtract

```
 2 10 17
  ̶3̶,̶1̶7̶9      last year's total
- 2,681      this year's total, so far
    498 + 1  difference
```

498 cans are needed to collect the same as last year.
So, 498 + 1, or 499, cans are needed to pass last year's total.

Check

You can check by adding. Since 2,681 + 499 = 3,180, the answer is correct. ✓

🏔 **3.4** The student will estimate solutions to and solve single-step and multistep problems involving the sum or difference of two whole numbers, each 9,999 or less, with or without regrouping.

- Solve a simpler problem.
- Choose an operation.
- Estimate or exact answer.

Use any strategy to solve each problem.

1. Some children took part in a penny hunt. About how many more pennies did Pat find than each of his two friends?

Penny Hunt	
Cynthia	133
Pat	182
Garcia	125

2. The attendance at a basketball game was 15,738. Records show that 6,385 people came through Gate A and 3,279 people came through Gate B. How many people came through Gate C, the last gate?

3. The library received 155 new books today. If there are now 7,842 books, how many were there before the new books arrived?

4. Mrs. Carpenter received a bill for $134 for car repairs. Should she pay an estimated amount or should she pay the exact amount? Explain your reasoning.

5. How much will all of the flowers cost?

Mr. White's Garden Shop		
Flower	Quantity	Cost Each
Daisy	7	$5
Rose	3	$10
Lily	4	$6
Petunia	9	$4
Marigold	9	$3

6. **Measurement** It took Kenya 1 hour and 37 minutes to ride in the car from her aunt's house to her grandmother's. Then she rode 3 hours and 14 minutes to her mom's house. To the nearest hundred, about how many minutes were spent riding in the car?

7. Hale has $20. He buys himself and two friends each a slice of pizza, a small salad, and water. How much money does he have left?

LUNCH MENU
SMALL SALAD $1
LARGE SALAD $2
SLICE OF PIZZA $2
GRILLED CHEESE ... $2
MILK $1
WATER $1

8. Mr. Roth's car cost $17,681. Mr. Randall's car cost $1,406 more than Mr. Roth's. How much did the cars cost together?

9. **WRITE MATH** Look at Exercise 8. Give an example of an answer that is not reasonable. Explain your reasoning.

Chapter Study Guide and Review

FOLDABLES®
Study Organizer

Be sure the following Key Concepts are noted in your Foldable.

Key Concepts

- Estimate sums and differences.

    (Lessons 1 and 2)

$$
\begin{array}{r}
566 \rightarrow 570 \\
+\,211 \rightarrow +\,210 \\
\hline
780
\end{array}
\qquad
\begin{array}{r}
735 \rightarrow 740 \\
-\,227 \rightarrow -\,230 \\
\hline
510
\end{array}
$$

- Add and subtract with regrouping.

    (Lessons 1 and 2)

$$
\begin{array}{r}
{\scriptstyle 1\ 1} \\
474 \\
+\,237 \\
\hline
711
\end{array}
\qquad
\begin{array}{r}
{\scriptstyle 3\ 1016} \\
4\!\!\!\backslash\!16 \\
-\,277 \\
\hline
139
\end{array}
$$

- Addition properties and subtraction rules help you add and subtract. (Lesson 1)

Commutative Property of Addition

$$4 + 3 = 7 \qquad 3 + 4 = 7$$

Identity Property of Addition

$$6 + 0 = 6 \qquad 0 + 6 = 6$$

Associative Property of Addition

$$(2 + 5) + 1 = 2 + (5 + 1)$$

Key Vocabulary

Associative Property of Addition

Commutative Property of Addition

compatible numbers

estimate

Identity Property of Addition

regroup

Vocabulary Check

Choose the vocabulary word that completes each sentence.

1. _____?_____ are numbers that are easy to add or subtract.

2. When you do not need an exact answer, you can _____?_____.

3. The _____?_____ states that grouping the addends does not change the sum.

4. To rename a number using place value is to _____?_____.

5. $2 + 4 = 6$ and $4 + 2 = 6$ is an example of the _____?_____.

6. The _____?_____ states that the sum of any number and zero is the number.

7. To find an answer that is close to the exact answer is to _____?_____.

Multi-Part Lesson Review

Lesson 1 — Add to Solve Problems

Algebra: Addition Properties (Lesson 1A)

Find each sum. Identify the property.

8. $0 + 10 = \blacksquare$

9. $11 + 2 = \blacksquare$
$2 + 11 = \blacksquare$

10. Algebra Find the missing number. Identify the property.

$$(6 + 9) + 5 = 6 + (\blacksquare + 5)$$

Find each sum mentally.

11.
$$\begin{array}{r} 4 \\ 6 \\ + 0 \\ \hline \end{array}$$

12.
$$\begin{array}{r} 8 \\ 6 \\ + 2 \\ \hline \end{array}$$

EXAMPLE 1

$2 + 7 = \blacksquare$ and $7 + 2 = \blacksquare$

The sum is 9. The order does not change the sum. This is the Commutative Property of Addition.

EXAMPLE 2

$8 + 0 = \blacksquare$

The sum is 8. The sum of any number and 0 is that number. This is the Identity Property of Addition.

Estimate Sums (Lesson 1B)

Estimate. Round to the indicated place value.

13. $765 + 121$; tens

14. $2,210 + 1,909$; thousands

Estimate. Use compatible numbers.

15. $333 + 585$

16. $4,128 + 470$

17. $311 + 681$

18. $970 + 241$

19. There are about 2,000 earthquakes each year in Yellowstone National Park. Is this an estimate or an exact number? Explain.

EXAMPLE 3

An artist created a piece of art with 675 round glass beads. There are also 179 beads in the shape of a heart. About how many beads are there altogether?

Estimate $675 + 179$. Round each number to the nearest hundred. Then add.

$$\begin{array}{r} 675 \longrightarrow 700 \\ + 179 \longrightarrow + 200 \\ \hline 900 \end{array}$$

So, there are about 900 beads.

Three-Digit Addition (Lesson 1D)

Add. Check for reasonableness.

20. 377
      + 26

21. 657
      + 245

22. $675
      +$255

23. $325
      +$256

24. Flavio and Felix bought airline tickets for $213. Their rental car and hotel are $378. How much will they spend on these vacation expenses?

25. Measurement One year Ithaca had a record snowfall of 124 inches. The next year it snowed 117 inches. What was the total snowfall for the two years?

EXAMPLE 4

Judy read one book with 175 pages and another with 409 pages. How many pages did Judy read in total?

Find 175 + 409. Add the ones.

```
  1
  175      5 ones + 9 ones = 14 ones
+ 409      14 ones = 1 ten + 4 ones
    4
```

Add the tens. Then hundreds.

```
  1
  175      1 ten + 7 tens = 8 tens
+ 409      1 hundred + 4 hundreds =
  584      5 hundreds
```

So, 175 + 409 = 584.

Judy read 584 pages.

Problem-Solving Skill: Estimate or Exact Answer (Lesson 1E)

Tell whether an estimate or exact answer is needed. Then solve.

26. For a dance team, Viviana needs $250 to join and $75 for her uniform. How much money does Viviana need?

27. To get to school each day, Yodi travels 53 minutes each way. About how many minutes does he travel to and from school over five days?

EXAMPLE 5

The Bonilla family spent $1,679 on their vacation. The Turner family spent $983. About how much money did the families spend together?

Estimate. Then add.

```
  $1,679  ⟶    $1,700
+ $983    ⟶  + $1,000
               $2,700
```

The families spent about $2,700.

Add Four-Digit Numbers (Lesson 1F)

Find each sum. Use estimation to check for reasonableness.

28. 9,432 + 1,360   **29.** 7,500 + 2,239

30. Mrs. Ruth donated $1,250 to a charity. Her sister donated $595. What is the total donation?

31. How much will two of each item cost?

 $444

 $587

EXAMPLE 6

Find 3,127 + 1,260.

Estimate

$$3,127 \longrightarrow 3,000$$
$$+ 1,260 \longrightarrow + 1,000$$
$$\overline{4,000}$$

Use Mental Math

$$3,127 = 3,000 + 100 + 20 + 7$$
$$+ 1,260 = 1,000 + 200 + 60 + 0$$
$$\overline{4,000 + 300 + 80 + 7 = 4,387}$$

Check for Reasonableness

4,387 is close to 4,000. The answer is reasonable. ✔

So, 3,127 + 1,260 = 4,387.

Lesson 2 ## Subtract to Solve Problems

Estimate Differences (Lesson 2A)

Estimate. Round to the given place.

32. 8,728 − 6,493; thousands

33. 7,659 − 696; hundreds

34. **Measurement** Derek is 3,285 days old. Tonisha is 4,015 days old. About how much older is Tonisha?

EXAMPLE 7

Estimate 7,045 − 2,871. Round to the nearest thousand.

$$7,045 \longrightarrow 7,000$$
$$- 2,871 \longrightarrow - 3,000$$
$$\overline{4,000}$$

So, 7,045 − 2,871 is about 4,000.

Subtract Three-Digit Numbers with Regrouping (Lesson 2C)

Subtract. Check your answer.

35. $431 − $252   **36.** 767 − 178

37. **Measurement** There are 365 days in one year. There were 173 sunny days this year. How many days were not sunny?

EXAMPLE 8

Find 233 − 198.

$$
\begin{array}{r}
{\scriptstyle 1\,12\,13} \\
\cancel{233} \\
- 198 \\
\hline
35
\end{array}
\qquad
\begin{array}{r}
{\scriptstyle 1} \\
35 \\
+ 198 \\
\hline
233
\end{array}
$$

Check 35 + 198 = 233 ✔

Subtract Four-Digit Numbers (Lesson 2D)

Subtract. Check your answer.

38. 4,246 − 1,781   **39.** 7,624 − 5,937

40. In which month were fewer raffle tickets sold? Explain.

TV Raffle Ticket Sales		
Day	March	April
Saturday	3,129	4,103
Sunday	3,977	3,001

EXAMPLE 9

Find 5,236 − 2,477.

```
   1112
  4 1216
   5,236          1 1 1
 − 2,477          2,759
   2,759        + 2,477
                  5,236
```

Check 2,759 + 2,477 = 5,236. ✓

Subtract Across Zeros (Lesson 2E)

Subtract. Use addition to check.

41. $4,006
   − $895

42. 9,000
   − 206

43. 28,600 − 11,165

44. Mr. Acosta had $2,003 in his bank account. He bought a laptop computer for $1,299. How much does he have left?

EXAMPLE 10

Find 2,005 − 593.

Step 1 Subtract ones.

```
   2,005
  − 593
      2
```

Step 2 Regroup thousands, hundreds, and tens. Then subtract.

```
     9
   1 1010
   2,005
  − 593
   1,412
```

Check 1,412 + 593 = 2,005

So, 2,005 − 593 = 1,412. ✓

Problem-Solving Investigation: Choose a Strategy (Lesson 2F)

Use any strategy to solve each problem.

45. Measurement Lunch period is 40 minutes. It takes 3 minutes for each child to get through the lunch line. How much time will be left after seven students go through the lunch line?

46. The Williams family saved $12,000 to make home improvements. They spent $7,320 to update their kitchen. How much money is left?

EXAMPLE 11

Students need to make 425 get well cards. Second graders made 75 cards and third graders made 90. How many cards still need to be made?

Step 1

Find the total cards made.

```
   75  second grade
 + 90  third grade total
  165
```

Step 2

Find the number still needed.

```
   312
   425  number needed
 − 165  number made
   260  number to be
        made
```

So, 260 cards still need to be made.

Practice Chapter Test

Tell whether each statement is *true* or *false*.

1. Always start with the ones place when adding.

2. When asked to find the sum, you are asked to subtract.

3. Use the table to solve. How many tickets were purchased the last two weeks?

Dolphin Watching Tickets

Week	Child Tickets	Adult Tickets
1	173	106
2	121	115

4. Rusty's book has 285 pages. He read 24 pages on Monday, 37 pages on Tuesday, and 41 pages on Wednesday. How many pages does he have left to read?

5. MULTIPLE CHOICE What is the sum of 12,048 and 37,251?

  A. 4,797   **C.** 89,399

  B. 49,299   **D.** 99,289

Estimate. Round to the given place.

6. 5,364 + 482; hundreds

7. 9,325 − 8,236; thousands

Tell whether an estimate or an exact answer is needed. Then solve.

8. Mrs. Murphey had $92. She bought a watch. Now she has $36. How much was the watch?

9. There are three office buildings on a block. About how many offices are in the three buildings?

Number of Offices by Building		
A	B	C
2,114	3,112	2,295

Complete each number sentence. Identify the property or rule used.

10. ■ + 73 + 79 = 73 + 79 + 65

11. ■ − 389 = 0

12. 2 + (3 + 9) = (2 + ■) + 9

Subtract. Use addition or estimation to check.

13. 4,005 − 273   **14.** 6,007 − 317

15. MULTIPLE CHOICE Val spent $378 at the mall. Her sister spent $291. Round to the nearest hundred, about how much did the sisters spend altogether?

  F. $700   **H.** $600

  G. $669   **J.** $400

16. WRITE MATH Explain how you can check to see if a difference is reasonable when subtracting.

TEST EXAMPLE

On a car trip, Jerry counted 125 white cars. Marla counted 67 red cars. How many more cars did Jerry count?

A. 58   **C.** 68

B. 62   **D.** 192

TEST-TAKING TIP

You can check the reasonableness of your sum or difference by first estimating.

Read the Test Question

You need to find the difference between 125 and 67.

Solve the Test Question

Find $125 - 67$.

Estimate

$$125 \longrightarrow 130$$
$$\underline{-67 \longrightarrow -70}$$
$$60$$

Subtract, regrouping when needed.

$$\begin{array}{r} \overset{11}{} \\ 0\,\overset{}{1}5 \\ \cancel{125} \\ -\ 67 \\ \hline 58 \end{array}$$

Check 58 is close to the estimate 60. The answer is reasonable. ✔

The answer is A.

Read each question. Then fill in the correct answer on the answer sheet provided by your teacher or on a separate sheet of paper.

1. Last year, the theater spent $7,625. This year the theater will spend $9,910. How much more will the theater spend this year?

    A. $2,285   **C.** $2,325

    B. $2,315   **D.** $2,395

2. What number makes this number sentence true?

$$2 + 5 + 8 = 2 + 8 + \blacksquare$$

    F. 2   **H.** 8

    G. 5   **J.** 15

3. If 84,702 pennies were placed in a line, the line would stretch a mile. How many pennies are needed to stretch two miles?

A. 68,404 **C.** 168,404

B. 69,404 **D.** 169,404

4. The River School sold 3,428 banners. The Gibson School sold 4,636 banners. How many banners were sold in all?

F. 7,252 **H.** 7,954

G. 7,952 **J.** 8,064

5. Which number is 10,000 less than 83,298?

A. 73,298 **C.** 83,298

B. 74,298 **D.** 84,298

6. Each year the Garden Club collects $1,200. So far, the club has collected $858. How much more does the club need to collect?

F. $342 **H.** $448

G. $352 **J.** $458

7. Estimate the difference to the nearest thousand.

$$2,812 - 1,356$$

A. 1,400 **C.** 1,500

B. 1,575 **D.** 2,000

8. The table shows the number of coupons mailed out by four large grocery stores.

Grocery Store Coupons	
Store	**Number of Coupons**
Fast Mart	35,411
Saver Center	35,408
Gardens	35,416
Big Value	35,420

Which store mailed out the most coupons?

F. Big Value **H.** Gardens

G. Fast Mart **J.** Saver Center

9. Which of the following is an example of the Commutative Property of Addition?

A. $421 + 0 = 421$

B. $421 + (76 + 4) = (421 + 76) + 4$

C. $421 + 76 = 76 + 421$

D. $421 - 0 = 421$

NEED EXTRA HELP?									
If You Missed Question . . .	1	2	3	4	5	6	7	8	9
Go to Chapter-Lesson . . .	2-2D	2-1A	2-1F	2-1F	2-2D	2-2E	2-2A	1-2B	2-1A
For help with . . .	SOL 3.4	SOL 3.4	SOL 3.4	SOL 3.4	SOL 3.4	SOL 3.4	SOL 3.1b	SOL 3.1c	SOL 3.20b

CHAPTER 3

Model Multiplication and Division Problems

connectED.mcgraw-hill.com

Investigate

 Animations

 Vocabulary

 Math Songs

 Multilingual eGlossary

Learn

 Personal Tutor

 Virtual Manipulatives

 Audio

 Foldables

Practice

 Self-Check Practice

 eGames

 Worksheets

 Assessment

The ☆BIG Idea

How can I develop an understanding of multiplication and division and their basic facts?

FOLDABLES
Study Organizer

Make this Foldable to help you organize information about multiplication and division concepts and facts. Begin with four sheets of $8\frac{1}{2}'' \times 11''$ paper.

Review Vocabulary

repeated addition *suma repetida* an addition sentence that shows adding the same number over and over again

$$4 + 4 + 4 + 4 + 4 = 20$$

Key Vocabulary

English	Español
multiply	multiplicar
product	producto
divide	dividir
quotient	cociente
inverse operations	operación inversa

When Will I Use This?

Nate in Pizza Puzzle

Your Turn!
You will solve this problem in the chapter.

Are You Ready for the Chapter?

You have two options for checking Prerequisite Skills for this chapter.

Text Option Take the Quick Check below.

QUICK Check

Find each sum.

1. 2 + 2 + 2 + 2

2. 4 + 4

3. 5 + 5 + 5

4. 10 + 10 + 10 + 10

5. 0 + 0 + 0

6. 1 + 1 + 1 + 1 + 1

Identify a pattern. Then find the missing numbers.

7. 5, 10, 15, ■, ■, 30

8. 12, ■, 8, 6, ■, 2

9. 3, 6, 9, ■, 15, ■

10. ■, 8, 12, 16, ■

11. 50, ■, 30, 20, ■

12. 6, 12, ■, 24, ■

Write an addition sentence for each picture.

13.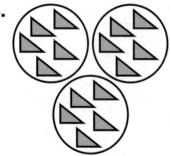

14.

15.

Solve. Use repeated addition.

16. Larisa has 2 cups with 4 crackers in each cup. How many crackers does she have in all?

17. On Monday and Tuesday, Lance rode his bike around the block 3 times each day. How many times in all did he ride his bike around the block?

 Online Option Take the Online Readiness Quiz.

Explore Model Multiplication

Main Idea

I will use models to explore the meaning of multiplication.

Materials

connecting cubes

Get Connect**ED**

3.5 The student will recall multiplication facts through the twelves table, and the corresponding division facts. **3.6** The student will represent multiplication and division, using area, set, and number line models, and create and solve problems that involve multiplication of two whole numbers, one factor 99 or less and the second factor 5 or less.

Multiplication is an operation on two numbers that can be thought of as *repeated addition.* The sign ($\times$) means to multiply. You can use models to explore multiplication.

 **ACTIVITY**

Find how many are in 4 groups of 5.

Step 1 **Model 4 groups of 5.**

Use connecting cubes to show 4 groups of 5 cubes.

There are 4 groups. There are 5 cubes in each group.

Step 2 **Find 4 groups of 5.**

Label the groups of cubes with numbers. Use repeated addition.

$$5 + 5 + 5 + 5 = 20$$

Step 3 Record the results.

Copy the table. Record the number of groups, the number in each group, and the total.

Explore other ways to group the 20 connecting cubes equally.

Number of Groups	Number in Each Group	Total
4	5	20

Think About It

1. How can addition help you find the total number when multiplying?

2. How did you find the total number of cubes in Step 2?

3. What do the numbers stand for in the number sentence in Step 2?

4. Explain another way to group 20 cubes equally.

Practice and Apply It

Use models to find the total number.

5. 2 groups of 3

6. 3 groups of 4

7. 1 group of 5

8. 8 groups of 2

9. 5 groups of 5

10. 6 groups of 4

Draw a model to find the total number.

11. 6 groups of 2

12. 4 groups of 5

13. 7 groups of 2

14. **WRITE MATH** Explain how addition and multiplication are similar.

Main Idea

I will relate multiplication and addition.

 Vocabulary

multiplication

multiply

factors

product

 Get Connect**ED**

3.5 The student will recall multiplication facts through the twelves table, and the corresponding division facts. **3.6** The student will represent multiplication and division, using area, set, and number line models, and create and solve problems that involve multiplication of two whole numbers, one factor 99 or less and the second factor 5 or less.

Multiplication as Repeated Addition

 **REAL-WORLD EXAMPLE** Use Models

1 **FOOD** For Gilberto's party, his mother made 4 small pizzas. Each pizza had 6 pieces of pepperoni. How many pieces of pepperoni did Gilberto's mother use to make 4 small pizzas?

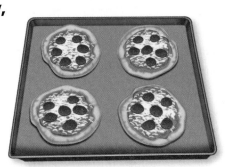

Find how many pieces of pepperoni are in 4 groups of 6.

One Way: **Counters**	Another Way: **Repeated Addition**
	Write an addition sentence to show equal groups.
	$6 + 6 + 6 + 6 = 24$
There are 4 groups. There are 6 counters in each group. This is a total of 24 counters.	

So, 4 groups of 6 is 24. Gilberto's mother used 24 pieces of pepperoni.

Put equal groups together to **multiply**. The numbers multiplied are **factors**. The result is the **product**.

 REAL-WORLD EXAMPLE   Use Models

2 **BEES** A honeycomb cell has 6 sides. How many sides do 5 separate honeycomb cells have altogether?

Find how many sides are in 5 groups of 6.

 **Remember**

When you multiply, you add the same number multiple times.

One Way: Repeated Addition

6 + 6 + 6 + 6 + 6 = 30

Another Way: Multiplication Sentence

number of cells (groups)		number of sides		total
5	×	6	=	30
factor		factor		product

So, there are 30 sides altogether.

✓ CHECK What You Know

Write an addition sentence and a multiplication sentence for each model. See Examples 1 and 2

1.

2.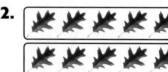

Multiply. Use models and repeated addition. See Examples 1 and 2

3. 2 × 6
4. 4 × 4
5. 5 × 3
6. 7 × 2

7. Marcos gave three friends 4 stickers each. How many stickers did he give away?

8. **TALK MATH** Can you write 2 + 3 + 5 = 10 as a multiplication sentence? Explain.

EXTRA PRACTICE
Begins on page EP2.

Write an addition sentence and a multiplication sentence for each model. See Examples 1 and 2

9.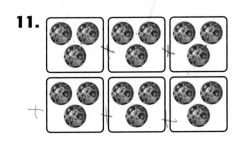

10.

11.

12.

13. 6 groups of 6   **14.** 8 groups of 4   **15.** 10 groups of 3

16. 7 groups of 5   **17.** 5 groups of 7   **18.** 9 groups of 4

Multiply. Use models and repeated addition. See Examples 1 and 2

19. 3×5 **20.** 5×2 **21.** 3×3

22. 6×2 **23.** 9×2 **24.** 10×6

25. 5×5 **26.** 4×7 **27.** 6×4

28. Adriano bought 3 boxes of paints. Each box has 8 colors. What is the total number of paints?

29. Leonora found 4 bags of buttons. Each bag has 10 buttons. How many buttons are there altogether?

30. Each boy has 5 balloons and each girl has 3 balloons. How many balloons do they have if there are 3 boys and 6 girls?

31. A starfish has 5 legs. There are 5 starfish on the beach. If 4 of the starfish are each missing 1 leg, how many legs are there?

H.O.T. Problems

32. OPEN ENDED Write a real-world multiplication problem whose product is greater than 40.

33. CHALLENGE What is 2 more than 5 groups of 3?

34. WRITE MATH Describe a real-world situation where you would use multiplication to solve a problem.

Explore **Multiplication with Arrays**

Main Idea

I will use arrays to explore and model multiplication.

Materials

color tiles

grid paper and plain paper

scissors and glue

Get ConnectED

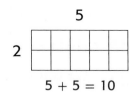
3.5 The student will recall multiplication facts through the twelves table, and the corresponding division facts. **3.6** The student will represent multiplication and division, using area, set, and number line models, and create and solve problems that involve multiplication of two whole numbers, one factor 99 or less and the second factor 5 or less. Also addresses 3.20a.

Parker bought 12 fishing hooks. How can he put them in his tackle box so they are in equal rows and columns?

🏃 📷 **ACTIVITY**

1 **Arrays and Repeated Addition**

Step 1 **Arrange 12 tiles in a rectangle.** Compare your rectangle to your neighbor's rectangle. How are they different? How are they alike?

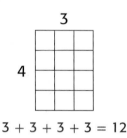

3 + 3 + 3 + 3 = 12

Step 2 **Write an addition sentence to show equal rows.**

ACTIVITY

2 **Arrays and Multiplication**

Step 1 **From the grid paper, cut an array that has 5 rows of 2 squares.**
  • Glue it on white paper, and then label it.
  • Write a repeated addition sentence to represent the array.

2 + 2 + 2 + 2 + 2 = 10

Step 2 **Cut an array of 2 rows of 5 squares.**
  • Glue and label it next to the first one.

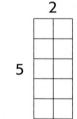

5 + 5 = 10

🔊 **124** *Model Multiplication and Division Problems*

Step 3 **Write a multiplication sentence for each array.**
The arrays show the **Commutative Property of Multiplication.**

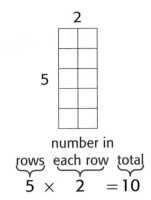

number in
rows   each row   total
5 ×   2   = 10

number in
rows   each row   total
2 ×   5   = 10

Think About It

1. What is the connection between repeated addition and an array?

2. Explain the Commutative Property of Multiplication.

3. How can you use an array to model the Commutative Property of Multiplication?

Practice and Apply It

Write an addition sentence and a multiplication sentence for each array.

4.

5.

6.

7.

Make an array to find the total number. Write the multiplication sentence.

8. 2 × 4   **9.** 1 × 4   **10.** 5 × 2   **11.** 4 × 4

12. Tyrone made a 4 × 6 array using stones. How many stones did Tyrone use?

13. If you made an array to find 3 × 5, how can you change the array to find 2 × 5?

14. 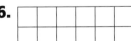 **WRITE MATH** List and explain the kind of everyday objects you find in an array.

Main Idea
I will use arrays to multiply.

**Vocabulary**
array

**Get Connect ED**

3.5 The student will recall multiplication facts through the twelves table, and the corresponding division facts. **3.6** The student will represent multiplication and division, using area, set, and number line models, and create and solve problems that involve multiplication of two whole numbers, one factor 99 or less and the second factor 5 or less. Also addresses 3.20a.

Arrays and Multiplication

The cups are arranged in equal rows and equal columns. This arrangement is an **array**. Arrays can help you multiply.

REAL-WORLD EXAMPLE Model an Array

1 **PARTY CUPS** Roberto places party cups on a table in 3 rows of 5 cups each. How many cups are on the table?

To find the total number of cups, use counters to model an array. The array shows 3 rows of 5.

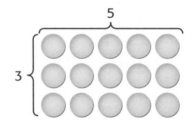

You can use addition or multiplication to find the total.

One Way: Add	Another Way: Multiply
$5 + 5 + 5 = 15$	$3 \times 5 = 15$ factor factor product

$3 \times 5 = 15$ ← Write a multiplication sentence.

So, 3 groups of 5 cups is 15 in all.

Commutative Property of Multiplication

2 PHOTOS One page of Elsa's photo album is shown. Write two multiplication sentences to find how many photos are on each page.

Remember

The models in Example 2 are also arrays since they have columns of equal number and rows of equal number.

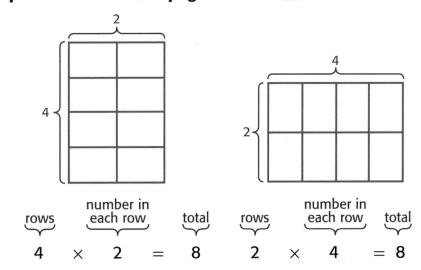

rows	number in each row	total	rows	number in each row	total
4	× 2	= 8	2	× 4	= 8

Vocabulary Link

Everyday Use

Commute To go back and forth.

Math Use

Commutative To change the order of factors.

Key Concept Commutative Property

Words The **Commutative Property of Multiplication** says the order in which numbers are multiplied does not change the product.

Examples
4	×	3	=	12	3	×	4	=	12
factor		factor		product	factor		factor		product

 **What You Know**

Write two multiplication sentences for each array.

See Examples 1 and 2

1. ○○○○○○○○
○○○○○○○○

2. [grid image]

3. Write two multiplication sentences to find how many puppies there are if 5 dogs each have 2 puppies.

4. 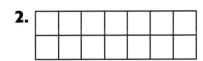 **TALK MATH** What other operation uses the Commutative Property? Explain.

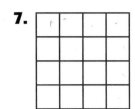
Write two multiplication sentences for each array.

See Examples 1 and 2

5.

6.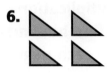

7.

8.

9.

10.

Algebra Use the Commutative Property of Multiplication
to find each missing number. See Example 2

11. $5 \times 2 = 10$
$2 \times \blacksquare = 10$

12. $3 \times 5 = 15$
$\blacksquare \times 3 = 15$

13. $3 \times 9 = 27$
$9 \times 3 = \blacksquare$

14. Geometry Hope drew the area
model at the right. Write a multiplication
sentence to represent her model.

Multiply. Use an array if needed. See Examples 1 and 2

15. Adult tickets to the talent show
cost $8. How much will 4 adult
tickets cost?

16. Tamika gives her dog 2 treats
every day. How many treats does
Tamika's dog get in one week?

**Use the Commutative Property of Multiplication to write two
multiplication sentences for each situation. Then solve.**

See Example 2

17. Baily made a 3 by 4 array with
number cards. How many number
cards are there?

18. There were 4 students with
5 balloons each. How many
balloons do the students have?

19. FIND THE ERROR Alyssa is using the numbers 3, 4, and 12 to show the Commutative Property of Multiplication. Find and correct her mistake.

$3 \times 4 = 12$
so, $12 \times 3 = 4$

20. 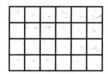 **WRITE MATH** Describe how an array can help you find the answer to a multiplication problem.

 Test Practice

21. Which multiplication sentence is modeled below? (Lesson 1D)

A. $5 \times 7 = 35$ **C.** $8 \times 3 = 24$

B. $6 \times 6 = 36$ **D.** $4 \times 6 = 24$

22. Dominic drew 7 lines. Each line is 5 inches long. The total length of all 7 lines is 35 inches. If Dominic drew 5 lines and each line was 7 inches long, what is the total length of all 5 lines? (Lesson 1B)

F. 30 **H.** 40

G. 35 **J.** 45

Spiral Review

Multiply. Use models and repeated addition. (Lesson 1B)

23. Jerome saw a group of 8 lizards. Each lizard had 2 stripes on its back. How many stripes were there in all?

Write an addition sentence and a multiplication sentence for each model. (Lesson 1B)

24.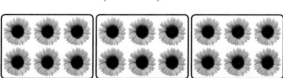

25.

Main Idea

I will recognize the comparison of two groups as another type of multiplication.

 Vocabulary

comparison problems
bar diagram

 *Get Connect*ED

 3.5 The student will recall multiplication facts through the twelves table, and the corresponding division facts. **3.6** The student will represent multiplication and division, using area, set, and number line models, and create and solve problems that involve multiplication of two whole numbers, one factor 99 or less and the second factor 5 or less.

Use Multiplication to Compare

Sometimes you have to look at a problem in a different way when a phrase like *times as many, times more,* and *times as much* is used. These kinds of problems are **comparison problems**.

REAL-WORLD EXAMPLE Use Models

1. **CAMP** **Mary attended camp for 7 days this summer. Tyler attended 3 times as many days as Mary. Find the number of days Tyler attended camp.**

Use models to help you compare the groups of days.

Step 1 Model Mary's days at camp as 1 group of 7 days.

Step 2 Tyler had 3 times as many days at camp. Model Tyler's days at camp as 3 groups of 7.

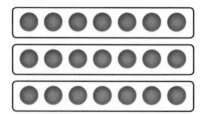

Step 3 Find the total of 3 groups of 7.

$$7 + 7 + 7 = 21$$
or
$$3 \times 7 = 21$$

So, Tyler attended camp 21 days.

A type of model drawing is the **bar diagram**. A bar diagram can help you understand a problem and plan to solve it.

 REAL-WORLD EXAMPLE Use a Bar Diagram

2 BEADS Cassady used 5 beads to make a bracelet. Suki used 3 times as many beads as Cassady. How many beads did Suki use?

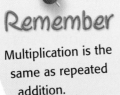
Remember

Multiplication is the same as repeated addition.

Step 1 Cassady's 5 beads are modeled as one part.

Cassady	5 beads

Step 2 Suki has 3 times as many beads as Cassady. So, the same part is modeled 3 times.

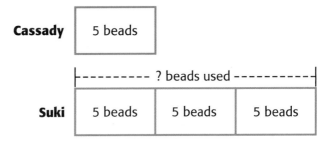

Step 3 Find the total number of Suki's beads.

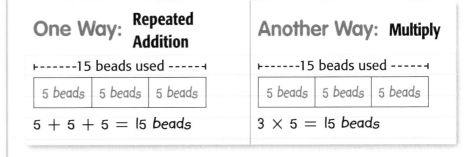

One Way: Repeated Addition	Another Way: Multiply
⊢------15 beads used -----⊣	⊢------15 beads used -----⊣
5 beads | 5 beads | 5 beads	5 beads | 5 beads | 5 beads
5 + 5 + 5 = 15 beads	3 × 5 = 15 beads

So, Suki used 15 beads.

Use the models to compare. Then write a multiplication sentence. See Example 1

1. 3 times as much

2. 2 times more

3. 4 times as many

Use the bar diagram to compare. Then write a multiplication sentence. See Example 2

4. twice as many boys

4 boys

5. 6 times as much money

$2

6. 3 times more pens

4 pens

Solve. Use a bar diagram if needed. See Example 2

7. | BAR | DIAGRAM | While on a trip, Sheri bought 3 postcards. Willa bought twice as many. How many postcards did Willa buy?

8.  **TALK MATH** Do you prefer to use the bar diagram or models to help you solve problems? Explain.

Practice and Problem Solving

EXTRA PRACTICE
Begins on page EP2.

Use the models to compare. Then write a multiplication sentence. See Example 1

9. 3 times as many

10. 5 times more

11. 4 times as much

12. 10 times as much

13. 2 times more

14. twice as many

15. 8 times as many

16. 4 times more

17. 5 times as much

Use the bar diagram to compare. Then write a multiplication sentence. See Example 2

18. 5 times as many balls

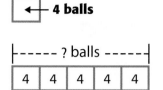

|------ ? balls ------|
| 4 | 4 | 4 | 4 | 4 |

19. 4 times as many fish

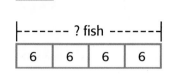

|------- ? fish -------|
| 6 | 6 | 6 | 6 |

20. 2 times as many bows

`3 bows`

|-- ? bows --|
| 3 | 3 |

21. 3 times more yo-yos

`5 yo-yos`

|-------- ? yo-yos --------|
| 5 | 5 | 5 |

22. 5 times as many stars

|------ ? stars ------|
| 1 | 1 | 1 | 1 | 1 |

23. 3 times as much money

`$6`

|------- ? $ -------|
| $6 | $6 | $6 |

Solve. Use a bar diagram if needed. See Example 2

24. `BAR DIAGRAM` There are 3 times as many blue balloons as green balloons. There are 4 green balloons. How many blue balloons are there?

25. `BAR DIAGRAM` Nan needs 4 times as much flour as sugar. She needs 4 cups of sugar. How much flour does she need?

26. `BAR DIAGRAM` Devi practiced her flute 6 days last month. How many days did she practice this month if she practiced 3 times as many days?

27. `BAR DIAGRAM` Perry paid 10¢ for a rubber snake. Sam paid 3 times as much for his snake. How much did Sam pay for his snake?

H.O.T. Problems

28. OPEN ENDED Write a real-world comparison problem using the numbers 2 and 5.

29. WHICH ONE DOESN'T BELONG? Identify the model that does not represent the number sentence $3 \times 4 = 12$. Explain.

$$4 + 4 + 4 = 12$$

$$12 - 4 = 8$$

30. 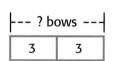 **WRITE MATH** Explain how a bar diagram can help you plan and solve a problem.

Main Idea

I will use multiplication to find the total number of combinations that can be made when given two groups of objects.

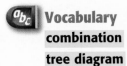 **Vocabulary**

combination

tree diagram

 *Get Connect**ED***

3.5 The student will recall multiplication facts through the twelves table, and the corresponding division facts. **3.6** The student will represent multiplication and division, using area, set, and number line models, and create and solve problems that involve multiplication of two whole numbers, one factor 99 or less and the second factor 5 or less.

Use Multiplication to Find Combinations

When you make a **combination** you make a new set that has one item from each set of items.

REAL-WORLD EXAMPLE   Make a Picture

1   **FOOTBALL** Amos' team has 3 jersey colors—green, red, and yellow. They can wear black or white socks. Find all of the jersey and sock combinations for the team.

To find the combinations, match each color of jersey with each color of socks.

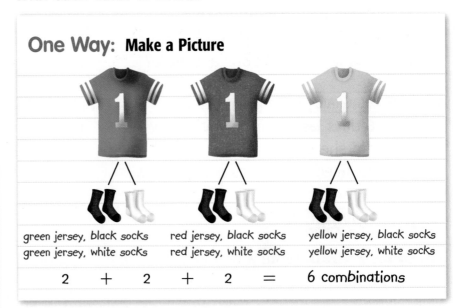

One Way: Make a Picture

green jersey, black socks
green jersey, white socks

red jersey, black socks
red jersey, white socks

yellow jersey, black socks
yellow jersey, white socks

2   +   2   +   2   =   6 combinations

Another Way: Write a Multiplication Sentence

There are 3 jersey colors and 2 sock colors.

Multiply to find the total number of combinations.

3   ×   2   =   6

jersey   sock   combinations

colors   colors

There are 6 jersey and sock combinations possible.

Another way to find combinations is a tree diagram.
A **tree diagram** uses "branches" to show all the possible combinations.

REAL-WORLD EXAMPLE Make a Tree Diagram

2 **ICE-CREAM SUNDAES**
What are the possible sundae combinations if one ice cream flavor and one topping is chosen?

Draw a "branch" to match each ice cream flavor with each topping.

Sundaes	
Ice Cream	**Toppings**
Chocolate	Sprinkles
Vanilla	Whipped Cream
Strawberry	Peanuts

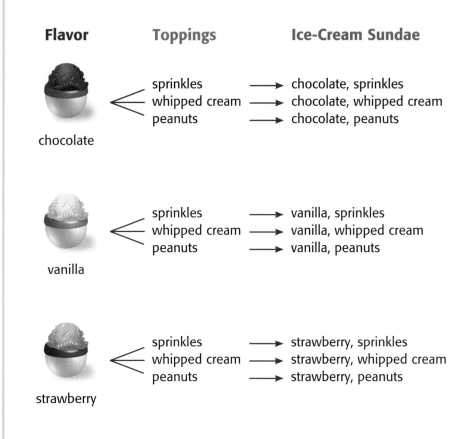

Flavor	Toppings	Ice-Cream Sundae
chocolate	sprinkles →	chocolate, sprinkles
	whipped cream →	chocolate, whipped cream
	peanuts →	chocolate, peanuts
vanilla	sprinkles →	vanilla, sprinkles
	whipped cream →	vanilla, whipped cream
	peanuts →	vanilla, peanuts
strawberry	sprinkles →	strawberry, sprinkles
	whipped cream →	strawberry, whipped cream
	peanuts →	strawberry, peanuts

Check Multiply to find the number of combinations.

3 flavors × 3 toppings = 9 combinations ✔

So, there are 9 possible sundae combinations.

Make a picture or tree diagram to find all the possible combinations. Write a multiplication sentence. See Examples 1 and 2

1. The music teacher told her students to run, walk, or hop while they clapped or snapped their fingers. What are the possible combinations of one hand and one foot motion?

2. There are green, blue, red, and orange balloons with silver or gold streamers. Find the possible combinations of one color balloon and one streamer.

3. Preston can buy in-line skates or roller skates in silver or black. Find Preston's choices.

4.  **TALK MATH** Explain how a tree diagram helps you find all the possible combinations without repeating any.

Practice and Problem Solving

EXTRA PRACTICE
Begins on page EP2.

Make a picture or tree diagram to find all the possible combinations. Write a multiplication sentence. See Examples 1 and 2

5. Jackie is playing a card game with triangles, circles, squares, and trapezoids. The shapes can be blue, red, yellow, or green. How many different colored shape-cards are there?

6. List all of the 2-digit numbers that can be made with 3, 4, 2, or 5 as the tens digit and 1, 6, 7, 8, or 9 as the ones digit.

7. What are the possible color combinations if one color from each spinner is spun?

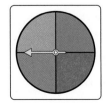 

8. The students will choose one piece of paper and one piece of chalk. What are the combinations they may get?

Use the information to solve the problems.

Pizza Puzzle

9. Draw a picture or tree diagram to show the different one-topping pizza and crust combinations.

10. Is Nate able to make 8 different one-topping pizzas? Write a multiplication sentence to show the total number of one-topping pizzas that can be made.

H.O.T. Problems

11. OPEN ENDED Write a real-world combination problem. Ask a neighbor to find all the possible combinations. Provide the answer.

12. WHICH ONE DOESN'T BELONG? Choose one fruit and one cheese to make all the possible combinations. Find the combination that does not belong. Explain.

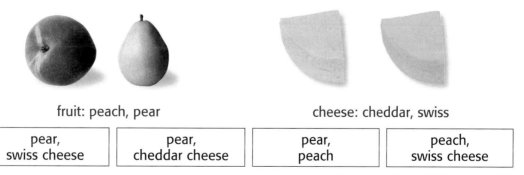

fruit: peach, pear   cheese: cheddar, swiss

pear, swiss cheese	pear, cheddar cheese	pear, peach	peach, swiss cheese

13. **WRITE MATH** Explain a situation when you may need to know how to find the total number of combinations that would result when putting two sets of things together.

Problem-Solving Strategy: Make a Table

Main Idea I will use the *make a table* strategy to solve a problem.

 Selma bought 3 shorts and 2 shirts. Her sister, Laura, bought 4 shorts and 2 shirts. How many different shirt and shorts combinations can each girl make?

Understand **What facts do you know?**

- You know what each girl bought.

What do you need to find?

- How many different shirt and shorts combinations they can each make.

Plan Organize the information in a table.

Solve

- Make a table for each girl. Make a row for each pair of shorts and a column for each shirt. List the possible shirt and shorts combinations.

Selma	Shirt 1	Shirt 2
Shorts A	A1	A2
Shorts B	B1	B2
Shorts C	C1	C2

Laura	Shirt 1	Shirt 2
Shorts A	A1	A2
Shorts B	B1	B2
Shorts C	C1	C2
Shorts D	D1	D2

Selma: 3 × 2 = 6
       shorts   shirts   combinations

Laura: 4 × 2 = 8

So, Selma can make 6 combinations, and Laura can make 8.

Check Since $3 \times 2 = 6$ and $4 \times 2 = 8$, you know that the number of clothing combinations is correct. ✓

3.5 The student will recall multiplication facts through the twelves table, and the corresponding division facts.

Refer to the problem on the previous page.

1. How did the *make a table* strategy help you find the answer to the problem?

2. Suppose Laura had 3 shirts instead of 2. How many combinations would she have?

3. Look back at your answer for Exercise 2. How do you know that the answer is correct? Show your work.

4. How are the problems on the previous page and Exercise 2 alike?

PRACTICE

EXTRA PRACTICE
Begins on page EP2.

Solve. Use the *make a table* strategy.

5. How many lunches can Malia make if she chooses one main item and one side item from the menu shown below?

Main Dishes
Pizza
Hamburger
Taco

Side Dishes
Bread
Fruit
Veggies

6. Amber has coins in a jar. The sum of the coins is 13¢. What are the possible coin combinations Amber could have?

7. Choose one bread and one meat.
bread: wheat or white
meat: turkey or chicken
What are all the possible combinations?

8. Look at the table. How many pens do Nestor and Pam have in all? How many more pens does Carra have than Pam?

Name	Pens
Pam	7
Nestor	9
Carra	20

9. The students in Mr. Robb's class are designing a flag. The flag's background can be red or green with a blue or a purple stripe. How many flags can they design? Explain how you solved the problem.

10. Geometry Rodrigo is putting up a fence in the shape of a triangle.

Side A	Side B	Side C
2 times as long as side B	18 feet	same as side A

How much fencing does he need?

11. **WRITE MATH** Write one real-world problem that would involve making a table to find the answer.

Lesson 1G Meaning of Multiplication **139**

OTS OF ARMS AND LEGS

Have you ever wondered why a cheetah has 4 legs instead of 3? Or why an octopus has 8 arms instead of 4? The number of arms or legs an animal has helps it hunt for food and escape from predators.

A cheetah has 4 legs that balance its body. Its legs help it run as fast as 70 miles per hour. An octopus has an unprotected body and no claws or teeth. So, 8 arms are more helpful to an octopus than only 4 or 6 arms.

ANIMAL	NUMBER OF LEGS OR ARMS
Sugar star (Sea star)	5
Ant	6
Ostrich	2
Hermit crab	10
Sea turtle	4

Model Multiplication and Division Problems

Real-World Math

Use the information on the previous page to solve each problem. Write a multiplication sentence to solve. Then write an addition sentence to check.

 1. Three ants are on a park bench. How many legs are there in all?

 2. You see 7 ostriches. How many legs do you see altogether?

 3. If you see a pack of 3 cheetahs, how many legs are there in all?

4. If there are 4 octopuses, how many octopus arms are there total?

 5. You count 30 sugar star arms in the aquarium. How many sugar stars are there? Explain.

 6. There are 3 sea turtles and 2 sugar stars in another aquarium. How many arms and legs are there altogether?

 7. How many legs in all do 6 hermit crabs have?

Did You Know?

An octopus has 240 suction cups on each of its 8 arms.

Game Time

You will need: 1 set of array cards for each player; one blank spinner

Get Ready!

Players: 2–3 players
Number the blank spinner 1–10.

Each player cuts a set of array cards on the dotted lines.

Get Set!

Each player places their set of cards faceup in an array of 4 rows and 4 columns.

Go!

 Player 1 spins the spinner two times and finds the product. The player finds an array card that matches the product and turns the card over. If there is no array card to match, the player's turn is over.

 The remaining players repeat the directions in turn.

☆ "Array" is exclaimed when one player has 1 complete row or 1 complete column turned over.

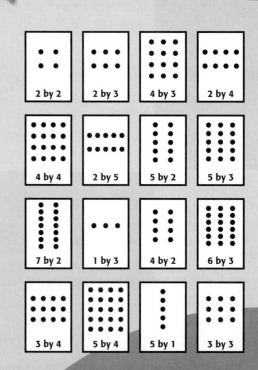

Array cards:
2 by 2 | 2 by 3 | 4 by 3 | 2 by 4
4 by 4 | 2 by 5 | 5 by 2 | 5 by 3
7 by 2 | 1 by 3 | 4 by 2 | 6 by 3
3 by 4 | 5 by 4 | 5 by 1 | 3 by 3

Mid-Chapter Check

Find the total number. (Lesson 1A)

1. 2 groups of 4   **2.** 4 groups of 5

3. 9 groups of 2   **4.** 5 groups of 3

Multiply. Use models and repeated addition. (Lesson 1B)

5. 2×6 **6.** 5×2

7. 3×3 **8.** 2×8

Write two multiplication sentences for each array. (Lesson 1D)

9.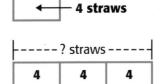

10.

Use the models to compare. Then write a multiplication sentence.

(Lesson 1E)

11. 2 times as many   **12.** 5 times as many

13. How many possible boy-girl pairs can be made if Ben, Lauren, Jamal, Ian, and Angela were chosen? Make a picture or diagram to find all the possible combinations. Write a multiplication sentence. (Lessons 1F, 1G)

14. MULTIPLE CHOICE Nine tigers each make 4 paw prints. Which of the following number sentences should be used to find the total number of paw prints? (Lesson 1D)

A. $9 + 4 = 13$ **C.** $9 \times 4 = 36$

B. $9 - 4 = 5$ **D.** $9 \times 4 = 40$

Use the bar diagram to compare. Then write a multiplication sentence. (Lesson 1E)

15. 3 times as many straws

← 4 straws

? straws
4	4	4

16. 5 times as many pencils

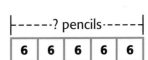
← 6 pencils

? pencils
6	6	6	6	6

17. MULTIPLE CHOICE Which of the following number sentences is related to this addition sentence? (Lesson 1B)

$$5 + 5 + 5 = 15$$

F. $3 \times 5 = 15$ **H.** $15 - 5 = 10$

G. $3 + 5 = 8$ **J.** $5 + 3 = 8$

18. **WRITE MATH** Explain how multiplication and addition are related. (Lesson 1B)

Explore **Model Division**

Main Idea

I will explore two meanings of division.

Materials

counters

paper plates

Get ConnectED

3.5 The student will recall multiplication facts through the twelves table, and the corresponding division facts. **3.6** The student will represent multiplication and division, using area, set, and number line models, and create and solve problems that involve multiplication of two whole numbers, one factor 99 or less and the second factor 5 or less.

Division is an operation with two numbers. One number tells you how many things you have. The other tells you how many equal groups to form or how many to put in each group.

$$10 \div 5 = 2$$

Read ÷ as *divided by*. 10 divided by 5 = 2.

To **divide** means to separate a number into equal groups, to find the number of groups, or find the number in each group.

ACTIVITY

① **Divide 12 counters into 3 equal groups.**

Step 1 Count out 12 counters. Using paper plates, show 3 groups.

Step 2 Place one counter at a time on each plate until all of the counters are gone.

Step 3 Twelve counters were divided into 3 groups. There are 4 counters in each group. So, $12 \div 3 = 4$.

② **Place 12 counters in groups of 3.**

Step 1 Count out 12 counters.

Step 2 Make groups of 3 until all the counters are gone.

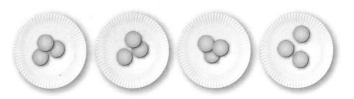

There are 4 groups of 3.
So, $12 \div 4 = 3$.

Think About It

1. Explain how you divided 12 counters into equal groups.

2. When you divided the counters into groups of 3, how did you find the number of equal groups?

Practice and Apply It

3. Make equal groups to find the number of counters in each group.

4. Find the number of equal groups of 5.

5. Copy the chart. Then use counters to help complete it.

Number of Counters	Number of Equal Groups	Number in Each Group	Division Sentence
9	3	3	$9 \div 3 = 3$
14	2	▪	▪
15	▪	5	▪
6	▪	3	▪

6. **WRITE MATH** Can 13 counters be divided equally into groups of 3? Explain.

Division as Equal Sharing

Activity 1 in the Explore lesson showed that one way to **divide** is to find the number in each group. This can be done by sharing equally.

REAL-WORLD EXAMPLE **Share Equally**

1. **RABBITS** Caley has 6 rabbits that she keeps in 3 hutches. She has an equal number of rabbits in each hutch. How many rabbits are in each hutch?

You can draw a picture. Place one rabbit at a time in each hutch until there are no more rabbits.

6	÷	3	=	2
rabbits		hutches (groups)		in each hutch

So, there are 2 rabbits in each hutch.

② CAMP Fifteen scouts are divided equally to sleep in 3 tents. How many scouts are in each tent?

You can use counters to model an array.

Remember

When you divide you share an equal number to all the groups.

Step 1 Place one counter (scout) in each row (tent).

Tent 1 ⬤_____

Tent 2 ⬤_____

Tent 3 ⬤_____

Step 2 Continue to place one counter (scout) in each row (tent) until all of the counters are gone.

Tent 1 ⬤⬤⬤⬤⬤ ←— 5 scouts

Tent 2 ⬤⬤⬤⬤⬤ ←— 5 scouts

Tent 3 ⬤⬤⬤⬤⬤ ←— 5 scouts

Step 3 Write a number sentence.

$15 \div 3 = 5$

So, 5 scouts are in each tent.

✓ CHECK What You Know

Use counters to model the total. Divide to find the number in each group. See Examples 1 and 2

1. 10 counters
2 equal groups

____ in each group

____ ÷ ____ = ____

2. 14 counters
7 equal groups

____ in each group

____ ÷ ____ = ____

3. 20 counters
5 equal groups

____ in each group

____ ÷ ____ = ____

4. Dexter had 30 blocks. He stacked them in equal rows on top of each other until he ran out of blocks. Dexter's towers stood 10 blocks tall. How many towers did Dexter make?

5. **TALK MATH** Explain what it means to share equally when dividing.

Use counters to model the total. Divide to find the number in each group. See Examples 1 and 2

6. 4 counters
2 equal groups
▨ in each group

▨ ÷ ▨ = ▨

7. 12 counters
2 equal groups
▨ in each group

▨ ÷ ▨ = ▨

8. 10 counters
5 equal groups
▨ in each group

▨ ÷ ▨ = ▨

9. 8 counters
4 equal groups
▨ in each group

▨ ÷ ▨ = ▨

10. 15 counters
5 equal groups
▨ in each group

▨ ÷ ▨ = ▨

11. 18 counters
2 equal groups
▨ in each group

▨ ÷ ▨ = ▨

12. Marla has $30. How many compact discs can she buy?

$10

13. There are 6 juice boxes in a package. How many packages need to be bought if 24 juice boxes are needed for the picnic?

14. Mrs. Miller needs 18 feet of fabric. How many yards of fabric will she need to buy? (*Hint:* 1 yard = 3 feet)

15. The bookstore had a sale. Every time you bought 3 books you got 1 free. Alberto bought 9 books. How many free books did he get?

Algebra **Find each missing number.**

16. 8 ÷ ▨ = 4

17. ▨ ÷ 3 = 3

18. 12 ÷ 3 = ▨

19. ▨ ÷ 2 = 6

20. 16 ÷ ▨ = 4

21. 20 ÷ 4 = ▨

Data File

There are many different kinds of saltwater fish off ocean beaches.

22. Together, 3 snooks weigh about 12 pounds. About how much does each snook weigh if each weighs about the same?

23. Draw a picture to show two different ways the fish could be divided equally. Then, write a number sentence for each picture.

24. OPEN ENDED Write a real-world division problem in which 5 would be the answer.

25. WHICH ONE DOESN'T BELONG? Identify the number sentence that does not belong. Explain.

$$12 \div 3 = 4 \qquad 15 \div 3 = 5 \qquad 12 \div 6 = 2 \qquad 12 \div 4 = 3$$

26. **WRITE MATH** Explain one meaning of division.

 **Test Practice**

27. Nathan wants to buy a clock. He can choose one shape and one color.

Shape	Color
Square	Red
Circle	Blue
	Green

How many different combinations are possible? (Lesson 1F)

A. 3　　　　**C.** 5

B. 4　　　　**D.** 6

28. Alma planted an equal number of seeds in each pot. How many seeds did Alma put in each pot?

(Lesson 2B)

F. 2　　　　**H.** 18

G. 9　　　　**J.** 36

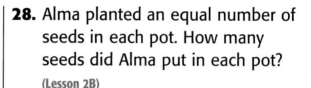 **Spiral Review**

29. The lunch menu choices are carrots or celery and an apple, orange, or banana. The students must choose one vegetable and one fruit. Make a table to find all the vegtable and fruit combinations. (Lesson 1G)

30. Find all the combinations that can be made with one number and one letter. Write a multiplication sentence. (Lesson 1F)

L, C, T, M　　5, 2, 7, 3

Main Idea

I will use models to relate division and subtraction.

 Vocabulary

repeated subtraction

 Get Connect ED

3.5 The student will recall multiplication facts through the twelves table, and the corresponding division facts. **3.6** The student will represent multiplication and division, using area, set, and number line models, and create and solve problems that involve multiplication of two whole numbers, one factor 99 or less and the second factor 5 or less.

Relate Division and Subtraction

Recall that to divide means to separate a number into equal groups, to find the number of groups, or find the number in each group.

🏃 ✏️ 📷 **REAL-WORLD EXAMPLE**   Use a Number Sentence

① **PENCILS There are 15 pencils in a box. Each pencil is either red, blue, or yellow. There are the same number of each color. How many pencils of each color are there? Use a number sentence to record the solution.**

Place one counter at a time on each plate until all 15 counters are gone.

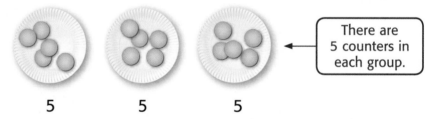

5   5   5

There are 5 counters in each group.

The number sentence that describes the model is 15 ÷ 3 = 5. So, there are 5 pencils of each color.

You can also divide using **repeated subtraction**. Subtract equal groups of 3 repeatedly until you get to zero.

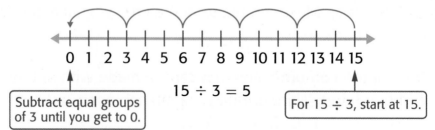

0 1 2 3 4 5 6 7 8 9 10 11 12 13 14 15

15 ÷ 3 = 5

Subtract equal groups of 3 until you get to 0.

For 15 ÷ 3, start at 15.

REAL-WORLD EXAMPLE Repeated Subtraction

2 SPORTS Andre wants to put his 10 baseball cards into equal groups of 2. How many groups can he make?

Use repeated subtraction to find $10 \div 2$. Write a number sentence.

One Way: Number Line	Another Way: Paper and Pencil
⑤ ④ ③ ② ① 0 1 2 3 4 5 6 7 8 9 10	① ② ③ ④ ⑤ $\begin{array}{r}10\\-2\\\hline8\end{array}$ $\begin{array}{r}8\\-2\\\hline6\end{array}$ $\begin{array}{r}6\\-2\\\hline4\end{array}$ $\begin{array}{r}4\\-2\\\hline2\end{array}$ $\begin{array}{r}2\\-2\\\hline0\end{array}$
Start at 10. Count back by 2s until you reach 0. How many times did you subtract?	Subtract groups of 2 until you reach 0. How many groups did you subtract?

So, the number sentence $10 \div 2 = 5$ shows that Andre will have 5 groups of cards.

✓ CHECK What You Know

Use models to divide. Write a number sentence. See Example 1

1. There are 16 flowers. Each vase has 4 flowers. How many vases are there?

2. There are 14 ears. Each dog has 2 ears. How many dogs are there?

Use repeated subtraction to divide. See Example 2

3.

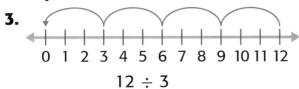

0 1 2 3 4 5 6 7 8 9 10 11 12

$12 \div 3$

4.

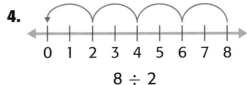

0 1 2 3 4 5 6 7 8

$8 \div 2$

5. $6 \div 2$

6. $12 \div 6$

7. $25 \div 5$

8. There are 16 mittens. Each student wears 2 mittens. How many students are there?

9. **TALK MATH** Explain how to use a number line to find $18 \div 9$.

Use models to divide. Write a number sentence. See Example 1

10. There are 16 orange slices. Each orange has 8 slices. How many oranges are there?

11. Measurement There are 16 miles. Each trip is 2 miles. How many trips are there?

12. There are 25 marbles, with 5 marbles in each bag. How many bags are there?

13. Four friends will share 12 muffins equally. How many muffins will each friend get?

Use repeated subtraction to divide. See Example 2

14.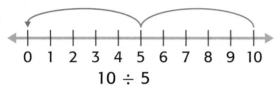
10 ÷ 5

15.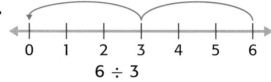
6 ÷ 3

16.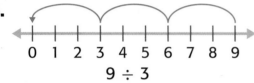
9 ÷ 3

17.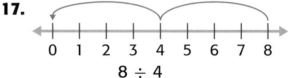
8 ÷ 4

18. 18 ÷ 3
19. 12 ÷ 2
20. 24 ÷ 6

21. 12 ÷ 3
22. 27 ÷ 3
23. 28 ÷ 7

24. There are 12 erasers. Tobias wants to share them equally among himself and his 2 friends. How many erasers will each person get?

25. Chester has 24 pencils. He kept 4 and shared the others equally among his 4 brothers. How many pencils did each brother get?

REAL-WORLD PROBLEM SOLVING

Social Studies Chicago's Ferris wheel is 10 stories tall. Each gondola can seat up to 6 people while they enjoy a 7-minute ride.

26. Suppose someone took a 21-minute ride. How many rides were taken?

27. If 30 students from a class wanted to ride, how many gondolas would they need?

28. It costs $24 for 4 people to ride. How much is each ticket?

29. OPEN ENDED Write a real-world problem that could be represented by 18 ÷ 6.

30.  **WRITE MATH** How is division related to subtraction?

Test Practice

31. Mr. Gomez bought the pizzas shown below. If 3 classes share the pizzas evenly, how many pizzas will each class get?

(Lesson 2B)

A. 2   **C.** 8

B. 3   **D.** 16

32. Hally biked 12 miles this week. She always rode the same 2-mile path. Which of the following number sentences shows the number of days she biked?

(Lesson 2C)

F. 6 ÷ 2 = 12

G. 24 ÷ 2 = 12

H. 12 ÷ 2 = 6

J. 12 ÷ 4 = 3

Spiral Review

Use counters to model the total. Divide to find the number in each group. (Lesson 2B)

33. 12 counters
4 equal groups
▨ in each group

▨ ÷ ▨ = ▨

34. 16 counters
4 equal groups
▨ in each group

▨ ÷ ▨ = ▨

35. 18 counters
3 equal groups
▨ in each group

▨ ÷ ▨ = ▨

Use counters to help complete the chart. (Lesson 2A)

	Total counters	Number of groups	Number in each group	Division sentence
36.	4	▨	2	▨
37.	10	▨	5	▨

Explore

Relate Division and Multiplication

Main Idea

I will explore how division and multiplication are related.

Materials

counters

Get ConnectED

3.2 The student will recognize and use the inverse relationships between addition/subtraction and multiplication/division to complete basic fact sentences. The student will use these relationships to solve problems.
3.5 The student will recall multiplication facts through the twelves table, and the corresponding division facts. Also addresses 3.6.

You can relate division and multiplication.

 **ACTIVITY**

① **Relate Division and Multiplication**

Step 1 **Find 21 ÷ 3.**

Model 21 counters divided into 3 equal groups.

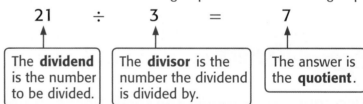

There are 7 counters in each row.

Step 2 **Write a division sentence.**

number in all   number of groups   number in each group

$$21 \div 3 = 7$$

The **dividend** is the number to be divided.

The **divisor** is the number the dividend is divided by.

The answer is the **quotient**.

Step 3 **Write a multiplication sentence.**

number of groups   number in each group   number in all

$$3 \times 7 = 21$$

Think About It

1. Explain how you used models to show 21 ÷ 3.

2. Explain how the array shows that 21 ÷ 3 = 7 is related to 3 × 7 = 21.

3. What pattern do you notice in the number sentences?

4. How can multiplication facts be used to divide?

Practice and Apply It

Use counters to model each problem. Then write related division and multiplication sentences to help find the answer.

5. 12 ÷ 6

6. 18 ÷ 3

7. 25 ÷ 5

8. 15 ÷ 3

9. 16 ÷ 2

10. 24 ÷ 8

Write a related division and multiplication sentence for each picture.

11.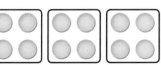

12.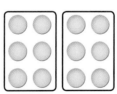

13.

14.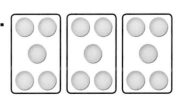

15. WRITE MATH How do you know what multiplication sentence to use to find 28 ÷ 4?

Main Idea
I will divide using related multiplication facts.

 Vocabulary

inverse operations

dividend

divisor

quotient

related facts

fact family

*Get Connect*ED

3.2 The student will recognize and use the inverse relationships between addition/subtraction and multiplication/division to complete basic fact sentences. The student will use these relationships to solve problems.
3.5 The student will recall multiplication facts through the twelves table, and the corresponding division facts. Also addresses 3.6.

Inverse Operations

In the Explore Activity, you used arrays to help you understand how division and multiplication are related. Operations that are related are **inverse operations**; they *undo* each other.

REAL-WORLD EXAMPLE Use an Array

1 **MUFFINS** The pan of blueberry muffins represents an array. The array shows 3 rows of muffins with 4 muffins in each row. Use the array to write a related multiplication and division sentence.

Multiplication	Division
number of rows — number in each row — number in all	number in all — number of rows — number in each row
$3 \times 4 = 12$	$12 \div 3 = 4$
factor — factor — product	**dividend divisor quotient**

The related multiplication and division sentences show how multiplication and division are inverse operations.
$3 \times 4 = 12$ is the inverse of $12 \div 3 = 4$.

A group of **related facts** using the same numbers is a **fact family**. Each fact family follows a pattern by using the same numbers.

Fact Family 3, 4, and 12	Fact Family 7 and 49
$3 \times 4 = 12$ $4 \times 3 = 12$ $12 \div 3 = 4$ $12 \div 4 = 3$	$7 \times 7 = 49$ $49 \div 7 = 7$

Remember

When a number is divided in half, it is the same as dividing a number by two.

 EXAMPLE   Write a Fact Family

② **Use the fact family 3, 6, and 18 to write four related multiplication and division sentences.**

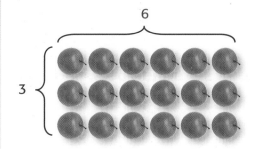

$3 \times 6 = 18$

$6 \times 3 = 18$

$18 \div 3 = 6$

$18 \div 6 = 3$

The pattern shows that 3, 6, and 18 are used in each number sentence.

✓ **CHECK What You Know**

Use the array to complete each pair of number sentences. See Example 1

1. ▢ $\times 5 = 15$
      ▢ $\div 3 = 5$

2. $4 \times$ ▢ $= 24$
      $24 \div$ ▢ $= 6$

Write the fact family for each set of numbers. See Example 2

3. 2, 6, 12

4. 4, 5, 20

5. 3, 9, 27

6. Isabella will divide 18 marbles equally into 2 bags. Show this with a number sentence.

7. 🗣️ **TALK MATH** Why are the product and the dividend the same in $3 \times 7 = 21$ and $21 \div 3 = 7$?

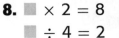
Practice and Problem Solving

Use the array to complete each pair of number sentences.

See Example 1

8. ■ × 2 = 8
■ ÷ 4 = 2

9. 2 × ■ = 4
4 ÷ ■ = 2

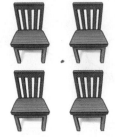

10. ■ × 2 = 14
■ ÷ 2 = 7

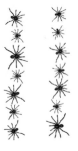

11. 4 × ■ = 20
20 ÷ ■ = 4

Write the fact family for each set of numbers. See Example 2

12. 2, 3, 6

13. 2, 7, 14

14. 4, 16

15. 4, 8, 32

16. 4, 3, 12

17. 4, 7, 28

Identify the pattern by writing the set of numbers for each fact family.

18. 5 × 9 = 45
9 × 5 = 45
45 ÷ 5 = 9
45 ÷ 9 = 5

19. 7 × 2 = 14
2 × 7 = 14
14 ÷ 2 = 7
14 ÷ 7 = 2

20. 3 × 3 = 9
9 ÷ 3 = 3

Solve. Write a number sentence.

21. All 5 members of the Malone family went to the movies. Their tickets cost a total of $30. How much was each ticket?

22. The petting zoo has 21 animals. There are an equal number of goats, ponies, and cows. How many of each animal are there?

23. Measurement Mr. Thomas travels 20 miles each week to and from work. If he works 5 days a week, how many miles does Mr. Thomas travel each day to go to work?

24. Stacia and her friend are each making a bracelet. They have 18 beads to share. If they use the same number of beads, how many beads will each bracelet have?

25. NUMBER SENSE What multiplication fact will help you find $27 \div 9$?

26. WHICH ONE DOESN'T BELONG? Identify the number sentence that does not belong. Explain.

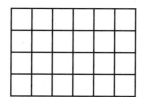

$3 \times 6 = 18$ $18 \div 2 = 9$ $18 \div 6 = 3$ $6 \times 3 = 18$

27. **WRITE MATH** Explain how multiplication facts can help you with division facts. Give an example.

Test Practice

28. The figure below is a model for $4 \times 6 = 24$.

Which number sentence is in the same fact family? (Lesson 2E)

A. $4 \div 6 = 24$ **C.** $24 \div 4 = 6$

B. $24 \div 3 = 8$ **D.** $24 \div 6 = 6$

29. Which number sentence is modeled by repeated subtraction on the number line? (Lesson 2C)

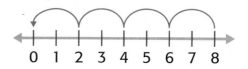

F. $4 \div 2 = 8$

G. $16 \div 2 = 8$

H. $8 \div 2 = 4$

J. $24 \div 8 = 3$

 **Spiral Review**

Use repeated subtraction to divide. (Lesson 2C)

30. $12 \div 4$ **31.** $18 \div 3$ **32.** $28 \div 7$ **33.** $25 \div 5$

34. One frog sat on a log for 18 minutes. A second frog sat for half as long. How long did the second frog sit on the log? (Lesson 2B)

Multiply. Use repeated addition. (Lesson 1B)

35. 8×3 **36.** 2×9 **37.** 3×10 **38.** 10×5

Problem-Solving Investigation

Main Idea I will choose the best strategy to solve a problem.

P.S.I. TEAM +

DENZELL: Our third-grade class will make 3 holiday baskets to give away. We have a total of 21 food items to equally fill the baskets with.

YOUR MISSION: Find how many items will fill each basket.

Understand

- You know the class will make 3 baskets.

- There are 21 items to equally fill the baskets with.

- Find the number of items that will fill each basket.

Plan
You can use models to solve the math problem.

Solve
Use counters to model the situation.

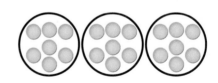

The model shows that $21 \div 3 = 7$.

So, the third-grade class will fill each basket with 7 items.

Check
Check by using repeated addition.
$7 + 7 + 7 = 21$
The answer is 21, so you know your answer is correct and reasonable. ✓

3.2 The student will recognize and use the inverse relationships between addition/subtraction and multiplication/division to complete basic fact sentences. The student will use these relationships to solve problems.

Mixed Problem Solving

EXTRA PRACTICE
Begins on page EP2.

- Make a table.
- Draw a picture.
- Make a model.

Use any strategy to solve each problem.

1. Solana buys two of each of the following items. She gives the cashier two $20-bills. How much change will she receive?

2. Dasan planted 30 tomato seeds in his garden. Three out of every 5 seeds grew into plants. How many tomato plants did he have?

3. Would it cost more to send 2 letters or 3 postcards? Explain.

4. Claudia and Danielle bought paint for their project. They chose 5 colors. Each bottle of paint costs $3. Find the total cost.

5. **Measurement** Alfonso exercised 20 minutes yesterday. Today he is going to exercise twice as long. How long does Alfonso plan to exercise today?

6. **Geometry** Blaine built a cube staircase. How many cubes does he need to build 6 steps?

7. Marjorie made 48 pancakes for the school breakfast. Elian ate some of the pancakes, and now Marjorie only has 43 pancakes. How many pancakes did Elian eat?

8. There are 3 children in line. Cami is right after Brock. Branden is third. What place is each child in line?

9. One campsite has 3 tents with 5 people in each tent. Another campsite has 3 tents with 4 people in each. How many campers are there in all?

10. Rachel sold 4 glasses of lemonade for 25¢ each. How much money did she make?

11. **WRITE MATH** Mrs. Felps read her students one book each day for 2 weeks. If there are 5 days in each school week, how many books did she read in all? Explain your reasoning.

Chapter Study Guide and Review

FOLDABLES Study Organizer

Be sure the following Key Concepts are noted in your Foldable.

Meaning of Multiplication

Arrays and Multiplication

Key Concepts

- **Multiplication** can be thought of as repeated addition. (Lesson 1)

$$4 \times 5 = 20$$

is the same as

$$5 + 5 + 5 + 5 = 20$$

- The **Commutative Property of Multiplication** states that the order in which numbers are multiplied does not change the product. (Lesson 1)

$$3 \times 2 = 6 \qquad 2 \times 3 = 6$$

- In the operation of **division**, one number tells you how many things you have. The other number tells you how many equal groups to form or how many to put in each group.

(Lesson 2)

$$8 \div 2 = 4$$

- Multiplication and division are **inverse operations**. They "undo" each other.

(Lesson 2)

Key Vocabulary

array

divisor

fact family

factors

product

quotient

Vocabulary Check

Choose the vocabulary word that completes each sentence.

1. An ____?____ is an arrangement of equal rows and equal columns.

2. The answer to a division problem is the ____?____.

3. In the multiplication sentence $2 \times 6 = 12$, 12 is the ____?____.

4. A ____?____ is a group of related facts using the same numbers.

5. In the division sentence $12 \div 3 = 4$, 3 is the ____?____.

6. Two ____?____ are multiplied together to get a product.

Multi-Part Lesson Review

Meaning of Multiplication

Multiplication as Repeated Addition (Lesson 1B)

Write an addition and a multiplication sentence for each model.

7.   **8.**

EXAMPLE 1

Write an addition sentence and a multiplication sentence.

$6 + 6 + 6 = 18$ $3 \times 6 = 18$

Multiply. Use repeated addition.

9. 4×6 **10.** 2×7

Arrays and Multiplication (Lesson 1D)

Write two multiplication sentences for each array.

11.   **12.**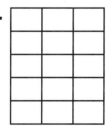

EXAMPLE 2

There are 3 rows of 4 muffins. How many muffins altogether? Write two multiplication sentences.

$3 \times 4 = 12$

$4 \times 3 = 12$

Use Multiplication to Compare (Lesson 1E)

Use the model and bar diagram to compare. Then write a multiplication sentence.

13. 4 times as many

14. twice as much money

$5

├------ ? $ ------┤

$5	$5

EXAMPLE 3

Timmy downloaded 5 songs. His sister downloaded three times as many. How many songs did she download?

3 times as many songs

5 songs

├------ ? songs ------┤

5	5	5

$3 \times 5 = 15$ songs

Use Multiplication to Find Combinations (Lesson 1F)

Make a picture or tree diagram to find all the possible combinations. Write a multiplication sentence.

15. Find the possible combinations of one yogurt and one topping.

Yogurt	Toppings
Strawberry	Granola
Peach	Strawberries
Vanilla	

16. Ian can buy a skateboard or a surfboard. Both come in yellow, orange, green, or red. Find Ian's choices of colored skateboards and surfboards.

EXAMPLE 4

Jane is buying a bike. List all of Jane's bike and color choices.

Bike Choices

Road Bike   **Mountain Bike**

green   silver   red
Color Choices

Jane has 6 choices of bikes.

Check   2   ×   3   =   6   ✓
                 types of   colors   combinations
                 bikes

Problem-Solving Strategy: Make a Table (Lesson 1G)

Solve. Use the *make a table* strategy.

17. Toya finishes reading a book every 3 days. How many books had she read after 21 days?

18. **Algebra** Polly is putting balloons in bunches. If Polly keeps her pattern going, how many balloons will be in the sixth bunch?

Balloon Bunches	
Bunch	**Number**
First	3
Second	5
Third	7

EXAMPLE 5

For the first day of school, Maggie can wear a yellow or a blue shirt. With her shirt she can wear a skirt, shorts, pants, or capris. How many possible outfits does Maggie have to wear?

Organize the information in a table.

	Yellow shirt	Blue shirt
Skirt	yellow shirt, skirt	blue shirt, skirt
Shorts	yellow shirt, shorts	blue shirt, shorts
Pants	yellow shirt, pants	blue shirt, pants
Capris	yellow shirt, capris	blue shirt, capris

Maggie has 8 possible outfits to wear.

Meaning of Division

Division as Equal Sharing (Lesson 2B)

Use counters to model the total. Divide to find the number in each group.

19. 12 counters
3 equal groups

_____ ÷ _____ = _____

20. 15 counters
5 equal groups

_____ ÷ _____ = _____

21. 8 counters
2 equal groups

_____ ÷ _____ = _____

EXAMPLE 6

Coach Shelton divided 27 players into 3 equal-sized teams. How many players are on each team?

Team 1 ◯◯◯◯◯◯◯◯◯ players

Team 2 ◯◯◯◯◯◯◯◯◯ players

Team 3 ◯◯◯◯◯◯◯◯◯ players

$27 \div 3 = 9$ players on each team.

Relate Division and Subtraction (Lesson 2C)

Use repeated subtraction to divide.

22.
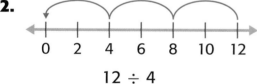
$12 \div 4$

23.
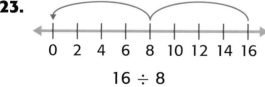
$16 \div 8$

24. $6 \div 2$ **25.** $27 \div 3$

26. $14 \div 2$ **27.** $4 \div 2$

28. Chang has 15 frogs in his pond. If he catches 3 a day, how many days will it take him to catch all of the frogs?

EXAMPLE 7

Find $8 \div 2$.

One Way: Number Line

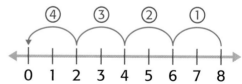

Start at 8. Count back by 2s until you reach 0. Count how many times you subtracted. So, $8 \div 2 = 4$.

Another Way: Repeated Subtraction

① ② ③ ④

$\begin{array}{cccc} 8 & 6 & 4 & 2 \\ -2 & -2 & -2 & -2 \\ \hline 6 & 4 & 2 & 0 \end{array}$

So, $8 \div 2 = 4$.

Inverse Operations (Lesson 2E)

Use the array to complete each pair of number sentences.

29. ■ × 2 = 8
    ■ ÷ 4 = 2

30. ■ × 6 = 24
    ■ ÷ 4 = 6

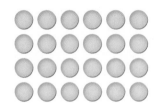

Write the fact family for each set of numbers.

31. 6, 7, 42   **32.** 8, 4, 2

33. 5, 4, 20   **34.** 4, 9, 36

EXAMPLE 8

Show division and multiplication as inverse operations. Write related multiplication and division facts.

3 × 7 = 21   21 ÷ 3 = 7

Write the fact family for the array.

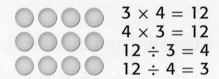

3 × 4 = 12
4 × 3 = 12
12 ÷ 3 = 4
12 ÷ 4 = 3

Problem-Solving Investigation: Choose a Strategy (Lesson 2F)

Use any strategy to solve.

35. Algebra One day, Juana received 2 gifts. The next day she received 4 gifts. The third day she received 6 gifts. If the pattern continues, how many gifts will she receive on the 6th day? How many gifts did she receive altogether?

36. You need to read 5 books a month during the school year. The school year is from August to May. How many books will you read in a school year?

EXAMPLE 9

Miriam bought 3 toys. Jamil bought 2 more toys than Miriam. How many toys did they buy?

You can model the problem with counters.

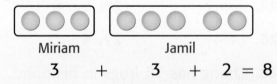

Miriam   Jamil

3   +   3   +   2 = 8

So, Miriam and Jamil bought 8 toys.

Tell whether each statement is *true* or *false*.

1. The Commutative Property of Multiplication says the order in which numbers are multiplied can change the product.

2. Repeated subtraction can help you solve a division problem.

Multiply. Use repeated addition.

3. 3×6

4. 3×9

5. 5×5

6. 6×4

Write two multiplication sentences for each array.

7.

8.

9. MULTIPLE CHOICE A cook boils 16 potatoes in 2 pots. Each pot has the same number of potatoes. Which number sentence shows how many potatoes are in each pot?

A. $16 + 2 = 18$

B. $16 - 2 = 18$

C. $16 \times 2 = 32$

D. $16 \div 2 = 8$

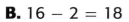

10. If Kathryn chooses 1 item from each menu, how many different combinations could she make? Make a table to explain.

Use the bar diagram to compare. Then write a multiplication sentence.

11. 4 times as many stars

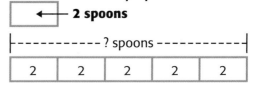

12. 5 times as many spoons

2	2	2	2	2

13. MULTIPLE CHOICE Benita did this division problem.

$$15 \div 5 = 3$$

Which problem could she do to check her answer?

F. $5 + 3$

H. 5×3

G. $3 - 5$

J. $3 \div 5$

14. **WRITE MATH** Can 6 roses be divided equally between 2 vases? Explain.

Test Practice

TEST EXAMPLE

Tyler rides his bicycle 2 miles a day. He rides 4 days a week. How many miles does Tyler ride in a week?

A. 4 miles   **C.** 8 miles

B. 6 miles   **D.** 10 miles

Read the Question

You need to find how many miles Tyler rides his bike in a week.

Solve the Question

You can draw an array to find 4 × 2.

So, Tyler rides 8 miles a week.
The answer is C.

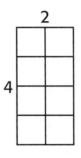

$4 \times 2 = 8$

Read each question. Then fill in the correct answer on the answer sheet provided by your teacher or on a separate sheet of paper.

1. The model shows 12 ÷ 3 = 4.

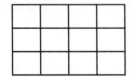

Which number sentence below is from the same family of facts?

   A. 3 + 4 = 7   **C.** 7 − 4 = 3

   B. 3 × 4 = 12   **D.** 6 ÷ 3 = 2

2. Which number sentence is modeled by the figure below?

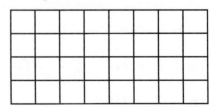

   F. 5 × 8 = 40   **H.** 8 + 8 + 8 = 24

   G. 4 × 8 = 32   **J.** 3 × 8 = 24

3. Bella arranged 24 shells in 6 equal-size groups. How many were in each group?

A. 3   **C.** 6

B. 4   **D.** 8

4. Marquez has 16 baseball cards. He puts the cards in piles of 8. How many piles does he make?

F. 2   **H.** 6

G. 4   **J.** 8

5. Ming-Su equally divides 6 fish into 3 fish tanks. Which picture shows Ming-Su's fish?

A.

B.

C.

D.

6. Evita swims 5 times a week for 2 hours. How many hours does Evita swim in a week?

F. 7

G. 10

H. 15

J. 25

7. Marcy ran 2 miles today. Brett ran 4 times as far as Marcy. How many miles did Brett run?

A. 4   **C.** 8

B. 6   **D.** 10

8. Seth arranged a group of buttons in rows and columns as shown.

What operation best shows how he arranged them?

F. 6 + 4   **H.** 4 − 6

G. 6 ÷ 4   **J.** 4 × 6

NEED EXTRA HELP?								
If You Missed Question . . .	1	2	3	4	5	6	7	8
Go to Chapter-Lesson . . .	3-2E	3-1D	3-2B	3-2C	3-2B	3-1B	3-1E	3-1D
For help with . . .	SOL 3.2	SOL 3.6	SOL 3.5	SOL 3.6	SOL 3.6	SOL 3.5	SOL 3.5	SOL 3.6

Solve Multiplication and Division Problems

connectED.mcgraw-hill.com

Investigate

 Animations

 Vocabulary

 Math Songs

 Multilingual eGlossary

Learn

 Personal Tutor

 Virtual Manipulatives

 Audio

 Foldables

Practice

 Self-Check Practice

 eGames

 Worksheets

 Assessment

The
⭐ BIG Idea

How can I develop strategies for solving basic multiplication facts and related division facts?

FOLDABLES®
Study Organizer

Make this Foldable to help you organize information about multiplication and division concepts and facts. Start with one sheet of 11″ × 17″ paper.

Multiply and Divide by 2 | Multiply and Divide by 3
Multiply and Divide by 5 | Multiply and Divide by 10
Multiply and Divide by 1 | Multiply and Divide with 0

Review Vocabulary

factor **factor** a number that is multiplied by another number

2 and 3 are factors of 6 because $2 \times 6 = 6$.

array **arregio** objects or symbols displayed in rows of the same length and columns of the same length

column

row

Key Vocabulary

English	Español
partition	separar

When Will I Use This?

A Leader For All

Your Turn!
You will solve this problem in the chapter.

You have two options for checking Prerequisite Skills for this chapter.

Text Option Take the Quick Check below.

QUICK Check

Multiply.

1. 6 × 4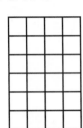

2. 1 × 5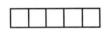

3. 5 × 2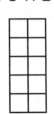

4. 7 × 2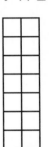

Draw an array for each fact. Multiply.

5. 5 × 4

6. 1 × 6

7. 4 × 7

8. 2 × 9

Solve.

9. Louis has 2 quarters. Yellow whistles cost 5¢ each. Louis wants to buy 8 whistles. Does he have enough money to buy 8 whistles? Explain.

10. There were 9 oak trees on each side of a street. After some trees were cut down, there were 7 trees left. How many trees were cut down?

Algebra Identify a pattern. Then find the missing numbers.

11. ▪, ▪, 30, 25, 20, 15

12. ▪, ▪, 16, 14, 12, 10

13. ▪, ▪, 41, 31, 21, 11

14. 60, 50, 40, 30, ▪, ▪,

 Online Option Take the Online Readiness Quiz.

Main Idea
I will use arrays and bar diagrams to multiply by 2.

3.5 The student will recall multiplication facts through the twelves table, and the corresponding division facts. **3.6** The student will represent multiplication and division, using area, set, and number line models, and create and solve problems that involve multiplication of two whole numbers, one factor 99 or less and the second factor 5 or less.

Multiply by 2

There are many different ways to multiply by 2. One way is to use an array. Another way is to draw a picture.

REAL-WORLD EXAMPLE Use an Array

1 **SCHOOL** The students in an art class are working on a project. How many students are there in the art class if there are 8 groups of 2?

You need to model 8 groups of 2 or 8 × 2.

One Way: Use an Array	**Another Way:** Draw a Picture
Show an array with 8 rows and 2 columns.	Draw 8 groups of 2.
2 + 2 + 2 + 2 + 2 + 2 + 2 + 2 or 16	2 + 2 + 2 + 2 + 2 + 2 + 2 + 2 or 16

So, there are 8 × 2 or 16 students in the art class.

You can also use a bar diagram to multiply by 2.

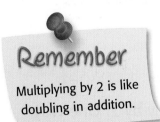
REAL-WORLD EXAMPLE   Use a Bar Diagram

2 **FRIENDS** **Sybil rides her bike to the park Monday, Wednesday, and Friday. It is a 2 mile round-trip. How many miles does she ride for the three days?**

Step 1   Model 2 miles a day as one part.

1 part = 2 miles

2 miles
⊢-1 day-⊣

Step 2   Since she rode the same amount for 3 days, model a total of 3 parts.

⊢------- ? miles -------⊣

2 miles	2 miles	2 miles

⊢--------3 days --------⊣

Step 3   Write a number sentence.

3 parts = 3 × 2

3 × 2 = 6   So Sybil rode 6 miles.

Check   Repeated addition shows that 3 × 2 = 6 is correct.

2 + 2 + 2 = 6 ✓

✓ **CHECK What You Know**

Multiply. See Examples 1 and 2

1.

4 groups of 2

2.

3 groups of 2

3.

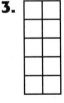

5 rows of 2

Multiply. Use a bar diagram if needed. See Example 2

4. 6 × 2   **5.** 2 × 2   **6.** 9 × 2   **7.** 8 × 2

8. BAR DIAGRAM Ten students each have 2 pieces of chalk. How many pieces of chalk are there?

9. TALK MATH Explain the different strategies you can use to remember the multiplication facts for 2.

Multiply. See Examples 1 and 2

10.

2 groups of 2

11.

6 groups of 2

12.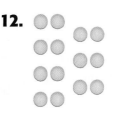

7 groups of 2

13.

3 rows of 2

14.

4 rows of 2

15.

5 rows of 2

Multiply. Use a bar diagram if needed. See Example 2

16. 2
     × 5

17. 2
     × 3

18. 5
     × 2

19. 4
     × 2

20. 2 × 7

21. 2 × 9

22. 6 × 2

23. 10 × 2

24. 2 × 4

25. 2 × 8

26. 2 × 2

27. 3 × 2

Solve. Use models if needed. See Examples 1 and 2

28. There are 2 squares. How many sides are there in all?

29. There are 2 dogs. How many eyes are there in all?

30. BAR DIAGRAM There are 2 spiders. Each has 8 legs. How many legs are there in all?

31. BAR DIAGRAM There are 3 students. Each has 2 pencils. How many pencils are there in all?

H.O.T. Problems

32. OPEN ENDED Write a real-world multiplication word problem with an answer between 11 and 19.

33. WRITE MATH Write a problem about a real-world situation in which a number is multiplied by 2.

Main Idea

I will use models to partition when dividing by 2.

Vocabulary

partition

Get ConnectED

3.5 The student will recall multiplication facts through the twelves table, and the corresponding division facts. 3.6 The student will represent multiplication and division, using area, set, and number line models, and create and solve problems that involve multiplication of two whole numbers, one factor 99 or less and the second factor 5 or less.

Divide by 2

In the previous chapter, you learned about the division symbol ÷. Another symbol for division is $)\overline{}$.

REAL-WORLD EXAMPLE   Use Models

① **FRUIT Javier and Alexis share an apple equally. If there are 8 slices, how many slices will each of them get?**

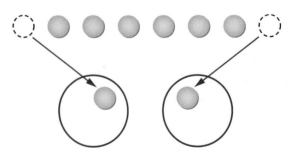

To share equally between 2 people means to divide by 2. So, find $8 \div 2$ or $2)\overline{8}$.

Share or **partition** one counter at a time into each group until the counters are gone.

The model shows $8 \div 2 = 4$ or $2)\overline{8}^{\,4}$.

Each person will get 4 apple slices.

② **SCHOOL** Twelve students are divided into 2 groups. How many students are in each group?

You can use a related fact to find 12 ÷ 2 or 2)‾12‾.

$2 \times \blacksquare = 12$ ◄——— You know that 2 × 6 = 12.

So, 12 ÷ 2 = 6 or 2)‾12‾ with 6 above.

There are 6 students in each group.

✓ CHECK What You Know

Divide. Write a related multiplication fact. See Examples 1 and 2

1.

2)‾4‾

2.

(two circles with stars)

10 ÷ 2

3. 6 ÷ 2

4. 14 ÷ 2

5. 2)‾8‾

6. Victor and his sister each read an equal number of books. Together they read 16 books. Write the number sentence to show how many books they each read.

7. 🗨 **TALK MATH** What are two different ways to find 16 ÷ 2?

Practice and Problem Solving

EXTRA PRACTICE
Begins on page EP2.

Divide. Write a related multiplication fact. See Examples 1 and 2

8.

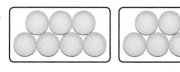

14 ÷ 2

9.

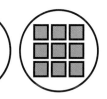

2)‾18‾

10. 4 ÷ 2

11. 16 ÷ 2

12. 18 ÷ 2

13. 2)‾2‾

14. 2)‾20‾

15. 2)‾6‾

Solve. Write a number sentence.

16. Damian will plant 12 seeds in groups of 2. How many groups of 2 will he have once they are all planted?

17. Kyle and Alan equally divide a package of 14 erasers. How many erasers will each person get?

18. Lydia shared her 16 pattern tiles equally with Pilar. Pilar then shared her tiles equally with Timothy. How many tiles does each student have?

19. Each car on the Supersonic Speed ride can hold 18 people. If the seats are in groups of 2, how many groups of two are there on 3 cars?

Algebra Copy and complete each table.

20.

Rule: Divide by 2.				
Input	10	▩	18	14
Output	▩	4	▩	7

21.

Rule: Multiply by 2.				
Input	7	▩	6	9
Output	▩	2	▩	▩

H.O.T. Problems

22. OPEN ENDED Write a number that when divided by 2 is more than 8.

CHALLENGE Divide.

23. $36 \div 2$ **24.** $50 \div 2$ **25.** $80 \div 2$ **26.** $42 \div 2$

27. FIND THE ERROR Carlos is finding $8 \div 2$. Find and correct his mistake.

$8 \div 2 = 16$
because
$2 \times 8 = 16$

28. WRITE MATH Can you divide 9 into equal groups of 2? Explain.

29. The owner wants to share the fish in the tank equally among 4 small fish bowls.

Which of the following could be used to find the number of fish in each bowl? (Lesson 1B)

A. 8 + 4   **C.** 8 × 4

B. 8 − 4   **D.** 8 ÷ 4

30. Ariel and Jonathan share some raisins for a snack. The raisins are shown.

How many raisins will each child get if they share them equally? (Lesson 1B)

F. 4   **H.** 16

G. 8   **I.** 32

31. What number makes this number sentence true? (Lesson 1A)

$$12 + 8 = \blacksquare \times 2$$

A. 5   **B.** 8   **C.** 9   **D.** 10

32. Which of the following is used to find how many legs are on 6 birds? (Lesson 1B)

F. 2 × 6   **H.** 2 + 6

G. 6 ÷ 6   **J.** 6 − 2

Spiral Review

Multiply. (Lesson 1A)

33.

2 rows of 5

34.

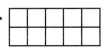

4 rows of 2

35.

7 groups of 2

Use any strategy to solve. (Lesson 1A)

36. Lolita read 10 pages in her book each of the last two nights. How many pages did Lolita read the last two nights altogether?

37. Julian bought 8 books this year. He gets a free book every time he buys 1. How many books did he get this year altogether?

Explore Find a Missing Factor

Main Idea

I will explore the multiplication table to look for patterns and find missing factors.

Materials

multiplication table

Get ConnectED

3.5 The student will recall multiplication facts through the twelves table, and the corresponding division facts. **3.19** The student will recognize and describe a variety of patterns formed using numbers, tables, and pictures, and extend the patterns, using the same or different forms.

You have learned different strategies for finding products. Patterns you find in the multiplication table can help you remember products and find missing factors.

🏃 ACTIVITY

① **Make a Multiplication Table**

Step 1 **Find the factors.**

To find the product of two factors, find the first factor in the left column and the second factor across the top row.

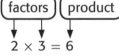

$$2 \times 3 = 6$$

factors

×	0	1	2	③	4	5	6	7	8	9	10
0											
1											
②				6							
3											
4											
5											
6											
7											
8											
9											
10											

factors

Write the product of 2 × 3 where row 2 and column 3 meet.

Step 2 **Find the products.**

Write the products of the multiplication facts you know. Remember that you can use the Commutative Property of Multiplication, a known fact, or patterns.

The multiplication table can also be used to help you find missing factors.

ACTIVITY

2) Find Missing Factors

Arlo was asked to bring 24 juice boxes to his scout meeting. He knows they come in packages of 4. How many packages will he need?

packages		number in each package		total
▧	×	4	=	24

Step 1 Find the row with 4 as a factor.

X	0	1	2	3	4	5	6
0	0	0	0	0	0	0	0
1	0	1	2	3	4	5	6
2	0	2	4	6	8	10	12
3	0	3	6	9	12	15	18
④	0	4	8	12	16	20	24
5	0	5	10	15	20	25	30

Step 2 Move across the row to find 24, the product.

X	0	1	2	3	4	5	6
0	0	0	0	0	0	0	0
1	0	1	2	3	4	5	6
2	0	2	4	6	8	10	12
3	0	3	6	9	12	15	18
④	0	4	8	12	16	20	㉔
5	0	5	10	15	20	25	30

Step 3 From 24, move straight up to find the missing factor, 6.

So, $6 \times 4 = 24$. Arlo needs 6 packages of juice boxes.

X	0	1	2	3	4	5	⑥
0	0	0	0	0	0	0	0
1	0	1	2	3	4	5	6
2	0	2	4	6	8	10	12
3	0	3	6	9	12	15	18
④	0	4	8	12	16	20	㉔
5	0	5	10	15	20	25	30

Think About It

1. Explain how patterns may help you find a missing factor.

2. How can you use the multiplication table to help find the quotient to a division fact?

3. How does the multiplication table show you that multiplication and division are related?

Main Idea

I will use different strategies to multiply by 3.

3.5 The student will recall multiplication facts through the twelves table, and the corresponding division facts. **3.6** The student will represent multiplication and division, using area, set, and number line models, and create and solve problems that involve multiplication of two whole numbers, one factor 99 or less and the second factor 5 or less. Also addresses 3.19.

Multiply by 3

In the previous lesson, you used a multiplication table to find factors and products.

×	0	1	2	3	4	5	6	7	8	9	10
0	0	0	0	0	0	0	0	0	0	0	0
1	0	1	2	3	4	5	6	7	8	9	10
2	0	2	4	6	8	10	12	14	16	18	20
3	0	3	6	9	12	15	18	21	24	27	30
4	0	4	8	12	16	20	24	28	32	36	40
5	0	5	10	15	20	25	30	35	40	45	50
6	0	6	12	18	24	30	36	42	48	54	60
7	0	7	14	21	28	35	42	49	56	63	70
8	0	8	16	24	32	40	48	56	64	72	80
9	0	9	18	27	36	45	54	63	72	81	90
10	0	10	20	30	40	50	60	70	80	90	100

There are other ways you can find products.

REAL-WORLD EXAMPLE   Use an Array

① **PETS There are 3 dogs. Each dog buried 4 bones in a yard. How many bones are buried in the yard?**

You can use an array to find 3 groups of 4 bones, or 3 × 4.

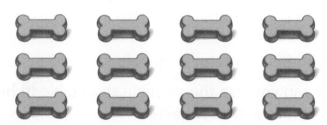

So, there are 12 bones buried in the yard.

You can use a number line to help you solve a problem.

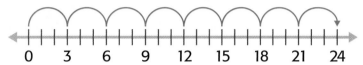 **REAL-WORLD EXAMPLE**   Skip Count

Remember

You use number patterns when you skip count.

2 **GAMES** **Eight friends have 3 marbles each. How many marbles are there in all?**

Each friend has a group of 3 marbles. There are 8 friends. Use a number line to find 8×3.

```
  ⌢   ⌢   ⌢   ⌢   ⌢   ⌢   ⌢   ⌢
←|||||||||||||||||||||||||||→
  0   3   6   9   12  15  18  21  24
```

Eight jumps of 3 is 24.

$8 \times 3 = 24$

So, there are 24 marbles in all.

EXAMPLE   Find a Missing Factor

3 **Find the missing factor.**

$$3 \times \blacksquare = 15$$

THINK 3 times what number equals 15?

Equally place 15 counters, one at a time, into 3 groups.

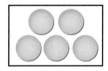 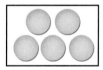 

Three groups of 5 are 15. The missing factor in the multiplication sentence is 5.

So, $3 \times 5 = 15$.

Key Concept   Multiplication Strategies

There are different strategies you can use to find the products of multiplication problems.

- Use models or draw a picture.
- Use repeated addition or skip count.
- Draw an array or a bar diagram.
- Use a related multiplication fact.
- Use patterns.

Multiply. Draw an array or skip count if needed. See Examples 1 and 2

1. 3
  × 1

2. 3
  × 5

3. 3 × 8

4. 3 × 6

Algebra **Find each missing factor.** See Example 3

5. 3 × ■ = 18

6. ■ × 5 = 15

7. ■ × 7 = 21

8. The branches on a tree have leaves that grow in groups of 3. How many leaves are on 9 branches?

9. 🗣 **TALK MATH** Explain two ways to find the product of 3 × 7.

Practice and Problem Solving

EXTRA PRACTICE
Begins on page EP2.

Multiply. Draw an array or skip count if needed. See Examples 1 and 2

10. 1
  × 3

11. 10
  × 3

12. 3
  × 4

13. 5
  × 3

14. 9 × 3

15. 3 × 7

16. 3 × 3

17. 6 × 3

18. 7 × 3

19. 3 × 4

20. 3 × 5

21. 3 × 10

Algebra **Find each missing factor.** See Example 3

22. 1 × ■ = 3

23. 3 × ■ = 9

24. ■ × 3 = 15

25. ■ × 3 = 27

26. 4 × ■ = 12

27. ■ × 3 = 6

28. There are 9 students. They each put 3 books on a shelf. How many books did they place on the shelf?

29. There are 7 daisies and 7 tulips. Each flower has 3 petals. How many petals are there in all?

30. Hoshi, Joan, and Kita each had 3 snacks packed in their lunch boxes. They each ate one snack in the morning. How many snacks are left in all?

31. Thom is buying 4 packages of seeds. Each package costs $3 and contains 5 envelopes of seeds. What will be the total cost? How many envelopes will he have?

H.O.T. Problems

32. **OPEN ENDED** Look at the 3s row in a multiplication table. Describe the pattern.

33. 🗣 **WRITE MATH** Write a real-world problem that contains groups of 3. Ask a classmate to solve. Check the answer.

34. In the pattern below, each number is 2 times greater than the number before it. What is the next number in the pattern? (Lesson 1A)

1, 2, 4, 8 ____

A. 10   **C.** 16

B. 12   **D.** 18

35. Jenny has 20 beads. Which number sentence shows how many bracelets Jenny can make if each has the number of beads shown below. (Lesson 1B)

F. 20 + 10 = 30

G. 20 ÷ 10 = 2

H. 20 − 10 = 10

J. 20 × 10 = 200

36. Which number sentence does the number line model? (Lesson 1D)

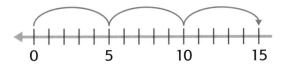

A. 5 × ▢ = 20   **C.** 3 × ▢ = 15

B. 2 × ▢ = 20   **D.** 15 × ▢ = 15

37. Jeslin bought 3 pairs of socks. Each pair of socks cost the same price. How much did each pair of socks cost? (Lesson 1D)

3/$18

F. $5   **H.** $7

G. $6   **J.** $8

Algebra Find each missing number. (Lesson 1B)

38. 16 ÷ ▢ = 2   **39.** 14 ÷ 2 = ▢   **40.** 6 ÷ ▢ = 3

Divide. Write a related multiplication fact. (Lesson 1B)

41. Each student in the Art Club must pay $2 for supplies. If $20 was collected, how many students are in the club?

42. Twelve students are going on a field trip. There are 2 vans that hold the same number of students. How many students will go in each van?

Main Idea

I will use multiplication and subtraction to divide by 3.

Get ConnectED

3.5 The student will recall multiplication facts through the twelves table, and the corresponding division facts. **3.6** The student will represent multiplication and division, using area, set, and number line models, and create and solve problems that involve multiplication of two whole numbers, one factor 99 or less and the second factor 5 or less. Also addresses 3.19.

Divide by 3

You have used the multiplication table to find missing factors. It can also be used to divide.

REAL-WORLD EXAMPLE

Use the Multiplication Table

1 **MARKERS** Marlo, Maria, and Tani have 24 markers in all. Each person has the same number of markers. How many markers does each person have?

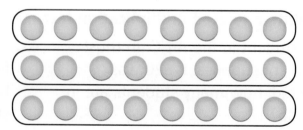

Divide a group of 24 into 3 equal groups. Find $24 \div 3$ or $3\overline{)24}$.

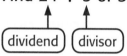
dividend   divisor

- Locate row 3.
- Follow row 3 to 24.
- Move straight up the column to the quotient.

×	1	2	3	4	5	6	7	⑧
1	1	2	3	4	5	6	7	8
2	2	4	6	8	10	12	14	16
③	3	6	9	12	15	18	21	㉔
4	4	8	12	16	20	24	28	32
5	5	10	15	20	25	30	35	40
6	6	12	18	24	30	36	42	48
7	7	14	21	28	35	42	49	56
8	8	16	24	32	40	48	56	64

So, $24 \div 3 = 8$ or $3\overline{)24}^{\,8}$. Each person has 8 markers.

Check The array below shows that $24 \div 3$ is 8. ✔

You can use related facts to help you divide.

 REAL-WORLD EXAMPLE   Use Related Facts

② **TRAVEL** **To travel to the beach, Angela and her 14 friends will divide up equally into 3 cars. How many friends will be in each car?**

You need to find 15 ÷ 3 or 3)‾15‾.

15 ÷ 3 = ■

3 × ■ = 15 ←⎯⎯ THINK 3 times what number equals 15?

3 × 5 = 15

So, 15 ÷ 3 = 5 or 3)‾15‾.
$$\overset{5}{}$$

There will be 5 friends in each car.

You can use repeated subtraction on a number line to divide.

 EXAMPLE   Use Repeated Subtraction

③ **Find 6 ÷ 3 or 3)‾6‾.**

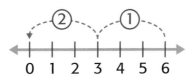

• Start at 6 and count back by 3s to 0.

• 3 was subtracted two times.

So, 6 ÷ 3 = 2 or 3)‾6‾.
$$\overset{2}{}$$

 **Remember**

A division sentence like 3)‾6‾ is read "six divided by three." Always read the dividend under the symbol first.

 CHECK What You Know

Divide. See Examples 1–3

1. 12 ÷ 3

2. 18 ÷ 3

3. 3)‾9‾

4. 3)‾27‾

5. Rosa spent $30 on 2 skirts and a purse. Each item costs the same. How much did each item cost?

6. **TALK MATH** How can you use 8 × 3 to find 24 ÷ 3?

Practice and Problem Solving

EXTRA PRACTICE
Begins on page EP2.

Divide. See Examples 1–3

7. 15 ÷ 3   **8.** 9 ÷ 3   **9.** 6 ÷ 3   **10.** 18 ÷ 3

11. 16 ÷ 2   **12.** 20 ÷ 2   **13.** 3$\overline{)12}$ **14.** 3$\overline{)3}$

15. 3$\overline{)30}$ **16.** 3$\overline{)27}$ **17.** 3$\overline{)21}$ **18.** 3$\overline{)24}$

Algebra **Copy and complete each table.**

19.

Rule: Divide by 3.				
Input	21	▓	30	▓
Output	▓	4	▓	6

20.

Rule: Subtract 3.				
Input	28	▓	33	▓
Output	▓	15	▓	16

21. A soccer coach buys 3 new soccer balls for $21. What is the price for each ball? Write a number sentence.

22. There are 27 bananas. They will be divided equally into 3 piles. How many will be in each pile?

23. Stanley is on a 3-day hike. He will hike a total of 18 miles. If he hikes the same number of miles each day, how many miles will he hike the first day?

24. Makenna placed 20 stickers in equal rows of 5. Then, she gave away 2 stickers. Can she make equal rows of 3 now? Explain.

Use the information to solve the problems.

A Leader For All

25. Mr. Martin wants to divide the students into groups of 3. How many groups will there be?

26. How many more adult volunteers are needed?

27. NUMBER SENSE Mr. Marcos buys 4 bottles of glue, 1 stapler, and 2 notebooks. Can the total amount spent be divided equally by 3? Explain.

Item	Cost
Glue	$2
Stapler	$5
Notebook	$3

28. WHICH ONE DOESN'T BELONG? Which fact does not belong? Explain.

$6 \div 3$ $3\overline{)6}$ $6 \div 2$ $6\overline{)18}$

29. **WRITE MATH** Explain how to find $9 \div 3$ two different ways.

 Test Practice

30. Mr. Lobo buys 3 of the same item at a store. The total is $27. What did he buy? (Lesson 1E)

A.
$8

C.
$4

B.
$9

D.
$3

31. Aiden and 2 of his friends each have 10 baseball cards. Which operation sign should be placed in the ■ to find out how many baseball cards the boys have altogether? (Lesson 1D)

$$3 \; \blacksquare \; 10 = 30$$

F. $+$

G. $-$

H. $\times$

J. $\div$

Multiply. (Lesson 1D)

32. 3×6 **33.** 3×3 **34.** 8×3

35. Marilyn has 12 shells in some bags. Each bag has 2 shells. How many bags are there in all? (Lesson 1B)

36. Chloe placed biscuit dough in 2 equal rows. There were 7 biscuits in each row. How many biscuits are there on the baking sheet? (Lesson 1A)

Problem-Solving Strategy: Work Backward

Main Idea I will solve a problem by working backward.

Frannie put some money in the bank to start a savings account. Last month she put in enough money to double that amount. Today, she put in more money and the total amount doubled again. Now she has $20. How much money did Frannie start with?

Understand **What facts do you know?**

- The money doubled two times.
- The total amount at the end is $20.

What do you need to find?

- Find the amount of money Frannie started with.

Plan Work backward from what you know, $20, to find the amount Frannie started with.

Solve Start with $20.

- Find the number that was doubled.
- Since the amount was doubled two times, find half of $10.

So, the amount of money Frannie started with was $5.

$20
↓
Half of $20 is $10.
↓
$10
↓
Half of $10 is $5.
↓
$5

Check When you double $5, the result is $5 × 2 or $10. When you double $10, the result is $10 × 2 or $20. So, the answer is correct. ✓

3.5 The student will recall multiplication facts through the twelves table, and the corresponding division facts.

EXTEND

Refer to the problem on the previous page.

1. Explain how the *work backward* strategy helped solve the problem.

2. Explain when to use the *work backward* strategy.

3. Suppose Frannie ended up with $36 after the amount doubled two times. How much did she start with?

4. How would you check your answer in Exercise 3?

PRACTICE

EXTRA PRACTICE
Begins on page EP2.

Solve. Use the *work backward* strategy.

5. Measurement Gerardo took one hour for lunch. Then he worked at a store for 3 hours. If he finished at 5:00 P.M., what time did he start lunch?

6. Flora, Alonso, and Luz went fishing. Find how many fish each caught.

Fish Caught

Name	Fish
Flora	3 more than Luz
Alonso	3 more than Flora
Luz	5 fish

7. Toya celebrated her birthday in March, 4 months after joining the swim team. Two months after joining the team, she swam in her first swim meet. What month did she swim in her first meet?

8. Whitney went to the craft store with $25. She bought 3 model airplanes for $4 each. She also bought 2 jars of model paint. She was given the change shown. How much did each jar of paint cost?

9. Mr. Robbins gave 9 students one pencil each. That afternoon, he gave 5 more students one pencil each. Now he has 15 pencils. How many pencils did he start with?

10. **WRITE MATH** Write a real-world problem that uses the *work backward* strategy to solve.

Extend

Model Multiplication

Main Idea

I will use technology to model multiplication.

3.5 The student will recall multiplication facts through the twelves table, and the corresponding division facts. **3.6** The student will represent multiplication and division, using area, set, and number line models, and create and solve problems that involve multiplication of two whole numbers, one factor 99 or less and the second factor 5 or less.

You can use the *Math Tool Chest* to model a multiplication problem.

REAL-WORLD EXAMPLE

1 **TOYS** A pet store sells dog bones. There are 3 bones in each package. How many bones are in 6 packages?

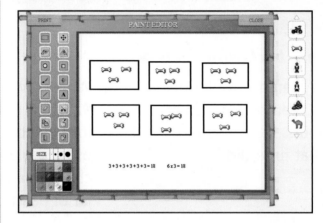

- Choose the rectangle tool. Make 6 rectangles.
- Choose the dog bone stamp. Stamp 3 dog bones in each rectangle.
- Choose the letter tool. Type an addition sentence and a multiplication sentence.

  So, 6 groups of 3 equals 18.

  $3 + 3 + 3 + 3 + 3 + 3 = 18$ or $6 \times 3 = 18$ bones

Practice and Apply It

Use the Math Tool Chest to model each situation. Write an addition sentence and a multiplication sentence.

1. Each hour there are 2 cartoons shown on television. How many cartoons are shown in 6 hours?

2. A car has 4 tires. How many tires are on 7 cars?

3. **TALK MATH** How do models help you solve multiplication problems?

Mid-Chapter Check

Multiply. (Lesson 1A)

1.

5 rows of 2

2.

4 rows of 2

3. 3×2

4. 2×2

5. $\begin{array}{r} 8 \\ \times\ 2 \\ \hline \end{array}$

6. $\begin{array}{r} 2 \\ \times\ 9 \\ \hline \end{array}$

Divide. Write a related fact. (Lesson 1B and 1E)

7.

$6 \div 3$

8.

$3\overline{)15}$

9. $12 \div 2$

10. $20 \div 2$

11. MULTIPLE CHOICE Three times as many students have a hot lunch than a packed lunch. There are 8 students with packed lunches. Which of the following could be used to find how many have hot lunch? (Lesson 1D)

A. $8 - 3$

C. 3×8

B. $3 + 8$

D. 8×4

12. Algebra Find a pattern. Complete the table. (Lesson 1B)

18	16	14	■	■	■
9	8	7	6	5	4

13. A postal worker has 18 packages to deliver to a school. She carries only 2 or 3 packages at a time. What is the fewest number of trips that she can make? What would be the most number of trips she can make? (Lesson 1F)

Algebra Find each missing factor.
(Lesson 1C)

14. $2 \times ■ = 16$

15. $2 \times ■ = 2$

16. $9 \times ■ = 27$

17. $■ \times 6 = 12$

18. MULTIPLE CHOICE Which number sentence is represented by the number line? (Lesson 1A)

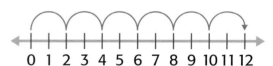

0 1 2 3 4 5 6 7 8 9 10 11 12

F. $2 \times 5 = 10$

G. $6 \times 2 = 12$

H. $6 \times 2 = 14$

J. $5 \times 4 = 20$

19. WRITE MATH Explain how patterns in a multiplication table can help you find 3×9. (Lesson 1D)

Main Idea

I will use different strategies, including patterns, to multiply by 5.

Get ConnectED

  3.5 The student will recall multiplication facts through the twelves table, and the corresponding division facts. **3.6** The student will represent multiplication and division, using area, set, and number line models, and create and solve problems that involve multiplication of two whole numbers, one factor 99 or less and the second factor 5 or less. Also addresses 3.19.

Multiply by 5

There is more than one way to multiply by 5.

REAL-WORLD EXAMPLE   Draw a Model

① **WATERMELONS**
A watermelon patch has 6 rows of watermelons. Each row has 5 watermelons. How many watermelons are in the farmer's patch?

You need to find 6 × 5.

One Way: Use a Bar Diagram	**Another Way:** Draw a Picture
5 melons ↓ 1 row ├──── ? melons ────┤ | 5 | 5 | 5 | 5 | 5 | 5 | ├──── 6 rows ────┤	(watermelons drawn in 6 rows of 5)
I part is 5 melons. 6 parts × 5 melons = 30 watermelons.	Use repeated addition. 5 + 5 + 5 + 5 + 5 + 5 = 30

So, 6 × 5 = 30 watermelons.

You can use patterns to multiply by 5.

 **REAL-WORLD EXAMPLE**   **Multiply Using Patterns**

2 **NICKELS** **Leandro has 7 nickels. How much money does he have?**

You know a nickel is 5¢. Count by fives to find $7 \times 5¢$.

5¢   10¢   15¢   20¢   25¢   30¢   35¢

Read   *5¢, 10¢, 15¢, 20¢, 25¢, 30¢, 35¢*

Notice the patterns in the answers.
$0 \times 5 = 0$ ← All of the products
$1 \times 5 = 5$ ← end in 0 or 5.
$2 \times 5 = 10$
$3 \times 5 = 15$

Extend the pattern.
$4 \times 5 = 20$
$5 \times 5 = 25$
$6 \times 5 = 30$
$7 \times 5 = 35$

So, Leandro has $7 \times 5¢$ or 35¢.

Remember

Multiplying by a number is the same as skip counting by that number.

CHECK What You Know

Multiply. Use a bar diagram or draw a picture if needed.

See Examples 1 and 2

1. $\begin{array}{r} 5 \\ \times 4 \\ \hline \end{array}$

2. $\begin{array}{r} 3 \\ \times 5 \\ \hline \end{array}$

3. $\begin{array}{r} 9 \\ \times 5 \\ \hline \end{array}$

4. $\begin{array}{r} 5 \\ \times 8 \\ \hline \end{array}$

5. $\begin{array}{r} 5 \\ \times 7 \\ \hline \end{array}$

6. $\begin{array}{r} 5 \\ \times 5 \\ \hline \end{array}$

7. BAR DIAGRAM Kai, Lakita, and Maxwell have a box of pretzels. If each gets 5 pretzels, how many pretzels did they have altogether? Explain.

8. TALK MATH Explain why the 5s facts might be easier to remember than other facts.

Multiply. Use a bar diagram or draw a picture if needed.

See Examples 1 and 2

9. 2 × 5

10. 3 × 5

11. 5 × 6

12. 7 × 5

13. 8 × 5

14. 5 × 10

15. 5 × 5

16. 5 × 9

17. 4 × 5

18. BAR DIAGRAM A pan of corn bread is cut into 5 rows with 7 pieces in each row. How many pieces are there in all?

19. A sunflower costs $6. Evelyn wants to buy 3. Does she have enough money if she has four $5-bills? Explain.

20. Bernardo's dad paid for his new roller blades with seven $5-bills. If his dad's change was $2, how much did the roller blades cost?

21. There are 82 members in a band. Part of the band divides into 5 groups of 9. How many members are not in a group of 9?

Data File

Almost all grapefruit grown in the United States is grown in Arizona, California, Florida, and Texas.

22. Grapefruit costs $3 a bag. How much would it cost to buy 5 bags?

23. Emily wants to buy 4 bags of grapefruit. Does she have enough money if she has two $5-bills? Explain.

24. A farmer picks 45 grapefruit equally from 5 trees in his orchard. What is the total number of grapefruit he picks from 2 trees?

H.O.T. Problems

25. WHICH ONE DOESN'T BELONG? Identify the strategy that will not help you find 5 × 6. Explain.

skip counting   rounding   make an array   draw a picture

26. WRITE MATH Can the ones digit in the product ever end in 2 when you are multiplying by 5? Explain.

Game Time

You will need: 20 index cards, crayons, 1-inch graph paper for each player

Get Ready!

Players: 2 players

Get Set!

Write the product of all the multiplication facts you have learned so far on each card. Then shuffle.

Go!

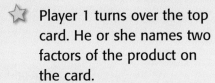 Player 1 turns over the top card. He or she names two factors of the product on the card.

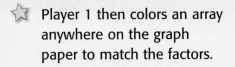 Player 1 then colors an array anywhere on the graph paper to match the factors.

  Player 2 checks to see if the product matches the number of squares colored in. If it is correct, Player 1 gets 1 point.

  The game continues, with players taking turns, until neither player can make a new array on their graph paper or until one player reaches 10 points after a complete round.

Main Idea

I will use multiplication and division as inverse operations to divide by 5.

Get ConnectED

3.5 The student will recall multiplication facts through the twelves table, and the corresponding division facts. **3.2** The student will recognize and use the inverse relationships between addition/subtraction and multiplication/division to complete basic fact sentences. The student will use these relationships to solve problems. Also addresses 3.6.

Divide by 5

There are different ways to divide by 5.

REAL-WORLD EXAMPLE

Use Subtraction

① **MONEY** A group of friends have a lemonade stand. The price of one glass of lemonade is 5¢. They earned 25¢ selling lemonade. How many glasses of lemonade did the group of friends sell?

Lemonade 5¢

You need to find 25¢ ÷ 5¢.

One Way: Use Models	Another Way: Repeated Subtraction

One Way: Use Models

There are 25 counters and 5 counters are in each group. There are 5 equal groups.

$$25¢ \div 5¢ = 5 \text{ or } 5¢\overline{)25¢}$$

Another Way: Repeated Subtraction

①	②	③	④	⑤
25	20	15	10	5
−5	−5	−5	−5	−5
20	15	10	5	0

Subtract groups of 5 until you reach 0. Count the number of groups you subtracted.

$$25¢ \div 5¢ = 5 \text{ or } 5¢\overline{)25¢}^{5}$$

So, the friends sold 5 glasses of lemonade.

In addition to using models and repeated subtraction, you can use related multiplication facts to divide.

REAL-WORLD EXAMPLE   Use Related Facts

2 **MONEY** The school store is selling pencils for 5¢ each. If Corey has 45¢, how many pencils can he buy with all his money?

Write a related multiplication fact to find 45¢ ÷ 5¢.

$45¢ ÷ 5¢ = \blacksquare$

$5¢ × \blacksquare = 45¢$ ← THINK What number times 5 is 45¢?

$5¢ × 9 = 45¢$

So, $45¢ ÷ 5¢ = 9$ or $5¢\overline{)45¢}$ with 9 above. Percy can buy 9 pencils.

Check The picture shows the number sentence 45¢ ÷ 5¢ = 9.

45¢ divided into groups of 5¢ forms 9 groups.
9 groups of 5¢ = 45¢. ✔

Pencils
5¢ each

Remember
Nickels can be used to represent the number 5.

✓ **CHECK What You Know**

Divide. Use models or related facts. See Examples 1 and 2

1. 35 ÷ 5

2. 5 ÷ 5

3. $5\overline{)20}$

4. $5\overline{)40}$

5. Measurement Lucia's classroom has rows of tables that are a total of 25 feet long. If 5 tables are in each row, how long is each table? Write a number sentence to show the solution.

6. TALK MATH How can you tell if a number is divisible by 5?

Divide. Use models or related facts. See Examples 1 and 2

7. 20 ÷ 5   **8.** 40 ÷ 5   **9.** 45 ÷ 5   **10.** 50 ÷ 5

11. 5)5   **12.** 5)15   **13.** 5)10   **14.** 5)35

Use the recipe for corn bread. Find how much of each is needed to make 1 loaf of corn bread.

15. cornmeal

16. flour

17. eggs

18. vanilla extract

Buttermilk Corn Bread	
10 cups cornmeal	3 cups butter
5 cups flour	8 cups buttermilk
1 cup sugar	5 tsp vanilla extract
5 Tbsp baking powder	15 eggs
4 tsp salt	2 tsp baking soda

Makes: 5 loaves

Solve. Write a number sentence.

19. **Measurement** Rose has a 30-inch piece of ribbon. She divides the ribbon into 5 equal pieces. How many inches long will each piece be?

20. Helen is reading a book with 50 pages. She reads 5 pages every day. How many days will it take her to finish the book?

21. **Measurement** Garrison has 45 minutes to do his homework. He has 9 problems left. How long can he spend on each problem if each one takes an equal amount of time?

22. Addison got 40 points on yesterday's 10-question math quiz. Each question is worth 5 points and there is no partial credit. How many questions did he miss?

REAL-WORLD PROBLEM SOLVING

Science The grizzly bear is one of the largest and most powerful animals.

23. About how long is a grizzly bear's foot?

24. What is the length of one grizzly bear?

25. The grizzly runs at a speed of about 35 miles per hour. What is that divided by 5?

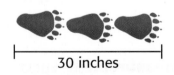

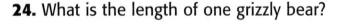

30 inches

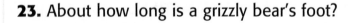

14 feet

26. OPEN ENDED Write a division sentence with a quotient of 9.

27. WHICH ONE DOESN'T BELONG? Identify the division sentence that does not belong. Explain your reasoning.

| $30 \div 5 = 6$ | $20 \div 2 = 10$ | $30 \div 6 = 5$ | $35 \div 5 = 7$ |

28.  **WRITE MATH** Explain the method you would use to find $30 \div 5$ and why you prefer that method.

Test Practice

29. This is an array for which number sentence? *(Lesson 1E)*

A. $15 \div 3 = 5$

B. $3 + 5 = 8$

C. $3 + 3 + 3 + 3 = 12$

D. $5 \times 5 = 25$

30. Robert solved this division problem.

$$20 \div 2 = 10$$

Which problem could he use to check his answer? *(Lesson 1B)*

F. $10 + 2 = \blacksquare$

G. $10 - 2 = \blacksquare$

H. $10 \times 2 = \blacksquare$

J. $10 \div 2 = \blacksquare$

Spiral Review

Divide. Write a related multiplication fact. *(Lesson 1B)*

31. $18 \div 2$ **32.** $16 \div 2$ **33.** $2\overline{)12}$

34. | BAR | DIAGRAM | Angelica had $40 to buy her mother some birthday gifts. She bought flowers for $16 and a new pen set for $8. Then she bought writing paper for $4. If this pattern continues, how much money will the next two gifts cost? How much money does she have after buying two more gifts? *(Lesson 1B)*

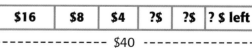

Main Idea

I will use patterns and models to multiply by 10.

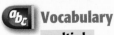 **Vocabulary**

multiple

 **Get Connect**ED

3.5 The student will recall multiplication facts through the twelves table, and the corresponding division facts. **3.6** The student will represent multiplication and division, using area, set, and number line models, and create and solve problems that involve multiplication of two whole numbers, one factor 99 or less and the second factor 5 or less. Also addresses 3.19.

Multiply by 10

Patterns can help you multiply by 10 to solve a problem.

REAL-WORLD EXAMPLE Use Patterns

① **TOES** Jason saw footprints on the beach. He counted 10 toes on each of the 3 sets of footprints. How many toes did Jason count in all?

Find 10 × 3.

Notice the pattern when multiplying by 10.

1 × 10 = 10 ← The ones digit of the product is zero.
2 × 10 = 20
3 × 10 = 30
4 × 10 = 40
5 × 10 = 50 ← same

The pattern can also be seen when skip counting on a number line. Count equal jumps of 10 three times.

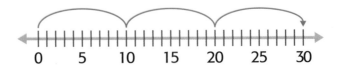

Read *10, 20, 30*

The pattern shows that 3 × 10 = 30.

So, Jason counted 30 toes.

Dimes can be used to model multiplying by 10.

 REAL-WORLD EXAMPLE Use Models

2 **MONEY** Orlando found 8 dimes under his bed while cleaning. How much money did Orlando find?

You need to find $8 \times 10¢$.
Dimes can be used as models to count by 10.

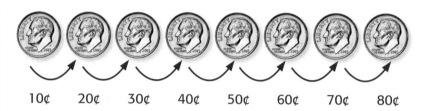

10¢   20¢   30¢   40¢   50¢   60¢   70¢   80¢

Read *10¢, 20¢, 30¢, 40¢, 50¢, 60¢, 70¢, 80¢*

8 dimes shows 80¢.

$8 \times 10¢ = 80¢$

So, Orlando found 80¢.

Check Use repeated addition to check.

$10 + 10 + 10 + 10 + 10 + 10 + 10 + 10 = 80$

So, the answer is correct. ✔

✓ CHECK What You Know

Multiply. Use patterns or models if needed. See Examples 1 and 2

1. 10
$\times 2$

2. 10
$\times 4$

3. 10
$\times 7$

4. 5×10

5. 3×10

6. 10×10

7. Mina bought a dress for $50. How many $10-bills will she need to pay for the dress?

8. **TALK MATH** How can knowing the 5s facts help you with your 10s facts?

Multiply. Use patterns or models if needed. See Examples 1 and 2

9. 10
    × 2

10. 10
    × 6

11. 10
    × 5

12. 10 × 3

13. 10 × 9

14. 10 × 1

15. 8 × 10

16. 10 × 5

17. 10 × 6

18. There are 10 cars. Each has 4 wheels. How many wheels are there altogether?

19. Ines has 6 packs of whistles. There are 10 whistles in each pack. How many whistles does she have altogether?

20. Measurement There are 3 feet in one yard. How many feet are in 10 yards?

21. There are 5 giraffes and 10 birds. How many legs are there altogether?

Use the Savings Accounts table.

22. How much money have the children saved altogether?

23. Algebra Write a multiplication sentence comparing the amount of money that Rebecca has saved with the amount Hakeem has saved.

24. What is the difference in the least amount of money saved and the greatest amount saved?

Savings Accounts	
Name	**$10 Bills**
Rebecca	7
Bret	3
Monsa	8
Hakeem	9

REAL-WORLD PROBLEM SOLVING

Art Some of the world's largest glass sculptures are found in the United States. Find the length of each sculpture.

25. Fiori di Como:
    5 less than 7 × 10.

26. Chihuly Tower:
    5 more than 10 × 5.

27. Cobalt Blue Chandelier:
    9 more than 2 × 10.

28. River Blue: 4 more than 10 × 1.

World's Largest Glass Sculptures	
Sculpture Name	**Length (feet)**
Fiori di Como, NV	■
Chihuly Tower, OK	■
Cobalt Blue Chandelier, WA	■
River Blue, CT	■

H.O.T. Problems

29. WHICH ONE DOESN'T BELONG? Identify the pair of multiplication sentences that is false.

| $2 \times 5 = 10 \times 1$ | $4 \times 3 = 6 \times 2$ | $5 \times 4 = 2 \times 10$ | $10 \times 3 = 5 \times 1$ |

30.  **WRITE MATH** Explain how you know that a multiplication fact with an answer of 25 cannot be a 10s fact.

More About Multiplying by 10 and 100

You can use a basic fact and patterns of zeros to mentally find the products of numbers multiplied by 10 and 100.

EXAMPLES Multiply by 10 and 100.

1 Use a basic fact and patterns of zeros to find 3×100.

$3 \times 1 = 3$ basic fact
$3 \times 10 = 30$ 3×1 ten $= 3$ tens
$3 \times 100 = 300$ 3×1 hundred $= 3$ hundreds

2 Use a basic fact and patterns of zeros to find 6×200.

$6 \times 2 = 12$ basic fact
$6 \times 20 = 120$ 6×2 tens $= 12$ tens
$6 \times 200 = 1,200$ 6×2 hundreds $= 12$ hundreds

A **multiple** is the product of a given number and any other whole number.

EXAMPLE Multiples of 10 and 100.

3 Use a basic fact and patterns of zeros to find 4×200.

$4 \times 2 = 8$ basic fact
$4 \times 20 = 80$ 4×2 tens $= 8$ tens
$4 \times 200 = 800$ 4×2 hundreds $= 8$ hundreds

Multiply. Use basic facts and patterns.

31. $2 \times 1 = $
$2 \times 10 = $
$2 \times 100 = $

32. $9 \times 1 = $
$9 \times 10 = $
$9 \times 100 = $

33. $7 \times 2 = $
$7 \times 20 = $
$7 \times 200 = $

34. 8×300 **35.** 5×30 **36.** 6×50

37. There are 200 hotel rooms in each of the two large hotels downtown. What is the total number of rooms?

3.5 The student will recall multiplication facts through the twelves table, and the corresponding division facts.
3.2 The student will recognize and use the inverse relationships between addition/subtraction and multiplication/division to complete basic fact sentences. The student will use these relationships to solve problems.

Divide by 10

You can use subtraction or multiplication to find the quotient to a division problem.

🏃 🖊 **REAL-WORLD EXAMPLE**

Use Subtraction or Multiplication

① **SCHOOL** There are 10 juice bars in a box. The third grade class needs 50 juice bars for a party treat. How many boxes of juice bars will the third grade class need?

Juice Bars

10 bars

You need to find $50 \div 10$.

One Way: Use Repeated Subtraction

$$
\begin{array}{ccccc}
① & ② & ③ & ④ & ⑤ \\
50 & 40 & 30 & 20 & 10 \\
-10 & -10 & -10 & -10 & -10 \\
\hline
40 & 30 & 20 & 10 & 0
\end{array}
$$

Subtract groups of 10 until you reach 0. Count the number of groups you subtracted. You subtracted groups of 10 five times.

Another Way: Use a Related Fact

You know that multiplication and division are inverse operations.

So, $10 \times 5 = 50$ and $50 \div 10 = 5$ or $10\overline{)50}$ with quotient 5.

They will need 5 boxes of juice bars.

Divide. See Example 1

1. $20 \div 10$

2. $40 \div 10$

3. $10\overline{)60}$

4. $10\overline{)10}$

5. There are 30 chairs at 10 tables. Each table has an equal number of chairs. How many chairs are at each table? Write a number sentence.

6. **TALK MATH** When you divide by 10, what do you notice about the quotient and dividend?

Practice and Problem Solving

EXTRA PRACTICE
Begins on page EP2.

Divide. See Example 1

7. $30 \div 10$

8. $50 \div 10$

9. $80 \div 10$

10. $90 \div 10$

11. $10\overline{)20}$

12. $10\overline{)70}$

13. $10\overline{)30}$

14. $10\overline{)40}$

Solve. Write a number sentence.

15. A vase holds 40 flowers. There are an equal number of daisies, roses, tulips, and lilies. How many of each kind of flower are there in the vase?

16. Rona went to the car show and saw 60 cars. If he saw 10 of each kind of car, how many different kinds of cars were there?

For Exercises 17–19, use the sign shown.

17. Julius spent 70¢ on sunflower seeds. How many packages did he buy?

18. How much did Neila pay for 1 yogurt?

19. How much would it cost to buy 1 of everything, including 1 piece of dried fruit?

HEALTH SHACK'S SNACKS

Sunflower seeds ......10¢ per package
Dried fruit................10 pieces for 50¢
Juice ....20¢ each
Yogurt..........................2 for 80¢

H.O.T. Problems

20. **OPEN ENDED** Use the numerals 7, 0, 8, and 5 to write two 2-digit numbers that can be divided by 10.

21. **WRITE MATH** Explain how counting by 10s can help you find $80 \div 10$.

22. Amado bought 30 frozen pizzas. They were equally packed with 5 in each box. Which number sentence shows how to find the number of boxes of pizza he bought? (Lesson 2B)

A. $30 - 5 =$ ▨

B. $30 + 5 =$ ▨

C. $30 \times 5 =$ ▨

D. $30 \div 5 =$ ▨

23. Look at the number sentence below.

$$90 \div \blacksquare = 9$$

Which number will make the number sentence true? (Lesson 2D)

F. 1

G. 10

H. 81

I. 100

24. Austin collected 9 shells every day while at the beach. How many shells did he collect over his 10-day vacation? (Lesson 2C)

A. 19

B. 90

C. 100

D. 190

25. Which number sentence is modeled by repeated subtraction on the number line? (Lesson 1B)

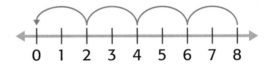

F. $4 \div 2 = 8$

G. $16 \div 2 = 8$

H. $8 \div 2 = 4$

J. $24 \div 8 = 3$

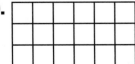 **Spiral Review**

Divide. (Lesson 2B)

26. $25 \div 5$

27. $45 \div 5$

28. $50 \div 5$

29. There are 40 soccer players. Each team will have 1 coach and an equal number of players. If there are 5 coaches, how many players will be on each team? Write a number sentence to record the solution. (Lesson 2B)

Write a multiplication sentence for each array. (Lesson 1D)

30.

31.

32.

Facts Practice

Multiply.

1. 2
 × 3

2. 2
 × 10

3. 6
 × 2

4. 2
 × 9

5. 5
 × 8

6. 4
 × 3

7. 5
 × 2

8. 5
 × 5

9. 2
 × 6

10. 7
 × 3

11. 5
 × 1

12. 2
 × 2

13. 5
 × 7

14. 3
 × 8

15. 2
 × 7

16. 3
 × 2

17. 5
 × 6

18. 2
 × 4

19. 5
 × 4

20. 3
 × 4

21. 2 × 5

22. 5 × 3

23. 5 × 10

24. 7 × 2

25. 2 × 8

26. 10 × 2

27. 2 × 9

28. 8 × 5

29. 10 × 10

30. 5 × 9

31. 4 × 5

32. 4 × 10

33. 10 × 7

34. 8 × 2

35. 9 × 2

36. 6 × 5

Problem Solving in Social Studies

Communities Within Communities

A community is a group of people who work, live, or play together. There are over 2,000 elementary schools in Florida, and each school is a community. Your classroom is also a community.

Often, a class works together on an art project. A mural is an art project that many people can work on together. It is a large painting that sometimes covers an entire wall.

There are many other examples of communities. In Florida, there are over 400 cities, towns, and villages. Each is a community. There are more than 1 million businesses in Florida that also form communities. Each of the families in Florida is a community, too.

Did You Know?

There are more than 33 million elementary students in the United States.

Real-World Math

Use the information on the previous page to solve each problem.

1 A group is painting a mural of their community. They have 14 pictures of places around their community. The mural is 7 feet wide. If they want to place the pictures evenly, how many will be placed in each foot of space?

2 A community has a Clean Up Litter Day. Thirty-five community members come to help. They divide into groups of five. How many groups are there?

3 There are 20 students in a class. A teacher forms 5 equal groups from the 20 students in her class. How many students are in each group?

4 There are about two times as many families in California as in Florida. California has more than 8 million families. About how many families are in Florida? Write a number sentence to represent your thinking.

5 A community has 45 stores. There are 5 stores on each street. How many streets are in the community?

6 Ten schools in a community donate a total of 30 boxes of clothes to a local charity. Each school donates the same number of boxes. How many boxes of clothes does each school donate?

Problem-Solving Investigation

Main Idea I will choose the best strategy to solve a problem.

P.S.I. TEAM +

ASHTON: My doctor saw 20 patients in 5 hours today. She saw the same number of patients each hour.

YOUR MISSION: Find the number of patients my doctor saw each hour.

Understand	In 5 hours, the doctor saw 20 patients.

Plan   Use division to find how many patients the doctor saw each hour in the 5 hours.

Solve   You need to find 20 ÷ 5.

total number of patients		number of hours		number of patients
20	÷	5	=	4

So, the doctor saw 4 patients each hour.

Check   You can use multiplication to check division.

$5 \times 4 = 20$ ✓

So, it makes sense that 4 patients would have been seen each hour.

3.5 The student will recall multiplication facts through the twelves table, and the corresponding division facts.

Mixed Problem Solving

EXTRA PRACTICE
Begins on page EP2.

- Choose an operation.
- Look for a pattern.
- Make a table.

Use any strategy to solve each problem.

1. Write a repeated addition sentence to find how many plants are in the garden. What other operation can help you solve this problem?

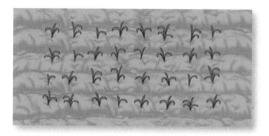

2. **Measurement** How much taller is the KVLY TV tower than the Prudential Tower? Explain.

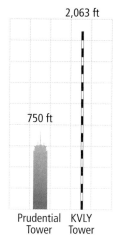

2,063 ft

750 ft

Prudential Tower   KVLY Tower

3. Shaun and Dean went to the park. The leaves were brown, red, and orange. They picked 7 of each color. How many leaves did they pick in all?

4. **Measurement** It rained 6 inches each month for the last 5 months. If it rains 6 more inches this month, what will be the total rainfall?

5. Sondra and Wanda were making jewelry for the school fundraiser. They each made the amount listed. How many items were made in all?

Jewelry Made

Item	Number
Earrings	5
Pins	4
Bracelets	6

6. **Measurement** Melody has 14 feet of string. She wants to make necklaces that are 2 feet long. How many necklaces can she make?

7. **Geometry** Jermaine has a square garden. Each side is 5 yards. How many yards of fence does he need to border the garden? Explain.

8. A group of 16 people want to go to the zoo. Use the sign below to find how they can get the lowest cost for admission.

Zoo Admission Prices

Per person.............. $6
Group rate........ $30 for 6

9. **WRITE MATH** Explain how to read a problem and decide what operation to use.

Main Idea

I will use number properties to multiply by 0 and 1.

3.5 The student will recall multiplication facts through the twelves table, and the corresponding division facts. **3.20** The student will **a)** investigate the identity and the commutative properties for addition and multiplication. Also addresses 3.19.

Multiply by 0 and 1

There are special properties for multiplying by 1 and 0.

The **Identity Property of Multiplication** says that when any number is multiplied by 1, the product is that number.

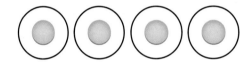 **REAL-WORLD EXAMPLE**   Multiply by 1

① **FLOWERS** There are 4 flowerpots. Each has 1 daisy. Find 4×1 to find how many daisies there are in all.

Model 4 groups of 1.

The model shows 4 groups of 1.

So, $4 \times 1 = 4$.

The **Zero Property of Multiplication** says that when you multiply a number by 0, the product is zero.

EXAMPLE   Multiply by 0

② **Find 6×0. Use the pattern shown.**

$1 \times 0 = 0$ ← Any number times zero equals 0.

$2 \times 0 = 0$

$3 \times 0 = 0$

$4 \times 0 = 0$

So, $6 \times 0 = 0$.

Multiply. See Examples 1 and 2

1.   9
    × 0

2.   1
    × 7

3.   5
    × 0

4.   8
    × 1

5. There is 1 student sitting at each of the 9 tables in the cafeteria. How many students are there altogether?

6. 📝 **TALK MATH** If 100 is multiplied by 0, what will be the answer? Explain your reasoning.

Practice and Problem Solving

EXTRA PRACTICE
Begins on page EP2.

Multiply. See Examples 1 and 2

7.   7
    × 1

8.   7
    × 0

9. 10
    × 1

10. 10
     × 0

11. 8×0

12. 1×2

13. 0×1

14. 6×1

Solve. Use models if needed.

15. How many pouches does 1 kangaroo have?

16. How many legs do 8 snakes have?

17. In a fantasy story, a pirate found 3 empty treasure chests with no jewels. How many jewels were there?

18. There is only 1 book on the shelf. It has 90 pages. How many pages are there altogether?

Algebra Find each missing factor.

19. ▉ $\times 6 = 6$

20. ▉ $\times 8 = 0$

21. $6 \times$ ▉ $= 0$

22. $1 \times$ ▉ $= 0$

H.O.T. Problems

23. OPEN ENDED Write a problem using one of the multiplication properties that you have just learned. Explain how to find the answer.

CHALLENGE Find the missing number.

24. $2{,}684 \times$ ▉ $= 2{,}684$

25. $1{,}039 \times 1 =$ ▉

26. $27 \times$ ▉ $= 0$

27. 📝 **WRITE MATH** Explain the Zero Property of Multiplication.

Main Idea

I will use division rules to divide with 0 and 1.

Get ConnectED

🔺 **3.5** The student will recall multiplication facts through the twelves table, and the corresponding division facts. **3.19** The student will recognize and describe a variety of patterns formed using numbers, tables, and pictures, and extend the patterns, using the same or different forms.

Divide with 0 and 1

There are rules you can use when 0 and 1 are divisors.

🏃 ✏️ 📷 **REAL-WORLD EXAMPLE**   Divide by 1

① **TOYS There are 3 toys. One storage box will hold 3 toys. How many boxes will you need for 3 toys?**

Find $3 \div 1$ or $1\overline{)3}$.
Since 3 toys fit in 1 box, make groups of 3, using counters.

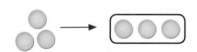

There is 1 group of 3.

So, $3 \div 1 = 3$ or $1\overline{)3}^{\,3}$.

Key Concept   Division Rules

Words	When you divide any number (except 0) by itself, the quotient is 1.
Example	$4 \div 4 = 1$ $4\overline{)4}^{\,1}$ ⚪ ⚪ ⚪ ⚪
Words	When you divide any number by 1, the quotient is the same as the dividend.
Example	$4 \div 1 = 4$ $1\overline{)4}^{\,4}$ ⚪⚪⚪⚪
Words	When you divide 0 by any number (except 0), the quotient is 0.
Example	$0 \div 4 = 0$ $4\overline{)0}^{\,0}$ ▢▢▢▢
Words	You cannot divide by 0.

Divide. See Example 1

1. $5 \div 1$ **2.** $0 \div 1$ **3.** $1 \div 1$ **4.** $1\overline{)9}$

5. $0 \div 7$ **6.** $10 \div 1$ **7.** $6\overline{)0}$ **8.** $7\overline{)7}$

9. If 6 people show up at the theater and there are 6 seats left, how many seats will each person get?

10. 🗣 **TALK MATH** Can you divide a number by 0? Can you divide 0 by a number other than 0? Explain.

Practice and Problem Solving

EXTRA PRACTICE
Begins on page EP2.

Divide. See Example 1

11. $2 \div 1$ **12.** $10 \div 10$ **13.** $0 \div 5$ **14.** $6 \div 1$

15. $0 \div 3$ **16.** $0 \div 9$ **17.** $1\overline{)4}$ **18.** $5\overline{)5}$

19. $1\overline{)7}$ **20.** $2\overline{)2}$ **21.** $1\overline{)10}$ **22.** $10\overline{)0}$

Solve. Write a number sentence.

23. There are 35 students in Mr. Macy's class. To play a game, each person needs 1 playing piece. How many playing pieces are needed for the class to play the game?

24. Mr. Carrington has a pack of paper with 5 different colors. If he gives 1 of each color to his students, how many pieces of paper will they each have?

25. Kari wants to give 5 friends an apple. She finds that she has no apples. How many apples can she give to her friends?

26. May and her 4 friends have 5 glasses of juice. How many glasses of juice will each person get?

H.O.T. Problems

27. OPEN ENDED Write a real-world division problem in which a number is divided by itself. Ask a classmate to answer it.

28. 🗣 **WRITE MATH** Explain how you could divide any number someone gives you, except 0, by 1 or itself.

🔬 Facts Practice

Multiply.

1.   0
     × 2

2. 10
     × 5

3.   0
     × 9

4.   2
     × 9

5.   6
     × 1

6.   2
     × 3

7. 10
     × 8

8.   0
     × 6

9.   1
     × 9

10.   5
      × 5

11.   4
      × 0

12.   2
      × 7

13. 10
      × 0

14.   5
      × 3

15.   1
      × 6

16.   2
      × 10

17.   4
      × 5

18.   2
      × 2

19.   1
      × 1

20.   5
      × 8

21. 4×3

22. 10×1

23. 0×3

24. 9×1

25. 0×8

26. 10×7

27. 1×4

28. 2×6

29. 5×10

30. 0×7

31. 1×0

32. 10×6

33. 1×0

34. 5×6

35. 10×3

36. 2×0

37. 10×10

38. 0×10

39. 1×5

40. 0×4

Chapter Study Guide and Review

FOLDABLES
Study Organizer

Be sure the following Key Concepts are noted in your Foldable.

Key Concepts

Multiplication Strategies (Lesson 1)

- models
- related facts
- repeated addition
- bar diagrams
- arrays
- patterns

Division Strategies (Lesson 1)

- models
- arrays
- related facts
- repeated subtraction

Multiplication Properties (Lesson 3)

- **Identity Property of Multiplication**
  The product of a number multiplied by 1 is that number.
  $$8 \times 1 = 8$$

- **Zero Property of Multiplication**
  The product of a number multiplied by 0 is 0.
  $$8 \times 0 = 0$$

Division Rules (Lesson 3)

- The quotient of a number divided by itself is 1.
  $$8 \div 8 = 1$$
- You cannot divide by 0.

Key Vocabulary

- divide
- dividend
- divisor
- factor
- partition
- quotient

Vocabulary Check

Choose the vocabulary word that completes each sentence.

1. ____?____ means to separate a number into equal groups, to find the number of groups, or the number in each group.

2. The number to be divided is the ____?____.

3. A ____?____ is a number that is multiplied by another number.

4. The number by which the dividend is divided is called the ____?____.

5. The ____?____ is the answer to a division problem.

6. To ____?____ means to divide or share equally among all groups.

Multi-Part Lesson Review

Lesson 1 **Multiplication and Division Facts for 2 and 3**

Multiply and Divide by 2 (Lessons 1A and 1B)

Multiply.

7. $\begin{array}{r} 2 \\ \times\, 1 \\ \hline \end{array}$ **8.** $\begin{array}{r} 7 \\ \times\, 2 \\ \hline \end{array}$ **9.** $\begin{array}{r} 2 \\ \times\, 4 \\ \hline \end{array}$

10. There are 9 birds. Each has 2 legs. How many legs are there in all?

11. There is one dog. How many ears in all?

Divide. Write a related fact.

12. $2\overline{)12}$ **13.** $2\overline{)14}$

14. $16 \div 2$ **15.** $20 \div 2$

16. Measurement Zoe and Koko will equally share an 18-inch long piece of paper. How long will each piece be?

Multiply and Divide by 3 (Lessons 1D and 1E)

Multiply or divide.

17. 3×8 **18.** 9×3

19. 6×3 **20.** $12 \div 3$

21. $3\overline{)3}$ **22.** $3\overline{)30}$

23. There are 4 trees with 3 rabbits under each tree. Two rabbits hop away. How many are left?

24. A van holds 6 people. How many vans are needed for 18 people?

EXAMPLE 1

How many wings are there on 5 butterflies?

? wings
2 wings | 2 wings | 2 wings | 2 wings | 2 wings
5 butterflies

$5 \times 2 = 10$ wings altogether.

EXAMPLE 2

Maros will share 6 dog biscuits between his 2 dogs. How many biscuits will each dog get?

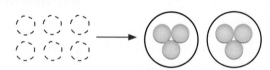

$6 \div 2 = 3$

Each dog will get 3 biscuits.

EXAMPLE 3

Lisa is 27 years old. She is 3 times older than her niece. How old is her niece?

Find $27 \div 3$.

Use related facts to divide.

$27 \div 3 = \blacksquare$

$3 \times \blacksquare = 27$ ◄── THINK 3 times what number equals 27?

$3 \times 9 = 27$

So, $27 \div 3 = 9$ or $3\overline{)27}$.

Problem-Solving Strategy: Work Backward (Lesson 1F)

Solve. Use the *work backward* strategy.

25. Leanne gave away 14 apples. She now has the apples shown. How many apples did she start with?

26. Some of the numbers from one row of Miss Smith's multiplication chart are lost.

___, ___, ___, 21, 24, ___, 30

In order, which numbers is she missing?

EXAMPLE 4

Three is subtracted from a number. The difference is multiplied by 2. Then, 4 is added to the product. Finally, 9 is subtracted to give a difference of 9. What is the number?

Work backward from the answer.

$9 + 9 = 18$

$18 - 4 = 14$

$14 \div 2 = 7$

$7 + 3 = 10$

The starting number is 10.

Lesson 2 **Multiplication and Division Facts for 5 and 10**

Multiply and Divide by 5 (Lessons 2A and 2B)

Multiply or divide.

27. 5×5 **28.** 7×5

29. $25 \div 5$ **30.** $5\overline{)50}$

31. How many triangles did Bob use if he repeated the design 3 times?

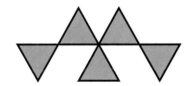

32. Each new student that comes to school during the year makes a handprint on the wall with paint. How many fingers are there?

EXAMPLE 5

Each day, Xavier saves the nickel he gets as change from his lunch money. How many nickels will he use if he wants to buy ice cream for 20¢?

Find $20 \div 5$.

Use repeated subtraction.

①   ②   ③   ④

$\begin{array}{c} 20 \\ -5 \\ \hline 15 \end{array}$ $\begin{array}{c} 15 \\ -5 \\ \hline 10 \end{array}$ $\begin{array}{c} 10 \\ -5 \\ \hline 5 \end{array}$ $\begin{array}{c} 5 \\ -5 \\ \hline 0 \end{array}$

There are 4 groups of 5. $20 \div 5 = 4$

So, Xavier will use 4 nickels.

Multiply and Divide by 10 (Lessons 2C and 2D)

Multiply or divide.

33. 10×5

34. 10×4

35. $10\overline{)60}$

36. $10\overline{)10}$

37. There are 40 baskets of grapes on store shelves. If there are 10 baskets on each shelf, how many shelves are there?

38. Curtis used 9 dimes to buy a drink. How much did he spend?

EXAMPLE 6

Find 7×10.

Use the pattern of counting by 10s.

Read: 10, 20, 30, 40, 50, 60, 70

So, $7 \times 10 = 70$.

Lesson 3 ## Multiply and Divide With 0 and 1

Problem-Solving Investigation: Choose a Strategy (Lesson 3A)

39. Benito had $20 in the bank. He took out $8 and later put back $6. How much money does he have in the bank now?

40. Of the 48 balls that sold, 2 times as many tennis balls were sold as soccer balls. How many soccer balls were sold?

EXAMPLE 7

Samir has $25. Does he have enough money to purchase 6 toy boats that cost $5 each?

Find the total cost of the toy boats.

$6 \times \$5 = \$30$

Since $\$25 < \$30$, he does not have enough money.

Multiply and Divide with 0 and 1 (Lessons 3B and 3C)

Multiply or divide.

41. 5×0

42. 1×9

43. $0 \div 8$

44. $1\overline{)2}$

45. Gisela gave 8 gifts to her friends. She gave each friend 1 gift. How many friends did Gisela give a gift to?

EXAMPLE 8

Terry did 4 pages of homework in 4 nights. He did the same number of pages each night. How many pages did he do each night?

Find $4 \div 4$.

4 pages $\div$ 4 nights = 1 page

So, $4 \div 4 = 1$ page each night.

Tell whether each statement is *true* or *false*.

1. When you divide any number by 1, the quotient is that number.

2. Repeated subtraction can help you solve a division problem.

Multiply.

3.
$$\begin{array}{r} 1 \\ \times\ 5 \\ \hline \end{array}$$

4.
$$\begin{array}{r} 9 \\ \times\ 5 \\ \hline \end{array}$$

Algebra Find each missing factor.

5. $7 \times \blacksquare = 35$

6. $\blacksquare \times 5 = 40$

7. $10 \times \blacksquare = 80$

8. $\blacksquare \times 9 = 90$

Divide. Write a related fact.

9. $5\overline{)30}$

10. $5\overline{)25}$

11. $0 \div 7$

12. $10 \div 1$

13. MULTIPLE CHOICE Ryder did this division problem.
$$70 \div 10 = 7$$
Which problem could he do to check his answer?

A. $70 + 10$ **C.** $10 + 7$

B. 10×7 **D.** $10 \div 70$

14. Five gardeners each picked the number of tomatoes shown. How many tomatoes were picked in all?

15. Kareem gave 25 football cards to Cindy, 13 to Naomi, and 14 to Brad. Kareem now has half the cards he started with. How many cards did he start with?

16. BAR DIAGRAM The movie theater has 6 rows of seats. Each row has 10 people. How many people are in the theater? Use a bar diagram to solve.

17. Five boys find 5 fishing poles. Do they have enough poles so that each boy has a pole? Solve. Write a number sentence.

18. A scout group sold boxes of popcorn for $10. How much money did Javier raise?

Scout	Money Raised							Total
Griffen	✪	✪	✪	✪	✪	✪	✪	$70
Bartolo	✪	✪	✪	✪				$40
Javier	✪	✪	✪	✪	✪	✪		■
key: ✪ = $10								

19. MULTIPLE CHOICE Twenty-seven students will divide into equal groups to play a game. Which problem below will give them equal groups?

F. $27 \div 3$ **H.** $27 \div 10$

G. $27 \div 5$ **J.** $27 \div 2$

20. WRITE MATH Can the product of a multiplication problem ever end in 2 when you are multiplying by 10? Explain.

Alma wants to place 15 star stickers in 3 equal rows. How many stickers will be in each row?

A. 2   **C.** 5

B. 3   **D.** 10

Multiplication and division are inverse operations so thinking of a related fact can help you solve a problem.

Read the Question

You need to find the number of star stickers that will be in each row.

Solve the Question

Draw a model to help you understand the question. Show 15 star stickers in 3 equal rows.

There are 5 star stickers in each row.

So, the answer is C.

Read each question. Then fill in the correct answer on the answer sheet provided by your teacher or on a separate sheet of paper.

1. Daniel has 40 baseball cards. He puts the cards in piles of 8. How many piles does he make?

     A. 2   **C.** 5

     B. 4   **D.** 8

2. What number can 8 be divided by to give the answer 8?

     F. 0   **H.** 8

     G. 1   **J.** 16

3. What does 2×5 mean?

A. $5 + 5$

B. $2 + 5 + 2 + 5 + 2$

C. $5 + 5 + 5 + 5 + 5$

D. $2 + 2$

---

4. Gabe works at a car wash 6 hours a day. It takes Gabe 1 hour to wash one car. Which number sentence shows the number of cars he washes in 1 day?

F. $6 - 6 = 0$

H. $6 \times 1 = 6$

G. $6 \times 0 = 0$

J. $6 + 1 = 7$

---

5. Which number sentence is modeled by the array?

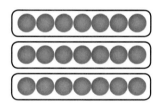

A. $24 \div 8 = 3$

C. $18 \div 3 = 6$

B. $21 \div 3 = 7$

D. $21 \div 4 = 5$

---

6. Which number will make the number sentence true?

$$\blacksquare \times 3 = 0$$

F. 0

H. 3

G. 1

J. 4

---

7. The product of 5 and another factor is 50. What is the missing factor?

A. 45

C. 9

B. 10

D. 5

---

8. Which number sentence is modeled by the figure below?

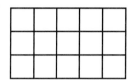

F. $3 + 3 + 3 = 9$

G. $4 \times 5 = 20$

H. $3 \times 6 = 18$

J. $3 \times 5 = 15$

---

9. Clara has 8 packs of gum. Each pack contains 5 pieces of gum. If Clara chews 3 pieces, how many pieces does she have left?

A. 37

C. 13

B. 32

D. 8

---

10. Which problem could Leo do to check $60 \div 10 = 6$?

F. $10 + 6 = \blacksquare$

H. $10 \times 6 = \blacksquare$

G. $10 - 6 = \blacksquare$

J. $10 \div 6 = \blacksquare$

NEED EXTRA HELP?										
If You Missed Question . . .	1	2	3	4	5	6	7	8	9	10
Go to Chapter-Lesson . . .	4-2B	4-3C	4-1A	4-3B	4-1E	4-3B	4-2C	4-1D	4-2A	4-2D
For help with . . .	SOL 3.5	SOL 3.5	SOL 3.6	SOL 3.6	SOL 3.6	SOL 3.5	SOL 3.5	SOL 3.6	SOL 3.6	SOL 3.5

CHAPTER 5

Solve More Multiplication and Division Problems

connectED.mcgraw-hill.com

Investigate

 Animations

 Vocabulary

 Math Songs

 Multilingual eGlossary

Learn

 Personal Tutor

 Virtual Manipulatives

 Audio

 Foldables

Practice

 Self-Check Practice

 eGames

 Worksheets

 Assessment

The ☆BIG Idea

How can I solve more basic multiplication facts and related division facts?

FOLDABLES® Study Organizer

Make this Foldable to help you organize information about multiplication and division concepts and facts. Start with three sheets of $8\frac{1}{2}" \times 11"$ paper.

More Multiplication and Division
- Multiply and Divide by 4
- Multiply and Divide by 6 and 7
- Multiply and Divide by 8 and 9
- Multiply and Divide by 11 and 12

Review Vocabulary

inverse operations operación inversa
Inverse operations undo each other. Multiplication and division are inverse operations.

$8 \times 3 = 24$, so $24 \div 3 = 8$

Key Vocabulary

English	Español
known fact	hecho conocido
double	doble
partial product	productus parciales
decompose	descomponer

When Will I Use This?

Kim and Jacob in
Hard Work Pays Off

Your Turn!
You will solve this problem in the chapter.

You have two options for checking Prerequisite Skills for this chapter.

Text Option Take the Quick Check below.

QUICK Check

Tell whether each pair of groups are equal.

1.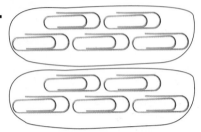

2.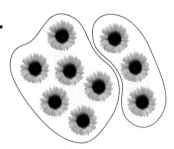

Algebra Use the array to complete each pair of number sentences.

3. $2 \times \blacksquare = 8$

$8 \div \blacksquare = 4$

4. $1 \times 4 = \blacksquare$

$4 \div \blacksquare = 4$

Divide.

5. $25 \div 5$

6. $18 \div 2$

7. $10\overline{)20}$

8. Luther and Sheila have 40 marbles. They are playing with 3 friends. Will there be enough marbles for each player to have an equal number of marbles? Explain.

Algebra Find each missing factor.

9. $4 \times \blacksquare = 20$

10. $3 \times \blacksquare = 30$

11. $5 \times \blacksquare = 45$

 Online Option Take the Online Readiness Quiz.

Explore

Double a Known Fact

Main Idea

I will explore doubling a known fact to multiply.

Materials

counters

grid paper, plain paper

scissors, glue

Get ConnectED

3.5 The student will recall multiplication facts through the twelves table, and the corresponding division facts. **3.6** The student will represent multiplication and division, using area, set, and number line models, and create and solve problems that involve multiplication of two whole numbers, one factor 99 or less and the second factor 5 or less.

A **known fact** is a fact you have memorized. You can use a known multiplication fact to solve a multiplication fact you do not know.

ACTIVITY

1. **Find 4 × 6.**

   Four is 2 **doubled.**

   So, 4 × 6 is the same as 2 × 6 plus 2 × 6.

   Step 1 **Model the known fact, 2 × 6.**

   Use counters to make an array.

   Show 2 × 6 or 2 rows of 6.

   $2 \times 6 = 12$

   Step 2 **Double the known fact.**

   Make one more 2 × 6 array.

   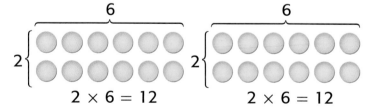

   $2 \times 6 = 12$ $2 \times 6 = 12$

   Step 3 **Find 4 × 6.**

   Put the arrays together to show 4 × 6.

   So, 4 × 6 = 24.

   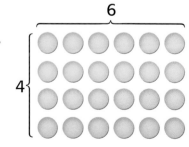

2 Find 6 × 5.

Six is 3 doubled.

So, 6 × 5 is the same as 3 × 5 plus 3 × 5.

Step 1 **Model the known fact 3 × 5 two times.**

Use grid paper to make two 3 × 5 arrays.

• Cut out the arrays.

• Write the product on each array.

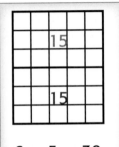

Step 2 **Double the known fact 3 × 5.**

• Put the arrays together.

• Glue on white paper.

• Add the products.

Step 3 **Find 6 × 5.**

Write the multiplication sentence.

6 × 5 = 30

6 × 5 = 30

Think About It

1. Why can you double the product of 2 × 6 to find 4 × 6?

2. What doubles fact would 3 × 6 help you find?

3. How can 2 × 9 help you find 4 × 9?

4. Give an example of doubling a known fact. Explain.

5. Draw two arrays you could put together to find 4 × 5.

Main Idea

I will double a known fact to multiply by 4.

 Vocabulary

known fact

double

 Get ConnectED

3.5 The student will recall multiplication facts through the twelves table, and the corresponding division facts. **3.6** The student will represent multiplication and division, using area, set, and number line models, and create and solve problems that involve multiplication of two whole numbers, one factor 99 or less and the second factor 5 or less.

Multiply by 4

To multiply by 4, you can use the same strategies you used to multiply by 2. Think about doubling the **known facts** of 2 to help you multiply by four.

REAL-WORLD EXAMPLE Use an Array

① **ORANGES** A box is packed with 4 rows of oranges. Each row has 9 oranges. How many oranges are in the box?

You need to find 4×9.

4 is 2 **doubled**. So, 4×9 is *double* 2×9.

4×9 = 2×9 + 2×9

= 18 + 18

$\begin{array}{r} 18 \\ + 18 \\ \hline 36 \end{array}$

So, $4 \times 9 = 36$. There are 36 oranges in the box.

2 **FRUIT** There are 4 bunches of bananas. Each bunch has 3 bananas. How many bananas in all?

Remember

To find the product of a 4s fact, double the product of a 2s fact that you know.

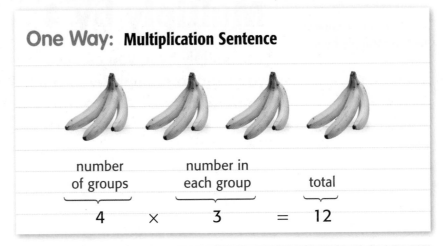

One Way: Multiplication Sentence

number of groups		number in each group		total
4	×	3	=	12

Another Way: Addition Sentence

Use repeated addition to show 4 groups of 3.
$3 + 3 + 3 + 3 = 12$

So, there are 12 bananas in all.

CHECK What You Know

Multiply. See Examples 1 and 2

1.   4
   × 1

2.   4
   × 2

3.   4
   × 4

Write a multiplication sentence for each situation. See Example 2

4. A bakery has 5 pies. Each pie is cut into 4 pieces. How many people can buy a piece of pie?

5. The library offers 4 activities on Saturday. Each activity table has room for 10 children. How many children can take part in the activities?

6. Arleta read 4 books. Each book has 8 chapters. How many chapters did she read in all?

7. **TALK MATH** Explain how knowing 2 × 7 can help you find 4 × 7.

Multiply. See Examples 1 and 2

8. $\begin{array}{r} 3 \\ \times\,4 \\ \hline \end{array}$

9. $\begin{array}{r} 4 \\ \times\,6 \\ \hline \end{array}$

10. $\begin{array}{r} 5 \\ \times\,4 \\ \hline \end{array}$

11. 2×4

12. 4×7

13. 4×4

14. 9×4

15. 8×4

16. 10×4

Write a multiplication sentence for each situation. See Example 2

17. Kendrick and Tyra each have an umbrella. How many umbrellas are there after 2 friends join them with their umbrellas?

18. There are 9 rows on a bus. Four children can sit in each row. If there are 48 children, how many will not be able to ride the bus?

19. [BAR | DIAGRAM] Write a multiplication sentence to show that 4 dimes equal 40 cents.

20. A factory packs 4 science kits in each box. They packed 7 boxes. How many kits did they pack?

H.O.T. Problems

21. OPEN ENDED Explain the strategy you would use to find 4×6. Why do you prefer this strategy?

22. FIND THE ERROR Jaime is finding 4×8. Find and correct his mistake.

> 4×8 is the same as $2 + 8 + 2 + 8$. The answer is 20.

23. CHALLENGE Mitch bought 4 bottles of suntan lotion for $6 each. Later the lotion went on sale for $4 each. How many more bottles could he have bought for the same amount of money if he waited for the sale?

24. WRITE MATH Write a real-world problem that involves multiplying by 4.

Main Idea

I will use related multiplication facts and repeated subtraction to divide by 4.

 Vocabulary

inverse operations

 **Get ConnectED**

3.2 The student will recognize and use the inverse relationships between addition/subtraction and multiplication/division to complete basic fact sentences. The student will use these relationships to solve problems. Also addresses 3.6.
3.5 The student will recall multiplication facts through the twelves table, and the corresponding division facts.

Divide by 4

You can use models and related multiplication facts to divide by 4.

REAL-WORLD EXAMPLE **Use Models**

1 **MEASUREMENT** The distance around a square window in Peter's house is 12 feet. What is the length of each side? Write a number sentence.

Divide 12 feet by the number of sides, 4.

There are 12 counters divided into 4 equal groups. There are 3 counters in each group.

So, $12 \div 4 = 3$. Each side is 3 feet long.

Multiplication and division are **inverse operations**. You can use a related multiplication fact to find the answer to a division fact.

REAL-WORLD EXAMPLE **Use Related Facts**

2 **BIRDS** An ostrich egg weighs 4 pounds. The total weight of the eggs in a nest is 28 pounds. Write a number sentence to show how many ostrich eggs are in the nest.

Use a related multiplication fact to find $28 \div 4$, or $4\overline{)28}$.

$$28 \div 4 = \blacksquare$$
$$4 \times \blacksquare = 28$$
$$4 \times 7 = 28$$

THINK What number times 4 equals 28?

So, $28 \div 4 = 7$, or $4\overline{)28}^{\,7}$. There are 7 eggs in the nest.

Remember

A number line can also be used for repeated subtraction.

③ MONEY Trevor has $20 to divide equally among 4 people. Write a number sentence to show how much each person will get.

You need to find $20 ÷ 4, or 4)$20.

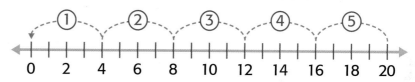

① ② ③ ④ ⑤

$20	$16	$12	$8	$4
− 4	− 4	− 4	− 4	− 4
$16	$12	$8	$4	$0

You subtracted 4 five times.

So, $20 ÷ 4 = $5, or 4)$20 with quotient $5. Each person will get $5.

Check The number line shows there are 5 groups of 4 in 20. ✔

① ② ③ ④ ⑤

```
0   2   4   6   8   10  12  14  16  18  20
```

Key Concept Division Strategies

There are several strategies you can use to divide.
- Use models or draw an array.
- Use repeated subtraction.
- Use a related multiplication fact.

✓ CHECK What You Know

Divide. Use models or related facts. See Examples 1–3

1. 16 ÷ 4

2. 4 ÷ 4

3. 32 ÷ 4

4. 4)8

5. 4)28

6. 4)40

7. Amel has 36 quarters. If each video game machine takes 4 quarters, how many games can he play?

8. 🗨 **TALK MATH** Without dividing, how do you know that the quotient of 12 ÷ 3 is greater than the quotient of 12 ÷ 4?

Divide. Use models or related facts. See Examples 1–3

9. $0 \div 4$ **10.** $4 \div 4$ **11.** $24 \div 4$ **12.** $36 \div 9$

13. $5\overline{)20}$ **14.** $3\overline{)12}$ **15.** $4\overline{)12}$ **16.** $4\overline{)40}$

Algebra **Find each missing number.**

17. $36 \div \blacksquare = 4$ **18.** $\blacksquare \div 4 = 6$ **19.** $4 \times \blacksquare = 40$ **20.** $\blacksquare \times 4 = 28$

Measurement **Find the measure of the shaded part.**

21.

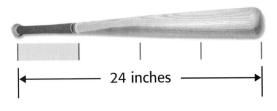

|← 24 inches →|

22.

|← 40 miles →|

Solve. Write a number sentence.

23. Gwen, Clark, Elvio, and Trent will be on vacation for 20 days. They are dividing the planning equally. How many days will Clark have to plan?

24. A bus has 36 pieces of luggage. If each person brought 4 pieces of luggage, how many people are on the trip?

25. It costs $40 for a family of 4 to ride go-carts for 1 hour. How much does it cost 1 person to ride for 2 hours?

26. There are 4 bananas, 3 apples, and 5 pears. An equal number of fruit is placed in 4 baskets. How many pieces will be in each basket?

Berto wants to make a graph from the data he collected.

27. He will use a key where each symbol equals 4 friends. How many symbols should he use to show the number of friends that marched in the parade? Explain.

28. Suppose the number of friends who watched the parade is put into groups of 4. How many groups are there?

Did You Go to Saturday's Parade?

Responses	Number
Marched	20
Watched	16
Did not go	4

29. FIND THE ERROR Kendra is finding $12 \div 4$. Find and correct her mistake.

$4 + 8 = 12$
so
$12 \div 4 = 8$

30. **WRITE MATH** Write a real-world problem that uses the division fact $36 \div 9$.

 Test Practice

31. Four friends bought a total of 20 computer games. Each friend bought the same number of games. Which number sentence shows how many games they each bought? (Lesson 1C)

A. $20 \times 4 = 80$

B. $20 \div 4 = 5$

C. $20 + 4 = 24$

D. $20 - 4 = 16$

32. There are 4 sheets of stickers. Each sheet has 7 stickers. Which symbol goes in the box to make the number sentence true? (Lesson 1B)

$7 \ \blacksquare \ 4 = 28$

F. $+$ **H.** $\times$

G. $-$ **J.** $\div$

Spiral Review

Divide. (Lesson 1C)

33. $4 \div 4$ **34.** $4 \div 1$ **35.** $36 \div 4$ **36.** $0 \div 4$

Multiply. (Lesson 1B)

37. 1×4 **38.** 3×4 **39.** 6×4 **40.** 7×4

41. Measurement Jamila practices her violin for 1 hour, 4 days a week. How many hours does she practice each week? (Lesson 1B)

Multiplication and Division Facts for 4

Problem-Solving Skill: Extra or Missing Information

Main Idea I will solve a problem by identifying extra or missing information.

The school's hayride starts at 6 P.M. There are 4 wagons that hold 9 children each. Half of the children going are girls. What is the total number of children that can ride on the 4 wagons?

Understand

What facts do you know?

- The hayride starts at 6 P.M.

- There are 4 wagons that hold 9 children.

- Half of the children are girls.

What do you need to find?

- Find the number of children that can ride on the 4 wagons.

Plan

Decide what facts are important to solve the question.

- the number of wagons

- the number of children each wagon holds

> **Extra Information**
> - The hayride starts at 6 P.M.
> - Half of the children are girls.

Solve

To find the total number, multiply the number of wagons by the number of children each wagon holds.

$4 \times 9 = $ ■

$4 \times 9 = 36$

So, 36 children can ride on the hay wagons.

Check

Since $9 + 9 + 9 + 9 = 36$, you know the answer is correct. ✓

3.5 The student will recall multiplication facts through the twelves table, and the corresponding division facts.

Refer to the problem on the previous page.

1. How did you know what information was important and what was not?

2. Suppose there are 36 children but only 3 wagons. How many children will ride on each wagon?

3. Look back at your answer for Exercise 2. How do you know that the answer is correct?

4. Draw an array to verify that your answer to Exercise 2 is correct.

PRACTICE

EXTRA PRACTICE
Begins on page EP2.

Solve. If there is missing information, tell what facts you need to solve the problem.

5. Bert bought the items below. How much change did he get back?

Item	Cost
Pencils	$2
Paper	$1
Binder	$3

6. Measurement Alejandra is 58 inches tall. Her sister is in the first grade and is 48 inches tall. How much taller is Alejandra than her sister?

7. Mrs. Friedman had 2 boxes of chalk. She bought 4 more boxes with 10 pieces each. She paid $2 per box. How much did she spend on the 4 boxes of chalk?

8. Ten of Eduardo's baseball cards are All Star cards. His friend has twice as many baseball cards. How many baseball cards does Eduardo's friend have?

9. The third grade class had four chicks hatch every day for 5 days. Nine of the chicks were yellow, and the rest were brown. How many chicks hatched in all?

10. An animal shelter has 23 cats and 14 dogs. How much would it cost to adopt 1 cat and 1 dog?

11. **WRITE MATH** Rewrite Exercise 5 so it has enough information to solve. Then solve.

Lesson 1D Multiplication and Division Facts for 4 **239**

Main Idea

I will make a bar diagram or double a known fact to multiply by 6.

Get ConnectED

3.5 The student will recall multiplication facts through the twelves table, and the corresponding division facts.

3.6 The student will represent multiplication and division, using area, set, and number line models, and create and solve problems that involve multiplication of two whole numbers, one factor 99 or less and the second factor 5 or less.

Multiply by 6

You can make a bar diagram to help you understand real-world multiplication problems. The diagram will help you make a plan to solve.

REAL-WORLD EXAMPLE   Use a Bar Diagram

1) **FROGS There are 4 frogs sitting on a log. Each frog eats 6 flies. How many flies are eaten altogether?**

There are 4 frogs and each frog eats 6 flies. Use a bar diagram to model 4 groups of 6.

Step 1 Draw one bar to represent the number of flies eaten by one frog.

6 flies

Step 2 There are 4 frogs, so model one bar 4 times.

|--------------------? flies-------------------|
| 6 flies | 6 flies | 6 flies | 6 flies |

Step 3 Write a multiplication sentence to find the total number of flies eaten.

$4 \times 6 = 24$

So, the frogs ate 24 flies altogether.

Check $6 + 6 + 6 + 6 = 24$

Repeated addition shows that $4 \times 6 = 24$ is correct. ✔

② MARCHING BAND A band marches in 6 rows with 7 members in each row. How many members are there altogether?

You can double a known fact to find 6 × 7.

Step 1 6 is the double of 3.
So, 6 × 7 is the double of 3 × 7.

Step 2 6 × 7 = 3 × 7   +   3 × 7

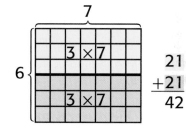

                21   +   21   = 42

So, 6 × 7 = 42. There are 42 members.

Check An array and partial products show that 6 × 7 = 42 is correct. ✔

Remember

There are many different ways to multiply.

✓ **CHECK What You Know**

Use the bar diagram to write a multiplication sentence. See Example 1

1. BAR DIAGRAM Marsha and her 2 brothers each saved $6. How much money did they save altogether?

```
|--------- ? $ ---------|
|  $6  |  $6  |  $6  |
```

2. BAR DIAGRAM Joey hit the ball 6 times farther than his friend. His friend hit the ball 8 feet. How far did Joey hit the ball?

```
|--------- ? feet ---------|
| 8 ft | 8 ft | 8 ft | 8 ft | 8 ft | 8 ft |
```

Multiply. Double a known fact if needed. See Example 2

3. 1 × 6   **4.** 0 × 6   **5.** 6 × 4   **6.** 6 × 6

7. Gil has 5 friends. He and each friend have 5 video games. How many video games do they have in all?

8. TALK MATH Explain why the product of 6 and 3 is double the product of 3 and 3.

Use the bar diagram to write a multiplication sentence. See Example 1

9. | BAR | DIAGRAM | Sometimes the sun shines only 2 hours a day in one part of the world. At the same time, if may shine 6 times longer somewhere else. How many hours would that be?

|← — — — — — — ? hours — — — — — — →|
| 2 h | 2 h | 2 h | 2 h | 2 h | 2 h |

10. | BAR | DIAGRAM | Felipe helped clean chalkboard erasers after school for 4 classrooms. Each room had 6 erasers. How many erasers did Felipe clean?

|← — — — — — ? erasers — — — — — →|
| 6 erasers | 6 erasers | 6 erasers | 6 erasers |

Multiply. Double a known fact if needed. See Example 2

11. $\begin{array}{r} 6 \\ \times\ 2 \\ \hline \end{array}$

12. $\begin{array}{r} 5 \\ \times\ 6 \\ \hline \end{array}$

13. $\begin{array}{r} 4 \\ \times\ 6 \\ \hline \end{array}$

14. $\begin{array}{r} 3 \\ \times\ 6 \\ \hline \end{array}$

15. $\begin{array}{r} 6 \\ \times\ 6 \\ \hline \end{array}$

16. $\begin{array}{r} 10 \\ \times\ 6 \\ \hline \end{array}$

17. $\begin{array}{r} 6 \\ \times\ 9 \\ \hline \end{array}$

18. $\begin{array}{r} 7 \\ \times\ 6 \\ \hline \end{array}$

19. 6×0

20. 6×3

21. 8×6

22. 6×5

Algebra Find each missing factor.

23. $4 \times \blacksquare = 24$

24. $\blacksquare \times 6 = 60$

25. $6 \times \blacksquare = 36$

26. $6 \times \blacksquare = 18$

Solve. Use a model if needed.

27. In the morning, 6 eggs hatched. By the evening, nine times as many had hatched. What is the total number of eggs that hatched?

28. If Ida has 6 dimes, does she have enough money for 8 pieces of bubble gum that cost 6¢ each? Explain.

29. Six students bought 5 pretzels each. If they gave away 6 of the pretzels, how many pretzels are left?

30. There are 7 vans that hold 6 students each. Is there enough room for 45 students? Explain.

H.O.T. Problems

31. OPEN ENDED Use one of the multiplication strategies to explain how you would find the product of 6×6.

32. **WRITE MATH** Write a real-world problem that can be solved by multiplying by 6.

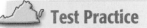

33. Sherry uses the pan below to bake blueberry muffins. She puts 10 blueberries into each muffin. How many muffins will she make if she uses 5 trays like the one shown? (Lesson 1D)

A. 6

B. 30

C. 50

D. 60

34. Malik had 20 fish in a large aquarium. He moved 4 of the fish to a 10-gallon aquarium. Which of the following number sentences could be used to find the number of fish Malik had left in the large aquarium? (Lesson 1D)

F. $\blacksquare - 10 = 20$ **H.** $20 - 10 = \blacksquare$

G. $20 - 4 = \blacksquare$ **J.** $\blacksquare - 4 = 20$

35. Mr. Baxter bought 6 boxes of light bulbs. Each box has 4 bulbs. Which number sentence shows how to find the total number of bulbs? (Lesson 2A)

A. $6 - 4 = 2$ **C.** $6 + 4 = 10$

B. $24 \div 6 = 4$ **D.** $6 \times 4 = 24$

36. Henry put the shells he collected into equal groups of 3 shells. Solve to find how many shells Henry collected. If there is missing information, tell what facts you need to solve the problem. (Lesson 1D)

Multiply. (Lessons 2A, 1B)

37. 0×6 **38.** 4×0 **39.** 4×1

40. 2×4 **41.** 6×2 **42.** 4×6

Solve. Write a number sentence. (Lesson 1C)

43. Jessica shares 28 stickers with 3 of her friends. How many stickers will Jessica and her friends each have if they are shared equally?

44. All 4 members of the Smith family went to the zoo. Their tickets cost a total of $32. How much was each ticket?

Main Idea

I will use repeated addition to multiply by 7.

 Get ConnectED

 3.5 The student will recall multiplication facts through the twelves table, and the corresponding division facts.

3.6 The student will represent multiplication and division, using area, set, and number line models, and create and solve problems that involve multiplication of two whole numbers, one factor 99 or less and the second factor 5 or less.

Multiply by 7

You can use repeated addition to multiply by 7.

🏃 ✏ **REAL-WORLD EXAMPLE**   **Use Repeated Addition**

① **RIDES** A ride at an amusement park has 7 cars. Each car has 5 seats. How many people can go on the ride at the same time?

Find 7×5. Use repeated addition to count 7 groups of 5 seats in each car. Add 5 seven times.

$$5 + 5 + 5 + 5 + 5 + 5 + 5 = 35$$

So, $7 \times 5 = 35$. The ride can hold 35 people at a time.

To multiply by 7, you can also use a known fact.

✏ **EXAMPLE**   **Use a Known Fact**

② **Find 7×6.**

You know $6 \times 7 = 42$.

So, $7 \times 6 = 42$. Commutative Property

Check Doubling a known fact shows that $6 \times 7 = 42$ is correct. ✔

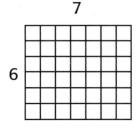

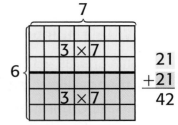

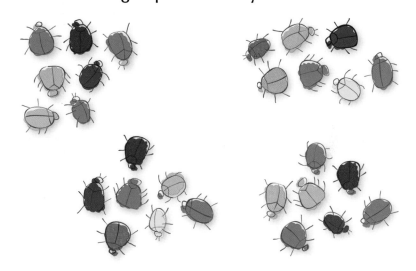

REAL-WORLD EXAMPLE   Find Missing Factors

3 **Algebra** **A bug box has a total of 28 beetles. There are an equal number of each size of beetle. There are 7 of each size. How many sizes are there?**

You can draw pictures to model and solve a multiplication sentence.

different sizes		number of each size		total
■	×	7	=	28

> THINK What number times 7 equals 28?

Draw beetles in groups of 7 until you have 28 beetles.

Four groups of 7 is 28. The missing **factor** in the multiplication sentence is 4.

So, 4 × 7 = 28. There are 4 sizes of beetles.

✓ CHECK What You Know

Multiply. Use repeated addition or a known fact, if needed.

See Examples 1 and 2

1.
$$\begin{array}{r} 2 \\ \times\ 7 \\ \hline \end{array}$$

2.
$$\begin{array}{r} 7 \\ \times\ 8 \\ \hline \end{array}$$

3. 9 × 7

4. 7 × 10

Algebra **Find each missing factor.** See Example 3

5. 7 × ■ = 0

6. ■ × 7 = 49

7. 7 × ■ = 70

8. Whitney gave 7 friends 4 pencils each. How many pencils did she give them in all?

9. **⬛ TALK MATH** Describe two different strategies for multiplying a number by 7.

Lesson 2B Multiplication and Division Facts for 6 and 7   **245**

Multiply. Use repeated addition or a known fact, if needed.

See Examples 1 and 2

10. 3
  × 7

11. 1
  × 7

12. 4
  × 7

13. 7
  × 2

14. 0
  × 7

15. 7
  × 7

16. 9
  × 7

17. 7
  × 6

18. 7 × 4

19. 5 × 7

20. 7 × 8

21. 10 × 7

22. 7 × 2

23. 10 × 7

24. 7 × 9

25. 7 × 5

Algebra Find each missing factor. See Example 3

26. 4 × ■ = 28

27. 7 × ■ = 49

28. 8 × ■ = 56

29. ■ × 7 = 63

30. ■ × 7 = 21

31. 7 × ■ = 42

32. Ryan and 6 friends played basketball. They made a total of 35 baskets. Each made the same number of baskets. How many baskets did each person make?

33. During the 9 weeks of summer vacation, Bradley spent 2 weeks at soccer camp. How many days was he not at camp?

34. Antonio has 5 packs of rubber spiders. Each pack has 7 spiders. How many spiders does he have in all?

35. Inez has 8 CDs. How many songs are there if each CD has 7 songs?

H.O.T. Problems

36. NUMBER SENSE Is the product of 3 × 7 greater than the product of 3 × 8? How do you know without multiplying? Explain.

37. WHICH ONE DOESN'T BELONG? Identify which multiplication sentence is incorrect. Explain.

| 7 × 9 = 63 | 7 × 7 = 48 | 5 × 7 = 35 | 7 × 0 = 0 |

38. WRITE MATH Explain why using repeated addition is not the best strategy for finding a product like 7 × 9.

🔬 Facts Practice

Multiply.

1. 4
  × 9

2. 5
  × 3

3. 6
  × 4

4. 3
  × 6

5. 3
  × 2

6. 4
  × 4

7. 2
  × 2

8. 4
  × 5

9. 4
  × 6

10. 2
  × 5

11. 2
  × 7

12. 8
  × 2

13. 8
  × 3

14. 2
  × 3

15. 6
  × 3

16. 4
  × 3

17. 6
  × 5

18. 3
  × 9

19. 6
  × 2

20. 4
  × 7

21. 7×2

22. 5×2

23. 5×9

24. 2×4

25. 8×5

26. 3×3

27. 5×6

28. 7×4

29. 3×4

30. 4×4

31. 7×3

32. 9×2

33. 5×5

34. 9×4

35. 2×6

36. 5×7

Main Idea

I will use arrays and repeated subtraction to divide by 6 and 7.

 Get ConnectED

 **3.2** The student will recognize and use the inverse relationships between addition/subtraction and multiplication/division to complete basic fact sentences. The student will use these relationships to solve problems. **3.5** The student will recall multiplication facts through the twelves table, and the corresponding division facts.

Divide by 6 and 7

You learned that arrays can help you understand how division and multiplication are inverse operations.

REAL-WORLD EXAMPLE

Inverse Operations

1. **PICNIC** Paco set each picnic table with 6 dinner plates. He used 24 plates to set the tables. How many tables did he set?

Use an array to find $24 \div 6$, or $6\overline{)24}$. It will help you relate division to multiplication.

In the array, each column represents one table of 6 plates. There are 4 columns. So, there will be 4 tables.

$$24 \div 6 = 4, \text{ or } 6\overline{)24}.$$

So, Paco set 4 tables.

Check The number line shows there are 4 groups of 6 in 24.

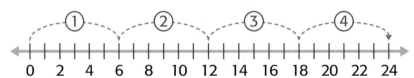

You can use many different methods to divide by 6 and 7.

EXAMPLES Relate Subtraction and Multiplication

Remember

Some division strategies are more useful than others when working with large numbers.

② **READING** Molly read 28 books in 7 months. She read the same number each month. How many books did she read each month?

Find how many groups of 7 are in 28.
Use repeated subtraction to find 28 ÷ 7, or $7\overline{)28}$.

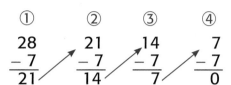

① ② ③ ④

$\begin{array}{c} 28 \\ -\ 7 \\ \hline 21 \end{array}$ $\begin{array}{c} 21 \\ -\ 7 \\ \hline 14 \end{array}$ $\begin{array}{c} 14 \\ -\ 7 \\ \hline 7 \end{array}$ $\begin{array}{c} 7 \\ -\ 7 \\ \hline 0 \end{array}$

The number 7 is subtracted four times to reach 0.

So, 28 ÷ 7 = 4, or $7\overline{)28}^{\,4}$. Molly read 4 books each month.

③ **TEACHING** Mr. Jeremiah has 21 reports to grade. He will grade the same number of reports each day for 7 days. How many reports will he grade each day?

Use the inverse operation of multiplication to find 21 ÷ 7, or $7\overline{)21}$.

21 ÷ 7 = ■

7 × ■ = 21 ← THINK 7 times what number equals 21?

7 × 3 = 21

So, 21 ÷ 7 = 3, or $7\overline{)21}^{\,3}$. He will grade 3 reports each day.

✓ CHECK What You Know

Divide. Use models or repeated subtraction. See Examples 1–3

1. 24 ÷ 6

2. 18 ÷ 6

3. $7\overline{)35}$

4. 21 ÷ 7

5. 14 ÷ 7

6. $6\overline{)30}$

7. Measurement One kite tail measures 7 feet long. Elena has 56 feet of tail fabric. How many kite tails can she make?

8. **TALK MATH** Are using related multiplication and division facts the same as using fact families? Explain.

Divide. Use models or repeated subtraction. See Examples 1–3

9. $6 \div 6$ **10.** $42 \div 6$ **11.** $28 \div 7$ **12.** $70 \div 7$

13. $6\overline{)36}$ **14.** $6\overline{)60}$ **15.** $7\overline{)0}$ **16.** $7\overline{)42}$

Algebra Find each missing number.

17. $7 \times \blacksquare = 63$ **18.** $7 \times \blacksquare = 35$ **19.** $7 \times \blacksquare = 70$

     $63 \div 7 = \blacksquare$ $35 \div 7 = \blacksquare$ $70 \div 7 = \blacksquare$

Algebra Copy and complete each table.

20.

Rule: Divide by 6.			
Input	36	12	48	$\blacksquare$
Output	$\blacksquare$	$\blacksquare$	$\blacksquare$	10

21.

Rule: Divide by 7.			
Input	28	42	$\blacksquare$	70
Output	$\blacksquare$	$\blacksquare$	7	$\blacksquare$

Solve. Write a number sentence.

22. A rosebush has 42 rosebuds. The 7 stems of the rosebush have an equal number of buds. How many buds are on each stem?

23. The sewing club is making a quilt with 63 squares. The squares are quilted in 7 equal rows. How many quilt squares are there in each row?

24. For every tree that is cut down, 7 new trees are planted. If 56 new trees have been planted, how many trees were cut down?

25. There are 7 groups of 5 students and 5 groups of 7 students at the tables in the cafeteria. What is the total number of students?

H.O.T. Problems

26. OPEN ENDED Write two numbers that cannot be divided by 7 evenly.

27. WHICH ONE DOESN'T BELONG? Identify the division sentence that does not belong with the others. Explain.

| $56 \div 7$ | $7\overline{)48}$ | $49 \div 7$ | $7\overline{)63}$ |

28. WRITE MATH When you know that $42 \div 6 = 7$, you also know that $42 \div 7 = 6$. Explain why.

Main Idea

I will use technology to model division.

3.5 The student will recall multiplication facts through the twelves table, and the corresponding division facts. **3.6** The student will represent multiplication and division, using area, set, and number line models, and create and solve problems that involve multiplication of two whole numbers, one factor 99 or less and the second factor 5 or less.

Model Division

You can use the *Math Tool Chest* to model division problems.

ACTIVITY

① **GAME** **Twenty-one students equally divided into 3 teams for a game. How many students were on each team?**

You want to find 21 ÷ 3.

Choose the counters icon from the *Math Tool Chest*.

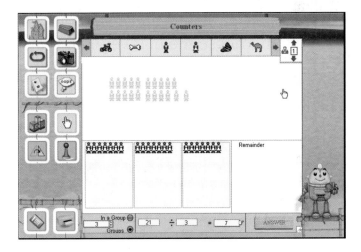

- Choose division for the mat type.
- Choose a boy or girl stamp.
- Stamp out 21 boys or girls.
- At the bottom of the screen, choose 3 and "Groups."

The number sentence shows you are finding 21 ÷ 3.

- Select and place one student at a time on a team.

Check Choose "Answer" to find how many students are on each team.

So, 21 ÷ 3 = 7 students on each team. ✔

2) **FOOD** The grocer is selling 24 bananas. There are 6 bananas in each bunch. How many bunches are there?

To find 24 ÷ 6, choose the counters icon from the *Math Tool Chest.*

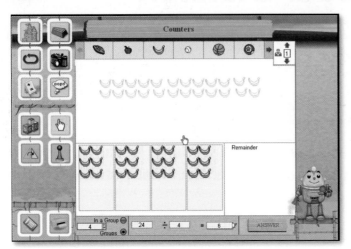

- Choose division for the mat type.
- Choose the banana stamp, and stamp out 24 bananas.
- At the bottom, choose the number 6 and "In a Group."

The number sentence shows that you are finding 24 ÷ 6, 24 bananas with 6 bananas in each bunch.

- Select and place one banana at a time in a bunch.

Check   Choose "Answer" to find how many bunches of bananas there are.

So, 24 ÷ 6 = 4 bunches. ✔

Practice and Apply It

Use *Math Tool Chest* to solve.

1. Thirty people are camping in 5 tents. Each tent holds the same number of people. How many people are in each tent?

2. The zoo has 18 monkeys. Each monkey will share its tree with only 2 other monkeys. How many trees are needed?

3. Each circus car holds 7 clowns. There are a total of 28 clowns. How many cars will be needed?

4. Forty-nine people are on floats at the parade. Each float holds 7 people. How many floats are there?

Mid-Chapter Check

Multiply. (Lesson 1B)

1. 4
$\times\ 4$

2. 8
$\times\ 3$

3. 5×4

4. 6×5

Write a multiplication sentence for each situation. (Lesson 1B)

5. Tory wrote 4 pages every day in his journal. After 9 days, how many pages did he write?

6. Four runners from a team each ran 7 times around the track. What is the total number of times the runners ran around the track?

Divide. Use models or related facts.
(Lesson 1C)

7. $8 \div 2$

8. $20 \div 4$

9. $4\overline{)24}$

10. $4\overline{)36}$

11. MULTIPLE CHOICE There are 4 quarts in one gallon of milk. One quart is equal to 2 pints. How many quarts of milk are in the gallons shown below? (Lesson 1D)

A. 3 **B.** 4 **C.** 8 **D.** 12

Use the bar diagram to write a multiplication sentence. (Lesson 2A)

12.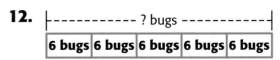

| — ? bugs — |
| 6 bugs | 6 bugs | 6 bugs | 6 bugs | 6 bugs |

13.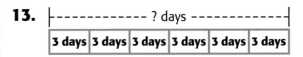

| — ? days — |
| 3 days | 3 days | 3 days | 3 days | 3 days | 3 days |

Find each missing factor. (Lesson 2B)

14. $7 \times \blacksquare = 49$

15. $7 \times \blacksquare = 70$

16. $\blacksquare \times 5 = 35$

17. $\blacksquare \times 7 = 28$

18. MULTIPLE CHOICE Aisha picked 42 apples. She placed an equal number in 7 bags. Which of the following could be used to find how many apples were in each bag? (Lesson 2C)

F. $42 + 7$ **H.** 42×7

G. $42 - 7$ **J.** $42 \div 7$

19. WRITE MATH Sophia said that if she knows $36 \div 4 = 9$, then she can find $36 \div 9$. What is the answer? Explain her reasoning. (Lesson 1C)

Mid-Chapter Check **253**

Main Idea

I will use arrays and known facts to multiply by 8.

Get Connect**ED**

3.5 The student will recall multiplication facts through the twelves table, and the corresponding division facts.
3.6 The student will represent multiplication and division, using area, set, and number line models, and create and solve problems that involve multiplication of two whole numbers, one factor 99 or less and the second factor 5 or less.

Multiply by 8

You can use an array or a known fact to multiply by 8.

 REAL-WORLD EXAMPLE   Use an Array

① **BIRDS** There are 8 trees lining a street. In each tree, there are 6 birds. How many birds are there in all?

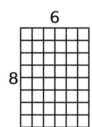

You need to find 8 × 6.

Think of each tree as a group of 6 birds.

So, 8 × 6 = 48 birds in all.

You can change the order of the factors to find a related fact.

REAL-WORLD EXAMPLE   Use a Known Fact

② **BUTTONS** Jaya has 8 shirts. There are 4 buttons on each shirt. How many buttons are there altogether?

Think of each shirt as a group with 4 buttons in each group. You need to find 8 × 4.

You know that 4 × 8 = 32.

So, 8 × 4 = 32.   Commutative Property

Jaya's shirts have 32 buttons altogether.

The 4s facts are helpful in remembering the 8s facts. The 8s facts are double the 4s.

Remember

When one of the factors is even, you can use the *double a known fact* strategy.

REAL-WORLD EXAMPLE   Double a Known Fact

(3) **ALLOWANCE Pearl earns $7 every week for doing her chores. How much money will she earn after 8 weeks?**

You can double a known fact to find 8 × $7.

8 is the double of 4. So, 8 × $7 is double 4 × $7.

8 × $7	=	4 × $7	+	4 × $7	
	=	$28	+	$28	= $56

So, 8 × $7 = $56. Pearl will earn $56 after 8 weeks.

Check   An array and partial products show that 8 × 7 is correct. ✔

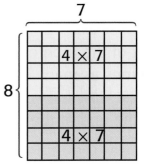

✓ CHECK What You Know

Multiply. Use an array or a known fact, if needed. See Examples 1–3

1. 8
  × 2

2. 0
  × 8

3. 4
  × 8

4. 8
  × 5

5. 8 × 1

6. 6 × 8

7. 8 × 3

8. 8 × 7

9. Nate spends $4 on 8 cans of dog food each week. How much does he spend in 4 weeks?

10. ❓ **TALK MATH** If there are 4 groups of 8 students and 8 groups of 8 students, how many students are there in all? Explain.

Multiply. Use an array or a known fact, if needed. See Examples 1–3

11.	12.	13.	14.
2	1	7	8
× 8	× 8	× 8	× 8

15. 0 × 8   **16.** 8 × 9   **17.** 10 × 8   **18.** 3 × 8

19. 8 × 6   **20.** 5 × 8   **21.** 8 × 4   **22.** 9 × 8

Algebra Find each missing factor.

23. $8 \times \blacksquare = 64$ **24.** $\blacksquare \times 8 = 40$ **25.** $8 \times \blacksquare = 56$ **26.** $8 \times \blacksquare = 80$

27. There are 3 large and 4 small spiders in a web. Each has 8 legs. How many legs are there altogether?

28. Admission for one person to the Science Center is $8. How much would it cost a family of 6?

29. BAR DIAGRAM Jolon worked 5 hours the first week of the month. By the end of the month, he had worked 8 times as many hours as the first week. How many hours did he work by the end of the month?

30. There are 9 crates, each with 8 cases of oranges, on a delivery truck. How many cases of oranges will be left if 5 crates are delivered at the first stop?

Data File

Mrs. Miller's class of 8 students decided to adopt an animal at the Central Florida Zoo.

31. From which adoption level could the students adopt if they each paid $5?

32. How much would each student need to pay in order to adopt from the Animal Lover level?

**Central Florida Zoo
Adopt An Animal**

Adoption Level............ Price	
Zoo Friend $35	
Animal Lover $56	
Kingdom Keeper.................$100	

33. If each student paid $10, would they be able to adopt from the Kingdom Keeper level? Explain.

34. Suppose one student decided *not* to be part of the Adopt an Animal program. Could the rest of the students still adopt from the Zoo Friend level for the same amount of money? Explain.

35. OPEN ENDED Explain a strategy that you would use to find 9 × 8. Why do you prefer this strategy?

36. NUMBER SENSE Explain how you can use the Commutative Property of Multiplication to find 8 × 7.

37. **WRITE MATH** Write a real-world problem that involves multiplying by 8.

Test Practice

38. What number makes this number sentence true? (Lesson 2B)

$$7 \times 5 < 4 \times \blacksquare$$

A. 3

B. 5

C. 7

D. 10

39. Which multiplication sentence is modeled below? (Lesson 3A)

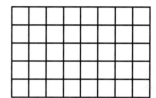

F. 5 × 8 = 40   **H.** 40 × 8 = 5

G. 5 × 9 = 40   **J.** 40 × 5 = 8

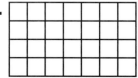 

Divide. Use models or repeated subtraction. (Lesson 2C)

40. 30 ÷ 6   **41.** 56 ÷ 7   **42.** 42 ÷ 7

43. There are 48 people attending an awards ceremony. There will be 6 chairs in each row. How many rows are needed for the ceremony?

Multiply. Use repeated addition or a known fact, if needed. (Lesson 2B)

44. 8 × 7   **45.** 7 × 7   **46.** 9 × 7

Write a multiplication sentence for each array. (Lesson 1B)

47.   **48.**   **49.**

Main Idea

I will use a known fact or patterns to multiply by 9.

 Get ConnectED

 3.5 The student will recall multiplication facts through the twelves table, and the corresponding division facts. **3.20** The student will **a)** investigate the identity and the commutative properties for addition and multiplication. Also addresses 3.19.

Multiply by 9

To multiply by 9, you can use a known fact.

🏃 ✍ **REAL-WORLD EXAMPLE**

Commutative Property of Multiplication

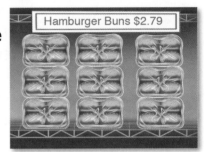
Hamburger Buns $2.79

① **BUNS** There are 9 packages of hamburger buns. There are 8 buns in each package. How many buns are there in all?

To solve the problem you can use a known fact.

number of packages	number in each package	total
9	× 8	= ■

You know $8 \times 9 = 72$. Commutative Property

So, $9 \times 8 = 72$. There are 72 buns.

Subtracting from a known fact will help you remember your 9s facts.

✍ **REAL-WORLD EXAMPLE**

Subtract from a Known Fact

② **STUDENTS** How many students are there in 9 groups with 5 students in each group?

To find 9×5, multiply the smaller factor by 10 and then subtract the smaller factor one time.

Step 1 9×5 is 9 groups of 5. Use the known fact of 10 groups of 5. $10 \times 5 = 50$

Step 2   Subtract 1 group of 5 to get $50 - 5$, or 45.

So, $9 \times 5 = 45$ students.

Remember

The Commutative Property of Multiplication allows you to change the order of factors to find a known fact.

You can use patterns to help remember the 9s facts. The first factor and the product in the 9s table create a pattern.

- The tens digit of the product is always 1 less than the factor that is multiplied by 9.

- The sum of the digits of the product equals 9.

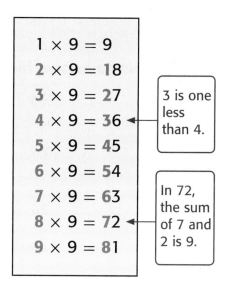

$1 \times 9 = 9$
$2 \times 9 = 18$
$3 \times 9 = 27$
$4 \times 9 = 36$ ◄ 3 is one less than 4.
$5 \times 9 = 45$
$6 \times 9 = 54$
$7 \times 9 = 63$
$8 \times 9 = 72$ ◄ In 72, the sum of 7 and 2 is 9.
$9 \times 9 = 81$

REAL-WORLD EXAMPLE — Use Patterns

③ MONEY Mr. Clancy bought 6 cans of paint. Each can costs $9. How much did he spend?

Since the total cost is needed, multiply. Find $6 \times \$9$.

$6 \times \$9 \rightarrow \$5$ ◄ THINK $6 - 1 = 5$

$6 \times \$9 = \$54$ ◄ THINK $5 + ? = 9$
$5 + 4 = 9$

So, $6 \times \$9 = \$54$. Mr. Clancy spent $54.

✓ CHECK What You Know

Multiply. Use a known fact or patterns, if needed. See Examples 1–3

1. 9
    × 1

2. 4
    × 9

3. 9
    × 2

4. 6
    × 9

5. 0×9

6. 9×3

7. 10×9

8. 7×9

9. Lyle has 63 rocks in his collection. He places them into bags. Each bag holds 9 rocks. How many bags are there?

10. **TALK MATH** How can patterns help you when multiplying by 9?

Multiply. Use a known fact or patterns, if needed. See Examples 1–3

11. 3
   × 9

12. 9
   × 6

13. 4
   × 9

14. 2
   × 9

15. 5
   × 9

16. 8
   × 9

17. 9
   × 10

18. 9
   × 9

19. 1 × 9

20. 7 × 9

21. 9 × 5

22. 10 × 9

23. 9 × 0

24. 9 × 3

25. 6 × 9

26. 9 × 7

Algebra Find each missing factor.

27. ■ × 9 = 18

28. 3 × ■ = 27

29. 5 × ■ = 45

30. 9 × ■ = 54

31. 6 × ■ = 54

32. 9 × ■ = 72

Solve. Use models, if needed.

33. Opal and Ela have 9 marbles each. How many marbles are there in all?

34. Cecilia sold 5 books for $9 each. How much money did she get?

35. There were 4 car races on Saturday and 3 on Sunday. If there were 9 cars racing in each race, how many cars raced over the two days?

36. **Measurement** Phil uses 9 yards of rope for each ladder he makes. He makes 4 rope ladders. How many yards of rope will he use?

H.O.T. Problems

37. NUMBER SENSE Is 9 × 2 the same as 3 × 3 × 2? Explain.

38. FIND THE ERROR Eva is finding 9 × 9. Find and correct her mistake.

If 9 × 8 = 72, then
9 × 9 must be
8 more, so 9 × 9 = 80.

39. **WRITE MATH** Describe how the number 10 can help you solve multiplication problems with 9 as a factor.

Facts Practice

Divide.

1. $4\overline{)24}$ 2. $6\overline{)42}$ 3. $3\overline{)27}$ 4. $5\overline{)45}$

5. $4\overline{)8}$ 6. $9\overline{)45}$ 7. $2\overline{)16}$ 8. $9\overline{)54}$

9. $7\overline{)56}$ 10. $7\overline{)28}$ 11. $3\overline{)24}$ 12. $4\overline{)32}$

13. $5\overline{)40}$ 14. $5\overline{)15}$ 15. $6\overline{)48}$ 16. $3\overline{)9}$

17. $4\overline{)20}$ 18. $7\overline{)21}$ 19. $2\overline{)14}$ 20. $5\overline{)40}$

21. $30 \div 6$ 22. $80 \div 10$ 23. $60 \div 6$ 24. $42 \div 7$

25. $36 \div 6$ 26. $32 \div 4$ 27. $40 \div 5$ 28. $36 \div 4$

29. $12 \div 6$ 30. $18 \div 2$ 31. $21 \div 3$ 32. $20 \div 10$

33. $1 \div 1$ 34. $49 \div 7$ 35. $25 \div 5$ 36. $54 \div 6$

Main Idea
I will use the inverse operations of multiplication and division to divide by 8 and 9.

3.5 The student will recall multiplication facts through the twelves table, and the corresponding division facts.

3.6 The student will represent multiplication and division, using area, set, and number line models, and create and solve problems that involve multiplication of two whole numbers, one factor 99 or less and the second factor 5 or less.

Divide by 8 and 9

You can apply division and multiplication as inverse operations to find a quotient.

REAL-WORLD EXAMPLE Inverse Operations

① **SCIENCE** The pictograph shows the number of times each student visited a science museum. If 32 students visited 2 or more times, how many symbols should be drawn in that row?

Science Museum Visits	
Number of Visits	**Number of Students**
Never	✋
1	✋ ✋
2 or more	
Key: ✋ = 8 students	

There are 32 students being divided into groups of 8.

One Way: Multiplication	Another Way: Division
32 ÷ 8 = ■	32 ÷ 8 = ■
8 × ■ = 32	32 ÷ ■ = 8
8 × 4 = 32	32 ÷ 4 = 8
So, 32 ÷ 8 = 4.	So, 32 ÷ 8 = 4.

So, there should be 4 symbols drawn in the row.

2 **ART** Kyra and 8 of her friends made 63 paper stars. They will each take home an equal number. How many paper stars will each take home?

Find $63 \div 9$, or $9\overline{)63}$.

Place 63 counters in 9 groups one at a time.

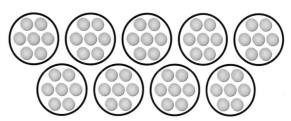

So, $63 \div 9 = 7$, or $9\overline{)63}^{\,7}$. Kyra and her friends will each take home 7 stars.

REAL-WORLD EXAMPLE   Repeated Subtraction

3 **QUARTERS** Bob collected 27 state quarters over the last 9 years. Each year he added the same number. How many quarters did he add each year?

Use repeated subtraction to find $27 \div 9$, or $9\overline{)27}$.

①	②	③
27	18	9
$-\ 9$	$-\ 9$	$-\ 9$
18	9	0

> 9 is subtracted three times to reach zero.

So, $27 \div 9 = 3$, or $9\overline{)27}^{\,3}$. Bob added 3 quarters each year.

Remember

Multiplication and division are inverse operations. Think of a multiplication fact to help you find a quotient.

✓ **CHECK What You Know**

Divide. Use related facts or repeated subtraction. See Examples 1–3

1. $8 \div 8$

2. $18 \div 9$

3. $8\overline{)64}$

4. Each art project uses 9 tiles. There are 81 tiles. How many projects can be made?

5. 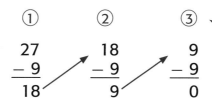 **TALK MATH** How do multiplication facts help you check to see if your division is correct?

Divide. Use related facts or repeated subtraction. See Examples 1–3

6. $16 \div 8$ **7.** $72 \div 8$ **8.** $63 \div 9$ **9.** $27 \div 9$

10. $8\overline{)80}$ **11.** $8\overline{)32}$ **12.** $9\overline{)90}$ **13.** $9\overline{)54}$

Algebra Find each missing number.

14. $9 \times \blacksquare = 36$
$36 \div 9 = \blacksquare$

15. $8 \times \blacksquare = 40$
$40 \div 8 = \blacksquare$

16. $8 \times \blacksquare = 48$
$48 \div 8 = \blacksquare$

Solve. Write a number sentence.

17. Tionna has 24 party favors to evenly divide between her 8 guests. How many favors will each get?

18. One baseball game has 9 innings. If 36 innings out of 54 have been played, how many games remain?

Use the information to solve the problems.

Hard Work Pays Off

Remember, Jacob wants to buy a skateboard. He earns $15 a week but wants to divide his money evenly 3 ways.

The red skateboard is $45.

Sale

Lightning Bolt!

19. How much money will Jacob save each week for the skateboard?

20. How many weeks will it take for Jacob to save enough money to buy the skateboard?

H.O.T. Problems

21. OPEN ENDED Choose two facts from Exercises 6–13. Explain a strategy for remembering them.

22. WRITE MATH Write a real-world multiplication problem in which you would divide by 8 or 9.

Game Time

Number Cubes
Multiply and Divide Numbers

You will need: one 0–5 number cube, one 5–10 number cube

Get Ready!

Players: 2 players

Get Set!

Make a chart to record each roll.

Go!

☆ Player 1 rolls the number cubes.

☆ Each player writes down the numbers.

☆ Each player uses the two numbers in number sentences that use multiplication and division facts.

☆ Each player gets 1 point for each correctly written number sentence.

☆ The game ends when 1 player earns 50 points.

Cube 1	Cube 2	Multiplication sentence	Division sentence
5	4	$5 \times 4 = 20$	$20 \div 5 = 4$

Problem-Solving Investigation

Main Idea I will choose the best strategy to solve a problem.

P.S.I. TEAM +

DOUGLAS: My sister gave me a package of drawing paper. There are 32 sheets. I want to make them last 8 days.

YOUR MISSION: Find how many sheets Douglas can use each day if he uses the same number each day.

Understand

Douglas has 32 sheets of paper for 8 days. Find how many sheets he can use each day.

Plan

You know the total number of sheets of paper and how many days they need to last. Act it out using counters.

Solve

Use 32 counters to represent the 32 sheets of paper. Make 8 equal groups, placing the counters one at a time into each group.

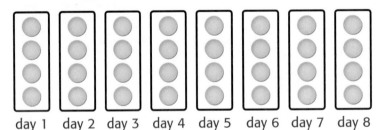

day 1　day 2　day 3　day 4　day 5　day 6　day 7　day 8

So, Douglas can use 4 sheets of paper each day.

Check

Use repeated addition to check the answer.

$$4 + 4 + 4 + 4 + 4 + 4 + 4 + 4 = 32 \checkmark$$

3.5 The student will recall multiplication facts through the twelves table, and the corresponding division facts.

- Act it out.
- Draw a picture.
- Choose an operation.

Use any strategy to solve each problem.

1. Jonas has 6 fish tanks with 5 fish in each. After he sold some, he had 22 fish left. How many fish did he sell? How much money did he make if he sold each fish for $5?

2. BAR DIAGRAM Grandmother picked 4 times as many apples as pears. What is the difference in the number of apples and pears picked?

4 times as many

| 8 pears |

|------------? apples-----------|
| 8 apples | 8 apples | 8 apples | 8 apples |

3. Measurement Paula put 6 books on one side of a balance scale. On the other side, she put 2 books and her baseball glove. The sides balanced. Each book weighs 3 pounds. How much does her glove weigh?

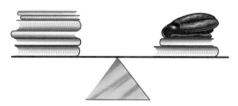

4. Marvina and Gustavo went to the grocery store. Marvina bought 5 items for $6 each. Gustavo bought 7 items for $8 each. How much did they spend together?

5. Angelina's mother knits gloves and mittens that are red, blue, green, or brown. How many different choices of gloves and mittens are there when she sells them? Explain.

6. Measurement Devon and his sister have 42 bottles of water. Devon drinks the amount shown each day. His sister drinks 4 bottles each day. How many days will the water last?

7. Selena, Ronnie, Jared, and Patty each have 5 books. Selena and Jared each read 4 of their books. Ronnie did not read 2 of his books. Patty read all of her books. How many books did they read in all?

8. Algebra What is the next number in the pattern?

    25, 26, 29, 30, 33, 34, ▮

9. WRITE MATH There are 42 students going on a picnic. Each car holds 6 students. Each van holds 7 students. Would it be less expensive to take cars or vans? Explain.

Picnic Transportation	
Vehicle	**Cost**
Car	$10
Van	$11

Main Idea

I will multiply by 11 and 12.

 Vocabulary

decompose

partial product

 **Get Connect**ED

 3.2 The student will recognize and use the inverse relationships between addition/subtraction and multiplication/division to complete basic fact sentences. The student will use these relationships to solve problems. Also addresses 3.6.

3.5 The student will recall multiplication facts through the twelves table, and the corresponding division facts.

Multiply by 11 and 12

When multiplying by 11, you can use patterns and models.

✏ 📷 **REAL-WORLD EXAMPLE**   Use Patterns or Models

1 **STRAWS** There are 11 straws in a package. Helen bought 4 packages. How many straws does Helen have?

Find 4 × 11.

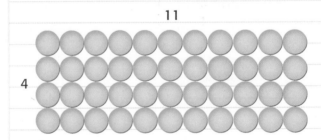

One Way: Use Patterns

Multiply by 11		
1	× 11 =	11
2	× 11 =	22
3	× 11 =	33
4	× 11 =	44

The pattern shows that when a single digit number is multiplied by 11, the product is the digit repeated.

Another Way: Use Models

Model 4 rows of 11 counters.

11

4

Use repeated addition. 11 + 11 + 11 + 11 = 44
The model shows that 4 × 11 = 44.

So, Helen has 44 straws.

2 **MEASUREMENT** There are 12 inches in one foot. How many inches are in 6 feet?

Find 6×12.

Step 1 Model 6×12 by **decomposing**, or breaking apart the 12 into easier numbers.

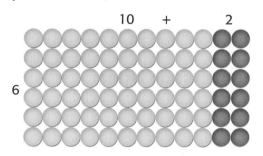

Step 2 Multiply each part.

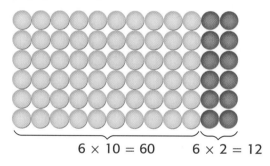

$6 \times 10 = 60$ $6 \times 2 = 12$

Step 3 Add each part or **partial product**.

$60 + 12 = 72$

So, there are 72 inches in 6 feet.

Remember

You can use expanded form to break a number into easier parts to work with.

✓ **CHECK** **What You Know**

Multiply. Use models or patterns, if needed. See Examples 1 and 2

1. 11
$\times\ 3$

2. 11
$\times\ 5$

3. 11
$\times\ 1$

4. 12
$\times\ 2$

5. 12
$\times\ 4$

6. 12
$\times\ 3$

7. Maurice bought 7 dozen eggs for his mother. How many eggs did he buy?

1 dozen eggs

8. **TALK MATH** Why does the pattern shown in Example 1 work only when multiplying 11 by a single-digit number?

Multiply. Use models or patterns, if needed. See Examples 1 and 2

9. 11
× 7

10. 11
× 3

11. 11
× 9

12. 11 × 2

13. 11 × 11

14. 11 × 10

15. 12
× 1

16. 12
× 6

17. 12
× 8

18. 12 × 5

19. 12 × 9

20. 12 × 12

Algebra Find each missing factor.

21. 4 × ■ = 48

22. 11 × ■ = 44

23. ■ × 12 = 84

Solve.

24. Math books are stacked in piles of 11. There are 6 piles. Are there enough books for two classes that have 35 students in each? Explain.

25. Today is Bethany's eighth birthday. How many months old is she? What is the difference, in months, between the ages of Bethany and her friend who turned 9 today?

26. How many holes are in 10 pretzels like the one shown?

27. A teacher gave 11 extra credit points to any student who brought in five different leaves for a project. Nine students brought five leaves each. Write a number sentence to show the number of extra credit points the teacher gave.

Data File

The Flatiron Building in New York City is thought to be one of the first skyscrapers.

28. Complete this number sentence to find the number of floors in the Flatiron Building.
11 × 2 = ■ floors

29. Josh's mother works on the sixth floor of this building. There are two flights of stairs between each floor. Each flight of stairs is 11 steps. How many steps are there to the floor Josh's mother works on?

Problems

30. NUMBER SENSE Answer this riddle. The product is 108. What are my factors?

31. OPEN ENDED Explain the strategy you prefer to use when finding the product of a multiplication fact of 12 you do not know.

32. **WRITE MATH** Explain what it means to break apart a factor and when you might use this strategy.

Test Practice

33. Each side of a 5-sided stadium is bordered by 12 flags. Which number sentence will tell you the total number of flags bordering the stadium? (Lesson 4A)

 A. $5 + 12 = 17$

 B. $12 - 5 = 7$

 C. $12 \times 5 = 60$

 D. $0 \div 12 = 0$

34. How many inches long is Moira's roll of tape? Use the table to help you answer the question. (Lesson 3D)

| 1 foot = 12 inches |
| 1 yard = 3 feet |

 F. 9 inches

 G. 15 inches

 H. 36 inches

 J. 108 inches

35. The cups shown can hold a total of 32 ounces of liquid. Ben needs 56 ounces of chicken broth for his soup. How many more cups of chicken broth does Ben need?

(Lesson 3C)

 A. 1

 B. 3

 C. 8

 D. 24

36. Madison can make two pies with the apples shown. If she has 9 times as many apples, how many pies can she make? (Lesson 3B)

 F. 11

 G. 18

 H. 45

 J. 54

Multiplication and Division Facts for 11 and 12

Main Idea

I will use models, repeated subtraction, and related facts to divide by 11 and 12.

 Get ConnectED

 3.5 The student will recall multiplication facts through the twelves table, and the corresponding division facts.

3.6 The student will represent multiplication and division, using area, set, and number line models, and create and solve problems that involve multiplication of two whole numbers, one factor 99 or less and the second factor 5 or less. Also addresses 3.2.

Divide by 11 and 12

You can use models, repeated subtraction, or related facts to divide by 11 and 12.

REAL-WORLD EXAMPLE

Divide by Subtracting

① **SCIENCE For a field trip, 33 students went to the science museum. There were 11 microscopes. Each was used by an equal number of students in a group. How many students were in each group?**

Find 33 ÷ 11, or 11)‾33‾.

One Way: Use Models	**Another Way: Use Repeated Subtraction**
Place 33 counters into 11 equal groups.	Count how many times 11 is subtracted from 33 until the difference is 0.
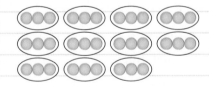	① ② ③ 33 22 11 −11 −11 −11 22 11 0
There are 3 counters in each group. So, 33 ÷ 11 = 3.	11 was subtracted from 33 3 times. So, 33 ÷ 11 = 3.

$$33 \div 11 = 3, \text{ or } 11\overset{3}{)33}.$$

So, 3 students were in each group.

Check You can use multiplication to check.
$3 \times 11 = 33$ ✔

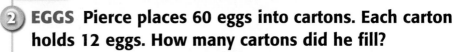

REAL-WORLD EXAMPLE   Make Equal Groups

2 **EGGS** Pierce places 60 eggs into cartons. Each carton holds 12 eggs. How many cartons did he fill?

Find $60 \div 12$, or $12\overline{)60}$. Put 60 counters in groups of 12.

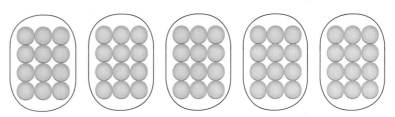

There are 5 equal groups of 12. $60 \div 12 = 5$, or $12\overline{)60}^{5}$.

So, Pierce filled 5 cartons.

Multiplication facts can be used to solve division problems.

Remember

In the previous lesson, you learned multiplication facts for 12.

EXAMPLE   Use Related Facts

3 **Find $48 \div 12$, or $12\overline{)48}$.**

$12 \times \blacksquare = 48$

The missing factor is 4.

$12 \times 4 = 48$

So, $48 \div 12 = 4$, or $12\overline{)48}^{4}$.

✓ **CHECK What You Know**

Divide. See Examples 1–3

1. $22 \div 11$

2. $77 \div 11$

3. $11\overline{)88}$

4. $36 \div 12$

5. $72 \div 12$

6. $12\overline{)48}$

7. Tonya shares 44 carnival tickets with 10 friends. Write a number sentence to show how many tickets Tonya and her friends will each get.

8.  **TALK MATH** Describe the quotients of two-digit numbers that are divided by 11.

Lesson 4B Multiplication and Division Facts for 11 and 12   **273**

Divide. See Examples 1–3

9. $11 \div 11$

10. $55 \div 11$

11. $44 \div 11$

12. $66 \div 11$

13. $11\overline{)99}$

14. $11\overline{)77}$

15. $24 \div 12$

16. $12 \div 12$

17. $36 \div 12$

18. $84 \div 12$

19. $12\overline{)96}$

20. $12\overline{)120}$

Algebra **Find each missing number.**

21. $22 \div \blacksquare = 2$

22. $48 \div \blacksquare = 4$

23. $\blacksquare \div 11 = 3$

24. $\blacksquare \div 12 = 5$

25. $\blacksquare \div 9 = 11$

26. $\blacksquare \div 11 = 12$

Solve. Write a number sentence.

27. The books below have a total of 66 chapters. Suppose each book has an equal number of chapters. How many chapters does each of the books have?

28. Darla made a gift bag for each guest at her party. Each bag had 12 gifts. There were a total of 84 gifts. Some of the bags are shown. How many bags are not shown?

29. Allen has a total of 60 sports cards. He divided them equally among his friends and himself. Each person got 12 cards. How many friends got sports cards?

30. A restaurant served 144 onion rings to 12 customers. Each customer got an equal number of onion rings. How many onion rings did each customer receive?

Problems

31. OPEN ENDED Describe a real-world situation in which you could divide by 12.

32. FIND THE ERROR Luke solved a division problem. Find and correct his mistake.

$144 \div 12 = 11$

33.  **WRITE MATH** Write about a situation in which the division problem has a quotient of 11.

Test Practice

34. Sandra planted 18 seeds. She put an equal number of seeds in 9 pots. Which number sentence shows how many seeds Sandra put in each pot? (Lesson 3C)

A. $18 \div 9 = 2$

B. $18 \times 9 = 162$

C. $18 + 9 = 27$

D. $18 - 9 = 9$

35. There were 77 flowers placed equally in 11 vases. Which number sentence shows how many flowers are in each vase? (Lesson 4B)

F. $77 \times 11 = 847$

G. $77 \div 11 = 7$

H. $77 + 11 = 88$

J. $77 - 11 = 66$

Spiral Review

Algebra **Find each missing number.** (Lesson 3C)

36. $56 \div 8 = \blacksquare$
$8 \times \blacksquare = 56$

37. $32 \div 8 = \blacksquare$
$8 \times \blacksquare = 32$

38. $81 \div 9 = \blacksquare$
$9 \times \blacksquare = 81$

39. There are 42 windows on the houses on a street. Each house has 2 windows on the front, 3 on the back, and 1 on each side. How many houses are there on the street? (Lesson 2C)

Not Just a Blanket

People have been making quilts for 2,000 years. The oldest existing quilt is between 1,000 and 1,500 years old.

Quilts are made of two layers of fabric, with padding in between. Different shapes of cloth are sewn together in detailed patterns.

Some quilts are very small, but others are very large. The largest quilt in the world weighs 800 pounds. It is 85 feet wide and 134 feet long. Quilts are much more than blankets. They are works of art!

Real-World Math

Use the information on the previous page and the picture of the quilt above to solve each problem.

1 How many feet longer is the length than the width of the largest quilt in the world?

2 How can you use repeated addition to find the number of large squares in the pictured quilt?

3 Suppose you need to make a quilt that uses twice as many large squares as the quilt shown. How many squares do you need to make your quilt?

4 How many squares do you need if you make 3 quilts with 9 squares each?

5 If you need to make 6 quilts, how many squares do you need?

6 Each quilt square is 7 inches wide and 7 inches long. How long is the quilt?

7 A quilt is 9 squares long and 7 squares wide. How many squares are there in all?

8 You have 7 quilts. Each quilt is 3 squares long and 3 squares wide. Do you have 63 squares? Explain.

Chapter Study Guide and Review

Be sure the following Key Concepts are noted in your Foldable.

More Multiplication and Division

Multiply and Divide by 4
Multiply and Divide by 6 and 7
Multiply and Divide by 8 and 9
Multiply and Divide by 11 and 12

Key Concepts

- Doubling a **known fact** can help you solve more difficult multiplication facts. (Lessons 1 and 2)

Find 4×7.

$$\begin{array}{r} 14 \\ +14 \\ \hline 28 \end{array}$$

4 2×7 2×7

- By using patterns you can multiply by 11. (Lesson 4)

Multiply by 11		
2	× 11	22
3	× 11	33
4	× 11	44

- Use models to **decompose**, or take apart, the number 12. Then find its **partial products**. (Lesson 4)

Find 3×12.

10   2

3

$3 \times 10 = 30$ $3 \times 2 = 6$

$30 + 6 = 36$ or $3 \times 12 = 36$

Key Vocabulary

decompose

double

inverse operations

known fact

partial products

quotient

Vocabulary Check

Choose the vocabulary word that completes each sentence.

1. A(n) _____?_____ is a fact you have memorized.

2. You ____?____ a factor when you multiply it by 2.

3. Multiplication and division are _____?_____ because they undo each other.

4. ____?____ means to take a number apart.

5. The ____?____ multiplication method is when you find the products of the ones, tens, and so forth, then add them together.

6. To check the ____?____ of a division problem, use multiplication.

Multi-Part Lesson Review

Lesson 1 **Multiplication and Division Facts for 4**

Multiply and Divide by 4 (Lessons 1B and 1C)

Multiply or divide.

7. 3 × 4

8. 24 ÷ 4

9. 4 × 9

10. 32 ÷ 4

11. Algebra Write a multiplication sentence to show that 4 nickels equal 20 cents.

EXAMPLE 1

How many legs are on 3 cats?

Use repeated addition and models.

Cat 1	Cat 2	Cat 3
○○○○	○○○○	○○○○

4 legs + 4 legs + 4 legs = 12

So, 3 × 4 = 12 legs.

Problem-Solving Skill: Extra or Missing Information (Lesson 1D)

Solve. If there is missing information, tell what facts you need to solve the problem.

12. The troop ordered pizza. Each pizza was cut into 8 slices. How many pizzas did they order?

13. There are 11 people in the troop. Their van has 4 rows of seats, and each row holds 3 people. How many people can the van hold?

EXAMPLE 2

A troop leader drives 5 miles each way to a troop meeting. He leaves at 4 P.M. How many miles does he drive there and back?

Decide what facts are important.

- He drives 5 miles to the meeting.
- He drives 5 miles from the meeting.

Multiply to solve. 2 × 5 = 10 miles

Lesson 2 **Multiplication and Division Facts for 6 and 7**

Multiply and Divide by 6 and 7 (Lessons 2A, 2B, and 2C)

Multiply or divide.

14. 7 × 2

15. 49 ÷ 7

16. 56 ÷ 7

17. 6 × 8

18. How many slices of pizza will Chantal need to buy when her 5 friends visit and each has 3 slices?

EXAMPLE 3

Forty-two students sat in 7 equal rows. How many students were in each row? Find 42 ÷ 7.

①	②	③	④	⑤	⑥
42	35	28	21	14	7
− 7	− 7	− 7	− 7	− 7	− 7
35	28	21	14	7	0

So, 42 ÷ 7 = 6 students.

Lessons 3 and 4

Multiplication and Division Facts for 8, 9, 11, and 12

Multiply and Divide by 8, 9, 11, and 12 (Lessons 3A, 3B, 3C, 4A, and 4B)

Multiply or divide.

19. $9\overline{)81}$

20. 8×11

21. 12×6

22. $4\overline{)48}$

23. Eight campers divide 64 large marshmallows. Each s'more uses 2 marshmallows. How many s'mores can each camper have?

24. Annie is celebrating her ninth birthday today. How old was Annie on her birthday 48 months ago? (*Hint:* There are 12 months in one year.)

EXAMPLE 4

Hugo equally passed out 54 pins to 9 people. How many pins did each get?

Use a related fact to find $54 \div 9$.

$9 \times \blacksquare = 54$ ← THINK 9 times what equals 54?

$9 \times 6 = 54$

So, $54 \div 9 = 6$ pins.

Problem-Solving Investigation: Choose a Strategy (Lesson 3D)

Use any strategy to solve.

25. Algebra Geraldo has twice as many coins as Lenny. Lenny has 12. How many do they have altogether?

26. Star gave each of her 6 friends 5 pieces of paper. There are 70 pieces of paper left. How much did she have to begin with?

27. A store is selling 5 packages of 8 pencils each. Another 6 packages has 10 pencils each. What is the total number of pencils the store has to sell?

EXAMPLE 5

Mrs. Lopez made tea. She used 3 tea bags for one pitcher. If she makes 4 pitchers, how many tea bags will she use?

Make a model to find 4×3.

$4 \times 3 = 12$ tea bags

Multiply.

1. $\begin{array}{r} 6 \\ \times\ 4 \\ \hline \end{array}$

2. $\begin{array}{r} 7 \\ \times\ 9 \\ \hline \end{array}$

3. 4×5

4. 9×4

Algebra **Find each missing factor.**

5. $3 \times \blacksquare = 24$

6. $\blacksquare \times 8 = 40$

7. $7 \times \blacksquare = 56$

8. $\blacksquare \times 9 = 54$

Write a multiplication sentence for each situation.

9. Mr. Thompson bought 6 of the same item at the store. He paid a total of $42. What did he buy?

$6 $2

$7 $75

10. An 80-member marching band stood in 10 equal rows. How many band members are in each row?

Divide. Write a related multiplication fact.

11. $5\overline{)30}$

12. $9 \div 1$

13. **MULTIPLE CHOICE** Which of the following would be used to find how many toes are on 7 people?

   A. $70 + 10$

   B. 7×10

   C. $10 + 7$

   D. $10 \div 70$

Solve. If there is missing information, tell what facts you need to solve the problem.

14. Morgan buys packages of 30 bookmarks. Each package costs $2. How many bookmarks did she buy?

15. Each playground slide has 7 steps. If the playground has 3 slides, how many steps are there altogether?

Divide.

16. $88 \div 8$

17. $12 \div 12$

18. $72 \div 9$

19. $80 \div 10$

20. There are 9 cans of tennis balls in a box. How much would 2 boxes of tennis balls cost?

$3

21. **MULTIPLE CHOICE** How many packages of fruit cups does Seth need to buy if he will give one fruit cup to each student in his class of 24?

   F. 4   H. 8

   G. 6   J. 9

22. **WRITE MATH** Explain what it means to decompose a number.

Test Practice

TEST EXAMPLE

Mrs. Kong took 8 boxes of lunches on a field trip. Each box has 6 lunches. How many lunches does she have for the students?

A. 42   **C.** 54

B. 48   **D.** 56

TEST-TAKING TIP

Read each problem carefully, underlining key words. Think about different ways to solve the problem.

Read the Question

You need to find the total number of lunches Mrs. Kong has for the students.

Solve the Question

Find 8 × 6.

You know that 6 × 8 = 48.

So, 8 × 6 = 48. Commutative Property

The answer is B.

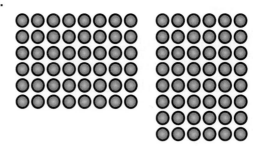

Read each question. Then fill in the correct answer on the answer sheet provided by your teacher or on a separate sheet of paper.

1. How many square holes are in Bev's breakfast waffles?

    A. 40   **C.** 63

    B. 56   **D.** 64

2. How many pattern blocks are in 7 sets?

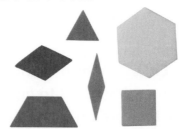

    F. 35   **H.** 42

    G. 36   **J.** 48

3. Tavis bought 4 packages of juice boxes. Each package has 4 juice boxes. Which number sentence shows how to find the total number of juice boxes?

A. $4 + 4 =$ ▪ **C.** $4 \times 4 =$ ▪

B. $4 - 4 =$ ▪ **D.** $16 - 4 =$ ▪

---

4. The figure below is a model for $5 \times 9 = 45$.

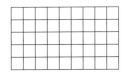

What division sentence is modeled by the same figure?

F. $36 \div 9 = 4$ **H.** $45 \div 5 = 9$

G. $36 \div 4 = 9$ **J.** $50 \div 5 = 10$

---

5. Adrian has 24 apples to equally divide among 4 baskets. How many apples will be in each basket?

A. 6 **C.** 4

B. 5 **D.** 3

---

6. Which sign will make the number sentence true?

$$9 \; \blacksquare \; 9 = 1$$

F. $+$ **H.** $\times$

G. $-$ **J.** $\div$

---

7. The box of paints is a model for which number sentence below?

A. $3 \times 5 = 15$ **C.** $18 \div 6 = 3$

B. $3 + 7 = 10$ **D.** $21 \div 7 = 3$

---

8. If $12 \times 9 = 108$, then what is ▪ $\div 9 = 12$?

F. 10 **H.** 108

G. 25 **J.** 180

---

9. Chandler works 4 hours each week. How many weeks will it take for him to work 36 hours?

A. 4 **C.** 7

B. 6 **D.** 9

---

10. How much will these 4 paperback books cost together?

F. $21 **H.** $27

G. $25 **J.** $28

NEED EXTRA HELP?										
If You Missed Question . . .	1	2	3	4	5	6	7	8	9	10
Go to Chapter-Lesson . . .	5-3A	5-2B	5-1B	5-3C	5-1C	4-3C	5-2C	5-4B	5-1C	5-2B
For help with . . .	SOL 3.6	SOL 3.5	SOL 3.6	SOL 3.5	SOL 3.2	SOL 3.20b	SOL 3.2	SOL 3.5	SOL 3.5	SOL 3.5

Collect and Analyze Data

connectED.mcgraw-hill.com

Investigate

- Animations
- Vocabulary
- Math Songs
- Multilingual eGlossary

Learn

- Personal Tutor
- Virtual Manipulatives
- Audio
- Foldables

Practice

- Self-Check Practice
- eGames
- Worksheets
- Assessment

The ☆BIG Idea

How can I collect data several ways and then organize and analyze it in a variety of graphs?

FOLDABLES
Study Organizer

Make this Foldable to help you organize information about data and graphs. Start with three sheets of $8\frac{1}{2}$" × 11" paper.

Collect and Analyze Data
Collect Data
Graphs with Pictures
Bar Graphs
Line Plots
Probability

Review Vocabulary

tally chart marcas(s) de conteo a way to keep track of data using tally marks to record the results

What Is Your Favorite Color?	
Color	**Tally**
Blue	☰☰☰ |||
Green	||||

Key Vocabulary

English	Español
frequency table	tabla de funciones
data	datos
probability	probabilidad
bar graph	gráfica de barras
line plot	esquema lineal

When Will I Use This?

Are You Ready for the Chapter?

You have two options for checking Prerequisite Skills for this chapter.

Text Option Take the Quick Check below.

QUICK Check

Write the number represented by the tally marks.

1. ||| **2.** ⲧⲏⲧ   **3.** ⲧⲏⲧ | **4.** ⲧⲏⲧ ⲧⲏⲧ

Identify a pattern. Then find the missing numbers.

5. 2, 4, 6, 8, ▪, ▪

6. 5, 10, 15, 20, ▪, ▪

7. 10, 20, 30, 40, ▪, ▪

8. 100, 200, 300, ▪, ▪

Find each sum.

9.	**10.**	**11.**
3	8	5
2	7	6
5	4	9
+ 6	+ 1	+ 2

How is each group of objects alike? Classify each set of objects.

12.

13.

 Online Option Take the Online Readiness Quiz.

Explore **Collect Data**

Main Idea
I will explore collecting data through observation, surveys, and experiments.

Materials
paper and pencil

connecting cubes:
8 red, 6 purple,
3 yellow, and 6 green

Get ConnectED

3.17 The student will **a)** collect and organize data, using observations, measurements, surveys, or experiments.

Data is collected information or facts. One way to collect data is by **observing** or watching.

ACTIVITY

1 **Collect Data Through Observation**

Step 1 **Choose an activity to observe.**

For example, you may choose to observe what your classmates do for lunch.

Step 2 **Make a list of choices.**

Buy	Pack	Go Home

Sample

Step 3 **Observe and record the data in a table.**

Record if your classmates buy, pack, or go home for lunch.

Buy	Pack	Go Home
Arnaldo	Howi	Toni
Julia	R...	William

Sample

You can also collect data by taking a **survey,** or asking a lot of people a question.

ACTIVITY

2 **Collect Data Through a Survey**

Step 1 **Choose a survey question.**

You may ask, "What kind of pet do you have?"

Step 2 **List possible choices.**

dog   cat   hamster   other

Step 3 **Record the data in a table.** Sample

Bill cat	Tom cat	Sue other	

Data is also collected when doing an **experiment,** or performing a test.

ACTIVITY

3 **Collect Data Through an Experiment**

Step 1 **Choose an experiment.**

Are there more red, purple, green, or yellow connecting cubes in the bag?

Step 2 **Conduct the experiment.**

Without looking, choose one cube at a time. Look at it and then return it to the bag. Do this 24 times.

Step 3 **Record the results in a table.**

Each time you choose a cube, record its color.

Sample

red	red	purple	yellow

Practice and Apply It

1. Collect data three different ways: observe an activity, take a survey, and conduct an experiment. Follow the steps from the Explore Lesson.

Main Idea

I will construct frequency tables to organize data.

 **Vocabulary**

frequency table
tally chart
data
survey
tally mark(s)

[Get Connect**ED**]

3.17 The student will **a)** collect and organize data, using observations, measurements, surveys, or experiments.

Construct Frequency Tables

A **frequency table** uses numbers to tell how many times something happens. You can make a **tally chart**, a type of frequency table, to record and organize a set of **data** using tally marks.

REAL-WORLD EXAMPLE   Organize Data

1 **SCOUTS** Mr. Alvarez took a **survey**. He asked each of his scouts, "What is your favorite camping activity?" The results are shown. Organize the data in a tally chart and a frequency table.

Swimming	Hiking	Fishing
Hunter	Amado	Julian
Eric	Avery	Chen
Ian	Omar	Lamarko
Jamal	Nicolas	
Alano		

Step 1   Draw a table with two columns. Include a title.

Step 2   List each activity in the first column.

Step 3   Use tally marks or numbers to record the results.

One Way: Tally Chart

Favorite Camping Activity	
Activity	**Tally**
Swimming	卌
Hiking	||||
Fishing	|||

Each **tally mark** represents one scout.

Another Way: Frequency Table

Favorite Camping Activity	
Activity	**Frequency**
Swimming	5
Hiking	4
Fishing	3

Numbers are used to record the results.

You can take a survey and collect and organize data on a tally chart and a frequency table.

Explore Mini Activity

Step 1 Write a survey question you can ask your classmates. An example is shown below.

What type of lunch is your favorite?

A. pizza   **C.** grilled cheese

B. hamburger   **D.** peanut butter and jelly

Step 2 Create a tally chart to record your results.

Step 3 Ask the question to each of your classmates. Organize the data as you collect it.

Step 4 Use the information on your tally chart to create a frequency table.

Analyze the data.

1. Write two sentences that describe your survey results.

2. Were the survey results what you expected? Explain.

> **Remember**
> The tally marks used to represent a value of 5 are ⅢⅠ, not ⅠⅠⅠⅠⅠ.

✓ CHECK What You Know

1. The data shows the sports cards more frequently traded in Mrs. Patton's class. Organize the data in a tally chart. See Example 1

Traded Sport Cards	
Sport	**Frequency**
Basketball	3
Baseball	6
Football	9
Hockey	5

2. Ishi lists all of the fish in her fish tank. Organize the data below in a frequency table. See Example 1

Ishi's Fish Tank	
jewelfish	tetra
jewelfish	tetra
jewelfish	tetra
catfish	loach
catfish	loach

3. Refer to Exercise 1. What is the most popular sport card to trade? What is the least popular? See Example 1

4. TALK MATH List three questions that you could ask in a survey.

EXTRA PRACTICE
Begins on page EP2.

Organize each set of data in a tally chart. See Example 1

5. Donna records the pizza toppings her friends like most.

Pizza Toppings		
cheese	cheese	veggie
cheese	pepperoni	veggie
cheese	pepperoni	
cheese	pepperoni	

6. Elisa took a survey to find out what breed of dog her classmates have.

Dog Breeds	
beagle	golden retriever
beagle	golden retriever
beagle	golden retriever
poodle	golden retriever

Organize each set of data in a frequency table. See Example 1

7. Measurement While observing temperatures for one week, Arnaldo recorded the following data.

Weekly Temperatures	
Temperature (°F)	Days
70–75	||
76–80	|||
81–85	|
86–90	|

8. Darla observed her friends. She collected data on the flavor of milk they drank at lunch.

Flavors of Milk		
chocolate	white	strawberry
chocolate	white	strawberry
chocolate	strawberry	chocolate
chocolate	strawberry	white
white	strawberry	strawberry

Use the tally chart that shows items sold at a school store.

9. Which item was the top seller? How many were sold?

10. Which item sold once?

11. How many items were sold altogether?

12. Organize the data in a frequency table.

Items Sold at School Store	
Item	Tally
Eraser	卌
Bottle of glue	
Pencil	卌 |||
Scissors	|

H.O.T. Problems

13. OPEN ENDED Experiment with tossing a quarter, nickel, dime, and penny 25 times. Use a tally chart to record the number of times each coin lands heads up.

14. ✏ **WRITE MATH** Suppose you are collecting and organizing data about attendance at the state fair. Would it be better to use a frequency table or a tally chart? Explain.

Problem-Solving Strategy: Make a List

 Ginger observed Kia, Kirk, and Shonda lining up to come in from recess. They are deciding the order they should line up. How many different ways can they line up?

Understand **What facts do you know?**

- There are three students.

What do you need to find?

- Find how many different ways they can line up.

Plan   Organize the different combinations in a list or table. Then use the data from the list to solve the problem.

Solve

- Observe the students and collect your data. Start with Kia. Create different combinations with her first. Then record the results.

- Repeat this method of making a list with each of the other students being first.

Possible Ways to Line Up		
First	**Second**	**Third**
1. Kia	Kirk	Shonda
2. Kia	Shonda	Kirk
3. Kirk	Shonda	Kia
4. Kirk	Kia	Shonda
5. Shonda	Kirk	Kia
6. Shonda	Kia	Kirk

- Count all the different combinations.

There are 6 possible ways for the students to line up.

Check   None of the ways repeat. So, the answer makes sense. ✓

 3.17 The student will **b)** construct a line plot, a picture graph, or a bar graph to represent the data.

Refer to the problem on the previous page.

1. Explain why the *make a list* strategy was helpful in solving this problem.

2. Explain how to organize all of the combinations in a table.

3. If there were four students, what is the number of possible line-up combinations?

4. How do you know your answer to Exercise 3 is correct?

PRACTICE

EXTRA PRACTICE
Begins on page EP2.

Solve. Use the *make a list* strategy.

5. Aleta has black pants and tan pants. She also has a striped shirt, a plaid shirt, and a flowered shirt. How many different outfits can Aleta make using one pair of pants and one shirt?

6. Gabriel asks for one scoop each of vanilla, chocolate, and strawberry ice cream. How many different ways can he order the scoops of ice cream on the cone?

7. Reid and Fata are making gift packages of toys. What are all of the different packages they can make if they put two toys together?

8. Adele will make a fan out of three different colors of paper. How many color combinations can Adele make if she uses blue, red, and green in a different order each time?

9. Five girls signed up for a table tennis tournament. Each girl has to play each of the other girls one time. How many games will the girls play in all? Show your work.

Table Tennis
Tournament

Amalia   Della
Bianca   Lori
Lizzy

10. Mr. Castillo asked his students to make as many different 3-digit number combinations as they could using the numbers 5, 7, and 8 without repeating numbers. How many numbers can be made?

11. **WRITE MATH** Give an example of a problem for which you would use the *make a list* strategy to solve.

Explore Picture Graphs and Pictographs

Main Idea

I will explore collecting, organizing, recording, and displaying data in picture graphs and pictographs.

Materials

11″ × 17″ paper

sticky notes

Get ConnectED

3.17 The student will **a)** collect and organize data, using observations, measurements, surveys, or experiments; **b)** construct a line plot, a picture graph, or a bar graph to represent the data.

Data recorded in a tally chart can be displayed in graphs with pictures. A **picture graph** uses different pictures to represent each tally. A **pictograph** uses the same symbol to represent more than one tally.

ACTIVITY

① **Construct Graphs with Pictures**

Step 1 **Collect data.**

Make a tally chart like the one shown. Ask 15 people to draw their favorite fruit on a sticky note. Mark each response with a tally.

Favorite Fruits		
Fruit	**Tally**	**Number**
Banana		
Orange		
Strawberry		
Apple		

Step 2 **Organize and record data.**

Count the tally marks in each row and write the number in the last column.

Favorite Fruits		
Fruit	**Tally**	**Number**
Banana	⅏		6
Orange	||||	4
Strawberry	||	2
Apple	|||	3

Step 3 **Display the results.**

• Fold 2 pieces of paper into sixths lengthwise. Give each graph a title and label each section as shown.

• Construct two different graphs with pictures.

One Way: Make a Picture Graph

Have each friend place their sticky note on the graph, lining them up under each other.

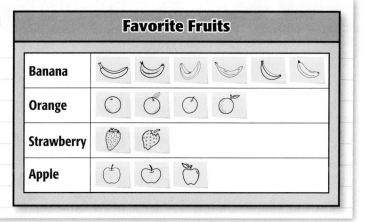

Another Way: Make a Pictograph

- Make a key. Have each basket represents 2 friends.
- Draw one basket for every two students.
- Put the baskets on the graph to show how many friends liked each fruit.

Think About It

1. What does half of a fruit basket represent in the pictograph? Explain whether or not you would ever need to use $\frac{1}{2}$ of a picture in a picture graph.

2. What do you notice about the number of pictures in the picture graph in comparison to the number of symbols in the pictograph?

Practice and Apply It

3. Use a tally chart to organize, record, and collect data from 10 students about their favorite music. Then use the data to make a picture graph and a pictograph.

4. **WRITE MATH** How are a picture graph and a pictograph similar? How are they different?

Main Idea

I will collect, organize, and analyze data in picture graphs and pictographs.

 Vocabulary

picture graph

pictograph

observe

key

analyze

interpret

experiment

Get ConnectED

3.17 The student will **a)** collect and organize data, using observations, measurements, surveys, or experiments; **b)** construct a line plot, a picture graph, or a bar graph to represent the data. Also addresses 3.17c.

Construct and Analyze Picture Graphs and Pictographs

A **picture graph** represents each tally of data with a picture. A **pictograph** uses a symbol to represent more than one tally of data.

REAL-WORLD EXAMPLE   Graphs with Pictures

1 **PRIZES** While at the fair, Brandy and Penny **observed** the prizes at a game booth. They made a tally mark for each stuffed animal they saw. They each displayed the data they collected in a graph.

Stuffed Animal Prizes

Stuffed Animal	Tally	Number
Teddy bear	卌 I	6
Cat	IIII	4
Dog	卌 II	7
Turtle	II	2

Brandy's Picture Graph

Stuffed Animal Prizes

Teddy bear	
Cat	
Dog	
Turtle	

Penny's Pictograph

Stuffed Animal Prizes

Teddy bear	☺ ☺ ☺
Cat	☺ ☺
Dog	☺ ☺ ☺ (
Turtle	☺
key: ☺ = 2 stuffed animals	

Step 1   The girls each made a table with a title and labels.

Step 2   Brandy used different pictures to represent the data in her graph. Each picture stands for 1. She does not need a key.

Step 3   Penny used a symbol to represent the data. Each symbol stands for 2. She made a **key** to show this.

The graphs display the same set of data two different ways.

When you read a graph, you study, or **analyze**, the data. Then you are able to **interpret** the data, or explain what you learned.

Read a Pictograph

2 **MOVIES** The pictograph shows the results of a survey Antoine conducted. Who saw two more movies than Grace during summer vacation?

Remember

A pictograph must have a key.

The key shows that each 🎟️ symbol represents 2 movies.

Grace saw 🎟️ + 🎟️ + 🎟️ or 2 + 2 + 2 = 6 movies

Carla saw 🎟️ + 🎟️ + 🎟️ + 🎟️ or

2 + 2 + 2 + 2 = 8 movies

So, Carla saw two more movies than Grace.

Analyze and Interpret a Pictograph

3 **RECYCLING** The pictograph shows the results of an experiment Darren's school conducted.

After analyzing the data, what did Darren's school learn?

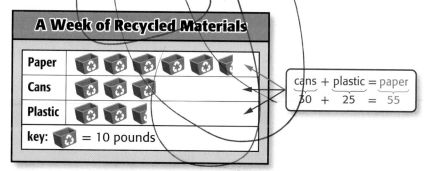

$$\underbrace{cans}_{30} + \underbrace{plastic}_{25} = \underbrace{paper}_{55}$$

Darren's school learned they recycled the same amount of paper as cans and plastic combined.

1. Display the set of data in a picture graph. Then write a sentence that interprets the data. See Examples 1 and 3

Two Weeks of Weather		
Type of Weather	Tally	Number of Days
Sunny	$\cancel{||||}\,|$	6
Cloudy	$|||$	3
Snow	$\cancel{||||}$	5

Read the pictograph that shows how many gallons of milk were sold. See Example 2

2. Which store sold the most milk?

3. Which store sold six gallons more than the small grocery store?

4. Suppose each gallon costs $2. How much money was spent on milk at the large grocery store?

5. A pictograph shows 2 ♪ symbols. Each symbol represents 3 people who enjoy rock music. How many people enjoy rock music?

6.  **TALK MATH** Explain why a pictograph must have a key.

EXTRA PRACTICE
Begins on page EP2.

7. Display the set of data in a picture graph. Then write a sentence that interprets the data.

See Examples 1 and 3

Sport Balls Sold on Saturday	
Type of Ball	Number Sold
Football	6
Baseball	4
Basketball	7

8. Display the set of data in a pictograph. Then write a sentence that interprets the data.

See Examples 1 and 3

Fish Caught on Sunday	
Type of Fish	Number of Fish
Trout	10
Bass	8
Catfish	17

Read the pictographs. See Example 2

Third-Grade Shoe Sizes	
size 2	🥿
size 4	🥿 🥿 🥿
size 6	🥿 🥿 🥿 🥿 🥿
size 8	🥿
key: 🥿 = 4 students	

Chores per Week	
Latisha	❚ ❚
Kelley	❚ ❚ ❚ ❚
Cruz	❚
Juan	❚ ❚ ❚
David	❚ ❚ ❚
key: ❚ = 2 chores	

9. What is the most common shoe size?

10. What is the second-most common shoe size?

11. How many students were asked for their shoe size? Explain.

12. Name two students who have a total of 10 chores altogether.

13. If each child earned $1 for each chore, how much money would Latisha earn? Explain.

14. A barn had 4 of each animal shown below and 5 pigs. Display the set of data in a picture graph. Then write a sentence that interprets the data.

See Examples 1 and 3.

15. Ask 10 people what state they would most like to visit. Display the data in a pictograph. Then write a sentence that interprets the data. See Examples 1 and 3

California   Colorado   New York

16. Collect data to find the number of students that have a blue, green, red or other color toothbrush. Make a picture graph to display the results.

17. A key shows that each symbol means 5 balls. How many symbols would there be to represent 10 balls? Explain.

H.O.T. Problems

18. OPEN ENDED Describe a real-world example of data that can be shown easily in a pictograph, but not in a picture graph. Explain.

19. 📝 **WRITE MATH** Is it possible to interpret a pictograph without a key? Explain.

Mid-Chapter Check

1. Organize the set of data in a frequency table. (Lesson 1B)

Students' Weekend Activities			
swim	shop	TV	jog
shop	TV	swim	TV
TV	shop	shop	jog

2. Display the set of data in a pictograph. Then write a sentence that interprets the data. (Lesson 2B)

Favorite Exercise		
Type of Exercise	Tally	Number of Students
Sit-ups	卌 卌	10
Push-ups	卌 II	7
Jumping jacks	卌 III	8

3. A pictograph shows 6 ✈ symbols. Each symbol represents 4 times someone has flown in the last year. How many times did all of the people fly in the last year? (Lesson 2B)

4. **MULTIPLE CHOICE** How many more students like pepperoni pizza than like cheese pizza? (Lesson 2B)

Favorite Pizza	
Cheese	🍪 🍪
Pepperoni	🍪 🍪 🍪
Vegetable	🍪 🍪 🍪
key: 🍪 = 2 students	

A. 1   **C.** 3

B. 2   **D.** 4

5. **MULTIPLE CHOICE** The pictograph shows favorite types of movies. How many more people like cartoons than like drama? (Lesson 2B)

Favorite Type of Movie	
Comedy	▢ ▢ ▢
Drama	▢
Cartoon	▢ ▢ ▢ ▢ ▢
key: ▢ = 3 people	

F. 4   **H.** 12

G. 8   **J.** 16

6. Draw a tally chart that may have been used to create this picture graph. (Lesson 1B)

Favorite Season	
Spring	🌸 🌸
Summer	☀ ☀ ☀ ☀
Fall	🍎 🍎 🍎
Winter	❄

7. Display the set of data in a picture graph. Then write a sentence that interprets the data. (Lesson 2B)

Favorite Place to Read a Book		
Place	Tally	Number of Students
Bed	卌 IIII	9
Outside	III	3
School	卌 III	8
Library	IIII	4

8. **WRITE MATH** How do you decide how many each symbol should stand for in a pictograph?

(Lesson 2B)

Game Time

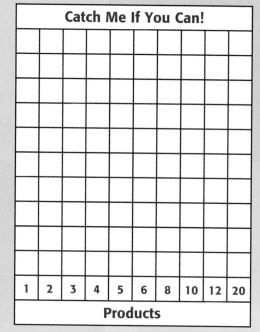

Catch Me If You Can!
Make a Graph

You will need: 2 spinners, grid paper, crayon

Get Ready!

Players: 2 players

Get Set!

☆ Divide one spinner into 3 equal parts. Label the parts 1, 2, and 4.

☆ Divide the other spinner into 4 equal parts. Label the parts 1, 2, 3, and 5.

☆ Make the game board shown.

Go!

☆ Player 1 spins each spinner and finds the product of the two numbers.

☆ Player 1 then colors in one square on the graph paper above the product.

☆ Player 2 takes a turn.

☆ The game continues, taking turns, until one bar reaches the top of the graph.

Catch Me If You Can!

1	2	3	4	5	6	8	10	12	20

Products

Explore Bar Graphs

Main Idea

I will explore collecting, organizing, recording, and displaying data in bar graphs.

Materials

grid paper

3 colored pencils

20 two-color counters

Get ConnectED

3.17 The student will **a)** collect and organize data, using observations, measurements, surveys, or experiments; **b)** construct a line plot, a picture graph, or a bar graph to represent the data.

Data in a tally chart can also be displayed in a bar graph. A **bar graph** uses bars of different lengths or heights to show data.

🏃 **ACTIVITY** Construct a Bar Graph

Milo surveyed five grades to find the number of May birthdays. He recorded the data in a tally chart.

May Birthdays	
Grade	**Tally**
First	ЖЖ
Second	ЖЖ ЖЖ I
Third	III
Fourth	IIII
Fifth	II

Step 1 **Draw and label.**
- Draw a rectangle. Separate it into equal rows.
- Label the side and bottom of the graph to describe the information.
- Give the graph a title.

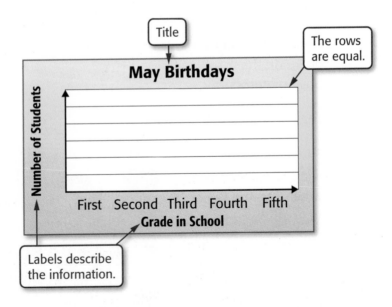

Title

The rows are equal.

Labels describe the information.

Step 2 **Choose a scale.**

Write a scale along the vertical arrow, or **axis**. A **scale** is a set of numbers that represents the data.

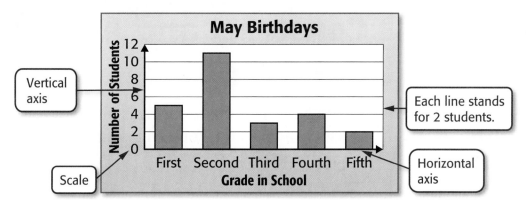

Vertical axis

Scale

May Birthdays

Number of Students

Grade in School

First Second Third Fourth Fifth

Each line stands for 2 students.

Horizontal axis

Step 3 **Draw the bars.**

Draw vertical bars to match each number from your data, leaving space between each bar.

Think About It

1. How would you decide what scale to use?

2. Why do you think the scale counts by 2?

3. Why do some bars stop between two numbers or two lines?

Practice and Apply It

Display each set of data in a bar graph.

4.

Favorite Meal	
Meal	**Tally**
Breakfast	IIII
Lunch	ⵉⵉⵉ ⵉⵉⵉ II
Dinner	ⵉⵉⵉ ⵉⵉⵉ ⵉⵉⵉ

5.

Beverage Chosen Most Often at Lunch	
Beverage	**Tally**
Apple Juice	ⵉⵉⵉ ⵉⵉⵉ ⵉⵉⵉ I
Milk	ⵉⵉⵉ ⵉⵉⵉ
Water	ⵉⵉⵉ III

6. Place 20 two-color counters in front of you, red side up. A partner keeps time. Experiment to see how many counters you can turn from red to yellow in 5, 10, and 15 seconds. Record the data in a tally chart, then display the results in a bar graph.

7. **WRITE MATH** Refer to Step 2. How will the bar graph change when the scale changes?

Main Idea
I will collect, organize, display, and analyze data in bar graphs.

 Vocabulary
bar graph
axis
scale

  **Get Connect_ED**

 3.17 The student will **a)** collect and organize data, using observations, measurements, surveys, or experiments; **b)** construct a line plot, a picture graph, or a bar graph to represent the data. Also addresses 3.17c.

Construct and Analyze Bar Graphs

You have learned that a survey is a way of collecting data by asking a question. You can display the collected data in a **bar graph**.

REAL-WORLD EXAMPLE Construct a Bar Graph

① **SPORTS Desmond surveyed his friends. He asked them to name their favorite summer sport. He recorded the data that he collected in a frequency table. Make a vertical bar graph to display the results of Desmond's survey.**

Favorite Summer Sports		
Sport	**Tally**	**Number**
Tennis	IIII	4
Swimming	HHT HHT	10
Baseball	HHT II	7
Biking	HHT I	6

In a *vertical* bar graph, the bars go up and down. It includes a title, labels, a scale, and bars. The scale in a vertical bar graph is along the vertical **axis**. There is a space between each bar.

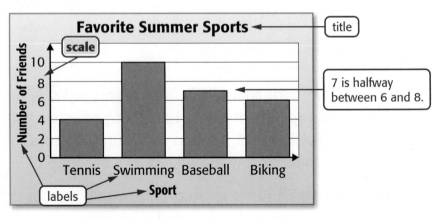

Remember

On a bar graph, there is a space between each bar.

② ANIMALS The bar graph shows how long some animals sleep. Which two animals sleep the most?

In a *horizontal* bar graph, the bars go from left to right. The scale is along the horizontal axis.

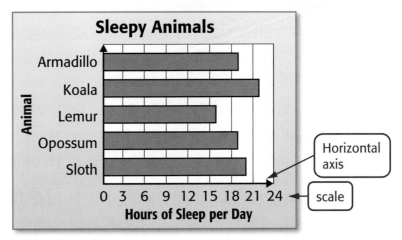

The lengths of the bars for the sloth and the koala are the longest. So, the sloth and the koala sleep the most.

③ HOBBIES The bar graph shows the results of a survey. How many more teachers like to read on the weekend than like to hike?

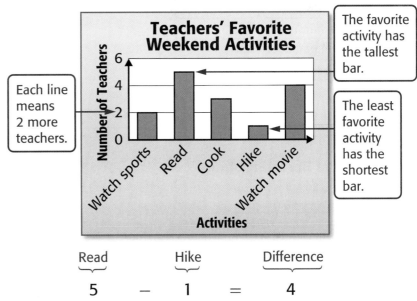

Read		Hike		Difference
5	−	1	=	4

So, 4 more teachers prefer to read on the weekend than hike.

1. Display the set of data below in a vertical bar graph. See Example 1

Favorite Birds to Watch	
Bird	**Tally**
Cardinal	⊬⊬ |||
Robin	||||
Goldfinch	⊬⊬ ||||

2. Display the set of data below in a horizontal bar graph. See Example 2

Animal Life Spans	
Animal	**Time (years)**
Lion	10
Hamster	2
Kangaroo	5
Rabbit	7

For Exercises 3–5, refer to Example 2. See Examples 2 and 3

3. Which animal sleeps the most?

4. Name one animal that sleeps three hours longer than the lemur.

5. Write one sentence that interprets the data.

6.  **TALK MATH** How are vertical and horizontal bar graphs alike? How are they different?

7. Display the set of data below in a vertical bar graph. See Example 1

Width of Birds' Nests	
Bird	**Width (ft)**
Bald eagle	8
Blue heron	5
Monk parakeet	3
Stork	6

8. Display the set of data below in a horizontal bar graph. See Example 2

World Series Wins	
Team	**Wins**
Cardinals	⊬⊬ ||||
Giants	⊬⊬
Yankees	⊬⊬ ⊬⊬ ⊬⊬ ⊬⊬ ⊬⊬	
Dodgers	⊬⊬	

For Exercises 9–12, refer to the graph. See Examples 2 and 3

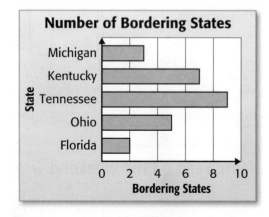

9. How many states border Tennessee?

10. How many more states border Ohio than Michigan?

11. Which states have 5 or fewer states bordering them?

12. Write one sentence that interprets the data.

Use the information to solve the problem.

Birthday Dilemma

Remember, Jamie is trying to figure out what activity to do during his birthday party.

This needs to be organized. It is making my brain hurt!

Alyssa-baseball
Jacob-swim
Kendra-picnic
Eva-swim
Luke-baseball
Kim-swim

13. Organize Jamie's data in a tally chart. Then display the data in a bar graph. Which activity was the most popular among Jamie's friends?

H.O.T. Problems

14. **OPEN ENDED** Observe the color of your classmates' hair. Collect and display the data in a horizontal bar graph. Write two sentences that interpret the data.

15. **WRITE MATH** How will the bars on a bar graph change if the numbers on the scale are made greater? Explain.

Test Practice

16. Which data is needed to complete the graph? (Lesson 3B)

Bead Colors in a Bracelet

Beads

Blue   Red   Orange   Green
Color

  A. The colors in a bracelet.

  B. The scale of the graph.

  C. The color with the least beads.

  D. The title of the graph.

17. The pictograph shows the favorite hiking trails of 24 third graders. How many shoes need to be added to finish the graph? (Lesson 2B)

Favorite Hiking Trails	
Blue Trail	👟
Red Trail	👟
Yellow Trail	👟 👟 👟
key: 👟 = 3 students	

  F. 3   **H.** 15

  G. 9   **J.** 19

EGGS!

Most eggs are white and about $1\frac{1}{2}$ inches long.

Did you know that eggs come in all sorts of colors, sizes, and shapes? Most birds that lay white eggs, like kingfishers and woodpeckers, lay their eggs in dark holes.

Birds that lay their eggs in open areas without a nest lay eggs that are colored like the soil. This keeps predators from finding them.

Did You Know?

Some birds lay their eggs in the nests of other birds so that the other birds will hatch them.

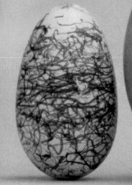

Real-World Math

Use the bar graph to solve each problem.

1 How much longer is an emperor penguin egg than a robin egg?

2 A hummingbird laid 4 eggs. What is the total length of the eggs?

3 What is the second longest egg?

4 How many eggs are being compared?

5 Which egg is half the length of an elephant bird egg?

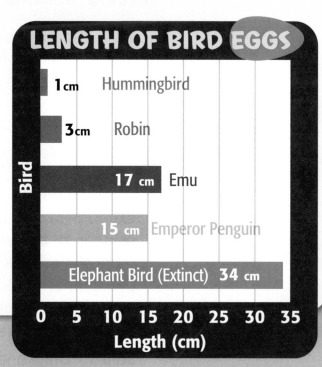

LENGTH OF BIRD EGGS

Bird

1 cm Hummingbird
3 cm Robin
17 cm Emu
15 cm Emperor Penguin
Elephant Bird (Extinct) **34** cm

0   5   10   15   20   25   30   35
Length (cm)

Main Idea
I will collect, organize, and analyze data in line plots.

 Vocabulary
line plot

 Get ConnectED

3.17 The student will **a)** collect and organize data, using observations, measurements, surveys, or experiments; **b)** construct a line plot, a picture graph, or a bar graph to represent the data. Also addresses 3.17c.

Construct and Analyze Line Plots

You can also organize data in a line plot. A **line plot** uses Xs above a number line to show how often something happens.

REAL-WORLD EXAMPLE   Construct a Line Plot

1 **SPINNER** Albert did an experiment. He spun a spinner 16 times. The table shows how often the spinner landed on each number. Construct a line plot for the results.

Numbers Spun			
0	1	2	1
1	2	0	1
2	1	4	1
0	1	1	3

Step 1 Draw and label a number line. Include all values of the data. Give it a title that describes the data.

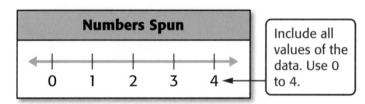

Include all values of the data. Use 0 to 4.

Step 2 Draw an X above the number for each result.

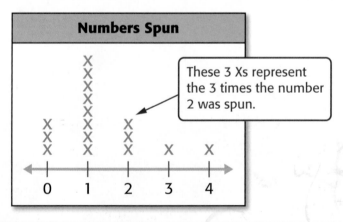

These 3 Xs represent the 3 times the number 2 was spun.

Remember

Start with the smallest number and end with the largest number of data when numbering a line plot.

② **EXPERIMENT** Use Albert's line plot to find the difference between the number spun most often and least often.

The number 1 was spun most often since the greatest number of Xs are above it. The numbers 3 and 4 were spun the least number of times. So, the difference is 8 − 1 = 7.

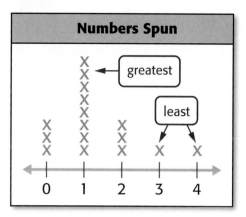

CHECK What You Know

Display each set of data in a line plot. See Example 1

1.

Frequency of Digits on a Math Page				
digit 0 4	digit 1 7	digit 2 3	digit 3 8	digit 4 0
digit 5 5	digit 6 4	digit 7 2	digit 8 1	digit 9 1

2.

Hours Spent on Homework Each Week	
Time (hours)	Tally
8				
9	ﬞ卌	
10	卌
11	卌 |||

For Exercises 3 and 4, refer to the line plot below.

See Example 2

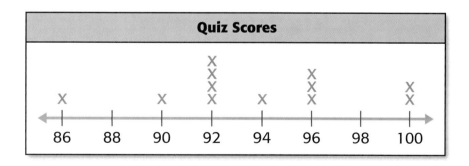

3. How many students' quiz scores are recorded? Explain.

4. What is one conclusion you can draw from this line plot? Explain.

5. **TALK MATH** Does a tally chart or a line plot make it easier to see how often numbers happen in a set of data? Explain.

Display each set of data in a line plot. See Example 1

6.

Chores per Week				
Tess 1	Cirilo 4	Nikita 3	Patrick 2	Raquel 3
Hao 2	Santos 5	Gia 2	Juwan 4	Pia 3
Demitri 2	Tammy 6	Sue 3	Shanti 1	Trey 2
Ayana 3	Jim 5	Maxine 4	Ellis 3	Burt 3

7.

Rollercoaster Rides				
Yuma 1	Barry 3	Rogelio 2	David 3	Toni 0
Camila 1	Jen 6	Jodie 0	Jean 3	Vince 3
Charles 0	Thea 3	Tito 1	Eric 1	Stuart 2
Irene 0	Sophie 3	Carl 2	Art 0	Skylar 1

8.

Hours of TV Watched	
Hours of TV	**Students**
0	|
1	||||
2	
3	||
4	|
5	||

9.

Number of Siblings	
Siblings	**Students**
0	卌 ||
1	卌
2	卌 ||||
3	|||
4	||
5 or more	||

For Exercises 10–13, refer to the line plot below. See Example 2

10. What do the Xs stand for on this line plot?

11. How many apples were in the most number of bags?

12. Were there more bags with 11 apples or 12 apples?

13. What conclusion could you draw?

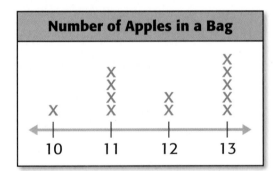

14. As a class, take a timed one-minute multiplication fact test, like the ones found in the multiplication chapters. Find the number of facts completed correctly. Record all student scores on a line plot. Write one sentence that interprets the data.

15. **OPEN ENDED** Give an example of a set of data that is not best displayed in a line plot. Explain.

16. **WRITE MATH** Explain how a tally chart and a line plot are alike and different.

Test Practice

17. Which sentence about the data below is true? (Lesson 4A)

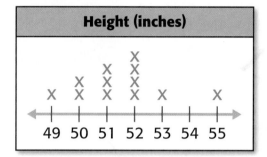

Height (inches)

49 50 51 52 53 54 55

A. All students are 55 inches.

B. Half of the students are 52 inches or greater.

C. Most students are 51 inches.

D. No one is 49 inches tall.

18. Use the graph. What is the difference between the least favorite and most favorite means of travel? (Lesson 3B)

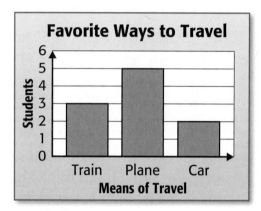

Favorite Ways to Travel

Train   Plane   Car
Means of Travel

F. 2   H. 5

G. 3   J. 7

Spiral Review

Display each set of data in a vertical bar graph. (Lesson 3B)

19.

Orchestra Instruments	
Instrument	**Tally**
Brass	|||
Woodwind	ЖΉ
Strings	ЖΉ
Percussion	ЖΉ ||

20.

Favorite After-School Snack	
Snack	**Tally**
Apple	|||
Granola Bar	||
Smoothie	ЖΉ |||
Yogurt	ЖΉ

21. Analyze the bar graphs you made for Exercises 19 and 20. Write a sentence for each that interprets the data. (Lesson 3B)

Problem-Solving Investigation

Main Idea I will choose the best strategy to solve a problem.

P.S.I. TEAM +

SHANE: I will do an experiment. I will roll a 0–5 number cube and a 5–10 number cube 20 times. The greatest possible sum is 15. I think half of my rolls will have the sum of 15. Is this a reasonable estimate?

YOUR MISSION: Find if half of the rolls could have the sum of 15. Then decide if that was a reasonable estimate.

Understand

When two number cubes are rolled, 15 is the highest possible sum. Shane thinks half of his rolls will have the sum of 15.

Plan

Make a line plot to display the number of times each sum is rolled. Then find half of 20 rolls.

Solve

Make a line plot. The scale should include all the possible sums.

Conduct the experiment. Display the results.

Sums Rolled

				X			X		
				X	X		X	X	
		X	X	X	X	X	X	X	X
		X	X	X	X	X	X	X	X

5 6 7 8 9 10 11 12 13 14 15

Next, find half of 20 rolls. 20 ÷ 2 = 10 rolls

The greatest possible sum 15 was rolled only twice. Half of the rolls did not have the sum of 15.

Check

The sum 15 was rolled only twice. The estimate was not reasonable. ✔

3.17 The student will **b)** construct a line plot, a picture graph, or a bar graph to represent the data. Also addresses 3.17c.

- Reasonable answers.
- Make a list.
- Solve a simpler problem.

Use any strategy to solve each problem.

1. Is 4,000 a reasonable estimate for the difference in attendance on Monday and Wednesday? Explain.

State Fair Attendance	
Monday	13,953
Tuesday	12,473
Wednesday	18,340

2. Anson swam 28 laps last week and 24 laps this week. He says he needs to swim the same number of laps each week for about two more weeks to swim a total of 100 laps. Is this a reasonable estimate? Explain.

3. Aubrey's class earned tokens for good behavior. The tally chart shows their votes for a reward.

Reward	Tally
Extra recess	ⅢⅢ Ⅰ
Game time	ⅢⅠ
Pizza treat	ⅢⅢ ⅢⅠ
Read-aloud time	ⅢⅢ ⅢⅢ

Is it reasonable to say about half of the class voted for a read-aloud time? Explain. Display this data in a picture graph.

4. Draw an example of a tally chart that may have been used to organize the information in the vertical bar graph below. How many people were surveyed for this graph? Explain.

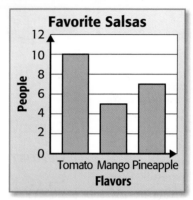

5. Mr. Gonzalez made a frequency table of the books he has collected. Display his data in a pictograph. Write one sentence to interpret the data.

Book Collection	
Mystery	15
Gardening	25
Biography	20
Fiction	15

6. Julina estimated that she needs to make 100 favors for the family reunion. Is this a reasonable estimate if 67 relatives will come on Friday and 42 will come on Saturday? Explain your reasoning.

7. **WRITE MATH** Explain an everyday situation when you would find putting data in a tally chart helpful.

Main Idea

I will tell whether events are certain, likely, unlikely, or impossible.

 **Vocabulary**
probability

 **Get Connect** ED

3.18 The student will investigate and describe the concept of probability as chance and list possible results of a given situation.

Identify Probability

You can use words to describe the probability or chance, that an event will happen.

Key Concept   Probability

Words   **Probability** describes how likely it is that an event will happen.

Examples

Certain to choose a marble.

Likely to choose red.

Unlikely to choose green.

Impossible to choose yellow.

▶ ✎ **REAL-WORLD EXAMPLES**   Describe Probability

① **Dana has a bag of 8 wristbands. Only one wristband is blue. Avery picks a wristband without looking. How likely is it that Avery will pick blue?**

There is only 1 blue wristband out of a total of 8. So, it is *unlikely* that Avery will pick a blue wristband.

② **How likely is it that Avery will pick green?**

There are 7 green wristbands out of a total of 8.

So, it is *likely* that a green one will be picked.

3 **SPINNERS** Andrea spins the spinner. How likely is it that she will spin a multiple of 3?

The numbers 3, 6, 9, and 12 are multiples of 3. So, it is *certain* that Andrea will spin a multiple of 3.

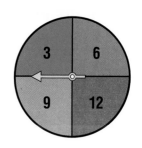

4 **GAMES** Theo and Yasmin are playing a card game. Yasmin needs to draw a 4 to win. The cards shown will be shuffled and placed facedown on a table. How likely is it that Yasmin will draw a 4?

There are no 4s. The probability that Yasmin will draw a 4 is *impossible*.

✓ **CHECK** **What You Know**

Describe the probability of landing on each color. Write *certain*, *likely*, *unlikely*, or *impossible*. See Examples 1–4

1. green

2. blue

3. yellow

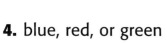

4. blue, red, or green

5. Jasmine is playing a game. She uses a number cube labeled 1, 2, 3, 4, 5, and 6. Describe the probability that she will roll a 7.

6. 🗨️ **TALK MATH** Explain the difference between an event that is *certain* and an event that is *likely*.

Describe the probability of choosing each color. Write *certain, likely, unlikely,* or *impossible.* See Examples 1–4

7. purple   **8.** green   **11.** yellow   **12.** red

9. white   **10.** blue or green   **13.** green   **14.** blue

Describe a bag of marbles that represents each statement.

15. Choosing a red marble is *impossible.*   **16.** Choosing a red marble is *certain.*

17. There are 7 letter tiles in a bag. Five of the tiles are labeled S. One tile is labeled R, and the other is labeled M. Describe the probability of choosing the letter S.

18. Francis asks Dan to choose a marble from a bag of 10 marbles. What is the probability of choosing the color blue if one marble is blue?

Data File

Maryland's state colors are red, gold, and black.

19. What color is the spinner *likely* to land on?

20. Is the spinner *likely* or *unlikely* to land on gold?

21. How could you change the spinner so that it is *certain* to land on red?

State Colors

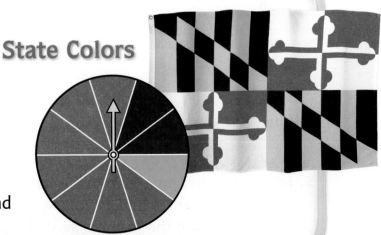

22. **FIND THE ERROR** Nate is spinning a spinner. The spinner is evenly divided into 4 sections. The colors are red, yellow, green, and blue. Find and correct his mistake.

> It is unlikely that the spinner will land on orange.

23. **WRITE MATH** Describe the probability of the following event. Explain.

   A cow can fly like a bird.

 **Test Practice**

24. How many shirt-pant outfits are possible? (Lesson 1C)

   A. 2   **C.** 6

   B. 4   **D.** 8

25. Lina has 7 cubes in a bag.

   She closes her eyes and picks one cube. Describe the probability that she picks a green cube. (Lesson 5A)

   F. certain   **H.** unlikely

   G. likely   **J.** impossible

Spiral Review

26. How many snack and drink combinations are possible if one snack and one drink is chosen? Explain your reasoning. (Lesson 1C)

27. Make a line plot for the data: (Lesson 4A)
   5, 7, 2, 1, 5, 2, 8, 9, 3, 5, 7, 3, 9, 7, 2, 10, 4, 4, 3

Cold Snacks
Juice bar
Ice cream cone
Pudding bar

Cold Drinks
Smoothie
Ice water
Ice tea

Main Idea
I will learn to use the results of probability experiments to predict future events.

 Vocabulary
prediction
outcomes

Get ConnectED

3.18 The student will investigate and describe the concept of probability as chance and list possible results of a given situation.

Make Predictions

You can use the results, or **outcomes**, from an experiment to make **predictions** about what is likely to happen next. When two outcomes have the same probability of happening, we say the outcomes are *equally likely*.

✏️ **REAL-WORLD EXAMPLE**   Make a Prediction

① **EXPERIMENT Cole picked one cube from a bag, recorded its color in a tally chart, and repeated his experiment. Then he displayed the results in a bar graph and in a line plot. Make two predictions based on the graphs.**

Cubes in a Bag		
Outcome	**Tally**	**Total**
1 Purple	|||	3
2 Green	﹢﹢﹢ ﹢﹢﹢	10
3 Red	|||	3

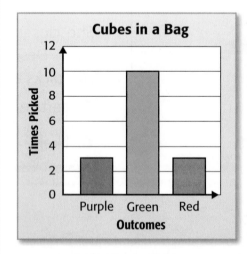

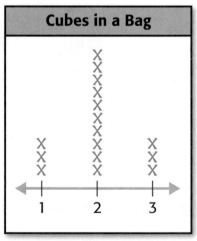

• Green cubes were picked more often than red or purple cubes. So, green is *more likely* to be picked than any other color.

• Purple and red were picked an equal number of times. They are *equally likely* to be picked.

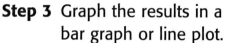 **Explore** Mini Activity

Step 1 Make a spinner and a tally chart like the ones shown.

Step 2 Perform an experiment. Spin the spinner 50 times. Record the result.

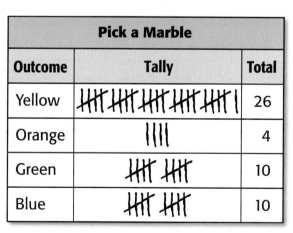

Step 3 Graph the results in a bar graph or line plot.

Remember

In order to make reliable predictions, probability experiments need to be performed many times.

1. Use the results to make a prediction for your next spin.

2. What kinds of things do you look for when making predictions?

Experiment		
Outcome	Tally	Number
1 Red		
2 Yellow		
3 Blue		
4 Green		

3. What information from your bar graph or line plot helped you make your predictions?

✓ CHECK What You Know

The tally chart shows the results of choosing a marble from a bag 50 times and then replacing it each time.

See Example 1

1. What color is likely to be chosen next? Why?

2. What two colors are equally likely to be picked? Explain.

Pick a Marble		
Outcome	Tally	Total
Yellow	卌 卌 卌 卌 卌 l	26
Orange	llll	4
Green	卌 卌	10
Blue	卌 卌	10

3. Is it reasonable to predict that twice as many marbles are yellow than any other color? Why?

4. **TALK MATH** There are 28 students. Of the students, 18 are girls. If the students put their names in a bag, do you think a boy's name or girl's name will be picked first? Explain.

The line plot shows the results of rolling a number cube labeled 1, 2, 3, 4, 5, and 6. See Example 1

5. How many times did Sari roll the cube?

6. Which numbers have been rolled so far?

7. What number do you predict Sari would roll next? Why?

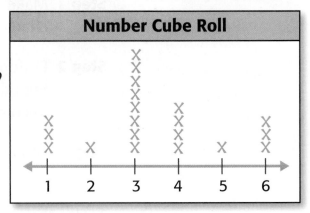

Number Cube Roll

The bar graph shows the number of letters in the third-grade spelling words. See Example 1

8. Explain whether it is *likely* or *unlikely* that an 8-letter word will be on the next spelling list.

9. How many letters do most of the spelling words have?

10. Predict the number of letters most of the words will have on the next spelling list.

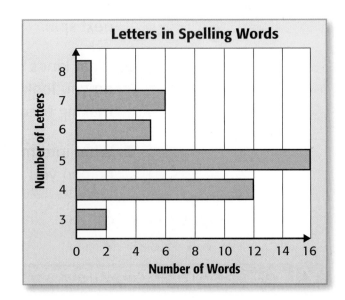

Letters in Spelling Words

Number of Letters

Number of Words

Weather To closely predict the weather each day, weather forecasters use data that has been gathered for a long period of time.

11. How many years does this data cover?

12. Predict a *likely* temperature for May 23 next year in central Ohio. Explain.

13. Predict an *unlikely* temperature for May 23 next year. Explain.

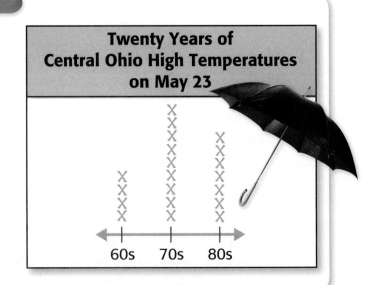

Twenty Years of Central Ohio High Temperatures on May 23

60s   70s   80s

H.O.T. Problems

14. CHALLENGE The table shows the results from spinning a spinner. Draw a spinner that could have produced these outcomes. Explain your decision for the spinner you drew.

15. 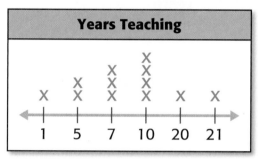 **WRITE MATH** Explain how graphs and line plots can be used to make predictions.

Spinner Results		
Outcomes	**Tally**	**Total**
Orange	ⅢⅢ ⅢⅢ |||	13
Red	||||	4
Green	|||	3

Test Practice

16. Which statement is true? (Lesson 4A)

Years Teaching

```
                    X
              X     X
        X     X     X
  X     X     X     X     X     X
  +-----+-----+-----+-----+-----+---->
  1     5     7     10    20    21
```

A. All teachers have been teaching 10 years, except one.

B. All have taught 7 years or more.

C. Most of the teachers have taught 7 years or more.

D. No one has taught 21 years.

17. What color is the spinner most likely to land on next time?
(Lesson 5B)

Color Spin		
Outcomes	**Tally**	**Number**
Red	|||	3
Blue	ⅢⅢ ⅢⅢ ⅢⅢ	15
Green	||	2
Yellow	ⅢⅢ	5

F. red   **H.** green

G. blue   **J.** yellow

Describe the probability of choosing each color(s). Write *certain*, *likely*, *unlikely*, or *impossible*. (Lesson 5A)

18. red

19. green

20. orange

21. red, green, or blue

22. Wesley bought 4 bags of beads. Each bag has 155 beads. If he gave away 111 beads, how many did he have left? (Lesson 4B)

To assess mastery of SOL 3.18, see your Virginia Assessment Book.

Chapter Study Guide and Review

Be sure the following Key Concepts are noted in your Foldable.

Collect and Analyze Data
Collect Data
Graphs with Pictures
Bar Graphs
Line Plots
Probability

Key Concepts

- **Data** is collected information or facts. It can be collected through surveys, experiments, and observation. (Lesson 1)
- **Frequency tables** help us to record and organize collected data. (Lesson 1)

Friends' Eye Color		
Color	**Tally**	**Frequency**
Blue	‖‖‖ ‖‖‖	9
Green	‖‖‖	3
Brown	‖‖‖ ‖	6

- **Data can be displayed several ways.** A **picture graph** and **pictograph** use a picture or symbol to show and compare data. (Lesson 2)
  A **bar graph** compares data with bars. (Lesson 3)
  A **line plot** uses a number line and Xs to show how often something happens. (Lesson 4)
- You can learn from the information in a graph when you **analyze** the data. (Lesson 2)

Key Vocabulary

- **bar graph**
- **data**
- **line plot**
- **pictograph**
- **probability**
- **scale**

Vocabulary Check

Choose the vocabulary word that completes each sentence.

1. A set of ____?____ is information or facts that have been collected.

2. The chance that an event will happen is ____?____.

3. A ____?____ is a graph that uses columns of Xs above a number line to show frequency of data.

4. A ____?____ compares data by using bars of different lengths or heights to show the values.

5. A ____?____ is a set of numbers that represent the data.

6. A ____?____ displays a symbol to represent data.

Multi-Part Lesson Review

Lesson 1 · Collect Data

Construct Frequency Tables (Lesson 1B)

Organize the set of data in a tally chart.

7. Jack took a survey to find his friends' favorite type of book.

Type of Book	
mystery	science fiction
mystery	sports stories
mystery	sports stories
mystery	sports stories

8. Which type of book is the most popular?

9. Which type of book is the least popular?

EXAMPLE 1

Make a tally chart to show the data.

Careta asked her friends to pick their favorite type of sandwich.

Favorite Type of Sandwich	
Sandwich	**Tally**
Ham and Cheese	⊪⊪ II
Peanut Butter	III
Turkey	⊪⊪

Problem-Solving Strategy: Make a List (Lesson 1C)

Solve. Use the *make a list* strategy.

10. Maya is making cards out of four different colors of paper. How many ways can she order the colors pink, red, yellow, and green?

11. Virginia is making AB patterns out of squares, triangles, trapezoids, and circles. If each pattern uses only two shapes, how many different patterns can she make?

12. Mia, Ned, and Sean are in line for lunch. How many different ways could they be ordered in line?

13. Mr. Diaz asked his students to list all the three-digit numbers they could make using the numbers 5, 9, and 3 once. How many three-digit numbers can be made?

EXAMPLE 2

Dalton has one notebook of each color—red, green, and purple. How many different ways can he order all three notebooks?

Possible Ways to Order			
	First	**Second**	**Third**
1.	Red	Green	Purple
2.	Red	Purple	Green
3.	Green	Red	Purple
4.	Green	Purple	Red
5.	Purple	Red	Green
6.	Purple	Green	Red

There are 6 ways to order the notebooks.

Check None of the ways repeat. So, the answer makes sense. ✔

Lesson 2 **Graphs with Pictures**

Construct and Analyze Picture Graphs and Pictographs (Lesson 2B)

14. Display the set of data in a pictograph. Let each symbol represent 2 coins.

Coins in Bank	
Type of Coin	**Number**
Penny	20
Nickel	12
Dime	8
Quarter	10

15. How many more pennies than nickels are there?

16. How many nickels and dimes are there altogether?

17. How much are the dimes worth?

18. Which group of coins equals the greatest amount of money?

EXAMPLE 3

Display the data in a picture graph.

Shirt Colors	
Color	**Number of Shirts**
Red	4
Blue	5
Green	3

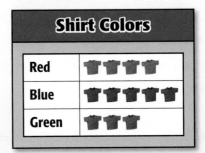

Each picture represents 1 shirt.

Lesson 3 **Bar Graphs**

Construct and Analyze Bar Graphs (Lesson 3B)

19. Display the set of data in a horizontal bar graph.

Location of Bird Nests	
Tree	7
Roof	3
Bush	4
Porch swing	1

20. Which location has the most bird nests?

21. Which location has 3 more bird nests than the porch swing?

EXAMPLE 4

The tallest bar represents hiking. So, the campers prefer hiking the most.

Lesson 4 — Line Plots

Construct and Analyze Line Plots (Lesson 4A)

Use the ages of the members of a swim team shown below.

22. Display this set of data in a line plot: 10, 10, 6, 7, 12, 8, 7, 7, 10, 7, 8, 10, 9, 9, 9, 8, 10, 9, 10

23. How many members are there?

24. **Algebra** Compare the number of members who are 6 years old and the number of members who are 8 years old. Use >, <, or =.

25. How many swimmers are 10 years old or older?

EXAMPLE 5

Display the number of home runs per game scored this season in a line plot. Write a sentence about the line plot.

3, 6, 1, 2, 2, 4, 3, 1, 1, 3, 2, 2, 2

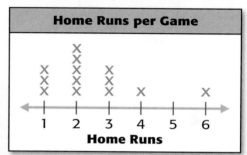

Only 1 home run was scored in three different games.

Problem-Solving Investigation: Choose a Strategy (Lesson 4B)

Use any strategy to solve.

26. Marcia has the money shown. Does she have more or less than $1? How much more or less than $1?

27. Suppose you add 25 to a number and then subtract 14. If the result is 48, what was the original number?

EXAMPLE 6

Sadie has 20 stuffed animals. She will keep 5 and divide the rest equally among 3 friends. How many stuffed animals will each friend get?

Subtract to find how many stuffed animals Sadie is giving away.

20	−	5	=	15
total		Sadie keeps		divide equally

Divide to solve the problem.

$15 \div 3 = 5$

So, each of Sadie's friends will get 5 stuffed animals.

Lesson 5 **Probability**

Identify Probability (Lesson 5A)

Describe the probability of the spinner landing on each number. Write *certain, likely, unlikely,* or *impossible.*

28. four   **29.** six

30. three   **31.** multiple of 3

EXAMPLE 7

Andy spins the spinner shown. How likely is it that he will spin a multiple of 4?

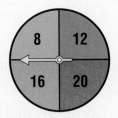

The numbers 8, 12, 16, and 20 are all multiples of 4, so it is *certain* Andy will spin a multiple of 4.

Make Predictions (Lesson 5B)

The tally chart shows the results from spinning a four-color spinner 50 times.

Spinner Results	
Color	**Tally**
Yellow	‖
Blue	ЖЖ ЖЖ ЖЖ ЖЖ ЖЖ ‖‖‖
Green	ЖЖ ЖЖ
Red	ЖЖ ЖЖ

32. What color is the spinner most likely to land on next? Why?

33. What two colors is the spinner equally likely to land on? Explain.

34. Is it reasonable to say that half of the colors on the spinner are blue? Explain.

EXAMPLE 8

The results from rolling a six-sided number cube 14 times are shown in the line plot. Predict the next number to be rolled.

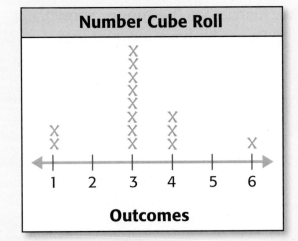

The next roll is likely to be a 3.

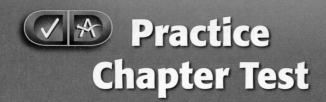

Practice Chapter Test

Tell whether each statement is *true* or *false*.

1. A line plot uses Xs above a number line to show how often something happens.

2. A bar graph does not need a scale.

3. Display the data in a horizontal bar graph.

Pick a Marble	
Color	**Tally**
Yellow	ЖΉ ЖΉ ЖΉ I
Orange	ЖΉ III
Green	ЖΉ ЖΉ II
Blue	ЖΉ III

4. **MULTIPLE CHOICE** The pictograph shows the number of ribbons earned in each gymnastics event. What is the total number of ribbons received?

Gymnastics Ribbons	
High bar	🎗 🎗
Parallel bars	🎗 🎗 🎗
Vault	🎗
Key: 🎗 = 2 ribbons	

A. 5 C. 11

B. 6 D. 12

5. Draw a tally chart that might have been used to collect the data for Exercise 4.

Use the tally chart in Exercise 3 to answer the following questions.

6. What is the total number of times a marble was picked?

7. Which two colors have an equally likely outcome?

8. Based on this information, which two colors does there seem to be more of?

9. **MULTIPLE CHOICE** The chart shows the results of spinning a spinner. What color is the spinner most likely to land on?

Color Spin	
Color	**Tally**
Red	ЖΉ ЖΉ ЖΉ
Blue	ЖΉ ЖΉ ЖΉ ЖΉ ЖΉ ЖΉ ЖΉ ЖΉ
Green	ЖΉ
Yellow	III

F. red H. green

G. blue J. yellow

10. **✏️ WRITE MATH** What does the tally chart of results from Exercise 9 tell you about the colors on the spinner?

How many students checked out more than 4 books?

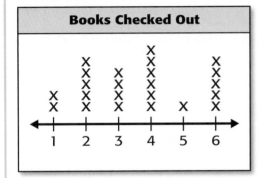

A. 6   **B.** 7   **C.** 10   **D.** 23

TEST-TAKING TIP

Eliminate answer choices that are unreasonable.

Read the Question

You need to find how many students checked out more than 4 books.

Solve the Question

More than 4 means 5 and 6. Use the line plot and count the number of Xs above the numbers 5 and 6.

So, 1 + 5, or 6, students checked out more than 4 books.

The answer is A.

Read each question. Then fill in the correct answer on the answer sheet provided by your teacher or on a separate sheet of paper.

1. A humpback whale weighs 2,558 pounds. What is the weight rounded to the nearest thousand?

    A. 1,000 pounds   **C.** 3,000 pounds

    B. 2,000 pounds   **D.** 4,000 pounds

2. Twenty-eight students separated into 7 equal groups. Which of the following could help you find the number of students in each group?

    F. 28 + 7   **H.** 28 × 7

    G. 28 − 7   **J.** 28 ÷ 7

3. The bar graph shows the number of students absent during a 5-day period. How many students were absent in all?

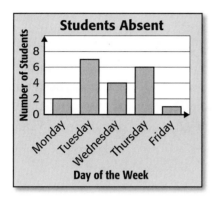

A. 1   **C.** 13

B. 7   **D.** 20

4. Which sentence about the data below is true?

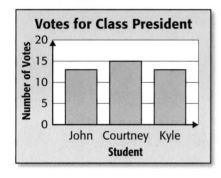

F. Kyle has more votes than John.

G. John and Courtney have equal votes.

H. John and Kyle's votes are equal.

J. Courtney has 5 more votes than Kyle.

5. The 2nd graders in the school district collected 4,539 canned goods for the food drive. The 3rd graders in the school district collected twice this amount. How many canned goods did the two grades collect altogether?

A. 4,539   **C.** 13,617

B. 8,068   **D.** 11,700

6. Tickets to a high school football game cost $6 for adults and $4 for students. How much would 3 adult and 4 student tickets cost?

F. $17   **H.** $36

G. $34   **J.** $70

7. Terrance scored 12 points. How many basketballs should be drawn next to Terrance's name?

Points Scored	
Raul	🏀 🏀 🏀 🏀 🏀
Don	🏀 🏀 🏀
Hugh	🏀 🏀 🏀 🏀
Terrance	
key: 🏀 = 2 points	

A. 4   **C.** 6

B. 7   **D.** 7

NEED EXTRA HELP?							
If You Missed Question . . .	1	2	3	4	5	6	7
Go to Chapter-Lesson . . .	1-3B	5-2C	6-3B	6-3B	2-1F	5-1B	6-2B
For help with . . .	SOL 3.1b	SOL 3.5	SOL 3.17c	SOL 3.17c	SOL 3.4	SOL 3.5	SOL 3.17b

CHAPTER 7

Geometric Figures and Spatial Reasoning

connectED.mcgraw-hill.com

Investigate

 Animations

 Vocabulary

 Math Songs

 Multilingual eGlossary

Learn

 Personal Tutor

 Virtual Manipulatives

 Audio

 Foldables

Practice

 Self-Check Practice

 eGames

 Worksheets

 Assessment

The ☆BIG Idea

How can I describe and analyze properties of two- and three-dimensional figures?

FOLDABLES Study Organizer

Make this Foldable to help you organize information about geometric figures. Start with one sheet of 11" × 17" paper.

Review Vocabulary

two-dimensional figure figura bidimensional

a figure which has only length and width

Key Vocabulary

English	Español
angle	ángulo
polygon	polígono
quadrilateral	cuadrilátero
congruent figures	figuras congruentes
symmetry	simetría

When Will I Use This?

Are You Ready for the Chapter?

You have two options for checking Prerequisite Skills for this chapter.

Text Option Take the Quick Check below.

QUICK Check

Identify the figure that does not belong with the other three. Explain.

1.

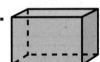

Figure A   Figure B   Figure C   Figure D

2.

Figure F   Figure G   Figure H   Figure I

3. Macy has a triangle, a square, a cube, and a rectangle. Which figure does not belong with the other three? Explain.

Tell how the figures in each pair differ.

4.

5.

6.

7.

8.

9.

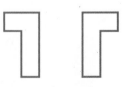

10. Devin and Tamia each drew a different figure that has 8 sides. Draw an example of what the figures could look like.

 Online Option Take the Online Readiness Quiz.

Main Idea

I will learn to identify lines, line segments, and rays and the ways in which they meet and cross each other.

 Vocabulary

point

line

line segment

endpoints

ray

intersecting lines

perpendicular lines

parallel lines

 *Get Connect ED*

3.15 The student will identify and draw representations of points, line segments, rays, angles, and lines.

Lines, Line Segments, and Rays

Lines, line segments, and points can be helpful when describing two-dimensional, or plane figures.

Key Concept Lines, Line Segments, and Rays	
Words	**Model**
A **point** is a location in space.	A
A **line** is a straight set of points that extend in opposite directions without ending.	A ⟵•————————•⟶ B
A **line segment** is part of a line between two **endpoints**.	A •————————• B
A **ray** is part of a line. It has one endpoint and extends in one direction without ending.	A •————————→ B

REAL-WORLD EXAMPLES   Line Segments and Rays

1 **TRIANGLE** Describe the figure Paul drew. Then label its parts.

Three line segments form the sides of the triangle. Each line segment has two endpoints.

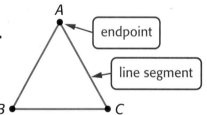

2 **SUN** Describe the path of sunshine as a line or a ray.

The path of light begins at the sun and extends without ending. So, the path of light is a ray, a ray of sunshine.

Lines can be classified by the way they meet or cross each other.

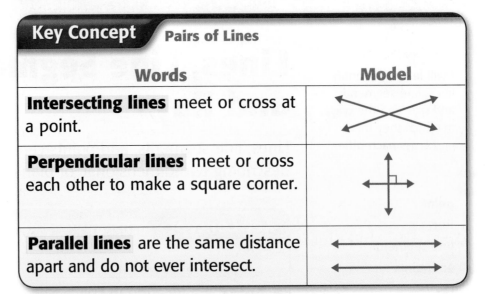

Key Concept — Pairs of Lines

Words	Model
Intersecting lines meet or cross at a point.	
Perpendicular lines meet or cross each other to make a square corner.	
Parallel lines are the same distance apart and do not ever intersect.	

REAL-WORLD EXAMPLE — Classify Pairs of Lines

3 **MAPS** Streets on a city map resemble line segments.

Oak Street and Pine Street are parallel to each other.

Oak Street and Queen Street are intersecting and perpendicular streets.

✓ CHECK What You Know

Describe each figure as a *point, line, ray,* or *line segment.*

See Examples 1 and 2

1.

2.

3. •
P

Classify each pair of lines as *intersecting, perpendicular,* or *parallel.* See Example 3

4.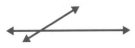

5.

6.

7. Draw and label an example of a ray and a line segment. See Examples 1 and 2

8. ✍ **TALK MATH** Discuss how intersecting and perpendicular lines are similar and different.

Describe each figure as a *point, line, ray,* or *line segment.*

See Examples 1 and 2

9.

10.

11.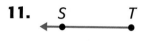

12.

13.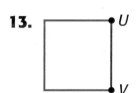

14.

Draw and label an example of each figure. See Examples 1 and 2

15. line

16. point

Classify each pair of lines as *intersecting, perpendicular,* or *parallel.* See Example 3

17.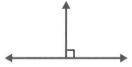

18.

19.

20.

21.

22.

23. Look at Exercises 17–22. Which objects have both intersecting and perpendicular lines?

24. Print and label three capital letters of the alphabet to show examples of intersecting, perpendicular, and parallel lines.

H.O.T. Problems

25. REASONING Why do you suppose the area where streets come together is called an *intersection*?

26. OPEN ENDED Draw a real world example of each pair of lines. Label your lines *parallel, perpendicular,* or *intersecting.*

27. WRITE MATH How is a line different from a line segment? How are they alike?

Explore Angles

Main Idea

I will explore angles of two-dimensional figures.

Materials

geoboard, rubber bands

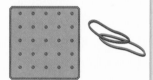

pattern blocks

index card

3.14 The student will identify, describe, compare, and contrast characteristics of plane and solid geometric figures (circle, square, rectangle, triangle, cube, rectangular prism, square pyramid, sphere, cone, and cylinder) by identifying relevant characteristics, including the number of angles, vertices, and edges, and the number and shape of faces, using concrete models.

3.15 The student will identify and draw representations of points, line segments, rays, angles, and lines.

An **angle** is made when two rays share the same endpoint. The shared endpoint is called the **vertex.**

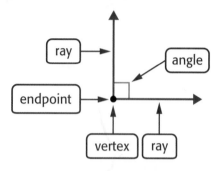

 **ACTIVITY**

① **Explore Angles**

Step 1 Make a large square similar to the orange pattern block.

Step 2 Use your index card to compare one angle formed by two sides of the square.

An angle that forms a *square corner* is called a **right angle.**

 ACTIVITY

② **Compare Angles**

Step 1 Make a large triangle similar to the green pattern block.

Step 2 Use your index card to compare one angle formed by two sides of the triangle.

This angle is *less than* a right angle.

ACTIVITY

③ Compare Angles

Step 1 Make a large hexagon similar to the yellow pattern block.

 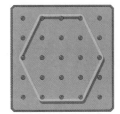

Step 2 Use your index card to compare an angle formed by two sides of the hexagon.

This angle is *greater than* a right angle.

Practice and Apply It

Tell whether each angle shown is a *right angle, less than* a right angle, or *greater than* a right angle. Use an index card if needed.

1.

2.

3.

4.

5.

6.

7. ☰ **WRITE MATH** Can a triangle have two right angles? Explain.

Main Idea
I will describe, analyze, and compare two-dimensional figures.

 Vocabulary

two-dimensional figure

polygon

quadrilateral

pentagon

hexagon

octagon

decagon

Get ConnectED

 3.14 The student will identify, describe, compare, and contrast characteristics of plane and solid geometric figures (circle, square, rectangle, triangle, cube, rectangular prism, square pyramid, sphere, cone, and cylinder) by identifying relevant characteristics, including the number of angles, vertices, and edges, and the number and shape of faces, using concrete models.
3.15 The student will identify and draw representations of points, line segments, rays, angles, and lines.

Two-Dimensional Figures: Polygons

A **two-dimensional figure**, or plane figure, has length and width. Circles and polygons are two-dimensional figures. A **polygon** is a closed two-dimensional figure of three or more line segments, called sides, and angles.

triangle
3 sides
3 angles

quadrilateral
4 sides
4 angles

pentagon
5 sides
5 angles

hexagon
6 sides
6 angles

octagon
8 sides
8 angles

decagon
10 sides
10 angles

REAL-WORLD EXAMPLES   Describe and Identify Polygons

TRAFFIC SIGNS Stop signs are plane figures that have eight sides. The shape of the stop sign is a polygon. Describe and identify each polygon.

1

There are 8 sides and 8 angles. So, it is an octagon.

2

There are 5 sides and 5 angles. So, it is a pentagon.

(3) **WINDOWS** The designs in the window are made of different polygons. How are the polygons lined in red alike? How are they different?

They both have an even number of sides.

One polygon has 4 sides. The other has 8 sides.

✓ CHECK What You Know

Describe each two-dimensional figure. Use the terms *sides* and *angles*. Then identify the figure. See Examples 1 and 2

1.

2.

3.

Compare each set of polygons. Explain how they are alike and different. See Example 3

4.

5.

6. Bryson used a square pattern block and a triangular pattern block. He placed the edges together. What new polygon did he create?

7.  **TALK MATH** Explain why the shape of the tambourine is not a polygon.

Describe each two-dimensional figure. Use the terms *sides* and *angles*. Then identify the figure. See Examples 1 and 2

8.

9.

10.

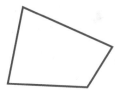

11.

12.

13.

Compare each set of polygons. Explain how they are alike and different. See Example 3

14.

15.

16.

17.

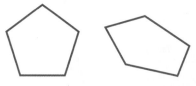

18. What is another name for a square, other than polygon?

19. Classify the polygon that has fewer angles than a quadrilateral.

20. Is the figure shown below a polygon? Explain.

21. What three-sided polygon do you get when you fold a square in half, corner to corner?

Use the information to solve the problems.

High-Flying Adventure

Remember, Luke is trying to figure out how to make right angles with 2 sticks.

Aha! Now, I get it.

Online Math Dictionary
right angle:

22. What are right angles?

23. Draw a figure to show what two sticks forming four right angles would look like. How would you classify the lines the sticks make in the figure you drew?

H.O.T. Problems

24. **OPEN ENDED** Describe an object in your classroom that is made of at least two polygons.

25. **WRITE MATH** A circle is a two-dimensional plane figure. Explain why it is not a polygon.

Test Practice

26. The teacher drew four figures on the board. Which figure appears to not have any parallel lines?
(Lesson 1A)

A.

C.

B.

D.

27. How many line segments does this cracker appear to have?
(Lesson 1A)

F. 5   **H.** 7

G. 6   **J.** 8

Main Idea

I will identify, describe, and classify quadrilaterals.

Vocabulary

parallelogram

rhombus

trapezoid

 3.14 The student will identify, describe, compare, and contrast characteristics of plane and solid geometric figures (circle, square, rectangle, triangle, cube, rectangular prism, square pyramid, sphere, cone, and cylinder) by identifying relevant characteristics, including the number of angles, vertices, and edges, and the number and shape of faces, using concrete models.

3.15 The student will identify and draw representations of points, line segments, rays, angles, and lines.

Quadrilaterals

All quadrilaterals have 4 sides and 4 angles.

Some quadrilaterals have two sets of sides that are parallel, or equal distance apart.

parallel line segments

These quadrilaterals are called parallelograms.

parallelogram

- opposite sides are the same length and are parallel
- opposite angles are the same

Key Concept   Quadrilaterals

square
- 4 sides of equal length
- opposite sides are parallel
- 4 right angles

rectangle
- opposite sides of equal length
- opposite sides are parallel
- 4 right angles

rhombus
- 4 sides of equal length
- opposite sides are parallel
- opposite angles are the same

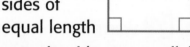

trapezoid
- one pair of parallel sides

The square, rectangle, and rhombus are quadrilaterals that are also parallelograms.

The trapezoid is a quadrilateral but is *not* a parallelogram. Explain why.

 **EXAMPLE** Describe and Identify Quadrilaterals

1 **Describe and identify the quadrilateral by its sides.**

The opposite sides are the same length and are parallel. So, it is a rectangle. It is also a parallelogram.

Remember

"Quad" in *quadrilateral* means "four."

 EXAMPLE Classify Angles

2 **Describe and identify the quadrilateral. Classify the angle shown as a *right*, *less than* a right, or *greater than* a right angle.**

Its sides are the same length and opposite sides are parallel.

So, it is a parallelogram called a *rhombus*.

This angle is greater than a right angle.

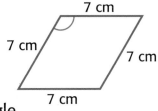

7 cm, 7 cm, 7 cm, 7 cm

✓ CHECK What You Know

Describe and identify each quadrilateral by its sides. See Example 1

1.

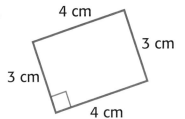

4 cm, 3 cm, 3 cm, 4 cm

2.

6 m, 7 m, 7 m, 6 m

3.

2 feet, 2 feet, 2 feet, 2 feet

Describe and identify each quadrilateral. Classify the angle shown as a *right*, *less than* a right, or *greater than* a right angle. See Example 2

4.

10 cm, 1 cm, 1 cm, 10 cm

5.

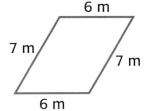

7 ft, 4 ft, 4 ft, 7 ft

6.

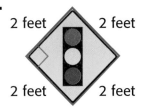

7. Kaila is thinking of a quadrilateral. Its opposite sides are parallel and the same length. There are 4 right angles. Name the quadrilateral.

8.  **TALK MATH** Describe how a rectangle and a square are alike and how they are different.

Describe and identify each quadrilateral by its sides.

See Example 1

9.
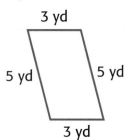
3 yd
5 yd   5 yd
3 yd

10.
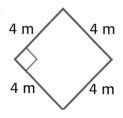
4 m   4 m
4 m   4 m

11.
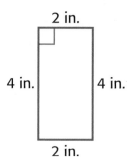
2 in.
4 in.   4 in.
2 in.

12.
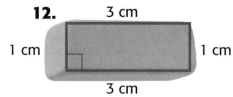
3 cm
1 cm   1 cm
3 cm

13.
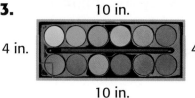
10 in.
4 in.   4 in.
10 in.

14.
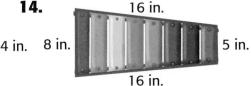
16 in.
8 in.   5 in.
16 in.

Describe and identify each quadrilateral. Classify the angle shown as a *right, less than* a right, or *greater than* a right angle. See Example 2

15.
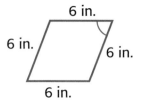
6 in.
6 in.   6 in.
6 in.

16.
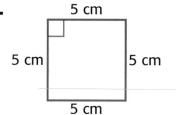
5 cm
5 cm   5 cm
5 cm

17.
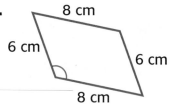
8 cm
6 cm   6 cm
8 cm

18.

1 ft
1 ft   1 ft
1 ft

19.

4 in.
6 in.   6 in.
3 in.

20.
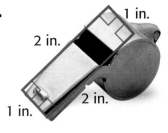
1 in.
2 in.
2 in.
1 in.

Identify each quadrilateral described.

21. This figure has opposite sides that are parallel and 4 right angles. Two sides are longer than the other sides.

22. This figure has two pairs of parallel sides of the same length and no right angles.

23. Mrs. Samson measured a rug. Each side is 6 feet long. All of the corners are right angles. What is the shape of the rug?

24. Look at the previous exercise. If Mrs. Samson put two of the rugs side by side, what shape would the rugs make?

25. OPEN ENDED Draw and identify a quadrilateral that has 4 equal sides with 2 angles that are greater than right angles.

CHALLENGE Find an object that represents each shape.

26. square   **27.** rectangle   **28.** parallelogram

29.  **WRITE MATH** Describe how a parallelogram and a square are alike and how they are different.

 Test Practice

30. In this figure, which two angles appear greater than a right angle? (Lesson 1B)

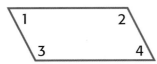

   A. Angles 1 and 2

   B. Angles 1 and 4

   C. Angles 2 and 3

   D. Angles 2 and 4

31. Which of these shapes appears to be a quadrilateral but not a parallelogram? (Lesson 1D)

Spiral Review

Compare each set of polygons. Explain how they are alike and different. (Lesson 1A and 1C)

32.

33.

Classify the angle shown as a *right, less than* a right, or *greater than* a right angle. (Lesson 1B)

34.

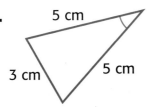

5 cm
3 cm
5 cm

35.

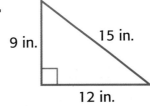

9 in.
15 in.
12 in.

36.

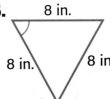

8 in.
8 in.
8 in.

To assess mastery of SOL 3.15, see your Virginia Assessment Book.

Problem-Solving Strategy: Guess, Check, and Revise

Main Idea I will solve a problem by using the guess, check, and revise strategy.

 Julianna has four polygons. The polygons have a total of 19 sides and 19 vertices. Two of the polygons are the same. One polygon has four sides of equal length. What are the names of the four polygons?

Understand **What facts do you know?**

- There are four polygons.
- You know the total number of sides and vertices.
- One polygon has four sides of equal length.
- Two polygons are the same.

What do you need to find?

- Find the names of the four polygons.

Plan Use the *guess, check, and revise* strategy.

Solve From the clues, you know that one polygon is a square.

$$19 - 4 = 15$$

The sides of the remaining polygons need to equal 15. Two polygons are the same. Make a guess, then check. Use what you find to revise.

Guess & Revise					Check
3 + 3	4		6		16 no
	4	5 + 5		8	22 no
3	4		6 + 6		19 yes ✓

So, Julianna has 1 triangle, 1 square, and 2 hexagons.

Check The answer makes sense with the facts of the problem. So, the answer is correct. ✓

3.14 The student will identify, describe, compare, and contrast characteristics of plane and solid geometric figures (circle, square, rectangle, triangle, cube, rectangular prism, square pyramid, sphere, cone, and cylinder) by identifying relevant characteristics, including the number of angles, vertices, and edges, and the number and shape of faces, using concrete models.

Refer to the problem on the previous page.

1. How did the answer from your first guess help you revise your second guess?

2. Suppose the total number of sides and vertices is 21. How would your answer be revised?

3. Continue the *guess, check, and revise* strategy. Use the same facts to find *another way* to name four polygons with 19 sides and vertices.

4. Explain when you would use the *guess, check, and revise* strategy to solve a problem.

PRACTICE

EXTRA PRACTICE Begins on page EP2.

Solve. Use the *guess, check, and revise* strategy.

5. A toy store sold $67 worth of bean-bag animals. How many of each size did they sell?

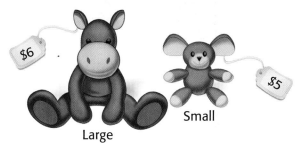

Large   Small

6. Ed has some hexagon and square pattern blocks. There are a total of 24 sides. How many of each polygon does he have?

7. There are 30 apples in a basket. Half are red. There are 5 more green apples than yellow apples. How many of each color are there?

8. Dawnita has 8 coins. The total is $1. What are the coins?

9. Kira is thinking of two numbers. Their difference is 12 and their sum is 22. What are the numbers?

10. For lunch, Nadia bought two different items. She spent exactly 70¢. What did she buy?

Food	Cost
Box of raisins	35¢
Apple	25¢
Granola bar	45¢
Grilled cheese	85¢

11.  **WRITE MATH** Camden, Holden, and Odell have 10 pencils in all. They each have more than 1 pencil. Camden has the most pencils. Holden has the fewest pencils. How many pencils does each boy have? Explain how you would use the *guess, check, and revise* strategy to solve.

Main Idea

I will identify, classify, and describe three-dimensional figures.

 Vocabulary

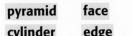
three-dimensional figure

cube	cone
rectangular prism	
pyramid	face
cylinder	edge
sphere	vertex

 Get ConnectED

3.14 The student will identify, describe, compare, and contrast characteristics of plane and solid geometric figures (circle, square, rectangle, triangle, cube, rectangular prism, square pyramid, sphere, cone, and cylinder) by identifying relevant characteristics, including the number of angles, vertices, and edges, and the number and shape of faces, using concrete models.

Three-Dimensional Figures

We see objects every day. They are three-dimensional figures.

A **three-dimensional figure** is a solid figure that has length, width, and height.

Key Concept **Three-Dimensional Figures**

cube **rectangular prism** **cone**

pyramid **cylinder** **sphere**

EXAMPLE Identify Three-Dimensional Figures

1) **Identify each three-dimensional figure.**

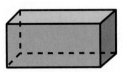

The figure is a rectangular prism.

A soup can looks like a cylinder.

A three-dimensional figure can be classified by its faces, edges, and vertices.

A **face** is a flat surface. Faces of solid figures are two-dimensional figures. These faces are square.

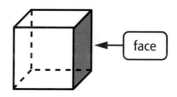

An **edge** is where 2 faces meet.

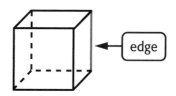

A **vertex** is the point, where 3 or more edges meet. When there is more than one vertex they are called *vertices.*

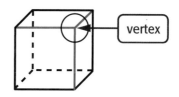

EXAMPLE Classify Three-Dimensional Figures

2 **A figure has 1 square and 4 triangular faces, 8 edges, and 5 vertices. Classify the figure.**

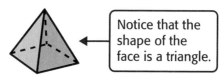

Notice that the shape of the face is a triangle.

So, the figure is a pyramid.

EXAMPLE Describe Three-Dimensional Figures

3 **Describe the figure shown.**

The figure has 6 square faces, 12 edges, and 8 vertices.

Identify each three-dimensional figure. See Example 1

1.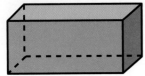

2.

3.

Classify each three-dimensional figure. See Example 2

4. This figure has 1 circular face.

5. This figure has 2 circular faces.

Describe each three-dimensional figure. Use the terms *faces, edges,* **and** *vertices.* See Example 3

6.

7.

8. Brandi and Ling are playing the drums. What solid figure do the drums represent?

9. 🗨 **TALK MATH** How are the three-dimensional figures of a cone and cylinder different? How are they alike?

Practice and **P**roblem **S**olving

EXTRA PRACTICE
Begins on page EP2.

Identify each three-dimensional figure. See Example 1

10.

11.

12.

13.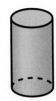

14.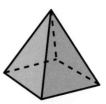

15.

Classify each three-dimensional figure. See Example 2

16. This figure has 6 faces. It is not a cube.

17. This figure has 1 face.

18. This figure has 0 faces, 0 edges, and 0 vertices.

19. This figure has 4 triangular faces and 1 square face. It also has 8 edges and 5 vertices.

Describe each three-dimensional figure. Use the terms *faces, edges,* **and** *vertices.* See Example 3

20.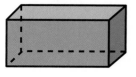
21.
22.
23.

24. Taye bought a box of cereal. What three-dimensional figure is a box of cereal?

25. Max threw his basketball through the hoop. What three-dimensional figure is a basketball?

26. A piece of clay is rolled into a sphere, then cut in half. How many faces does each half have?

27. If a cube is cut in half as shown, what three-dimensional figures are made?

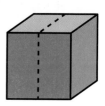

H.O.T. Problems

28. OPEN ENDED Name three real-world objects that you would find at home or in your classroom that resemble a cylinder.

29. WHICH ONE DOESN'T BELONG? Identify the figure that does not belong with the others. Explain.

30. **WRITE MATH** What do a cube and a rectangular prism have in common?

31. School begins at 8:00 A.M. Classify the angle formed by the hands on the clock. (Lesson 1B)

A. right angle
B. greater than a right angle
C. less than a right angle
D. there is no angle

32. Bruce's skates were packed in the box shown. Identify the shaded face as a two-dimensional figure. (Lesson 1C)

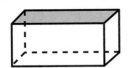

F. triangle   **H.** circle
G. square   **I.** rectangle

33. Marshall bought oatmeal in a container shaped like a cylinder. Which figure is a cylinder? (Lesson 1F)

A.   **C.**

B.   **D.**

34. Choose the best answer. What do a cube and a rectangular prism have in common? (Lesson 1F)

F. They both have four faces.
G. They are both two-dimensional figures.
H. The faces of each solid are equal size.
I. They both have the same number of edges and vertices.

Spiral Review

Solve. (Lesson 1D)

35. Norika has 3 pattern blocks. The polygons have a total of 13 sides and 13 vertices. One polygon has 4 sides, but only 2 sides are equal in length. What are the 3 polygons? (Lesson 1G)

Describe and identify each quadrilateral by its sides. (Lesson 1C)

36.    **37.**    **38.**

To assess mastery of SOL 3.14, see your Virginia Assessment Book.

Mid-Chapter Check

Describe each two-dimensional figure. Use the terms *sides* and *angles*. Then identify the figure. (Lesson 1C)

1.

2.

Identify each three-dimensional figure. (Lesson 1F)

3.

4.

5.

6.

7. Collin is flying a kite. What type of a polygon is this kite? (Lesson 1C)

8. MULTIPLE CHOICE Each tile in Mick's mosaic has a right angle. Which tile below seems to have a right angle? (Lesson 1B)

A.

B.

C.

D.

Describe each figure by classifying the angle shown as a *right, less than a right, or greater than a right angle.* (Lesson 1B)

9.

10.

Classify each set of lines as *intersecting, perpendicular, or parallel.* (Lesson 1A)

11.

12.

13. Describe and identify the quadrilateral buttons on Rhonda's coat. Classify the angles. (Lesson 1D)

14. MULTIPLE CHOICE Identify the figure that is a trapezoid. (Lesson 1C)

F.

H.

G.

J.

15. **WRITE MATH** What is the connection between the number of sides and number of angles in a polygon? (Lesson 1C)

Explore Congruent Figures

Main Idea

I will build and draw two-dimensional figures to explore congruency.

Materials

pattern blocks

paper

Get ConnectED

3.16 The student will identify and describe congruent and noncongruent plane figures.

Figures that are the same shape but a different size are **similar** figures.

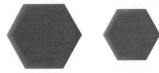

These figures are similar.

Congruent figures have the same shape *and* the same size.

These figures are congruent.

ACTIVITY

1. **Congruent Figures**

Step 1 Trace a yellow hexagon pattern block.

Using green triangle pattern blocks, try to make a figure that is congruent.

Step 2 Trace the outside of the figure you created.

Cut it out. Place the cut-out hexagon on top of your outline.

The hexagons fit exactly. They are congruent.

2 Similar Figures

Step 1 Make a parallelogram with two red trapezoids.
Make a parallelogram with two blue rhombuses.

Step 2 Place the blue parallelogram on top of the red parallelogram.

The parallelograms are the same shape but not the same size. They are similar.

Practice and Apply It

Tell if each pair of figures is *congruent* or *similar*. If needed, trace over the second figure in each pair. Place the tracing over the first figure.

1.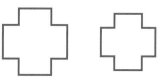

2.

3.

4.

5. **WRITE MATH** If two figures are the same size and same shape, but turned in different directions, are they congruent? Explain.

Main Idea
I will analyze two-dimensional figures in order to identify congruency.

 **Vocabulary**
congruent
similar

 **Get ConnectED**

3.16 The student will identify and describe congruent and noncongruent plane figures.

Congruency

 REAL-WORLD EXAMPLE   Congruent Figures

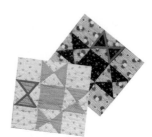

1. **QUILTS** The quilt squares have a pattern of triangles and squares. What do you notice about the red triangles on each quilt square?

If you lay them on top of each other you would find they are the same size and shape.

Figures that have the same size and same shape are **congruent**.

 EXAMPLES   Identify Congruent Figures

Tell whether the two-dimensional figures in each pair are congruent.

2.

The figures have the same size and shape. So, they are congruent.

3.

The figures are the same shape but not the same size. So, they are **similar**.

✓ **CHECK What You Know**

Tell whether each pair of figures is *congruent* or *similar*. See Examples 1–3

1.

2.

3.

4. **TALK MATH** Can a rectangle and a square be congruent? Explain your reasoning.

Tell whether each pair of figures is *congruent* or *similar*.

See Examples 1–3

5.

6.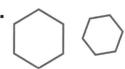

7.

8.

9.

10.

11. One pool measures 16 feet long and 12 feet wide. Another pool measures 12 feet wide and 6 feet long. Are the pools congruent? Explain.

12. All of the rectangular doors in Ani's house are the same size. Ani says they are congruent. Is she correct? Explain.

13. A rectangle has two sides that measure 3 feet and 5 feet. What are the measurements of the other two sides?

14. The sides of a square are each 9 feet long. If there is another square that is congruent to the one described, how long are its sides? Explain how you know.

H.O.T. Problems

15. OPEN ENDED Draw two triangles that are not congruent.

16. WHICH ONE DOESN'T BELONG? Which figure is not congruent to the others? Explain.

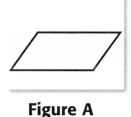

Figure A

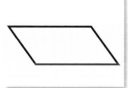

Figure B

Figure C

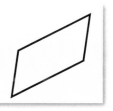

Figure D

17. **WRITE MATH** Do figures have to be in the same position to be congruent? Explain. Draw a picture to support your answer.

Explore Lines of Symmetry

When a figure is folded in half and the sides match exactly, the figure has **symmetry.** The line that the figure was folded on is the **line of symmetry.**

Main Idea

I will explore symmetry of two-dimensional figures.

Materials

paper cutouts of symmetrical and non-symmetrical two-dimensional figures

white paper, scissors

Get ConnectED

ACTIVITY

1 **Find a Line of Symmetry**

Step 1 Hold the paper figure of a square. Bring the top point down to the bottom point. Make a fold.

Step 2 Look at both sides. Do both sides match exactly? The sides match exactly. So, the figure has symmetry.

Step 3 Look for more lines of symmetry by folding the paper in different ways.

Step 4 Look for a line of symmetry on the remaining paper figures. Record your findings on the chart.

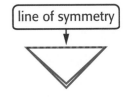

line of symmetry

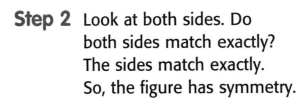

Symmetry	No Symmetry

Think About It

1. Does the square have more than one line of symmetry? Explain.

2. Does the line of symmetry always run from top to bottom? Explain.

3. What are the sides called if they match exactly when folded on a line of symmetry?

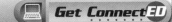

2 Draw Figures with Symmetry

Sonja wants to make a mask. Both sides need to be exactly the same. How can a line of symmetry help?

Step 1 Fold a piece of paper lengthwise.

Step 2 With the fold on the left side, draw the outline of half of the mask. Start at the fold and end at the fold.

Step 3 Cut out the mask. Start at the fold and end at the fold. Carefully poke the scissors through the paper to cut out the eyes.

Step 4 Open up the mask and refold. Do the sides match exactly? Are they congruent?

Think About It

4. Explain why both sides of the mask are exactly the same.

5. You can fold paper to find a line of symmetry. How can you find a line of symmetry in something that cannot be folded, such as a flower?

6. How is the fold line, or line of symmetry, like a mirror?

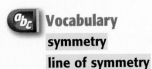

Main Idea

I will analyze two-dimensional figures in order to identify symmetry.

 **Vocabulary**

symmetry

line of symmetry

Get Connect**ED**

Draw Lines of Symmetry

Explore Mini-Activity

Step 1 Trace a hexagon pattern block. Then trace it again to make one figure as shown.

Step 2 Cut out the figure. Fold it in half. Open the figure and trace the fold with a pencil. This is a **line of symmetry**.

Step 3 Fold the figure a different way to find a different line of symmetry.

1. Use the pattern blocks at the right to build a figure with symmetry.

2. Are there any other lines of symmetry? Explain.

Some figures, like the one above, are exact matches when cut in half. This is called **symmetry**. The dashed line is called the **line of symmetry**.

🏃 🖊 **EXAMPLES** Line of Symmetry

Tell whether each figure has a line of symmetry. Write *yes* or *no*. If yes, tell how many lines of symmetry it has.

①

②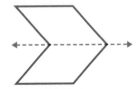

Yes; The figure has one line of symmetry.

Yes; The figure has two lines of symmetry.

When two halves of a figure do not match, the figure does *not* have a line of symmetry.

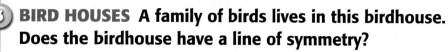

REAL-WORLD EXAMPLE   Line of Symmetry

③ BIRD HOUSES **A family of birds lives in this birdhouse. Does the birdhouse have a line of symmetry?**

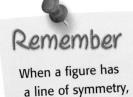

Remember

When a figure has a line of symmetry, the two sides are congruent.

The two halves of the birdhouse do not match.

The birdhouse does not have a line of symmetry.

✓ CHECK **What You Know**

Tell whether each figure has a line of symmetry. Write *yes* or *no*. If yes, tell how many lines of symmetry the figure has.

See Examples 1–3

1.

2.

3.

4.

5.

6.

7. Draw the letter *T,* and draw its lines of symmetry.

8. **TALK MATH** Draw three objects that show examples of symmetry.

Tell whether each figure has a line of symmetry. Write *yes* or *no*. If yes, tell how many lines of symmetry the figure has. See Examples 1–3

9.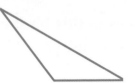

10.

11.

12.

13.

14.

15. Name three capital letters that have a line of symmetry.

16. Name three digits that have a line of symmetry.

17. Explain why Circle A has more than one line of symmetry and Circle B does not.

18. Explain why this line is not the figure's line of symmetry.

A   B

Data File

Each state flag is unique and different. Ohio's flag is the only state flag that is shaped like a pennant, not a rectangle.

19. Which flags at the right have a line of symmetry that runs top to bottom?

20. Which flag at the right does not have any line of symmetry?

21. Which flag at the right has two lines of symmetry?

22. What is the greatest number of lines of symmetry that a rectangle, such as a flag, can have?

Alabama

Arizona

Florida

Ohio

23. OPEN ENDED Draw a picture of half of a figure that shows symmetry. Have a classmate draw the other half.

24. CHALLENGE Look at this picture. How would you test this object to make sure that it shows symmetry?

25. WRITE MATH Can a figure have more than one line of symmetry? Explain.

Test Practice

26. Carolina's charm bracelet has 4 charms. Which charm has more than two lines of symmetry?

(Lesson 2D)

A. moon   **C.** oval

B. pentagon   **D.** heart

27. Which two pieces of the circle are congruent? (Lesson 2B)

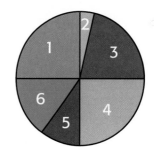

F. 1 and 3   **H.** 3 and 6

G. 1 and 4   **J.** 3 and 4

 Spiral Review

Tell whether each pair of figures is *congruent* or *similar*. (Lesson 2B)

28.

29.

30.

Solve. (Lesson 1F)

31. Christy is painting the walls in three rooms. Each room is shaped like a rectangular solid. How many walls will Christy paint altogether? Explain.

Extend Symmetry

Main Idea

I will use technology to build and draw two-dimensional figures in order to apply symmetry.

REAL-WORLD EXAMPLE

① **Becky has a rectangle. She wants to find its line of symmetry.**

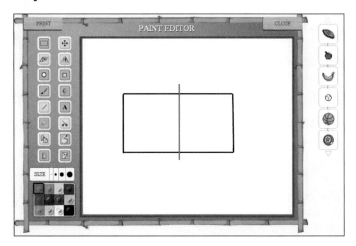

Use the *Math Tool Chest Paint Editor* to draw a rectangle and its line of symmetry.

- Choose the line tool to create a rectangle.
- Choose the line tool to draw one line of symmetry on the rectangle.
- Does the rectangle have other lines of symmetry? Draw them.

Practice and Apply It

Use technology to draw each polygon. Then draw one or more lines of symmetry.

1. triangle
2. rectangle
3. circle
4. pentagon
5. hexagon
6. octagon
7. Name five capital letters of the alphabet that have a line of symmetry. Draw each line of symmetry.
8. **TALK MATH** Explain how to find the line of symmetry of a geometric figure.

Game Time

Art is Shaping Up
Draw Figures

You will need: 10 index cards, white board, marker, or paper and pencil

Get Ready!

Players: 2

Get Set!

Cut the cards in half. Then label the cards with the terms shown.

Go!

⭐ Shuffle the cards. Then spread the cards facedown on the table.

⭐ Player 1 turns over a card and draws the shape. If the drawing is correct, Player 1 keeps the card.

⭐ If Player 1 cannot draw the figure, Player 2 is given a chance to draw the figure.

⭐ Player 2 keeps the card if he or she can draw the figure. If he or she cannot, the card is put back.

⭐ Player 2 selects a card.

⭐ Continue playing until all cards are gone. The player who collects more cards wins.

polygon	octagon
quadrilateral	right angle
triangle	rectangle
pentagon	square
hexagon	rhombus
parallelogram	decagon
trapezoid	irregular polygon

GARDENS UNDER GLASS

There are three large gardens close to the United States Capitol building in Washington, D.C. The Botanic Garden is right across the street. It has more than 4,000 kinds of plants. It also includes a conservatory.

This conservatory is amazing! It is made mostly of glass and aluminum. The conservatory is divided into 10 rooms.

Did You Know?

The Jungle Room is over 80 feet high and has a walkway that is 96 feet long!

Use the diagram below to solve each problem.

1 What two-dimensional figure does the shape of the east and west galleries represent?

2 Which of the labeled rooms do not have a line of symmetry?

3 If a triangle was placed above Oasis to create a two-dimensional figure with five vertices, what polygon would be made?

4 Suppose the Oasis room was cut in half diagonally. What polygons would be created?

5 What two-dimensional figure does the shape of the Meditation Garden and Children's Garden represent? What do you notice about these two rooms?

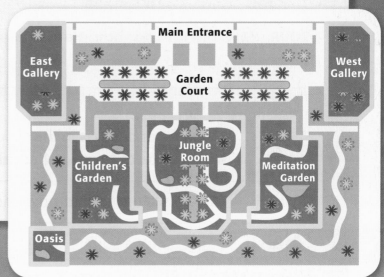

Problem-Solving Investigation

Main Idea I will choose the best strategy to solve a problem.

P.S.I. TEAM +

MATILDA: I made a peanut butter and jelly sandwich in the shape of a square. I cut the bread twice to make 4 equal pieces in the shape of triangles.

YOUR MISSION: Find how Matilda cut her sandwich.

Understand	Matilda's sandwich is in the shape of a square. She cut the sandwich twice to make 4 equal pieces in the shape of triangles.
Plan	Draw a picture to find how she cut her sandwich.
Solve	• First, draw a square to represent the sandwich. • Draw two lines of symmetry to make triangles of equal shape and size. 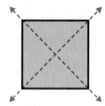 Matilda cut two diagonal lines to make 4 pieces in the shape of triangles.
Check	Since the picture shows 4 congruent triangles, you know the answer is correct. ✓

3.16 The student will identify and describe congruent and noncongruent plane figures.

- Draw a picture.
- Choose an operation.
- Make a table.
- Work backward.

Use any strategy to solve each problem.

1. Brady is planning a party. He sends invitations to 3 friends from his soccer team, 5 friends from school, and 9 neighbors. Seven friends tell him they cannot come. How many friends will come to the party?

2. Ana drew the figures shown. How many figures in Ana's drawing have more than one line of symmetry?

3. Kip shares apple juice with his friends. He drinks 1 cup. His friends each drink one more cup than him. They drink 13 cups of juice in all. How many friends are there?

4. | BAR | DIAGRAM | Tierra ran 4 blocks to her friend's house. Then she ran twice as far to the grocery store. How many blocks did she run in all?

5. Dario runs 2 miles each day for a week. Jordan runs twice as much as Dario. At the end of 7 days, how many miles have Jordan and Dario run altogether?

6. Michelle bought 2 orange juices and 1 bottle of water. Carly bought a bottle of water, milk, and a soda. Who spent more money?

Item	Cost
Orange juice	$1
Milk	$2
Soda	$1
Bottled water	$2

7. Julianna has 3 three-dimensional figures. The figures have a total of 17 flat faces, 32 edges, and 21 vertices. Two of the figures have 6 equally-shaped faces each. What are the names of the three figures?

8. A store is having a sale on fruit at half the original price. Tyson buys 1 cantaloupe, 2 mangos, and 1 apple. How much money did he spend?

Original Fruit Price

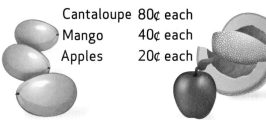

Cantaloupe	80¢ each
Mango	40¢ each
Apples	20¢ each

9. 📝 **WRITE MATH** Look back at Exercise 5. Change the wording so that the *work backward* strategy would have to be used.

Chapter Study Guide and Review

Be sure the following Key Concepts are noted in your Foldable.

Key Concepts

- A **three-dimensional figure** is a solid figure that has length, width, and height. (Lesson 1)

- **Polygons** are closed **two-dimensional figures** that have three or more line segments and angles. (Lesson 1)

quadrilateral   pentagon   octagon

- **Angles** are classified as a right, less than a right, or greater than a right angle. (Lesson 1)

- Polygons can be **congruent** and have **symmetry**. (Lesson 2)

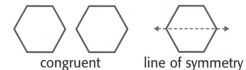

congruent   line of symmetry

Key Vocabulary

- **angle**
- **congruent figures**
- **parallel lines**
- **polygon**
- **quadrilateral**
- **ray**
- **symmetry**

Vocabulary Check

Choose the vocabulary word that completes each sentence.

1. Figures that have the same size and shape are ____?____.

2. A figure has ____?____ when the sides match exactly when cut in half.

3. ____?____ are the same distance apart and never intersect.

4. All ____?____ have 4 sides and 4 angles.

5. A ____?____ has three or more line segments and angles.

6. A ____?____ is part of a line. It has one endpoint and extends in one direction forever.

7. A right ____?____ forms the corner of a square.

Multi-Part Lesson Review

Geometric Figures

Lines, Line Segments, and Rays (Lesson 1A)

Describe each figure as a *point, line, ray,* or *line segment.*

8.
C
D

9.
• *X*

10.

O ●————● *P*

11. ● *F*

12. Draw a pair of perpendicular lines.

Classify the pair of lines as *intersecting, perpendicular,* or *parallel.*

13.

14.

EXAMPLE 1

Describe the figure as a *point, line, ray,* or *line segment.*

B
A ●

The figure has one endpoint. It extends in only one direction without ending. This figure is a *ray.*

EXAMPLE 2

Classify the pair of lines as *intersecting, perpendicular,* or *parallel.*

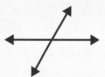

The pair of lines cross. When the lines cross they *do not* make a square corner. These lines are *intersecting.*

Two-Dimensional Figures: Polygons (Lesson 1C)

Describe each two-dimensional figure. Use the terms *sides* and *angles.* Then identify the figure.

15.

16.

17.
4 in.   7 in.
7 in.   4 in.

18.

EXAMPLE 3

The flag of Jamaica is shown. Describe and identify the green polygons.

Each polygon has 3 sides and 3 angles. So, they are triangles.

Quadrilaterals (Lesson 1D)

Describe and identify each quadrilateral by its sides.

19.

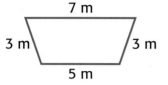

20.

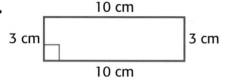

EXAMPLE 4

Describe and identify the figure.

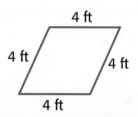

- Opposite angles are the same.
- It has two sets of parallel lines.
- All four sides are the same length.

So, it is a rhombus and a parallelogram.

Problem-Solving Strategy: Guess, Check, and Revise (Lesson 1E)

21. The playhouse windows are polygons with a total of 10 right angles, 1 less than right, and 2 greater than right angles. How many windows are there, and what shapes are they?

22. Mei bought two items. She spent exactly 93¢. What did she buy?

School Supplies	Cost
Eraser	32¢
Pencil	15¢
Pen	20¢
Ruler	61¢

23. There are 20 crayons in a bag. The crayons are red, yellow, and blue. There is the same number of red as yellow. There are twice as many blue as yellow. How many of each color are there?

EXAMPLE 5

Chloe and Dawn are the same age. Tonya is 3 years older than Chloe. The sum of their ages is 39.

Add different combinations of numbers. Check and revise to solve.

Guess			Check
Chloe	Dawn	Tonya	Total
10	10	12	32 No
15	15	17	47 No
12	12	15	39 Yes ✔

So, Chloe and Dawn are each 12 years old and Tonya is 15 years old.

Three-Dimensional Figures (Lesson 1F)

Identify each three-dimensional figure.

24.

25.

26.

27.

28. This figure has 6 faces. All 6 faces are equal in size and shape.

EXAMPLE 6

Identify each three-dimensional figure.

The figure is a pyramid.

A party hat looks like a cone.

Lesson 2 **Spatial Reasoning**

Congruency (Lesson 2B)

Tell whether each pair of figures is _congruent_ or _similar._

29.

30.

31.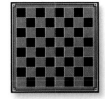

EXAMPLE 7

The figures have the same size and same shape. So, they are congruent.

The figures have the same shape but _not_ the same size. So, they are similar.

Draw Lines of Symmetry (Lesson 2D)

Tell whether each figure has a line of symmetry. Write *yes* or *no.* If yes, tell how many lines of symmetry it has.

32.

33.

EXAMPLE 8

The figure has one line of symmetry.

Problem-Solving Investigation: Choose a Strategy (Lesson 2F)

Solve. Use any strategy.

34. A sidewalk surrounds a rectangular park. What is the total length of the sidewalk?

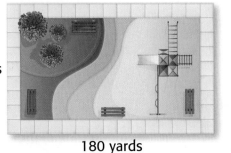

120 yards

180 yards

35. Tanner grabbed a handful of pattern blocks. There are 6 blocks with a total of 26 sides. None of the pattern blocks have a right angle. Which blocks could Tanner have grabbed?

36. Marty says that the hands on her clock form a right angle. What time could it be?

EXAMPLE 9

The school spent $5,585 on math books, $4,090 on a scoreboard, and $3,500 on computers. There is $2,000 left. How much money did the school begin with?

When you have the ending number you need to work backward to find the starting number.

$$
\begin{array}{ll}
\$2,000 & \text{left} \\
\$3,500 & \text{computers} \\
\$4,090 & \text{scoreboard} \\
+\,\$5,585 & \text{math books} \\
\hline
\$15,175 & \text{money at start}
\end{array}
$$

The school began with $15,175.

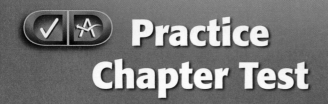

1. Draw and label an example of a line segment.

Classify each pair of lines as *intersecting*, *perpendicular*, or *parallel*.

2.

3.

Describe each two-dimensional figure. Use the terms *sides* and *angles*. Then identify each figure.

4.

5.

Describe each figure by classifying the angle as a *right, less than* a right, or *greater than* a right angle.

6.

7.

8. MULTIPLE CHOICE Which statement about these figures is true?

A. There is one polygon.

B. These are all polygons.

C. There are two polygons.

D. None of these are polygons.

Describe and identify each quadrilateral.

9.

10.

11. There are 3 dogs in the park. Fido is 5 pounds heavier than Buttercup. Buttercup is three times as heavy as Jupiter. Jupiter weighs 8 pounds. How much do Fido and Buttercup each weigh? Use any strategy.

12. Compare the set of polygons. Explain how they are alike and different.

 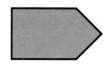

13. MULTIPLE CHOICE Which picture best represents a cone?

F.

H.

G.

J.

14. **WRITE MATH** Tell if these two figures are congruent. Explain.

TEST EXAMPLE

Angie drew a figure that has 8 sides and 8 angles. Which figure did she draw?

A. right triangle

B. trapezoid

C. pentagon

D. octagon

Read the Question

You need to use the description to identify the figure.

Solve the Question

The figure has 8 sides and 8 angles.

So, the figure is an octagon.

The answer is D.

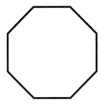

Read each question. Then fill in the correct answer on the answer sheet provided by your teacher or on a separate sheet of paper.

1. Which figure is a hexagon?

A.

C.

B.

D.

2. Which polygon has fewer angles than a quadrilateral?

F. hexagon

G. pentagon

H. square

J. triangle

3. Which pair of figures is congruent?

A.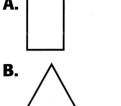

B.

C.

D.

4. Three friends were playing a basketball game. Diego won by 15 points. Marissa had 10 points more than Hannah. If Hannah had 20 points, how many points did Diego and Marissa have?

F. Diego 15; Marissa 10

G. Diego 15; Marissa 30

H. Diego 35; Marissa 10

J. Diego 45; Marissa 30

5. Which angle appears to be a right angle?

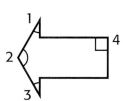

A. 1   **B.** 2   **C.** 3   **D.** 4

6. The outline of which road sign appears to have only one line of symmetry?

F.   **H.** CALIFORNIA U S 66

G.  STOP   **J.**  REST AREA 2 km

7. Which of the following describes the shape of the globe?

A. sphere   **C.** cone

B. cube   **D.** pyramid

8. How could you classify the pair of lines below?

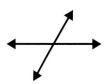

F. intersecting and perpendicular

G. parallel and intersecting

H. perpendicular but not intersecting

J. intersecting but not perpendicular

NEED EXTRA HELP?

If You Missed Question . . .	1	2	3	4	5	6	7	8
Go to Chapter-Lesson . . .	7-1C	7-1D	7-2B	7-1E	7-1B	7-2D	7-1F	7-1A
For help with . . .	SOL 3.14	SOL 3.14	SOL 3.16	SOL 3.1c	SOL 3.15	SOL 3.14	SOL 3.14	SOL 3.15

Use Patterns and Algebraic Thinking

connectED.mcgraw-hill.com

Investigate

Animations

Vocabulary

Math Songs

Multilingual eGlossary

Learn

Personal Tutor

Virtual Manipulatives

Audio

Foldables

Practice

Self-Check Practice

eGames

Worksheets

Assessment

The ☆BIG Idea

How can I use words, variables, tables, and graphs to create and analyze patterns and relationships?

FOLDABLES
Study Organizer

Make this Foldable to help you organize information about patterns and algebraic thinking. Begin with one sheet of 11″ × 17″ paper.

Geometric Patterns | Number Patterns
Number Sentences | Function Tables

Review Vocabulary

graph grafica an organized drawing that shows sets of data and how they are related to each other

Key Vocabulary

English	Español
pattern	patrón
rule	regla
function	función
variable	variable

When Will I Use This?

The Team in A Successful Season

Game 1

Good game, Tigers! We scored 35 points!

During the season I am going to keep track of the points everyone scores.

Then we can see if there are any patterns.

Game 3

Great game, Tigers! We scored 40 points!

Before Game 5

Our last game is tomorrow. Let's review your scores from the first 4 games.

Jaime, you doubled your points in each game. Carlos and Luke each made the same number of points in each game.

If our pattern continues, how many points should we score tomorrow?

Your Turn!
You will solve this problem in the chapter.

Are You Ready for the Chapter?

You have two options for checking Prerequisite Skills for this chapter.

Text Option Take the Quick Check below.

QUICK Check

Identify a pattern. Then fill in the missing numbers.

1. 30, 40, 50, ■, 70, ■

2. 20, 25, ■, 35, ■

3. 43, 45, ■, ■, 51

4. 105, ■, 85, ■, 65

Add or subtract.

5. 9 + 3

6. 12 + 7

7. 16 + 5

8. 32 + 43

9. 11 − 4

10. 20 − 6

11. 25 − 8

12. 38 − 22

Multiply or divide.

13. 5 × 6

14. 3 × 8

15. 18 ÷ 2

16. 28 ÷ 4

17. Abia sold 1 more candle for the fundraiser than Melanie. Together, they sold 15 candles. Draw a picture that shows how many candles they each sold.

18. Daniela spent $20 at the grocery store and $15 at the toy store. How much did she spend in all? Show how you can solve this problem using numbers.

19. Each toy shown costs $5. Show how you can find the total cost using an addition sentence.

 Online Option Take the Online Readiness Quiz.

Main Idea

I will analyze, represent, and extend geometric patterns using words.

 **Vocabulary**

pattern

Get Connect**ED**

3.19 The student will recognize and describe a variety of patterns formed using numbers, tables, and pictures, and extend the patterns, using the same or different forms.

Geometric Patterns

A **pattern** is a series of numbers or figures that follow a rule.

REAL-WORLD EXAMPLES   Extend a Pattern

TILES Maddie's mom is installing a tile floor in their kitchen. What colors of tiles will continue the pattern in the next row?

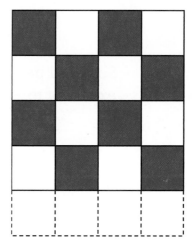

① **Represent the geometric pattern using words.**

Maddie's mom installs a row of blue, white, blue, white tiles. This is followed by a row of white, blue, white, blue tiles.

② **Extend the pattern using words.**

The next row will be blue, white, blue, white tiles.

3 SCHOOL Mrs. Pembroke shows her students the pattern below. She asks them to represent the pattern using words. Then she asks, "How many red pattern blocks will be used if the pattern extends until there are a total of 14 polygons?"

Remember

There may be more than one pattern in a row of numbers or figures.

The pattern is yellow, green, red, green.

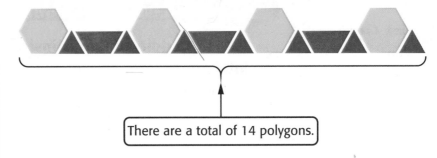

There are a total of 14 polygons.

So, 3 red pattern blocks will be used when the pattern is extended to a total of 14 polygons.

CHECK What You Know

Represent and extend each pattern using words. See Examples 1 and 2

1.

2.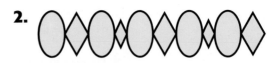

Represent each pattern using words. Then solve. See Example 3

3. **Geometry** How many triangles will be used if this pattern continues until there are a total of 30 polygons?

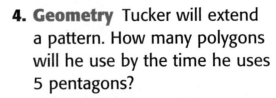

4. **Geometry** Tucker will extend a pattern. How many polygons will he use by the time he uses 5 pentagons?

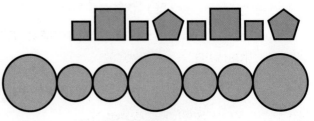

5. **TALK MATH** Explain why the pattern of circles to the right can be described as an ABBA pattern.

Represent and extend each pattern using words.

See Examples 1 and 2

6. 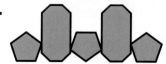   **7.**    **8.**

9. 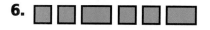   **10.** 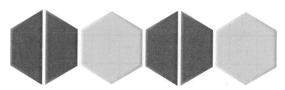   **11.**

Represent each pattern using words. Then solve. See Example 3

12. How many red pattern blocks will be used if the pattern is extended until there are a total of 13 polygons?

13. How many hexagons will be used if the pattern is extended until there are a total of 25 polygons?

Solve.

14. Geometry A banner has a pattern of 4 triangles and 2 squares. How many polygons will there be if this pattern is shown 5 times?

15. Geometry Susie painted a row of 15 circles. The pattern is 2 red circles and 3 blue circles with a green circle after each blue circle. How many green circles are there?

16. Geometry A pattern shows 2 triangles and 1 square. A hexagon is placed between each triangle. How many triangles are there when the pattern is extended to a total of 17 shapes?

17. Measurement Each side of each polygon is 1 inch. As the pattern is extended, how many polygons are needed so that the distance around the polygons equals 32 inches?

H.O.T. Problems

18. OPEN ENDED Create a pattern using three different shapes. Explain your pattern.

19. WRITE MATH Explain where you see geometric patterns in real-world objects.

Main Idea

I will identify and extend number patterns.

3.19 The student will recognize and describe a variety of patterns formed using numbers, tables, and pictures, and extend the patterns, using the same or different forms.

Number Patterns

Number patterns are everywhere. Look at the speed limit signs shown. What number pattern do you see?

A hundred chart shows many number patterns.

1	2	3	4	5	6	7	8	9	10
11	12	13	14	15	16	17	18	19	20
21	22	23	24	25	26	27	28	29	30
31	32	33	34	35	36	37	38	39	40
41	42	43	44	45	46	47	48	49	50
51	52	53	54	55	56	57	58	59	60
61	62	63	64	65	66	67	68	69	70
71	72	73	74	75	76	77	78	79	80
81	82	83	84	85	86	87	88	89	90
91	92	93	94	95	96	97	98	99	100

EXAMPLE   Identify a Number Pattern

① **Identify a pattern in 15, 25, 35, 45, ■. Then find the missing number.**

The pattern shows that 10 is added to each number.

15,   25,   35,   45,   ■
  +10   +10   +10   +10

The missing number is 55.

REAL-WORLD EXAMPLE — Identify a Number Pattern

2 **READING** Lakeisha is reading a book. If the pattern continues, how many pages will she read on Saturday?

Each day, Lakeisha reads 3 more pages than the day before.

Pages Lakeisha Read

Day	Pages
Monday	3
Tuesday	6
Wednesday	9
Thursday	12
Friday	15
Saturday	▨

3,   6,   9,   12,   15,   18

+3   +3   +3   +3   +3

So, Lakeisha will read 18 pages on Saturday.

REAL-WORLD EXAMPLE — Extend a Number Pattern

3 **SPORTS** Meg's bowling scores are 150, 145, 140, ▨, 130, ▨. Find the missing numbers in the pattern.

Notice that 5 is subtracted from each number before it.

150, 145, 140, 135, 130, 125

−5   −5   −5   −5   −5

The missing numbers are 135 and 125.

✓ CHECK What You Know

Identify a pattern. Then find the missing numbers. See Examples 1–3

1. 10, 12, 14, 16, ▨, 20

2. 5, 10, 15, 20, ▨, 30

3. 20, ▨, 40, 50, ▨, 70

4. 110, 107, ▨, 101, 98, ▨

5. A track team runs 4 laps on Day 1, 6 laps on Day 2, and 8 laps on Day 3. The pattern continues. How many laps will they run on Day 5?
See Example 3

6. **TALK MATH** Suppose you start at 20 and skip count to 36. Are you skip counting by 3s? Explain.

Identify a pattern. Then find the missing numbers. See Examples 1–3

7. 10, 14, 18, ■, 26, 30

8. 13, 18, 23, ■, 33, 38

9. 28, 24, 20, ■, 12, 8

10. 63, 60, ■, 54, 51, 48

11. 34, 36, ■, 40, ■, 44

12. 71, 76, 81, ■, 91, ■

13. 105, 100, ■, 90, ■, 80

14. 100, 110, 120, ■, ■

15. Each soccer player below has a number. If the pattern continues, what is Takisha's number?

Soccer Players' Numbers	
Name	**Number**
Kisho	3
Kayla	5
Michael	7
Lenora	9
Takisha	■

16. Christian is saving his allowance. How much money will he have saved at week 5? at week 10?

Dillon's Savings	
Week	**Total Saved**
1	$4
2	$8
3	$12
4	$16
5	■

17. Elki draws 6 stars, 10 stars, 14 stars, and 18 stars. He continues the pattern. How many stars will he draw next?

18. **Measurement** A school bell rings at 8:15, 8:45, 9:15, and 9:45. The pattern continues when the next bell rings. What time is it?

Use the information to solve the problem.

A Successful Season

Remember, Coach is sharing our individual stats for the season.

Tiger Basketball Team Points					
Player	Game 1	Game 2	Game 3	Game 4	Game 5
Jaime	1	2	4	8	
Carlos	6	6	6	6	
Nate	8	10	12	14	
Luke	10	10	10	10	
Jacob	14	13	12	11	
Total	35	37	40	45	

19. If the scoring pattern continues, how many points should each player on the Tigers team score at tomorrow's game? What will be the total for the game?

H.O.T. Problems

20. OPEN ENDED Create a number pattern. Explain your pattern.

21.  **WRITE MATH** Describe the pattern that can produce
the numbers 104, 99, 94, 89, ... What number is next?

Test Practice

22. The triangles decrease in size.
If the pattern is extended, what is
the measure of the height of the
next triangle? (Lesson 1A)

17 in.   12 in.   8 in.   5 in.

A. 4 in.

B. 3 in.

C. 2 in.

D. 1 in.

23. All of these figures are *pulanes.*

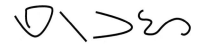

None of these figures are *pulanes.*

Which of these is NOT a *pulane*?
(Lesson 1A)

F. ⬜ (trapezoid)   **H.** ⬜ (rounded rectangle)

G. ⬭ (oval)   **J.** 〽 (curve)

Spiral Review

24. Ella is making a pattern with chalk. The pattern is 1 pink,
3 yellow, 2 blue, and 1 green piece of chalk. How many
yellow pieces of chalk will she use if she extends this pattern
until there are 30 pieces of chalk? (Lesson 1B)

Represent each pattern using words. Then solve. (Lesson 1A)

25. , , ___ , ,

26. , , , ___

Problem-Solving Strategy: Look for a Pattern

Main Idea I will solve a problem by looking for a pattern.

 Christina is making a pattern with colored tiles. In the first row, she uses 2 tiles. She uses 4 tiles in the second row and 8 tiles in the third row. If she continues the pattern, how many tiles will be in the sixth row?

Understand **What facts do you know?**

- There will be 2 tiles in the first row, 4 tiles in the second row, and 8 tiles in the third row.

What do you need to find?

- How many tiles will be in row six?

Plan You can first make a table of the information. Then look for a pattern.

Solve

- First, put the information in a table.

- Look for a pattern. The numbers double.

- Once you know the pattern, you can continue it.

So, there will be 64 tiles in the sixth row.

1st	2nd	3rd	4th	5th	6th
2	4	8			

+2 +4 +8

$8 + 8 = 16$

$16 + 16 = 32$

$32 + 32 = 64$

Check Complete the table using the pattern.

There are 64 tiles in the sixth row. ✓

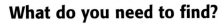

1st	2nd	3rd	4th	5th	6th
2	4	8	16	32	64

+2 +4 +8 +16 +32

 3.19 The student will recognize and describe a variety of patterns formed using numbers, tables, and pictures, and extend the patterns, using the same or different forms.

EXTEND

Refer to the problem on the previous page.

1. Look back at the Example. Check your answer. How do you know that it is correct? Show your work.

2. Explain how you identified the pattern for this problem.

3. Suppose there are 4 tiles in the first row, 8 in the second, and 16 in the third. How many tiles are in row 6?

4. Why is it a good idea to put the information in a table first?

PRACTICE

EXTRA PRACTICE
Begins on page EP2.

Solve. Use the *look for a pattern* strategy.

5. Algebra A set of bowling pins is shown. If there are 3 more rows, how many pins are there in all?

6. Yutaka is planting 24 flowers. He uses a pattern of 1 daisy and then 2 tulips. If the pattern continues, how many tulips will he use?

7. Measurement Adelina makes 3 hops forward and then 1 hop back. Each hop is 1 foot. How many hops does she make before she has gone 2 yards forward? (*Hint:* There are 3 feet in 1 yard.)

8. Jacy mows lawns every other day. He earns $5 the first day. After that, he earns $1 more than the time before. If he starts mowing on the first day of the month, how much money will he earn on day 19?

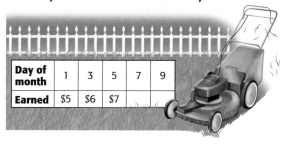

Day of month	1	3	5	7	9
Earned	$5	$6	$7		

9. Algebra Shandra is collecting cans for a recycling drive. If the pattern continues, how many cans will she collect in week 5?

Week	1	2	3	4	5
Cans	6	12	24		

10. **WRITE MATH** Explain how the *look for a pattern* strategy helps you solve problems.

Explore Represent Patterns

Main Idea

I will explore how to represent patterns with words and numbers and in graphs.

Materials

plain paper

scissors

pattern blocks: squares and triangles

3.19 The student will recognize and describe a variety of patterns formed using numbers, tables, and pictures, and extend the patterns, using the same or different forms.

Mrs. Parker is cutting colored paper into equal-sized pieces. First, she cuts one piece of paper in half. Then she cuts each of those pieces in half. Mrs. Parker cuts the pieces into halves one more time. How many pieces of paper will she have after the third set of cuts?

ACTIVITY

1 **Represent a Pattern**

Step 1 **Model the paper cuts.**

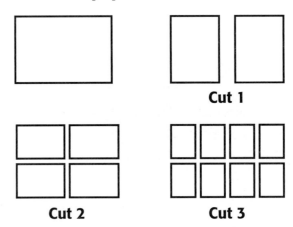

Cut 1

Cut 2

Cut 3

Step 2 **Use words to represent the pattern.**
The number of pieces of paper doubles as each new set of cuts is made.

Step 3 **Use a table to represent the pattern.**

Set of cuts	1	2	3
Pieces	2	4	8

So, the number of pieces of paper after the third set of cuts is 8.

Think About It

1. How many pieces of paper will there be after the fourth set of cuts? How do you know?

Mr. Hess is arranging tables and chairs for Family Math Night. There are 6 square tables. One chair will fit on each side of the table. How many people can be seated at all the tables?

ACTIVITY

2 **Use Words and a Graph**

Step 1 **Find how many people can sit at each table.** Model one set of tables and chairs.

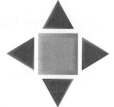

Step 2 **Use words to represent the pattern.** Four people will sit at each table.

Step 3 **Use a pictograph to represent and extend the pattern.**

Family Math Night	
1 Table	🧍
2 Tables	🧍 🧍
3 Tables	🧍 🧍 🧍
4 Tables	🧍 🧍 🧍 🧍
5 Tables	🧍 🧍 🧍 🧍 🧍
6 Tables	🧍 🧍 🧍 🧍 🧍 🧍
key: 🧍 = 4 people	

🧍 × 6 = 24

So, 24 people can sit at 6 tables.

Think About It

2. Suppose Mr. Hess found another square table. How many more people can be seated? What is the total number of people that can be seated now?

3. Mr. Hess decided he would like to use longer tables. Each long table will be made by pushing 2 of the square tables together. One person can still sit at each open end and two on each side of each long table. How many people can be seated with this arrangement? Use pattern blocks to model the problem.

4. **WRITE MATH** Does using a graph help you recognize a pattern? Explain.

Main Idea

I will create, analyze, and represent patterns using graphs and words.

 Get ConnectED

 **3.19** The student will recognize and describe a variety of patterns formed using numbers, tables, and pictures, and extend the patterns, using the same or different forms.

Patterns in Graphs

Graphs can be helpful in analyzing patterns.

🏃 ✏️ **REAL-WORLD EXAMPLE**   **Use a Pictograph**

① **PATTERNS** The grocery store has a special on apples. If you buy 2 apples, you get 1 free. If you buy 3 apples, you get 2 free. You get 3 free apples if you buy 4. Represent the pattern with words. Use the pictograph to find the number of free apples you get when you buy 5.

Apple Special	
Buy 2	🍎
Buy 3	🍎
Buy 4	🍎 🍎
Buy 5	🍎 🍎
key: 🍎 = 2 free apples	

Words The pattern is the number of free apples equals the number of apples bought minus 1.

So, if you buy 5 apples, you get 4 free.

✏️ **REAL-WORLD EXAMPLE**   **Use a Bar Graph**

② **SPORTS** The yards gained by the football team on 4 plays are shown. Represent the pattern in a bar graph and with words.

5, 10, 15, 20

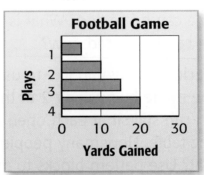

Words The pattern is add five.

3 **WEATHER** The number of sunny and cloudy days in a row make a pattern. Represent the pattern with words. Then extend the graph.

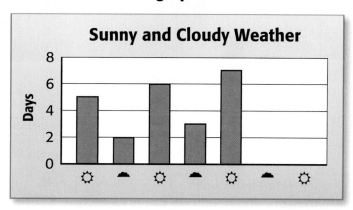

Sunny and Cloudy Weather

Remember

When a bar stops between two lines, its value is between the numbers before and after the end of the bar.

Words The number of cloudy days is 3 less than the sunny days before it. The number of sunny days is 4 more than the cloudy days before it.

Extend the pattern.

$$5 - 3 = 2$$
$$2 + 4 = 6$$
$$6 - 3 = 3$$
$$3 + 4 = 7$$
$$7 - 3 = 4$$
$$4 + 4 = 8$$

✓ CHECK What You Know

Represent each pattern using words. Then extend the graph.

See Examples 1 and 3

1.

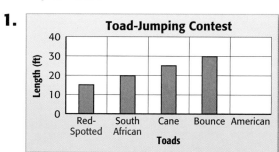

Toad-Jumping Contest

2.

Family Members					
Wilkins	☺	☺	☺	☺	☺
Laynes	☺	☺	☺	☺	
Millers	☺	☺	☺		
Estafans	☺	☺			
Pitzers					
key: ☺ = 2 family members					

3. Represent the pattern in a graph and with words. See Example 2

22, 24, 27, 31, 36, ■

4. **TALK MATH** What does it mean to extend a pattern? Can a pattern be extended forever?

Represent each pattern using words. Then extend the graph.

See Examples 1 and 3

5.

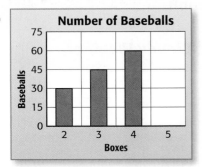

6.

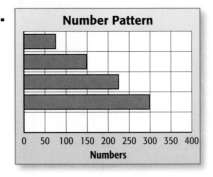

7.

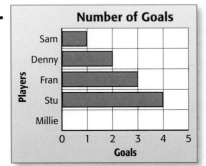

8.

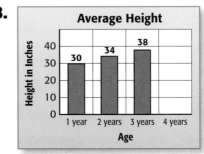

Represent the pattern in a graph and with words. See Example 2

9. 25, 23, 20, 18, 15, ▦

10. 15, 20, 30, 35, 45, ▦

11. There are 10 pencils and 2 red pens in each package. How many packages would you have to buy to get 24 red pens?

12. The border of a bulletin board has a pattern of 35 blue and orange stars. Every fourth star is orange. How many blue stars are there?

13. How many weeks will it take Becca to save enough money to buy a $20 CD? She has saved a total of $3 the first week. By the second week she has a total of $6, and a total of $9 the third week.

14. How many boxes will a large and an extra large bag hold together?

Bag size	Small	Medium	Large	X Large
Boxes	4	7	10	▦

H.O.T. Problems

15. CHALLENGE Create a pattern and represent it in a graph.

16. 📝 **WRITE MATH** Suppose you wanted to extend this pattern ten more steps: 2, 6, 12, 20, 30
Is there a way to extend it without writing each step?

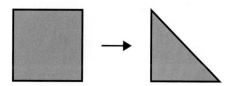

17. Pacho folded a square piece of paper in half on the diagonal.

He continued to fold the paper in half 3 more times. How many triangles were there once he unfolded the paper? (Lesson 1D)

A. 4   **C.** 12

B. 8   **D.** 16

18. A roller coaster ride has 6 cars. Each car has 2 benches and each bench holds 2 people. The ride lasts 3 minutes. How many people can ride the roller coaster in 30 minutes? (Lesson 1C)

F. 30 people

G. 72 people

H. 240 people

J. 720 people

Solve. (Lesson 1C)

19. Dwayne rolled a number cube 5 times. What pattern do you see?

20. Alvin is training for a race. The first week he runs 2 miles. The next week he runs 5 miles, and the third week he runs 8 miles. How many weeks will it be when he reaches 20 miles?

Identify a pattern. Then find the missing numbers. (Lesson 1B)

21. 1,020; ▇; 1,060; 1,080; ▇

22. 107, 101, ▇, 89, ▇

23. Identify the pattern of Byron's stamp collection.

24. Extend the pattern until 7 squares have been drawn. What is the total number of polygons? (Lesson 1A)

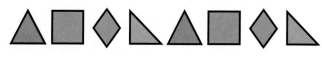

Game Time

Pick a Pattern
Geometric Patterns

You will need: pattern blocks and a brown paper lunch bag

Get Ready!

Players: 2 players

Get Set!

Place about 50 pattern blocks in a brown paper bag.

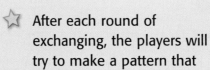

Go!

⭐ Each player takes 15 pattern blocks from the bag without looking. Then each player lays them out on the table.

⭐ Looking at the blocks, each player tries to make a shape or color pattern with his or her own 15 blocks.

⭐ Player 1 may take one unwanted pattern block, return it to the bag, and take a new one without looking.

⭐ Player 2 does the same.

⭐ After each round of exchanging, the players will try to make a pattern that includes their new block.

⭐ The players will continue with rounds of exchanging until 1 player has a pattern of 15 blocks.

Mid-Chapter Check

Represent and extend each pattern using words. (Lesson 1A)

1.

2.

Represent each pattern using words. Then solve. (Lesson 1A)

3. How many sticks will there be by the time there are 20 circles?

4. What will be the total number of polygons by the time the stick is on top of the triangle again?

Identify a pattern. Then find the missing numbers. (Lesson 1B)

5. 0, 5, 15, 20, 30, ■, 45, ■

6. ■, 46, 50, ■, 58, 62

7. **MULTIPLE CHOICE** Erasers are sold in packages of 3. Which number could NOT be a total of erasers bought?
(Lesson 1B)

   A. 6   **C.** 13

   B. 9   **D.** 15

8. Devesh takes care of his two dogs. He feeds each dog 3 treats each day. How many treats does he give the dogs in one week? (Lesson 1C)

9. For his first lost tooth, Hernan received one quarter. He gets 10¢ more every time he loses another tooth. He received 3 quarters for the last tooth he lost. How many teeth has he lost? (Lesson 1C)

10. Represent the pattern using words. Then extend the graph. (Lesson 1E)

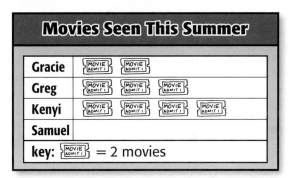

11. **MULTIPLE CHOICE** How wide will the next quadrilateral be if the pattern continues? (Lesson 1B)

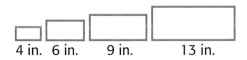

   F. 17 in.   **H.** 19 in.

   G. 18 in.   **J.** 20 in.

12. **WRITE MATH** Write a number pattern that is add 3 then subtract 2. Extend it so it has 5 numbers.
(Lesson 1B)

Explore Model Expressions

Main Idea

I will explore modeling expressions using pictures, numbers, and words.

Materials

counters

 Get ConnectED

3.19 The student will recognize and describe a variety of patterns formed using numbers, tables, and pictures, and extend the patterns, using the same or different forms.
3.20 The student will **a)** investigate the identity and the commutative properties for addition and multiplication; and **b)** identify examples of the identity and commutative properties for addition and multiplication.

An **expression** is a combination of numbers and operations that represents a quantity. An expression does not have an equals sign.

ACTIVITIES

① **Alice invited three friends to play in her backyard.**

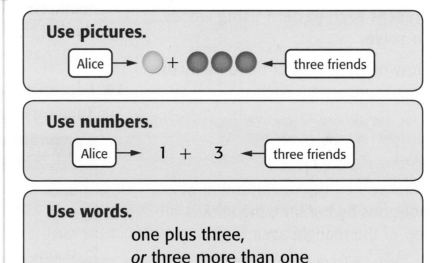

Use pictures.

Alice → ○ + ●●● ← three friends

Use numbers.

Alice → 1 + 3 ← three friends

Use words.

one plus three,
or three more than one

② **There were five cartons of milk. Joe drank one.**

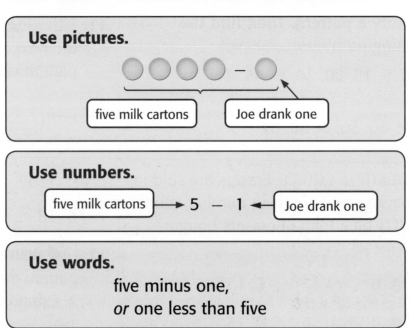

Use pictures.

○○○○ – ○

five milk cartons   Joe drank one

Use numbers.

five milk cartons → 5 – 1 ← Joe drank one

Use words.

five minus one,
or one less than five

3 **Tracy has four pretzels. Scott has two times as many.**

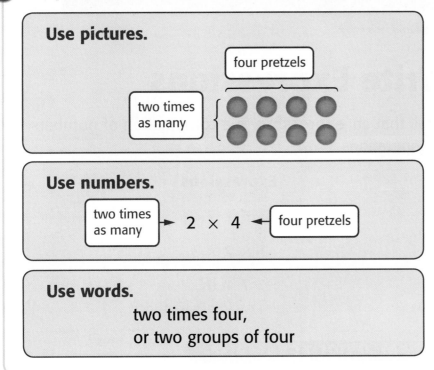

Use pictures.

four pretzels

two times as many

Use numbers.

two times as many → 2 × 4 ← four pretzels

Use words.

two times four,
or two groups of four

Think About It

1. In Activity 2, why is one of the counters separate from the others?

2. How did you know what operation to use in Activity 3?

3. Model the following with pictures, numbers, and words.

six fish were equally caught by two fishermen

Practice and Apply It

Model each expression with pictures, numbers, and words.

4. Jeff had 12 crayons. He lost 5 of them.

5. The soccer team scored 1 point. They gained 4 more points.

6. A carpenter had 6 nails. She went to the store to buy 8 more.

7. 10 sandwiches were served. 6 sandwiches were eaten.

8. **WRITE MATH** Write an expression using numbers. Model the expression using words and pictures.

Main Idea
I will write expressions.

Vocabulary
expression

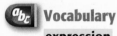

3.19 The student will recognize and describe a variety of patterns formed using numbers, tables, and pictures, and extend the patterns, using the same or different forms.
3.20 The student will
a) investigate the identity and the commutative properties for addition and multiplication; and **b)** identify examples of the identity and commutative properties for addition and multiplication.

Write Expressions

Recall that an **expression** is a combination of numbers and operations.

Expressions

$$6 + 7$$

$$1 \times 2 \times 3$$

$$7 - 0$$

REAL-WORLD EXAMPLES   **Model and Write Expressions**

1. **MONEY** Tomás has $10. Aisha has $5 more than Tomás. Use numbers and an operation to write an expression that shows the amount of money Aisha has.

Aisha	more than	Tomás
$5	+	$10

The expression is $5 + $10.

2. **AGE** Omar's age is Tiffany's age minus 7 years. Tiffany is 12 years old. Write an expression to show Omar's age.

Tiffany's age	minus	years
12	−	7

The expression is 12 − 7.

Remember

Read carefully to understand what operation you should use.

3 SWINGS There are 5 swing sets at a playground. Each swing set has 3 swings. Use numbers and an operation to write an expression for the total number of swings.

swing sets	groups of	swings
5	×	3

The expression is 5 × 3.

4 DOGS A group of dogs has a total of 36 legs. Write an expression for the number of dogs.

total legs	equal number	legs per dog
36	÷	4

The expression is 36 ÷ 4.

✓ CHECK What You Know

Use numbers and an operation to write each phrase as an expression. See Examples 1–4

1. 4 more than 7

2. the total of 5 rows of 6 chairs

3. half of 18

4. 3 people equally divide $21

5. Each package of muffin mix makes 8 muffins. When Taryn makes 3 packages, how many muffins will she have altogether? Write an expression.

6. **TALK MATH** Explain how you know what operation to use when writing an expression for the phrase *total of 7 teams of 8 players each.*

Practice and Problem Solving

Use numbers and an operation to write each phrase as an expression. See Examples 1–4

7. difference between 89 and 80

8. 6 groups have 6 people

9. 8 more than 45

10. the product of 8 and 4

11. 12 more than 18

12. 5 people equally share 10 apples

13. walk 2 blocks 3 times a day

14. 7 pencils and 5 pens in a box

There are 6 pinwheels in the ground. Write an expression to tell how many there will be when there are: See Examples 1–4

15. 2 fewer pinwheels

16. 4 times as many pinwheels

17. half as many pinwheels

18. 10 more pinwheels

19. 3 equal groups of pinwheels

Write an expression for each situation.

20. There were 6 groups of scouts. Each group earned 9 badges. How many badges did the scouts earn in all?

21. Mr. Lewis bought 3 flats of flowers for a total of $22. How much change should he receive if he paid with two $20 bills?

REAL-WORLD PROBLEM SOLVING

Shopping There is a sale on school supplies. Write an expression for each situation.

22. the cost of 5 bottles of glue

23. the difference between the price of flash cards and a pack of pens

24. the number of notebooks for $1.00

25. the total cost of crayons, markers, and glue

BIG

School Supplies Sale

Item	Price
Glue	20¢
Markers	50¢
Flash cards	$1.00
Crayons	10¢
Pens	50¢
Notebook	10¢

H.O.T. Problems

OPEN ENDED Write one phrase for each expression.

26. 35 ÷ 5   **27.** 9 + 18   **28.** 3 × 7   **29.** 36 − 12

30. WHICH ONE DOESN'T BELONG? Identify the expression that does not belong. Explain.

| $25 more than $30 | total of 16 and 17 | number of cats that have 20 legs | the total of 12, 15, and 17 |

31. **WRITE MATH** Write two word phrases for the expression 18 ÷ 3.

 **Test Practice**

32. Seven cars on the ferris wheel have five people each. Which sign completes the expression?

(Lesson 2B)

7 ▢ 5

A. +

B. −

C. ×

D. ÷

33. Six mother ducks are in a pond. Each duck has 6 ducklings. Which expression shows how to find the total number of ducklings?

(Lesson 2B)

F. 6 − 6

G. 6 ÷ 6

H. 6 + 6

J. 6 × 6

Spiral Review

34. Silvia rode her bike 3 laps around the block on Sunday. Monday she rode 6 laps. She made 15 laps on Thursday. With this pattern, how many laps did she ride on Tuesday and Wednesday? Represent the pattern in a graph and with words.

(Lessons 1E and 1C)

Identify a pattern. Then find the missing numbers. (Lesson 1B)

35. 28, 32, 36, ___, ___   **36.** 732, 727, ___, 717, ___   **37.** 185, 235, 285, ___, ___

Main Idea
I will write and solve number sentences.

 Vocabulary
number sentence

 Get ConnectED

 3.20 The student will **a)** investigate the identity and the commutative properties for addition and multiplication; and **b)** identify examples of the identity and commutative properties for addition and multiplication.
3.19 The student will recognize and describe a variety of patterns formed using numbers, tables, and pictures, and extend the patterns, using the same or different forms.

Write Number Sentences

A **number sentence** is an expression using numbers and the equals sign (=).

REAL-WORLD EXAMPLE

Write Number Sentences

septagon   decagon

① **POLYGONS** A decagon is a polygon that has ten sides. Another polygon, septagon, has seven sides. Model and write a number sentence that shows the difference in the number of sides.

To find the difference, you can subtract.

Models

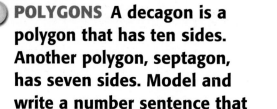

> The model shows 10 cubes. Subtract 7 cubes.

Words   After subtracting 7 cubes from 10, there are 3 cubes left. 10 minus 7 equals 3.

Number Sentence $10 - 7 = 3$

The number sentence $10 - 7 = 3$ shows the difference in the number of sides of the polygons.

REAL-WORLD EXAMPLE

Write Number Sentences

② **RECESS** There are 12 students on the playground. They are equally grouped playing ball, jumping rope, and playing on swings. Model and write a number sentence to show how many students are in each group.

Pictures

Words Twelve students equally divided into three groups equals four students in each group.

Number Sentence $12 \div 3 = 4$

Sometimes a number may be unknown, or missing, in a number sentence.

Explore Mini-Activity

Find 4 + ▦ = 9.

Step 1 Model the left side of the number sentence. The cup represents the unknown.

Step 2 Model the right side of the number sentence.

Step 3 Put counters in the cup until the number on each side of the equals sign is the same.

The number sentence is solved when you find the unknown.

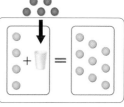

$4 + ▦ = 9$

$4 + 5 = 9$

Remember

When looking for an unknown number, try inverse operations.

 EXAMPLE Solve Number Sentences

3 **Solve the number sentence 2 × ▦ = 8 by finding the unknown.**

$2 × ▦ = 8$

$2 × 4 = 8$

> THINK 2 times what number equals 8?

So, the number sentence is $2 × 4 = 8$.

✓ CHECK What You Know

Write a number sentence for each situation. Use models, if needed. See Examples 1–2

1. On Monday 12 newspapers are delivered on my street. On Tuesday, 18 papers are delivered. How many papers are delivered altogether?

2. Felisha had $20. She spent $3 on her lunch, $5 at the movies, and $9 at the toy store. How much money was left?

Solve each number sentence by finding the unknown. See Example 3

3. $14 + ▦ = 21$

4. $30 - ▦ = 18$

5. $12 + 3 + ▦ = 19$

6. Mark has 25 toys. Draw a picture and write a number sentence to show how many toys Mark will give away if he keeps 4.

7. **TALK MATH** Describe a real-world problem that uses a number sentence with several numbers.

Write a number sentence for each situation. Use models, if needed. See Examples 1–2

8. Jessie picked 85 strawberries and 72 blueberries. How many berries did Jessie pick altogether?

9. A truck driver drove 548 miles one day and 163 miles the next day. How much farther did the truck driver travel on the first day?

10. Al gave his iguana 15 beans. The iguana ate 4 beans by lunch, 7 more by dinner, and 3 more by bedtime. How many beans were left at the end of the day?

11. Twenty customers ordered a turkey sandwich. Three ordered a ham sandwich. Thirteen ordered a chicken sandwich. How many customers were there in all?

Solve each number sentence by finding the unknown. See Example 3

12. $14 - \blacksquare = 6$

13. $24 + \blacksquare = 33$

14. $36 = 32 + \blacksquare$

15. $\blacksquare + 4 + 11 = 21$

16. $12 + 3 + \blacksquare = 17$

17. $\blacksquare - 7 - 6 = 22$

For Exercises 18–20, use the table.

18. Write a number sentence using subtraction.

19. Write a number sentence using addition.

20. Write a problem using the number sentence $258 - 75 = 183$.

Miles Between Cities in New York		
From	**To**	**Miles**
Albany	Buffalo	258
Rochester	Ithaca	75
Buffalo	New York City	297
New York City	Syracuse	199

H.O.T. Problems

21. OPEN ENDED Complete the number sentence with two different numbers to solve. $874 - \blacksquare = 444 - \blacksquare$

22. FIND THE ERROR Morgan wrote a number sentence. Find and correct her mistake.

56 − 40

23. ![] **WRITE MATH** Write a problem that uses the number sentence $48 + \blacksquare = 55$. Solve.

24. Kelly downloaded 3 songs on her MP3 player. Later that day she downloaded 5 more songs. How many songs did Kelly download that day? Which number sentence represents the problem above? (Lesson 2C)

A. $3 + 5 = 8$

B. $8 - 5 = 3$

C. $3 \times 5 = 15$

D. $15 \div 5 = 3$

25. Which pattern is represented by the graph? (Lesson 1E)

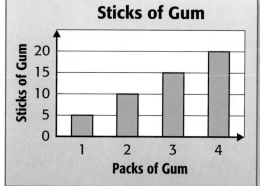

F. Add 1. **H.** Subtract 1.

G. Add 5. **J.** Multiply by 1.

26. If the pattern continues, which numbers will be the sixth and seventh numbers in the pattern? (Lesson 1B)

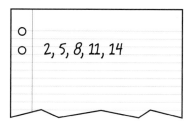

2, 5, 8, 11, 14

A. 16, 18 **C.** 17, 21

B. 17, 20 **D.** 18, 22

27. Irena wrote this number pattern.

24, 26, 28, 30, ___

What would be a reasonable answer for the next number? (Lesson 1B)

F. 28

G. 32

H. 35

J. 40

Spiral Review

Solve.

28. Rachel sold 4 glasses of lemonade the first hour, 8 glasses the second hour, and 12 glasses of lemonade the third hour. If the pattern continues, how many glasses of lemonade will she sell the next hour? What is the pattern? (Lesson 1C)

Algebra Identify the pattern. Then find the missing numbers. (Lesson 1B)

29. 19, ■, 23, ■, 27

30. 4, 10, ■, 22, 28, ■

Main Idea

I will write and solve expressions and equations.

 Vocabulary

equation

is not equal to (≠)

 Get Connect**ED**

3.20 The student will **a)** investigate the identity and the commutative properties for addition and multiplication; and **b)** identify examples of the identity and commutative properties for addition and multiplication.
3.19 The student will recognize and describe a variety of patterns formed using numbers, tables, and pictures, and extend the patterns, using the same or different forms.

Expressions and Equations

There are 16 apples in a basket. Lenora buys 4 apples. The expression $16 - 4$ tells how many apples were left.

(total apples) → $16 - 4$ ← (apples sold)

You have learned that an expression is a combination of numbers and operations. A few examples of expressions are shown.

$$5 + 7 \qquad 3 + 2 + 5 \qquad 12 - 8$$

An **equation**, or number sentence, is an expression using numbers and the equals sign (=). Equations show that the amount on both sides of the equals sign have the same value. A few examples are shown.

$$5 + 7 = 12 \qquad 3 + 2 + 5 = 10 \qquad 12 - 8 = 4 + 0$$

 **REAL-WORLD EXAMPLE**

Write Expressions and Equations

1 **APPLES** Use the information shown. Write an expression about the total number of red and green apples. Then write an equation to solve.

Apples
Red.........5
Yellow....3
Green......4

Use counters to model the expression.

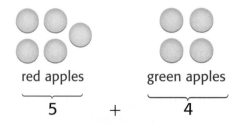

red apples   green apples

        5   +   4

So, the expression is $5 + 4$.

The equation is $5 + 4 = 9$ red and green apples.

Remember

In an equation, the value on each side of the equals sign is the same.

② **Tell whether + or − makes the equation 4 ● 3 = 7 true. Use counters to model.**

$4 ● 3 = 7$
$4 − 3 = 7$
$1 = 7$
The equation is false.
$4 − 3 ≠ 7$
$4 − 3$ **is not equal to** 7.

$4 ● 3 = 7$
$4 + 3 = 7$
$7 = 7$
The equation is true.
$4 + 3 = 7$
$4 + 3$ is equal to 7.

So, the symbol + makes the equation $4 ● 3 = 7$ true.

③ **Find the unknown to make the equation 2 + 8 = ▩ × 2 true.**

$2 + 8 = ▩ × 2$
$10 = ▩ × 2$
$10 = 5 × 2$
$10 = 10$

THINK $2 + 8 = 10$
What times 2 is 10?

So, the number 5 will make the equation true.

✓ CHECK What You Know

Write an expression. Then write an equation to solve. See Example 1

1. Jin wrote 3 letters today and 2 letters yesterday. How many letters did she write in all?

2. The animal shelter had 6 puppies. They sold 3 of them. How many puppies are left?

Tell whether + or − makes each equation true. See Example 2

3. $9 ● 2 = 11$

4. $18 = 28 ● 10$

5. $14 ● 7 = 10 + 11$

Tell whether the equation is true or false. Write = or ≠. See Example 2

6. $18 + 9 ● 9$

7. $18 + 20 ● 38$

8. $45 + 40 ● 5$

Algebra   Find the unknown to make the equation true. See Example 3

9. $3 + 4 = ▩ − 9$

10. $18 − ▩ = 6 × 2$

11. $▩ × 5 = 7 + 8$

12. 📖 **TALK MATH** What is the difference between an expression and an equation?

Write an expression. Then write an equation to solve. See Example 1

13. A basketball team won 11 games. A soccer team won 14 games. How many games were won in all?

14. Of the girls in a group, 14 have long hair and 9 have short hair. How many more have long hair?

15. Monisha scored 15 points Monday and 13 today. How many fewer points were made today?

16. Mori needs 4 yellow beads, 16 red, 2 white, and 14 green. How many beads are needed?

17. Caitlyn caught 37 fish and threw 9 back. How many fish were left?

18. There are 143 goats and 291 cows. How many animals are there?

Tell whether + or − makes each equation true. See Example 2

19. $44 \bullet 6 = 60 - 10$

20. $30 \bullet 3 = 17 + 10$

21. $12 \div 1 = 5 \bullet 7$

22. $26 - 13 = 17 \bullet 4$

Tell whether the equation is true or false. Write = or ≠. See Example 2

23. $60 - 50 \bullet 40 + 15$

24. $71 - 61 \bullet 85 - 75$

25. $19 + 8 \bullet 3 \times 9$

26. $32 \div 4 \bullet 9 \times 4$

Algebra Find the unknown to make the equation true. See Example 3

27. $8 \div 1 = 18 - \blacksquare$

28. $4 \times \blacksquare = 20 \div 5$

29. $60 - 10 = 10 \times \blacksquare$

30. $\blacksquare - 8 = 3 \times 4$

REAL-WORLD PROBLEM SOLVING

Ice Cream Use the data to write an equation for each phrase.

31. difference of votes for the two most favorite flavors

32. sum of votes for vanilla and cookie dough flavors

33. difference of votes for vanilla and strawberry flavors

34. sum of all the votes

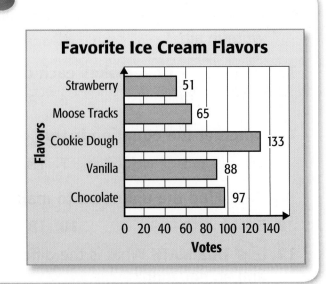

Favorite Ice Cream Flavors

Flavor	Votes
Strawberry	51
Moose Tracks	65
Cookie Dough	133
Vanilla	88
Chocolate	97

35. CHALLENGE Use the numbers 13, 16, and 29 to write two expressions. Then use <, >, or = to compare the expressions.

36. WHICH ONE DOESN'T BELONG? Identify the example that is not an expression. Explain.

| 41 + 66 | 17 + 3 | 28 − 9 = 19 | 12 + 2 + 6 |

37. WRITE MATH Write a real-world problem that can be solved using a subtraction equation.

 **Test Practice**

38. Solve this number sentence.

(Lesson 2C)

$$352 - 199 = \blacksquare$$

A. 1,153   **C.** 153

B. 157   **D.** 147

39. Which sign makes the equation true? (Lesson 2D)

$$79 \;\blacksquare\; 26 = 105$$

F. +   **H.** ×

G. −   **J.** ÷

Spiral Review

Write a number sentence for each situation. (Lesson 2C)

40. There are 20 drummers in the parade. Eleven of them are men. How many are women?

41. Measurement In a race, Joseph ran 206 feet and Iago ran 181 feet. How much farther did Joseph run than Iago?

42. Audrey had 73¢. She found one quarter under the sofa. How much money does she have now?

Represent each pattern with words. Then extend the graph. (Lesson 1E)

43.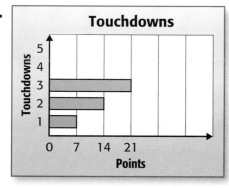

44.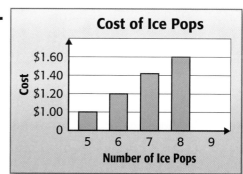

Main Idea
I will look for a rule and extend it to solve a problem.

 **Vocabulary**
rule

 Get ConnectED

3.19 The student will recognize and describe a variety of patterns formed using numbers, tables, and pictures, and extend the patterns, using the same or different forms.

Make a Table to Find a Rule

A pattern is called a rule. A **rule** tells you what to do to the first number (input) to get the second (output).

🏃 ✏️ **REAL-WORLD EXAMPLE** Find and Extend a Rule

① **GEOMETRY** Katie is building 5 separate triangles with straws. The first triangle used 3 straws, and the second triangle used another 3 straws. Find the total number of straws Katie needs to make 5 triangles.

Make a table to find and extend the rule.

Step 1 Find the rule.
You know that 1 triangle = 3 straws.

$1 \times 3 = 3$
2 triangles = 6 straws
$2 \times 3 = 6$
3 triangles = 9 straws
$3 \times 3 = 9$
The rule is to multiply the number of triangles by 3.

Rule: Multiply by 3.	
Number of Triangles	**Number of Straws**
1	3
2	6
3	9
4	■
5	■

Step 2 Extend the rule.

4 triangles = 4×3, or 12 straws
5 triangles = 5×3, or 15 straws

So, Katie will need 15 straws to make 5 triangles.

REAL-WORLD EXAMPLE

Find and Extend the Rule

② **PLANTS** Mateo found one four-leaf clover. He then found another. Now, he has 2 clovers and there are a total of 8 leaves. How many leaves will there be if he finds 5 clovers with 4 leaves each?

Step 1 Find the rule.

Rule: Multiply by 4.	
Clover	**Leaves**
1	4
2	8
3	▪
4	▪
5	▪

Step 2 Extend the rule.

$$3 \times 4 = 12$$
$$4 \times 4 = 16$$
$$5 \times 4 = 20$$

So, there are 20 leaves on 5 clovers.

✓ **CHECK What You Know**

1. The table shows how many shoes are needed for different numbers of people. Find and extend the rule for the table. Then copy and complete.

See Examples 1 and 2

Rule: ▢				
Input	1	2	3	4
Output	2	4	6	▪

2. There are 2 books about Italy, 4 books about Japan, 6 books about China, and 8 books about Russia. If the pattern continues, and the next set of books is about England, how many books will there be about England? Make a table to solve the problem.

3. 📝 **TALK MATH** Explain how multiplication can be used to help you extend a pattern.

Find and extend the rule for each table. Then copy and complete. See Examples 1 and 2

4. The table shows the number of sails needed for several boats. Each boat has the same number of sails.

Rule: ▮	
Input	**Output**
7	63
▮	36
3	▮
▮	18

5. The table shows how much movie tickets cost for different numbers of people.

Rule: ▮				
Input	6	4	9	▮
Output	$30	$20	▮	$35

Make a table to find a rule. Then extend the rule to solve.

See Examples 1 and 2

6. The amusement park sold ride tickets in packs of 5, 10, 15, and 20 tickets. What would a pack of 5 tickets cost if 20 tickets cost $4?

7. Mrs. Glenn planted 5 flowers in the front row of her garden. The second row had 10 flowers, and the third row had 15. How many flowers will be in the 5th row?

Data File

Aaron wants to save his money so he can go to space camp at the U.S. Space and Rocket Center. Each week he puts more money into his savings account.

8. How much extra money is Aaron putting into his savings account each week?

9. If the pattern continues, how much money will Aaron put into his account in Week 5?

10. How many weeks will it take Aaron to put in $23, if this pattern continues?

11. What is the total amount of money Aaron will have saved after 5 weeks?

Week	Money Saved Each Week
1	$5
2	$7
3	$9
4	$11
5	▮

12. CHALLENGE Create a table that uses a multiplication rule. Write input and output pairs.

13. WHICH ONE DOESN'T BELONG? Identify the number pair that would not be found in a table with a rule of × 6. Explain.

| 5 and 30 | 8 and 24 | 10 and 60 | 7 and 42 |

14. ✏️ **WRITE MATH** Explain how to find a rule when given a pattern.

Test Practice

15. The table shows the number of crayons needed. (Lesson 3A)

Crayons Needed	
Students	**Crayons**
3	15
4	20
6	30

Each student gets the same number of crayons. How many are needed for 8 students?

A. 20   **C.** 35

B. 30   **D.** 40

16. Tell which sign makes the equation true. (Lesson 2C)

$$6 \bullet 4 = 24$$

F. +   **H.** ×

G. −   **J.** ÷

17. One pencil costs $2. Two pencils cost $4. Three pencils cost $6. How much will 4 pencils cost?

(Lesson 1C)

A. $7   **C.** $10

B. $8   **D.** $12

 **Spiral Review**

Represent the pattern in a graph. Then represent the pattern using words. (Lesson 1E)

18. 10, 14, 12, 16, 14, ▥

19. 24, 23, 20, 19, 16, ▥

20. Rafael is making a pattern with pattern blocks. In the first row he uses 1 block. He uses 4 blocks in the second row and 7 in the third row. If the pattern continues, how many pattern blocks will be in the fifth row? (Lesson 1C)

Main Idea
I will use addition and subtraction to complete function tables.

Vocabulary
function
variable
function table

Get ConnectED

3.19 The student will recognize and describe a variety of patterns formed using numbers, tables, and pictures, and extend the patterns, using the same or different forms.

Make a Function Table (+, −)

A relationship where one quantity depends upon another quantity is a **function**.

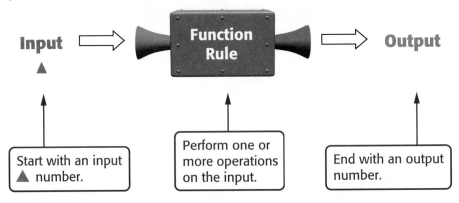

Input ⇒ **Function Rule** ⇒ **Output**
▲

Start with an input ▲ number.

Perform one or more operations on the input.

End with an output number.

A symbol such as ▲ represents an unknown number. It is called a **variable**. The input, output, and function rule can be shown in a table called a **function table**.

REAL-WORLD EXAMPLE

Make a Function Table

1 **MONEY** The table shows the amount of money four children each have saved. Make a function table to find how much money each child will have in savings after receiving $5 more.

Savings Accounts	
Name	Amount(s)
Lorena	$25
Valeria	$23
Sharon	$22
Isaiah	$21

Rule: Add $5.		
Input (△)	△ + $5	Output
$25	$25 + $5	$30
$23	$23 + $5	$28
$22	$22 + $5	$27
$21	$21 + $5	$26

REAL-WORLD EXAMPLE

2 AGE Isaac is 3 years older than his brother. Find Isaac's age when his brother is 2, 3, 4, and 5 years old. Use the rule to extend the function table.

The rule is brother's age + 3, or add 3.

Start with each input (△) number. Apply the rule to find the output number.

Rule: △ + 3	
Input (△)	Output
2	▨
3	▨
4	▨
5	▨

Rule: △ + 3		
Input (△)	△ + 3	Output
2	2 + 3	5
3	3 + 3	6
4	4 + 3	7
5	5 + 3	8

Remember

To check your answer, reverse the operation of your function and see if it works.

5 − 3 = 2
6 − 3 = 3
7 − 3 = 4
8 − 3 = 5

You can use subtraction to complete a function table.

 REAL-WORLD EXAMPLE

3 CHAIRS Each third-grade class always has 2 extra chairs in the room. Find how many students there are based on the number of chairs. Use the rule to extend the function table.

The rule is △ − 2 or, subtract 2.

Start with each input (△) number. Apply the rule to find the output number.

Rule: △ − 2	
Input (△)	Output
20	▨
21	▨
22	▨
23	▨

Rule: △ − 2		
Input (△)	△ − 2	Output
20	20 − 2	18
21	21 − 2	19
22	22 − 2	20
23	23 − 2	21

Lesson 3B Function Tables **419**

Copy the function table and extend the pattern. See Examples 1–3

1. Trinity is 5 years older than her sister. Use the function table to find Trinity's age when her sister is 1, 2, 3, or 4 years old.

Rule: △ + 5	
Input (△)	Output
1	▢
2	▢
3	▢
4	▢

For Exercises 2 and 3, use the following information.

Kelsey is four years older than her pet turtle.

2. Make a function table to find how old her pet turtle will be when she is 13, 14, 15, or 16 years old.

3. Write the function rule.

4. 📋 TALK MATH How do function tables show patterns?

EXTRA PRACTICE
Begins on page EP2.

Copy each function table and extend the pattern. See Examples 1–3

5. Ignacio always rides his bike 6 miles farther than Mason. Use the function table to find how many miles Ignacio rides when Mason rides 1, 3, 5, or 7 miles.

Rule: △ + 6	
Input (△)	Output
1	▢
3	▢
5	▢
7	▢

6.

Rule: △ − 9	
Input (△)	Output
17	▢
18	▢
19	▢
20	▢

7.

Rule: △ − 4	
Input (△)	Output
15	▢
12	▢
9	▢
6	▢

Find the rule for the function table.

8. A book has 44 pages. Ely read the same number of pages each day until he finished. The table shows how many pages were left to read before and after he read each day.

Rule:	
Input (△)	**Output**
44	33
33	22
22	11
11	0

Make a function table for each situation. Write the function rule.

9. Pasqual and his friends will each get $7 for allowance. How much money will each child have if they already have $1, $2, $3, or $4?

10. A store orders 3 more boxes of strawberries than oranges. How many boxes of oranges will the store order if they order 8, 9, 10, or 11 boxes of strawberries?

11. Jayla is reading a book that has 122 pages. If she reads 25 pages every day, how many pages will she have left to read after 1, 2, 3, or 4 days?

12. Every week, Mr. Montoya pays $3 to send a package. He began with $30. How much money will he have after 4 weeks?

H.O.T. Problems

13. **OPEN ENDED** Make a function table for the rule add 5.

14. **FIND THE ERROR** Nate is making a function table for △ + 9. Find and correct his mistake.

Rule: △ + 9		
Input (△)	7	5	6
Output	16	13	15

I made a function table for △ + 9.

15. **WRITE MATH** Write a real-world problem that would result in the function table to the right. What is the function rule?

Rule:			
Input (△)	250	251	252
Output	260	261	262

Problem-Solving Investigation

Main Idea I will choose the best strategy to solve a problem.

🏃 ✎ P.S.I. TEAM ➕

ELAN: My school is having a book swap. The first day, 8 books were brought to school. The second day, 12 were brought. Yesterday, my friends brought 16 books.

YOUR MISSION: Suppose the pattern continues. Find the total number of books after 7 days.

Understand

You know the number of books brought the first three days. Find the total number of books after 7 days.

Plan

Use the *make a table* strategy. Find and extend the pattern to solve the problem.

Solve

The pattern is to add 4 books each day. To find the total, add the number of books from each day.

Day	1	2	3	4	5	6	7
Books	8	12	16	20	24	28	32

+4 +4 +4 +4 +4 +4

$$\begin{array}{cccccc} 8 & 20 & 36 & 56 & 80 & 108 \\ +12 & +16 & +20 & +24 & +28 & +32 \\ \hline 20 & 36 & 56 & 80 & 108 & 140 \end{array}$$

So, the total number of books is 140.

Check

The answer makes sense for the facts given in the problem. ✓

🏔 **3.19** The student will recognize and describe a variety of patterns formed using numbers, tables, and pictures, and extend the patterns, using the same or different forms.

- Make a table.
- Act it out.
- Work backward.

Use any strategy to solve each problem.

1. Orlan has 40 comic books. He keeps 10 comic books for himself and divides the rest equally among his 5 friends. How many comic books does each friend get?

2. Two teams scored a total of 20 points. The Bears scored 6 more points than the Seahawks. How many points did each team score?

3. Darnell ran for 4 minutes on Monday. He ran 8 minutes on Tuesday and 12 minutes on Wednesday. If the pattern continues, how many minutes will he run on Thursday and Friday? Copy and complete the function table.

Rule:				
Days of the Week	Mon.	Tues.	Wed.	Thurs.	Fri.
Miles Ran	4	8	12		

4. Suppose you add 35 to a number, then subtract 10. The result is 26. What was the original number?

5. The graph shows the number of people in each car that drove by Niguel's house. What is the total number of people who drove by?

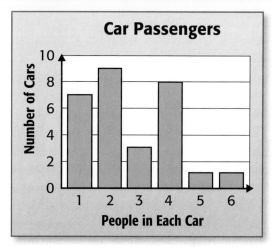

Car Passengers

6. The pictograph below shows how many bundles of yarn Mrs. Finn bought. How many bundles did she buy altogether?

Mrs. Finn's Yarn

Red	🧶 🧶 🧶
Blue	🧶
White	🧶 🧶 🧶
Each	🧶 = 2 bundles of yarn

7. **WRITE MATH** There are 48 oranges in a box and half as many grapefruit. To find the total number of pieces of fruit, would you use the *make a table* strategy? Explain.

Main Idea

I will use multiplication and division to complete function tables.

 Get ConnectED

3.19 The student will recognize and describe a variety of patterns formed using numbers, tables, and pictures, and extend the patterns, using the same or different forms.

Make a Function Table (×, ÷)

Function rules can also involve multiplication or division.

REAL-WORLD EXAMPLE — Make a Function Table

1 **PET** Christine has a piglet for a pet. It cost her $6 the first week to feed her piglet. How much will Christine pay for feed in week 5? Make a function table to find the cost of feeding Christine's piglet in week 5.

Pet Piglet Food

Week Input (△)	Cost Output
1	$6
2	$12
3	$18
4	$24
5	

To find the output values, multiply each input value (△) by $6.

Pet Piglet Food

Input (△)	Rule: △ × $6	Output
1	1 × $6	$6
2	2 × $6	$12
3	3 × $6	$18
4	4 × $6	$24
5	5 × $6	$30

So, the cost of feeding the piglet in week 5 is $30.

You can identify or describe the rule, or pattern, in a function table.

 REAL-WORLD EXAMPLE   Identify the Rule

2 QUARTERS The table shows how many quarters are in different numbers of dollar bills (△). Use the function table to identify the rule.

Start with each input (△) number. Identify the rule that gives the output number.

So, the rule is △ × 4.

Rule: ☐	
Input (△)	Output
1	4
2	8
3	12
4	16

Rule: △ × 4		
Input (△)	△ × 4	Output
1	1 × 4	4
2	2 × 4	8
3	3 × 4	12
4	4 × 4	16

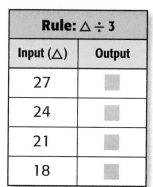 **REAL-WORLD EXAMPLE**   Complete a Function Table (÷)

3 TRICYCLES The table shows how many tricycles can be made with different numbers of wheels (△). Describe the rule.

Start with each input (△) number. Apply the rule to find the output number.

The pattern shows that as △ decreases by 3, the output decreases by 1.

Rule: △ ÷ 3	
Input (△)	Output
27	▨
24	▨
21	▨
18	▨

Rule: △ ÷ 3		
Input (△)	△ ÷ 3	Output
27	27 ÷ 3	9
24	24 ÷ 3	8
21	21 ÷ 3	7
18	18 ÷ 3	6

1. The table shows how many pairs of socks can be matched up after different numbers of socks (△) are taken out of the clothes dryer. Copy the function table and extend the pattern. See Example 1

Rule: △ ÷ 2	
Input (△)	Output
8	■
10	■
12	■
14	■

2. A butterfly has 2 wings. Make a function table to show the total number of wings for 4, 5, 6, or 7 butterflies. Then write the rule and describe the pattern. See Examples 2–3

3. 💬 **TALK MATH** Can you look only at the input numbers in a function table to determine the function rule? Explain.

Practice and Problem Solving

EXTRA PRACTICE Begins on page EP2.

Copy each function table and extend the pattern. See Example 1

4. Each ladybug that Karley sees has 6 spots on it. Use the table to find the total number of spots for different numbers of ladybugs (△).

Rule: △ × 6	
Input (△)	Output
5	■
6	■
7	■
8	■

5. Each week the total number of snacks (△) are divided evenly among 9 students in the travel club. Use the table to find how many snacks each student gets when different numbers of snacks are served.

Rule: △ ÷ 9	
Input (△)	Output
18	■
27	■
36	■
45	■

Make a function table for each situation. Write the rule.

See Example 2

6. The price for admission to a zoo is $7. How many tickets can you buy for $63, $56, $49, or $42?

7. Each box holds 12 water bottles. How many boxes are there if there are 60, 48, 36, or 24 bottles?

8. Rama bought 6 bags of chips. He spent $12. How many bags of chips would he have bought if he spent $14, $16, $18, or $20?

9. Dorian and her friends went to the movies. Each ticket cost $5. How much would they spend if Dorian went with 2, 3, 4, or 5 friends?

Describe the pattern of each function table. See Example 3

10.

Rule: △ ÷ 3	
Input (△)	Output
27	9
21	7
15	5
9	3

11.

Rule: △ ÷ 6	
Input (△)	Output
72	12
54	9
36	6
18	3

12.

Rule: △ × 2	
Input (△)	Output
12	24
13	26
14	28
15	30

13.

Rule: △ × 4	
Input (△)	Output
6	24
7	28
8	32
9	36

H.O.T. Problems

14. CHALLENGE Look at the function table shown. What is the function rule?

Input (△)	15	25	40	50
Output	4	6	9	11

15. NUMBER SENSE In the function rule △ + 3, the output value is 8. How can you determine the value of △?

16. WRITE MATH Write a real-world math problem where using a function table for multiplication or division will help you solve the problem.

Problem Solving in Science

A Visit to the
Supermarket

A supermarket is a busy place. Some people shop at a supermarket every day of the week. Today, some supermarkets are as big as 4 football fields!

Supermarkets sell many kinds of food, including healthy foods. Some of the healthiest foods you can buy are yogurt, broccoli, citrus fruits, nuts, oatmeal, and orange juice.

These foods come in different containers and sizes. The prices of some foods are based on size. For example, 1 kilogram of pears costs around $2. The price of a liter of soda is around $3.

Did You Know?

Tomatoes are the most widely grown fruit in the world.

Real-World Math

Use the items on the shelf above to solve each problem.

1 Suppose a customer buys 1 item from the shelf. The next customer buys 2 items. The next buys 3 items. If this pattern continues, how many items would be bought in all after the fifth customer?

2 Write an equation to show how many items are on the bottom shelf.

3 A function table shows that 4 more containers of yogurt are sold than apples. What is the rule?

4 Write an equation to show how many more apples are shown than boxes of spaghetti.

5 A store receives twice as many tomato sauce cans as orange juice bottles. Write a number sentence to show how many juice bottles are received if 12 cans of tomato sauce are received.

6 A bottle of water costs $1, and a package of 6 bottles costs $5. How much money is saved if you buy 4 packages instead of 24 bottles?

Be sure the following Key Concepts are noted in your Foldable.

Geometric Patterns

Number Patterns

Number Sentences

Function Tables

Key Concepts

- A series of numbers or figures that follow a rule is called a **pattern**. (Lesson 1)

$$10, 20, 30, 40, 50$$

- Patterns can be represented with words. (Lesson 1)

The pattern is one figure with a pointed top, one figure with a flat top.

- Patterns can be represented in a **graph**.

Apples for Sale		
1	🪙🪙🪙	
2	🪙🪙🪙🪙	
3	🪙🪙🪙🪙🪙🪙	
4	🪙🪙🪙🪙🪙🪙🪙🪙	
key: 🪙 = 10¢		

The pattern is add 25¢ (Lesson 1)

- A **function table** can help you find and extend a pattern. (Lesson 3)

abc Key Vocabulary

equation

function

function table

graph

rule

variable

Vocabulary Check

Choose the vocabulary word that completes each sentence.

1. A _____?_____ organizes data and shows how sets of data relate to each other.

2. A relationship that shows one quantity depending on another quantity is a _____?_____.

3. "Subtract three" is an example of a _____?_____ because it shows what to do to the input number to get the output number.

4. A _____?_____ may be shown as a ▲ to represent a number that is unknown.

5. An _____?_____ is an expression using numbers and the equals sign.

6. A table that lists pairs of numbers that follow a rule is a _____?_____.

Multi-Part Lesson Review

Lesson 1 Patterns

Geometric and Number Patterns (Lessons 1A and 1B)

7. Represent and extend the pattern using words.

8. How many pentagons will be used if this pattern extends until there is a total of 18 polygons?

9. Identify a pattern. Then find the missing numbers.

200, 400, ■, ■, 1,000; 1,200

10. As the pattern continues, what are the next four numbers?

27, 30, 33, 36

11. How much money will Sue owe on her overdue library books after week 6 and week 7?

25¢, 50¢, 75¢, $1.00, $1.25, ■, ■

EXAMPLE 1

How many stars will be used if this pattern extends until there is a total of 16 shapes?

The pattern is star, moon, star, circle. There will be a total of 8 stars.

EXAMPLE 2

Liam has 140 points. The pattern shows the points he lost each time he missed hitting the ball. What is the pattern of lost points? How many points did he have after the third and fifth miss?

140, 135, 130, 125, 120, 115
−5   −5   −5   −5   −5

Five points are lost (subtracted) after each miss. After the third and fifth miss his points are 125 and 115.

Problem-Solving Strategy: Look for a Pattern (Lesson 1C)

Solve.

12. Lisa cuts pies in a pattern. She cuts the first pie in half, the second into fourths, and the third into eighths. How will she cut the fourth pie?

13. Continue the pattern of house numbers if the first three are 77, 89, and 101.

EXAMPLE 3

Rich's test scores follow a pattern. What are his last two scores?

Test	1	2	3	4	5
Score	79	84	89	94	99

+5   +5   +5   +5

Rich's last two scores are 94 and 99.

Patterns in Graphs (Lesson 1E)

Represent the pattern in a graph and with words.

14. Carter cut boards that are 2 yards, 4 yards, 6 yards, and 8 yards long. How many feet long will each board be? (*Hint:* 3 feet = 1 yard)

15. Laurie counted the times her heart beat for 10 seconds. Laurie counted 8 beats. What is the total number of times Laurie's heart would beat after 1 minute, 2 minutes, 3 minutes, and 4 minutes? (*Hint:* 60 seconds = 1 minute)

EXAMPLE 4

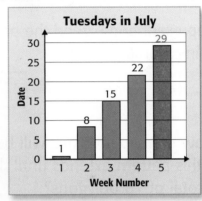

The dates of the Tuesdays in July make a pattern. Extend the pattern by adding 7. The last Tuesday in July is the 29th.

Lesson 2 ## Number Sentences

Write Expressions, Number Sentences, and Equations (Lessons 2B, 2C, and 2D)

Write an expression. Then write a number sentence to solve.

16. TJ picked 69 raspberries. He gave his sister 29 of them. How many raspberries does TJ have left?

17. Rashid hit 27 baseballs yesterday. Today he hit 41. How many baseballs did he hit in all?

Tell whether + or − makes each equation true.

18. 52 ● 13 = 99 − 34

19. 47 + 32 = 6 ● 73

20. Tell whether the equation is true or false. Write = or ≠.

10 + 12 ● 12 − 10

EXAMPLE 5

There are 2 ladybugs and 3 butterflies. How many insects are there?

Pictures

Words   Two insects plus three insect equals five insects.

Expression   2 + 3

Number Sentence   2 + 3 = 5

Make a Table to Find a Rule (Lesson 3A)

Find and extend the rule for each table.

21. The table shows the number of cups in a given number of pints.

Rule: ▦	
Input (△)	Output
1	2
2	4
3	▦
4	▦

EXAMPLE 6

Each new bookcase the library buys has the same number of shelves. How many shelves will they have after they buy 6 bookcases?

Rule: Multiply by 4.	
Input (△)	Output
3	12
4	16
5	20
6	24

So, the library will have 24 shelves after they buy 6 bookcases.

Make a Function Table (+, −) (Lesson 3B)

Copy and complete.

22. For every bead project, Mariana will use 5 fewer red beads than blue beads. How many blue beads will she need if she uses the given number of red beads?

Rule: △ + 5	
Input (△)	Output
10	▦
20	▦
30	▦
40	▦

EXAMPLE 7

Tom is in fourth grade. His brother is in first grade. What grade will Tom be in when his brother is in fourth, fifth, sixth, and seventh grade?

Rule: △ + 3		
Input (△)	△ + 3	Output
4	4 + 3	7
5	5 + 3	8
6	6 + 3	9
7	7 + 3	10

Problem-Solving Investigation: Choose a Strategy (Lesson 3C)

Solve.

23. Hailey planted 30 tomato seeds in her garden. Three out of every 5 seeds grew into tomato plants. How many tomato plants does Hailey have?

24. Alvar, Brian, Charlotte, Diana, and Ethan line up in the order of their ages. Diana was born after Alvar but before Brian. Charlotte is the oldest. Ethan is younger than Brian. In what order are they lined up if the first child is the oldest?

EXAMPLE 8

Connie gave 6 baseball cards to Lily, 4 to Nesto, and 7 to Augustine. She has 7 baseball cards left. How many cards did Connie start with?

You know the number of cards Connie gave to each of her friends and how many were left over.

Choose addition to solve the problem.

Lily   Nesto   Augustine   left

6   +   4   +   7   +   7   =   24 cards

So, Connie started with 24 cards.

Make a Function Table (×, ÷) (Lesson 3D)

Make a function table. Write the rule.

25. There are 6 eggs in my cake recipe. If I used 48, 42, 36, or 30 eggs, how many cakes would I have made?

26. There are 3 sticks of clay in one package. How many sticks of clay are in 3, 5, and 7 packages?

27. There are 2 socks in each pair. How many pairs of socks would Alisa have folded if she folded 20, 16, 12, and 8 socks?

EXAMPLE 9

Alek is making paper cubes. How many faces will there be when the given number of cubes are finished?

Rule: $\triangle \times 6$	
Input ($\triangle$)	Output
2	12
3	18
4	24
5	30

So, there are 12 faces on 2 cubes, 18 on 3 cubes, 24 on 4 cubes, and 30 on 5 cubes.

Tell whether each statement is *true* or *false*.

1. An equation never has an equals sign.

2. A pattern is the same as a rule.

3. Tell whether + or − makes the number sentence true.
$$36 + 14 = 56 \bullet 6$$

4. Tell whether the equation is true or false. Write = or ≠.
$$5 + 4 \bullet 3 \times 3$$

5. Identify a pattern. Then find the missing numbers.
85, ■ , 105, 115, ■ , 135

Represent and extend each pattern using words.

6.

7.

8. Write an expression. Then write an equation to solve. Alexa picked 20 daffodils and 16 daisies. How many flowers did she pick in all?

9. **MULTIPLE CHOICE** The table below shows the cost of movie tickets.

Movie Tickets					
Input	1	2	3	4	5
Output	$8	$16	$24	?	?

What is the cost for 5 movie tickets?

A. $31 **C.** $48

B. $40 **D.** $56

Make a function table for the situation. Write the function rule.

10. Sol runs 3 miles in 21 minutes. If he continues to run at the same speed, how many minutes will it take him to run 6, 9, and 10 miles?

11. Use the graph. Represent the pattern with words. Then extend the graph.

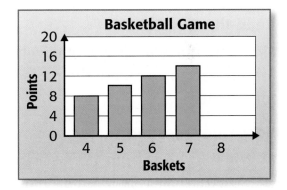

12. Landon is buying ping-pong balls. Each package contains 4 balls. How many balls will he have if he buys 7, 8, 9, or 10 packages? Represent the pattern in a graph and with words.

13. **MULTIPLE CHOICE** Timothy draws 27 squares. He colors every fourth square blue. How many blue squares are there?

F. 3 **H.** 5

G. 4 **J.** 6

14. 📝 **WRITE MATH** Can △ = 2 and △ = 5 be in the same problem? Why or why not?

An art teacher has planned a project that uses 2 wiggle eyes for each student. The eyes come in packages of 12. How many packages will she need to buy so that she has 84 wiggle eyes?

A. 6   **C.** 8

B. 7   **D.** 9

TEST-TAKING TIP

When looking for a pattern, see how a number changes from the one before it.

Read the Question

Find how many packages of wiggle eyes are needed to complete the project. Look for a pattern.

Solve the Question

Packages	1	2	3	4	5	6	7
Eyes	12	24	36	48	60	72	84

+12 +12 +12 +12 +12 +12

So, 7 packages are needed to have 84 wiggle eyes. The answer is B.

Read each question. Then fill in the correct answer on the answer sheet provided by your teacher or on a seperate sheet of paper.

1. Rico writes these five numbers on a chalkboard.

15, 12, 9, 6, 3

Which rule describes the numbers?

    A. Add 3.   **C.** Add 2.

    B. Subtract 3.   **D.** Subtract 2.

2. Gail has 22 marbles, Taran has 29 marbles, and Leon has 34 marbles. Which expression will help you find the total number of marbles?

    F. 34 + 29   **H.** 22 + 29 − 34

    G. 22 + 29 + 34   **J.** 22 − 29 − 34

3. Jimmy is buying bottled water.

Bottles of Water				
Number of Cases	2	4	6	8
Number of Bottles	20	40	60	80

Based on the table, how many bottles come in one case?

A. 10   **C.** 20

B. 15   **D.** 25

4. How many hexagons will be used if the pattern below extends until there are a total of 25 polygons?

F. 4   **H.** 10

G. 8   **J.** 12

5. A store has different size packages of invitations. The chart shows how the number of invitations increases from one package to the next.

Packages of Invitations				
Small	Medium	Large	Extra Large	Jumbo
6	12	?	24	30

How many invitations are in a large package of invitations?

A. 14   **C.** 18

B. 16   **D.** 20

6. The graph below represents the number of lemons needed for each quart of lemonade.

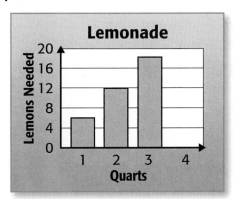

How many lemons are needed to make 4 quarts of lemonade?

F. 24   **H.** 30

G. 26   **J.** 32

7. Tao counted the triangles in each part of his design. Then he found the total number of sides.

Rule: ■	
Input (△)	Output
3	9
5	15
7	21
9	27

What rule describes the pattern?

A. Add 3.   **C.** Multiply by 3.

B. Subtract 3.   **D.** Divide by 3.

NEED EXTRA HELP?							
If You Missed Question . . .	1	2	3	4	5	6	7
Go to Chapter-Lesson . . .	8-1B	8-2B	8-3D	8-1A	8-3B	8-1E	8-3A
For help with . . .	SOL 3.19	SOL 3.19	SOL 3.19	SOL 3.19	SOL 3.19	SOL 3.19	SOL 3.19

Fractions

connectED.mcgraw-hill.com

Investigate

 Animations

 Vocabulary

 Math Songs

 Multilingual eGlossary

Learn

 Personal Tutor

 Virtual Manipulatives

 Audio

 Foldables

Practice

 Self-Check Practice

 eGames

 Worksheets

 Assessment

The ☆**BIG Idea**

How can I use models to understand fractions and equivalent fractions?

 FOLDABLES Study Organizer

Make this Foldable to help you organize information about fraction concepts. Begin with four sheets of $8\frac{1}{2}'' \times 11''$ paper.

Fractions
Parts of a Whole
Parts of a Set
Compare Fractions
Order Fractions
Equivalent Fractions
Add Like Fractions
Subtract Like Fractions

Review Vocabulary

is equal to (=)   es igual a (=)   having the same value

$$2 + 3 = 4 + 1$$

Key Vocabulary

English	Español
fraction	fracción
numerator	numerador
denominator	denominador
benchmark fractions	fracciones de referencia
equivalent fractions	fracciones equivalentes

When Will I Use This?

Luke and Eva in Weather Talk

Are You Ready for the Chapter?

You have two options for checking Prerequisite Skills for this chapter.

Text Option Take the Quick Check below.

QUICK Check

Write the number of parts. Then tell whether each figure shows *equal* or *not equal* parts.

1.

2.

3.

4.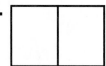

5. Draw a circle that is divided into 6 equal parts.

Tell the number of equal parts. Write *halves*, *thirds*, or *fourths*.

6.

7.

8.

9.

10. Jill draws a figure and divides it into fifths. What could her figure look like?

Tell which point represents each given number.

11. 380

300   320   340

12. 169

173   175   177

13. How many units are between each tick mark on the number line?

82 91   109   136   163

 Online Option Take the Online Readiness Quiz.

Explore Model Fractions

Main Idea
I will explore fractions using linear models.

Materials
paper

ruler

scissors

Get ConnectED

3.3 The student will
a) name and write fractions (including mixed numbers) represented by a model.
b) model fractions (including mixed numbers) and write the fractions' names.

A **fraction** is a number that represents part of a whole or part of a set. You can make models to represent fractional parts of a whole.

ACTIVITY

Step 1 **Make a Model**

Cut 4 strips of paper that are each 1 inch wide and 8 inches long. Label one strip 1.

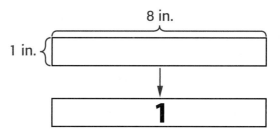

Step 2 Make a Fraction Model

Fold the second strip in half. Cut on the fold. Label each part $\frac{1}{2}$.

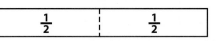

Step 3 Make More Fraction Models

Fold the third strip in half twice. Cut on the folds, and label each part $\frac{1}{4}$.

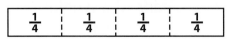

Step 4 Fold the last strip in half three times. Cut on the folds, and label each part $\frac{1}{8}$.

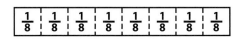

Think About It

1. How many strips are labeled $\frac{1}{2}$? $\frac{1}{4}$? $\frac{1}{8}$?

2. How many strips labeled $\frac{1}{2}$ are needed to equal the strip labeled 1?

3. Is $\frac{1}{2}$ greater than or less than $\frac{1}{8}$? Explain.

Practice and Apply It

Model each pair of fractions. Then write the greater fraction.

4. $\frac{1}{8}, \frac{1}{2}$

5. $\frac{1}{2}, \frac{1}{4}$

6. $1, \frac{1}{4}$

7. $\frac{1}{2}, 1$

8. $\frac{1}{4}, \frac{1}{8}$

9. $\frac{1}{8}, 1$

10. **WRITE MATH** Describe how you would construct fraction models that show $\frac{1}{16}$.

Main Idea
I will use area and linear models to represent fractions that name part of a whole.

 Vocabulary
fraction
unit fraction
numerator
denominator

 Get Connect**ED**

3.3 The student will **a)** name and write fractions (including mixed numbers) represented by a model. **b)** model fractions (including mixed numbers) and write the fractions' names.

Part of a Whole

A **fraction** is a number that names part of a whole. A **unit fraction** is a number that names *one* part of a whole. Some unit fractions are $\frac{1}{2}$, $\frac{1}{3}$, and $\frac{1}{4}$.

 **REAL-WORLD EXAMPLE**

Model Fractions

① **RUGS** This rug has 5 equal sections. The sections are red, orange, purple, yellow, and green. What fraction of the rug is red?

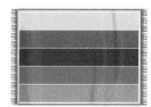

One Way: Use Models	**Another Way:** Draw a Picture
The rug above represents one whole. The whole is divided into 5 equal parts, or fifths.	Draw the rug with 5 equal parts. One part is red.

One Way column:

$$\boxed{1}$$
$$\boxed{\tfrac{1}{5}}\ \boxed{\tfrac{1}{5}}\ \boxed{\tfrac{1}{5}}\ \boxed{\tfrac{1}{5}}\ \boxed{\tfrac{1}{5}}$$

Write $\frac{1}{5}$

Read one-fifth

Another Way column:

$\frac{1}{5}$ ← part that is red
← total number of equal parts

So, $\frac{1}{5}$, or one-fifth, of the rug is red.

The **numerator** tells the number of equal parts being used.

The **denominator** tells the total number of equal parts.

$\frac{1}{5}$ ← numerator
← denominator

unit fraction

 **ACTIVITY** Write and Read Fractions

2 **What fraction of the figure is green?**

$\frac{2}{3}$ ← parts that are green
← total number of equal parts

Write $\frac{2}{3}$

Read *two-thirds*

So, $\frac{2}{3}$, or two-thirds, of the figure is green.

$\frac{2}{3}$ is *not* a unit fraction.

Sometimes parts of a whole cannot easily be named by fractions because the parts are not equal.

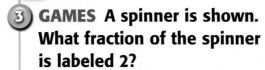 **REAL-WORLD EXAMPLE** Unequal Parts

3 **GAMES A spinner is shown. What fraction of the spinner is labeled 2?**

There are 4 parts, but the parts are not equal. So, you cannot easily write a fraction.

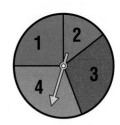

✓ CHECK What You Know

Write the fraction for the part that is yellow. Then write the fraction for the part that is *not* yellow. Label your answers.

See Examples 1–3

1.

2.

3.

4. What fraction of the pizza has cheese only?

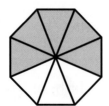

5. **TALK MATH** What is a fraction? How does a fraction describe the shaded part of a whole?

EXTRA **PRACTICE**
Begins on page EP2.

Write the fraction for the part that is blue. Then write the fraction for the part that is *not* blue. Label your answers.

See Examples 1–3

6.

7.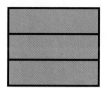

8.

9.

10.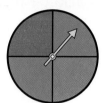

11.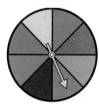

12. What fraction of the honeycomb has bees?

13. What fraction of the pizza has pepperoni?

Draw a picture for each fraction. Shade the fraction.

14. $\frac{2}{5}$ **15.** $\frac{1}{7}$ **16.** three-eighths   **17.** two-halves

REAL-WORLD PROBLEM SOLVING

Art The primary colors are red, blue, and yellow. The secondary colors are green, orange, and violet.

18. What fraction of the primary and secondary colors is red?

19. What fraction is blue or orange?

20. What fraction is not violet?

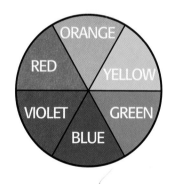

H.O.T. Problems

21. OPEN ENDED Draw a picture for which you cannot easily write a fraction to describe the shaded parts of the whole. Explain your thinking.

22. WRITE MATH Explain how to write a fraction to describe part of a whole.

Main Idea

I will use set models to represent fractions that name part of a set.

Get ConnectED

3.3 The student will
a) name and write fractions (including mixed numbers) represented by a model.
b) model fractions (including mixed numbers) and write the fractions' names.

Part of a Set

Explore Mini-Activity

Fractions can also be used to name part of a set. You can use counters to help you represent fractional parts of a set of objects.

1. What counter color is represented by the fraction *three out of five*?

2. Use a fraction to represent the fractional part of the yellow counters.

$$\frac{\bigcirc\bigcirc}{\bigcirc\bigcirc\bigcirc\bigcirc\bigcirc}$$ ← yellow counters (numerator)
← total counters (denominator)

3. What color of the counters is represented by $\frac{3}{5}$?

4. Write the fraction that shows two out of five.

EXAMPLE Write and Read Fractions

1 **COUNTERS** What fraction of the set of counters is yellow?

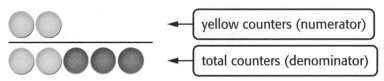

Each counter is a fraction of the set of counters.

There are 3 yellow counters out of a total of 7 counters.

Write $\frac{3}{7}$ ← use numbers

Read *three-sevenths* ← use words

So, $\frac{3}{7}$, or three-sevenths, of the counters are yellow.

DOGS Cody told his four dogs to sit.

 **Remember**

The "d" in denominator will help you remember which number in a fraction is the denominator. The denominator is down.

② **What fraction of the set of dogs listened to Cody?**

The yellow counters represent the sitting dogs. The red counter represents the standing dog.

3 dogs, out of a total of 4 dogs, are sitting down.

Write $\frac{3}{4}$ ← dogs sitting
← total dogs

Read *three-fourths*

So, $\frac{3}{4}$, or three-fourths, of the dogs obeyed.

③ **What fraction of the set of dogs did *not* listen to Cody?**

1 dog, out of a total of 4 dogs, is standing. So, $\frac{1}{4}$, or one-fourth, of the dogs did *not* listen to Cody.

✓ CHECK What You Know

Write the fraction for the part of the set that is yellow. Then write the fraction for the part of the set that is *not* yellow. Label your answers. See Examples 1–3

1.

2.

3.

4. Moria has three blue counters, four red counters, and three yellow counters. What fraction of the set of counters is red?

5. **TALK MATH** What do the numerator and denominator in a fraction represent?

 **EXTRA PRACTICE**
Begins on page EP2.

Write the fraction for the part of the set that is yellow. Then write the fraction for the part of the set that is *not* yellow. Label your answers. See Examples 1–3

6.

7.

8.

9.

10.

11.

12. What fraction of the set of items shown below are living things?

13. There are 3 red paintbrushes and 5 green. What fraction of the set of paintbrushes is red?

Use the information to solve the problem.

🏃 **Weather Talk**

Remember, they are reporting the fraction of sunny days during morning announcements.

It rained 4 days this week!

Thursday was the only sunny day!

WEEKLY WEATHER REPORT

| Monday | Tuesday | Wednesday | Thursday | Friday |

14. How many days was it sunny? What fraction of the school week was sunny?

15. OPEN ENDED Draw a set of objects that represent a fraction with a numerator of 4. Write the fraction.

16. 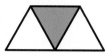 **WRITE MATH** Write a problem involving a fraction of a set. Solve.

Test Practice

17. Which figure is $\frac{2}{3}$ shaded?
(Lesson 1B)

A.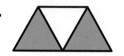

B.

C.

18. Which group shows $\frac{5}{7}$ of the flowers shaded? (Lesson 1C)

F.

G.

H.

J.

D.

Spiral Review

Write the fraction for the part that is blue. Then write the fraction for the part that is *not* blue. Label your answers.

(Lesson 1B)

19.

20.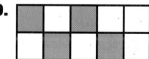

21.

Draw a picture for each fraction. Shade the fraction. (Lesson 1B)

22. five-sixths

23. $\frac{6}{10}$

24. two-sevenths

Problem-Solving Strategy: Draw a Picture

Main Idea I will solve a problem by drawing a picture.

Anessa and her brother have 8 insects in a jar. One-half of the insects are beetles. One is a firefly and the rest are crickets. How many of the insects are crickets?

Understand **What facts do you know?**

- There are 8 insects.

- One is a firefly.

- One-half are beetles.

- The rest are crickets.

What do you need to find?

- Find how many of the insects are crickets.

Plan You can draw a picture to solve the problem.

Solve

- First, draw a figure that is divided into 8 equal parts. This shows 8 insects.

- To show the beetles, shade $\frac{1}{2}$ of the figure. Shade 1 part to show the firefly.

- There are 3 parts not shaded. This is the number of crickets.

So, 3 of the insects are crickets.

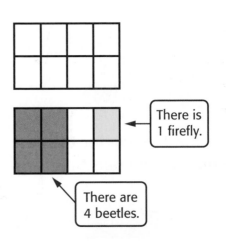

There is 1 firefly.

There are 4 beetles.

Check 4 beetles + 1 firefly + 3 crickets = 8 insects. There are 8 insects.

So, the answer is correct. ✓

3.3 The student will **b)** model fractions (including mixed numbers) and write the fractions' names.

Refer to the problem on the previous page.

1. Explain why the figure was divided into 8 equal parts.

2. Explain why 4 of the 8 boxes were shaded to show the number of beetles.

3. Suppose Anessa had 10 insects. How many would be crickets?

4. Look back at Exercise 3. Check your answer. How do you know it is correct? Show your work.

PRACTICE

EXTRA PRACTICE
Begins on page EP2.

Solve. Use the *draw a picture* strategy.

5. There are 12 books. Four-twelfths of the books are Willow's. Two belong to Basilio. The others belong to Tyree. How many books belong to Tyree?

6. **Measurement**
   Mill Park is 5 miles directly east of Bear Cabin. Nature Museum is 5 miles directly south of Bear Cabin. Glacier Lake is 5 miles directly west of Mill Park. Is this possible? Explain.

7. Lucy and Nicole have equal-sized pieces of pizza. The table shows how much of each piece Lucy and Nicole ate. Who ate more?

Lucy	Nicole
$\frac{1}{2}$	$\frac{3}{4}$

8. Four students are standing in line. Evan is ahead of Kamilah. Chad is behind Kamilah. Tariq is behind Evan. In what order are they standing?

9. There are 4 houses on a block. The table shows what fraction of the houses have a dog or cat. How many of the houses have a dog?

Dogs	Cats
$\frac{3}{4}$	$\frac{1}{2}$

10. Berta rides the elevator 3 floors up from her home to meet her friend Devan. They go down 7 floors, where they meet Celeste. How many floors is Berta from her home?

11. Ali is playing jacks. She tosses 10 jacks on the floor. She then picks up $\frac{4}{10}$ of them. How many jacks are left on the floor?

12. **WRITE MATH** Explain what it means to draw a picture to solve a problem. How is a picture helpful in solving a problem?

Explore **Compare Fractions**

To compare fractions, make a model or a picture. Think about what each number in the fraction means.

Main Idea

I will explore how to compare fractions with like and unlike denominators.

Materials

fraction circles

fraction tiles

number line WorkMat 2

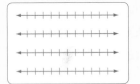

Get ConnectED

3.3 The student will
c) compare fractions having like and unlike denominators, using words and symbols (>, <, or =).

ACTIVITY

① Ajay has $\frac{3}{6}$ of his homework done. Yuki finished $\frac{4}{6}$ of hers. Who has finished a larger part of their homework? Compare $\frac{3}{6}$ and $\frac{4}{6}$.

Step 1 Represent each fraction with fraction tiles.

Completed Homework

Ajay | $\frac{1}{6}$ $\frac{1}{6}$ $\frac{1}{6}$ | $\frac{3}{6}$ done

Yuki | $\frac{1}{6}$ $\frac{1}{6}$ $\frac{1}{6}$ $\frac{1}{6}$ | $\frac{4}{6}$ done

Step 2 Since each whole is divided into 6 parts, look at the numerator.

Three equal-sized parts is less than 4. → $\frac{1}{6}$ $\frac{1}{6}$ $\frac{1}{6}$ $\frac{3}{6} < \frac{4}{6}$ $\frac{1}{6}$ $\frac{1}{6}$ $\frac{1}{6}$ $\frac{1}{6}$

Ajay   Yuki

or $\frac{4}{6} > \frac{3}{6}$

So, Yuki has finished a larger part of her homework.

ACTIVITY

② Alex is in a class that is $\frac{3}{5}$ boys and $\frac{2}{5}$ girls. Are there more boys or girls? Compare $\frac{3}{5}$ and $\frac{2}{5}$.

Represent each fraction on a number line.

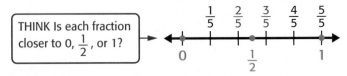

THINK Is each fraction closer to 0, $\frac{1}{2}$, or 1?

$\frac{3}{5}$ is closer to one whole. So, $\frac{3}{5} > \frac{2}{5}$ or $\frac{2}{5} < \frac{3}{5}$.

So, there are more boys in Alex's class.

③ Abby ate $\frac{1}{4}$ of a granola bar. Randall ate $\frac{1}{6}$ of the same-sized granola bar. Who ate more? Compare $\frac{1}{4}$ and $\frac{1}{6}$.

Step 1 Represent each whole fraction with fraction circles.

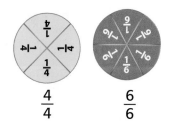

$$\frac{4}{4} \qquad \frac{6}{6}$$

Step 2 Pull away the fractional part you are comparing.

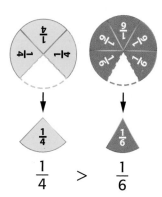

$$\frac{1}{4} \quad > \quad \frac{1}{6}$$

Both fractions represent 1 part of the whole. You can look at the size of the parts to compare. So, $\frac{1}{4} > \frac{1}{6}$ or $\frac{1}{6} < \frac{1}{4}$.
So, Abby ate more of the granola bar.

Practice and Apply It

Use models to compare. Use >, <, or =.

1. $\frac{1}{5} \bullet \frac{1}{3}$

2. $\frac{1}{10} \bullet \frac{1}{8}$

3. $\frac{1}{2} \bullet \frac{1}{4}$

4. Roshonda put $\frac{1}{3}$ pound of apples and $\frac{1}{2}$ pound of grapes in her fruit salad. Which is heavier, the apples or the grapes?

5. **WRITE MATH** How does the denominator help you decide which fraction is greater when the numerator is the same?

6. **TALK MATH** Can you easily compare two fractions that have the same denominator? Explain.

Main Idea

I will compare fractions using models and strategies.

 Vocabulary

benchmark fractions

 Get ConnectED

3.3 The student will **c)** compare fractions having like and unlike denominators, using words and symbols (>, <, or =).

Compare Fractions

You can use models to compare fractions and see whether a fraction is greater than (>), less than (<), or equal to (=) another fraction.

REAL-WORLD EXAMPLE   Use a Model

1 **READING** Camille and Pete were reading a book. Camille read $\frac{5}{8}$ of the book, while Pete read $\frac{3}{8}$ of the same book. Use models to find who read more of the book.

Pages Read	
Camille	$\frac{5}{8}$
Pete	$\frac{3}{8}$

Compare $\frac{5}{8}$ and $\frac{3}{8}$. Use >, <, or =.

Camille | $\frac{1}{8}$ | $\frac{1}{8}$ | $\frac{1}{8}$ | $\frac{1}{8}$ | $\frac{1}{8}$ |

Pete | $\frac{1}{8}$ | $\frac{1}{8}$ | $\frac{1}{8}$ |

There are 5 one-eighth tiles and 3 one-eighth tiles.

So, $\frac{5}{8}$ is greater than $\frac{3}{8}$.

$$\frac{5}{8} > \frac{3}{8} \text{ or } \frac{3}{8} < \frac{5}{8}$$

So, Camille read more of the book than Pete.

A number line with benchmarks of 0, $\frac{1}{2}$, and 1 can be used to compare fractions. Common fractions you use often, such as $\frac{1}{4}$, $\frac{1}{3}$, $\frac{1}{2}$, $\frac{2}{3}$, and $\frac{3}{4}$ are **benchmark fractions**.

REAL-WORLD EXAMPLE   Use a Number Line

2) **MEASUREMENT** A whirligig beetle is about $\frac{3}{8}$ inch long. A lightning bug is about $\frac{1}{2}$ inch long. Which insect is longer?

Use a number line and benchmarks to compare $\frac{1}{2}$ and $\frac{3}{8}$.

To find which insect is longer, place each fraction on a number line. Then, ask yourself which fraction is closer to 1.

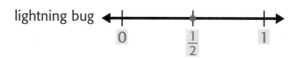

$\frac{1}{2}$ is closer to 1.

So, $\frac{1}{2} > \frac{3}{8}$ or $\frac{3}{8} < \frac{1}{2}$.

The lightning bug is longer than the whirligig beetle.

Remember

When you compare fractions, be sure the wholes are the same size.

REAL-WORLD EXAMPLE   Draw a Picture

3) **FOOD** Keri and Hank each have mini pizzas that is the same size. Keri ate $\frac{1}{2}$ of her pizza. Hank ate $\frac{3}{4}$ of his pizza. Who ate less?

Draw a picture to compare $\frac{1}{2}$ and $\frac{3}{4}$.

So, $\frac{1}{2} < \frac{3}{4}$ or $\frac{3}{4} > \frac{1}{2}$. Keri ate less pizza than Hank.

Use the models to compare. Use >, <, or =. See Examples 1–3

1.

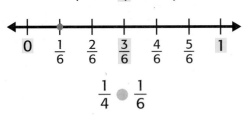

$$\frac{4}{5} \bullet \frac{3}{5}$$

2.

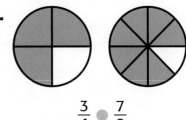

$$\frac{3}{4} \bullet \frac{7}{8}$$

Use the number line and benchmarks to compare.

Use >, <, or =. See Example 2

3.

$$\frac{1}{4} \bullet \frac{1}{6}$$

4.

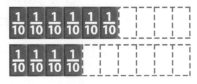

$$\frac{2}{3} \bullet \frac{5}{6}$$

5. Alister makes a party mix with $\frac{1}{3}$ cup of raisins and $\frac{2}{3}$ cup of cereal. Are there more raisins or cereal? Explain.

6. 🗨 **TALK MATH** Tell how you know that $\frac{1}{4}$ is less than $\frac{3}{4}$.

Practice and Problem Solving

EXTRA PRACTICE Begins on page EP2.

Use the models to compare. Use >, <, or =. See Examples 1–3

7.

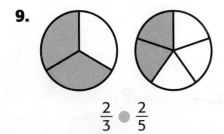

$$\frac{1}{3} \bullet \frac{2}{3}$$

8.

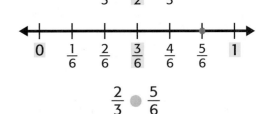

$$\frac{6}{10} \bullet \frac{4}{10}$$

9.

$$\frac{2}{3} \bullet \frac{2}{5}$$

10.

$$\frac{3}{4} \bullet \frac{3}{5}$$

Use the number line and benchmarks to compare.

Use >, <, or =. See Example 2

11.

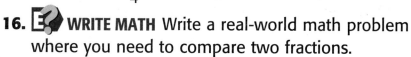

0          $\frac{1}{2}$ 1

0    $\frac{1}{6}$ $\frac{2}{6}$ $\frac{3}{6}$ $\frac{4}{6}$ $\frac{5}{6}$ 1

$\frac{1}{2}$ ⚫ $\frac{3}{6}$

12.

0 $\frac{1}{8}$ $\frac{2}{8}$ $\frac{3}{8}$ $\frac{4}{8}$ $\frac{5}{8}$ $\frac{6}{8}$ $\frac{7}{8}$ 1

0 $\frac{1}{8}$ $\frac{2}{8}$ $\frac{3}{8}$ $\frac{4}{8}$ $\frac{5}{8}$ $\frac{6}{8}$ $\frac{7}{8}$ 1

$\frac{7}{8}$ ⚫ $\frac{6}{8}$

Solve.

13. Nat has 6 toy planes. Two of them are red. Are more or less than $\frac{3}{6}$ of the planes red?

14. Otis plays soccer, basketball, football, and runs track. Do more or less than $\frac{2}{4}$ of the sports use a ball?

 H.O.T. Problems

15. NUMBER SENSE Is $\frac{1}{4}$ of the smaller waffle the same as $\frac{1}{4}$ of the larger waffle? Explain.

16. 🖹❓ **WRITE MATH** Write a real-world math problem where you need to compare two fractions.

Test Practice

17. Debbie realized that more than $\frac{4}{8}$ of her summer vacation is gone. Which fraction is more than $\frac{4}{8}$? *(Lesson 2B)*

A. $\frac{3}{8}$ **C.** $\frac{1}{2}$

B. $\frac{2}{4}$ **D.** $\frac{3}{4}$

18. Dayle has 4 goldfish, 2 guppies, and 1 tetra. What fraction of Dayle's fish is *not* goldfish? *(Lesson 1C)*

F. $\frac{1}{7}$ **H.** $\frac{3}{7}$

G. $\frac{2}{7}$ **J.** $\frac{4}{7}$

Spiral Review

19. Alaina is drawing the pattern shown. What fraction of the pattern is triangles? *(Lesson 1D)* △⬠⬠△⬠⬠

20. Hayden has 6 pets. One-third of them are cats. One is a hamster, and the rest are turtles. How many are turtles? *(Lesson 1C)*

Main Idea
I will order fractions using models and strategies.

 Get ConnectED

3.3 The student will
c) compare fractions having like and unlike denominators, using words and symbols (>, <, or =).

Order Fractions

You can use models to order fractions.

REAL-WORLD EXAMPLE   **Use Models**

1 **GYM** Third graders ran three days during gym class this week. The table shows the fraction of students that completed one mile each day. Order the fraction of students from greatest to least. Which day did the most students complete one mile?

Ran One Mile	
Day	Fraction of Students
Monday	$\frac{4}{8}$
Wednesday	$\frac{5}{6}$
Friday	$\frac{3}{4}$

One Way: Fraction Tiles

Monday $\frac{1}{8}$ $\frac{1}{8}$ $\frac{1}{8}$ $\frac{1}{8}$ $\frac{4}{8}$

Wednesday $\frac{1}{6}$ $\frac{1}{6}$ $\frac{1}{6}$ $\frac{1}{6}$ $\frac{1}{6}$ $\frac{5}{6}$

Friday $\frac{1}{4}$ $\frac{1}{4}$ $\frac{1}{4}$ $\frac{3}{4}$

The fraction tiles show that $\frac{4}{8} < \frac{3}{4} < \frac{5}{6}$.

Another Way: Draw a Diagram

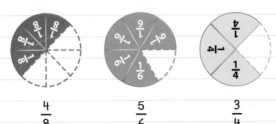

Monday   Wednesday   Friday

$\frac{4}{8}$ $\frac{5}{6}$ $\frac{3}{4}$

The drawings show that $\frac{4}{8} < \frac{3}{4} < \frac{5}{6}$.

So, most students completed one mile on Wednesday.

2 Use benchmarks of 0, $\frac{1}{2}$, and 1 to order $\frac{3}{8}$, $\frac{3}{6}$, and $\frac{1}{4}$ from least to greatest.

Ask yourself which fraction is closest to 0, which is closest to $\frac{1}{2}$, and which is closest to 1.

Remember

When the denominators are the same, look at the numerators. The greater the numerator, the greater the fraction.

$\frac{3}{8}$　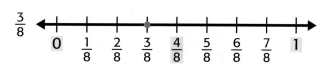

$\frac{3}{6}$　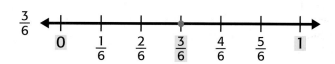

$\frac{1}{4}$　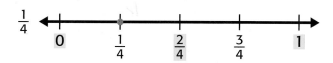

$\frac{1}{4}$ is closest to 0, $\frac{3}{6}$ is closest to 1, and $\frac{3}{8}$ comes between $\frac{1}{4}$ and $\frac{3}{6}$.

So, the number lines and benchmarks show that $\frac{1}{4} < \frac{3}{8} < \frac{3}{6}$.

 **What You Know**

Use models to order each set of fractions from least to greatest. See Examples 1 and 2

1. $\frac{1}{2}$, $\frac{2}{8}$, $\frac{3}{4}$

2. $\frac{3}{5}$, $\frac{4}{10}$, $\frac{2}{10}$

3. $\frac{1}{4}$, $\frac{1}{6}$, $\frac{1}{8}$

4. Owen bought $\frac{5}{8}$ pound of ham, $\frac{1}{2}$ pound of chicken, and $\frac{3}{4}$ pound of turkey at the store. Order the deli meat from greatest to least amount bought.

5. **TALK MATH** Explain how a number line can be used to order fractions.

Use models to order each set of fractions from least to greatest. See Examples 1 and 2

6. $\frac{1}{10}$, $\frac{1}{5}$, $\frac{4}{5}$

7. $\frac{4}{8}$, $\frac{7}{8}$, $\frac{1}{8}$

8. $\frac{5}{8}$, $\frac{3}{4}$, $\frac{1}{4}$

9. $\frac{2}{3}$, $\frac{2}{6}$, $\frac{3}{6}$

10. $\frac{6}{12}$, $\frac{1}{3}$, $\frac{3}{3}$

11. $\frac{3}{4}$, $\frac{1}{2}$, $\frac{1}{3}$

12. Measurement Order the amount of rainfall in the following cities from greatest to least.

Rainfall in July	
City	**Amount of Rain**
Las Vegas, NV	$\frac{1}{5}$ inch
St. Louis, MO	$\frac{9}{10}$ inch
Milwaukee, WI	$\frac{1}{2}$ inch

13. Measurement Order the amount of each ingredient in the recipe from greatest to least.

SNACK MIX

$\frac{1}{4}$ cup walnuts

$\frac{5}{8}$ cup granola

$\frac{3}{8}$ cup yogurt chips

Mix and enjoy.

14. Measurement Order the fractions of an inch from least to greatest.
$\frac{7}{8}$, $\frac{2}{8}$, $\frac{2}{4}$

H.O.T. Problems

15. NUMBER SENSE Are these fractions ordered from greatest to least? Explain.

$$\frac{1}{3}, \frac{1}{4}, \frac{1}{5}$$

16. FIND THE ERROR Morgan is ordering three fractions from greatest to least. Find and correct her mistake. Explain.

$\frac{4}{10}$, $\frac{3}{5}$, $\frac{1}{2}$

17. WRITE MATH Explain what it means to use benchmarks to compare and order fractions.

Write the fraction for the part that is green. Then write the fraction for the part that is *not* green. (Lesson 1B)

1.

2.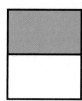

Draw a picture for each fraction. Shade the fraction. (Lesson 1B)

3. $\frac{1}{6}$

4. $\frac{3}{5}$

5. A cake is divided equally into 8 pieces. If two pieces are eaten, what fraction of the cake is left? (Lesson 1B)

6. MULTIPLE CHOICE What fraction of the figure is shaded? (Lesson 1B)

A. $\frac{1}{2}$

B. $\frac{5}{9}$

C. $\frac{5}{8}$

D. $\frac{3}{8}$

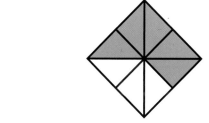

7. Sydney has 7 packages of sticky notes. Five of the packages are pink, one is green, and one is blue. Write a fraction to show what part of the set of sticky notes is *not* pink.

(Lesson 1C)

Compare. Use >, <, or =. (Lesson 2B)

8.

$\frac{5}{6}$ $\frac{2}{3}$

9.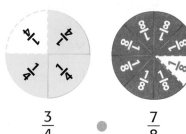

$\frac{3}{4}$ $\frac{7}{8}$

10. Measurement Kenyon poured $\frac{3}{4}$ cup of water and $\frac{3}{8}$ cup of vegetable oil in a mixing bowl. Did he use more water or vegetable oil? (Lesson 2B)

11. Algebra Clem is thinking of two numbers. The sum of the numbers is 8. The product is 15. What are the numbers? (Lesson 1D)

Order each set of fractions from least to greatest. (Lesson 2C)

12. $\frac{3}{10}, \frac{4}{5}, \frac{1}{5}$

13. $\frac{1}{2}, \frac{1}{3}, \frac{1}{4}$

14. **WRITE MATH** Sarah did three sets of jumping jacks. She finished the first set in $\frac{1}{2}$ of a minute. She finished the second set in $\frac{5}{6}$ of a minute, and the last set in $\frac{2}{3}$ of a minute. Order her times from greatest to least. Explain. (Lesson 2C)

Problem-Solving Investigation

Main Idea I will choose the best strategy to solve a problem.

P.S.I. TEAM +

CARLOTA: Last night, I played a board game. On one turn, I rolled two number cubes. The sum of the numbers was 9. The difference was 3.

YOUR MISSION: Find the two numbers Carlota rolled.

Understand

Carlota rolled two number cubes. The sum of the numbers was 9. The difference was 3. Find the two numbers rolled.

Plan

Make a table to show all of the possible rolls and their sums.

Solve

The table shows that to get a sum of 9, Carlota must have rolled 5 and 4, or 6 and 3.

$6 + 3 = 9$ $3 + 6 = 9$

$5 + 4 = 9$ $4 + 5 = 9$

Find the difference.

$6 - 3 = 3$

$5 - 4 = 1$

Since $6 + 3 = 9$ and $6 - 3 = 3$, Carlota must have rolled 6 and 3.

+	0	1	2	3	4	5	6
0	0	1	2	3	4	5	6
1	1	2	3	4	5	6	7
2	2	3	4	5	6	7	8
3	3	4	5	6	7	8	9
4	4	5	6	7	8	9	10
5	5	6	7	8	9	10	11
6	6	7	8	9	10	11	12

Check

Since $3 + 6 = 9$ and $6 - 3 = 3$, you know the answer is correct. ✓

 3.3 The student will **b)** model fractions (including mixed numbers) and write the fractions' names.

- Make a table.
- Draw a picture.
- Guess, check, and revise.
- Work backward.

Use any strategy to solve each problem.

1. **Measurement** Paige is finishing the third grade. She weighs 77 pounds. During the school year she gained 8 pounds. What did Paige weigh at the start of third grade?

2. A family of four goes bowling. Find the total cost if each person rents a ball and shoes and plays two games.

BOWLING
$4 per game
$2 shoe rental
$1 ball rental

3. **Measurement** A moose weighs about 1,300 pounds. A cougar weighs about 250 pounds. How much more does the moose weigh than the cougar?

4. Emil is drawing the pattern shown. What fraction of the pattern is squares?

5. Pablo, Annie, and Roman each have a pet. One has a cat, one has a turtle, and another has a mouse. Annie and Pablo each have a pet with fur. Pablo and Roman each have a pet that lives in an aquarium. Who has the mouse?

6. Suppose you buy the items shown for lunch. If you pay with a $10-bill, how much change will you receive?

Lunch
Soda $1
Pizza $2

7. **Algebra** There are two numbers whose sum is 8 and quotient is 3. Find the numbers.

8. Lulu's parents took Lulu and two of her friends to the zoo. How much money did they pay for admission and parking?

Zoo Admission Prices
Adults $8
Children $5
Groups of 10 or more.................... $7 each
Parking $3

9. Alejandro's family has a hamster, 2 dogs, and 4 fish. What fraction of his family's pets is dogs?

10. **WRITE MATH** A cake has 4 layers. One layer is orange, one is vanilla, and the others are peach. What fraction of the cake is peach? Explain.

Explore Equivalent Fractions

Main Idea

I will model equivalent fractions.

Materials

fraction tiles

Get ConnectED

Fraction models can help you find fractions that name the same amount, or **equivalent fractions**.

ACTIVITY

Step 1 **Model $\frac{1}{2}$.**

Start with 1 whole and a $\frac{1}{2}$ fraction tile.

1
$\frac{1}{2}$	

Step 2 **Find one fraction equivalent to $\frac{1}{2}$.**

Use $\frac{1}{4}$ fraction tiles to equal the length of the $\frac{1}{2}$ fraction tile. Count the number of $\frac{1}{4}$ fraction tiles. So, $\frac{1}{2} = \frac{2}{4}$.

1			
$\frac{1}{2}$			
$\frac{1}{4}$	$\frac{1}{4}$		

Step 3 **Find another fraction equivalent to $\frac{1}{2}$.**

Use $\frac{1}{8}$ fraction tiles to equal the length of the $\frac{1}{2}$ fraction tile. Count the number of $\frac{1}{8}$ fraction tiles. So, $\frac{1}{2} = \frac{4}{8}$.

1							
$\frac{1}{2}$							
$\frac{1}{4}$		$\frac{1}{4}$					
$\frac{1}{8}$	$\frac{1}{8}$	$\frac{1}{8}$	$\frac{1}{8}$				

Think About It

1. How many of the $\frac{1}{4}$ fraction tiles are equal to the length of the $\frac{1}{2}$ fraction tile?

2. How many of the $\frac{1}{8}$ fraction tiles are equal to the length of the $\frac{1}{2}$ fraction tile?

3. Write two fractions that name the same amount as $\frac{1}{2}$.

4. Copy and complete $\frac{1}{2} = \frac{\blacksquare}{4} = \frac{\blacksquare}{8}$.

5. Use fraction models to find two fractions equivalent to $\frac{1}{3}$.

Practice and Apply It

Use models to complete the equivalent fractions.

6. = How many $\boxed{\frac{1}{8}}$?

$\frac{1}{4} = \frac{\blacksquare}{8}$

7. $\boxed{\frac{1}{5}}$ = How many $\boxed{\frac{1}{10}}$?

$\frac{1}{5} = \frac{\blacksquare}{10}$

8. $\boxed{\frac{1}{3}}$ = How many $\boxed{\frac{1}{6}}$?

$\frac{1}{3} = \frac{\blacksquare}{6}$

9. = How many $\boxed{\frac{1}{12}}$?

$\frac{2}{6} = \frac{\blacksquare}{12}$

Use fraction models to determine whether each pair of fractions is equivalent or not equivalent. Write *yes* or *no*.

10. $\frac{1}{2}$ and $\frac{3}{6}$

11. $\frac{1}{4}$ and $\frac{2}{4}$

12. $\frac{3}{4}$ and $\frac{6}{8}$

13. $\frac{3}{3}$ and $\frac{6}{6}$

14. $\frac{3}{5}$ and $\frac{5}{10}$

15. $\frac{2}{3}$ and $\frac{4}{6}$

16. **WRITE MATH** How do you know whether two fractions are equivalent? Explain how you know whether two fractions are not equivalent.

Main Idea

I will use models to find equivalent fractions.

Vocabulary

equivalent fractions

 Get ConnectED

Equivalent Fractions

Two or more different fractions that name the same amount are called **equivalent fractions**.

REAL-WORLD EXAMPLE Use Models

① **BOOKS** Kwan has a bookshelf. One of the 3 shelves has books. Kwan says that $\frac{1}{3}$ of the shelves have books. What other fraction has the same value as $\frac{1}{3}$? Complete $\frac{1}{3} = \frac{\blacksquare}{6}$ to find an equivalent fraction.

One Way: Use Models	**Another Way:** Draw a Diagram
Think about the number of equal parts in the fraction tiles.	The rectangle is divided into thirds. One part is shaded.
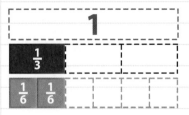	A rectangle of equal size is divided into sixths. The same amount is shaded.
There are 2 sixths in $\frac{1}{3}$. So, $\frac{1}{3} = \frac{2}{6}$.	There are 2 sixths in $\frac{1}{3}$. So, $\frac{1}{3} = \frac{2}{6}$.

Complete each number sentence to find equivalent fractions.

See Example 1

1.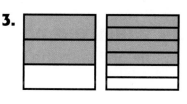

$$\frac{1}{2} = \frac{\blacksquare}{4}$$

2.

$$\frac{\blacksquare}{4} = \frac{2}{8}$$

3.

$$\frac{\blacksquare}{3} = \frac{\blacksquare}{6}$$

4. Wayne ate two fifths of an apple pie. Write another fraction that names $\frac{2}{5}$.

5. 🗒️ **TALK MATH** What pattern do you see in the fractions $\frac{1}{2} = \frac{2}{4} = \frac{4}{8}$?

Practice and Problem Solving

EXTRA **PRACTICE**
Begins on page EP2.

Complete each number sentence to find equivalent fractions.

See Example 1

6.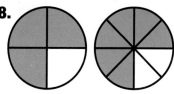

$$\frac{1}{2} = \frac{\blacksquare}{6}$$

7.

$$\frac{1}{5} = \frac{\blacksquare}{10}$$

8.

$$\frac{\blacksquare}{4} = \frac{6}{8}$$

9.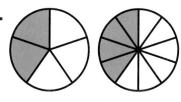

$$\frac{\blacksquare}{5} = \frac{4}{10}$$

10.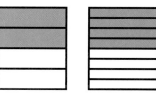

$$\frac{\blacksquare}{4} = \frac{\blacksquare}{8}$$

11.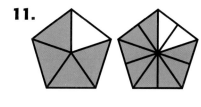

$$\frac{\blacksquare}{5} = \frac{\blacksquare}{10}$$

Algebra **Find each missing value. Use models if needed.**

12. $\frac{1}{2} = \frac{\blacksquare}{8}$

13. $\frac{1}{3} = \frac{\blacksquare}{12}$

14. $\frac{3}{\blacksquare} = \frac{6}{8}$

15. $\frac{\blacksquare}{5} = \frac{8}{10}$

Write an equivalent fraction for each fraction name.

16. One-sixth of a game spinner is red.

17. Amy read two-thirds of a book.

H.O.T. Problems

18. OPEN ENDED Give an example of two fractions that are not equivalent. Draw a picture to support your answer.

19. WHICH ONE DOESN'T BELONG? Which fraction does not belong with the other three? Explain your reasoning.

$\frac{4}{8}$ $\frac{1}{2}$ $\frac{5}{10}$ $\frac{3}{5}$

20.  **WRITE MATH** Explain how you would find a fraction equivalent to $\frac{1}{2}$.

Test Practice

21. What fraction of the figure is shaded? (Lesson 1B)

   A. $\frac{1}{8}$

   B. $\frac{5}{8}$

   C. $\frac{6}{8}$

   D. $\frac{5}{6}$

22. Which figure is equivalent to $\frac{2}{3}$? (Lesson 3C)

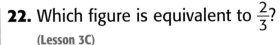

F.   **H.**

G.   **J.**

Spiral Review

23. Phillip has 8 marbles. One-fourth of the marbles are red. One is multi-colored, and the rest are green. How many are green? (Lesson 3A)

24. In Luanda's neighborhood, 8 children have scooters and 2 do not. Write a fraction to show how many children do *not* have scooters. (Lesson 1C)

25. What fraction of the set of paints is red?
(Lesson 1C)

26. What fraction of the items shown is round?
(Lesson 1C)

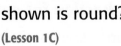 **468** Fractions

Extend Equivalent Fractions

Main Idea

I will use technology to model equivalent fractions.

ACTIVITY

Use *Math Tool Chest* to model equivalent fractions.

Savanna played 4 video games. If Savanna won $\frac{1}{2}$ of the games, how many games did she win?

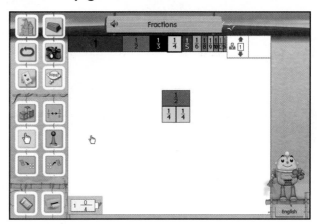

- Stamp out a $\frac{1}{2}$-fraction tile.
- Underneath, stamp out enough $\frac{1}{4}$-fraction tiles to equal $\frac{1}{2}$.
- The model shows that $\frac{1}{2} = \frac{2}{4}$.

How many games did Savanna win?

✓ CHECK What You Know

Use Math Tool Chest to model each fraction and find one equivalent fraction.

1. $\frac{1}{5}$

2. $\frac{3}{6}$

3. $\frac{3}{9}$

4. $\frac{4}{12}$

5. Oscar cut a loaf of bread into 12 slices. Each slice is $\frac{1}{12}$ of the loaf. He used $\frac{1}{3}$ of the loaf to make sandwiches. How many slices of bread did he use?

6. Raheem was at bat 8 times during a baseball game. He struck out 2 times. What fraction of times at bat did Raheem strike out?

To assess partial mastery of SOL 3.3, see your Virginia Assessment Book.

Problem Solving in Science

The BUZZ on Insects

Insects have been around for 250 million years . . . long before the dinosaurs. Today, there are over 800,000 known species of insects! These species represent $\frac{1}{12}$ of all the animal species on Earth.

Insects have different sizes and shapes, but they all have four things in common. Insects have
- three body parts,
- six jointed legs,
- two antennae, and
- an outside skeleton.

Real-World Math

Use the information on these two pages to solve each problem.

1. Is the length of the firefly greater than or less than the length of the housefly?

2. Is the length of the lady beetle greater than or less than $\frac{1}{2}$ inch?

3. Of Earth's animal species, $\frac{1}{12}$ are insects. What part are not insects? Draw a model to show your work.

4. What part of all animals on Earth are not beetles?

5. Round the number of bugs to the nearest ten thousand.

6. What fraction of the insects shown are longer than $\frac{1}{2}$ inch?

7. Suppose you put one lady beetle in front of another. Which insect would have this same length?

8. Which two insects are the same length?

Six-Spotted Green Tiger Beetle
$\frac{5}{8}$ inch

Firefly
$\frac{3}{4}$ inch

Honeybee
$\frac{4}{8}$ inch

Lady Beetle
$\frac{3}{8}$ inch

Housefly
$\frac{1}{2}$ inch

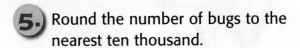

That's a Lot of Insects!

Insect	Number of Species
Beetle	350,000
Butterfly & Moth	170,000
Fly	120,000
Bee & Ant	110,000
Bug	82,000
Grasshopper	20,000
Dragonfly	5,000

Did You Know?

Of all the animals on Earth, $\frac{1}{4}$ are beetles.

Explore **Add Like Fractions**

Main Idea

I will use models to add like fractions.

Materials

fraction tiles

Get ConnectED

 **3.7** The student will add and subtract proper fractions having like denominators of 12 or less.

Two fractions, such as $\frac{2}{5}$ and $\frac{1}{5}$, are called **like fractions** because they have the same denominator. Fraction models can be used to explore adding like fractions.

ACTIVITY

1) Find $\frac{2}{5} + \frac{1}{5}$.

Step 1 Model $\frac{2}{5}$.

Use two $\frac{1}{5}$ fraction tiles to show $\frac{2}{5}$.

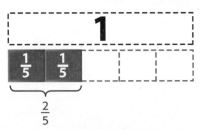

Step 2 Model $\frac{1}{5}$.

Use one $\frac{1}{5}$ fraction tile to show $\frac{1}{5}$.

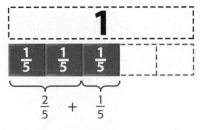

Step 3 Add.

Count the total number of $\frac{1}{5}$ fraction tiles. So, $\frac{2}{5} + \frac{1}{5} = \frac{3}{5}$.

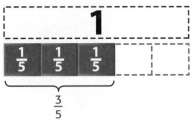

(2) Find $\frac{3}{8} + \frac{4}{8}$.

Step 1 **Model $\frac{3}{8}$.**

Start with 1 whole.
Use three $\frac{1}{8}$ fraction
tiles to show $\frac{3}{8}$.

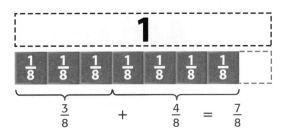

Step 2 **Model $\frac{4}{8}$.**

Use four $\frac{1}{8}$ fraction tiles to show $\frac{4}{8}$.

Step 3 **Add.**

Count the total number of $\frac{1}{8}$ fraction tiles.
So, $\frac{3}{8} + \frac{4}{8} = \frac{7}{8}$.

Think About It

1. How did you use fraction models to show the addends?

2. How did you find each sum?

Practice and Apply It

Add.

3.

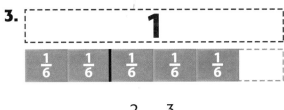

$\frac{2}{6} + \frac{3}{6}$

4.

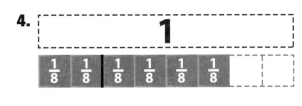

$\frac{2}{8} + \frac{4}{8}$

5. ✍ **WRITE MATH** Look at the numerators and the denominators in each exercise above. Can you find each sum without using fraction models? Explain.

Main Idea

I will add like fractions.

Vocabulary

like fractions

3.7 The student will add and subtract proper fractions having like denominators of 12 or less.

Add Like Fractions

To add two **like fractions** such as $\frac{1}{5}$ and $\frac{3}{5}$, you add the numerators the same way you add whole numbers. You keep the same denominator.

REAL-WORLD EXAMPLE   Add Like Fractions

1 **GARDENS** Tamera planted beans in $\frac{1}{5}$ of the garden. Her sister Cecelia planted carrots in $\frac{3}{5}$ of the garden. What fraction of the garden did they plant with beans and carrots?

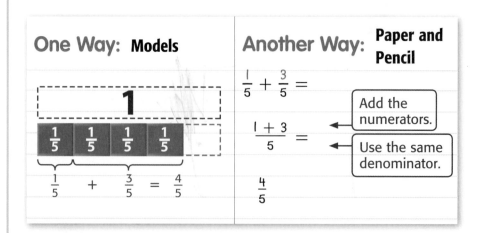

One Way: Models	Another Way: Paper and Pencil
1 $\frac{1}{5}$ $\frac{1}{5}$ $\frac{1}{5}$ $\frac{1}{5}$ $\frac{1}{5} + \frac{3}{5} = \frac{4}{5}$	$\frac{1}{5} + \frac{3}{5} =$ Add the numerators. $\frac{1+3}{5} =$ Use the same denominator. $\frac{4}{5}$

So, they planted $\frac{4}{5}$ of the garden with beans and carrots.

② **WEATHER A local weather report showed the rainfall for Wednesday and Thursday. How much rain fell in these two days?**

How Much Rain Did We Get?

Wednesday   Thursday

$\frac{3}{8}$ inch $\frac{5}{8}$ inch

You need to find $\frac{3}{8} + \frac{5}{8}$.

$\frac{3}{8} + \frac{5}{8} =$

$\frac{3+5}{8} =$

$\frac{8}{8} = 1$ ← THINK $\frac{8}{8} = 1$

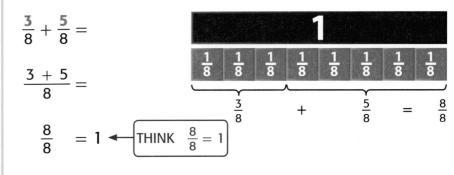

Remember

If a fraction has the same numerator and denominator, write the fraction as 1.

$\frac{8}{8} = 1$

So, $\frac{8}{8}$, or 1, inch of rain fell in the two days.

Key Concept   Add Like Fractions

Words   To add fractions with the same denominator, add the numerators and keep the same denominator.

Example $\frac{5}{7} + \frac{1}{7} = \frac{5+1}{7} = \frac{6}{7}$

✓ **CHECK What You Know**

Add. Use fraction models if needed. See Examples 1 and 2

1. $\frac{1}{8} + \frac{2}{8}$

2. $\frac{1}{10} + \frac{2}{10}$

3. $\frac{5}{12} + \frac{2}{12}$

4. $\frac{1}{6} + \frac{5}{6}$

5. Alister uses $\frac{1}{3}$ cup of cereal to make one batch of party mix. How much cereal will he use to make 2 batches?

6. 📝 **TALK MATH** Describe the numerator and denominator of a fraction that can be written as 1.

Add. Use fraction models if needed. See Examples 1 and 2

7. $\frac{1}{8} + \frac{4}{8}$

8. $\frac{1}{6} + \frac{4}{6}$

9. $\frac{1}{4} + \frac{3}{4}$

10. $\frac{2}{3} + \frac{1}{3}$

11. $\frac{1}{3} + \frac{1}{3}$

12. $\frac{2}{5} + \frac{2}{5}$

13. $\frac{1}{7} + \frac{4}{7}$

14. $\frac{3}{9} + \frac{2}{9}$

15. $\frac{2}{9} + \frac{7}{9}$

16. $\frac{4}{10} + \frac{6}{10}$

17. $\frac{2}{10} + \frac{7}{10}$

18. $\frac{7}{12} + \frac{4}{12}$

19. Barb paints $\frac{2}{5}$ of a wall. Her dad paints $\frac{1}{5}$ of the wall. How much of the wall did they paint in all?

20. A recipe uses $\frac{1}{4}$ cup of cheese. How much cheese would you use if you doubled the recipe?

21. Write an addition sentence that can be used to find what fraction of the weekdays had sunshine or rain.

22. What is the total length of the turtle?

Monday	Tuesday	Wednesday	Thursday	Friday

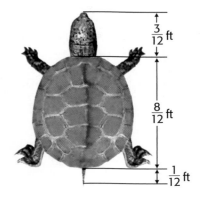

$\frac{3}{12}$ ft

$\frac{8}{12}$ ft

$\frac{1}{12}$ ft

23. Steven has $\frac{3}{10}$ of one dollar. Rob has $\frac{6}{10}$ of one dollar. Together, what part of one dollar do they have?

Algebra Find each missing value.

24. $\frac{3}{8} + \frac{\blacksquare}{8} = \frac{5}{8}$

25. $\frac{\blacksquare}{7} + \frac{2}{7} = \frac{6}{7}$

26. $\frac{5}{6} + \blacksquare = 1$

Data File

The state bird of California is the valley quail.

27. How much would two of the smallest quails weigh?

28. Find the total weight of two of the largest quails.

Valley Quail	
Size	9–10 inches
Weight	smallest: $\frac{1}{4}$ pound largest: $\frac{1}{2}$ pound

29. FIND THE ERROR Carlos is adding fractions. Find and correct his mistake.

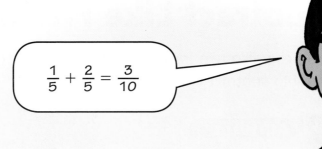

$$\frac{1}{5} + \frac{2}{5} = \frac{3}{10}$$

30. **WRITE MATH** Explain how to find $\frac{2}{9} + \frac{4}{9}$.

Test Practice

31. Lorenzo used $\frac{5}{8}$ of a cup of raisins in a recipe. Which fraction is more than $\frac{5}{8}$? (Lesson 2B)

A. $\frac{3}{8}$ **C.** $\frac{1}{2}$

B. $\frac{2}{4}$ **D.** $\frac{3}{4}$

32. A pie was divided into eighths. Kaylee ate $\frac{1}{8}$ of the pie. Orlando ate $\frac{2}{8}$ of the pie. How much of the pie did they eat? (Lesson 4B)

F. $\frac{1}{8}$ **H.** $\frac{1}{2}$

G. $\frac{3}{8}$ **J.** $\frac{5}{8}$

Spiral Review

Complete each number sentence to find equivalent fractions.

(Lesson 3C)

33. $\frac{1}{2} = \frac{\blacksquare}{6}$ **34.** $\frac{2}{3} = \frac{4}{\blacksquare}$ **35.** $\frac{3}{5} = \frac{\blacksquare}{10}$

36. Measurement It takes Stefanie 30 minutes to get to school. What fraction of an hour is this? (Lesson 3A)

Use models to compare. Use >, <, or =. (Lesson 2B)

37. $\frac{1}{4} \bullet \frac{3}{4}$ **38.** $\frac{1}{3} \bullet \frac{1}{2}$ **39.** $\frac{2}{3} \bullet \frac{3}{5}$

40. Gus bought a package of baseball cards for $4.00. He paid with a $10 bill. What fraction of the $10 bill did he receive as change? (Lesson 1B)

Explore Subtract Like Fractions

Main Idea
I will use models to subtract like fractions.

Materials
fraction tiles

Get ConnectED

3.7 The student will add and subtract proper fractions having like denominators of 12 or less.

You can also use fraction models to help you understand how to subtract like fractions.

ACTIVITY

① Find $\frac{5}{6} - \frac{2}{6}$.

Step 1 **Model $\frac{5}{6}$.**
Use five $\frac{1}{6}$ fraction tiles to show $\frac{5}{6}$.

Step 2 **Subtract $\frac{2}{6}$.**
Remove two $\frac{1}{6}$ fraction tiles to show the subtraction of $\frac{2}{6}$. Count the fraction pieces left.
So, $\frac{5}{6} - \frac{2}{6} = \frac{3}{6}$.

2 Find $\frac{7}{12} - \frac{3}{12}$.

Step 1 Model $\frac{7}{12}$.

Use seven $\frac{1}{12}$ fraction tiles to show $\frac{7}{12}$.

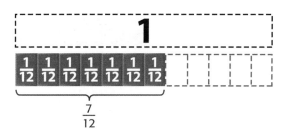

Step 2 Subtract $\frac{3}{12}$.

Remove three $\frac{1}{12}$ fraction tiles. Count the fraction tiles left.

So, $\frac{7}{12} - \frac{3}{12} = \frac{4}{12}$.

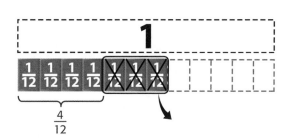

Think About It

1. How did you use fraction models to show $\frac{7}{12}$?

2. What did you do to find the difference?

Practice and Apply It

Write the subtraction sentence for each model.

3.
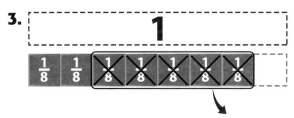

4.
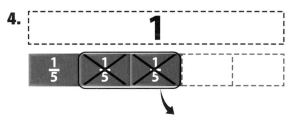

5. $\frac{5}{6} - \frac{1}{6}$ **6.** $\frac{8}{9} - \frac{7}{9}$ **7.** $\frac{4}{4} - \frac{2}{4}$

8. **WRITE MATH** Look at the numerators and the denominators in each exercise. What do you notice about the difference?

Main Idea

I will subtract like fractions.

Get Connect**ED**

3.7 The student will add and subtract proper fractions having like denominators of 12 or less.

Subtract Like Fractions

Subtracting like fractions is similar to adding like fractions. You subtract the numerators instead of adding them. Keep the same denominator.

REAL-WORLD EXAMPLE   Subtract Like Fractions

1) **MEASUREMENT** To make a pitcher of lemonade, Vanessa needs $\frac{2}{4}$ cup of lemonade mix. She has $\frac{3}{4}$ cup of mix. How much mix will Vanessa have left after making one pitcher of lemonade?

You need to find $\frac{3}{4} - \frac{2}{4}$.

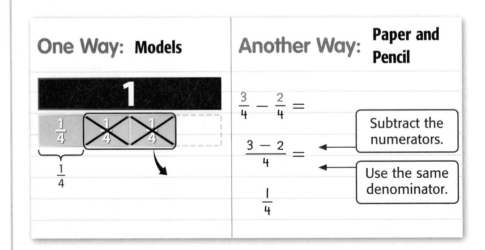

One Way: Models	Another Way: Paper and Pencil
1 $\frac{1}{4}$ $\frac{1}{4}$ $\frac{1}{4}$ $\frac{1}{4}$	$\frac{3}{4} - \frac{2}{4} =$ ← Subtract the numerators. $\frac{3-2}{4} =$ ← Use the same denominator. $\frac{1}{4}$

So, Vanessa will have $\frac{1}{4}$ cup of lemonade mix left.

Subtract Like Fractions

2) SCIENCE About $\frac{9}{10}$ of an iceberg is below water. Subtract $1 - \frac{9}{10}$ to find what part of the iceberg is above water.

Remember

When subtracting a fraction from 1, write 1 as a fraction.

Find $1 - \frac{9}{10}$.

$1 - \frac{9}{10}$

THINK $1 = \frac{10}{10}$

$\frac{10}{10} - \frac{9}{10} = \frac{10 - 9}{10}$

$= \frac{1}{10}$

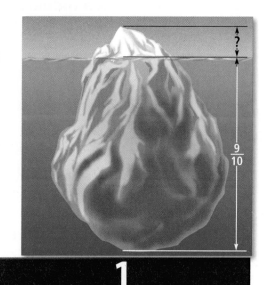

$\frac{9}{10}$

1

$\frac{1}{10}$ ❌❌❌❌❌❌❌❌❌

$\frac{1}{10}$

So, $\frac{1}{10}$ of the iceberg is above water.

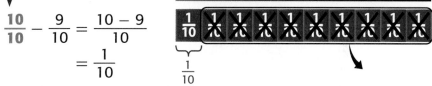

Key Concept Subtract Like Fractions

Words To subtract fractions with the same denominator, subtract the numerators and use the same denominator.

Example $\frac{6}{8} - \frac{1}{8} = \frac{6 - 1}{8} = \frac{5}{8}$

✓ CHECK What You Know

Subtract. Use fraction models if needed. See Examples 1 and 2

1. $\frac{5}{6} - \frac{4}{6}$ **2.** $\frac{7}{8} - \frac{3}{8}$ **3.** $\frac{6}{9} - \frac{4}{9}$ **4.** $\frac{1}{3} - \frac{1}{3}$

5. Sonia has 1 cup of juice. She drinks $\frac{3}{4}$ cup. How much juice is left?

6. **TALK MATH** To find $1 - \frac{7}{8}$, why do you write 1 as $\frac{8}{8}$?

Subtract. Use fraction models if needed. See Examples 1 and 2

7. $\frac{2}{3} - \frac{1}{3}$

8. $\frac{4}{5} - \frac{1}{5}$

9. $\frac{4}{6} - \frac{3}{6}$

10. $\frac{6}{8} - \frac{5}{8}$

11. $\frac{1}{2} - \frac{1}{2}$

12. $\frac{5}{6} - \frac{5}{6}$

13. $\frac{7}{8} - \frac{2}{8}$

14. $\frac{8}{9} - \frac{2}{9}$

15. $\frac{7}{10} - \frac{3}{10}$

16. $\frac{9}{12} - \frac{5}{12}$

17. $1 - \frac{1}{5}$

18. $1 - \frac{7}{9}$

19. There is $\frac{3}{5}$ of a pan of lasagna. A family eats $\frac{1}{5}$ of the lasagna. What fraction of the lasagna is left?

20. A box is divided into 10 equal sections. If $\frac{7}{10}$ of the sections are filled, what fraction is not filled?

21. The fish is 1 inch long. Write a subtraction expression you can use to find the length of the fish's tail.

22. A pizza shop cuts a pizza into eighths. They sell $\frac{3}{8}$ of the slices to one customer and $\frac{1}{8}$ to another customer. What fraction of the pizza is left?

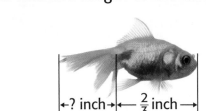

←? inch→←$\frac{2}{3}$ inch→

Algebra **Find each missing value.**

23. $\frac{4}{5} - \frac{\blacksquare}{5} = \frac{1}{5}$

24. $\frac{\blacksquare}{8} - \frac{1}{8} = \frac{6}{8}$

25. $1 - \blacksquare = \frac{2}{5}$

H.O.T. Problems

26. OPEN ENDED Write a real-world word problem that contains subtraction of fractions.

27. FIND THE ERROR Kim is finding $1 - \frac{3}{3}$. Find and correct her mistake.

$1 - \frac{3}{3} = \frac{2}{3}$

28. **WRITE MATH** Write two ways you may use subtraction of fractions each day.

29. Marc grew $\frac{4}{12}$ of a foot last year, this year he grew another $\frac{1}{12}$ of a foot. How much has Marc grown over the last two years? (Lesson 4B)

A. $\frac{5}{24}$ foot

B. $\frac{3}{12}$ foot

C. $\frac{4}{12}$ foot

D. $\frac{5}{12}$ foot

30. A loaf of bread is cut into ten equal slices. Mora and Adriana each eat $\frac{2}{10}$ of the bread slices. How much of the bread is left? (Lesson 4D)

F. $\frac{3}{10}$

G. $\frac{4}{10}$

H. $\frac{6}{10}$

J. $\frac{8}{10}$

Spiral Review

Add. Use fraction models if needed. (Lesson 4B)

31. $\frac{1}{5} + \frac{2}{5}$

32. $\frac{3}{8} + \frac{5}{8}$

33. $\frac{1}{12} + \frac{3}{12}$

Complete each number sentence to find equivalent fractions. (Lesson 3C)

34. $\frac{\blacksquare}{6} = \frac{2}{12}$

35. $\frac{3}{4} = \frac{\blacksquare}{8}$

36. $\frac{\blacksquare}{6} = \frac{2}{3}$

Use models to order each set of fractions from greatest to least. (Lesson 2C)

37. $\frac{1}{5}, \frac{1}{4}, \frac{1}{3}$

38. $\frac{5}{8}, \frac{1}{8}, \frac{1}{2}$

39. $\frac{3}{6}, \frac{2}{3}, \frac{3}{3}$

40. A dessert recipe uses $\frac{2}{3}$ cup of berries and $\frac{3}{4}$ cup of grapes. Which is the greater amount, the berries or the grapes? (Lesson 2B)

Solve. (Lesson 1C)

41. Heath drew four times as many pictures as his brother. Heath's brother drew 2 pictures. What fraction of the boys' pictures did Heath draw?

42. There are 7 tiles in a bag. Six tiles are blue, and 1 tile is red. Write the fraction for the part of the set that is blue. Write the fraction for the part of the set that is *not* blue.

Game Time

Fraction Concentration
Find Equivalent Fractions

You will need: 10 index cards; scissors; marker

Get Ready!
Players: 2 players

Get Set!
Cut each index card in half. Then label as shown.

Go!

☆ Shuffle the cards. Then spread out the cards facedown.

☆ Player 1 turns over any two of the cards.

☆ If the fractions are equivalent, Player 1 keeps the cards and continues his or her turn.

☆ If the fractions are not equivalent, the cards are turned over and Player 2 takes a turn.

☆ Continue playing until all fraction matches are made. The player with more cards wins.

$\frac{1}{2}$	$\frac{1}{3}$	$\frac{1}{4}$	$\frac{1}{5}$
$\frac{3}{4}$	$\frac{2}{5}$	$\frac{2}{3}$	$\frac{3}{9}$
$\frac{4}{5}$	$\frac{4}{8}$	$\frac{4}{10}$	$\frac{2}{12}$
$\frac{1}{6}$	$\frac{6}{10}$	$\frac{2}{8}$	$\frac{3}{5}$
$\frac{2}{10}$	$\frac{8}{10}$	$\frac{4}{6}$	$\frac{6}{8}$

Chapter Study Guide and Review

Be sure the following Key Concepts are noted in your Foldable.

Fractions
Parts of a Whole
Parts of a Set
Compare Fractions
Order Fractions
Equivalent Fractions

Key Concepts

- A **fraction** names part of a whole or part of a set. (Lesson 1)

  numerator

  $$\frac{2}{3} \qquad \frac{3}{5}$$

  denominator

- Use models or draw a picture to compare and order fractions. (Lesson 2)

- **Equivalent fractions** name the same amount. (Lesson 3)

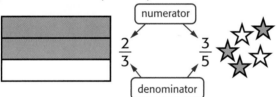

  $$\frac{2}{4} = \frac{4}{8}$$

- To add **like fractions**, add the numerators. (Lesson 4)

  $$\frac{3}{8} + \frac{2}{8} = \frac{3+2}{8} = \frac{5}{8}$$ ← Keep the same

- To subtract like fractions, subtract the numerators. (Lesson 4)

  $$\frac{7}{9} - \frac{4}{9} = \frac{7-4}{9} = \frac{3}{9}$$ ← Keep the same

Key Vocabulary

denominator

equivalent fractions

fraction

like fractions

numerator(s)

Vocabulary Check

Choose the vocabulary word that completes each sentence.

1. The number $\frac{1}{2}$ is a(n) ____?____.

2. When adding ____?____, such as $\frac{1}{5}$ and $\frac{3}{5}$, the denominator stays the same.

3. In the fraction $\frac{3}{4}$, the 3 is called the ____?____.

4. The fractions $\frac{1}{3}$ and $\frac{2}{6}$ are ____?____.

5. The ____?____ tells the total number of equal parts.

6. Subtract only the ____?____ when solving a problem such as $\frac{3}{4} - \frac{2}{4}$.

Multi-Part Lesson Review

Understand Fractions

Part of a Whole and Part of a Set (Lessons 1B and 1C)

Write the fraction for the part that is blue. Then write the fraction for the part that is *not* blue.

7.

8.

9.

10.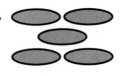

Draw a picture for each fraction. Shade the fraction.

11. $\frac{2}{3}$

12. $\frac{3}{8}$

EXAMPLE 1

What fraction of the figure is blue?

$\frac{3}{4}$ ← numerator
← denominator

Write $\frac{3}{4}$ ← use numbers

Read *three-fourths* ← use words

So, $\frac{3}{4}$ or three-fourths is blue.

Problem-Solving Strategy: Draw a Picture (Lesson 1D)

13. A music CD tower can hold 16 CDs. One-half of the slots are filled with CDs. How many CDs are in the CD tower?

14. A boat ride has 15 boats. The boats are yellow, purple, or orange. One-fifth are yellow. Five are purple. How many of the boats are orange?

15. Melinda and Ruben are playing tic-tac-toe. Melinda has Xs in one-third of the 9 squares. Ruben has Os in 2 of the squares. How many squares are empty?

EXAMPLE 2

There are 12 trucks. One-third are red. Two are blue. The rest are green. How many trucks are green?

Divide a figure into 12 equal parts. Shade $\frac{1}{3}$ to show the red trucks and 2 parts to show the blue trucks.

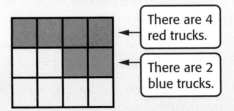

There are 4 red trucks.

There are 2 blue trucks.

There are 6 parts left. So, 6 are green.

Compare and Order Fractions

Compare and Order Fractions (Lessons 2B and 2C)

16. Compare. Use >, <, or =.

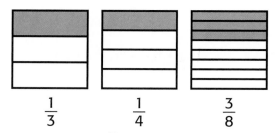

$\frac{2}{5}$ ● $\frac{3}{4}$

17. Order the set of fractions from least to greatest.

$\frac{1}{3}$ $\frac{1}{4}$ $\frac{3}{8}$

18. Lucita walks $\frac{3}{4}$ mile. Sergio walks $\frac{3}{6}$ mile. Who walks farther?

EXAMPLE 3

Compare $\frac{2}{3}$ and $\frac{3}{5}$. Use fraction models.

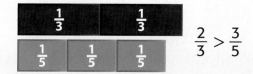

$\frac{2}{3} > \frac{3}{5}$

Order $\frac{4}{6}$, $\frac{2}{4}$, and $\frac{1}{6}$ from least to greatest. Use a number line.

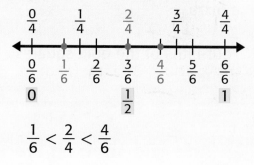

$\frac{1}{6} < \frac{2}{4} < \frac{4}{6}$

Equivalent Fractions

Problem-Solving Investigation: Choose a Strategy (Lesson 3A)

19. Sodas cost $2. Salads cost $4. Lia buys 1 soda and 1 salad. Trish orders 1 soda and 2 salads. How much money is spent in all?

20. Mrs. Cook drove 7 hours each day for 2 days. Then she drove 4 hours each day for 2 days. How many hours did she drive in all?

21. Paloma needs 5 wall tiles for each mural she makes. She has 15 tiles. How many murals can she make?

EXAMPLE 4

Zane saves $6 in coins each month. How long will it take him to save $48 in coins?

To solve the problem, you can use the *guess, check, and revise* strategy.

$6 × 7 = $42   no
$6 × 9 = $54   no
$6 × 8 = $48   yes

It will take Zane 8 months to save $48.

Equivalent Fractions (Lesson 3C)

Complete each number sentence to find an equivalent fraction.

22. $\frac{1}{2} = \frac{\blacksquare}{4}$

23. $\frac{2}{2} = \frac{\blacksquare}{6}$

24. $\frac{1}{3} = \frac{\blacksquare}{6}$

25. $\frac{3}{5} = \frac{\blacksquare}{10}$

Write an equivalent fraction for each fraction name.

26. Harish put extra cheese on $\frac{1}{5}$ of a pizza.

27. Four-fifths of the quilt squares are red.

EXAMPLE 5

Complete $\frac{2}{3} = \frac{\blacksquare}{6}$ to find an equivalent fraction.

One Way: Use Fraction Models

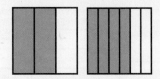

Another Way: Draw a Picture

There are 4 sixths in $\frac{2}{3}$. So, $\frac{2}{3} = \frac{4}{6}$.

Lesson 4 **Add and Subtract Fractions**

Add and Subtract Like Fractions (Lessons 4B and 4D)

Add or subtract. Use fraction models, if needed.

28. $\frac{5}{9} + \frac{2}{9}$

29. $\frac{3}{7} + \frac{1}{7}$

30. $\frac{3}{5} - \frac{1}{5}$

31. $\frac{8}{10} - \frac{2}{10}$

32. $\frac{9}{12} - \frac{7}{12}$

33. $\frac{3}{6} + \frac{3}{6}$

34. The tail of a squirrel is about $\frac{1}{2}$ of its length from its nose to the tip of its tail. What fraction does the squirrel's body represent?

EXAMPLE 6

Find $\frac{3}{8} + \frac{1}{8}$.

Use fraction models.

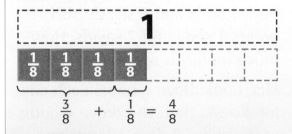

$\frac{3}{8} + \frac{1}{8} = \frac{4}{8}$

EXAMPLE 7

Find $\frac{4}{8} - \frac{3}{8}$. Use paper and pencil.

$\frac{4}{8} - \frac{3}{8} = \frac{4-3}{8} = \frac{1}{8}$

Tell whether each statement is *true* or *false*.

1. The numerator is the top number in a fraction.

2. The fractions $\frac{3}{5}$ and $\frac{5}{10}$ are equivalent fractions.

Complete each number sentence to find equivalent fractions.

3. $\frac{1}{4} = \frac{\blacksquare}{8}$

4. $\frac{3}{5} = \frac{\blacksquare}{10}$

5. What fraction of the spinner is purple?

6. There are 2 groups of 5 students and 2 groups of 7 students on a field trip. How many students are there altogether?

7. MULTIPLE CHOICE Which figure is equivalent to $\frac{3}{4}$?

A.

C.

B.

D.

8. Of the fish in an aquarium, $\frac{8}{12}$ are orange and $\frac{4}{12}$ are striped. Are more fish orange or striped?

9. MULTIPLE CHOICE Which fraction of the leaves is shaded?

F. $\frac{2}{6}$

H. $\frac{4}{6}$

G. $\frac{2}{4}$

J. $\frac{4}{2}$

Use the number lines to help you order from greatest to least.

10. $\frac{2}{5}, \frac{7}{8}, \frac{4}{6}$

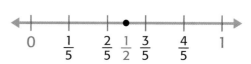

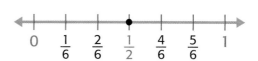

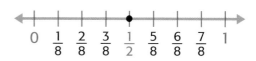

Add or subtract.

11. $\frac{5}{9} - \frac{3}{9}$

12. $\frac{4}{10} + \frac{5}{10}$

13. $\frac{3}{6} + \frac{1}{6}$

14. $\frac{4}{7} - \frac{1}{7}$

15. WRITE MATH There are 9 students. Four-ninths of them are carrying backpacks. Are more students carrying backpacks or not carrying backpacks? Explain.

A container is divided into fifths. Paul fills $\frac{1}{5}$ of the container with peanuts, $\frac{2}{5}$ with popcorn, and $\frac{1}{5}$ with pretzels. What fraction of the container is empty?

A. $\frac{1}{5}$ **C.** $\frac{3}{5}$

B. $\frac{2}{5}$ **D.** $\frac{4}{5}$

Read the Question

Find the fraction of the container that is empty.

Solve the Question

Draw a picture to solve the problem.

$$\frac{1}{5} + \frac{2}{5} + \frac{1}{5} = \frac{4}{5}$$

So, $\frac{4}{5}$ of the container is filled and $\frac{1}{5}$ of the container is empty.
The answer is A.

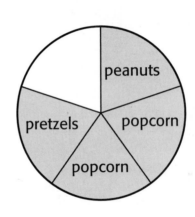

$\frac{1}{5}$ peanuts

$\frac{2}{5}$ popcorn

$\frac{1}{5}$ pretzels

Read each question. Then fill in the correct answer on the answer sheet provided by your teacher or on a separate sheet of paper.

1. If $\frac{3}{5}$ of a wheel of cheese has been eaten, what fraction of the cheese has not been eaten?

A. $\frac{1}{4}$ **C.** $\frac{2}{5}$

B. $\frac{3}{8}$ **D.** $\frac{2}{4}$

2. Edgar divided a piece of paper into 9 equal-sized rectangles. He shaded $\frac{2}{3}$ of the paper. How many rectangles are not shaded?

F. 3   **H.** 6

G. 5   **J.** 8

3. A pie is cut into 8 equal slices. Some friends eat 6 pieces. What fractional part of the pie have they eaten?

A. $\dfrac{3}{4}$ **C.** $\dfrac{2}{3}$

B. $\dfrac{4}{6}$ **D.** $\dfrac{6}{6}$

---

4. Casey drew smiley faces on her paper. Which face appears to have a line of symmetry?

F.   **H.**

G.   **J.**

---

5. A sandwich is divided into eighths.

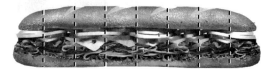

Antonio ate $\dfrac{3}{8}$ of the sandwich. Mandy and Anita each ate $\dfrac{1}{8}$ of the sandwich. How much is left?

A. $\dfrac{3}{8}$ **C.** $\dfrac{5}{8}$

B. $\dfrac{4}{8}$ **D.** $\dfrac{6}{8}$

---

6. Of the following, which set is ordered from greatest to least?

F. $\dfrac{4}{8}, \dfrac{5}{8}, \dfrac{3}{4}$ **H.** $\dfrac{3}{4}, \dfrac{4}{8}, \dfrac{5}{8}$

G. $\dfrac{3}{4}, \dfrac{5}{8}, \dfrac{4}{8}$ **J.** $\dfrac{5}{8}, \dfrac{4}{8}, \dfrac{3}{4}$

---

7. Emma has 3 black cats and 1 gray cat. What fraction of Emma's cats is gray?

A. $\dfrac{1}{4}$ **C.** $\dfrac{2}{3}$

B. $\dfrac{1}{2}$ **D.** $\dfrac{3}{4}$

---

8. Tony made tacos for dinner using the recipe below. Tony used the least amount of which topping?

Tempting Tacos
F. $\dfrac{3}{4}$ cup   peppers
G. $\dfrac{1}{2}$ cup   tomatoes
H. $\dfrac{1}{4}$ cup   green onions
J. 1 cup   cheddar cheese

NEED EXTRA HELP?								
If You Missed Question . . .	1	2	3	4	5	6	7	8
Go to Chapter-Lesson . . .	9-4D	9-4D	9-3C	7-3D	9-4B	9-2C	9-1C	9-2B
For help with . . .	SOL 3.7	SOL 3.7	SOL 3.3a	SOL 3.14	SOL 3.7	SOL 3.3c	SOL 3.3a	SOL 3.3c

CHAPTER
10

Mixed Numbers

connectED.mcgraw-hill.com

Investigate

 Animations

 Vocabulary

 Math Songs

 Multilingual eGlossary

Learn

 Personal Tutor

 Virtual Manipulatives

 Audio

 Foldables

Practice

 Self-Check Practice

 eGames

 Worksheets

 Assessment

The ☆BIG Idea

How can I use models to understand mixed numbers?

FOLDABLES
Study Organizer

Make this Foldable to help you organize information about fractions. Begin with one sheet of $8\frac{1}{2}'' \times 11''$ paper.

| Mixed Numbers | Compare and Order Mixed Numbers | Equivalent Mixed Numbers |

Review Vocabulary

equivalent fractions fracciones equivalentes

fractions that have the same value

$$\frac{2}{4} = \frac{1}{2}$$

| $\frac{1}{4}$ | $\frac{1}{4}$ | | |

| $\frac{1}{2}$ | |

Key Vocabulary

English	Español
fraction	fracción
mixed number	número mixto

When Will I Use This?

Are You Ready for the Chapter?

You have two options for checking Prerequisite Skills for this chapter.

Text Option Take the Quick Check below.

QUICK Check

Write a fraction for the part shaded yellow.

1.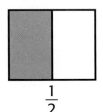

2.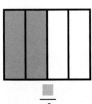

3.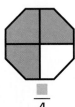

Write an equivalent fraction.

4.

$$\frac{1}{2} \qquad \frac{\blacksquare}{4}$$

5.

$$\frac{6}{8} \qquad \frac{\blacksquare}{4}$$

6. Jenna's mom cut an apple into 4 pieces. She gave Jenna 3 pieces. Then she cut another apple of the same size into 8 pieces and gave Ian 6 pieces. Who has more apple? Explain.

7. Taka painted $\frac{1}{4}$ of the room. What fraction of the room does Taka have left to paint?

Use >, <, or =.

8. $\frac{5}{10} \ \bullet \ \frac{6}{10}$

9. $\frac{2}{3} \ \bullet \ \frac{2}{6}$

10. $\frac{1}{3} \ \bullet \ \frac{3}{4}$

Tell which point represents each given number.

11. 36

30 32 34

12. 123

127 129 131

Online Option Take the Online Readiness Quiz.

Explore Mixed Numbers

Main Idea

I will use area and linear models to explore mixed numbers.

Materials

fraction circles

fraction tiles

Get ConnectED

3.3 The student will **b)** model fractions (including mixed numbers) and write the fractions' names.

You have learned that a fraction is a number that names part of a whole or part of a set. Sometimes a fraction names 1 whole.

ACTIVITY

1 **Steven cut an orange into 8 pieces.**

Step 1 Use a fraction circle to model 1 whole orange.

Step 2 Model 1 whole orange cut into 8 equal pieces.

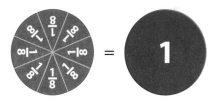

Step 3 Write the fraction.
Write $\frac{8}{8} = 1$
Read eight-eighths equals one

Think About It

1. How many sixths are in 1 whole that is divided into 6 equal parts?

2. Model 1 whole that has been divided equally into fifths.

3. What does a fraction look like that names 1 whole?

A number that names a whole and part of another whole is
a **mixed number.**

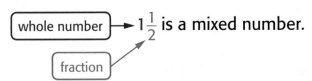

whole number → $1\frac{1}{2}$ is a mixed number.

fraction

ACTIVITY

2 **Delmar drank 1 whole glass of milk and half of another.**

Step 1 Use a fraction tile to model 1 whole.

1

Step 2 Use fraction tiles marked $\frac{1}{2}$. Model 1 whole
and one-half.

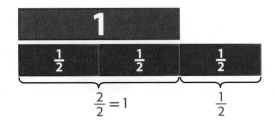

1
$\frac{1}{2}$ $\frac{1}{2}$ $\frac{1}{2}$

$\frac{2}{2} = 1$ $\frac{1}{2}$

Step 3 Write the fraction.
Write $1\frac{1}{2}$
Read one *and* one-half

Practice and Apply It

Model each number.

4. 2

5. $1\frac{4}{6}$

6. $2\frac{1}{10}$

7. Look back at Activity 2. How many halves make the mixed
number $1\frac{1}{2}$?

8. Domingo cuts his piece of toast into 4 pieces. Emilio cuts
his equal-sized piece of toast into 6 pieces. Does Emilio
have more toast than Domingo? Explain.

9. **WRITE MATH** How can you tell if a fraction is less than
1 whole, is 1 whole, or is more than 1 whole?

Main Idea

I will represent mixed numbers using area and linear models.

 Vocabulary

proper fraction

mixed number

improper fraction

 **Get Connect ED**

 **3.3** The student will **a)** name and write fractions (including mixed numbers) represented by a model; **b)** model fractions (including mixed numbers) and write the fractions' names; **3.7** The student will add and subtract proper fractions having like denominators of 12 or less.

Mixed Numbers

A fraction that names part of a whole is also known as a **proper fraction**. A **mixed number** names a whole number and part of another whole.

Proper Fractions	Mixed Numbers
$\frac{1}{2}$ $\frac{3}{4}$ $\frac{2}{6}$	$1\frac{3}{4}$ $2\frac{1}{2}$ $3\frac{2}{6}$

 **REAL-WORLD EXAMPLE**   Use Area Models

1 **FOOD** Julia made two peanut butter and jelly sandwiches. She cut the sandwiches into 4 pieces each. After eating some, she has 5 pieces left. What fraction of the sandwiches does Julia have left?

Each sandwich has 4 pieces. There are 5 pieces left. Count the wholes and the parts.

$$\frac{4}{4} \quad + \quad \frac{1}{4} \quad = \quad 1\frac{1}{4}$$

whole   part

So, $1\frac{1}{4}$ of the sandwiches are left.

2 MEASUREMENT Porcupine quills can be as short as 1 inch and as long as 12 inches.

Write the length of this quill as a mixed number.

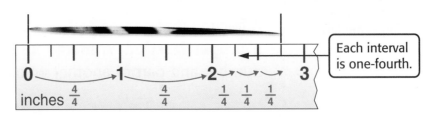

Each interval is one-fourth.

inches $\frac{4}{4}$ $\frac{4}{4}$ $\frac{1}{4}$ $\frac{1}{4}$ $\frac{1}{4}$

> **Remember**
>
> When the numerator and the denominator are the same, the fraction equals 1.

Count the wholes.

$$\frac{4}{4} + \frac{4}{4} = 2$$

Count the parts.

$$\frac{1}{4} + \frac{1}{4} + \frac{1}{4} = \frac{3}{4}$$

$$2 + \frac{3}{4} = 2\frac{3}{4} \text{ inches}$$

So, the quill is $2\frac{3}{4}$ inches long.

3 Identify point A as a mixed number.

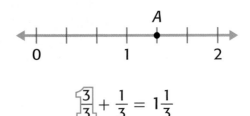

$$\frac{3}{3} + \frac{1}{3} = 1\frac{1}{3}$$

Each interval on the number line is one-third.

So, point A is $1\frac{1}{3}$.

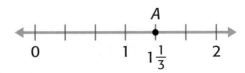

Write a mixed number for each model. See Examples 1 and 2

1.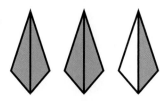

2.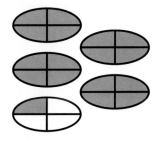

3.

Identify each point. Write as a mixed number. See Example 3

4. $B = $ ▢

5. $G = $ ▢

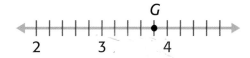

6. Does *Point C* represent the mixed number $1\frac{1}{4}$ or $1\frac{3}{4}$? Explain.

7. 🅴 **TALK MATH** Explain how to model $2\frac{3}{5}$.

Practice and Problem Solving

EXTRA **PRACTICE**
Begins on page EP2.

Write a mixed number for each model. See Examples 1 and 2

8.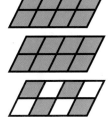

9.

10.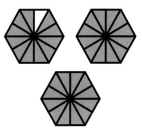

11.

12.

Identify each point. Write as a mixed number. See Example 3

13. A = ■ B = ■

1   2   3

14. C = ■ D = ■

2   3

15. S = ■ T = ■

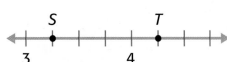

3   4

16. U = ■ V = ■

6   7

17. Measurement Enrique needs $1\frac{1}{2}$ cups of flour for pancakes, and $1\frac{3}{4}$ cups for bread. Using a one-fourth cup measure he filled it 7 times. Did he measure flour for the pancakes or the bread. Explain.

18. Measurement Bailey ate $2\frac{4}{6}$ cups of popcorn during the first half of the movie. On a number line, is $2\frac{4}{6}$ closer to the number 2 or the number 3.

REAL-WORLD PROBLEM SOLVING

Animal Tracks You can identify animals by the tracks they make.

19. Draw a model to represent the length of a black bear's track.

20. When counting on a number line is the length of a deer's track before or after the length of a lynx's track? Draw a model to explain.

Length of Animal Tracks	
Animal	**Length (inches)**
Black bear	$7\frac{1}{10}$
Deer	$3\frac{1}{2}$
Lynx	$3\frac{7}{10}$

21. Identify each butterfly by its length.

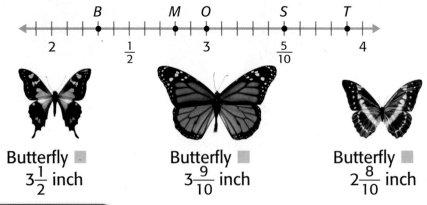

Butterfly ■
$3\frac{1}{2}$ inch

Butterfly ■
$3\frac{9}{10}$ inch

Butterfly ■
$2\frac{8}{10}$ inch

H.O.T. Problems

22. OPEN ENDED Name two mixed numbers that have the same value.

23. 📝 **WRITE MATH** Compare a fraction and a mixed number.

More About **Mixed Numbers**

You know that a proper fraction is a fraction that has a value less than 1. Its numerator is smaller than its denominator.

You also know that a mixed number has a whole number part and a proper fraction part.

| **Mixed Numbers** |
| $1\frac{4}{5}$ $2\frac{1}{3}$ |

Sometimes a fraction has a numerator greater than, or equal to, the denominator. This is an **improper fraction**

Fractions that are greater than, or equal to one, may be named as a mixed number or an improper fraction.

| **Improper Fractions** |
| $\frac{9}{5}$ $\frac{7}{3}$ |

EXAMPLE Write Mixed Numbers and Improper Fractions

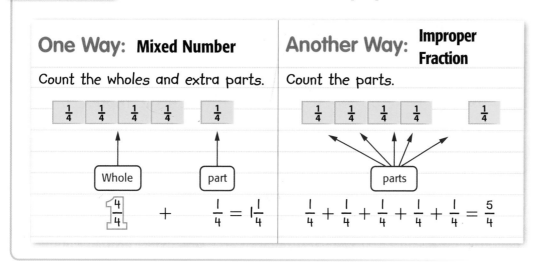

One Way: Mixed Number

Count the wholes and extra parts.

$$1\frac{4}{4} + \frac{1}{4} = 1\frac{1}{4}$$

Another Way: Improper Fraction

Count the parts.

$$\frac{1}{4} + \frac{1}{4} + \frac{1}{4} + \frac{1}{4} + \frac{1}{4} = \frac{5}{4}$$

Write a mixed number and an improper fraction for each model.

24.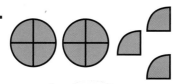

25.

26.

27. Jay baked two apple pies. He cut them into equal pieces. Jay ate one piece, which was $\frac{1}{8}$ of the pie. What fraction of the pies are left?

(Lesson 1B)

28. A dessert recipe uses $1\frac{2}{3}$ cups of berries, $\frac{3}{4}$ cup of grapes, $1\frac{1}{2}$ cups of sliced peaches, and $2\frac{1}{2}$ cups of kiwi. Which of these is not a mixed number? (Lesson 1B)

Problem-Solving Strategy: Make a Model

Main Idea I will solve a problem by using the make a model strategy.

Nora's class is making 3 colors of clay: red, blue, and green. It takes $2\frac{1}{4}$ cups of flour to make each color. How many cups of flour will be used for all three colors?

Understand **What facts do you know?**

- $2\frac{1}{4}$ cups of flour are needed for each color.

- They will make three colors of clay.

What do you need to find?

- The total cups of flour needed.

Plan You can use the *make a model* strategy. Use models to represent the cups of flour for each color.

Solve Model $2\frac{1}{4}$ cups of flour for the red clay.

Model $2\frac{1}{4}$ cups of flour for the blue clay.

Model $2\frac{1}{4}$ cups of flour for the green clay.

There are a total of 6 whole cups and $\frac{3}{4}$ cup of flour.

So, $6\frac{3}{4}$ cups of flour are needed.

Check Count the full cups. $1 + 1 + 1 + 1 + 1 + 1 = 6$

Count the left-over one-fourth cups. $\frac{1}{4} + \frac{1}{4} + \frac{1}{4} = \frac{3}{4}$

$6 + \frac{3}{4} = 6\frac{3}{4}$. So, the answer is correct. ✔

3.3 The student will **a)** name and write fractions (including mixed numbers) represented by a model; **b)** model fractions (including mixed numbers) and write the fractions' names;

Refer to the problem on the previous page.

1. Why was $2\frac{1}{4}$ cups modeled 3 times?

2. Suppose the amount of flour needed was $4\frac{1}{2}$ cups for each color. How would the answer change?

3. Describe a situation when you may have to put mixed numbers together to find a total.

4. Why is the *make a model* strategy helpful when working with fractions?

PRACTICE

EXTRA PRACTICE
Begins on page EP2.

Solve. Use the *make a model* strategy.

5. Measurement It takes one hour to make 4 pizzas. How many pizzas can be made in $4\frac{1}{2}$ hours?

6. Measurement Rudy left for the Florida shore at 5 A.M. If the trip takes 10 hours, will he be at his destination by 3 P.M.? Explain.

7. There are 4 packs of yogurt. Each pack has 6 yogurts. How many more packs are needed for a total of 30 yogurts?

8. How much will lunch cost for 5 people if each person buys all of the items on the menu?

Lunch	
Item	**Cost**
Chicken	$2
Apple	$1
Milk	$1

9. Brice catches 3 more fish than Damon. Sarita catches 3 more fish than Brice. Brice catches 5 fish. How many fish did each person catch?

10. Algebra If Rita draws 15 more shapes in her pattern, how many of those shapes would be triangles?

11. There are 36 frogs swimming in a pond. Four more are on lily pads than are on the banks of the pond. There are a total of 58 frogs. How many frogs are on the lily pads and on the banks?

12. Darin has 17 apples in a basket. He wants to share them with three of his friends. How many will Darin and each friend get if the apples are shared equally? How many will be left?

13. WRITE MATH How many 8-ounce packages of dog bones are in a box that weighs 200 ounces? Explain the strategy you found most helpful in solving this problem.

Red, White, and Blueberries!

The blueberry is one of the few fruits native to North America. For centuries, Native Americans used blueberries to dye baskets and cloth and to eat. Blueberries were also used as medicine.

North America grows and uses more blueberries than people from any other continent. Blueberries are found in all types of food, such as pancakes, muffins, smoothies, salsas, and salads.

Blueberry and Strawberry Parfait

5 cups vanilla frozen yogurt

$1\frac{1}{4}$ cups strawberries

$1\frac{1}{4}$ cups blueberries

$3\frac{1}{3}$ cups granola

$6\frac{1}{4}$ teaspoons honey

whipped cream

5 parfait glasses

Blend blueberries until almost smooth. Put blended berries in a bowl and set aside. Repeat with strawberries. Layer each parfait glass with $\frac{1}{2}$ cup of yogurt, $\frac{1}{4}$ cup of blended blueberries and $\frac{1}{3}$ cup of granola. Add $\frac{1}{2}$ cup of yogurt, $\frac{1}{4}$ cup of blended strawberries and $\frac{1}{3}$ cup of granola. Top with whipped cream. Spoon $1\frac{1}{4}$ teaspoons of honey on top and enjoy!

Blueberry Pancakes

2 eggs, separated

$1\frac{1}{2}$ cups flour

$2\frac{1}{4}$ cups baking powder

3 tablespoons sugar

$\frac{1}{2}$ teaspoon salt

1 cup milk

3 tablespoons butter, melted

1 cup blueberries

In a small bowl, beat egg whites until stiff. In a separate bowl, mix together flour, baking powder, sugar, and salt. Beat egg yolks in a medium-size bowl; add milk and butter. Stir egg mixture into dry ingredients; mix until batter is smooth. Stir in blueberries. Fold in egg whites. Pour batter on a hot, greased griddle.

Real-World Math

Use the information on the previous page to solve each problem.

1. Look at the pancake recipe. List the ingredients that have fractions greater than 1.

2. Suppose you had $1\frac{3}{4}$ cups of flour. Would you have enough flour to make the pancake recipe? Explain.

3. Does the pancake recipe call for more than or less than 1 cup of flour? Explain.

4. Look at the parfait recipe. List the ingredients made up of fractions greater than 1.

5. Would you need more granola or blueberries to make the parfaits?

6. Would 2 cups of strawberries be enough to make the parfait recipe? Explain.

7. Would 1 cup of blueberries be enough to make the parfait recipe? Explain.

8. Suppose you spooned 1 teaspoon of honey onto each parfait. How much more honey do you need to add to each parfait?

Game Time

★ Mixed Number Match
Match Mixed Numbers and Models

You will need: 1 set of model cards, 1 set of mixed-number cards

Get Ready!

Players: 2 players

Get Set!

☆ Cut out the model cards and the mixed-number cards.

☆ Shuffle the cards separately and place in 2 piles.

☆ Deal the players 5 of each card.

Go!

☆ Players place matches on the table.

☆ Round 1 begins. Player 1 replaces the cards that were made into matches, taking an even number of model and mixed-number cards from the piles.

☆ Player 1 continues matching and replacing cards until no more matches can be made.

☆ Player 2 takes a turn.

☆ Round 2 begins. Player 1 may discard 1 model card and 1 mixed-number card and then choose a replacement for each from the piles. If matches can be made, play will continue as in Round 1.

☆ The game continues until both players have had an equal number of turns and one player is rid of all their cards. The player with more matches wins.

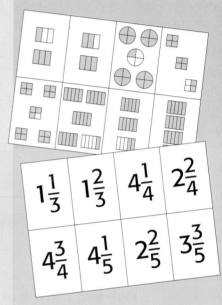

$1\frac{1}{3}$ $1\frac{2}{3}$ $4\frac{1}{4}$ $2\frac{2}{4}$

$4\frac{3}{4}$ $4\frac{1}{5}$ $2\frac{2}{5}$ $3\frac{3}{5}$

Mid-Chapter Check

Write a mixed number and an improper fraction for each model.
(Lesson 1B)

1.

2.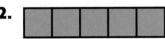

3.

4. MULTIPLE CHOICE While making a dessert for his family, Will almost forgot to put in the one ingredient that was not listed as a mixed number. What was that ingredient? (Lesson 1B)

  A. 1 teaspoon cinnamon

  B. $1\frac{1}{2}$ teaspoons baking soda

  C. $1\frac{1}{4}$ teaspoons salt

  D. $1\frac{3}{4}$ teaspoons honey

5. Maverick drew a line $1\frac{2}{3}$ yards long. The line that Carissa drew was $2\frac{3}{6}$ yards long. Who drew the line that was less than 2 yards long? (Lesson 1C)

Identify each point. Write as a mixed number. (Lesson 1B)

6. $A = \blacksquare$

7. $B = \blacksquare$

8. Identify the point that represents $2\frac{1}{2}$.
$2\frac{1}{2} = \blacksquare$

9. MULTIPLE CHOICE The model represents the length of the nails that Jeffery needs for the wood box he is making. How long are the nails that he needs? (Lesson 1B)

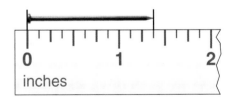

  F. $1\frac{6}{8}$ inches   **H.** $1\frac{3}{8}$ inches

  G. $1\frac{7}{8}$ inches   **J.** $\frac{3}{8}$ inches

10. **WRITE MATH** Explain what $2\frac{5}{8}$ means. (Lesson 1C)

Main Idea

I will use models and strategies to compare and order mixed numbers.

Get ConnectED

3.3 The student will **c)** compare fractions having like and unlike denominators, using words and symbols (>, <, or =).

Compare and Order Mixed Numbers

You can use models to compare mixed numbers.

REAL-WORLD EXAMPLE Compare Mixed Numbers

1 **BAKING** **Susana is making oatmeal bars. Does the recipe call for more flour or oatmeal?**

Oatmeal Bars

$1\frac{1}{2}$ cups oatmeal   1 teaspoon vanilla
$1\frac{3}{4}$ cups flour   1 teaspoon baking soda
2 eggs

Mix well. Pour into a 13" x 9" pan. Bake at 350°.

Step 1 Model the fractions.

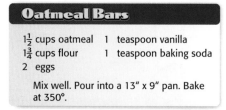

Step 2 Compare the whole numbers.

The oatmeal and flour have the same whole number. 1 = 1

Step 3 Compare the fraction part.

$$\frac{1}{2} < \frac{3}{4}$$

So, Susana needs more flour than oatmeal.

To order mixed numbers you can use a number line.

REAL-WORLD EXAMPLE   Use a Number Line

2 **CRAFTS** Tammie is making bows to sell at the craft fair. She uses $3\frac{2}{6}$ yards of red ribbon, $3\frac{5}{6}$ yards of blue ribbon, and $1\frac{4}{6}$ yards of green ribbon. **Order the ribbon lengths from least to greatest.**

Compare, then order the mixed numbers by placing them on the number line.

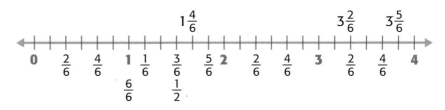

So, the order of the ribbon lengths from least to greatest is $1\frac{4}{6}$, $3\frac{2}{6}$, and $3\frac{5}{6}$ yards.

CHECK What You Know

Compare the mixed numbers. Use >, <, or =. See Example 1

1.

$2\frac{3}{4}$ ● $1\frac{3}{4}$

2.

$1\frac{2}{5}$ ● $1\frac{4}{5}$

Use the number line to order the mixed numbers from least to greatest. See Example 2

3. $2\frac{1}{3}$, $2\frac{2}{3}$, $1\frac{2}{3}$

4. ? **TALK MATH** Explain why $2\frac{3}{4}$ is called a mixed number.

Compare the mixed numbers. Use >, <, or =. See Example 1

5.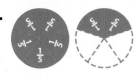

$1\frac{7}{8}$ ● $1\frac{2}{3}$

6.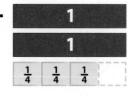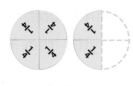

$2\frac{3}{4}$ ● $2\frac{3}{6}$

7.

$1\frac{2}{5}$ ● $1\frac{2}{4}$

8.

$2\frac{1}{4}$ ● $1\frac{3}{4}$

Use the number line to order the mixed numbers from least to greatest. See Example 2

9. $1\frac{2}{8}, 1\frac{3}{4}, 1\frac{2}{4}$

10. $2\frac{1}{5}, 1\frac{4}{5}, 2\frac{3}{5}$

11. Measurement Margie's frog leaped $1\frac{2}{3}$ feet. Sylvestor's frog leaped $1\frac{6}{8}$ feet. Whose frog leaped farther? Explain.

12. Measurement Kim weighed $5\frac{3}{4}$ pounds at birth. Her twin weighed $5\frac{3}{8}$ pounds. Did Kim or her twin weigh more at birth? Explain.

13. Measurement Order the number of inches the children grew from least to greatest.

Child	Gavin	Miki	Nakos
Growth (inches)	$2\frac{2}{10}$	$3\frac{1}{5}$	$2\frac{1}{2}$

14. Measurement Order the runners in the table from fastest to slowest.

Runner	Sara	Berkley	Jed
Time (min)	$10\frac{4}{5}$	$10\frac{3}{4}$	$10\frac{6}{10}$

15. NUMBER SENSE What two whole numbers does $2\frac{3}{4}$ come between on a number line? Explain.

16. 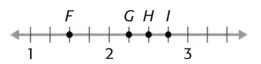 **WRITE MATH** Explain how to compare two mixed numbers.

Test Practice

17. A hummingbird grows to only $2\frac{1}{2}$ inches in length. Identify the point that represents this number. (Lesson 1B)

```
          F       G H I
      ←+──┼──┼──┼──┼─┼─┼──┼──→
         1       2       3
```

A. F

B. G

C. H

D. I

18. Compare and order the lengths of some of the world's smallest animals from least to greatest.
(Lesson 2A)

Animal	Length (in.)
Bumblebee bat	$1\frac{3}{10}$
Thread snake	$4\frac{1}{4}$
Bee hummingbird	$2\frac{2}{10}$

F. $1\frac{3}{10}, 4\frac{1}{4}, 2\frac{2}{10}$

G. $4\frac{1}{4}, 2\frac{2}{10}, 1\frac{3}{10}$

H. $2\frac{2}{10}, 1\frac{3}{10}, 4\frac{1}{4}$

J. $1\frac{3}{10}, 2\frac{2}{10}, 4\frac{1}{4}$

Spiral Review

Solve. (Lesson 1C)

19. Mel's dog is $8\frac{3}{4}$ inches tall. Trina's dog is $9\frac{1}{4}$ inches tall. Whose dog is shorter?

Write a mixed number for each model. (Lesson 1B)

20.

21.

Identify each point. Write as a mixed number. (Lesson 1B)

22. $A = $ ▓ $B = $ ▓

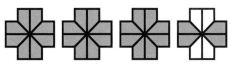
```
        A   B
   ←+──┼─●─●─┼──┼──┼──→
    3              4
```

23. $D = $ ▓ $E = $ ▓

```
      D                    E
  ←+─●─┼──┼──┼──┼──┼──●──→
   7          8
```

Problem-Solving Investigation

Main Idea I will choose the best strategy to solve a problem.

P.S.I. TEAM +

IAN: As a final project on our study of France, we each made one French food to share with the class. I made crepes that I cut into 8 pieces each. Delmar ate $1\frac{5}{8}$ crepes and Brenda ate $1\frac{1}{2}$ crepes.

YOUR MISSION: Find who ate more.

Understand

You know how much Delmar and Brenda each ate. Find who ate more crepes.

Plan

Use the *act it out* strategy with fraction tiles.

Solve

Show that Delmar ate $1\frac{5}{8}$ crepes.

Show that Brenda ate $1\frac{1}{2}$ crepes.

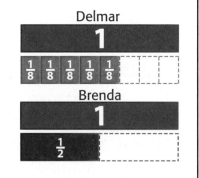

Compare. They both ate 1 whole.

Compare the fractions.

$$\frac{5}{8} > \frac{1}{2}$$

Delmar   Brenda

So, Delmar ate more crepes.

Check

You can check using a number line. The answer is correct. ✔

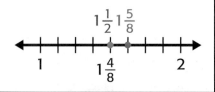

3.3 The student will **c)** compare fractions having like and unlike denominators, using words and symbols (>, <, or =).

EXTRA PRACTICE
Begins on page EP2.

- Act it out.
- Draw a picture.
- Work backward.

Use any strategy to solve each problem.

1. There are 136 guests coming to the party. The guests are equally seated at each table. Should 5, 6, or 8 guests be seated at each table? Explain.

2. Measurement A potato-sack race will be held inside a rectangular area that is 50 meters long and 40 meters wide. Dorothy has a piece of rope 200 meters long to mark the area. How much rope will be left?

3. Izzie and her family buy the items shown. They want to make 4 equal payments to pay for the items. If each payment is $213, how much money did they already pay?

Computer Items	
Item	**Cost**
Computer	$676
Printer	$177
Software	$99

4. Measurement A community garden is 50 yards long and 14 yards wide. It is equally divided into 10 smaller gardens in 2 rows of 5. What is the distance around one of the smaller gardens?

5. Measurement The length of a football field is 100 yards. Santiago ran 20 yards in one play and another 40 yards in the next play. Suppose he started at his 10-yard line. How many more yards does he need to run to make a touchdown?

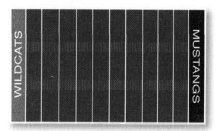

6. Measurement There are 1,440 minutes in one day. How many minutes are in one week?

7. Measurement The table shows Janna and Gilbert's finishing times for races they were in. Suppose they each walked at the same pace for each mile of the race. How many minutes per mile did each walk? Who walked faster per mile? Explain.

Finishing Time		
Walker	**Distance**	**Time (min)**
Janna	5 miles	45
Gilbert	7 miles	56

8. ✍ **WRITE MATH** Look back at Exercise 6. Which strategy did you use to solve it? Explain.

Explore

Find Equivalent Mixed Numbers

Main Idea

I will use models to explore equivalent mixed numbers.

Materials

fraction tiles

fraction circles

Get Connect**ED**

Equivalent fractions are fractions that name the same number. Two equivalent fractions are $\frac{1}{2}$ and $\frac{2}{4}$.

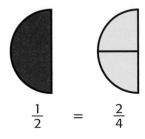

$$\frac{1}{2} \quad = \quad \frac{2}{4}$$

To find equivalent mixed numbers, keep the whole number the same. Find an equivalent fraction for the fraction part of the mixed number.

ACTIVITY

1. **Find a fraction equivalent to $1\frac{1}{3}$.**

Step 1 Model $1\frac{1}{3}$.

Use a 1 whole and a $\frac{1}{3}$ fraction tile.

Step 2 Find same-sized fraction tiles to equal the length of the $\frac{1}{3}$ fraction tile.

Step 3 Count the wholes. Count the fraction pieces.

So, $1\frac{2}{6}$ is equal to $1\frac{1}{3}$.

ACTIVITY

2 Which mixed number is equivalent to $1\frac{1}{4}$? $1\frac{2}{4}$ or $1\frac{2}{8}$?

Step 1 Model $1\frac{1}{4}$.

$1\frac{1}{4}$

Step 2 Model $1\frac{2}{4}$.

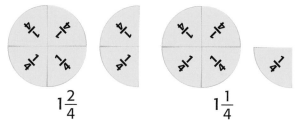

$1\frac{2}{4}$ $1\frac{1}{4}$

The whole numbers are equivalent. The fractions are not equivalent. So, $1\frac{1}{4}$ and $1\frac{2}{4}$ are not equivalent.

Step 3 Model $1\frac{2}{8}$.

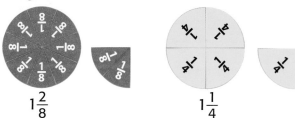

$1\frac{2}{8}$ $1\frac{1}{4}$

The whole numbers are equivalent and the fractions are equivalent. So, the mixed numbers $1\frac{1}{4}$ and $1\frac{2}{8}$ are equivalent.

So, $1\frac{1}{4} = 1\frac{2}{8}$.

Practice and Apply It

Use fraction models to find an equivalent mixed number.

1. $1\frac{4}{6}$ **2.** $2\frac{3}{5}$ **3.** $2\frac{6}{8}$

Use fraction models to determine whether each pair of mixed numbers is equivalent. Write *yes* or *no*.

4. $2\frac{2}{6}$ and $2\frac{2}{3}$ **5.** $1\frac{1}{2}$ and $2\frac{2}{4}$ **6.** $2\frac{8}{10}$ and $2\frac{4}{5}$

Equivalent Mixed Numbers

These are all equivalent mixed numbers.

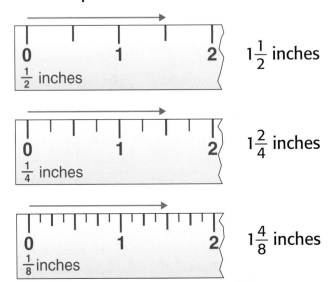

$1\frac{1}{2}$ inches

$1\frac{2}{4}$ inches

$1\frac{4}{8}$ inches

REAL-WORLD EXAMPLE

Equivalent Mixed Numbers

1 **ORANGES** Two groups of scouts each cut 3 large oranges. One group cut each of their oranges into five slices. The other group cut their oranges into 10 slices each. The models show that both groups ate an equal amount of oranges. How much did the second group eat?

The first group ate $2\frac{2}{5}$ of their oranges.

The second group ate $2\frac{4}{10}$ of their oranges.

So, $2\frac{2}{5} = 2\frac{4}{10}$. They are equivalent mixed numbers.

Remember

There are many ways to name the same number.

2 **SMOOTHIES** Stu's recipe for a strawberry smoothie calls for $1\frac{3}{4}$ cups strawberries. He only has a 1-cup measure and a $\frac{1}{8}$-cup measure. How can Stu measure the strawberries?

Stu models 1 whole cup and $\frac{3}{4}$ of another whole cup.

Then, Stu lays $\frac{1}{8}$ pieces on top of the $\frac{3}{4}$ circle until it is covered.

So, Stu could use the 1-cup measure once and the $\frac{1}{8}$-cup measure 6 times to measure the strawberries.

✓ CHECK What You Know

1. Complete the number sentence to name the equivalent mixed number.

See Example 1

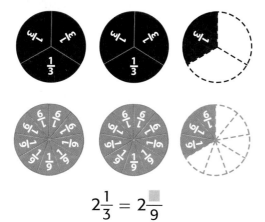

$$2\frac{1}{3} = 2\frac{\blacksquare}{9}$$

2. Write the mixed number for the part that is shaded. Then find the equivalent mixed number.

See Example 2

A. $1\frac{3}{6}$ **B.** $1\frac{4}{6}$

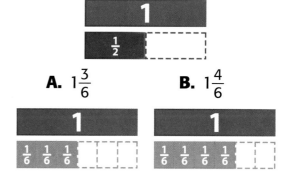

3. Measurement Mr. Franz has a piece of rope that is $7\frac{4}{8}$ feet long. He needs another piece the same length. Should he buy the piece marked $7\frac{3}{4}$ feet or the one marked $7\frac{1}{2}$ feet?

4. 📝 **TALK MATH** Explain why $1\frac{3}{4}$ and $1\frac{6}{8}$ are equivalent mixed numbers, but $2\frac{9}{12}$ is not.

Lesson 2D Compare and Order Mixed Numbers   **517**

Complete the number sentence to name the equivalent mixed number. See Example 1

5.

$$2\frac{4}{6} = 2\frac{\blacksquare}{3}$$

6.

$$1\frac{2}{4} = 1\frac{\blacksquare}{2}$$

Write the mixed number for the part that is shaded. Then find the equivalent mixed number. See Example 2

7.

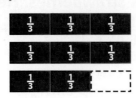

A. $1\frac{1}{3}$ **B.** $1\frac{2}{10}$

8.

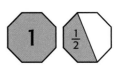

A. $1\frac{4}{8}$ **B.** $1\frac{6}{8}$

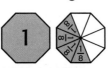 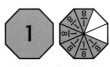

9. Which two ribbons are the same length?

Ribbon	Length
Striped	$3\frac{3}{4}$ ft
Silver	$3\frac{6}{8}$ ft
Green	$3\frac{2}{4}$ ft

10. Bernice has only a $\frac{1}{4}$-cup measure. How will Bernice measure correctly if the recipe lists ingredients written in whole cups?

Use the information to solve the problem.

11. Compare the fractions. Is there enough cereal in the box for the trail mix? Explain.

12. OPEN ENDED Write a real-world word problem where $2\frac{5}{8}$ is equivalent to another mixed number.

13. WHICH ONE DOESN'T BELONG? Choose the mixed number that does not belong. Explain.

| $7\frac{5}{6}$ | $7\frac{4}{8}$ | $7\frac{2}{4}$ | $7\frac{1}{2}$ |

14. **WRITE MATH** Explain how you would go about finding an equivalent mixed number.

 **Test Practice**

15. Sebastian lives $1\frac{3}{4}$ miles from the library. How many miles does Seth live from the library if he says it is the same distance as Sebastian? (Lesson 2D)

A. $1\frac{1}{2}$　　**C.** $1\frac{6}{8}$

B. $1\frac{2}{4}$　　**D.** $1\frac{3}{8}$

16. Marina's sticker book has 10 pages. Each page holds 6 stickers. She has $9\frac{1}{2}$ pages filled. How many more stickers does Marina need to fill up the book? (Lesson 2B)

F. 1　　**H.** 4

G. 3　　**J.** 6

Spiral Review

Solve. (Lesson 2B)

17. There are 12 dogs for sale at a pet store. One-half of the dogs are Collies and four are Beagles. The rest of the dogs are Dalmatians. How many dogs are Dalmatians?

Compare the mixed numbers. Use >, <, or =. (Lesson 2A)

18. $3\frac{3}{4} \bullet 3\frac{2}{3}$　　　　**19.** $2\frac{4}{12} \bullet 2\frac{1}{3}$　　　　**20.** $2\frac{3}{4} \bullet 4\frac{5}{10}$

21. Edmund and Lloyd are planning to cut the grass. Lloyd says he will cut $\frac{1}{2}$ of the grass. Edmund says he will cut $\frac{4}{8}$ of the grass. Who will cut more? Explain. (Lesson 1C)

Chapter Study Guide and Review

Be sure the following Key Concepts are noted in your Foldable.

Key Concepts

- A **mixed number** names a whole number and part of a whole number or part of a set. **(Lesson 1)**

$1\frac{2}{6}$

- Use models or a number line to compare and order mixed numbers. **(Lesson 2)**

Step 1 Compare the whole numbers.

$$1\frac{1}{2}, \ 1\frac{1}{4}, \ 1\frac{3}{4}$$

The whole numbers are the same.

Step 2 Compare the **fractions**.

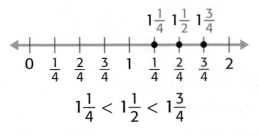

$$1\frac{1}{4} < 1\frac{1}{2} < 1\frac{3}{4}$$

abc Key Vocabulary

equivalent fractions
fraction
improper fraction
mixed number

Vocabulary Check

Choose the vocabulary word that completes each sentence.

1. A number that names part of a whole or part of a set is a(n) _____?_____.

2. An example of _____?_____ greater than one are $1\frac{2}{4}$ and $1\frac{1}{2}$.

3. Fractions that name the same amount are _____?_____.

4. A(n) _____?_____ has a whole number part and a fraction part.

5. $\frac{5}{8}$ is an example of a _____?_____.

6. An example of a(n) _____?_____ is $\frac{8}{3}$.

Multi-Part Lesson Review

Understand Mixed Numbers

Mixed Numbers (Lesson 1B)

Write a mixed number and an improper fraction for each model.

7.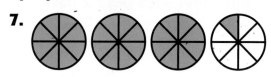

8.

9.

EXAMPLE 1

Miranda is $4\frac{3}{4}$ feet tall when she has her shoes on. The model shows how tall she is when her shoes are off. How tall is Miranda?

Write a mixed number and an improper fraction for the model.

| $\frac{1}{4}$ | $\frac{1}{4}$ | $\frac{1}{4}$ | $\frac{1}{4}$ | | $\frac{1}{4}$ | $\frac{1}{4}$ | $\frac{1}{4}$ | $\frac{1}{4}$ |

| $\frac{1}{4}$ | $\frac{1}{4}$ | $\frac{1}{4}$ | $\frac{1}{4}$ | | $\frac{1}{4}$ | $\frac{1}{4}$ | $\frac{1}{4}$ | $\frac{1}{4}$ |

| $\frac{1}{4}$ | $\frac{1}{4}$ | | |

With her shoes off, Miranda is $4\frac{2}{4}$, or $\frac{18}{4}$ feet tall.

Problem-Solving Strategy: Make a Model (Lesson 1C)

Solve. Use the *make a model* strategy.

10. Janise and Sheldon each modeled how far they walked. Janise drew 2 circles and divided them into halves. Sheldon also drew 2 circles but divided them into thirds. They each colored 1 full circle and 1 part of the second circle. If each circle equals 1 mile, how far did Janise walk? How far did Sheldon walk? Who walked farther?

EXAMPLE 2

Ken cut 5 apples into 8 pieces each. His soccer team ate $4\frac{3}{8}$ apples. What fraction of the apples was left? How many pieces is that?

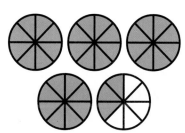

$\frac{5}{8}$ of the apples are left. That is 5 pieces.

Lesson 2 Compare and Order Mixed Numbers

Compare and Order Mixed Numbers (Lesson 2A)

Compare the mixed numbers. Use >, <, or =.

11.

$1\frac{2}{3}$ $1\frac{2}{5}$

Use the number line to order the mixed numbers from least to greatest.

12. $1\frac{4}{5}$, $1\frac{3}{5}$, $1\frac{1}{5}$

0   1   2

EXAMPLE 3

Compare the mixed numbers.

Ross and Jewel each have 2 packs of gum. Each pack had 5 sticks. Ross chewed $\frac{2}{5}$ of one pack and Jewel chewed $\frac{4}{5}$ of one pack. Who has more gum left?

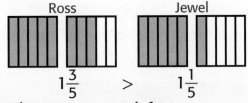

Ross   Jewel

$1\frac{3}{5}$ > $1\frac{1}{5}$

Ross has more gum left.

Problem-Solving Investigation: Choose a Strategy (Lesson 2B)

Solve.

13. Tadeo bought an oatmeal bar that weighs $5\frac{1}{3}$ ounces. Marisa's oatmeal bar weighs $5\frac{1}{4}$ ounces. Whose oatmeal bar weighs less?

14. April used $1\frac{2}{3}$ cups of apples and $1\frac{3}{4}$ cups of raisins in her recipe. Model each ingredient. Which ingredient did April use more?

EXAMPLE 4

There are $3\frac{1}{2}$ gallons of milk on the grocer's shelf. The milk is in $\frac{1}{2}$-gallon cartons. How many cartons are there?

7 halves = 3 whole and $\frac{1}{2}$

There are seven cartons of milk.

Equivalent Mixed Numbers (Lesson 2D)

Complete each number sentence.

15. $3\frac{2}{6} = 3\frac{\blacksquare}{3}$ 16. $1\frac{3}{5} = 1\frac{\blacksquare}{10}$

17. $2\frac{2}{7} = 2\frac{\blacksquare}{14}$ 18. $1\frac{4}{8} = 1\frac{\blacksquare}{2}$

EXAMPLE 5

Find an equivalent mixed number.

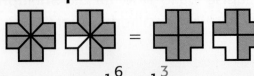

$1\frac{6}{8} = 1\frac{3}{4}$

Tell whether each statement is *true* or *false*.

1. A mixed number names part of a whole.

2. Four fourths equals 1 whole.

3. The mixed number $1\frac{1}{3}$ means there is one whole and one-third of another whole.

Write a mixed number and an improper fraction for each.

4.

5.

Identify each point. Write as a mixed number.

6. $A = $

2   3   4   5

7. $B = $

5   6   7   8

8. MULTIPLE CHOICE Mrs. Collins put $2\frac{4}{8}$ cups of chicken in the soup. Which mixed number is equivalent?

A. $\frac{1}{2}$ **C.** $2\frac{1}{2}$

B. $1\frac{3}{4}$ **D.** $2\frac{3}{4}$

9. Write the mixed number for the part that is shaded. Then find the equivalent mixed number.

A. $2\frac{1}{6}$ **B.** $2\frac{2}{6}$

10. MULTIPLE CHOICE Which ingredient does Ty need most of for his pasta salad recipe?

F. $1\frac{1}{8}$ cups salad dressing

G. $1\frac{3}{8}$ cups tomatoes

H. $3\frac{2}{4}$ cups pasta

J. $2\frac{3}{4}$ cups lettuce

11. Three friends stood in a line. Order them so they are standing shortest to tallest.

Friends	Height
Tawny	$3\frac{3}{8}$ feet
Baron	$3\frac{1}{2}$ feet
Ollie	$3\frac{2}{8}$ feet

12. A dessert recipe uses $1\frac{2}{3}$ cups of berries and $1\frac{3}{4}$ cups of grapes. Which is the lesser amount, berries or grapes?

13. **WRITE MATH** Explain the difference between a proper fraction and an improper fraction.

TEST EXAMPLE

Identify the point that represents $1\frac{4}{6}$ on the number line below.

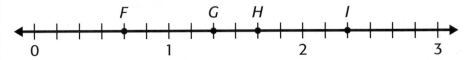

A. F   **C.** H

B. G   **D.** I

Read the Test Question

You need to find the point that represents $1\frac{4}{6}$.

Solve the Test Question

The 1 in the mixed number $1\frac{4}{6}$ means that it is more than 1 but less than 2. The denominator tells you the space between 1 and 2 is equally divided into 6 parts. Each part is $\frac{1}{6}$.

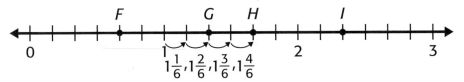

Start at 1, move to the right, and count 4 parts.

This is $1\frac{4}{6}$.

The answer is C.

TEST-TAKING TIP

Look at the denominator of the mixed number to determine the number of equal parts the whole is divided into.

Read each question. Then fill in the correct answer on the answer sheet provided by your teacher or on a separate sheet of paper.

1. Which statement about the mixed number $2\frac{2}{4}$ is true?

    A. $2\frac{1}{2} > 2\frac{2}{4}$ **C.** $2\frac{6}{8} = 2\frac{2}{4}$

    B. $2\frac{2}{4} < 3$ **D.** $2\frac{2}{4} < 2\frac{1}{4}$

2. Which of the following is greater than $\frac{9}{10}$?

    F. $1\frac{1}{10}$ **H.** $\frac{1}{2}$

    G. $\frac{8}{10}$ **J.** $\frac{1}{12}$

3. Which improper fraction is represented by the figures below?

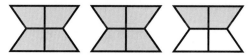

A. $\frac{7}{4}$ **C.** $\frac{8}{3}$

B. $\frac{16}{6}$ **D.** $\frac{5}{2}$

4. Alita cut a piece of felt that was $1\frac{2}{3}$ yards long. Which figure represents this mixed number?

F. ▭
H. ▭
G. ▭
J. ▭

5. Two boys and a girl share $80. The girl gets twice as much money as each of the boys. How much money does each of the children get?

A. $20, $20, $40

B. $15, $15, $30

C. $25, $25, $25

D. $25, $25, $50

6. There are $2\frac{4}{10}$ ounces of hot chocolate mix in the package. Which mixed number is equivalent?

F. $2\frac{2}{10}$ **G.** $2\frac{8}{10}$ **H.** $2\frac{1}{5}$ **J.** $2\frac{2}{5}$

7. Identify the mixed number that point *M* represents.

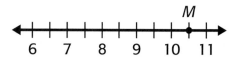

A. $\frac{10}{11}$ **B.** $10\frac{1}{2}$ **C.** $9\frac{3}{4}$ **D.** $8\frac{5}{6}$

8. Judie had $8,000 in her savings account. She spent $4,537 on a used car. How much does she have left in her account?

F. $3,463 **H.** $4,363

G. $3,467 **J.** $5,473

9. There are 50 third-grade students at Greensdale Elementary School. One out of every 5 third-grade students takes the bus to school. How many third graders take the bus to school?

A. 1 **B.** 10 **C.** 20 **D.** 25

NEED EXTRA HELP?									
If You Missed Question . . .	1	2	3	4	5	6	7	8	9
Go to Chapter-Lesson . . .	10-2A	10-2A	10-1B	10-1B	2-2F	10-2D	10-1B	2-2E	10-1C
For help with . . .	SOL 3.3c	SOL 3.3c	SOL 3.7	SOL 3.3a	SOL 3.4	SOL 3.3c	SOL 3.3a	SOL 3.4	SOL 3.7

CHAPTER 12

connectED.mcgraw-hill.com

Investigate

 Animations

 Vocabulary

 Math Songs

 Multilingual eGlossary

Learn

 Personal Tutor

 Virtual Manipulatives

 Audio

 Foldables

Practice

 Self-Check Practice

 eGames

 Worksheets

 Assessment

Measurement

The ☆BIG Idea

How can I select appropriate linear units, strategies, and tools to measure the length of objects and distances?

 FOLDABLES®
Study Organizer

Make this Foldable to help you organize information about measurement. Begin with one sheet of 11″ × 17″ paper.

abc eG

Review Vocabulary

inch pulgada a customary unit for measuring length
The length of a paper clip is about one inch long.

one inch

Key Vocabulary

English	Español
perimeter	perímetro
unit	unidad
centimeter (cm)	centímetro (cm)
meter (m)	metro (m)
kilometer (km)	kilómetro (km)

When Will I Use This?

Carlos and Kim in
Extreme Park Makeover!

Planting this flower garden at school is such a cool volunteer project!

Yeah, but I'm ready for a lemonade break soon!

Not so fast! We haven't finished the edging yet.

I'm one step ahead of you. I drew this plan last night.

That looks great, but we have to use these sections of garden fencing.

Oh, yeah. This is going to be hard work. Let's measure to find out how many we need.

Looks like each side of our square garden is 6 feet long. Now what?

Well, we need to find how much fencing we need. Let's discuss it over lemonade.

Your Turn!
You will solve this problem in the chapter.

Are You Ready for the Chapter?

You have two options for checking Prerequisite Skills for this chapter.

Text Option Take the Quick Check below.

QUICK Check

Identify which figure or object is shorter.

1.

Figure A

Figure B

2.

3. Sancho walked 15 miles, and Alberto walked 15 yards. Who walked farther? Explain.

Identify which sides are the same length.

4.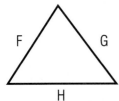

F   G

H

5.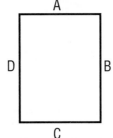

A

D   B

C

6.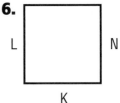

M

L   N

K

Choose the most appropriate unit to measure each length.

7.

centimeter or meter

8.

inch or foot

9. Bernard made a 2-foot paper clip chain. Erin's paper clip chain was 2 yards long. Whose chain was longer?

 Online Option Take the Online Readiness Quiz.

Explore Length to the Nearest Inch and Half Inch

Main Idea

I will use models to explore length to the nearest inch and half inch.

Materials

inch ruler

small paper clips

pencil

connecting cubes

Get ConnectED

3.9 The student will estimate and use U.S. Customary and metric units to measure **a)** length to the nearest 12-inch, inch, foot, yard, centimeter, and meter.

Length is the measure of the distance between two points. Length is measured in specific amounts called **units**. You can estimate and measure length with a nonstandard unit.

ACTIVITY

1. Estimate and measure length using a paper clip.

Step 1 **Estimate.**

Estimate the length of a pencil in paper clips.

Step 2 **Measure.**

Arrange paper clips end-to-end, as shown. Count the paper clips.

How close was your estimate to the actual length in paper clips?

An inch (in.) is a standard unit of measure in the customary measurement system.

inches

2 **Estimate and measure length using a ruler.**

Step 1 **Estimate.**

Estimate the length of the comb in inches.

Step 2 **Measure.**

Line up one end with the 0 mark, as shown. Find the closest inch mark at the other end of the comb. How close was your estimate to the actual length?

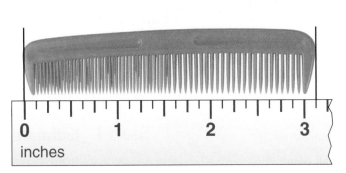
inches

Think About It

1. In both activities, how did you estimate length?

2. Is a paper clip or a ruler more accurate for measuring? Explain.

Practice and Apply It

Estimate. Then measure each length to the nearest inch.

3.
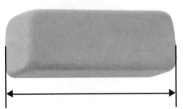

4.

5. Find objects in your classroom that measure about 1 inch, 4 inches, and 6 inches. Then copy and complete the table shown.

Measure	Object
1 inch	?
4 inches	?
6 inches	?

6. **WRITE MATH** How did you decide which objects to choose?

A fraction is a number that names part of a whole. Sometimes when you measure the length of an object, you use a fraction to be more precise.

There are two $\frac{1}{2}$ **inches** in 1 inch.

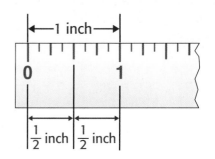

ACTIVITY

③ **Measure length to the nearest half inch.**

Step 1 Connect 3 cubes in a line.

Step 2 Estimate the total length of the cubes to the nearest $\frac{1}{2}$ inch.

Step 3 Measure to find the closest $\frac{1}{2}$-inch mark at the end of the cubes. How close was your estimate to the actual length?

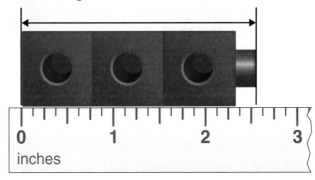

To the nearest $\frac{1}{2}$ inch, the cubes are $2\frac{1}{2}$ inches in length.

Practice and Apply It

Estimate. Then measure each length to the nearest $\frac{1}{2}$ inch.

7.

8.

9. **WRITE MATH** Can an object be 2 inches in length when measured to the nearest inch and nearest half inch? Explain.

Main Idea

I will select the most appropriate units, strategies, and tools to estimate and measure length to the nearest half inch.

Vocabulary

length

half inch $\left(\frac{1}{2}\right)$

Get ConnectED

3.9 The student will estimate and use U.S. Customary and metric units to measure **a)** length to the nearest 12-inch, inch, foot, yard, centimeter, and meter.

Length to the Nearest Half Inch

When you measure **length** in $\frac{1}{2}$ inches, your measurements are more precise. There are two $\frac{1}{2}$ **inches** in one inch.

Half-inch marks come halfway between two inch marks.

🏃 ✍️ REAL-WORLD EXAMPLE

① **TOYS** Jamari has a rubber bug collection. What is the length of Jamari's rubber bug to the nearest $\frac{1}{2}$ inch?

Estimate The bug is a little longer than the length of a paper clip. So, the bug is a little longer than 1 inch.

Line up one end of the bug with the 0 mark. Find the $\frac{1}{2}$-inch mark that is closest to the other end of the bug.

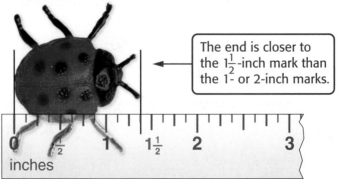

The end is closer to the $1\frac{1}{2}$-inch mark than the 1- or 2-inch marks.

To the nearest $\frac{1}{2}$ inch, the bug is $1\frac{1}{2}$ inches long.

Check Since the measurement is close to the estimate of a little more than 1 inch, the answer is reasonable. ✔

Sometimes when measuring to the nearest $\frac{1}{2}$ inch, the length is a whole number.

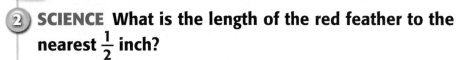

REAL-WORLD EXAMPLE — Nearest $\frac{1}{2}$ Inch

2 **SCIENCE** **What is the length of the red feather to the nearest $\frac{1}{2}$ inch?**

Estimate The feather is a little less than the length of 3 paper clips. So, the feather is about 3 inches long.

Even though you measure to the nearest $\frac{1}{2}$ inch, the end of the feather is closer to a whole inch.

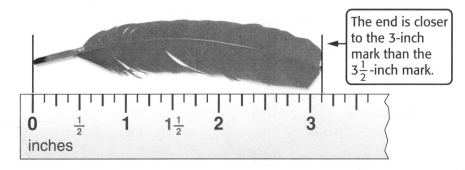

The end is closer to the 3-inch mark than the $3\frac{1}{2}$-inch mark.

So, to the nearest $\frac{1}{2}$ inch, the red feather is 3 inches long.

Check Since the measurement is close to the estimate of a little more than 3 inches, the answer is reasonable. ✔

✓ CHECK What You Know

Estimate each length. Then measure each to the nearest $\frac{1}{2}$ inch.

See Examples 1 and 2

1.

2.

3. Winston has a carrot that is $5\frac{1}{2}$ inches long. After he cuts off $\frac{1}{2}$ inch, how long is the carrot?

4. **TALK MATH** Tell how to find a $\frac{1}{2}$-inch mark on a ruler.

Estimate each length. Then measure each to the nearest $\frac{1}{2}$ inch.

See Examples 1 and 2

5.

6.

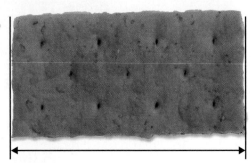

7.

8.

9.

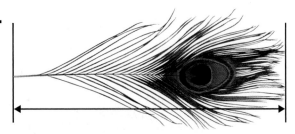

10. Ramiro needs two pieces of string that are $2\frac{1}{2}$ inches long and 3 inches long. What is the total length of string needed?

11. Tia's hair ribbon is 10 inches long, and Mallory's is $8\frac{1}{2}$ inches long. What is the difference in the lengths of the two ribbons?

12. Kerri's comb is $4\frac{1}{2}$ inches long. What are the inch marks on either side of this measurement?

13. Jody's ruler is broken and starts at $2\frac{1}{2}$ inches. Can she use her ruler to draw a line 5 inches long? Explain.

H.O.T. Problems

14. CHALLENGE Explain how you could use a piece of string to measure this line.

15. OPEN ENDED Draw a design using straight lines. Measure the total length of all the lines.

16. **WRITE MATH** Explain how you would use a ruler to measure the length of the stick bug.

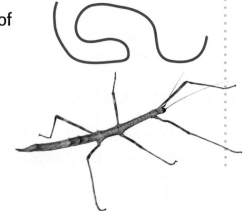

Game Time

Hit the Target
Standard Measurement

You will need: game card, inch ruler, a target (i.e., an eraser), and 1 square pattern block

Get Ready!

Players: 2 players

Get Set!

Copy the game card shown.

Player's Name	Toss #1	Toss #2	Toss #3	Toss #4	Total Score

Go!

 Player 1 tosses the pattern block at the target.

 Player 2 measures the distance between the target and the pattern block to the nearest $\frac{1}{2}$ inch.

 Player 1 records the distance on the game card.

 Player 2 stands the same distance from the target as Player 1 and tosses the pattern block. Player 1 measures the distance.

 Move the target and toss again.

 Both players will take four turns at tossing the pattern block at the target. Add the distances of the four tosses for each player. The player with the lower total wins.

Main Idea

I will choose the most appropriate tools and units to estimate and measure customary units of length.

 Vocabulary

units
foot (ft)
yard (yd)
mile (mi)

Get ConnectED

3.9 The student will estimate and use U.S. Customary and metric units to measure **a)** length to the nearest 12-inch, inch, foot, yard, centimeter, and meter.

Customary Units of Length

To measure longer lengths and distances, you need to use customary **units** of measure other than inch.

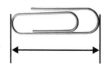

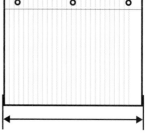

The length of a paper clip is about 1 inch (in.) long.

A sheet of notebook paper is about 1 **foot (ft)** long.

A baseball bat is about 1 **yard (yd)** long.

A **mile (mi)** equals 4 times around a football field.

Customary Units of Length
1 foot (ft) = 12 inches (in.)
1 yard (yd) = 36 inches or 3 feet
1 mile (mi) = 1,760 yards or 5,280 feet

REAL-WORLD EXAMPLE   Choose Units of Length

① **MEASUREMENT** Patterson stood with his feet together and then jumped as far as he could. What unit should Patterson use to measure the distance he jumped?

An inch is too short. A mile is too long. Even a yard is too long. The most appropriate unit to use is the foot.

You can estimate length.

 **REAL-WORLD EXAMPLE** Estimate Length

② **BOOKS Choose the better estimate for the width of your math book, 10 inches or 10 feet.**

Think about an inch and a foot.

A paper clip is
about 1 inch.

A ruler is 1 foot.

The width of your math book is about 10 paper clips, not 10 rulers. So, the better estimate is 10 inches.

You can use estimation to check if your actual measurement is reasonable.

REAL-WORLD EXAMPLE Estimate and Measure Length

③ **MONEY Measure the width of a quarter.**

Estimate A quarter is about the same width as a paper clip, so it is probably about 1 inch wide.

Remember

Estimating helps
you check for
reasonableness.

So, the width of a quarter is 1 inch.

Check Based on the estimate, the answer
is reasonable. ✔

Choose the most appropriate unit to measure each length.
Write *inch, foot, yard,* or *mile*. See Example 1

1. height of a calculator

2. width of your desk

Choose the better estimate. See Example 2

3. length of a cricket
   1 inch or 1 foot

4. the height of a chair
   3 miles or 3 feet

Estimate. Then measure each length. Use *inch, foot,* or *yard*. See Example 3

5. your shoe length

6. width of your smile

7. width of a door

8. Mrs. Frisk is measuring the length of her cat. What unit should she use to measure the cat? Why?

9. TALK MATH Describe a situation when it may be helpful to know how to estimate units of length.

Practice and Problem Solving

EXTRA PRACTICE
Begins on page EP2.

Choose the most appropriate unit to measure each length.
Write *inch, foot, yard,* or *mile*. See Example 1

10. the length of a pencil

11. the height of a boy

12. the distance between two cities

13. the length of a swing set

Choose the better estimate. See Example 2

14. the length of your foot
   8 inches or 8 feet

15. the width of a computer screen
   16 yards or 16 inches

16. the height of a wall
   11 inches or 11 feet

17. the width of a window
   3 miles or 3 feet

Estimate. Then measure each length. Use *inch, foot,* or *yard*. See Example 3

18. your pencil

19. your height

20. your arm

21. A piece of rope can stretch from the front of a classroom to the back. Are there 25 miles of rope or 25 feet of rope? Explain.

22. The distance from Zach's home to school is 100 units. What is the most appropriate unit to measure the length? Explain.

23. OPEN ENDED Give an example of an object that is a little longer than 1 yard.

24. WHICH ONE DOESN'T BELONG? Identify the length that does not belong. Explain your reasoning.

36 inches	3 feet	48 inches	1 yard

25.  **WRITE MATH** Explain why a yardstick is a better choice than a ruler for measuring the distance around a playground.

Test Practice

26. Melissa's ruler is broken and starts at the 2-inch mark. If she wants to draw a line that is 4 inches long, at what inch mark will she stop drawing? (Lesson 1A)

A. 2-inch

B. $4\frac{1}{2}$-inch

C. 6-inch

D. 7-inch

27. Which real-life object is longer than 1 foot? (Lesson 1C)

F.

G.

H.

J.

Spiral Review

Measure each to the nearest half inch. (Lesson 1B)

28.

29.

30.

Problem-Solving Strategy: Solve a Simpler Problem

Main Idea I will solve a problem by first solving a simpler problem.

Paul and his dad have 75 feet of lights to decorate the restaurant's outside seating area with. Each of the two railings and one door will need 25 feet of lights. The roof is 50 feet across and each of its two sides is 25 feet. What is the length of additional lights needed to complete the job?

Understand	**What facts do you know?**
	• They have 75 feet of lights.
	• The length of lights needed for each section is given.
	What do you need to find?
	• Find the total length of lights needed for decorating.
	• Find how many feet of additional lights they need to buy.
Plan	Use the *solve a simpler problem* strategy to solve the problem.
Solve	First, solve the simpler problem.

Find the total length of lights needed for decorating.

25 feet + 25 feet = 50 feet railings
                     25 feet door
                     50 feet roof
25 feet + 25 feet = 50 feet sides of roof
                 175 feet needed for decorating

Next, find the length of additional lights they need to buy.

         175 feet of lights needed
      − 75 feet of lights they have
         100 feet needed to buy

Paul and his dad need to buy 100 feet of lights to finish the job.

Check	Check by adding. 100 + 75 = 175. So, the answer is correct. ✔

3.9 The student will estimate and use U.S. Customary and metric units to measure **a)** length to the nearest 12-inch, inch, foot, yard, centimeter, and meter.

1. Explain how the *solve a simpler problem* strategy is helpful.

2. Suppose Paul and his dad had 75 *yards* of lights instead of 75 feet. Would they have to buy more or less lights? Explain.

3. Explain another strategy you could have used to solve this problem.

4. What is the total length of lights they would have to buy if there were four railings instead of two? Explain.

PRACTICE

EXTRA PRACTICE
Begins on page EP2.

Solve. Use the *solve a simpler problem* strategy.

5. **Geometry** Ramos is putting up a fence in the shape of a triangle. How much fencing is needed?

Side A	Side B	Side C
36 feet	half of side A	same as side A

6. Star gave 6 friends 5 pieces of paper each. She kept the rest of the paper. Star has 70 pieces of paper left. How many sheets of paper did she have to begin with?

7. Caleb wrote 80 riddles in the last five years. The second year he wrote 23 more riddles than he did the first year. He wrote 5 riddles each in the third and fourth years. The fifth year he wrote 7 riddles. How many riddles did he write the first and second year?

8. The total length of four walls of a rectangular room is 72 feet. One wall measures 16 feet. What is the length of the other three walls?

?
? [ ] 16 feet
?

9. A bus drops students at three schools on Brown St: **PSE**lementary, **PSM**iddle, and **PSH**igh. Use the facts to determine the order of the schools on the street.
   • PSE is 15 miles from PSM.
   • PSH and PSE are 5 miles apart.
   • PSH is 20 miles from PSM.

10. The Carpet Company is replacing the carpeting on a set of steps and its top landing. What is the total width and length of the piece of carpeting needed?

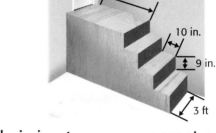

11. Admission to an amusement park is $25. Bus fare is $3 one way. Find the total cost for Kali and her friend for admission and bus fare to and from the park.

12. **WRITE MATH** Explain another problem-solving strategy or skill you used with the *solve a simpler problem* strategy to solve Exercise 9.

Explore Centimeter

Main Idea

I will measure length to the nearest centimeter.

Materials

centimeter ruler

0 1 2 3 4 5 6
centimeters

crayon

crayon

small paper clip

centimeter cubes or base-ten unit cubes

meterstick

Get Connect ED

3.9 The student will estimate and use U.S. Customary and metric units to measure **a)** length to the nearest 12-inch, inch, foot, yard, centimeter, and meter.

You can use metric units to measure length. One metric unit is the **centimeter (cm).** A centimeter is about the width of your index finger.

ACTIVITY

① **Estimate and Measure in Centimeters**

Step 1 **Estimate.**

About how many finger-widths long would you estimate the crayon to be?

crayon

Step 2 **Measure.**

Use the width of your finger to measure the length of the crayon.

- How close was your estimate to the actual finger-width measure?

Step 3 **Measure.**

Align the left end of the crayon with the 0 at the end of a centimeter ruler. Find the tick mark closest to the other end of the crayon.

crayon
0 1 2 3 4 5 6 7 8 9
centimeters

1. What is the length in centimeters?

2. How close was your finger-width measure to the actual number of centimeters?

A **meter (m)** is longer than a centimeter. It is used to measure longer lengths.

② Compare Metric Units

Step 1 Lay a meterstick on the floor.

Step 2 Lay centimeter cubes along the edge of the meterstick. Count the cubes.

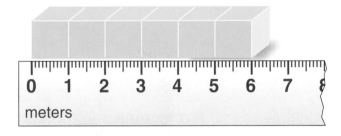

3. How many centimeter cubes did you lay along the edge of the meterstick?

4. What can you conclude from this activity?

Practice and Apply It

Estimate. Then measure each length to the nearest centimeter.

5.

6.

7.

Choose the better estimate.

8. length of a marker
   10 cm or 10 m

9. width of your thumb
   2 cm or 2 m

10. length of a hallway
   30 cm or 30 m

11. ❓ **WRITE MATH** When you compare the centimeter and meter measurements, which is more accurate? Explain.

Get ConnectED

Main Idea
I will choose the most appropriate tools and units to estimate and measure metric units of length.

 Vocabulary
centimeter (cm)
meter (m)
kilometer (km)

 **3.9** The student will estimate and use U.S. Customary and metric units to measure **a)** length to the nearest 12-inch, inch, foot, yard, centimeter, and meter.

Metric Units of Length

To measure short lengths, you can use the **centimeter (cm)**. To measure longer lengths, use the **meter (m)** or the **kilometer (km)**.

A centimeter is about the width across your index finger.

A meter is about the width of a door.

It takes about 10 minutes to walk 1 kilometer.

Metric Units of Length
1 meter (m) = 100 centimeters
1 kilometer (km) = 1,000 meters

REAL-WORLD EXAMPLE   Choose Metric Units

① **SPORTS** Moses' big sister runs high school track. She runs one time around the track. Choose the unit that should be used to find how far Moses' big sister runs around the track one time.

You need to determine whether to use *centimeter*, *meter*, or *kilometer*.

A centimeter is too short. A kilometer is too long to measure one time around the track. Use a meter.

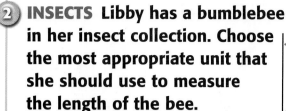

2 INSECTS Libby has a bumblebee in her insect collection. Choose the most appropriate unit that she should use to measure the length of the bee.

You need to determine whether it is best to use *centimeter, meter,* or *kilometer.*

A meter and kilometer are too long. A centimeter is the most appropriate unit to measure very short lengths.

So, use centimeters to measure the length of a bee.

Use what you know about meter and kilometer to estimate.

REAL-WORLD EXAMPLE   Estimate Length

3 LONG JUMP The world record for jumping the greatest distance in the long jump has not been broken in many years. Choose the better estimate for the distance jumped, 9 meters or 9 kilometers.

Think about a meter and a kilometer. A meter is about the width of a door and it takes about 10 minutes to walk 1 kilometer.

It would be reasonable to jump 9 meters, but not reasonable to jump 9 kilometers.

So, 9 meters is the better estimate.

Remember

There are 100 cents in a dollar. There are 100 *centi*meters in a meter.

**Choose the most appropriate unit to measure each length.
Write *centimeter*, *meter*, or *kilometer*.** See Examples 1 and 2

1. length of a goldfish

2. length of a car

3. length of a hiking trail

4. length of a pencil

Estimate. Then measure each length. Use centimeter or meter.

5. width of a math book

6. width of your classroom

7. Choose the best estimate for the length of a chalkboard, 5 m or 5 km. See Example 3

8.  **TALK MATH** Why is it important to know both the customary and metric systems of measurement?

Practice and Problem Solving

EXTRA PRACTICE
Begins on page EP2.

**Choose the most appropriate unit to measure each length.
Write *centimeter*, *meter*, or *kilometer*.** See Examples 1 and 2

9. height of a flagpole

10. distance a plane travels

11. length of an insect

12. length of a crayon

Choose the better estimate. See Example 3

13. distance you could travel on a train 500 km or 5,000 cm

14. length of a sofa 2 m or 20 cm

Estimate. Then measure each length. Use centimeter or meter.

15. width of your hand

16. height of a door

The table shows the wood needed to build a fort.

17. The wood for the floor needs to be cut into 4 pieces. Two of the pieces will be 1 meter long. If the remaining wood is cut equally in half, how long will the remaining boards be?

18. The wood for the walls will be cut into 5 equal pieces. How long will each piece be in centimeters?

Build a Fort

Amount of Wood Needed

Floor	6 m
Walls	5 m
Roof	6 m

H.O.T. Problems

Algebra **Compare. Use >, <, or =.**

19. 30 cm ● 30 m

20. 4 m ● 400 cm

21. 20 m ● 2 km

22. Measurement Reggie is in a race that is 5 kilometers long. Marta is in a race that is 500 meters long. Whose race is longer? Explain.

23.  **WRITE MATH** Suppose you are measuring the length of an object in centimeters. What should you do if the object does not line up exactly with a centimeter mark on the ruler?

Test Practice

24. Mr. Rockwell gave 9 students one pencil each. That afternoon, he gave 5 more students one pencil each. He has 15 pencils left. How many pencils did he start with? (Lesson 1D)

A. 14   **C.** 20

B. 15   **D.** 29

25. Choose the best unit for measuring the distance across the United States. (Lesson 1F)

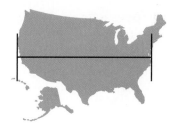

F. yard   **H.** centimeter

G. meter   **J.** kilometer

Spiral Review

26. Kareem gave 25 football cards to Mali, 13 cards to Millie, and 14 cards to Kevin. He has half of the cards he started with. How many cards did he start with? (Lesson 1D)

Choose the most appropriate unit to measure each length. Write *inch, foot, yard,* or *mile.* (Lesson 1C)

27. distance between two countries

28. distance from floor to ceiling

29. Tina drew a chalk line 4 feet long. Then she erased $8\frac{1}{2}$ inches of it. In inches, what is the length of Tina's chalk line? (Lesson 1B)

To assess partial mastery of SOL 3.9a, see your Virginia Assessment Book.

The Life and Lengths of Leap Frogs

Frogs come in all different colors and sizes. One of the world's smallest frogs, the Cuban pygmy, only grows to be $\frac{1}{2}$ inch long. The largest frog in the world is the Goliath frog. Goliath frogs can grow up $12\frac{1}{2}$ inches in length and weigh up to 7 pounds!

A frog's life begins inside an egg that a female frog lays. When the egg hatches, out comes a tadpole. Tadpoles swim around like fish while they slowly grow into frogs.

Did You Know?

Frogs do not need to drink water to survive. Their skin absorbs all the water they need.

Life Cycle of a Frog

Egg

Tadpole

Tadpole with legs

Young frog

Adult Frog

Real-World Math

Use the information on the previous page and the diagram above to solve each problem.

1 How much longer is the Goliath frog than the Cuban pygmy frog?

2 Look at the picture of a frog's egg. Measure its length. About how many frog eggs would equal the length of the tadpole without legs?

3 Measure the length of the tadpole with legs to the nearest centimeter.

4 How much longer is the tadpole with legs than the tadpole without legs?

5 Estimate. Then measure the length of the young frog to the nearest inch.

6 Estimate. Then measure the length of the adult frog to the nearest $\frac{1}{2}$ inch.

Mid-Chapter Check

Choose the better estimate. (Lesson 1C)

1. height of a ladder: 4 miles or 4 yards

2. length of a spoon: 6 feet or 6 inches

3. distance driven in a car trip
30 meters or 30 kilometers

Estimate each length. Then measure each to the nearest $\frac{1}{2}$ inch. (Lesson 1B)

4.

5.

6. MULTIPLE CHOICE Mrs. Conner took her children to the water park on Thursday. Her ticket cost $10. She spent a total of $38 after she used the coupon below.

How many children did Mrs. Conner take to the water park? (lesson 1D)

A. 3   **C.** 5

B. 4   **D.** 7

Estimate each length. Then measure to the nearest centimeter.
(Lesson 1F)

7.

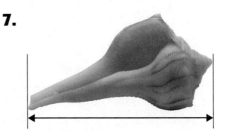

8.

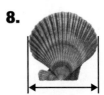

9. MULTIPLE CHOICE Which of the following is longer than 1 yard?
(lesson 1C)

F. a crayon   **H.** a toy car

G. your bed   **J.** a notebook

10. Some children offered to clean Ms. Dawson's garage. It took 2 days. She paid each child $4 per day. If she paid them $24 total, how many children were there?
(Lesson 1D)

11. **WRITE MATH** Name something you would measure in meters. Explain why you would not use centimeters to measure it. (Lesson 1F)

Explore Finding Perimeter

Main Idea

I will explore finding the perimeter of a figure.

Materials

base-ten cubes

centimeter ruler

3.9 The student will estimate and use U.S. Customary and metric units to measure **d)** area and perimeter. **3.10** The student will **a)** measure the distance around a polygon in order to determine perimeter.

Perimeter is the distance around the *outside of a figure,* or shape. You can estimate and measure perimeter.

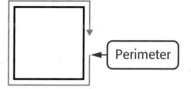

Perimeter

 **ACTIVITY**

1 **Measure Perimeter**

Step 1 Copy the table shown below.

Object	Estimate (cm)	Exact Measure (cm)	
		cubes	ruler
Math book			
Desktop			
Chalkboard eraser			

Step 2 Estimate the perimeter of your math book.

Step 3 Use centimeter cubes to measure the perimeter.

Step 4 Use a centimeter ruler to find the exact perimeter.

Step 5 Record the results. Repeat the steps for each object listed.

1. Write a number sentence for the perimeter of your math book.

2. What operation did you use to find perimeter?

Think About It

3. What other tools might you have used to measure the perimeter of the objects above?

4. Why do you estimate the perimeter before finding its exact measurement?

5. How would your answers have been different if you used an inch ruler? Explain.

Main Idea

I will choose the most appropriate unit, strategy, and tool to measure the perimeter of figures.

Vocabulary
perimeter

Get Connect**ED**

3.9 The student will estimate and use U.S. Customary and metric units to measure **d)** area and perimeter. **3.10** The student will **a)** measure the distance around a polygon in order to determine perimeter.

Perimeter

The distance around the *outside of a figure* or shape is its **perimeter**. You can measure perimeter using units of length, such as inch or meter.

🏃 ✏️ **EXAMPLES** Find the Perimeter

1 **Find the perimeter of the triangle.**

To find the perimeter if you already know the length of the sides, add the lengths of the sides.

5 in. + 3 in. + 5 in. = 13 in.

So, the perimeter is 13 inches.

3 in. / 5 in. \ 5 in.

2 **Find the perimeter of the shaded rectangle.**

To find the perimeter, add the units around *the outside of the figure.*

4 units + 5 units + 4 units + 5 units = 18 units

So, the perimeter is 18 units.

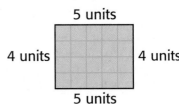

5 units

4 units 4 units

5 units

Key Concept **Find Perimeter**

Words The perimeter of a figure is the sum of the side lengths.

Model

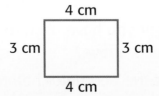

4 cm

3 cm   3 cm

4 cm

Symbols Perimeter = 3 cm + 4 cm + 3 cm + 4 cm
= 14 cm

③ **PHOTO** Leah framed a photo of her dog. What tool would she use to find the perimeter of the frame?

Leah's frame is not very big. She can find its perimeter with an inch ruler or a centimeter ruler.

④ **PUPPY** Warren and his dad will fence in the backyard for his new puppy. What is the most appropriate tool for them to use to find the perimeter of the backyard?

An inch ruler is much too small to measure the distance around a backyard. They should use a tape measure or a yardstick to measure the perimeter of a large area.

✓ **CHECK What You Know**

Find the perimeter of each figure. See Examples 1 and 2

1.
3 ft
10 ft

2.
6 cm
2 cm
3 cm
5 cm

3.

Select the most appropriate tool to find the perimeter of each.

See Examples 3 and 4

4. computer screen
centimeter ruler or yardstick

5. walls around a bedroom
inch ruler or tape measure

6. 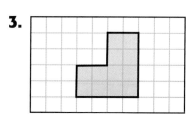 **TALK MATH** A triangle has three equal sides. Its perimeter is 15 units. How would you find the length of each side?

Find the perimeter of each figure. See Examples 1 and 2

7.
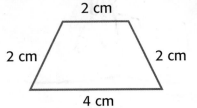

8.
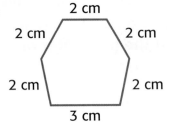

9.
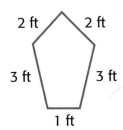

10.
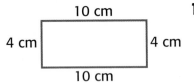

11.
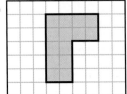

12.
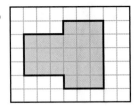

Select the most appropriate tool to find the perimeter of each.

See Examples 3 and 4

13. piece of writing paper
yardstick or inch ruler

14. greeting card
tape measure or centimeter ruler

15. length of football field
tape measure or inch ruler

16. height of a door
centimeter ruler or yardstick

17. Algebra A fountain has 3 sides. Its perimeter is 120 feet. One side is 40 feet and another is 50 feet, what is the length of the third side?

18. Mila's house has a 6-sided deck. Each side of the deck is 12 feet long. What is its perimeter?

19. Algebra The figure shown to the right has a perimeter of 21 feet. Find the length of the missing side.

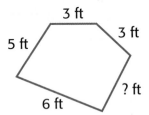

Data File

All professional baseball teams' playing fields are the same size.

20. The three bases and home plate make a diamond that is 90 feet on each side. What is the perimeter of the diamond?

21. Each side of each base is 15 inches long. What is the total perimeter of all three bases?

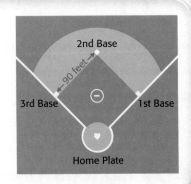

554 Measurement

Extreme Park Makeover!

Remember, we need to find how much fencing we need to go around our garden.

It looks like each piece of fence is 24 inches.

22. What is the perimeter of the garden space, in feet?

23. How many feet long is each piece of fence?

24. How many pieces of fence will Kim and Carlos need for the perimeter of the garden?

 H.O.T. Problems

25. OPEN ENDED Draw and label a figure that has a perimeter of 24 inches.

26. Geometry Two squares are shown. The length of each side is 8 feet. Find the total perimeter if the squares are put together to make a rectangle.

8 feet

27. **WRITE MATH** How can you find the perimeter of a rectangle if you know the length and width? Explain.

Test Practice

28. The garden shown below has a perimeter of 56 meters. What is the length of one side of this garden in centimeters? (Lesson 1F)

A. 56 cm   **C.** 560 cm

B. 80 cm   **D.** 700 cm

29. What is the perimeter of the figure? (Lesson 2B)

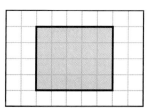

F. 11 units   **H.** 18 units

G. 12 units   **J.** 20 units

Problem-Solving Investigation

Main Idea I will solve a problem by choosing the best strategy.

P.S.I. TEAM ＋

CASSIE: My father is making a rectangular sandbox. It has a width of 4 feet and a length of 6 feet. The wood that goes around the sandbox costs $2 for each foot.

YOUR MISSION: Will $50 be enough money to pay for the wood?

Understand What facts do you know?

- The sandbox is 4 feet by 6 feet.
- The wood costs $2 a foot.
- They have $50.

What do you need to find?

- Is $50 enough money?

Plan   Use the *draw a picture* strategy to help you solve the problem.

Solve   First, draw a picture to represent the sandbox. Find the perimeter of the sandbox.

Then, multiply the perimeter by the cost per foot.

$20 \times \$2 = \$40$
The wood will cost $40.

Since $40 is less than $50, Cassie has enough money to buy the wood.

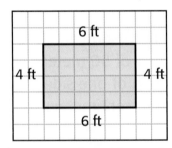

perimeter = 4 ft + 6 ft + 4 ft + 6 ft

Check $40 < $50. So, the answer is correct. ✓

3.10 The student will **a)** measure the distance around a polygon in order to determine perimeter.

- Solve a simpler problem.
- Draw a picture.
- Choose an operation.

Use any strategy to solve each problem.

1. Measurement Greenland, the largest island in the world, is 840,000 square miles. Iceland is 39,800 square miles. How much smaller is Iceland than Greenland?

2. During round one of a game, Elio, Nida, and Geoffrey each scored 4 points. In round two, they each scored twice as many points. Find the total number of points.

3. A frame is 2 inches longer and 2 inches wider than the photo below. What is the perimeter of the frame?

4 in.

6 in.

4. Lamar wants to buy two gallons of milk. One gallon costs $3. A half-gallon costs $2. Should Lamar buy two one-gallon jugs of milk or four half-gallon jugs to spend the least amount of money? Explain.

5. Phil cut a piece of yellow yarn that was 7 feet long. Kittia cut a piece of red yarn that was 78 inches long. Write an equation to show the total length of the yellow and red yarn in feet.

6. Look back at the problem on the previous page. Suppose there is also a square sandbox. One side measures 5 feet. Write an equation to show the total cost of the wood for the two sandboxes.

7. There were 17 bottles, 6 mugs, and 5 glasses on a shelf. Ron uses 2 bottles. Anne uses 1 mug and 1 glass. How many items are left?

8. Both Duane and Rajeev followed the homework schedule in the table. What is the total number of hours both boys spent on homework?

Homework Schedule	
Day	**Time (minutes)**
Monday	45
Tuesday	30
Wednesday	15

9. Lannetta will buy balloons for a party. She invited 6 friends from school, 3 friends from soccer, and 2 cousins. How many balloons will she need to buy if everyone gets two?

10. **WRITE MATH** Explain the strategy and steps you used to solve Exercise 4.

To assess partial mastery of SOL 3.10a, see your Virginia Assessment Book.

Explore **Measure Area**

Area is the number of square units needed to cover a figure without overlapping. You can use grid paper to explore area.

1 square unit

ACTIVITY

1 **Estimate Area**

Step 1 **Estimate.**

How many square units do you think will cover the side view of a connecting cube?

Step 2 **Trace.**

Trace one side of the connecting cube onto grid paper.

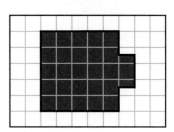

Step 3 **Determine Area.**

One whole square is 1 square unit.

Each of these is a $\frac{1}{2}$ square unit.

Count the number of whole square units. How many half-square units are there? Estimate the area. How does the estimate compare with your first estimate?

3.9 The student will estimate and use U.S. Customary and metric units to measure **d)** area and perimeter.
3.10 The student will **b)** count the number of square units needed to cover a given surface in order to determine area.

 **ACTIVITY**

2 **Estimate Area**

Step 1 **Use a geoboard.**

Use a rubber band to make a rectangle on a geoboard.

Step 2 **Estimate.**

Use what you learned in Activity 1 to estimate the area of the rectangle.

Step 3 **Determine the area.**

Count the squares in the rectangle.

Think About It

1. Is it easier to find the actual area of a rectangle on grid paper or to estimate? Explain.

2. How did you make your estimate for the area of the rectangle? How close is it to the actual area?

Practice and Apply It

Estimate and determine the area in square units of each figure.

3.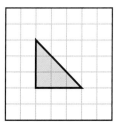

4.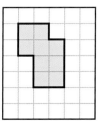

5.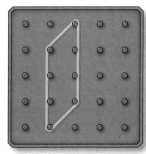

6. Make a polygon on a geoboard. Find the area in square units.

7. Draw a polygon on a piece of grid paper. Estimate the area in square units.

8. **WRITE MATH** Explain the difference between area and perimeter.

Main Idea

I will determine the area of a figure.

 Vocabulary

area

Get ConnectED

 3.9 The student will estimate and use U.S. Customary and metric units to measure **d)** area and perimeter.
3.10 The student will **b)** count the number of square units needed to cover a given surface in order to determine area.

Measure Area

Area is the number of square units needed to cover a figure without overlapping. In the Explore Activity, you estimated area. You can also find the actual area of a figure.

REAL-WORLD EXAMPLES **Determine Area**

1) **ART** **In art class, Halley drew figures on grid paper. One figure is shown at the right. What is the area of the figure Halley drew?**

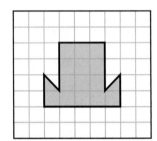

Count the number of whole squares. There are 14 whole squares.

There are 2 half-squares. Notice that two halves equal one whole.

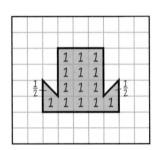

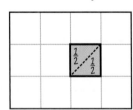

14 squares units + 1 square unit = 15 square units

So, the area is 15 square units.

2) **Find the area of the figure.**

Count the number of whole squares.

The area of this figure is 4 square units.

3 **GEOMETRY** Rafeal created the geoboard polygon shown. What is the area of the polygon?

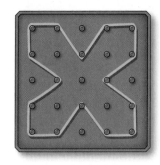

Step 1 Count the number of whole squares. There are 8 of them.

Step 2 Count the half-squares. There are 8 halves. Eight halves equal 4 whole squares.

Step 3 Add.

8 square units + 4 square units = 12 square units

So, the area of the polygon is 12 square units.

Remember
Two half-squares equal one whole square.

✓ **CHECK What You Know**

Find the area of each figure. See Examples 1–3

1.

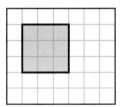

2.

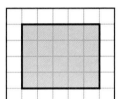

3.

4. Denitra plans to cover a desk with decorative tiles. What is the area of the space she will cover?

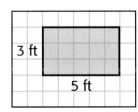

3 ft

5 ft

5. The frame is covered with squares of colored glass. What is the area covered by the colored glass?

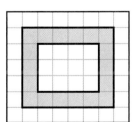

6. 📣 **TALK MATH** Explain how to find the area of a rectangle.

Find the area of each figure. See Examples 1–3

7.

8.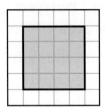

9.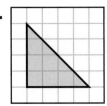

10.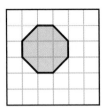

11.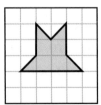

12.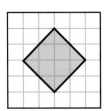

Find the area and perimeter of each figure.

13.

14.

15.

Find the area. Use a geoboard and rubber bands if needed.

16. Luisa is helping to put tile in a hallway. How many square tiles will be needed to fill the area?

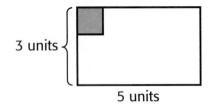

3 units
5 units

17. Elaine is finding the area of her closet. The size is shown. What is the area of her closet?

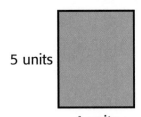

5 units
4 units

H.O.T. Problems

18. OPEN ENDED On grid paper, draw two rectangles that have different lengths and widths, but the same area.

19. CHALLENGE A room is 12 units wide by 24 units long. Find the area and the perimeter of the floor of the room.

20. 📝 **WRITE MATH** Write how to find the area of a rectangle that is 5 units long and 7 units wide.

To assess partial mastery of SOL 3.9d, see your Virginia Assessment Book.

Chapter Study Guide and Review

FOLDABLES
Study Organizer

Be sure the following Key Concepts are noted in your Foldable.

Key Concepts

- Estimate and measure **length** using customary and metric units. (Lesson 1)
- You can measure to fractions of an inch for more precise measurements. (Lesson 1)

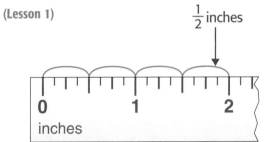

$\frac{1}{2}$ inches

- **Perimeter** is the distance around the *outside* of a figure. (Lesson 2)
- **Area** is the number of square units needed to cover a figure without overlapping. (Lesson 3)

Perimeter = 16 units
Area = 12 square units

Key Vocabulary

area

half inch $\left(\frac{1}{2}\right)$

length

meter

perimeter

units

Vocabulary Check

Choose the vocabulary word that completes each sentence.

1. The customary units of _____?_____ are inches, feet, yards, and miles.

2. To put a fence around your backyard, you would need to find the _____?_____.

3. The number of square units needed to cover a figure without overlapping is called the _____?_____.

4. Inch and meter are examples of specific amounts called _____?_____ of length.

5. A door's width measures about one _____?_____.

6. _____?_____ marks come halfway between two inch marks.

Multi-Part Lesson Review

Lesson 1 **Measure Length**

Length to the Nearest Half Inch (Lesson 1B)

7. Estimate the length. Then measure to the nearest half inch.

8. Tavio needs one piece of string that is $3\frac{1}{2}$ inches long and another one that is 4 inches longer. What is the total length of string?

EXAMPLE 1

What is the length of the piece of yarn to the nearest half inch?

The yarn is about the length of one paper clip and half of another.

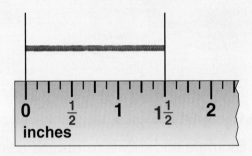

To the nearest half inch, the yarn is $1\frac{1}{2}$ inches long.

Customary Units of Length (Lesson 1C)

Choose the most appropriate unit to measure each length. Write *inch*, *foot*, *yard*, or *mile*.

9. the distance between cities

10. the height of a bike

Measure each length. Use *inch*, *foot*, or *yard*.

11. crayon   **12.** chalkboard

Choose the better estimate.

13. length of a fork
6 inches or 6 yards

EXAMPLE 2

What unit would you use to measure the width of a door? Write *inch*, *foot*, *yard*, or *mile*.

An inch and foot are too short. A mile is too long. A door is about 1 yard wide.

Problem Solving Strategy: Solve a Simpler Problem (Lesson 1D)

Solve.

14. The cat toys shown cost $6 altogether. Each toy is the same price. How much would 5 cat toys cost?

15. Colin bought 4 packs of trading cards for $2. How much would 6 packs of trading cards cost?

Mick hit a home run. The distance between the bases and home plate are equal. How far did he run?

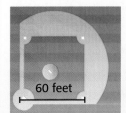

60 feet

Use a basic fact and pattern.

$4 \times 6 = 24$

$4 \times 60 = 240$

So, Mick ran 240 feet.

Metric Units of Length (Lesson 1F)

Choose the most appropriate unit to measure each length. Write *centimeter, meter,* or *kilometer.*

16. an unwound ball of yarn

17. a dragonfly

Choose the better estimate.

18. length of a football field
90 cm or 90 m

Olinda will travel to another state. What metric unit should be used to measure the distance she will travel?

The centimeter and meter are too short.

So, use the kilometer to measure the distance Olinda will travel.

Lesson 2 Perimeter

Perimeter (Lesson 2B)

Find the perimeter of each figure.

19.

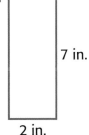

7 in.

2 in.

20.

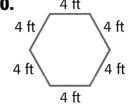

4 ft

4 ft   4 ft

4 ft   4 ft

4 ft

Find the perimeter of the triangle.

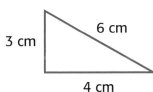

3 cm

6 cm

4 cm

$3 \text{ cm} + 4 \text{ cm} + 6 \text{ cm} = 13 \text{ cm}$

The perimeter of the triangle is 13 cm.

Problem-Solving Investigation: Choose a Strategy (Lesson 2C)

Solve. Use any strategy.

21. Angelo's book is $2\frac{1}{2}$ inches thick. He stacked it with another book that is 3 inches thicker. How tall was the stack of books?

22. **Geometry** There is a sculpture of wire shapes. There are 4 triangles, 2 squares, and 5 circles. What is the total length of wire used in meters?

Sculpture of Shapes	
Shape	**Length of Wire Used**
Triangle	25 cm
Square	50 cm
Circle	20 cm

EXAMPLE 6

Kelvin doubles the distance he runs each week. After 3 weeks he runs 8 miles. How many miles did Kelvin run the first week?

Use the *work backward* strategy to find the number of miles Kelvin ran the first week.

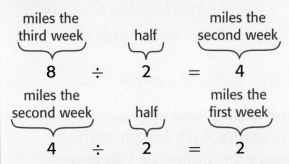

So, Kelvin ran 2 miles the first week.

Lesson 3

Measure Area (Lesson 3B)

23. Find the area of the figure.

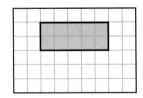

24. Tam is using a shoebox for an art project. What is the area of the bottom of the shoebox?

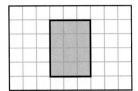

EXAMPLE 7

What is the area of the patio?

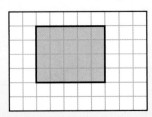

Count the number of squares the figure covers.

The figure covers 20 squares.

So, the area of the patio is 20 square units.

Practice Chapter Test

Tell whether each statement is *true* or *false*.

1. A centimeter is about the width of your index finger.

2. Area is the distance around a figure.

Measure each object to the nearest half inch.

3.

4.

Choose the most appropriate unit to measure each length. Write *inch, foot, yard,* or *mile*.

5. length of your bedroom

6. length of your finger

Choose the better estimate.

7. the height of a ladder
2 centimeters or 2 meters

8. length of a bridge
100 km or 1 km

9. MULTIPLE CHOICE Which of the following is longer than a centimeter?

A. ladybug   **C.** pen

B. staple   **D.** thumbtack

10. Lena's dad is building a fence with 28 sections. There will be one post between each section and one on each end. How many posts will he need?

11. Sandy is drawing a wall border. She draws a star every 6 inches. She draws 20 stars. How many feet long is Sandy's wall border?

Find the perimeter of each figure.

12.
12 ft
9 ft
11 ft

13.
9 in.
13 in.   13 in.
5 in.

Find the area of the figure.

14. The diagram shows the shape of a room. What is the area?

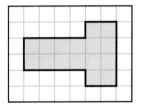

15. MULTIPLE CHOICE Choose the best estimate for the length of a soccer field.

F. 90 km   **H.** 90 inches

G. 90 m   **J.** 90 miles

16. WRITE MATH Can you find the perimeter of your desk if you know the length and width? Explain.

Test Practice

TEST EXAMPLE

A roll of wrapping paper is 48 inches wide and 12 feet long. If the paper was unrolled and layed flat, what would be its perimeter in feet?

A. 16 feet

B. 32 feet

C. 120 feet

D. 120 inches

TEST-TAKING TIP

Read the question carefully. Eliminate answer choices that are unreasonable.

Read the Question

You need to find the perimeter of the paper.

Solve the Question

48 inches equals 4 feet.

4 feet + 12 feet + 4 feet + 12 feet = 32 feet

So, the perimeter of the paper is 32 feet.

The answer is B.

Read each question. Then fill in the correct answer on the answer sheet provided by your teacher or on a separate sheet of paper.

1. Which is the most appropriate unit to measure the length of a shoe?

A. centimeter

B. liter

C. meter

D. kilometer

2. Estimate 8,732 + 4,903 to the nearest thousand.

F. 10,000

G. 12,000

H. 14,000

J. 14,600

3. Sheri's birdhouse is the shape of a pentagon. Which shape below is a pentagon?

A.

C.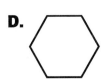

B.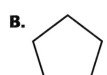

D.

---

4. What is the perimeter of a house that measures 34 feet long and 24 feet wide?

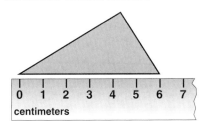

F. 58 feet

H. 92 feet

G. 82 feet

J. 116 feet

---

5. What is the length of the triangle to the nearest centimeter?

A. 4 centimeters   C. 6 centimeters

B. 5 centimeters   D. 7 centimeters

---

6. What is a reasonable estimate of the length of one side of the square?

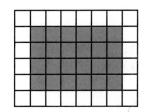

F. 1 inch   H. 3 inches

G. 2 inches   J. 4 inches

---

7. The shaded part of the figure below represents Molly's family room. What is the area of the room?

A. 18 square units

B. 24 square units

C. 36 square units

D. 48 square units

---

8. What is the length of Marc's crayon to the nearest $\frac{1}{2}$ inch?

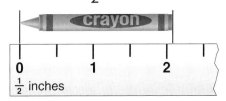

F. 1 inch   H. $2\frac{1}{2}$ inches

G. 2 inches   J. 3 inches

NEED EXTRA HELP?								
If You Missed Question . . .	1	2	3	4	5	6	7	8
Go to Chapter-Lesson . . .	11-1F	2-1B	7-1C	11-2B	11-1F	11-1B	11-3B	11-1B
For help with . . .	SOL 3.9a	SOL 3.4	SOL 3.14	SOL 3.9d	SOL 3.9a	SOL 3.9a	SOL 3.10	SOL 3.9a

More Measurement

connectED.mcgraw-hill.com

Investigate

 Animations

 Vocabulary

 Math Songs

 Multilingual eGlossary

Learn

 Personal Tutor

 Virtual Manipulatives

 Audio

 Foldables

Practice

Self-Check Practice

eGames

Worksheets

Assessment

The ☆BIG Idea

How can I select appropriate units, strategies, and tools to measure capacity, weight, mass, time, and temperature?

 FOLDABLES®
Study Organizer

Make this Foldable to help you organize information about measurement. Start with one sheet of 11" × 17" paper.

| Capacity | Weight and Mass |
| Time | Temperature |

Review Vocabulary

weight (peso) A measurement that tells how heavy an object is.

A bucket balance compares the weight of objects.

Key Vocabulary

English	Español
capacity	capacidad
mass	masa
decade	década
elapsed time	tiempo transcurrido

When Will I Use This?

Alyssa & Luke in **Time Flies**

More Measurement **571**

You have two options for checking Prerequisite Skills for this chapter.

Text Option Take the Quick Check below.

QUICK Check

Identify the object that holds more.

1.

2.

3. Which should hold more water, a swimming pool or a bathtub?

Identify which object weighs more.

4.

5.

6. Consuela took two equal-sized glasses of milk to the table. One of the glasses was full, and the other was half full. Which glass weighed less?

Write the time shown on each clock.

7.

8.

9. The mall opens at 8:00 in the morning. Suppose a customer began shopping when it opened and left three hours later. What time did the customer leave?

 Online Option Take the Online Readiness Quiz.

Explore Capacity

Main Idea

I will explore estimating and measuring capacity.

Materials

any cup, pint, quart, and gallon container

water

containers in a variety of sizes

Get Connect ED

3.9 The student will estimate and use U.S. Customary and metric units to measure **b)** liquid volume in cups, pints, quarts, gallons, and liters.

The amount a container can hold is called its **capacity**. Common containers and units for capacity are shown.

about 1 cup (c)   about 1 pint (pt)   about 1 quart (qt)   gallon (gal)

ACTIVITY

1 Estimate and Measure Capacity

Step 1 Cup, Pint, Quart, and Gallon

- Estimate how many cups a pint, quart, and gallon will hold.

- Use the cup to fill the pint, quart, and gallon containers.

- How many cups are in a pint, quart, and gallon? Record the results in the first row of the table.

Units of Capacity			
	Pint	**Quart**	**Gallon**
Cups	2		
Pints			
Quarts			

Step 2 Pint, Quart, and Gallon

- Make an estimate. How many pints do you think a quart container holds? a gallon container? How many quarts do you think a gallon container holds?

- Use an empty pint container to fill the quart and gallon containers. Use an empty quart container to fill the gallon container.

- How many pints are in a quart? in a gallon? How many quarts are in a gallon? Record the results.

2 Estimate and Measure Capacity

Step 1 **Estimate.**
- Estimate and record the capacity of each container.

Container	Estimate				Actual			
	c	pt	qt	gal	c	pt	qt	gal
A								
B								
C								
D								

Step 2 **Measure.**
- Use the cup, pint, quart, and gallon container to measure the actual capacity of each container.
- Record the results in the table.

Think About It

1. In Activity 1, how close were your estimates to the exact answers?

2. Name some containers from around your home that would have about the same capacity as a cup, pint, quart, and gallon.

3. What happens to the number of containers needed as the capacity of the container gets larger? smaller?

Practice and Apply It

Compare. Use >, <, or =.

4. 1 cup ● 1 gallon

5. 1 gallon ● 1 pint

6. 1 quart ● 1 cup

7. 1 cup ● 1 pint

8. 1 quart ● 1 gallon

9. 2 cups ● 1 pint

10. 2 pints ● 2 gallons

11. 4 pints ● 4 cups

12. 9 quarts ● 9 cups

13. 2 cups ● 1 gallon

14. 1 pint ● 10 cups

15. 2 quarts ● 2 pints

16. **WRITE MATH** How do you know that 10 gallons is equal to 40 quarts?

Main Idea

I will estimate and measure liquid volume using customary units of capacity.

 Vocabulary

capacity
cup (c)
pint (pt)
quart (qt)
gallon (gal)

 Get ConnectED

3.9 The student will estimate and use U.S. Customary and metric units to measure **b)** liquid volume in cups, pints, quarts, gallons, and liters.

Customary Units of Capacity

The amount of liquid a container can hold is its **capacity** or liquid volume. The customary units of capacity are the **cup (c)**, **pint (pt)**, **quart (qt)**, and **gallon (gal)**.

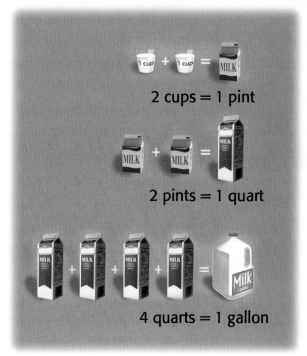

2 cups = 1 pint

2 pints = 1 quart

4 quarts = 1 gallon

🏃 ✍ **REAL-WORLD EXAMPLE**   **Choose Units of Capacity**

1️⃣ **POOLS Armando is filling his younger sister's wading pool. Choose the most appropriate unit Armando should use to measure the amount of water it takes to fill the pool.**

A cup, pint, and quart are too small. The most appropriate unit to use is the gallon.

Estimate Capacity

Remember

A *unit* is a fixed quantity used for measurement; for example, cup, pint, quart, and gallon.

2 **SOUP** Choose the better estimate for the capacity of a soup bowl, 2 cups or 2 gallons.

Think about the units of capacity, cup and gallon.

It makes sense that the capacity of a soup bowl is about 2 cups, not 2 gallons.

So, the better estimate for the capacity of a soup bowl is 2 cups.

✓ CHECK What You Know

Choose the most appropriate unit to measure each capacity. Write *cup, pint, quart,* or *gallon.* See Example 1

1.

2.

3.

Choose the better estimate. See Example 2

4. bucket of water
3 c or 3 gal

5. flower vase
2 c or 2 gal

6. Megan has 12 cups of punch. Does she have more or less than a quart?

7. Arturo is making hot chocolate for himself. Should he use 1 cup or 1 quart of milk? Explain.

8. 📝 **TALK MATH** How do you decide which unit of capacity to use?

Choose the most appropriate unit to measure each capacity.
Write *cup*, *pint*, *quart*, or *gallon*. See Example 1

9.

10.

11.

Choose the better estimate. See Example 2

12. watering can
2 qt or 2 pt

13. fish aquarium
5 gal or 10 qt

14. punch bowl
1 pt or 8 c

15. Choose the better estimate for the capacity of a pickle jar, 4 cups or 4 gallons.

16. Is the better estimate for the amount of water a person drinks each day 8 cups or 8 gallons?

17. Jackson showers for 10 minutes. Has he used about 15 cups or 150 gallons of water?

18. Would it be faster to fill a sink with a gallon container or a quart container?

19. Would 7 pints or 7 cups hold more?

20. Would 24 pints be more or less than 2 gallons?

H.O.T. Problems

21. OPEN ENDED Name three items from the grocery store that are measured by capacity.

22. CHALLENGE What two units of capacity does the table show?

First Unit	1	2	3	4	5	6
Second Unit	4	8	12	16	20	24

23. **WRITE MATH** Sumey and Terri are each filling equal-sized pails with water. Sumey is using a pint container. Terri is using a quart container. Who will fill her pail first? Explain.

Problem-Solving Strategy: Guess, Check, and Revise

Main Idea I will solve a problem by using the guess, check, and revise strategy.

Octavia's class is making homemade clay. The same amount of flour is used to make red clay and green clay. They use 5 more cups of flour to make blue clay. The total amount of flour used is 29 cups. How much flour is used for each color of clay?

Understand **What facts do you know?**

- The total amount of flour is 29 cups.
- The red and green clay use the same amount of flour.
- The blue clay uses 5 more cups of flour than the other two colors.

What do you need to find?

- The amount of flour used for each color of clay.

Plan

You can use the *guess, check, and revise* strategy. Guess different combinations of numbers and check to see if they fit the facts in the problem.

Solve

The red and green clay use the same amount of flour. The blue clay uses 5 more cups than the others. The total flour used is 29 cups.

Guess			Check
Red	Green	Blue	Total
10	10	15	35 no
9	9	14	32 no
8	8	13	29 yes

So, the green and the red clay use 8 cups of flour each, and the blue clay uses 13 cups of flour.

Check **Look back.**

$8 + 8 + 13 = 29$, and 13 is 5 more 8.

So, the answer is correct. ✔

3.9 The student will estimate and use U.S. Customary and metric units to measure **b)** liquid volume in cups, pints, quarts, gallons, and liters.

EXTEND

1. Explain what it means to use the *guess, check, and revise* strategy.

2. Suppose the total number of cups of flour is 29, but each color of clay uses a different amount. The blue clay uses 5 more cups of flour than the green clay. How much flour is used for each color?

3. You know that the sum of 9 cups, 9 cups and 11 cups are 29 cups. Explain why it is an incorrect guess for this problem.

4. Should you always use the *guess, check, and revise* strategy? Explain.

PRACTICE

EXTRA **PRACTICE**
Begins on page EP2.

Solve. Use the *guess, check, and revise* strategy.

5. Alfonso bought some packages of 8 markers and some packages of 12 markers. He has a total of 48 markers. How many packages of each set of markers did he buy?

6. Three friends talk about the number of family members they each have.

- Two have the same number in their family.
- Each has an odd number of family members but, no double digit number in a family.
- The total number is 17.

How many are in each family?

7. Griffin jogs two days each week. He jogs the same distance each of the two days each week. This week he jogged twice as far as last week. If he jogged a total of 18 miles this week and last, how many miles did he jog each of the two days last week and this week?

8. Guess this riddle. I am thinking of four numbers between 1 and 9 whose sum is 23. What numbers am I thinking of?

9. For homework, Granger's class was asked to create a design using the directions and shapes shown below.

- The total number of sides of the shapes used must be 32.
- 2 of the shapes are triangles
- Use the following shapes:

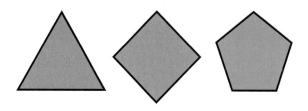

How many of each shape was used for the students' homework designs?

10. Dustin shares apple juice with his friends. He drinks 1 cup. His friends each drink one more cup than Dustin. There were 13 cups of juice in all. How many friends are there?

11. **WRITE MATH** Explain how the *guess, check, and revise* strategy and the work *backwards* strategy are alike and how they are different.

Main Idea
I will estimate and measure liquid volume using metric units of capacity.

 Vocabulary
liter (L)
milliliter (mL)

 Get Connect ED

3.9 The student will estimate and use U.S. Customary and metric units to measure **b)** liquid volume in cups, pints, quarts, gallons, and liters.

Metric Units of Capacity

In this activity, you will explore metric units of capacity.

Explore Mini Activity

Materials: eyedropper, penny, bottle cap, empty 1-liter bottle, and pail

Step 1 Use an eyedropper to find how many milliliters of water fit on the surface of a penny and a bottle cap. Count every 10 drops as 1 milliliter.

Step 2 Use an empty 1-liter plastic soda bottle to find how many liters of water fit in a bucket.

You have learned that capacity refers to the amount a container can hold. The metric units of capacity are **milliliter (mL)** and **liter (L)**.

milliliter (mL)

A dropper holds about 1 milliliter of liquid. This is about 10 drops. Use this unit to measure containers of small capacity.

liter (L)

This water bottle holds about 1 liter of liquid. Use this unit to measure containers of greater capacity.

Metric Units of Capacity
1 liter (L) = 1,000 milliliters (mL)

REAL-WORLD EXAMPLE   Choose Metric Units

1 BIRDS Choose the most appropriate unit to measure the amount of water a bird drinks each day.

A liter is too large. A bird would drink a small amount of water. So, milliliters should be used.

REAL-WORLD EXAMPLE   Estimate Capacity

2 FISH Choose the better estimate for the amount of water in the aquarium, 50 mL or 5 L.

50 mL is a small amount. It is not reasonable. Since 5 L is a larger amount of water, 5 L is reasonable.

✓ CHECK What You Know

Choose the most appropriate unit to measure each capacity. Write *milliliter* or *liter*. See Example 1

1. bucket

2. wading pool

3. spoon

Choose the better estimate. See Example 2

4.

3 mL or 3 L

5.

40 L or 40 mL

6.

50 mL or 50 L

7. Karl is using a spoon to measure honey for his tea. Is each spoonful 5 mL or 5 L?

8. 🗨 **TALK MATH** Describe some items sold in a grocery store that are packaged in liter containers.

Choose the most appropriate unit to measure each capacity.
Write *milliliter* or *liter*. See Example 1

9. pot of soup

10. juice box

11. pitcher of lemonade

12. bottle of glue

13. water bottle

14. fish tank

Choose the better estimate. See Example 2

15.

250 L or 250 mL

16.

100 mL or 100 L

17.

10 mL or 10 L

18.

2 mL or 2 L

19.

5 mL or 5 L

20.

200 mL or 200 L

REAL-WORLD PROBLEM SOLVING

Food A punch recipe is shown.

21. How many liters of punch will this recipe make?

22. How many liters of punch did the guests drink if there were 650 milliliters left after the party?

23. Mona used seven 500-milliliters bottles of grape juice. How many milliliters of grape juice did she use altogether?

Party Punch

3 L pineapple juice
1 L apple juice
1500 mL soda water
500 mL grape juice

Pour into a large punch bowl and chill.

H.O.T. Problems

24. OPEN ENDED Name an item that has a capacity of 1 liter.

25. **WRITE MATH** Think about a liter and a milliliter. What do you think the prefix "milli-" means? Explain.

To assess mastery of SOL 3.9b, see your Virginia Assessment Book.

Game Time

Capacity Guess
Estimate Capacity

You will need: labeled measuring containers (cup, pint, quart, and gallon); empty containers of different sizes and shapes

Get Ready!

Players: 2 or more

Get Set!

Place a variety of empty containers on a table.

Go!

☆ Player 1 chooses an empty container and gives it to Player 2.

☆ Player 2 estimates its capacity and guesses which measuring container to use to check the capacity.

☆ Player 2 fills the measuring container with water and then pours the water into the empty container.

☆ If the capacity is incorrect, Player 1 will get to estimate the capacity and check.

☆ Continue, switching roles each time. Each player scores one point for each correct answer.

Main Idea
I will estimate and measure using customary units of weight.

 Vocabulary
weight
ounce (oz)
pound (lb)

 Get Connect**ED**

 **3.9** The student will estimate and use U.S. Customary and metric units to measure **c)** weight/mass in ounces, pounds, grams, and kilograms.

Customary Units of Weight

Explore Mini Activity

Materials: bucket balance, 1-ounce weight, and 1-pound weight

Step 1 Use a bucket balance and weights to find objects that weigh about 1 ounce.

Step 2 Use a bucket balance and weights to find objects that weigh about 1 pound.

A scale is often used to measure how heavy something is, or to find its **weight**. A balance scale compares the weight of objects. The customary units of weight are **ounce (oz)** and **pound (lb)**.

A golf ball weighs about 1 ounce.

A soccer ball weighs about 1 pound.

1 pound   =   16 ounces

A soccer ball has about the same weight as 16 golf balls.

REAL-WORLD EXAMPLE   Choose Units of Weight

1 **FOOD** **Choose the unit to use to measure the weight of a slice of bread. Write *ounce* or *pound*.**

A pound is too heavy. The most appropriate unit to use is ounce.

So, use ounces to measure the weight of the slice of bread.

Remember

An ounce is a unit of measure for light objects. A pound is a unit of measure for heavy objects.

REAL-WORLD EXAMPLE   Estimate Weight

2 **BOOKS** **Choose the better estimate for the weight of these books, 3 ounces or 3 pounds.**

Think about an ounce and a pound. It makes sense that the weight of the books is about 3 pounds, not 3 ounces.

✓ CHECK What You Know

Choose the most appropriate unit to measure the weight of each object. Write *ounce* or *pound*. See Example 1

1.

2.

3.

Choose the better estimate. See Example 2

4. compact disc
2 oz or 2 lb

5. pineapple
5 lb or 5 oz

6. A price tag was placed over the unit of weight on a television box. Is the unit *ounce* or *pound*? Explain.

7. **TALK MATH** Explain how you can use a bucket balance and golf balls to measure the weight of items.

EXTRA PRACTICE
Begins on page EP2.

Choose the unit you would use to measure the weight of each object. Write *ounce* or *pound*. See Example 1

8.

9.

10.

11. bag of soil

12. paper clip

13. pencil

Choose the better estimate. See Example 2

14.

pair of socks
2 lb or 2 oz

15.

seahorse
7 oz or 7 lb

16.

light bulb
3 lb or 3 oz

17. Marshal's bag of peanuts weighs 5 pounds. His box of crackers weighs 6 ounces. Which weighs more?

18. Cam bought 5 bananas. Would they weigh 5 pounds or 5 ounces in all?

19. An ostrich egg weighs 4 pounds. Is this about the same weight as 4 soccer balls or 4 golf balls?

20. One bag of grapefruit weighs 3 pounds 8 ounces. A bag of oranges weighs 2 pounds 2 ounces. What is the difference between the weights?

Data File

Many animals are native to South Carolina.

21. Which weighs more, an American alligator or a white-tailed deer?

22. Which animal weighs about twice as much as a soccer ball? Explain.

South Carolina Wildlife		
Animal	**Weight**	**Length**
American alligator	600 lb	8 feet
Eastern cottontail	2 lb	15 inches
White-tailed deer	30 lb	6 feet

23. OPEN ENDED Name four objects that would weigh more than 1 pound.

24. CHALLENGE How many ounces are in 3 pounds?

25. **WRITE MATH** Explain what would happen to a balance scale if a 2-pound weight was on one side and a 24-ounce weight was on the other side.

Test Practice

26. Which of the following objects weighs more than 1 pound?
(Lesson 2A)

A.

B.

C.

D.

27. Sumi has 4 cups of punch left. Holly drank 3 cups, Brandon drank 2 cups, and 7 cups were spilled. How many pints of punch did Sumi have to start with? (Lesson 1B)

F. 2 pints

G. 4 pints

H. 6 pints

J. 8 pints

Spiral Review

Choose the most appropriate unit to measure each capacity. Write *milliliter* or *liter*. (Lesson 1D)

28. bowl of soup   **29.** fish aquarium   **30.** hamster waterbottle

31. Aida planted 8 flowers in 5 pots. She put 2 flowers in the red pots and 1 in each of the blue pots. How many red pots does Aida have? How many blue pots are there? (Lesson 1C)

Algebra Find and extend the rule for each table. Then copy and complete. (Lesson 1B)

32.

Rule: ■					
Pints	2	4	6	8	12
Cups	4	■	12	■	■

33.

Rule: ■					
Quarts	8	4	12	20	28
Gallons	■	1	■	5	■

Lengths, Heights, and Weights Oh My!

Animals come in different shapes and sizes. For example, a ruby-throated hummingbird is a little more than $3\frac{1}{2}$ inches long and weighs less than an ounce. On the other end of the scale, a rhinoceros can weigh 2,200 pounds. A beetle is less than an inch long, but a giraffe can be more than 18 feet tall.

Animals also have different characteristics to help them live in their environments. Elephants can hold up to 3 gallons of water in their trunks. A pelican's stomach can hold up to one gallon of food at a time.

Amazing Animals		
Animal	**Size**	**Weight (lb)**
Zebra	6 ft	530
Ostrich	9 ft	345
Alligator	9 ft	1,000
Tree frog	13 in.	6

Did You Know?

One of the heaviest living animals was a blue whale that weighed 389,760 pounds!

Real-World Math

Use the information on the previous page to solve each problem.

1. What is the length of a ruby-throated hummingbird rounded to the nearest inch?

2. What is the most appropriate unit to measure the height of a rhinoceros?

3. How many yards tall is a giraffe?

4. About how many feet longer is an alligator than a tree frog?

5. How many pints of food can a pelican hold in its stomach?

6. How many more quarts of water can an elephant hold in its trunk than a pelican can hold food in its stomach?

7. How many ounces does a tree frog weigh? (*Hint:* 16 ounces = 1 pound)

8. An alligator is about 8 inches long when it is born. Is a tree frog twice that length? Explain.

9. Which animal is almost two times the weight of the zebra?

PART   A   B

Main Idea

I will estimate and measure using metric units of mass.

 Vocabulary

mass

gram (g)

kilogram (kg)

 *Get Connect ED*

3.9 The student will estimate and use U.S. Customary and metric units to measure **c)** weight/mass in ounces, pounds, grams, and kilograms.

Metric Units of Mass

Mass is the amount of matter, or material in an object. The most common metric units used to measure the mass of an object are the **gram (g)** and **kilogram (kg)**.

A paper clip has a mass of about 1 gram.

A baseball bat has a mass of about 1 kilogram.

=

1,000 paper clips have about the same mass as one baseball bat.

Metric Units of Mass
1,000 grams (g) = 1 kilogram (kg)

 REAL-WORLD EXAMPLE   Choose Units of Mass

(1) **SNACKS** A store in the mall sells fresh baked pretzels. Choose the unit you would use to measure the mass of a pretzel.

Pretzels do not have much matter. It would be more reasonable to measure a pretzel's mass in grams.

Explore Mini-Activity

Materials: bucket balance, 1-kilogram mass

Step 1 Choose three small objects. Estimate if each one is *less than, more than,* or *about* 1 kilogram. Explain why you made the estimate that you did. Record your estimates in a table like the one shown.

Less Than 1 kilogram	1 kilogram	More Than 1 kilogram

Step 2 Check your estimates using the bucket balance and a 1-kilogram mass.

Step 3 Identify an object from the classroom that would have about the same mass as each object above.

Remember

A kilogram is a little more than 2 pounds.

You can use what you know about the gram and kilogram to estimate and compare mass.

 REAL-WORLD EXAMPLE   Estimate Mass

2 VEGETABLES Choose the better estimate for the mass of a large squash, 500 grams or 500 kilograms.

Think about a gram and a kilogram.

Since a large squash does not have the same mass as 500 baseball bats, we can see that the estimate should be 500 grams. So, the best estimate is 500 grams.

Choose the most appropriate unit to measure each mass.
Write *gram* or *kilogram*. See Example 1

1. toothbrush

2. orange

3. shovel

Choose the better estimate. See Example 2

4.

5 g or 5 kg

5.

50 g or 5,000 g

6.

4 g or 4 kg

7. **TALK MATH** Does a large object always have a greater mass than a small object? Explain.

Practice and Problem Solving

EXTRA PRACTICE
Begins on page EP2.

Choose the most appropriate unit to measure each mass.
Write *gram* or *kilogram*. See Example 1

8. teddy bear

9. lawn mower

10. child

11. bag of pretzels

12. pair of sunglasses

13. pencil

Choose the better estimate. See Example 2

14.

15 g or 15 kg

15.

900 g or 900 kg

16.

2 g or 2 kg

17. large ball
500 g or 50 kg

18. apple
160 g or 160 kg

19. cordless phone
200 g or 200 kg

20. **OPEN ENDED** A bag of potatoes has a mass of about 3 kilograms. Name two other items that have about the same mass. Explain your reasoning.

21. **WHICH ONE DOESN'T BELONG?** Identify the unit that does not belong. Explain.

| liter | Kilogram | Kilometer | milliliter |

22. **WRITE MATH** Explain how to change from kilograms to grams.

Test Practice

23. A package of flour weighs 5 pounds, and a package of sugar weighs 48 ounces. How much more does the package of flour weigh? (Lesson 2A)

    A. 1 pound   **C.** 40 ounces

    B. 2 pounds   **D.** 48 ounces

24. There are 1,000 grams in 1 kilogram. How many grams are in 7 kilograms? (Lesson 2B)

    F. 70 grams

    G. 700 grams

    H. 1,000 grams

    J. 7,000 grams

Solve.

25. The soup that Alaina is making needs 8 liters of water. She only has a 500-milliliter container. How can she use that container to measure 8 liters? (Lesson 1D)

26. Elton has 3 more rocks in his rock collection than Curtis. Together they have 35 rocks. How many rocks does each boy have? (Lesson 1C)

Choose the most appropriate unit to measure each weight. Write *ounce* or *pound*. (Lesson 1B)

27. pencil   28. bumblebee   29. dog

Mid-Chapter Check

Choose the most appropriate unit to measure each capacity. Write *cup, pint, quart,* or *gallon.* (Lesson 1B)

1.

2.

Choose the better estimate. (Lesson 1B)

3.

2 c or 1 qt

4.

2 gal or 3 qt

Solve. Use the *guess, check, and revise* strategy. (Lesson 1C)

5. Find the number.
  - It is less than 30 and greater than 10.
  - It is a multiple of 3.
  - It is an odd number.
  - The sum of its digits is 9.

6. MULTIPLE CHOICE Eva went on vacation 6 days longer than Suzie. Which of these shows the number of days that could have been Eva's and Suzie's vacations? (Lesson 1C)

  A. Eva 9, Suzie 6

  B. Eva 12, Suzie 7

  C. Eva 15, Suzie 9

  D. Eva 17, Suzie 9

Choose the better estimate. (Lesson 2B)

7.

8.

145 g or 145 kg   2 g or 2 kg

9. MULTIPLE CHOICE Which can hold more than one liter? (Lesson 1D)

  F. eyedropper   **H.** bathtub
  G. cereal bowl   **J.** water balloon

Solve.

10. Fillipa poured a half liter of milk into her glass. How many milliliters of milk does Fillipa have? (Lesson 1D)

11. Which container can hold about 1 gallon of liquid? (Lesson 1B)

bowl   paint can

Choose the most appropriate unit to measure each weight. Write *ounce* or *pound.* (Lesson 2A)

12. spoon   **13.** table

14. brick   **15.** feather

16. WRITE MATH Explain how you know that 1 gallon is greater than 1 milliliter. (Lessons 1B and 1D)

Main Idea
I will tell time to the nearest minute.

 Vocabulary
digital clock
analog clock

 Get Connect**ED**

3.11 The student will
a) tell time to the nearest minute, using analog and digital clocks.

Time to the Minute

Jake's watch is digital. A **digital clock** shows the time in numbers.

REAL-WORLD EXAMPLE Use a Digital Clock

① **TIME** Jake looked at his watch at the end of soccer practice. Write the time shown on Jake's digital watch.

The digits before the colon (:) show the hour.

The digits after the colon (:) show the minutes.

Read twelve fifteen   **Write** 12:15

An **analog clock** has an hour hand and a minute hand.

 **EXAMPLE** Use an Analog Clock

② **TIME** Write the time shown on the analog clock.

Step 1 **Find the hour.**

The shorter hand is the hour hand. It has passed the 5. But it has not reached the 6. So, the hour is 5.

Step 2 **Count the minutes.**

The longer hand is the minute hand. Start at 12. Count by fives, then count on by ones.
5, 10, 15, 20, 25, 30, 35, 40, 45 then 46, 47
There are 47 minutes.

Read five forty-seven   **Write** 5:47

Write the time shown on each digital or analog clock.

See Examples 1 and 2

1.

2.

3.

4. If the minute hand is pointing to the number 2, how many minutes past the hour is the clock showing?

5. [?] **TALK MATH** Which do you think is more difficult to read, an analog clock or a digital clock? Explain.

Practice and Problem Solving

EXTRA **PRACTICE**
Begins on page EP2.

Write the time shown on each digital or analog clock.

See Examples 1 and 2

6.

7.

8.

9.

10.

11.

12. If the minute hand is pointing to the number 7, how many minutes is it past the hour?

13. The clock on the wall showed 8:45. What time did it show 7 minutes later?

14. It was 12:53 when the basketball team came onto the court. Draw the hour hand and minute hand on the clock to show 12:53.

15. The third grade class walks to the lunch room at 11:16 each day. Draw the hour hand and minute hand on the clock to show 11:16.

16. OPEN ENDED Draw a digital clock with a time on it. Then describe in writing where the hour hand and minute hand would be pointing on an analog clock set at the same time.

17. FIND THE ERROR Kendra read the clock on the wall. Find her mistake and correct it.

It is 9:18.

18. **WRITE MATH** Does the minute hand or the hour hand move faster on an analog clock? How do you know?

Test Practice

19. Which of the following clocks represent 25 minutes past the hour? (Lesson 3A)

A.

C.

B.

D.

20. Choose the most appropriate unit to measure the mass of an apple. (Lesson 2B)

F. milliliter   H. liter

G. cup   J. gram

21. Angelo caught a 3 pound fish. Which of the following is equivalent? (Lesson 2A)

A. 48 milliters   C. 32 kilograms

B. 48 ounces   D. 32 quarts

Spiral Review

Choose the most appropriate unit to measure each mass.
Write *gram* or *kilogram* (Lesson 2B)

22.

23.

24.

Problem-Solving Investigation

Main Idea I will choose the best strategy to solve a problem.

P.S.I. TEAM +

BILLY: My family is going to a picnic at 6:15. I will bake 3 dozen cookies. It takes 10 minutes to bake one dozen cookies. We will need another 20 minutes to get ready and 15 minutes to walk there.

YOUR MISSION: Find the latest time Billy and his family can start to prepare in order to be on time to the picnic.

Understand

You know what time the party starts. You also know how long it takes to bake cookies, get ready, and walk there.

Plan

Use the *work backward* strategy to solve this problem.

Solve

Use a picture to help you work backward.

Mark everything on a time line in reverse order.
Mark the start time and how long each activity takes.

Party starts	Walk there	Get ready		Bake		Start time?
6:15	−15 min.	−20 min.	−10	−10	−10 min.	?
6:15	6:00	5:40	5:30	5:20	5:10	

So, Billy and his family need to start by 5:10.

Check

Use addition to check. 5:10 + 65 min. = 6:15.

So, the answer is correct. ✓

 3.11 The student will **b)** determine elapsed time in one-hour increments over a 12-hour period.

- Work backward.
- Make a table.
- Draw a picture.

Use any strategy to solve each problem.

1. Ms. Dunn bought 6 sheets of plywood, a box of nails, and a hammer from the hardware store. She spent $195. How much did the hammer cost?

Item   Cost

Plywood........$30 each

Box of nails....$5 each

Hammer........   each

2. Three friends are fishing. Francisco caught 3 times as many fish as Haley. Haley caught 7 fewer fish than Petra. Petra caught 15 fish. How many fish did Francisco and Haley catch?

3. Measurement Ciro played at the park with 5 friends for 30 minutes, 7 friends for 1 hour, and 2 friends for 15 minutes. He arrived at the park at 1:00 P.M., what time did he leave?

4. At an amusement park, the Ghost Castle ride can hold 4 children in each car. How many cars are needed for 43 children to ride?

5. Measurement The blue figures are windows. How many meters wide is missing the window?

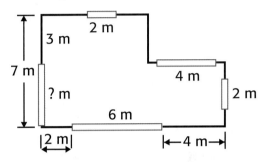

6. When you add 8 to a number, subtract 10 from the sum, and double the difference, you get 44. What is the number?

7. Salvador paid $140 for the cable, phone, and Internet bills. The cable bill was $62. The phone bill was $59. How much was the Internet bill?

8. Measurement Jocelyn wants to install a fence around a garden. How many feet of fence will be needed?

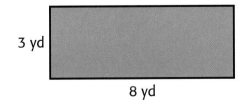

3 yd

8 yd

9. **WRITE MATH** Explain how the *work backward* strategy helped you solve Exercise 6.

Main Idea

I will determine the amount of elapsed time to solve problems.

Materials

2 student clocks

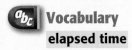**Vocabulary**

elapsed time

Get Connect**ED**

3.11 The student will **b)** determine elapsed time in one-hour increments over a 12-hour period.

Elapsed Time

To determine **elapsed time**, find the amount of time that passes from the start of an activity to the end of the activity.

Brooke got in line for the roller coaster at 12:20. It was 1:45 when it was her turn to ride. How much time elapsed while Brooke stood in line?

Explore Mini-Activity

Determine Elapsed Time

Step 1 Set one clock to the start time. Write the time. Set the second clock to the end time. Write the time.

12:20   1:45

Step 2 Rotate the minute hand of the first clock. Every time the hand passes the start time, without passing the end time, count one hour.

1 hour

12:20   1:45

Step 3 Continue to rotate the minute hand until the time matches the end time. Count by fives. Then count on by ones, if needed.

25
20   5
15   10

12:20   1:45

So, Brooke stood in line for 1 hour and 25 minutes.

🏃 ✏️ 📷 **REAL-WORLD EXAMPLES** Elapsed Time

① TRAVEL It takes Louisa one hour and 30 minutes to travel to her aunt's house. She leaves at 4:00 P.M. What time will she get to her aunt's house?

Add 1 hour and 30 minutes to 4:00 P.M.

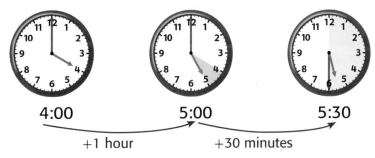

4:00   5:00   5:30
      +1 hour   +30 minutes

So, Louisa will get to her aunt's house at 5:30 P.M.

② CHOIR The clock shows the time June's choir practice started. It ended at 5:30 P.M. Find the elapsed time.

Find the elapsed time between 3:15 P.M. and 5:30 P.M.

3:15   4:15   5:15   5:30
      1 hour   1 hour   15 minutes

1 hour + 1 hour + 15 minutes = 2 hours 15 minutes
So, the elapsed time is 2 hours 15 minutes.

Remember
1 hour = 60 minutes
1 day = 24 hours

✓ **CHECK** **What You Know**

The following are movie times. Find the length of each movie.

See Examples 1 and 2

1. Start Time   End Time

2. Start time   End time

3. Jose's family went to the library at the time shown. How much time elapsed if they stayed until 4:00?

See Examples 1 and 2

4. 🗣️❓ **TALK MATH** Lupe went to sleep at the time shown at the right and awoke at 6:30 A.M. Explain how to find how long Lupe slept. See Examples 1 and 2

The following are times of baseball games. Find the length of each game. See Examples 1 and 2

5. Start Time   End Time

6. Start Time   End Time

7. Start Time   End Time

8. Start Time   End Time

Find each elapsed time. See Examples 1 and 2

9. The clock shows when Malina began reading her book. It is 12:50 when she stops.

10. The clock shows when Chris went to the park. He stays until 5:15 P.M.

Use the information to solve the problems.

Time Files

11. How much longer did Alyssa read?

12. Will she get to Book Buddies on time? Explain.

13. WHICH ONE DOESN'T BELONG? Which set of digital clocks does *not* show an elapsed time of 1 hour 25 minutes? Explain.

14. **WRITE MATH** Explain how working backward helps you find the amount of time elapsed.

 **Test Practice**

15. The clock shows the time Terrell finished downloading music.

If he downloaded music for 45 minutes, what time did he begin? (Lesson 3C)

A. 9:30　　**C.** 10:00

B. 9:45　　**D.** 10:30

16. Patricio subtracted two numbers and got a difference of 23,839. To get that difference he subtracted 83,381 from the total. What was the total? (Lesson 3B)

F. 59,542

G. 60,558

H. 106,110

J. 107,220

Spiral Review

Solve. (Lesson 3B)

17. Malika is shooting baskets. She makes a basket every 6th shot. If she makes a total of 9 baskets, how many shots did she take?

Write the time shown on each clock. (Lesson 3A)

18.

19.

20.

Main Idea

I will use a calendar and time line to determine longer periods of elapsed time.

Vocabulary

decade

century

time line

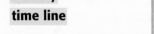Get Connect**ED**

 3.12 The student will identify equivalent periods of time, including relationships among days, months, and years, as well as minutes and hours.
3.11 The student will
b) determine elapsed time in one-hour increments over a 12-hour period.

Calendars and Time Lines

A calendar is helpful when finding how much time has elapsed in days, weeks, and months.

Periods of Time		
1 hour	=	60 minutes
1 day	=	24 hours
1 week	=	7 days
1 month	=	4 weeks
1 year	=	12 months, 52 weeks, or 365 days

REAL-WORLD EXAMPLE   Use a Calendar

1 **DAYS OFF Pepita would like to go skating her next day off from school. Today is September 15. Use the calendars to find how much time will elapse before her next day off.**

Pepita's free days are shaded.

Step 1   Start at September 15.

Step 2   Count down the rows until the week of her next day off.

There are 3 weeks.

Step 3   Count on the days from October 6 to October 10.

6 + 4 = 10

There are 4 days.

SEPTEMBER						
S	M	T	W	T	F	S
	1	2	3	4	5	6
7	8	9	10	11	12	13
14	15	16	17	18	19	20
21	22	23	24	25	26	27
28	29	30				

OCTOBER						
S	M	T	W	T	F	S
			1	2	3	4
5	6	7	8	9	10	11
12	13	14	15	16	17	18
19	20	21	22	23	24	25
26	27	28	29	30	31	

So, 3 weeks and 4 days will elapse before Pepita's next day off.

A time line is helpful to find longer periods of elapsed time.
A **time line** is a number line that shows years or dates.

Longer Periods of Time	
1 **decade**	= 10 years
1 **century**	= 100 years

REAL-WORLD EXAMPLE   Use a Time Line

② **INVENTIONS** Neil's time line shows some popular inventions. How many years elapsed between the invention of the first telephone and the cell phone?

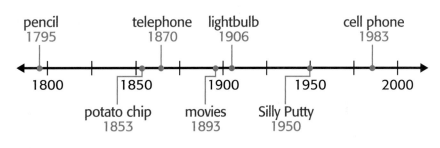

Inventions

pencil 1795   telephone 1870   lightbulb 1906   cell phone 1983

1800   1850   1900   1950   2000

potato chip 1853   movies 1893   Silly Putty 1950

```
 1983 cell phone
-1870 telephone
  113 years
```

So, 113 years, more than a century, elapsed.

✓ CHECK What You Know

Use the calendar or time line to solve. See Examples 1 and 2

1. Sabrina has a swimming class on June 5 and June 11. How many days will elapse before the next class?

JUNE						
S	M	T	W	T	F	S
	1	2	3	4	5	6
7	8	9	10	11	12	13
14	15	16	17	18	19	20
21	22	23	24	25	26	27
28	29	30				

2. Sabrina's last day of school is June 2. How many weeks of summer vacation will she have in June? How many days does that equal?

3. What happened between 2005 and 2009?

4. How many decades are represented by this time line?

5. 📱 **TALK MATH** Can events that happen in a month's time be shown on a time line? Explain.

Odell's Time Line

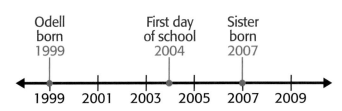

Odell born 1999   First day of school 2004   Sister born 2007

1999   2001   2003   2005   2007   2009

Use the calendars and time line to solve. See Examples 1 and 2

| JANUARY |
S	M	T	W	T	F	S
		1	2	3	4	5
6	7	8	9	10	11	12
13	14	15	16	17	18	19
20	21	22	23	24	25	26
27	28	29	30	31		

| FEBRUARY |
S	M	T	W	T	F	S
					1	2
3	4	5	6	7	8	9
10	11	12	13	14	15	16
17	18	19	20	21	22	23
24	25	26	27	28		

| MARCH |
S	M	T	W	T	F	S
					1	2
3	4	5	6	7	8	9
10	11	12	13	14	15	16
17	18	19	20	21	22	23
24/31	25	26	27	28	29	30

6. The Pets and Pals Dog Show is on the third Sunday of March. Mara needs 5 weeks to prepare her dog. When should she start?

7. Frank's grandparents are visiting January 18 through February 10. It is January 22. How much time is left until they leave?

8. Brynn's library book was due February 27. Today is March 15. Overdue fines are 5¢ a day. How much money will Brynn owe if she returns the book today?

9. Martin Luther King, Jr. Day is January 21. President's Day is the third Monday in February. How much time elapses between the two holidays?

10. How many Sundays are in the months of February and March?

11. Find what day of the week is April 10. Explain.

Decades of Computer Firsts

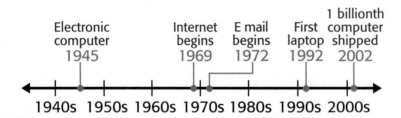

12. How many decades are represented by this timeline? How many more are needed to represent a century?

13. How many full decades elapsed between the beginning of the Internet and the 1 billionth computer?

14. How many years passed between the first computer and the first laptop?

15. In what decade was e-mail introduced?

Use the tables on the previous pages to convert each unit of time.

16. 3 hours = ■ minutes

17. ■ hours = 1 day

18. 14 days = ■ weeks

19. 120 minutes = ■ hours

20. 2 years = ■ months

21. 2 years = ■ days

22. OPEN ENDED Write a real-world problem in which you use *month*, *year*, *decade*, or *century* to show elapsed time.

23. FIND THE ERROR Nate is finding how many weeks are in 3 years. Find and correct his mistake.

There are 36 weeks in three years.

24. **WRITE MATH** Explain how you know that 4 weeks and 3 days is the same as 31 days.

Test Practice

25. Natasha was supposed to be home at 3:30. How late is she?

(Lessons 3A and 3C)

A. 13 minutes

B. 17 minutes

C. 47 minutes

D. 1 hour and 13 minutes

26. Tanya bought four items on sale. She spent $90 and saved $30. The table below shows the original and sale prices of each item. Of the four items she bought, how many were jeans? (Lesson 3B)

Item	Original	Sale
T-shirt	$20	$10
Jeans	$40	$35
Mirror	$15	$13
Blanket	$25	$10

F. 1   **G.** 2   **H.** 3   **J.** 4

27. Meg's cat, Pepper, was 6 weeks old when Meg got him. Now Pepper is 2 months old. How many weeks old is Meg's cat?

(Lesson 3C)

A. 8 weeks   **C.** 10 weeks

B. 9 weeks   **D.** 12 weeks

28. The label that showed the mass of a small package of pretzels was partly covered. All Michaela could read was 450. What unit of measure was used to determine the mass of the package? (Lesson 2B)

F. liter   **H.** gram

G. centimeter **J.** kilogram

Main Idea
I will use a Fahrenheit and Celsius thermometer to measure temperature.

 Vocabulary
temperature
degrees
Fahrenheit (°F)
Celsius (°C)

Get ConnectED

 **3.13** The student will read temperature to the nearest degree from a Celsius thermometer and a Fahrenheit thermometer. Real thermometers and physical models of thermometers will be used.

Fahrenheit and Celsius

A thermometer is an instrument that measures **temperature**, which tells how hot or cold something is. The customary unit of measure for temperature is **degrees Fahrenheit (°F)**.

REAL-WORLD EXAMPLE Measure Temperature

① **MEASUREMENT** On a July day in Virginia, Mike checks the temperature outside. Write the temperature shown in degrees Fahrenheit (°F).

Think of the numbers and tick marks as a vertical number line. On this thermometer each tick mark stands for one degree. Find the number closest to the top of the red line.

The number at the top of the red line is 90.

°Fahrenheit
120°
110°
100°
90°
80°
70°
60°

So, the temperature is 90°F.

Temperature can also be measured on the metric scale in **degrees Celsius (°C)**.

REAL-WORLD EXAMPLE Read a Thermometer

② **SCIENCE** Ashton's class is finding the temperature of a liquid being used in an experiment in degrees Celsius (°C) and degrees Fahrenheit (°F).

Find the numbers just below the top of the red line. Count up by ones to the top of the red line.

Celsius → °C   °F ← Fahrenheit

100°   220°
210°
200°
90°   190°
82°C   180°   180°F
80°   170°
70°   160°
150°
60°   140°

So, the temperature is about 82°C, or 180°F.

Write each temperature in degrees Fahrenheit (°F). See Example 1

1.

2.

3.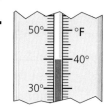

Write each temperature in degrees Fahrenheit (°F) and degrees Celsius (°C). See Example 2

4.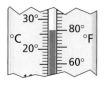

5.

6.

7. Drew's thermometer shows 25°C. Using the thermometer in Exercise 4, what is that temperature in °F?

8.  **TALK MATH** Comfortable room temperature is 72°F. What is comfortable room temperature on a Celsius scale? Explain.

Practice and Problem Solving

EXTRA PRACTICE
Begins on page EP2.

Write each temperature in degrees Fahrenheit (°F). See Example 1

9.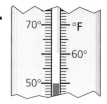

10.

11.

Write the temperature in degrees Fahrenheit (°F) and degrees Celsius (°C). See Examples 1 and 2

12.

13.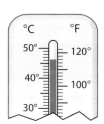

14.

H.O.T. Problems

15. OPEN ENDED Describe a real world situation where you see a thermometer being used.

16. **WRITE MATH** Write a problem that compares temperatures in °F and °C.

To assess mastery of SOL 3.13, see your Virginia Assessment Book.

FOLDABLES
Study Organizer

Be sure the following Key Concepts are noted in your Foldable.

Key Concepts

- Some customary units of **capacity** are

Units of Capacity	(Lesson 1)
1 pint = 2 cups	
1 quart = 2 pints	
1 gallon = 4 quarts	

- Some metric units of capacity are

Metric Units of Capacity	(Lesson 1)
1 liter = 1,000 milliliters	

- Some customary units of **weight** are

Units of Weight	(Lesson 2)
1 pound = 16 ounces	

- Some metric units of **mass** are

Metric Units of Mass	(Lesson 2)
1 kilogram = 1,000 grams	

- Temperature is measured in degrees Fahrenheit (°F) or degrees Celsius (°C). (Lesson 3)

Key Vocabulary

capacity

elapsed time

liter

mass

ounce

pound

weight

Vocabulary Check

Choose the vocabulary word that completes each sentence.

1. ___?___ is a customary unit of weight.

2. The amount of time that passes from the start of an activity to the end of the activity is ___?___.

3. 1 ___?___ is the same as 1,000 milliliters.

4. Ounces and pounds measure ___?___, and grams and kilograms measure ___?___.

5. Sixteen ounces equals 1 ___?___.

6. The most appropriate metric unit to measure the ___?___ of a fish tank is liter.

Multi-Part Lesson Review

Lesson 1 **Measure Capacity**

Customary and Metric Units of Capacity (Lessons 1B and 1D)

Choose the better estimate.

7.

1 c or 1 qt

8.

2 qt or 2 pt

Choose the most appropriate unit, *milliliter* or *liter*.

9. bottle of bubbles

10. cooler

EXAMPLE 1

Choose the better estimate for the capacity of a glass of juice, 1 cup or 1 gallon.

Think of a cup of yogurt and a gallon of milk.

It makes sense that a glass of juice is about 1 cup, not 1 gallon.

EXAMPLE 2

Choose the most appropriate unit to measure the capacity of a paper cup, *milliliter* or *liter*.

A paper cup holds a small amount of liquid. A liter is too large. So, use a milliliter to measure a paper cup's capacity.

Problem-Solving Strategy: Guess, Check, and Revise (Lesson 1C)

Solve. Use the *guess, check, and revise* strategy.

11. Hector picked 40 raspberries for his friends. He gave 8 of his friends the same number of raspberries. How many raspberries did each friend receive?

12. Andrew has a combination of 8 coins–quarters, dimes, and nickels–that add up to a value of 95¢. How many of each coin does he have?

EXAMPLE 3

The value of an even number is more than 10 and less than 20. The sum of its digits is 5. What is the number?

Guess numbers between 10 and 20.

Guess		Check	
Number	Even?	Sum	Correct?
11	no	2	No
16	yes	7	No
14	yes	5	Yes

So, the number is 14.

Lesson 2 **Measure Weight and Mass**

Customary Units of Weight (Lesson 2A)

Choose the most appropriate unit to measure the weight of each object. Write *ounce* or *pound*.

13.

14.

Choose the better estimate.

15. polar bear
900 oz or
900 lb

16. empty milk jug
4 oz or 4 lb

EXAMPLE 4

Choose the better estimate for the weight of a shoe, 5 ounces or 5 pounds.

Think of an ounce and a pound.

about an ounce   about a pound

It would make sense that a shoe weighs about 5 ounces.

Metric Units of Mass (Lesson 2B)

Choose the most appropriate unit to measure each mass. Write *gram* or *kilogram*.

17. bulldozer   **18.** person

19. large dog   **20.** greeting card

Choose the better estimate.

21.

8 kg or 800 kg

EXAMPLE 5

Lakita's dad put some strawberries in a bag for a snack. Choose the unit you would use to measure their mass.

You need to determine whether to use *grams* or *kilograms*.

Strawberries are small, so it would not make sense to measure their mass with kilograms.

So, use grams to measure their mass.

Time to the Minute (Lessson 3A)

Write the time shown on each clock.

22.

23.

24. The minute hand is pointing to the number 9. How many minutes is it past the hour?

EXAMPLE 6

Devin is learning to tell time.

Find the hour.

The hand is past 6.
So, the hour is 6.

Count the minutes.

Start at 12. Count by fives. Count on the single minutes. The time is 6:23.

Problem-Solving Investigation: Choose a Strategy (Lesson 3B)

25. The hour hand is between the four and five. The minute hand is on the nine. What time is it?

26. Chia starts school at 8:30. It takes her 30 minutes to get dressed and 15 minutes to eat. Her walk to school is 5 minutes long. What is the latest time she can get up and still be to school on time?

EXAMPLE 7

Every 10 seconds William can do 8 jumping jacks. How many jumping jacks can he do in 1 minute?

Draw a picture.
So, he can do
48 jumping jacks
in one minute.

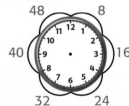

Elapsed Time (Lesson 3C)

Find each elapsed time.

27. Start Time   End Time

28. Pedro's 9th birthday is in 3 weeks and 4 days. Today is May 10. In what month is Pedro's birthday? Explain.

EXAMPLE 8

What time will it be in 3 hours and 45 minutes?

12:15   1:15   2:15   3:15   4:00

+ 1 hour + 1 hour + 1 hour + 45 minutes

So, it will be 4:00.

Calendars and Time Lines (Lesson 3D)

Use the calendar to solve.

FEBRUARY						
S	**M**	**T**	**W**	**T**	**F**	**S**
					1	2
3	4	5	6	7	8	9
10	11	12	13	14	15	16
17	18	19	20	21	22	23
24	25	26	27	28		

29. Micah has play practice every other Friday. If play practice starts on February 1, how many play practices will he have in February?

30. Lyn's aunt arrives for a visit on February 4 and leaves on February 18. How long is her visit?

Convert each unit of time.

31. 2 decades = ■ years

32. ■ centuries = 500 years

EXAMPLE 9

Use the time line to solve.

During which month did Milton receive the Spelling Bee Award?

Milton received the Spelling Bee Award in December.

Fahrenheit and Celsius (Lesson 3E)

Write each temperature in degrees Fahrenheit (°F) and degrees Celsius (°C).

33.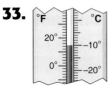

34.

35.

36.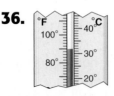

EXAMPLE 10

The thermometer shows the outside temperature. What is the temperature in degrees Fahrenheit (°F) and degrees Celsius (°C)?

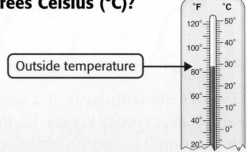

It is 85°F, about 29°C, outside.

Practice Chapter Test

Tell whether each statement is *true* or *false*.

1. Capacity can be measured in inches.

2. There are 365 days in one year.

3. Temperature can be measured in °F or °C.

Choose the most appropriate unit to measure each capacity. Write *cup*, *pint*, *quart*, or *gallon*.

4.

5.

6. It is Dillon's job at school to record the morning temperature in both degrees Fahrenheit (°F) and degrees Celsius (°C). What temperature should Dillon record?

A. 33°C; about 92°F

B. 17°C; about 62°F

C. 18°C; about 64°F

D. 5°C; about 42°F

Choose the most appropriate unit to measure each capacity. Write *milliliter* or *liter*.

7. trash can

8. juice glass

Choose the better estimate.

9.

9 g or 9 kg

10.

32 oz or 32 pounds

11. **MULTIPLE CHOICE** Art class began at 11:45. It ended 45 minutes later. What time did art class end?

F. 11:30   **H.** 1:15

G. 12:30   **J.** 1:45

Choose the most appropriate unit to measure each weight. Write *ounce* or *pound*.

12.

13.

Solve.

14. Kim ordered 3 gallons of punch for the party. Should each person get a cup that holds 8 ounces or 8 quarts?

15. Nolan is 22 years old. Braden is 24 years old. Have they been alive for the same number of decades? Explain.

16. **WRITE MATH** How would you explain elapsed time to someone?

The hockey team practice started at 6:30 A.M. and ended at 8:00 A.M.

TEST-TAKING TIP

Check your answer for reasonableness. Ask yourself if your answer choice makes sense with the question.

What was the total amount of time that hockey practice lasted?

A. 1 hour   **C.** 2 hours

B. 1 hour 30 minutes **D.** 2 hours 30 minutes

Read the Question

You need to find how long practice lasted.

Solve the Question

6:30 A.M. to 7:30 A.M. is 1 hour.

7:30 A.M. to 8:00 A.M. is 30 minutes.

So, hockey practice lasted 1 hour 30 minutes. The answer is B.

Read each question. Then fill in the correct answer on the answer sheet provided by your teacher or on a separate sheet of paper.

1. Lina baby-sat for 8 hours each week for 5 weeks. How many hours did she baby-sit in all?

   A. 13 hours   **C.** 32 hours

   B. 20 hours   **D.** 40 hours

2. Which is the most appropriate unit to measure the distance a ball was thrown?

   F. millimeter   **H.** yard

   G. inch   **J.** mile

3. The clocks show the times at which Morena began and finished soccer practice. How long did soccer practice last?

Began

Finished

A. 1 hour

C. 2 hours

B. $1\frac{1}{2}$ hours

D. $2\frac{1}{2}$ hours

4. Which is the most appropriate unit of measurement to use to find the capacity of a bathtub?

F. milliliter

H. cup

G. gallon

J. yard

5. Daily practice for the school play is 90 minutes long. The clock below shows the time practice ends.

What time does play practice begin?

A. 6:30

C. 3:30

B. 5:30

D. 2:30

6. Which is most likely to be the mass of a bicycle?

F. 15 centimeters

G. 15 grams

H. 15 liters

J. 15 kilograms

7. New Year's Day is January 1st. Jonathon's birthday is 3 weeks and 3 days after New Year's Day.

JANUARY						
S	M	T	W	T	F	S
			①	2	3	4
5	6	7	8	9	10	11
12	13	14	15	16	17	18
19	20	21	22	23	24	25
26	27	28	29	30	31	

What is the date of Jonathon's birthday?

A. January 4

C. January 25

B. January 22

D. January 29

8. Which is most likely to be the capacity of a cocoa mug?

F. 10 milliliters

H. 2 liters

G. 100 milliliters

J. 5 liters

NEED EXTRA HELP?								
If You Missed Question . . .	1	2	3	4	5	6	7	8
Go to Chapter-Lesson . . .	12-3B	11-1C	12-3C	12-1B	12-3C	12-2B	12-3D	12-1D
For help with . . .	SOL 3.12	SOL 3.9a	SOL 3.11b	SOL 3.9b	SOL 3.11b	SOL 3.9c	SOL 3.12	SOL 3.9b

CHAPTER 13

Multiply by a One-Digit Number

connectED.mcgraw-hill.com

 Investigate

 Animations

 Vocabulary

 Math Songs

 Multilingual eGlossary

 Learn

 Personal Tutor

 Virtual Manipulatives

 Audio

 Foldables

 Practice

 Self-Check Practice

 eGames

Worksheets

Assessment

The ☆BIG Idea

How can I use models and the standard algorithm to multiply whole numbers?

 FOLDABLES Study Organizer

Make this Foldable to organize information about multiplying by a one-digit number. Begin with one sheet of 11" × 17" paper.

Multiply by One-Digit Numbers — Multiply Two-Digit Numbers — Multiply Greater Numbers

Review Vocabulary

estimate estimacion a number close to an exact value, which indicates *about* how much

3 × 22 is about 3 × 20 or 60.

Key Vocabulary

English	Español
multiples	multiplo
partial product	productos parciales

618

You have two options for checking Prerequisite Skills for this chapter.

Text Option Take the Quick Check below.

QUICK Check

Write a multiplication sentence for each array.

1. ★ ★ ★ ★
   ★ ★ ★ ★
   ★ ★ ★ ★

2. ♥ ♥ ♥
   ♥ ♥ ♥
   ♥ ♥ ♥
   ♥ ♥ ♥

3.

Multiply.

4. $\begin{array}{r} 4 \\ \times\ 7 \\ \hline \end{array}$

5. $\begin{array}{r} 5 \\ \times\ 6 \\ \hline \end{array}$

6. $\begin{array}{r} 9 \\ \times\ 2 \\ \hline \end{array}$

7. 5×5

8. 9×1

9. 10×8

10. Two space shuttles are docked at the space station. Each shuttle has 8 astronauts. How many astronauts are there altogether?

11. For every pound of play clay Reynaldo makes, he needs 6 cups of flour. How many cups of flour does he need to make 6 pounds of play clay?

Estimate. Round to the indicated place value.

12. $422 + 39$; tens

13. $409 - 259$; hundreds

14. $86 - 56$; tens

15. $372 + 349$; hundreds

 Online Option Take the Online Readiness Quiz.

Main Idea
I will multiply multiples of 10, 100, and 1,000.

 **Vocabulary**
multiples

 Get ConnectED

 **3.5** The student will recall multiplication facts through the twelves table, and the corresponding division facts. **3.6** The student will represent multiplication and division, using area, set, and number line models, and create and solve problems that involve multiplication of two whole numbers, one factor 99 or less and the second factor 5 or less.

Multiples of 10, 100, and 1,000

You can use basic facts and patterns of zeros to help you multiply a number mentally by 10, 100, and 1,000.

Key Concept Multiples of 10, 100, and 1,000	
Multiplication Sentence	**Model and Words**
$3 \times 1 = 3$	3 ones
$3 \times 10 = 30$	3 tens
$3 \times 100 = 300$	3 hundreds
$3 \times 1,000 = 3,000$	3 thousands

 **EXAMPLE** Use Facts and Patterns

1 **Find 7 × 100.**

Use basic facts and patterns of zeros.

$7 \times 1 = 7$	7×1 one = 7 ones
$7 \times 10 = 70$	7×1 ten = 7 tens
$7 \times 100 = 700$	7×1 hundred = 7 hundreds

You can also multiply a number mentally by multiples of 10, 100, and 1,000. A **multiple** is the product of a given number and any other whole number.

2**0** is a multiple of 1**0**.
2**00** is a multiple of 1**00**.
2,**000** is a multiple of 1,**000**.

 REAL-WORLD EXAMPLE   Use Facts and Patterns

2 **CRAFT** Bags of 3,000 craft beads are on sale. Ellie bought 5 bags. How many beads did Ellie buy?

You need to find 5 × 3,000.

5 × 3 = 15	5 × 3 ones = 15 ones
5 × 3**0** = 15**0**	5 × 3 tens = 15 tens
5 × 3**00** = 1,5**00**	5 × 3 hundreds = 15 hundreds
5 × 3,**000** = 15,**000**	5 × 3 thousands = 15 thousands

So, 5 × 3,000 = 15,000. Ellie bought 15,000 beads.

Check for Reasonableness

Use repeated addition to prove your answer is reasonable.

3,000 + 3,000 + 3,000 + 3,000 + 3,000 = 15,000 ✔

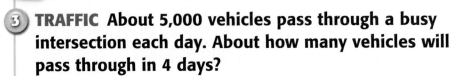 **REAL-WORLD EXAMPLE**   Use Facts and Patterns

3 **TRAFFIC** About 5,000 vehicles pass through a busy intersection each day. About how many vehicles will pass through in 4 days?

You need to find 4 × 5,000.

4 × 5 = 20
4 × 5**0** = 20**0**
4 × 5**00** = 2,0**00**
4 × 5,**000** = 20,**000**

THINK Sometimes the basic fact has a zero. Keep that zero, then add the others.

So, 4 × 5,000 = 20,000. About 20,000 vehicles will pass through in 4 days.

Check for Reasonableness

Use repeated addition to prove your answer is reasonable.

5,000 + 5,000 + 5,000 + 5,000 = 20,000 ✔

Multiply. Use basic facts and patterns. See Examples 1–3

1. $3 \times 1 = $ ■
$3 \times 10 = $ ■
$3 \times 100 = $ ■
$3 \times 1,000 = $ ■

2. $7 \times 4 = $ ■
$7 \times 40 = $ ■
$7 \times 400 = $ ■
$7 \times 4,000 = $ ■

3. $5 \times 6 = $ ■
$5 \times 60 = $ ■
$5 \times 600 = $ ■
$5 \times 6,000 = $ ■

4. 4×90

5. $4 \times 4,000$

6. 500×8

7. Hunter's Pizza Shop sold 3,000 pizzas each month for 6 months. Find the total number of pizzas sold for the 6 months.

8. TALK MATH Explain the pattern of zeros that you see when you multiply by 10, 100, or 1,000.

Practice and Problem Solving

EXTRA PRACTICE
Begins on page EP2.

Multiply. Use basic facts and patterns. See Examples 1–3

9. $2 \times 1 = $ ■
$2 \times 10 = $ ■
$2 \times 100 = $ ■
$2 \times 1,000 = $ ■

10. $6 \times 4 = $ ■
$6 \times 40 = $ ■
$6 \times 400 = $ ■
$6 \times 4,000 = $ ■

11. $7 \times 8 = $ ■
$7 \times 80 = $ ■
$7 \times 800 = $ ■
$7 \times 8,000 = $ ■

12. 5×50

13. 30×8

14. 4×30

15. 900×7

16. 600×9

17. 60×8

18. Demont's card album has 20 pages, and 6 trading cards are on each page. How many cards are there in all?

19. There are 100 houses. Each house has 10 windows. How many windows are there in all?

20. Cristina sold 200 trays of flowers each day for 9 days. Each tray holds 4 flowers. How many flowers did she sell?

21. Carlita has 3 boxes of teddy bears. Each box holds 20 bears. She sells each bear for $4. How much money did she earn?

H.O.T. Problems

22. OPEN ENDED Write a multiplication sentence that uses a multiple of 10 and has a product of 24,000.

23. WRITE MATH Write a real-world problem that involves multiplying by a multiple of 10.

Main Idea

I will estimate products and describe the reasonableness of the estimates.

 Get Connect**ED**

3.1 The student will
b) round whole numbers, 9,999 or less, to the nearest ten, hundred, and thousand.
3.6 The student will represent multiplication and division, using area, set, and number line models, and create and solve problems that involve multiplication of two whole numbers, one factor 99 or less and the second factor 5 or less.

Estimate Products

When you do not need an exact answer, you can estimate. One way to estimate is to round.

🏃 ✎ **REAL-WORLD EXAMPLE**   Estimate by Rounding

1 **SCHOOL Each of the 26 schools in Fair City sends 6 of their best spellers to the city spelling bee. About how many students go to the spelling bee?**

Estimate 6 × 26 by rounding to the nearest ten.

Step 1 Round the factor that is greater than 10 to the nearest ten.

6 × 26

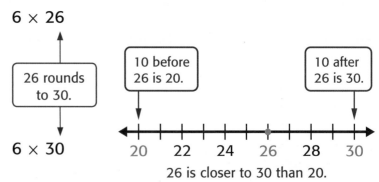

| 26 rounds to 30. | 10 before 26 is 20. | 10 after 26 is 30. |

6 × 30   20 22 24 26 28 30

26 is closer to 30 than 20.

Step 2 Multiply mentally.

6 × 30 = 180

So, about 180 students go to the spelling bee.

Remember

Round the factor that is greater than 10.

2 **PLAYS** There are 140 students. Each student can invite 3 people to a play. About how many people can be invited?

Estimate 3 × 140 by rounding to the nearest hundred.

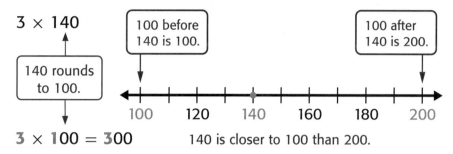

3 × 140

140 rounds to 100.

100 before 140 is 100.

100 after 140 is 200.

3 × 100 = 300   140 is closer to 100 than 200.

So, about 300 people can be invited to the play.

REAL-WORLD EXAMPLE   **Check for Reasonableness**

3 **SCHOOL BUS** A school bus holds about 52 students. Will 4 buses be enough to transport 175 students?

Estimate 4 × 52. Then compare to 175.

4 × 52   Round 52 to 50.

4 × 50 = 200   Multiply mentally.

The buses can hold about 200 students. 200 > 175 ✓ So, 4 buses will be enough to transport 175 students.

✓ CHECK What You Know

Estimate. Round to the nearest ten. See Example 1

1. 47
  × 4

2. 51
  × 8

3. 58
  × 2

Estimate. Round to the nearest hundred. See Example 2

4. 315 × 3

5. 189 × 5

6. 150 × 6

7. Measurement Jan estimated she spends about 5 hours each week in math class. Is her estimate reasonable if each math class is 55 minutes long? See Example 3

8. **TALK MATH** Is estimating 878 × 9 to the nearest hundred greater than the actual product? Explain.

Estimate. Round to the nearest ten. See Example 1

9.   27
       × 4

10.   17
        × 6

11.   36
        × 3

12. 28 × 8

13. 32 × 5

14. 43 × 4

Estimate. Round to the nearest hundred. See Example 2

15. 180
       × 9

16. 197
       × 6

17. 306
       × 3

18. 271 × 4

19. 290 × 7

20. 114 × 8

21. Hiking burns about 288 Calories each hour. About how many Calories can be burned if someone hikes 3 hours?

22. A restaurant keeps track of the paper goods it uses for one day, as shown below. Is it reasonable to estimate 2,500 napkins, cups, and bags are used in one week? Explain. See Example 3

23. Corrine uses 27 sheets of paper for a book she makes. About how many sheets would she need if she makes 8 books?

24. Measurement Hernando studies about 3 hours each day. Is it reasonable to estimate that is equal to about 100 hours in 4 weeks? Explain. See Example 3

Daily Paper Use

bags 532

hamburger wrappers 875

cups 1,091

napkins 913

Data File

Mrs. Shelby's Nature Club is visiting an apple orchard in the Blue Ridge Mountains of Virginia.

25. About how many third graders are going on the field trip? Round to the nearest hundred.

26. Is it reasonable to estimate that 3 times more fourth graders than second graders are going on the trip? Explain.

Apple Orchard Field Trip Attendance	
Grade	**Number**
Second	47
Third	189
Fourth	150

27. FIND THE ERROR Luke is estimating 458 × 4.
Find and correct his mistake.

> **Here is how I estimated:**
> 458 × 4
> ↓   ↓
> 400 × 4 = 1,600

28. 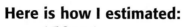 **WRITE MATH** Explain how you would estimate 77 × 6.

 **Test Practice**

29. Kome made a large mat out
of carpet squares by putting
the squares in 3 equal rows of
21 squares each. About how many
squares did Kome use?

(Lessons 1A and 1B)

A. 40   **C.** 65

B. 60   **D.** 80

30. Which product woud be a
reasonable estimate for this
number sentence? (Lesson 1B)

82 × 9 = ▦

F. 70

G. 700

H. 720

J. 810

Spiral Review

Multiply. Use basic facts and patterns. (Lesson 1A)

31. 2 × 80   **32.** 400 × 3   **33.** 600 × 7

34. It takes Conner's computer one minute to download 1 song.
How many seconds does it take his computer to download
3 songs?

35. Angelina collects stickers. She can fit 300 stickers in
one sticker book. Write a number sentence that
could be used to find the total number of stickers
in 4 books.

STAMP COLLECTING

The U.S. government began issuing stamps in 1847. People began saving and collecting them. During the Civil War, unused Union stamps were actually used as money. At first, small engraving and printing companies produced stamps for the government. Many of the same images—American leaders and symbols—appeared on stamps.

In 1924, a new era of stamp making began in response to collectors' great interest in stamps. Stamp makers began producing colorful, exotic stamps with a wide variety of subjects and many different colors of ink. Today, you can see everything from comic-book characters to your favorite musicians on stamps.

Real-World Math

Use the stamps on the next page to solve each problem.

1 What was the original cost of three Elvis stamps rounded to the nearest ten?

2 What is the greatest number of 24¢ stamps that could have been bought for less than $1?

3 Find the cost of ten 6¢ stamps.

4 Estimate the cost of two Elvis stamps and three Man on the Moon stamps.

5 If 78 stamp collectors each have one of each of the five stamps, about how many stamps are there altogether?

6 What combination of stamps would be needed for 44¢ postage?

7 Suppose the Man on the Moon stamp was issued in sheets of 10 stamps. What would have been the value of one sheet of Man on the Moon stamps?

Did You Know?

The most valuable U.S. stamp was sold for about $930,000.

Problem-Solving Strategy: Use Logical Reasoning

Main Idea I will solve a problem by using logical reasoning.

Three friends all have on different shirts. Hallie's shirt is white. Jimar's shirt is not green. Marisol's shirt is not red. What is the color of each of their shirts?

Understand **What facts do you know?**

- Hallie is wearing a white shirt.
- Jimar's shirt is not green.
- Marisol's shirt is not red.

What do you need to find?

- The color of each person's shirt.

Plan Make a table to show what you know. Then use logical reasoning to find the color of each person's shirt.

Solve Hallie is wearing white. So, write *yes* by her name under *white.* Place an X in all the rest of the *white* column and the other colors for Hallie.

	White	Red	Green
Hallie	yes	X	X
Marisol	X	X	yes
Jimar	X	yes	X

Marisol's shirt is not red and cannot be white, so it is green. The color that is left is red. Jimar's shirt must be red.

So, Hallie is wearing white, Marisol is wearing green, and Jimar is wearing red.

Check The answer makes sense for the facts given. So, the answer is correct. ✓

3.6 The student will represent multiplication and division, using area, set, and number line models, and create and solve problems that involve multiplication of two whole numbers, one factor 99 or less and the second factor 5 or less.

Refer to the problem on the previous page.

1. Explain how making a table helped in solving the problem.

2. What does it mean to use logical reasoning?

3. If the colors of shirts changed, how would the problem be different? How would it be the same?

4. How would the results be different if Marisol's shirt was not green?

PRACTICE

EXTRA PRACTICE
Begins on page EP2.

Solve. Use logical reasoning.

5. Marilee places her math book next to her reading book and language book. Her language book is next to her science book, which is next to her history book. What is a possible order?

6. Emerson, Thi, Joyce, and Lawanda each have one of four different pets. Emerson has a cat. Thi does not have a dog or a fish. Joyce does not have a bird or a fish. What pet does each person have?

7. Paulita, Shaheed, and Drake each play one of three different sports. According to the information in the table, what sport does each student play?

Sports Students Play	
Student	**Sport**
Paulita	soccer
Drake	not basketball
Shaheed	not soccer or football

8. Larrisa, Jo, and Callie went to lunch. They each ordered something different. Larrisa does not like hamburgers. Jo and Callie do not like salad. Who ordered the salad?

> **LUNCH MENU**
> * SALAD
> * FRUIT PLATE
> * HAMBURGER

9. Three friends want to buy the game shown below. Dexter has 5 quarters and 6 dimes. Belle has 6 quarters and 8 dimes. Emmett has 5 coins. If they will receive 10 cents in change, what coins does Emmett have?

10. WRITE MATH Write two sentences describing how you would use logical reasoning to help solve a real-world situation.

Main Idea

I will multiply two-digit numbers by a one-digit number with no regrouping.

 Get Connect ED

3.5 The student will recall multiplication facts through the twelves table, and the corresponding division facts. **3.6** The student will represent multiplication and division, using area, set, and number line models, and create and solve problems that involve multiplication of two whole numbers, one factor 99 or less and the second factor 5 or less.

Multiply by a One-Digit Number

You can use what you know about multiplying lesser numbers to find products of facts such as 3×13.

REAL-WORLD EXAMPLE   **Use Partial Products**

1 **MARBLES** Finn and his two brothers each have 13 marbles. How many marbles do they have altogether?

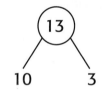

The array shows 3×13. Break the grid into tens and ones.

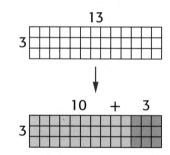

The part shaded orange shows 3×10.
The part shaded blue shows 3×3.

First, find the product of each part, or the partial products. Then add the partial products.

Step 1

$3 \times 10 = 30$

$3 \times 3 = 9$

$3 \times 13 = 39$

Step 2

$30 + 9 = 39$

So, Finn and his brothers have 39 marbles altogether.

You can also multiply by a one-digit number without models.

Remember

You can also use base-ten blocks and area models to help you multiply by one-digit numbers.

REAL-WORLD EXAMPLE   Use Paper and Pencil

2 PATTERNS Reese used 4 shapes to create a pattern around the border of a picture she drew. She repeated the pattern 22 times. What is the total number of shapes in Reese's border? Find 4 × 22.

Step 1   Multiply ones.

$$\begin{array}{r} 22 \\ \times\ 4 \\ \hline 8 \end{array}$$ ← 4×2 ones = 8 ones

Step 2   Multiply tens.

$$\begin{array}{r} 22 \\ \times\ 4 \\ \hline 88 \end{array}$$ ← 4×2 tens = 8 tens

Check The area model shows that 4 × 22 = 88. ✔

	20	+	2
4	4 × 20 = 80		4 × 2 = 8

$$\begin{array}{r} 22 \\ \times\ 4 \\ \hline 8 \\ +80 \\ \hline 88 \end{array}$$

$4 \times 2 = 8$
$4 \times 20 = 80$

✓ CHECK What You Know

Multiply. Use estimation to check. See Examples 1 and 2

1. $\begin{array}{r} 12 \\ \times\ 4 \\ \hline \end{array}$

2. $\begin{array}{r} 41 \\ \times\ 2 \\ \hline \end{array}$

3. $\begin{array}{r} 32 \\ \times\ 3 \\ \hline \end{array}$

4. 3 × 22

5. 3 × 21

6. 5 × 11

7. A classroom has 23 desks. Each desk has 3 books on it. How many books are on the desks altogether?

8. 🗨 **TALK MATH** Explain how area models help you multiply.

Practice and Problem Solving

EXTRA PRACTICE
Begins on page EP2.

Multiply. Use estimation to check. See Examples 1 and 2

9. 21
   × 4

10. 32
   × 2

11. 44
   × 2

12. 31
   × 2

13. 21
   × 2

14. 20
   × 3

15. 43
   × 2

16. 33
   × 3

17. 2×23

18. 2×33

19. 2×22

20. 2×14

21. There are 21 bags of bagels, with 4 bagels in each. If the third graders ate all but 9 bagels, how many did they eat?

22. Measurement Miranda cut 4 pieces of yarn that measured 9 inches each. How many feet of yarn did she use?

REAL-WORLD PROBLEM SOLVING

School The table shows the number of classes and students in grades 3, 4, and 5.

23. Write a number sentence for the total number of students in the fourth grade.

24. How many more students are in grade 4 than grade 3?

25. Write a number sentence that compares the total number of students in the 3rd grade and 5th grade. Use < or >.

26. What is the total number of students in grades three, four, and five?

Fair Street School
Student Count

Grade	Number of Classes	Students per Class
3	3	23
4	4	22
5	2	31

H.O.T. Problems

27. OPEN ENDED Explain the strategy you would use to find 82×4. Why do you prefer this strategy?

28. WRITE MATH Is the product of 3 and 32 the same as the product of 32 and 3? Explain your reasoning.

Mid-Chapter Check

Multiply. Use basic facts and patterns.

(Lesson 1A)

1. $4 \times 6 = \blacksquare$
$4 \times 60 = \blacksquare$
$4 \times 600 = \blacksquare$
$4 \times 6{,}000 = \blacksquare$

2. $8 \times 4 = \blacksquare$
$8 \times 40 = \blacksquare$
$8 \times 400 = \blacksquare$
$8 \times 4{,}000 = \blacksquare$

Multiply. Use mental math. (Lesson 1A)

3. 2×60

4. $3 \times 3{,}000$

5. $6 \times 8{,}000$

6. $4 \times 5{,}000$

7. MULTIPLE CHOICE The calendar shows how often Mr. Henry plans to teach math each week. About how many math lessons does he plan to teach in 22 weeks? (Lesson 1B)

Monday	Tuesday	Wednesday	Thursday	Friday
MATH		MATH		MATH

A. 40

C. 70

B. 60

D. 80

Solve. Use logical reasoning. (Lesson 2A)

8. Marco, Alfred, and Lee each like a different type of book—mystery, science fiction, or sports stories. What type of book does each boy like?

Favorite Types of Books	
Student	**Type of Book**
Marco	science fiction
Alfred	not science fiction or sports
Lee	not mysteries

Estimate. Round to the nearest ten.

(Lesson 1B)

9. $\begin{array}{r} 78 \\ \times\ 8 \\ \hline \end{array}$

10. $\begin{array}{r} 23 \\ \times\ 2 \\ \hline \end{array}$

Estimate. Round to the nearest hundred. (Lesson 1B)

11. $\begin{array}{r} 173 \\ \times\ 5 \\ \hline \end{array}$

12. $\begin{array}{r} 168 \\ \times\ 6 \\ \hline \end{array}$

13. MULTIPLE CHOICE A third grade class has 178 students. Each student needs 4 folders. About how many folders do the third graders need? (Lesson 1B)

F. 200

H. 600

G. 400

J. 800

Multiply. Use estimation to check.

(Lesson 2B)

14. $\begin{array}{r} 22 \\ \times\ 3 \\ \hline \end{array}$

15. $\begin{array}{r} 32 \\ \times\ 2 \\ \hline \end{array}$

16. Kisho made a quilt out of squares by putting the squares in 6 equal rows of 11 squares each. How many squares did Kisho use? (Lesson 2B)

17. **WRITE MATH** Explain the steps in estimating the product of 88×3 by rounding to the nearest ten. (Lesson 1B)

Explore **Multiply with Regrouping**

Main Idea

I will use models to explore multiplication with regrouping.

Materials

base-ten blocks

Get Connect ED

3.5 The student will recall multiplication facts through the twelves table, and the corresponding division facts. **3.6** The student will represent multiplication and division, using area, set, and number line models, and create and solve problems that involve multiplication of two whole numbers, one factor 99 or less and the second factor 5 or less.

Sometimes you need to regroup when adding. You might also need to regroup when multiplying.

ACTIVITY

Find 2 × 16.

Step 1 **Model 2 × 16**

Model 2 groups of 16.
Use 1 ten and
6 ones in each group.

2 groups of 16

Step 2 **Combine the Models**   2 groups of 10   2 group of 6

Combine the ones.
Combine the tens.

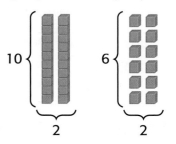

10   6

2   2

Step 3 **Regroup**

Regroup 12 ones as
1 ten and 2 ones.

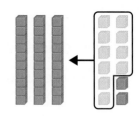

12 ones = 1 ten, 2 ones

Step 4 **Add the Partial Products**

3 tens = 30
2 ones = 2
30 + 2 = 32

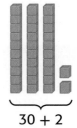

30 + 2

So, 2 × 16 = 32.

Think About It

1. How did you model each factor?

2. Why did you regroup?

3. How did the number of tens and ones change after you regrouped?

4. Will you always have to regroup in multiplication? Explain.

5. If you have 4 groups of 16, what would be the product?

Practice and Apply It

Write a multiplication sentence for each model.

6.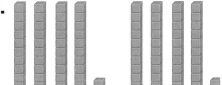

7.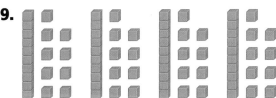

8.

9.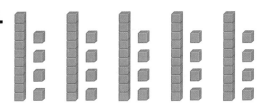

Multiply. Use base-ten models.

10. 5 × 18   **11.** 12 × 6   **12.** 4 × 24   **13.** 17 × 3

14. **WRITE MATH** Explain why knowing how to estimate is useful when multiplying greater numbers.

Main Idea

I will regroup while multiplying a two-digit number by a one-digit number.

Get ConnectED

3.5 The student will recall multiplication facts through the twelves table, and the corresponding division facts. 3.6 The student will represent multiplication and division, using area, set, and number line models, and create and solve problems that involve multiplication of two whole numbers, one factor 99 or less and the second factor 5 or less.

Multiply Two-Digit Numbers

You can connect multiplication models to paper and pencil.

REAL-WORLD EXAMPLE Use Models

① **BUILDINGS A new apartment building will have 5 floors, with 13 apartments on each floor. How many apartments will there be in the building?**

Use models to help you find the product of 5 × 13.

One Way: Base-Ten Models	**Another Way:** Paper and Pencil
Step 1 Model 5 × 13.	**Step 1** Multiply ones.
5 groups of 13	$\begin{array}{r} 1 \\ 13 \\ \times 5 \\ \hline 5 \end{array}$ 5 × 3 ones = 15 ones 15 ones = 1 ten and 5 ones
Step 2 Combine models.	**Step 2** Multiply tens.
15 ones = 1 ten, 5 ones	$\begin{array}{r} 1 \\ 13 \\ \times 5 \\ \hline 65 \end{array}$ 5 × 1 ten = 5 tens 5 tens + 1 ten = 6 tens
Step 3 Find 5 × 13.	
60 + 5 = 65	

So, the building will have 65 apartments.

2 **REPTILES** A female desert tortoise can lay as many as 8 eggs at one time. How many eggs could 12 female desert tortoises lay?

Find 8 × 12.

Estimate 8 × 12 ⟶ 8 × 10 = 80

Step 1   Multiply ones.

$$\begin{array}{r} 1 \\ 12 \\ \times\ 8 \\ \hline 6 \end{array}$$

8 × 2 ones = 16 ones = 1 ten and 6 ones

Step 2   Multiply tens.

$$\begin{array}{r} 1 \\ 12 \\ \times\ 8 \\ \hline 96 \end{array}$$

8 × 1 ten = 8 tens
8 tens + 1 ten = 9 tens

> **Remember**
> Do not multiply the regrouped tens again; add them once the tens are multiplied.

The area model shows that 8 × 12 is 96.

	10	+	2
8	8 × 10 = 80		8 × 2 = 16

$$\begin{array}{r} 12 \\ \times\ 8 \\ \hline 16 \\ +80 \\ \hline 96 \end{array}$$

16   Multiply ones.
+80   Multiply tens.
96   Add partial products.

So, 12 female tortoises could lay 96 eggs.

Check for Reasonableness

96 is close to the estimate of 80, so the answer is reasonable. ✔

✓ **CHECK What You Know**

Multiply. Use models if needed. See Examples 1 and 2

1. $\begin{array}{r} 13 \\ \times\ 4 \end{array}$

2. $\begin{array}{r} 27 \\ \times\ 3 \end{array}$

3. $\begin{array}{r} 13 \\ \times\ 8 \end{array}$

4. Measurement A construction crew finished 14 miles of highway in 1 week. At this rate, how many miles could they finish in 4 weeks?

5. **TALK MATH** What is the greatest number of ones that could be in the ones column without having to regroup? Explain.

Practice and Problem Solving

EXTRA PRACTICE
Begins on page EP2.

Multiply. Use models if needed. See Examples 1 and 2

6. 46
      × 2

7. 17
      × 4

8. 53
      × 2

9. 92
      × 3

10. 13
       × 6

11. 18
       × 9

12. 15
       × 4

13. 12
       × 5

14. 18 × 8

15. 14 × 9

16. 28 × 4

17. 31 × 8

18. Measurement A stick insect can measure 22 inches in length. How many inches long would 3 stick insects measure?

19. Measurement A gecko can grow close to 35 centimeters in length. How many centimeters would 4 geckos measure?

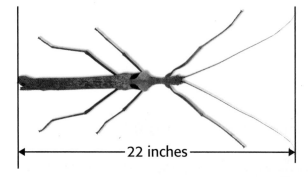

22 inches

35 centimeters

20. Eating 5 servings of grains each day is recommended. How many servings is this in a 31-day month?

21. A pizza parlor puts 65 pieces of pepperoni on each pizza. How many pieces of pepperoni are on 6 pizzas?

REAL-WORLD PROBLEM SOLVING

Airships The first airship, which was a blimp, was built more than 80 years ago. Today, television viewers get a bird's-eye view of many events from cameras in blimps.

22. Rounded to the nearest hundred, what is the blimp's fuel tank capacity?

23. At top speed, how many miles could a blimp travel in 3 hours?

24. What is the maximum height a blimp can rise if it is 5 times its average cruising height?

Blimp Facts
• A blimp cruises at 30–40 miles per hour, but its maximum speed is 65 miles per hour.
• The average cruising height of a blimp is 2,000 feet.
• The capacity of a blimp's fuel tank is 426 gallons.

25. OPEN ENDED Write a multiplication sentence whose product is less than 52.

26. NUMBER SENSE Without multiplying, how do you know that 21×3 is greater than 60?

27. WHICH ONE DOESN'T BELONG? Identify the multiplication expression that does not belong. Explain.

3×33	4×23	5×15	7×18

28. WRITE MATH Describe the steps you would take to multiply 76 and 4.

 **Test Practice**

29. Tyron's bookcase has 6 shelves. Each shelf holds 14 books. How many books does Tyron have in his bookcase? (Lesson 3B)

  A. 14   **C.** 84

  B. 64   **D.** 120

30. James made 23 paper airplanes. Lewis made twice as many. How many paper airplanes do the boys have altogether? (Leeson 2B)

  F. 23   **H.** 49

  G. 46   **J.** 69

Spiral Review

Multiply. Use estimation to check. (Lesson 2B)

31.   24
   $\times\ 2$

32.   33
   $\times\ 3$

33.   21
   $\times\ 4$

34. Lee's grandmother is making 3 baby quilts. Each quilt's squares will be sewn in an array of 8 rows, with 4 squares in each row. How many squares will she need to cut out?

35. On Thursday, 132 people visited the library. Three times as many people visited over the weekend. About how many people visited over the weekend? (Lesson 1B)

Problem-Solving Investigation

Main Idea I will choose the best strategy to solve a problem.

P.S.I. TEAM +

RYDELL: I need to fill 3 pitchers and
2 punch bowls with punch. It takes
11 cans of punch to fill one pitcher and
24 cans of punch to fill the punch bowl.

YOUR MISSION: Find how many cans of
punch are needed in all.

Understand

It takes 11 cans of punch to fill one pitcher. It takes 24 cans of punch to fill one punch bowl. Find how many cans of punch are needed in all.

Plan

Solve a simpler problem. Solve for each part of the problem, then add.

Solve

1 pitcher = 11 cans of punch
So, it takes 11 × 3, or 33, cans to fill 3 pitchers.

1 punch bowl = 24 cans
So, it takes 24 × 2, or 48, cans to fill 2 bowls.

Now find the total.

33 + 48 = 81

So, 81 cans of punch are needed in all.

Check

Use addition to check the reasonableness of the results.

bowl + bowl + pitcher + pitcher + pitcher
24 + 24 + 11 + 11 + 11 = 81

So, the answer is correct. ✓

3.6 The student will represent multiplication and division, using area, set, and number line models, and create and solve problems that involve multiplication of two whole numbers, one factor 99 or less and the second factor 5 or less.

- Solve a simpler problem.
- Make an organized list.
- Act it out.
- Use logical reasoning.

Use any strategy to solve each problem.

1. Terez and Freda collected tin cans for recycling. Terez collected 3 times as many as Freda. The total number collected by their class was 500 cans. Terez and Freda collected $\frac{1}{5}$ of that. How many cans did they each collect?

2. Measurement A log is shown. Suppose a piece that measures 11 inches is cut off. How many 5-inch pieces can be made from the part of the log that is left?

|← 46 inches →|

3. A number has two digits. The first digit is odd. The difference of the two digits is 2, and their sum is 12. What is the number?

4. Winnie lives down the street from Roger. Dakota lives next door to Roger. Regina lives between Winnie and Dakota. In what order do the friends live on the block?

5. Gloria, Roxana, and Beatriz are playing a game. Gloria has 88 points. Roxana has 26 points more than Gloria. Beatriz wins with 50 points more than Roxana. How many points does each person have?

6. Anthony and Juanna are playing a game with one 0–5 number cube and one 5–10 number cube. Each cube is rolled twice. The total of their rolls is 25. What could be the other three numbers rolled if one was a 5?

7. Logan, Rodolfo, Emanuel, and Corbin were waiting for the bus. Logan was next to Emanuel, who was not next to Corbin. Corbin was next to Rodolfo, but not next to Logan. In what order were they standing?

8. **WRITE MATH** Serena ran the distances shown. She ran 2 miles more than the total of these on Sunday. Explain how to find how many miles she ran for the four days.

Day	Distance
Monday	4 miles
Thursday	6 miles
Saturday	8 miles

Main Idea

I will regroup while multiplying three- and four-digit numbers by a one-digit number.

Multiply Greater Numbers

You have learned how to multiply two-digit numbers. Use what you know to multiply greater numbers.

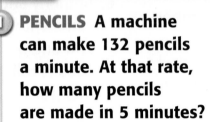 **REAL-WORLD EXAMPLE**   **Standard Algorithm**

1) **PENCILS** A machine can make 132 pencils a minute. At that rate, how many pencils are made in 5 minutes?

Find 5 × 132.   **Estimate** 5 × 132 ⟶ 5 × 100 = 500

Step 1   Multiply ones.

$$
\begin{array}{r}
\overset{1}{1}32 \\
\times\ 5 \\
\hline
0
\end{array}
$$
5 × 2 ones = 10 ones

Step 2   Multiply tens.

$$
\begin{array}{r}
\overset{1\,1}{1}32 \\
\times\ 5 \\
\hline
60
\end{array}
$$
5 × 3 tens = 15 tens
Add the regrouped amount. 15 + 1 = 16 tens

Step 3   Multiply hundreds.

$$
\begin{array}{r}
\overset{1\,1}{1}32 \\
\times\ 5 \\
\hline
660
\end{array}
$$
5 × 1 hundred = 5 hundreds
Add the regrouped amount. 5 + 1 = 6 hundreds

So, 660 pencils are made in 5 minutes.

Check for Reasonableness

Since 660 is close to the estimate of 500, the answer is reasonable. ✔

② **DUCKS** A duck eats about 1,960 grams of food in one week. How much would it eat in 4 weeks?

Find 1,960 × 4.

Step 1 Multiply ones.

$$\begin{array}{r} 1,960 \\ \times\ \ 4 \\ \hline 0 \end{array}$$ 4 × 0 one = 0 ones

Step 2 Multiply tens.

$$\begin{array}{r} {}^{2} \\ 1,960 \\ \times\ \ 4 \\ \hline 40 \end{array}$$ 4 × 6 tens = 24 tens

Step 3 Multiply hundreds.

$$\begin{array}{r} {}^{3\,2} \\ 1,960 \\ \times\ \ 4 \\ \hline 840 \end{array}$$
4 × 9 hundreds = 36 hundreds
Add the regrouped amount.
36 hundreds + 2 hundreds = 38 hundreds

Step 4 Multiply thousands.

$$\begin{array}{r} {}^{3\,2} \\ 1,960 \\ \times\ \ 4 \\ \hline 7,840 \end{array}$$
4 × 1 thousand = 4 thousands
Add the regrouped amount.
4 thousands + 3 thousands = 7 thousands

So, 1,960 × 4 = 7,840.

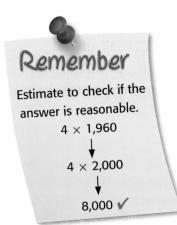

Remember

Estimate to check if the answer is reasonable.

4 × 1,960
↓
4 × 2,000
↓
8,000 ✓

✓ **CHECK What You Know**

Multiply. See Examples 1 and 2

1. $\begin{array}{r} 125 \\ \times\ 5 \\ \hline \end{array}$

2. $\begin{array}{r} 248 \\ \times\ 3 \\ \hline \end{array}$

3. $\begin{array}{r} 1,276 \\ \times\ \ \ 4 \\ \hline \end{array}$

4. $\begin{array}{r} 1,342 \\ \times\ \ \ 7 \\ \hline \end{array}$

5. If there are 365 days in one year, how many days are in 3 years?

6. ❓ **TALK MATH** How is multiplying a three-digit number with regrouping similar to multiplying a two-digit number with regrouping?

Multiply. See Examples 1 and 2

7. 518
× 2

8. 222
× 5

9. 159
× 3

10. 293
× 7

11. 1,042
× 8

12. 1,513
× 9

13. 2,278
× 3

14. 3,150
× 6

15. 170 × 4

16. 821 × 4

17. 1,122 × 9

18. 1,189 × 5

Algebra **Copy and complete each table.**

19.

Rule: Multiply by 6.	
Input	Output
112	
821	
145	

20.

Rule: Multiply by 4.	
Input	Output
38	
29	
417	

21.

Rule: Multiply by ☐.	
Input	Output
60	120
17	
75	

22. Measurement A jet is 232 feet long. What is the length of 7 jets lined up end-to-end on the runway?

23. Each page of a photo album holds 6 pictures. The album has 125 pages. How many photos can it hold?

Use the information to solve the problems.

A Pressing Problem

Remember, we are trying to figure out how many jelly beans the machine can press in 5 seconds.

The guidebook says that this machine can press 1,260 jellybeans in just one second!

24. How many jellybeans would Kendra like to go home with?

25. Suppose both Alyssa and Kendra went home with that many jellybeans. How many jellybeans would that be altogether?

H.O.T. Problems

26. OPEN ENDED Write a real-world multiplication word problem that has a product greater than 1,000.

27. WHICH ONE DOESN'T BELONG? Identify the multiplication problem that does not belong. Explain.

134	217	123	452
× 3	× 2	× 2	× 2
402	434	246	904

28. **WRITE MATH** Is the product of a two-digit number and a one-digit number always a three-digit number? Explain.

Test Practice

29. Tessa collected $125. Ariana collected 3 times as much. How much money did Ariana collect? (Lesson 3D)

 A. $128   **B.** $375

 C. $275   **D.** $500

30. Liana earned $70 each week for 7 weeks. She spent $125 and saved the rest. How much money did Liana save? (Lesson 3C)

 F. $365   **H.** $490

 G. $375   **J.** $700

Estimate. Round to the nearest hundred. (Lesson 1B)

31. 125
   × 8

32. 233
   × 4

33. 158
   × 3

34. Give a reasonable estimate for 82 × 9.

Multiply. Use basic facts and patterns. (Lesson 1A)

35. 5 × 300 = ▪

36. 8 × 9,000 = ▪

37. 400 × 6 = ▪

To assess mastery of SOL 3.6, see your Virginia Assessment Book.

Game Time

High and Low
Find a Product

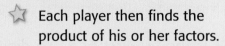

You will need: blank number cube, 1 game sheet per player

Get Ready!

Players: 2 or more

Get Set!

Label a number cube 1–6. Make game sheets like the one shown.

Go!

⭐ Decide if the goal for the game is a HIGH or a LOW product.

⭐ Player 1 rolls the number cube and records the number in any of the factor spaces on the game sheet.

⭐ Player 2 rolls the number cube and records the number in any of the factor spaces on their game sheet.

⭐ Play continues until players have filled in all the factor spaces on their game sheets.

⭐ Each player then finds the product of his or her factors.

⭐ The winner is the player with the greatest or least product, depending on the goal.

factor spaces

FOLDABLES
Study Organizer

Be sure the following Key Concepts are noted in your Foldable.

Key Concepts

- **Multiply Multiples of 10, 100, and 1,000**
  Use basic facts and patterns. (Lesson 1)

$4 \times 6 = 24$	4×6 ones
$4 \times 60 = 240$	4×6 tens
$4 \times 600 = 2,400$	4×6 hundreds
$4 \times 6,000 = 24,000$	4×6 thousands

- **Estimate Products** (Lesson 1)

  $5 \times 58 \rightarrow 5 \times 60 = 300$
  $5 \times 212 \rightarrow 5 \times 200 = 1,000$

- **Multiply Two-Digit Numbers** (Lesson 3)
  You can multiply many ways.
  An area model can help you find 24×4.

	20	4
4	$4 \times 20 = 80$	$4 \times 4 = 16$

  Multiply the ones and tens.
  Add the partial products.

  $$80 + 16 = 96$$

  So, $24 \times 4 = 96$.

Key Vocabulary

estimate

multiples

partial products

Vocabulary Check

Choose the vocabulary word that completes each sentence.

1. 15, 20, and 25 are _____?_____ of 5.

2. When you do not need an exact answer, you can _____?_____.

3. A _____?_____ of a number is the product of that number and any whole number.

4. When you find the product of each part, you are finding _____?_____.

5. To _____?_____ products, round factors to their greatest place value.

Multi-Part Lesson Review

Lesson 1 Multiples of 10, 100, and 1,000

Multiples of 10, 100, and 1,000 (Lesson 1A)

Multiply. Use basic facts and patterns.

6. 2 × 300   **7.** 7 × 8,000

8. 6 × 3,000   **9.** 9 × 900

10. Measurement One ton is equal to 2,000 pounds. How many pounds are equal to 5 tons?

11. Shannon has four books she wants to read. Each book is 100 pages long. How many pages are there altogether?

EXAMPLE 1

The school sold out their last 3 football games. There were 5,000 people at each game. How many tickets were sold for the three games?

You need to find 3 × 5,000.

3 × 5	= 15	3 × 5 ones
3 × 50	= 150	3 × 5 tens
3 × 500	= 1,500	3 × 5 hundreds
3 × 5,000	= 15,000	3 × 5 thousands

Estimate Products (Lesson 1B)

Estimate. Round to the nearest ten.

12. 68 × 2   **13.** 83 × 6

14. 7 × 44   **15.** 92 × 3

Estimate. Round to the nearest hundred.

16. 733 × 7   **17.** 6 × 478

18. 911 × 2   **19.** 8 × 675

20. Cathy reads 39 pages each hour. About how many pages will she read in 4 hours?

EXAMPLE 2

Each third grade class has 28 students. There are 8 third grade classes. About how many third grade students are in the school?

Estimate 8 × 28 by rounding to the nearest ten.

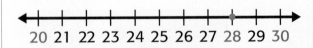

$$8 \times 30 = 240$$

So, there are about 240 third grade students.

Problem-Solving Strategy: Use Logical Reasoning (Lesson 2A)

Solve. Use logical reasoning.

21. Pilan, Harry, and Devin's jersey numbers are 12, 17, and 35. Pilan's number is a multiple of three. Harry's number is a multiple of five. Which jersey belongs with each boy?

22. Carrie has three cats named Stormy, Lucky, and Lani. Stormy is not black. Lucky is not orange or striped. Lani is striped. What colors are Stormy and Lucky?

23. Guido, Stan, Marc, and Cal are in line for lunch. Guido is next to Stan. Stan is behind Cal. Marc is last. Write the names of the boys in order from first in line to last.

EXAMPLE 3

Jerri's family has 3 people. Kaneesha does not have 4 or 7 people. Savannah does not have 5 or 7 people. How many people are in each family?

Use a table and logical reasoning.

Girl	3	4	5	7
Jerri	yes	✗	✗	✗
Kaneesha	✗	✗	yes	✗
Savannah	✗	yes	✗	✗
Johanna	✗	✗	✗	yes

So, Jerri has 3 family members, Kaneesha has 5, Savannah has 4, and Johanna has 7.

Multiply by a One-Digit Number (Lesson 2B)

Multiply. Use estimation to check.

24. 31
      × 3

25. 11
      × 6

26. 20
      × 3

27. 31
      × 2

28. 12 × 3

29. 4 × 11

30. 21 × 4

31. 33 × 3

32. Ms. Torsel bought three bags of carrots. Each bag has 21 mini carrots. How many carrots does Ms. Torsel have altogether?

EXAMPLE 4

Jamie read 3 books. Each book was 33 pages long. How many pages did she read?

Find 3 × 33. Think of 33 as 30 + 3.

	30	+	3
3	3 × 30 = 90		3 × 3 = 9

$$\begin{array}{r} 33 \\ \times\ 3 \\ \hline 9 \\ +\ 90 \\ \hline 99 \end{array}$$

So, Jamie read 99 pages.

Lesson 3 Multiply with Regrouping

Multiply Two-Digit Numbers (Lesson 3B)

Multiply. Use models if needed.

33. 35
× 4

34. 64
× 5

35. 28
× 2

36. 19
× 6

37. Measurement Nicolás made a long chalk line on the sidewalk. He traced along a one-foot ruler 8 times. How many inches long was Nicolás's chalk line?

EXAMPLE 5

Cletus has 5 photo albums. There are 65 pictures in each album. How many pictures does he have altogether?

Find 5 × 65.

Step 1 2
65
× 5
5

Step 2 2
65
× 5
325

So, Cletus has 325 pictures.

Problem-Solving Investigation: Choose a Strategy (Lesson 3C)

Use any strategy to solve.

38. Measurement Suppose you ride a bus 15 miles each day. How many miles will you ride in three days?

39. A book has 300 pages. A second book has 3 times as many pages. How many pages are in both books?

EXAMPLE 6

Harold earns $15 each time he mows a lawn. How much money did Harold earn after mowing 9 lawns?

$15 × 9 = $135

So, Harold earned $135.

Multiply Greater Numbers: Choose a Strategy (Lesson 3D)

Multiply.

40. 327 × 3

41. 465 × 4

42. 639 × 2

43. 1,347 × 5

44. The first 2,525 people at the game each received four coupons for a free beverage. How many coupons were given away?

EXAMPLE 7

It will cost each third grade class $128 to go on a trip to the zoo. How much will it cost 4 classes of the same size to go on the field trip?

Step 1 1 3
$128
× 4
12

Step 2 1 3
$128
× 4
$512

So, the field trip will cost $512.

Tell whether each statement is *true* or *false*.

1. When an exact answer is not needed, estimate to find an answer that is close to the exact answer.

2. Regrouped tens are not added after multiplying the tens.

3. Multiply. Use facts and patterns.

   $5 \times 6 =$ ▨
   $5 \times 60 =$ ▨
   $5 \times 600 =$ ▨
   $5 \times 6,000 =$ ▨

Multiply.

4. 115×4 5. 43×9

6. 270×3 7. 421×2

8. **MULTIPLE CHOICE** The Philadelphia Mint is one of several places where coins are made. The Mint has a machine that can produce 850 coins per minute. How many coins can be produced in 5 minutes?

   A. 850   **C.** 4,250

   B. 4,050   **D.** 5,000

Estimate. Round to the nearest ten.

9. $\begin{array}{r} 42 \\ \times\ 6 \\ \hline \end{array}$ 10. $\begin{array}{r} 75 \\ \times\ 4 \\ \hline \end{array}$

11. **Algebra** Copy and complete.

Rule: Multiply by 6.	
Input	**Output**
251	▨
332	▨
469	▨
102	▨

Estimate. Round to the nearest hundred.

12. 289×5 13. 350×6

14. The table shows how much money each class collected for a fundraiser. Which class collected about 3 times as much as the first grade class?

Class	Amount Raised
First grade	$211
Second grade	$399
Third grade	$604

15. **MULTIPLE CHOICE** There are 12 months in one year. About how many months are in 7 years?

   F. 70   **H.** 150

   G. 74   **J.** 200

16. **WRITE MATH** Explain why it is important to estimate the answer before finding the exact answer.

TEST EXAMPLE

There are 40 nickels in one roll of nickels. How many nickels are in 4 rolls of nickels?

A. 16 nickels   **C.** 80 nickels

B. 44 nickels   **D.** 160 nickels

Read the Question

There are 40 nickels in one roll of nickels. Multiply to find how many nickels there are in 4 rolls.

Solve the Question

Use a basic fact and patterns of zeros to to find 40 × 4.

$4 \times 4 = 16$ Use a basic fact.

$40 \times 4 = 160$ Use the pattern of zeros.

So, there are 160 nickels in 4 rolls. The answer is D.

Read each question. Then fill in the correct answer on the answer sheet provided by your teacher or on a separate sheet of paper.

1. Sancho spent 24 days at camp. He hiked 3 miles each day. How many miles did he hike in all?

   A. 72 miles   **C.** 27 miles

   B. 60 miles   **D.** 8 miles

2. Sonia has 30 shells. Brenda has 5 times as many shells as Sonia. How many shells does Brenda have?

   F. 35   **H.** 350

   G. 150   **J.** 1,500

3. Which expression describes the array below?

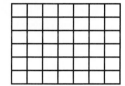

A. 8×6 **C.** 6×7

B. 7×8 **D.** 6×6

---

4. Two triangles have a perimeter of 44 centimeters each. What is the total perimeter of the two triangles?

F. 46 cm   **H.** 176 cm

G. 88 cm   **J.** 264 cm

---

5. About how many leaves would be on 21 similar clovers?

A. 21 leaves   **C.** 50 leaves

B. 24 leaves   **D.** 60 leaves

---

6. Jewel's mom baked 120 treats each day for 3 days. How many treats did she bake over the 3 days?

F. 120 treats   **H.** 360 treats

G. 320 treats   **J.** 400 treats

7. Amiri walked up and down the stairs of the Eiffel Tower in France 4 times. About how many steps did he walk up and down altogether?

1,060 steps

A. 1,000 steps   **C.** 4,000 steps

B. 1,060 steps   **D.** 8,000 steps

---

8. Dunn Elementary has 300 students. Each student will receive 5 new pencils on the first day of school. How many pencils will be given out on the first day?

F. 300 pencils   **H.** 800 pencils

G. 500 pencils   **J.** 1,500 pencils

---

9. Suppose you meet 5 friends and you all shake hands with each other. How many handshakes will there be?

A. 5 handshakes

B. 9 handshakes

C. 10 handshakes

D. 15 handshakes

NEED EXTRA HELP?									
If You Missed Question . . .	1	2	3	4	5	6	7	8	9
Go to Chapter-Lesson . . .	13-3B	13-1A	8-2D	13-2B	13-1B	13-3D	13-1B	13-1A	13-2A
For help with . . .	SOL 3.6	SOL 3.6	SOL 3.6	SOL 3.6	SOL 3.1b	SOL 3.6	SOL 3.1b	SOL 3.5	SOL 3.6

Problem-Solving Projects

When will I ever use this?

Have you ever said that? Did you wonder when you would use the math you are learning?

The Problem-Solving Projects apply the math you have learned so far in school to everyday events. Try them!

PROJECT 1 I Want to Go There **658**

PROJECT 2 Basket-Golf **660**

PROJECT 3 Crazy Cooks **662**

PROJECT 4 I Have Always Wanted a Llama **664**

I Want to Go THERE

As a team member of a travel agency, you will create a travel brochure for a 5-day trip for 4 people. The trip should be to a destination at least 100 miles away. Your brochure should include information about how the customers will travel; the sites they will visit; and the cost of hotels, food, and other expenses.

Getting Started

Day 1 The Best Place in the World

- Choose a location at least 100 miles away and 3 sites to visit there.
- Estimate all costs for the trip.
- Create a table to organize and display this data.

Day 2 Travel and Sightseeing

- Create a bar graph comparing travel costs.
- Draw two analog clocks showing the time of departure and time of arrival.
- Determine round-trip mileage in miles and kilometers.
- Construct a function table for the admission cost to each site for 1, 2, 3, and 4 people.
- Create a pictograph comparing the total cost of visiting each site.

Day 3 Lodging and Food

- Construct a function table for lodging costs for 1, 2, 3, 4, and 5 nights.
- The budget for food is $500.
- Plan 3 meals a day for 4 people for 5 days.

Day 4 Advertise the Trip

- Collect and organize your data, graphs, and tables.
- Create a brochure to show your client. Record and display the data.

Day 5 Convince Your Client

- Present your brochure to the class. Communicate why your trip is reasonably priced. Present your data.

Wrap Up ···

- Compare your estimated costs to your researched costs. What is the difference?
- Choose one part of the trip. Use what you have learned and tell how you could save money.
- Identify the mathematics you used in this project that could help you in everyday situations.

Basket-Golf

Have you ever wondered who created your favorite sport? Or what would happen if two sports were combined? You will create a new sport. You can either invent a new sport or combine two sports that already exist.

Getting Started

Day 1 Create It

- Create a class table. List 6 sports and 5 characteristics of each sport.
- Determine which of the characteristics you want for the new sport.

Day 2 Equipment, Playing Surface, and Area

- Design the equipment needed.
- Create a two-dimensional drawing of each piece of equipment.
- Label all measurements with standard units.

- Create a two-dimensional drawing of the playing surface. Describe it. Label its dimensions with standard units. Indentify the perimeter.
- Decide whether the playing surface will be divided into halves, quarters, or another fractional part. Label this on your drawing.

Day 3 Rules and Scoring

- Write the rules and procedures.
- Determine the playing time. Draw a clock for each playing period.
- Explain how to score and win. Make a function table to show the point system.

Day 4 Design the Uniforms

- Draw a picture of the uniform.
- Label each item with a reasonable price.
- Find the total cost of uniforms for a team. Write this as a number sentence.

Day 5 Introduce Your New Sport

- Present your new sport to the class.
- Describe one problem-solving strategy you used.

Wrap Up

- Reflect on the math involved in playing sports. Give three examples of how math is connected to sports.
- Describe parts of this project that remind you of an everyday situation in which you use math.

Crazy Cooks

Have you ever volunteered to help a charity? In this project, your class will form groups of 4 and prepare a recipe, sell the product, and then donate the proceeds to a local charity.

Getting Started

Day 1 Who Needs Your Help?

- Survey the class for charity ideas. Vote to select one. Set a donation goal.
- Survey classmates about their favorite baked goods. Record the results in a tally chart. Display the top 5 responses in a bar graph.
- Make a table to show the estimated total servings needed and the estimated price to be charged for each serving to reach the goal.

Days 2 and 3 Plan and Prepare

- Find the number of servings your recipe makes.
- Determine the number of batches needed.

- Create a function table to show the number of servings for 1, 2, 3, 4, and 5 batches.
- Determine the total amount of each ingredient needed.
- Use grocery ads or the Internet to research the cost of each ingredient. Calculate the cost of each ingredient for multiple batches. Find the total cost.
- Determine a reasonable price to charge. How does it compare to your estimate?
- Make the recipe.
- Determine how to divide the whole into equal servings.

Day 4 Sell

- Each group decides how much change is needed to start with and in what denominations.
- Sell the food at lunchtime. Make the change. Count the change back.

Day 5 Display Results

- Create a bar graph to show how many of each type of baked good was sold.
- Create another bar graph to show the money earned from each item.
- Analyze the data. Use the bar graph to find the profit. Did you meet your goal? Explain.
- Write a letter to the leaders of the charity and explain what you did. Send the letter with the money you made.

Wrap Up

- Identify other ways you could make money to support a charity.
- Identify several steps you took that were similar to steps you take when solving word problems.
- Identify the mathematics you used in this project that may help you in everyday experiences.

I Have Always Wanted a Llama

You will collect data needed to choose your class pet. Research the needs and costs of taking care of a class pet. Design a habitat for your pet. Then, present your research to your class.

Getting Started ······································

Day 1 So Many to Choose From

- Survey the class for ideas for a class pet. Record the data in a tally chart and display the data in a bar graph.
- Choose one pet to research. Make a table with two columns. Label one *Estimate* and the other *Actual.* Estimate the pet's length and weight in standard units. Find the actual length and weight. Find the difference between the estimate and the actual.

Day 2 and 3 Food and Home

- Create a function table to show what the pet eats and how much it eats for 1–7 days. Draw clocks to show when it should be fed.
- Design the pet's home. Make a three-dimensional sketch. Label the dimensions.
- Determine what accessories will be needed. Include pictures of at least one three-dimensional object, one symmetrical object, and two congruent objects.

Day 4 Costs

- Suppose you have $50 to spend on the pet's needs you identified on Day 3. Decide what you must have and what is extra. Create a table to show what must be bought and what you can buy with leftover money.
- Create a poster to show the most important parts of your research.

Day 5 Presentation

- Present your poster to the class.
- Describe one way math helped you with this project.

Wrap Up ···

- Did you have enough money on Day 4? How did you decide how to spend the money? Explain.
- How will this project help you make future decisions about money?

Student Handbook

Extra Practice **EP2**

Facts Practice **EP46**

Reference

Photo Credits **R1**

English-Spanish Glossary **R3**

Index **R29**

Quick Reference . . . **Inside Back Cover**

How to Use the Student Handbook

The Student Handbook is the additional skill and reference material found at the end of books. The Student Handbook can help answer these questions.

What If I Need More Practice?

You, or your teacher, may decide that working through some additional problems would be helpful. The **Extra Practice** section provides these problems for each lesson so you have ample opportunity to practice new skills.

What If I Forget a Vocabulary Word?

The **English-Spanish Glossary** provides a list of important, or difficult words used throughout the textbook. It provides a definition in English and Spanish.

What If I Need to Find Something Quickly?

The **Index** alphabetically lists the subjects covered throughout the entire textbook and the pages on which each subject can be found.

What If I Forget Multiplication Facts or Measurement Conversions?

Inside the back cover of your math book is a **Quick Reference** of a multiplication table. You will also find a list of measurement conversions inside the back cover.

Extra Practice

Multi-Part Lesson 1-1 Identify Place Value

PART A B   PAGES 13–19

Write the place of the underlined digit. Then write the value of the digit.

1. 7<u>0</u>6

2. 2,<u>4</u>32

3. 5,68<u>2</u>

4. <u>6</u>,734

5. 8,<u>0</u>98

6. <u>3</u>,365

Write each number in expanded form and word form.

7. 4,371

8. 2,988

9. 5,654

10. 7,702

11. 6,520

12. 8,906

PART C   PAGES 20–23

Write the place of the underlined digit. Then write its value.

1. 4,3<u>2</u>2

2. <u>8</u>0,761

3. 3,<u>0</u>00

4. 67,02<u>3</u>

5. 5<u>1</u>,089

6. <u>2</u>7,055

Write each number in expanded form and word form.

7. 8,954

8. 14,523

9. 81,306

10. 27,621

11. 9,909

12. 50,345

Multi-Part Lesson 1-2 Compare and Order Numbers

PART A   PAGES 24–25

Solve. Use the four-step plan.

1. Maria ate 7 grapes and 5 strawberries. How many pieces of fruit did she eat?

2. There were 22 people at the park. 7 people left. How many people were still at the park?

3. John has 18 more toy airplanes than Soto does. Soto has 13 toy airplanes. How many toy airplanes does John have?

4. During a treasure hunt, Megan walked 12 yards left, 6 yards forward, and 7 yards left. How many yards did Megan walk altogether?

Multi-Part Lesson 1-2 Compare and Order Numbers (continued)

PART B
PAGES 26–29

Compare. Use >, <, or =.

1. 177 ● 67

2. $455 ● $545

3. 610 ● 610

4. 234 ● 342

5. 404 ● 440

6. 908 ● 889

7. 756 ● 765

8. 3,576 ● 3,567

9. 4,222 ● 5,232

10. 1,045 ● 1,450

11. 2,357 ● 2,357

12. 2,787 ● 2,878

PART C
PAGES 30–32

Order the numbers from least to greatest.

1. 888; 8,008; 81

2. 146; 149; 143

3. 678; 768; 5,667

4. 1,790; 1,978; 1,843

5. 3,438; 896; 2,122

6. 1,222; 2,221; 1,022

Order the numbers from greatest to least.

7. 765; 7,650; 79

8. 999; 3,221; 4,000

9. 368; 386; 833

10. 2,567; 2,982; 2,199

11. 4,235; 4,325; 3,443

12. 616; 6,116; 16,611

Multi-Part Lesson 1-3 Round Numbers

PART A
PAGES 36–38

Round to the nearest ten.

1. 68

2. 23

3. 84

4. 233

5. 397

6. 408

7. 1,656

8. 2,492

Round to the nearest hundred.

9. 231

10. 778

11. 645

12. 1,282

13. 442

14. 581

15. 4,774

16. 987

Multi-Part Lesson 1-3 Round Numbers (continued)

PART B   PAGES 40–43

Round to the nearest thousand.

1. 3,810   **2.** 1,221   **3.** 5,989

4. 8,297   **5.** 3,099   **6.** 6,572

7. 1,100   **8.** 2,667   **9.** 1,589

10. 4,088   **11.** 7,476   **12.** 2,821

PART C   PAGES 44–45

Use the four-step plan to solve each problem.

1. Tony has 7 games, Allison has 9 games, and Jarrod has 12 games. They each bought 3 more games. How many games does each child have now?

2. Carlos jogged for 30 minutes today. Tomorrow he plans to jog 3 times as long as he did today. How long does he plan to jog tomorrow?

3. Gina bought a sweater for $14. She paid with a $20 bill. How much change did Gina get?

4. Sara picked 48 cherries. She ate 9 cherries. Her sister ate 12 cherries. How many cherries are left?

Multi-Part Lesson 1-4 Coins and Bills

PART A   PAGES 46–49

Find the value of the coins.

1.

2.

Find the value of the bills and coins.

3.

4.

Multi-Part Lesson 1-4 Coins and Bills (continued)

PAGES 50–53

A $5-bill was used to buy each item. Determine the change.
Use coins and bills if needed.

1.
$4.55

2.
$0.78

3.
$3.98

Solve. Write the amount of change that should be received.

4. Bernie buys a plant for $3.75. He pays with four $1-bills.

5. Pam buys a cupcake for $0.35. She pays with a $5-bill.

6. The printer charges $0.10 for each copy it makes. Jill has 6 copies made. She pays with a $1-bill.

7. Cal buys one rubber spider. They are on sale at two for $1.00. He pays with a $5-bill.

Multi-Part Lesson 2-1 Add to Solve Problems

PAGES 65–67

Find each sum. Identify the property.

1. $8 + 0 = $ ▨

2. $7 + 3 = $ ▨
$3 + 7 = $ ▨

3. $(4 + 5) + 3 = $ ▨
$4 + (5 + 3) = $ ▨

4. $6 + 5 = $ ▨
$5 + 6 = $ ▨

5. $0 + 5 = $ ▨

6. $9 + (4 + 3) = $ ▨
$(9 + 4) + 3 = $ ▨

Find each missing number. Identify the property.

7. $0 + 7 = 7 + $ ▨

8. $6 + (3 + 5) = (6 + $ ▨$) + 5$

9. $8 + 4 = $ ▨$ + 8$

10. $5 + $ ▨$ = 7 + $ ▨

11. $(9 + 3) + 4 = $ ▨$ + (3 + 4)$

12. ▨$ + 0 = 5 + $ ▨

Multi-Part Lesson 2-1 Add to Solve Problems (continued)

Estimate. Round to the indicated place value.

1. 43 + 29; tens

2. 664 + 49; tens

3. 1,329 + 755; hundreds

4. 9,488 + 2,061; thousands

5. $4,163 + $9,982; hundreds

6. 9,234 + 3,340; thousands

Estimate. Use compatible numbers.

7. 315 + 299

8. 152 + 280

9. 1,890 + 1,103

10. 2,790 + 6,265

Solve.

11. The cafeteria had 16 tuna sandwiches and 23 ham sandwiches left over. About how many sandwiches were left over?

12. On Monday, 1,759 vehicles crossed a bridge. On Tuesday, 2,801 vehicles crossed the same bridge. Together, how many vehicles crossed the bridge both days?

Add. Check for reasonableness.

1.   35
       + 46

2.   53
       + 38

3. $124
       + $49

4.   237
       + 57

5. $425
       + $272

6.   436
       + 288

7. $719
       + $255

8.   409
       + 354

9.   73
       + 236

10. 174 + 349

11. $384 + $567

12. 439 + 211

13. $563 + $398

14. 277 + 562

15. $478 + $335

Tell whether an estimate or an exact answer is needed. Then solve.

1. Each sandwich has two slices of bread. How many sandwiches can be made with 3 loaves of bread that have 18 slices each?

2. Maya has 90 beads. She uses about 25 beads to make a necklace. Does she have enough beads to make 4 necklaces?

3. A box of cookies costs $1.85. Milk costs $2.10. About how much will milk and 2 boxes of cookies cost?

4. Carmen walked 12 blocks forward and 25 blocks to the left. How many blocks did she walk in all?

Multi-Part Lesson 2-1 Add to Solve Problems (continued)

Find each sum. Use estimation to check for reasonableness.

1. 2,298
   + 367

2. 3,245
   + 107

3. $4,366
   + $523

4. 648
   + 751

5. 1,988
   + 3,766

6. $1,375
   + $817

7. 4,543
   + 2,376

8. $2,640
   + $3,765

9. 3,905
   + 4,227

10. 3,465 + 5,555

11. 2,988 + 2,675

12. 6,042 + 2,309

13. $1,991 + $2,685

14. 4,768 + 2,644

15. 1,548 + 5,673

Multi-Part Lesson 2-2 Subtract to Solve Problems

Estimate. Round to the given place value.

1. 273 − 228; tens

2. 886 − 558; hundreds

3. 243 − 89; hundreds

4. 2,921 − 2,349;
   thousands

5. 5,137 − 1,148;
   hundreds

6. 8,010 − 3,781;
   thousands

Estimate each difference using compatible numbers.

7. 7,698 − 4,322

8. 7,819 − 2,735

9. 5,424 − 3,869

10. 2,910 − 758

11. 3,620 − 1,250

12. 9,764 − 5,299

Subtract. Check your answer.

1. 267
   − 154

2. 498
   − 207

3. $634
   − $321

4. 867
   − 89

5. $576
   − $283

6. 755
   − 448

7. $234
   − $97

8. 923
   − 542

9. $744
   − $452

10. $353 − $86

11. 824 − 619

12. 563 − 227

Multi-Part Lesson 2-2 Subtract to Solve Problems (continued)

PART D PAGES 96–99

Subtract. Check your answer.

1.   2,453
    − 1,231

2.   5,691
    − 207

3. $8,732
    − $6,215

4.   4,863
    − 3,788

5.   7,239
    − 908

6.   9,999
    − 3,455

7. $4,891
    − $1,637

8.   2,472
    − 848

9.   3,643
    − 1,784

10. $7,278 − $3,495

11. 5,664 − 2,659

12. $7,221 − $4,833

PART E PAGES 102–105

Subtract. Use addition to check.

1. $400
    − $298

2.   800
    − 567

3.   1,000
    − 703

4.   3,600
    − 1,695

5.   5,000
    − 2,367

6. $9,000
    − $4,890

7.   7,000
    − 5,804

8.   6,400
    − 3,166

9.   9,600
    − 1,879

10. $2,200 − $883

11. $4,700 − $2,864

12. 8,600 − 7,621

13. 7,000 − 4,386

PART F PAGES 106–107

Use any strategy to solve each problem.

1. There were 123 people in line to ride a roller coaster. Forty-eight people got on the roller coaster for the next ride. How many people were left in line?

2. Mei collected 240 seashells. Of the shells, 128 were spiral-shaped. The rest were scallop-shaped. About how many scallop-shaped shells did Mei collect?

3. Jesse bought a baseball bat for $16 and a baseball for $5. He paid for them with a $20-bill and a $10-bill. How much change did he get back?

4. Jim had 583 baseball cards. He gave 212 of his cards to his brother. How many baseball cards does Jim have left?

Multi-Part Lesson 3-1 Meaning of Multiplication

PART A B   PAGES 119–123

Write an addition sentence and a multiplication sentence for each model.

1.    **2.**

3. 7 groups of 4   **4.** 4 groups of 8   **5.** 2 groups of 10

6. 3 groups of 9   **7.** 5 groups of 5   **8.** 3 groups of 6

PART C D   PAGES 124–129

Write two multiplication sentences for each array.

1. 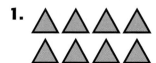   **2.** 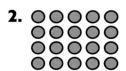   **3.**

Use the Commutative Property of Multiplication to find each missing number.

4. $4 \times 5 = 20$ **5.** $4 \times 9 = 36$ **6.** $5 \times 7 = 35$
   ■ $\times 4 = 20$ $9 \times$ ■ $= 36$ $7 \times 5 =$ ■

PART E   PAGES 130–133

Use the models to compare. Then write a multiplication sentence.

1. 4 times as many   **2.** 5 times more   **3.** twice as many

Use the bar diagram to compare. Then write a multiplication sentence.

4. 3 times as many hats   **5.** 2 times as many crayons **6.** twice as many bugs

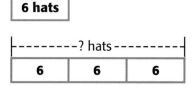   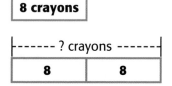   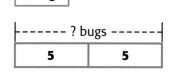

Multi-Part Lesson 3-1 Meaning of Multiplication (continued)

Make a picture or tree diagram to find all the possible combinations. Write a multiplication sentence.

1. Arianna is planning a party for five of her friends. She has red, pink, and green cups and 4 different designs of paper plates: balloons, ribbons, panda bears, and kittens. How many different cup and plate combinations are there?

2. Jonah is picking out his shirt and pants for school picture day. He has 5 shirts to choose from: green, red, light blue, navy, and striped. His pants are tan, denim, and grey. How many different combinations could he wear?

3. The third graders are picking the snack for their monthly birthday celebration. The food choices are veggie sticks, grapes, cheese cubes, and pretzels. They can choose either fruit punch or chocolate milk to drink. How many possible snack combinations are there if they choose one food and one drink?

4. For a craft project, students need to pick from 3 colors of pipe cleaners and 2 colors of craft paper. How many craft combinations are there?

Solve. Use the *make a table* strategy.

1. A swim team has 9 members. Five members of the team each swam 3 laps. The other members each swam twice as many laps as the first 5. How many laps did the team members swim altogether?

2. A camp leader packed 8 sandwiches and 6 apples in each picnic basket. She packed 36 apples altogether. How many sandwiches did she pack? How many picnic baskets did she use?

3. A flower shop charges $5 for 6 roses. Tulips cost $4 for 9. How much more would it cost to buy 24 roses than 36 tulips?

4. Rick is making a square pen for his turtle. Each side of the pen will be 3 feet long. Rick will use 4 posts for each foot of the pen. How many posts will he need?

Multi-Part Lesson 3-2 Meaning of Division

PART A B

PAGES 144–149

Use counters to model the total. Divide to find the number in each group.

1. 6 counters
2 equal groups
■ in each group
■ ÷ ■ = ■

2. 16 counters
4 equal groups
■ in each group
■ ÷ ■ = ■

3. 28 counters
4 equal groups
■ in each group
■ ÷ ■ = ■

Find each missing number.

4. $12 \div ■ = 4$

5. $■ \div 3 = 5$

6. $14 \div ■ = 7$

7. $■ \div 2 = 10$

8. $18 \div ■ = 6$

9. $■ \div 5 = 6$

10. Mrs. Martinez needs 24 snack bags of pretzels. The bags come in packages of 6. How many packages does she need to buy?

11. Coach Lewis needs to buy uniform socks for the 12 players on his soccer team. There are 4 pairs of socks in a package. How many packages does he need for his team?

PART C

PAGES 150–153

Use models to divide. Write a number sentence.

1. $12 \div 3$

2. $9 \div 3$

3. $16 \div 2$

4. $15 \div 5$

5. $24 \div 4$

6. $10 \div 2$

Use repeated subtraction to divide.

7. $21 \div 3$

8. $16 \div 4$

9. $8 \div 1$

10. $14 \div 2$

11. $20 \div 5$

12. $27 \div 9$

13. $18 \div 9$

14. $24 \div 3$

15. $12 \div 6$

PART D E

PAGES 154–159

Draw an array to complete each pair of number sentences.

1. $2 \times 3 = ■$
$6 \div ■ = 2$

2. $1 \times ■ = 7$
$7 \div 7 = ■$

3. $4 \times ■ = 16$
$■ \div 4 = 4$

4. $■ \times 4 = 12$
$12 \div ■ = 3$

5. $5 \times 4 = ■$
$20 \div 4 = ■$

6. $8 \times ■ = 24$
$24 \div ■ = 3$

Write the fact family for each set of numbers.

7. 2, 4, 8

8. 3, 7, 21

9. 1, 5, 5

10. 2, 9, 18

11. 4, 3, 12

12. 4, 5, 20

Multi-Part Lesson 3-2 Meaning of Division (continued)

Use any strategy to solve each problem.

1. Tennis balls are on sale for $3 a can or 4 cans for $10. If you buy 4 cans of tennis balls, how much will you save on each can?

2. Sara collected 32 red, orange, and yellow leaves to make a collage. She collected 9 orange leaves and 7 yellow leaves. How many red leaves did she collect?

3. There are about 18 soccer players on each team. There are 6 soccer teams in the league. About how many soccer players are in the league?

4. There are 7 spiders in a display at the zoo. Each spider has 8 legs. Each spider also has 2 body segments. How many spider legs are there altogether?

Multi-Part Lesson 4-1 Multiplication and Division Facts for 2 and 3

Multiply.

1.

2.

3.

4 groups of 2   7 groups of 2   8 groups of 2

Multiply. Use a bar diagram if needed.

4. $\begin{array}{r} 2 \\ \times\,6 \\ \hline \end{array}$

5. $\begin{array}{r} 8 \\ \times\,2 \\ \hline \end{array}$

6. $\begin{array}{r} 9 \\ \times\,2 \\ \hline \end{array}$

7. $\begin{array}{r} 10 \\ \times\,2 \\ \hline \end{array}$

8. $\begin{array}{r} 5 \\ \times\,2 \\ \hline \end{array}$

9. $\begin{array}{r} 2 \\ \times\,4 \\ \hline \end{array}$

10. $\begin{array}{r} 2 \\ \times\,2 \\ \hline \end{array}$

11. $\begin{array}{r} 2 \\ \times\,3 \\ \hline \end{array}$

Divide. Write a related multiplication fact.

1. $18 \div 2$

2. $4 \div 2$

3. $8 \div 2$

4. $12 \div 2$

5. $14 \div 2$

6. $10 \div 2$

7. $10 \div 2$

8. $16 \div 2$

9. $18 \div 2$

10. $6 \div 2$

11. $2 \div 2$

12. $12 \div 2$

PART C D

PAGES 180–185

Multiply. Draw an array or skip count if needed.

1. 7
$\times 3$

2. 3
$\times 8$

3. 6
$\times 3$

4. 5
$\times 3$

5. 10
$\times 3$

6. 1
$\times 3$

7. 0
$\times 3$

8. 9
$\times 3$

9. 8×3

10. 3×2

11. 3×7

12. 4×3

13. 3×9

14. 3×0

PART E

PAGES 186–189

Divide.

1. $9 \div 3$

2. $12 \div 3$

3. $0 \div 3$

4. $15 \div 3$

5. $3 \div 3$

6. $21 \div 3$

7. $3\overline{)24}$

8. $3\overline{)6}$

9. $3\overline{)30}$

Copy and complete each table.

10.

Rule: Divide by 2			
Input	12	■	20	■
Output	■	8	■	7

11.

Rule: Divide by 3			
Input	15	■	21	■
Output	■	1	■	6

PART F

PAGES 190–191

Solve. Use the *work backward* strategy.

1. Tara had 5 more homework problems yesterday than today. Yesterday she had 10 homework problems. How many problems does she have today?

2. Jamal received 9 CDs for his birthday. Then he bought 7 more CDs. Now he has 37 CDs. How many CDs did Jamal have before his birthday?

3. Ms. McCoy packed 6 coolers with equal numbers of juice and water bottles. She packed 36 bottles of juice altogether. How many bottles of juice and water did she pack in each cooler?

4. Tom had some money in his piggy bank. Last week he put twice as much money in his bank as he already had. This week he put 3 times as much in as he did last week. Now he has $27 in his bank. How much did he start with?

Multi-Part Lesson 4-2 Multiplication and Division Facts for 5 and 10

PART A
PAGES 194–196

Multiply. Use a bar diagram or draw a picture if needed.

1. 2
$\times$ 5

2. 5
$\times$ 5

3. 5
$\times$ 6

4. 9
$\times$ 5

5. 8
$\times$ 5

6. 10
$\times$ 5

7. 5
$\times$ 1

8. 5
$\times$ 7

9. 5×8

10. 10×5

11. 5×0

12. 5×9

13. 6×5

14. 7×5

PART B
PAGES 198–201

Divide. Use models or related facts.

1. $35 \div 5$

2. $20 \div 5$

3. $50 \div 5$

4. $40 \div 5$

5. $25 \div 5$

6. $45 \div 5$

Copy and complete each table.

7.

Rule: − 5	
Input	Output
45	
35	
20	
	10

8.

Rule: ÷ 5	
Input	Output
50	
30	
	4
	1

9.

Rule: × 5	
Input	Output
9	
8	
6	
	25

PART C
PAGES 202–205

Multiply. Use patterns or models if needed.

1. 10
$\times$ 2

2. 10
$\times$ 5

3. 10
$\times$ 1

4. 10
$\times$ 7

5. 10
$\times$ 6

6. 10
$\times$ 9

7. 10
$\times$ 4

8. 10
$\times$ 8

9. 5×10

10. 10×7

11. 10×4

12. 3×10

13. 10×9

14. 8×10

Multi-Part Lesson 4-2 Multiplication and Division Facts for 5 and 10 (continued)

PART D PAGES 206–208

Divide.

1. 40 ÷ 10

2. 20 ÷ 10

3. 70 ÷ 10

4. 30 ÷ 10

5. 100 ÷ 10

6. 90 ÷ 10

Solve. Write the number sentence.

7. ■ ÷ 10 = 6

8. 50 ÷ 10 = ■

9. ■ ÷ 10 = 9

10. 80 ÷ 10 = ■

11. ■ ÷ 4 = 10

12. ■ ÷ 10 = 3

Multi-Part Lesson 4-3 Multiply and Divide with 0 and 1

PART A PAGES 212–213

Use any strategy to solve each problem.

1. Sung made 3 equal-sized sets of frozen lemon treats and 2 equal-sized sets of frozen cherry treats. He made 25 treats altogether. How many treats were in each set?

2. Jaime ordered 4 pizzas for himself and 5 of his friends. Each pizza had 6 slices. How many slices of pizza did each boy have?

3. Each mother duck has 4 ducklings. There are 4 mother ducks. How many ducks and ducklings are there altogether?

4. Mrs. Diaz has five rows of peppers in her garden. There are 30 pepper plants in all. How many pepper plants are in each row?

PART B PAGES 214–215

Multiply.

1. 9
     × 0

2. 10
      × 1

3. 8
      × 1

4.   0
       × 6

5.   0
       × 8

6. 1
      × 5

7. 10
      × 0

8. 7
      × 1

9. 5 × 0

10. 0 × 4

11. 1 × 9

12. 0 × 7

13. 1 × 6

14. 3 × 0

Multi-Part Lesson 4-3 Multiply and Divide with 0 and 1 (continued)

PART C PAGES 216–217

Divide.

1. 9 ÷ 1 **2.** 0 ÷ 6 **3.** 10 ÷ 10 **4.** 8 ÷ 1

5. 5 ÷ 5 **6.** 4 ÷ 1 **7.** 0 ÷ 8 **8.** 2 ÷ 1

9. 10)‾0 **10.** 8)‾0 **11.** 9)‾9 **12.** 1)‾7

13. 2)‾2 **14.** 1)‾1 **15.** 4)‾0 **16.** 1)‾5

Multi-Part Lesson 5-1 Multiplication and Division Facts for 4

PART A B PAGES 229–233

Multiply.

1. $\begin{array}{r} 4 \\ \times\,3 \\ \hline \end{array}$ **2.** $\begin{array}{r} 4 \\ \times\,6 \\ \hline \end{array}$ **3.** $\begin{array}{r} 5 \\ \times\,4 \\ \hline \end{array}$ **4.** $\begin{array}{r} 10 \\ \times\,4 \\ \hline \end{array}$

5. $\begin{array}{r} 8 \\ \times\,4 \\ \hline \end{array}$ **6.** $\begin{array}{r} 4 \\ \times\,7 \\ \hline \end{array}$ **7.** $\begin{array}{r} 9 \\ \times\,4 \\ \hline \end{array}$ **8.** $\begin{array}{r} 1 \\ \times\,4 \\ \hline \end{array}$

9. 6 × 4 **10.** 4 × 0 **11.** 7 × 4

12. 4 × 8 **13.** 3 × 4 **14.** 4 × 9

PART C PAGES 234–237

Divide. Use models or related facts.

1. 16 ÷ 4 **2.** 8 ÷ 4 **3.** 20 ÷ 4

4. 24 ÷ 4 **5.** 0 ÷ 4 **6.** 32 ÷ 4

7. 4)‾12 **8.** 4)‾28 **9.** 4)‾40

Find each missing number.

10. 20 ÷ ■ = 4 **11.** ■ ÷ 4 = 10 **12.** 4 × ■ = 28

Multi-Part Lesson 5-1 Multiplication and Division Facts for 4 (continued)

**Solve. If there is missing information, tell what facts you need
to solve the problem.**

1. A vegetable garden has 4 rows of corn. There are 7 corn plants in each row. There are 5 rows of tomato plants next to the corn. How many corn plants are there?

2. Mark wants to buy a CD player that costs $45. He has saved $20. How many hours will he have to work before he has enough money for the CD player?

3. Zina played soccer for 30 minutes. Then she played basketball. How many minutes did Zina play sports?

4. Tony bought 5 boxes of crayons. There were 8 crayons in each box. Each box of crayons cost $2. How many crayons did Tony buy?

Multi-Part Lesson 5-2 Multiplication and Division Facts for 6 and 7

Multiply. Double a known fact if needed.

1. 6 $\times 2$	**2.** 3 $\times 6$	**3.** 5 $\times 6$	**4.** 6 $\times 9$
5. 1 $\times 6$	**6.** 7 $\times 6$	**7.** 10 $\times 6$	**8.** 6 $\times 8$

9. 4×6 **10.** 0×6 **11.** 6×7

12. 8×6 **13.** 5×6 **14.** 6×6

Multiply. Use repeated addition or a known fact if needed.

1. 4 $\times 7$	**2.** 6 $\times 7$	**3.** 7 $\times 7$	**4.** 1 $\times 7$
5. 7 $\times 9$	**6.** 10 $\times 7$	**7.** 5 $\times 7$	**8.** 7 $\times 8$

9. 2×7 **10.** 7×6 **11.** 0×7

12. 7×10 **13.** 9×7 **14.** 7×3

Multi-Part Lesson 5-2 Multiplication and Division Facts for 6 and 7 (continued)

PART C D PAGES 248–252

Divide. Use models or repeated subtraction.

1. $12 \div 6$ **2.** $28 \div 7$ **3.** $24 \div 6$

4. $35 \div 7$ **5.** $0 \div 7$ **6.** $21 \div 7$

7. $42 \div 6$ **8.** $30 \div 6$ **9.** $36 \div 6$

10. $6\overline{)6}$ **11.** $7\overline{)14}$ **12.** $6\overline{)18}$

13. $7\overline{)63}$ **14.** $6\overline{)48}$ **15.** $7\overline{)56}$

Multi-Part Lesson 5-3 Multiplication and Division Facts for 8 and 9

PART A PAGES 254–257

Multiply. Use an array or a known fact if needed.

1. $\begin{array}{r} 8 \\ \times 3 \\ \hline \end{array}$ **2.** $\begin{array}{r} 8 \\ \times 1 \\ \hline \end{array}$ **3.** $\begin{array}{r} 7 \\ \times 8 \\ \hline \end{array}$ **4.** $\begin{array}{r} 8 \\ \times 5 \\ \hline \end{array}$

5. $\begin{array}{r} 8 \\ \times 0 \\ \hline \end{array}$ **6.** $\begin{array}{r} 10 \\ \times 8 \\ \hline \end{array}$ **7.** $\begin{array}{r} 8 \\ \times 6 \\ \hline \end{array}$ **8.** $\begin{array}{r} 9 \\ \times 8 \\ \hline \end{array}$

9. 2×8 **10.** 8×4 **11.** 8×7

12. 8×9 **13.** 5×8 **14.** 8×10

PART B PAGES 258–260

Multiply. Use a known fact or patterns if needed.

1. $\begin{array}{r} 9 \\ \times 4 \\ \hline \end{array}$ **2.** $\begin{array}{r} 3 \\ \times 9 \\ \hline \end{array}$ **3.** $\begin{array}{r} 9 \\ \times 0 \\ \hline \end{array}$ **4.** $\begin{array}{r} 5 \\ \times 9 \\ \hline \end{array}$

5. $\begin{array}{r} 7 \\ \times 9 \\ \hline \end{array}$ **6.** $\begin{array}{r} 9 \\ \times 9 \\ \hline \end{array}$ **7.** $\begin{array}{r} 9 \\ \times 8 \\ \hline \end{array}$ **8.** $\begin{array}{r} 10 \\ \times 9 \\ \hline \end{array}$

9. 6×9 **10.** 9×2 **11.** 0×9

12. 7×9 **13.** 1×9 **14.** 9×5

PART C

PAGES 262–264

Divide. Use related facts or repeated subtraction.

1. $32 \div 8$

2. $27 \div 9$

3. $45 \div 9$

4. $40 \div 8$

5. $24 \div 8$

6. $36 \div 9$

7. $0 \div 9$

8. $16 \div 8$

9. $63 \div 9$

10. $9 \overline{)27}$

11. $9 \overline{)81}$

12. $8 \overline{)80}$

13. $9 \overline{)72}$

14. $8 \overline{)64}$

15. $9 \overline{)54}$

Solve. Write a number sentence.

16. There are 9 apples left to buy. If a different person bought 1 apple each, how many people bought an apple?

17. Six identical strings of lights have a total of 48 lights. How many lights are on each string?

PART D

PAGES 266–267

Use any strategy to solve each problem.

1. Dillon is picking lemons and oranges. For every 2 lemons he picks, he picks 4 oranges. When Dillon has picked 6 lemons, how many oranges will he have picked?

2. Colored markers are on sale at a store for $0.20 each or a set of 6 for $1. How much would you save if you bought 5 sets of colored markers instead of buying the markers individually?

3. John is putting cans of food on a shelf. He can fit 6 large cans on each shelf. How many cans could be fit on 4 shelves?

4. Scott earns $4 per hour doing yard work. He works 2 hours a day. How many days did it take him to earn $32?

5. Eight equally-sized teams were formed from the 56 players who showed up for the meeting. Another 16 players came on the first day of practice. How many players are now on the equally-sized teams?

6. A tray in the cafeteria has 48 bowls of soup arranged in an array. Name three possible arrays in which the bowls of soup could be arranged.

Multi-Part Lesson 5-4 Multiplication and Division Facts for 11 and 12

PART **A**

PAGES 268–271

Multiply. Use patterns or models if needed.

1. 4×11

2. 2×12

3. 11×5

4. $\begin{array}{r} 2 \\ \times\ 11 \\ \hline \end{array}$

5. $\begin{array}{r} 12 \\ \times\ 3 \\ \hline \end{array}$

6. $\begin{array}{r} 5 \\ \times\ 12 \\ \hline \end{array}$

7. $\begin{array}{r} 12 \\ \times\ 7 \\ \hline \end{array}$

8. $\begin{array}{r} 11 \\ \times\ 9 \\ \hline \end{array}$

9. $\begin{array}{r} 11 \\ \times\ 11 \\ \hline \end{array}$

10. The band members made 7 equal rows of 12 members each. What is the total number of band members?

11. Cups of apple cider are arranged in 11 rows with 8 cups in each row. What is the total number of cups of cider?

PART **B**

PAGES 272–275

Divide.

1. $77 \div 11$

2. $24 \div 12$

3. $55 \div 11$

4. $36 \div 12$

5. $33 \div 11$

6. $99 \div 11$

7. $60 \div 12$

8. $144 \div 12$

9. $11 \div 11$

Find each missing number.

10. $120 \div \blacksquare = 10$

11. $\blacksquare \div 12 = 12$

12. $\blacksquare \div 12 = 11$

13. There are 144 eggs to be placed in cartons of 12. How many egg cartons will be filled completely?

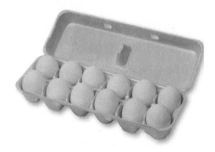

14. Manuel has 88 pennies in his bank. His dad gave him 22 more pennies. He will divide the pennies into equal groups as shown. How many groups of pennies will Manuel have?

Multi-Part Lesson 6-1 Collect Data

PART **A** **B**

PAGES 287–291

Organize each set of data in a tally chart and a frequency table.

1. The gym teacher gave her students assorted sports balls to use in class. They are listed below.

Sports Balls Used in Gym Class		
Mandy football	Twyla soccer ball	Steph basketball
Clem basketball	Devon football	Paula basketball
Norm basketball	Allen soccer ball	Denzel golf ball

2. Caley conducted a survey to find out where her friends went last time they were in the car. Her results are listed.

Most Recent Car Trip		
dentist	school	store
store	baseball practice	baseball practice
school	store	store

3. Refer to Exercise 1. Which type of sports ball was used least often in class? What is the difference between the number of sports balls used most often and the number used least?

4. How many friends were surveyed in Exercise 2? The same number of friends responded for which two car trips?

PART **C**

PAGES 292–293

Solve. Use the *make a list* strategy.

1. The coins in Marta's pocket add up to 15¢. How many combinations of coins could there be in her pocket?

2. Nita has a white scarf, a blue scarf, and a pink scarf. She also has purple mittens, pink mittens, and green mittens. How many combinations of scarves and mittens can Nita make?

3. Paul has a red pen, a blue pen, a green pen, and a purple pen. He told his friend to take two pens. How many different pairs of pens could his friend take?

4. Mr. Williams asked his students to make as many three-digit numbers as they could using the digits 3, 5, and 7 one time in each number. How many three-digit numbers could his students make?

Multi-Part Lesson 6-2 Graphs with Pictures

PART Ⓐ Ⓑ

1. Display the set of data in a picture graph. Then write a sentence that interprets the data.

Favorite Vegetable	
Vegetables	**Students**
Green beans	6
Carrots	5
Corn	8
Potatoes	7
Broccoli	5

2. Display the set of data in a pictograph. Then write a sentence that interprets the data.

Instruments Played by Third Graders	
Instrument	**Students**
Piano	10
Flute	3
Guitar	6
Drums	7

For Exercises 3–6, refer to the pictograph.

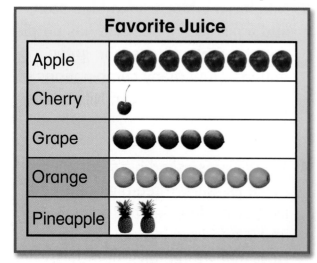

3. How many students does the pictograph represent?

4. How many students liked the least favorite pet?

5. What are the two favorite pets?

6. What is the difference in the number of students who like cats the best and those who like birds the best?

For Exercises 7–10 refer to the picture graph.

Favorite Juice

Apple	🍎🍎🍎🍎🍎🍎🍎🍎
Cherry	🍒
Grape	🍇🍇🍇🍇🍇
Orange	🍊🍊🍊🍊🍊🍊
Pineapple	🍍🍍

7. How many students does the picture graph represent?

8. How many more students like apple juice more than orange juice?

9. Could you say that more students like cherry and grape juice than like orange juice? Explain.

10. How would the pictures on the graph change if this was a pictograph and the key showed each piece of fruit stood for 2?

Multi-Part Lesson 6-3 Bar Graphs

PART Ⓐ Ⓑ

PAGES 302–307

1. Display the set of data in a vertical bar graph.

Average Length of Adult Male Animals	
Animal	**Length**
Alligator	11 feet
Hippopotamus	15 feet
Otter	3 feet
Tiger	9 feet

2. Display the set of data in a horizontal bar graph.

Most Popular Pets	
Animal	**Tally**
Bird	卌 ‖
Cat	卌 卌 卌 ‖
Dog	卌 卌 卌 卌 卌
Snake	‖

3. If you lined up the animals from Exercise 1 end-to-end, how far would they stretch?

4. In Exercise 2, can you tell what the most popular pet is without counting tallies? Explain.

For Exercises 5–7, refer to the bar graph.

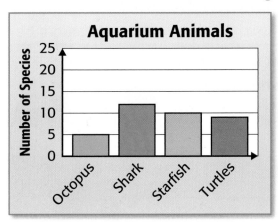

5. There are twice as many starfish species as what sea animal at the aquarium?

6. How would you find the total number of species represented by the graph?

7. Which two sea animals have close to the same number of species at the aquarium?

Multi-Part Lesson 6-4 Line Plots

PART Ⓐ

PAGES 310–313

Display each set of data in a line plot.

1.

Books Read in One Week	
Number of Books	**Students**
None	0
One	4
Two	9
Three	5
Four	4
Five	2

2.

Hours Spent on the Computer on the Weekend	
Hours	**Students**
None	卌 ‖
One	卌
Two	卌 ‖‖
Three	‖
Four	‖‖
Five	

Multi-Part Lesson 6-4 Line Plots (continued)

PART B   PAGES 314–315

Use any strategy to solve each problem.

1. Julie had a pizza party for 7 of her friends. She ordered 4 large pizzas. Each pizza was cut into 10 slices. Is it reasonable to say that each person got at least 6 slices of pizza? Explain.

2. Joey bought a notebook for $2 and paint set for $4. He paid for them with two $5-bills. Is it reasonable to say that Joey has enough money left over to buy 2 sets of paintbrushes for $3 each? Explain.

3. At soccer camp, there are 220 drinks in coolers. There are 3 kinds of drinks. There are 64 bottles of water and 78 bottles of sports drinks. Is it reasonable to say that there are about 115 bottles of juice? Explain.

4. Juan walks to and from school every day. His school is 9 blocks from his house. Is it reasonable to say that Juan walks about 150 blocks to and from school every 5 days? Explain.

Multi-Part Lesson 6-5 Probability

PART A   PAGES 316–319

Describe the probability of landing on each number or color. Write *certain, likely, unlikely,* or *impossible.*

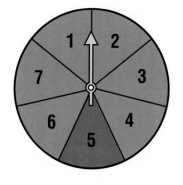

1. a number that is less than 5

2. a number that is between 0 and 8

3. an odd number

4. a number that is less than 2

5. orange

6. red

7. blue

8. not yellow

PART B   PAGES 320–323

The line plot shows the results from Miguel spinning a spinner with 6 numbers.

1. How many times did Miguel spin the spinner?

2. Which numbers would it be reasonable to say are on the spinner?

3. Which number do you think the spinner will land on next?

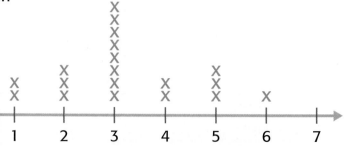

Spin the Spinner

Multi-Part Lesson 7-1 Geometric Figures

PART A   PAGES 335–337

Describe each figure as a *point, line, ray,* or *line segment*.

1.

2.

3.

4.

5.

6.

Classify each pair of lines as *intersecting, perpendicular,* or *parallel*.

7.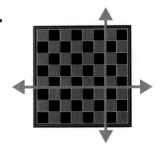

8.

9.

PART B C   PAGES 338–343

Describe each two-dimensional figure. Use the terms *sides* and *angles*. Then identify the figure.

1.

2.

3.

4.

5.

6.

Identify each polygon.

7. A closed figure that has 6 sides and 6 angles.

8. A polygon that has 5 sides and 5 angles.

Multi-Part Lesson 7-1 Geometric Figures (continued)

Describe and identify each quadrilateral. Classify the angle shown as a *right, less than* a right, or *greater than* a right angle.

1.

2.

3.

4.

5.

6.

Solve. Use the *guess, check, and revise* strategy.

1. Sara made 8 putts at the miniature golf course. Each putt was about 50 cm long. About how many meters was the total length of all the putts?

2. Each car on an amusement park ride holds 15 people. There are 20 cars on the ride. How many people can the ride hold?

3. Each week David practices his violin for 9 hours. Monday through Friday he practices the same number of minutes. He practices twice as long Saturday and Sunday. How long does he practice each day?

4. There are 12 dog pens in an animal shelter. Each pen can hold about 6 large dogs or 10 small dogs. Is there enough room for 90 small dogs and 20 large dogs? Explain.

Identify each three-dimensional figure.

1.

2.

3.

Classify each three-dimensional figure.

4. This figure has 1 edge, 1 face, and 1 vertex.

5. This figure has 6 square faces.

Multi-Part Lesson 7-2 Spatial Reasoning

PART **A** **B**

PAGES 356–359

Tell whether each pair of figures is *congruent* or *similar*.

1.    **2.**    **3.**

4.    **5.**    **6.**

7. Each side of a hexagon measures 6 inches. What will each side of a congruent hexagon measure?

8. Explain why the figures below are not congruent.

PART **C** **D** **E**

PAGES 360–366

**Tell whether each figure has a line of symmetry. Write *yes* or *no*.
If yes, tell how many lines of symmetry the figure has.**

1.    **2.** 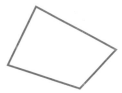   **3.**

4.   **5.**   **6.**

Multi-Part Lesson 7-2 Spatial Reasoning (continued)

PART F

Use any strategy to solve each problem.

1. Louis stopped working at 5:00. He pulled weeds for 2 hours, and he took a $\frac{1}{2}$-hour break. He raked leaves for $1\frac{1}{2}$ hours. What time did he start working?

2. Mei has 7 green marbles, 8 blue marbles, and 3 times as many red marbles as green ones. How many marbles does she have altogether?

3. Bailey wants to buy yo-yos to give as party favors. Each yo-yo costs $2. She has $25. Will she have enough money to buy 10 yo-yos? How much will it cost?

4. Cameron collected 80 stamps in the last 5 years. In the second year he collected 23 more stamps than he did the first year. He collected 5 stamps in his third and fourth years. His fifth year he collected 7 stamps. How many stamps did Cameron collect his first year?

Multi-Part Lesson 8-1 Patterns

PART A

Represent and extend each pattern using words.

1.

2.

Represent each pattern using words. Then solve.

3. Glenda makes a tile pattern. The first row has 2 blue tiles. The second row has 4 blue tiles and the third row has 8 blue tiles. How many blue tiles are in each of the next two rows?

4. If the pattern below continues until there are 20 polygons, how many squares will there be altogether?

Multi-Part Lesson 8-1 Patterns (continued)

Identify a pattern. Then find the missing numbers.

1. 9, 12, 15, ■, 21, 24

2. 26, 31, ■, 41, 46, 51

3. 77, 71, 65, ■, 53, 47

4. 11, 15, ■, 23, 27, 31

5. 99, ■, 85, 78, 71, ■

6. 55, ■, 45, ■, 35, 30

7. 20, ■, 60, 80, ■

8. 86, 94, 102, ■, 118, ■

9. 700, 600, ■, 400, ■, 200

10. 85, ■, ■, 112, 121, 130

Identify the pattern from a hundred chart. Then find the missing numbers.

11.

	57	
	67	
76		

12.

51			
		63	

13.

31		
		43

Solve. Use the *look for a pattern* strategy.

1. An oak tree was 3 feet tall after 1 year. After 3 years, it was 9 feet tall. If the tree grows the same amount each year, how tall will the tree be after 5 years?

2. Carlos is making a castle. For each tower, he uses 6 triangle blocks and 8 square blocks. If Carlos makes 4 towers on his castle, how many more square blocks than triangle blocks will he use?

3. Suki ran one lap on a track in 84 seconds. The next week, she ran the same lap in 81 seconds. If she continues to decrease her time by 3 seconds each week how many seconds will it take her to run the lap on the 4th week?

4. The dancers in a play are arranged in a pattern by height. The first student is 50 inches tall, the second is 47 inches tall, the third is 52 inches tall, and the fourth is 49 inches tall. If the pattern continues, how tall is the fifth student?

Multi-Part Lesson 8-1 Patterns (continued)

PART (D) (E)

PAGES 392–397

1. Represent the pattern in a graph and with words.
   6, 11, 16, 21, 26, 31, ■, ■

2. Jeff kept a log of the miles he ran each time he trained for the upcoming marathon. The first five entries in the log are 12, 10, 14, 12, and 16. Write the pattern in words. If the pattern continues, what will the next two entries be?

Represent each pattern with words. Then extend the graph.

3.
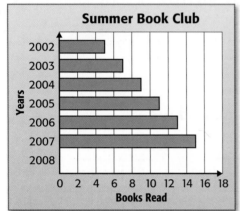

4.
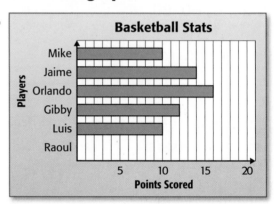

Multi-Part Lesson 8-2 Number Sentences

PART (A) (B)

PAGES 400–405

Use numbers and an operation to write each phrase as an expression.

1. the product of 7 and 4
2. 24 pens divided among 4 people
3. 5 groups of 8 people each
4. 9 more than 16
5. difference between 30 and 6
6. 8 less than 23
7. 22 and 10 more
8. 4 times as many as 5
9. 4 bunches with 3 bananas in each
10. 81 campers in 9 equal groups

PART (C)

PAGES 406–409

Write a number sentence for each situation. Use models if needed.

1. Last year, Pedro was 48 inches tall. Now he is 53 inches tall. How many inches did Pedro grow since last year?

2. How much change will Anwon receive if he buys two boxes of baseball cards for $19 each and he pays with a $50-bill?

Solve each number sentence by finding the unknown.

3. $21 + 40 = $ ■
4. $27 - $ ■ $ = 9$
5. $19 + 11 + 5 = $ ■
6. $17 + $ ■ $ = 24$
7. $35 - 7 = $ ■
8. $37 + 4 = $ ■

Multi-Part Lesson 8-2 Number Sentences (continued)

PART **D** PAGES 410–413

Write an expression. Then write an equation to solve.

1. A pet store has 32 hamsters and 17 turtles. How many more hamsters than turtles are there?

2. Thomas had $97 in his piggy bank. His uncle put $15 more into the piggy bank. How much does Thomas have in his piggy bank now?

3. Jocelyn's mother has 75 apples. She uses 23 of the apples to make pies. How many apples are left?

4. There are 116 dogs in a park. Of these dogs, 28 are Labrador Retrievers. How many dogs are not Labrador Retrievers?

Multi-Part Lesson 8-3 Function Tables

PART **A** PAGES 414–417

Find and extend the rule for each table. Then copy and complete.

1.

Rule:	
Input	**Output**
4	20
6	▨
8	40
9	▨

2.

Rule:	
Input	**Output**
3	21
▨	28
5	▨
6	42

3.

Rule:	
Input	**Output**
4	▨
▨	20
6	24
7	28

PART **B** PAGES 418–421

Copy each function table and extend the pattern.

1.

Rule: $\triangle + 9$	
Input $\triangle$	**Output**
3	▨
4	▨
5	▨
6	▨

2.

Rule: $\triangle - 6$	
Input $\triangle$	**Output**
20	▨
18	▨
16	▨
14	▨

3.

Rule: $\triangle + 11$	
Input $\triangle$	**Output**
9	▨
10	▨
11	▨
12	▨

Make a function table for each situation. Write the function rule.

4. Hannah is 10 years old. Her brother is 3 years younger than she is. How old will her brother be when Hannah is 11, 12, 13, and 14 years old?

5. Each book Quincy writes has 5 extra pages for drawings. How many pages will a book have that has 8, 9, 10, and 11 pages of writing?

Multi-Part Lesson 8-3 Function Tables (continued)

PART **C** PAGES 422–423

Use any strategy to solve each problem.

1. Four teams in a tournament have to play every team once. The top two teams then play each other. How many games will the top two teams play?

2. Hugo has 8 baseballs left. He gave 3 baseballs to each of his 5 brothers. He gave 4 baseballs to his sister. How many baseballs did Hugo have at first?

3. Shani is making a bracelet. She will use 2 different colored beads. She can choose from a blue, green, yellow, purple, and pink bead. How many different bead combinations could she choose?

4. The perimeter of a rectangular yard is 24 feet. What are the possible lengths of the sides in whole units?

PART **D** PAGES 424–427

Copy each function table and extend the pattern.

1.

Rule: △ × 6	
Input △	Output
7	
8	
9	
10	

2.

Rule: △ ÷ 8	
Input △	Output
40	
32	
24	
16	

3.

Rule: △ × 3	
Input △	Output
9	
10	
11	
12	

Multi-Part Lesson 9-1 Understand Fractions

PART **A** **B** PAGES 441–445

Write the fraction for the part that is blue. Then write the fraction for the part that is *not* blue. Label your answers.

1.

2.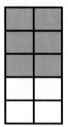

3.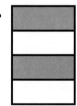

4.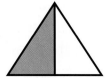

5.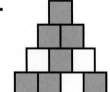

6.

Multi-Part Lesson 9-1 Understand Fractions (continued)

PART C PAGES 446–449

Write the fraction for the part of the set that is yellow. Then write the fraction for the part of the set that is *not* yellow. Label your answers.

1.

2.

PART D PAGES 450–451

Solve. Use the *draw a picture* strategy.

1. John and Ben played 8 games of checkers. John won 2 more games than Ben did. What fraction of the games did each boy win?

2. There were 24 cherries in a bowl. Tara took $\frac{1}{4}$ of them. Yuri took $\frac{1}{8}$ of them. How many cherries were left in the bowl?

3. Carli practiced dancing for $\frac{3}{6}$ of an hour. Lauren practiced for $\frac{3}{4}$ of an hour. Who practiced longer?

4. Alisha sliced a pizza into 10 pieces. She ate $\frac{3}{5}$ of the pizza. How many slices are left?

Multi-Part Lesson 9-2 Compare and Order Fractions

PART A B PAGES 452–457

Use the models to compare. Use >, <, or =.

1.

$\frac{1}{4}$	$\frac{1}{4}$		

$\frac{1}{4}$	$\frac{1}{4}$	$\frac{1}{4}$	

$\frac{2}{4}$ ● $\frac{3}{4}$

2.

$\frac{1}{6}$	$\frac{1}{6}$	$\frac{1}{6}$	$\frac{1}{6}$		

$\frac{1}{6}$	$\frac{1}{6}$				

$\frac{4}{6}$ ● $\frac{2}{6}$

Use the number line and benchmarks to compare. Use >, <, or =.

3.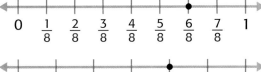

$\frac{6}{8}$ ● $\frac{4}{6}$

4.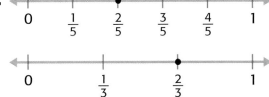

$\frac{2}{5}$ ● $\frac{2}{3}$

Multi-Part Lesson 9-2 Compare and Order Fractions (continued)

PART **C** PAGES 458–460

Use models to order each set of fractions from least to greatest.

1. $\frac{7}{8}, \frac{3}{4}, \frac{1}{4}$

2. $\frac{3}{6}, \frac{5}{6}, \frac{1}{6}$

3. $\frac{5}{12}, \frac{3}{4}, \frac{2}{4}$

4. $\frac{2}{5}, \frac{3}{10}, \frac{7}{10}$

5. $\frac{1}{3}, \frac{1}{8}, \frac{1}{6}$

6. $\frac{1}{2}, \frac{3}{5}, \frac{3}{10}$

7. Jordan bought three pieces of wood to repair the fence gate. The pieces were $\frac{1}{2}$, $\frac{2}{3}$, and $\frac{5}{8}$ of an inch thick. List the thicknesses in order from the least to the greatest.

8. Hamburger Haven is $\frac{2}{3}$ mile from Quenten's house. The grocery store is $\frac{1}{2}$ mile from his house, and the library is $\frac{3}{8}$ mile from his house. List the three distances, in order, from the least to the greatest.

Multi-Part Lesson 9-3 Equivalent Fractions

PART **A** PAGES 462–463

Use any strategy to solve each problem.

1. Josh rolled two number cubes at once. The sum of the numbers was 10. The difference was 2. What two numbers did Josh roll?

2. Lille bought a salad for $2 and a bowl of soup for $1. She has $7 left. How much money did she have before she bought lunch?

3. For every blue headband Kitty has, she has 3 white ones and 2 red ones. Kitty has 3 blue headbands. How many white and red headbands does she have?

4. Alex delivered 26 papers on one block. He delivered half as many on another block. How many papers did Alex deliver?

PART **B** **C** **D** PAGES 464–469

Complete each number sentence to find equivalent fractions.

1.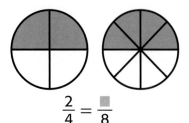

$$\frac{2}{4} = \frac{\blacksquare}{8}$$

2.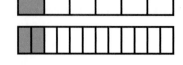

$$\frac{1}{6} = \frac{\blacksquare}{12}$$

3.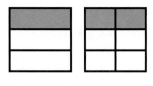

$$\frac{\blacksquare}{3} = \frac{\blacksquare}{6}$$

Find each missing value. Use models if needed.

4. $\frac{2}{3} = \frac{\blacksquare}{12}$

5. $\frac{3}{5} = \frac{\blacksquare}{10}$

6. $\frac{2}{6} = \frac{\blacksquare}{3}$

Multi-Part Lesson 9-4 Add and Subtract Fractions

PAGES 472–477

PART **A** **B**

Add. Use fraction models if needed.

1. $\frac{2}{4} + \frac{1}{4}$

2. $\frac{3}{6} + \frac{2}{6}$

3. $\frac{5}{10} + \frac{3}{10}$

4. $\frac{3}{12} + \frac{4}{12}$

5. $\frac{3}{9} + \frac{5}{9}$

6. $\frac{2}{7} + \frac{3}{7}$

7. $\frac{3}{4} + \frac{1}{4}$

8. $\frac{3}{5} + \frac{1}{5}$

9. $\frac{5}{8} + \frac{2}{8}$

PART **C** **D**

PAGES 478–483

Subtract. Use fraction models if needed.

1. $\frac{5}{8} - \frac{2}{8}$

2. $\frac{7}{12} - \frac{4}{12}$

3. $\frac{5}{10} - \frac{2}{10}$

4. $1 - \frac{2}{5}$

5. $\frac{4}{6} - \frac{3}{6}$

6. $\frac{1}{4} - \frac{1}{4}$

7. $\frac{7}{8} - \frac{5}{8}$

8. $\frac{8}{9} - \frac{4}{9}$

9. $\frac{3}{7} - \frac{2}{7}$

Multi-Part Lesson 10-1 Understand Mixed Numbers

PART **A** **B**

PAGES 495–501

Write a mixed number and an improper fraction for each model.

1.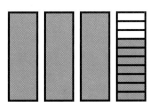

2.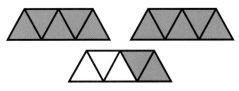

3.

4.

Identify each point. Write as a mixed number.

5.  $A =$

$B =$

6. $C =$

$D =$

Multi-Part Lesson 10-1 Understand Mixed Numbers (continued)

PART C PAGES 502–503

Solve. Use the *make a model* strategy.

1. The measurements for Marcy's outdoor turtle pen are shown. She wants to lengthen the longest sides of the pen by adding $2\frac{1}{2}$ feet of fencing to each of these sides. How long will each of those sides be?

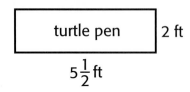

turtle pen | 2 ft

$5\frac{1}{2}$ ft

3. A recipe for peach pie uses $1\frac{1}{8}$ cups of sugar. How much sugar is needed for 4 pies?

2. If this pattern unit repeats, how many triangles will there be after 12 more shapes are added?

4. Elizabeth feeds her hamster in the morning each day. She feeds her cat every morning and evening. Her lizard eats once every three days. In 6 days, how many times will she feed her pets?

Multi-Part Lesson 10-2 Compare and Order Mixed Numbers

PART A PAGES 508–511

Compare the mixed numbers. Use >, <, or =.

1.   ●

$1\frac{3}{4}$ ● $2\frac{1}{4}$

2.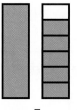

$1\frac{5}{6}$ ● $1\frac{3}{4}$

3.

$2\frac{3}{5}$ ● $2\frac{3}{4}$

Use the number line to order the mixed numbers from least to greatest.

4. $2\frac{5}{6}, 2\frac{2}{6}, 2\frac{1}{2}$

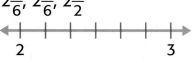

2   3

5. $3\frac{4}{8}, 3\frac{3}{4}, 3\frac{1}{4}$

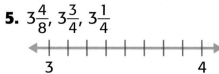

3   4

PART (B)

Use any strategy to solve each problem.

1. A book is the middle book on a shelf. There are 7 books to the right of this book. How many books are on the shelf in all?

2. Janet made 2 out of every 5 basketball shots she took. She made 12 shots. How many shots did she take?

3. Freddie ate 3 pieces of pizza. Tim ate 2 more pieces than Freddie. Half of the pizza is left. How many pieces were there to begin with?

4. Three friends have 8 video games each. If each friend sells 2, how many video games are left altogether?

PART (C) (D)

Complete the number sentence to name the equivalent mixed number.

1.

$$2\frac{1}{3} = 2\frac{\blacksquare}{6}$$

2.

$$1\frac{1}{2} = 1\frac{2}{\blacksquare}$$

Write the mixed number for the part that is shaded. Then find the equivalent mixed number.

3.

4.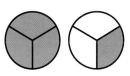

A.

A.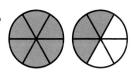

B.

B.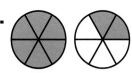

Multi-Part Lesson 11-1 Measure Length

PART (A) (B)   PAGES 529–534

Estimate each length. Then measure each to the nearest $\frac{1}{2}$ inch.

1.

2.

PART (C)   PAGES 536–539

**Choose the most appropriate unit to measure each length.
Write *inch, foot, yard,* or *mile.***

1. length of a bicycle

2. distance from Texas to Georgia

3. width of a book

4. length of a semi-truck

Choose the better estimate.

5. width of a TV screen
19 yards or 19 inches

6. length of a slide
4 yards or 4 miles

7. length of a fork
8 feet or 8 inches

8. distance to the grocery store
3 inches or 3 miles

PART (D)   PAGES 540–541

Solve. Use the *solve a simpler problem* strategy.

1. A chessboard is a square with eight squares on each side. Each player begins with a playing piece on each square in the two rows closest to him or her. How many pieces are in a chess set?

2. There are 16 peaches, 8 plums, and 24 carrot sticks in the refrigerator. Toni took out 2 peaches, 3 plums, and 10 carrot sticks. Ali took out 2 plums, 8 carrot sticks, and one peach. How many of each is left?

3. Ben has 50 toy airplanes. Half of them are silver. There are 4 times as many blue planes as white planes. How many blue and white planes does Ben have?

4. Diego is using bricks to make a border around a flower bed. His border is a rectangle with 6 bricks on each of two sides and 8 bricks on each of the other two sides. How many bricks will he use altogether if he stacks two more bricks on top of each brick?

Multi-Part Lesson 11-1 Measure Length (continued)

PART E F

PAGES 542–549

Choose the most appropriate unit to measure each length. Write *centimeter, meter,* or *kilometer.*

1. length of a crayon

2. length of a rake

3. length of a soccer field

4. length of an ocean shoreline

Choose the better estimate.

5. length of an alligator
2 m or 2 cm

6. length of a pencil
13 km or 13 cm

7. width of California
480 cm or 480 km

8. length of a jet
62 km or 62 m

Multi-Part Lesson 11-2 Perimeter

PART A B

PAGES 551–555

Find the perimeter of each figure.

1.
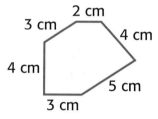

2.
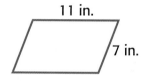

3.
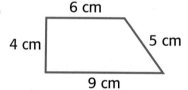

4.
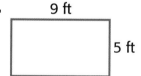

5.
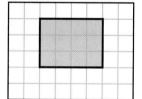

6.
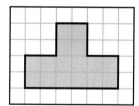

PART C

PAGES 556–557

Use any strategy to solve each problem.

1. A mall has 3 levels. Each level has 15 stores. Each store has 4 windows. How many windows are in the mall?

2. Ana is 120 cm tall. Her father is 200 cm tall. How much taller is Ana's father?

3. For every $5 that Henry saves, his dad gives him $3. When Henry has saved $100, how much will he have in all?

4. Stella bought 12 stickers and 4 posters. The stickers cost 3 for $0.25. The posters cost 2 for $6. How much did Stella spend?

Multi-Part Lesson 11-3 Area

PART **A** **B** PAGES 558–562

Find the area of each figure.

1.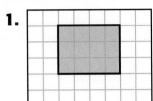

2.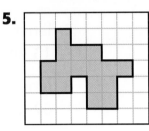

3.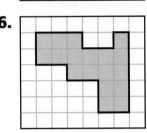

4.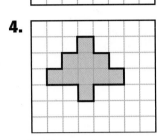

5.

6.

Multi-Part Lesson 12-1 Measure Capacity

PART **A** **B** PAGES 573–577

**Choose the most appropriate unit to measure each capacity.
Write *cup, pint, quart,* or *gallon.***

1. dog dish

2. milk bottle

3. cocoa

Choose the better estimate.

4. bathtub
50 c or 50 gal

5. bottle of shampoo
2 c or 2 qt

6. bottle of glue
1 gal or 1 c

7. can of wall paint
1 gal or 1 c

PART **C** PAGES 578–579

Solve. Use the *guess, check, and revise* strategy.

1. Ken bought some pencils for $0.60. He used 5 coins. What coins could Ken have used?

2. Mrs. Martinique will sew 8 buttons on 5 shirts and skirts. Each shirt will get 2 buttons and each skirt will get 1 button. How many shirts are there?

3. By the end of the game, the Wildcats had doubled their score and the Cheetahs had increased their score by 3 points. What was the total number of points scored by the end of the game?

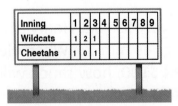

EP40 Extra Practice

Multi-Part Lesson 12-1 Measure Capacity (continued)

PART D

PAGES 580–582

**Choose the most appropriate unit to measure each capacity.
Write *milliliter* or *liter*.**

1. washing machine

2. test tube

3. drinking glass

4. shark aquarium

5. watering can

6. juice box

Choose the better estimate.

7. bathroom sink
8 mL or 8 L

8. tablespoon
15 mL or 15 L

9. large bottle of soda
2 mL or 2 L

Multi-Part Lesson 12-2 Measure Weight and Mass

PART A

PAGES 584–587

**Choose the most appropriate unit to measure the weight
of each object. Write *ounce* or *pound*.**

1. tennis ball

2. tiger

3. cell phone

4. pencil

5. television

6. fly

Choose the better estimate.

7. baseball bat
3 oz or 3 lb

8. frisbee
12 oz or 12 lb

9. an orange
6 oz or 6 lb

PART B

PAGES 590–593

**Choose the most appropriate unit to measure each mass.
Write *gram* or *kilogram*.**

1. bowling ball

2. grasshopper

3. wheelbarrow

4. golf ball

5. bag of pretzels

6. piece of chalk

Choose the better estimate.

7. zebra
300 g or 300 kg

8. penny
3 g or 3 kg

9. pumpkin
10 g or 10 kg

10. baseball
145 g or 145 kg

11. CD
15 g or 15 kg

12. microwave
20 g or 20 kg

Multi-Part Lesson 12-3 Measure Time and Temperature

PART A

PAGES 595–597

Write the time shown on each digital or analog clock.

1.

2.

3.

4.

5.

6.

PART B

PAGES 598–599

Use any strategy to solve each problem.

1. Kiri picks 500 g of blueberries every $\frac{1}{2}$ hour. How many hours will it take her to pick 3,000 g of blueberries?

2. Potatoes cost $2 for 3 kg at the grocery store. How much will 12 kg of potatoes cost?

3. Deanna walked 7 blocks to get to school. She took a different route on the way home that was 3 times as many blocks. How many blocks did Deanna walk that day?

4. Carmen and Rob played 60 games of checkers. Rob won twice as many games as Carmen did. How many games did each person win?

PART C

PAGES 600–603

The following are times of tennis matches. Find the length of each match.

1. Start Time   End Time

2. Start Time   End Time

Find each elapsed time.

3. The clock shows when Lydia started ice skating. It is 12:45 when she stops.

4. The clock shows when Helki's hockey practice started. It is 6:30 when practice ends.

Multi-Part Lesson 12-3 Measure Time and Temperature (continued)

PART D

PAGES 604–607

Use the calendars to solve.

			March			
S	M	T	W	T	F	S
		1	2	3	4	5
6	7	8	9	10	11	12
13	14	15	16	17	18	19
20	21	22	23	24	25	26
27	28	29	30	31		

			April			
S	M	T	W	T	F	S
					1	2
3	4	5	6	7	8	9
10	11	12	13	14	15	16
17	18	19	20	21	22	23
24	25	26	27	28	29	30

1. Peach Tree Elementary serves pizza for lunch on the second and fourth Friday of each month. What dates will pizza be served in the months of March and April?

2. Compare the number of Sundays to the number of Wednesdays in March and April. Use >, <, or =.

3. Marla begins spring break on March 25. She returns to school on April 4. How long is Marla's spring break?

4. What will be the date of the second Tuesday in May?

PART E

PAGES 608–609

Write the temperature in degrees Fahrenheit and degrees Celsius.

1.

2.
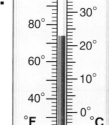

3. Use the thermometer above. Gabrielle's Fahrenheit thermometer shows that the temperature outside is 65°F. Mark lives next door and has a Celsius thermometer. What temperature should his thermometer show?

4. Water freezes at 0°C. Use the thermometer in Exercise 1 to determine the temperature at which water freezes on the Fahrenheit scale.

Multi-Part Lesson 13-1 Multiples of 10, 100, and 1,000

PART A
PAGES 621–623

Multiply. Use basic facts and patterns.

1. $3 \times 7 =$ ■
$3 \times 70 =$ ■
$3 \times 700 =$ ■
$3 \times 7,000 =$ ■

2. $5 \times 9 =$ ■
$5 \times 90 =$ ■
$5 \times 900 =$ ■
$5 \times 9,000 =$ ■

3. $8 \times 6 =$ ■
$8 \times 60 =$ ■
$8 \times 600 =$ ■
$8 \times 6,000 =$ ■

4. $9 \times 4 =$ ■
$9 \times 40 =$ ■
$9 \times 400 =$ ■
$9 \times 4,000 =$ ■

5. $7 \times 7 =$ ■
$7 \times 70 =$ ■
$7 \times 700 =$ ■
$7 \times 7,000 =$ ■

6. $6 \times 5 =$ ■
$6 \times 50 =$ ■
$6 \times 500 =$ ■
$6 \times 5,000 =$ ■

PART B
PAGES 624–627

Estimate. Round to the nearest ten.

1. $\begin{array}{r} 28 \\ \times\ 5 \\ \hline \end{array}$

2. $\begin{array}{r} 42 \\ \times\ 4 \\ \hline \end{array}$

3. $\begin{array}{r} 37 \\ \times\ 7 \\ \hline \end{array}$

Estimate. Round to the nearest hundred.

4. $\begin{array}{r} 170 \\ \times\ 6 \\ \hline \end{array}$

5. $\begin{array}{r} 210 \\ \times\ 8 \\ \hline \end{array}$

6. $\begin{array}{r} 390 \\ \times\ 5 \\ \hline \end{array}$

7. $\begin{array}{r} 289 \\ \times\ 3 \\ \hline \end{array}$

8. $\begin{array}{r} 113 \\ \times\ 9 \\ \hline \end{array}$

9. $\begin{array}{r} 274 \\ \times\ 6 \\ \hline \end{array}$

Multi-Part Lesson 13-2 Multiply Without Regrouping

PART A
PAGES 630–631

Solve. Use *logical reasoning.*

1. Four friends have different types of pets. Tina has a cat. Suni does not have a turtle. Ed does not have a dog. Mark does not have a dog or a snake. What type of pet does each person have?

2. Cameron got on the elevator and rode down 5 floors. Then she rode up 7 floors. She rode down 6 floors and got off on the 10th floor. What floor did she start on?

3. Curtis and Anna have change that has the same value. The value is under $1. Curtis has 7 coins. Anna has 4 coins. What two possible combinations could they have?

4. Andy drew 4 different shapes. A rectangle is on top. A triangle is on top of a square. A circle is not at the bottom. What is the order of the shapes from top to bottom?

Multi-Part Lesson 13-2 Multiply Without Regrouping (continued)

PART B   PAGES 632–634

Multiply. Use estimation to check.

1. 22
        × 3

2. 12
        × 4

3. 32
        × 3

4. 21 × 4

5. 43 × 2

6. 22 × 4

7. 2 × 34

8. 2 × 41

9. 3 × 31

Multi-Part Lesson 13-3 Multiply with Regrouping

PART A B   PAGES 636–641

Multiply. Use models if needed.

1. 29
        × 5

2. 33
        × 6

3. 51
        × 9

4. 25 × 4

5. 13 × 8

6. 23 × 5

7. 52 × 3

8. 24 × 7

9. 23 × 4

PART C   PAGES 642–643

Use any strategy to solve each problem.

1. Diana put 7 plums on one side of a scale. To balance the scale, she put 4 plums and 1 apple on the other side of the scale. Each plum weighs 2 ounces. How much does the apple weigh?

2. Troy, Andre, and Ana gathered 450 acorns. Troy gathered 5 times as many acorns as Ana. Andre gathered 3 times as many as Ana. How many acorns did each person collect?

3. Ms. McCoy has 3 pitchers of tea. Each pitcher holds 1 gallon of tea. How many cups of tea can she fill with the pitchers?

4. Alicia, Katie, and Megan each play a sport. Megan does not play soccer, Katie does not play basketball or tennis, and Alicia plays basketball. Which sport does each girl play?

PART D   PAGES 644–647

Multiply.

1. 214
       × 2

2. 128
       × 3

3. 405
       × 8

4. 160
       × 4

5. 391
       × 7

6. 286
       × 3

7. 622 × 3

8. 153 × 5

9. 112 × 9

Facts Practice

Addition

1. 2
  + 4

2. 6
  + 6

3. 1
  + 8

4. 9
  + 7

5. 3
  + 5

6. 4
  + 9

7. 7
  + 6

8. 10
  + 1

9. 7
  + 0

10. 2
  + 9

11. 3
  + 4

12. 6
  + 4

13. 5
  + 8

14. 1
  + 4

15. 2
  + 7

16. 9
  + 3

17. 5
  + 7

18. 9
  + 0

19. 10
  + 6

20. 8
  + 8

21. 5 + 4

22. 1 + 3

23. 6 + 5

24. 1 + 2

25. 10 + 3

26. 8 + 3

27. 4 + 7

28. 0 + 8

29. 6 + 8

30. 1 + 5

31. 3 + 6

32. 7 + 3

33. 0 + 4

34. 5 + 2

35. 7 + 8

36. 9 + 6

37. 0 + 3

38. 8 + 4

39. 10 + 7

40. 8 + 9

Addition

1. $\begin{array}{r} 6 \\ + 3 \\ \hline \end{array}$ **2.** $\begin{array}{r} 1 \\ + 9 \\ \hline \end{array}$ **3.** $\begin{array}{r} 2 \\ + 5 \\ \hline \end{array}$ **4.** $\begin{array}{r} 0 \\ + 10 \\ \hline \end{array}$

5. $\begin{array}{r} 1 \\ + 7 \\ \hline \end{array}$ **6.** $\begin{array}{r} 3 \\ + 7 \\ \hline \end{array}$ **7.** $\begin{array}{r} 3 \\ + 9 \\ \hline \end{array}$ **8.** $\begin{array}{r} 9 \\ + 9 \\ \hline \end{array}$

9. $\begin{array}{r} 5 \\ + 3 \\ \hline \end{array}$ **10.** $\begin{array}{r} 2 \\ + 10 \\ \hline \end{array}$ **11.** $\begin{array}{r} 4 \\ + 1 \\ \hline \end{array}$ **12.** $\begin{array}{r} 6 \\ + 7 \\ \hline \end{array}$

13. $\begin{array}{r} 9 \\ + 5 \\ \hline \end{array}$ **14.** $\begin{array}{r} 8 \\ + 1 \\ \hline \end{array}$ **15.** $\begin{array}{r} 4 \\ + 4 \\ \hline \end{array}$ **16.** $\begin{array}{r} 3 \\ + 8 \\ \hline \end{array}$

17. $\begin{array}{r} 10 \\ + 10 \\ \hline \end{array}$ **18.** $\begin{array}{r} 4 \\ + 3 \\ \hline \end{array}$ **19.** $\begin{array}{r} 7 \\ + 2 \\ \hline \end{array}$ **20.** $\begin{array}{r} 6 \\ + 0 \\ \hline \end{array}$

21. $5 + 1$ **22.** $4 + 6$ **23.** $3 + 3$ **24.** $8 + 7$

25. $2 + 6$ **26.** $0 + 5$ **27.** $10 + 4$ **28.** $9 + 8$

29. $7 + 7$ **30.** $8 + 5$ **31.** $9 + 10$ **32.** $3 + 2$

33. $10 + 8$ **34.** $1 + 6$ **35.** $8 + 10$ **36.** $5 + 5$

37. $2 + 2$ **38.** $7 + 9$ **39.** $10 + 5$ **40.** $8 + 6$

Facts Practice

Subtraction

1. $\begin{array}{r} 4 \\ -2 \\ \hline \end{array}$ 　　2. $\begin{array}{r} 11 \\ -2 \\ \hline \end{array}$ 　　3. $\begin{array}{r} 8 \\ -0 \\ \hline \end{array}$ 　　4. $\begin{array}{r} 12 \\ -9 \\ \hline \end{array}$

5. $\begin{array}{r} 10 \\ -5 \\ \hline \end{array}$ 　　6. $\begin{array}{r} 8 \\ -3 \\ \hline \end{array}$ 　　7. $\begin{array}{r} 13 \\ -6 \\ \hline \end{array}$ 　　8. $\begin{array}{r} 5 \\ -1 \\ \hline \end{array}$

9. $\begin{array}{r} 12 \\ -3 \\ \hline \end{array}$ 　　10. $\begin{array}{r} 7 \\ -1 \\ \hline \end{array}$ 　　11. $\begin{array}{r} 10 \\ -9 \\ \hline \end{array}$ 　　12. $\begin{array}{r} 6 \\ -4 \\ \hline \end{array}$

13. $\begin{array}{r} 10 \\ -1 \\ \hline \end{array}$ 　　14. $\begin{array}{r} 14 \\ -5 \\ \hline \end{array}$ 　　15. $\begin{array}{r} 7 \\ -7 \\ \hline \end{array}$ 　　16. $\begin{array}{r} 5 \\ -2 \\ \hline \end{array}$

17. $\begin{array}{r} 15 \\ -9 \\ \hline \end{array}$ 　　18. $\begin{array}{r} 8 \\ -2 \\ \hline \end{array}$ 　　19. $\begin{array}{r} 6 \\ -3 \\ \hline \end{array}$ 　　20. $\begin{array}{r} 13 \\ -9 \\ \hline \end{array}$

21. $7 - 2$ 　　**22.** $17 - 8$ 　　**23.** $10 - 3$ 　　**24.** $6 - 2$

25. $13 - 7$ 　　**26.** $15 - 6$ 　　**27.** $8 - 5$ 　　**28.** $5 - 3$

29. $11 - 4$ 　　**30.** $9 - 0$ 　　**31.** $12 - 8$ 　　**32.** $10 - 7$

33. $13 - 5$ 　　**34.** $7 - 3$ 　　**35.** $10 - 4$ 　　**36.** $6 - 0$

37. $10 - 2$ 　　**38.** $18 - 9$ 　　**39.** $14 - 7$ 　　**40.** $16 - 9$

Subtraction

1.   3
    − 2

2.   19
    − 10

3.   13
    − 4

4.   9
    − 7

5.   15
    − 5

6.   5
    − 5

7.   16
    − 8

8.   7
    − 5

9.   6
    − 1

10.   18
    − 10

11.   9
    − 6

12.   17
    − 9

13.   8
    − 4

14.   9
    − 1

15.   20
    − 10

16.   14
    − 6

17.   11
    − 3

18.   4
    − 3

19.   12
    − 7

20.   10
    − 8

21. $7 - 6$

22. $19 - 9$

23. $16 - 7$

24. $9 - 4$

25. $17 - 7$

26. $11 - 5$

27. $6 - 6$

28. $8 - 1$

29. $5 - 0$

30. $15 - 8$

31. $10 - 6$

32. $14 - 9$

33. $12 - 5$

34. $10 - 0$

35. $9 - 8$

36. $6 - 5$

37. $7 - 0$

38. $8 - 6$

39. $14 - 7$

40. $12 - 6$

Facts Practice

Multiplication

1. 2
   $\times\ 2$

2. 4
   $\times\ 3$

3. 5
   $\times\ 8$

4. 4
   $\times\ 0$

5. 8
   $\times\ 8$

6. 7
   $\times\ 8$

7. 9
   $\times\ 7$

8. 1
   $\times\ 6$

9. 4
   $\times\ 10$

10. 6
   $\times\ 8$

11. 5
   $\times\ 3$

12. 0
   $\times\ 2$

13. 9
   $\times\ 9$

14. 5
   $\times\ 1$

15. 8
   $\times\ 3$

16. 5
   $\times\ 7$

17. 0
   $\times\ 5$

18. 6
   $\times\ 3$

19. 10
   $\times\ 1$

20. 9
   $\times\ 6$

21. 4×7

22. 3×1

23. 2×8

24. 6×7

25. 8×4

26. 3×3

27. 6×0

28. 2×5

29. 5×6

30. 4×6

31. 3×9

32. 7×10

33. 9×2

34. 4×1

35. 0×10

36. 4×5

37. 1×7

38. 8×9

39. 6×6

40. 10×9

Multiplication

1. 1
  × 1

2. 10
  × 2

3. 5
  × 5

4. 8
  × 6

5. 7
  × 4

6. 3
  × 0

7. 9
  × 8

8. 5
  × 2

9. 8
  × 1

10. 6
  × 5

11. 7
  × 2

12. 9
  × 3

13. 5
  × 9

14. 6
  × 10

15. 7
  × 7

16. 0
  × 6

17. 4
  × 2

18. 2
  × 9

19. 10
  × 0

20. 7
  × 5

21. 1×9

22. 3×6

23. 4×8

24. 5×10

25. 2×3

26. 10×8

27. 7×0

28. 6×4

29. 4×10

30. 6×2

31. 0×4

32. 4×4

33. 1×0

34. 7×6

35. 9×4

36. 3×5

37. 8×0

38. 10×7

39. 8×7

40. 7×3

Multiplication **EP51**

Facts Practice

Division

1. $5\overline{)5}$ **2.** $10\overline{)20}$ **3.** $7\overline{)28}$ **4.** $9\overline{)18}$

5. $3\overline{)21}$ **6.** $6\overline{)60}$ **7.** $5\overline{)0}$ **8.** $8\overline{)56}$

9. $4\overline{)24}$ **10.** $10\overline{)30}$ **11.** $5\overline{)45}$ **12.** $1\overline{)3}$

13. $8\overline{)80}$ **14.** $10\overline{)0}$ **15.** $2\overline{)2}$ **16.** $5\overline{)30}$

17. $2\overline{)20}$ **18.** $6\overline{)18}$ **19.** $3\overline{)27}$ **20.** $5\overline{)35}$

21. $16 \div 2$ **22.** $72 \div 9$ **23.** $3 \div 3$ **24.** $48 \div 8$

25. $9 \div 1$ **26.** $12 \div 3$ **27.** $8 \div 4$ **28.** $2 \div 1$

29. $40 \div 4$ **30.** $27 \div 9$ **31.** $0 \div 9$ **32.** $6 \div 2$

33. $54 \div 6$ **34.** $63 \div 7$ **35.** $36 \div 4$ **36.** $15 \div 5$

37. $32 \div 8$ **38.** $36 \div 4$ **39.** $6 \div 3$ **40.** $35 \div 7$

Division

1. $4\overline{)16}$

2. $10\overline{)50}$

3. $1\overline{)1}$

4. $6\overline{)48}$

5. $3\overline{)0}$

6. $7\overline{)56}$

7. $9\overline{)27}$

8. $5\overline{)25}$

9. $9\overline{)90}$

10. $6\overline{)36}$

11. $2\overline{)14}$

12. $4\overline{)32}$

13. $1\overline{)5}$

14. $8\overline{)72}$

15. $3\overline{)15}$

16. $7\overline{)0}$

17. $10\overline{)70}$

18. $2\overline{)18}$

19. $8\overline{)64}$

20. $1\overline{)8}$

21. $12 \div 4$

22. $10 \div 2$

23. $45 \div 9$

24. $36 \div 9$

25. $60 \div 10$

26. $10 \div 1$

27. $42 \div 7$

28. $9 \div 3$

29. $8 \div 8$

30. $81 \div 9$

31. $36 \div 6$

32. $20 \div 4$

33. $10 \div 5$

34. $54 \div 9$

35. $8 \div 2$

36. $49 \div 7$

37. $4 \div 1$

38. $40 \div 8$

39. $0 \div 6$

40. $100 \div 10$

Facts Practice

Mixed Operations

1. $\begin{array}{r} 12 \\ -\ 7 \\ \hline \end{array}$

2. $\begin{array}{r} 8 \\ +\ 3 \\ \hline \end{array}$

3. $\begin{array}{r} 5 \\ \times\ 8 \\ \hline \end{array}$

4. $\begin{array}{r} 3 \\ -\ 1 \\ \hline \end{array}$

5. $\begin{array}{r} 4 \\ \times\ 3 \\ \hline \end{array}$

6. $\begin{array}{r} 2 \\ +\ 5 \\ \hline \end{array}$

7. $\begin{array}{r} 13 \\ -\ 7 \\ \hline \end{array}$

8. $\begin{array}{r} 4 \\ +\ 8 \\ \hline \end{array}$

9. $\begin{array}{r} 9 \\ -\ 9 \\ \hline \end{array}$

10. $\begin{array}{r} 8 \\ +\ 6 \\ \hline \end{array}$

11. $\begin{array}{r} 6 \\ \times\ 5 \\ \hline \end{array}$

12. $\begin{array}{r} 3 \\ +\ 9 \\ \hline \end{array}$

13. $\begin{array}{r} 4 \\ +\ 4 \\ \hline \end{array}$

14. $\begin{array}{r} 9 \\ \times\ 4 \\ \hline \end{array}$

15. $\begin{array}{r} 7 \\ \times\ 6 \\ \hline \end{array}$

16. $\begin{array}{r} 11 \\ -\ 4 \\ \hline \end{array}$

17. $\begin{array}{r} 3 \\ \times\ 0 \\ \hline \end{array}$

18. $\begin{array}{r} 13 \\ -\ 9 \\ \hline \end{array}$

19. $\begin{array}{r} 15 \\ -\ 8 \\ \hline \end{array}$

20. $\begin{array}{r} 4 \\ \times\ 7 \\ \hline \end{array}$

21. $5\overline{)15}$

22. $8 + 8$

23. 2×7

24. $25 \div 5$

25. $13 - 6$

26. $9\overline{)63}$

27. $49 \div 7$

28. 6×6

29. $5 + 8$

30. $15 - 9$

31. $4\overline{)20}$

32. $9 - 0$

33. $9\overline{)54}$

34. $3\overline{)0}$

35. 8×0

36. 1×2

37. $17 - 8$

38. $7 + 0$

39. $10 - 8$

40. $10 \div 5$

Photo Credits

iv Comstock Images/Getty Images; vi (tl tr)The McGraw-Hill Companies, (bl br)Doug Martin; ix David R. Frazier Photolibrary, Inc./Alamy; x Dynamic Graphics Group/PunchStock; xi James Balog/age fotostock; xii Robert McGouey/Alamy; xiii Glowimages/Getty Images; xiv Tom Brakefield/Stockbyte/Getty Images; xv Allan Baxter/Photodisc/Getty Images; xvi Getty Images; xviii (bl)Burke/Triolo Productions/Brand X Pictures/Getty Images, (br)Siede Preis/Getty Images; xix (honeybee)Frank Greenaway/Dorling Kindersley/Getty Images, (housefly)James Cotier/Stone/Getty Images, (lightning bug)Burke/Triolo Productions/Brand X Pictures/Getty Images, (ladybug)Photodisc/Getty Images; xx The McGraw-Hill Companies; xxi (br) The McGraw-Hill Companies, (bc)Getty Images, (cr)Spike Mafford/Getty Images; xxii Tom Brakefield/Digital Vision/Getty Images; xxiii Cre8tive Studios/Alamy; 0 Ed-Imaging; 1 Creatas/PunchStock; 4 CORBIS; 6 Ryan McVay/Getty Images; 7 (t)C Squared Studios/Getty Images, (b)Mark Steinmetz; 8 (t)Dynamic Graphics Group/PunchStock, (c)PhotoAlto/PunchStock, (b)Mark Steinmetz; 9 (c cl)Mark Steinmetz, (cr)Comstock/Punchstock, (br)Photodisc/Getty Images; 13 Ed-Imaging; 16 Image Source/Getty Images; 20 Steve Allen/Brand X Pictures/Getty Images; 21 Photodisc Collection/Getty Images; 24 David Kjaer/Nature Picture Library; 25 Steve Allen/Brand X Pictures/Getty Images; 26 Digital Vision, Ltd.; 32 (cl)Car Culture/Collection Mix: Subjects/Getty Images, (cr)G.K. & Vikki Hart/Getty Images; 34–35 CORBIS; 36 Ken Karp/The McGraw-Hill Companies; 39 (tr)PhotoLink/Getty Images, (br)Ed-Imaging; 41 James Balog/age fotostock; 43 (bl)Photos.com/Jupiterimages, (bcl)Getty Images, (bcr)Siede Preis/Getty Images, (br)Ryan McVay/Getty Images; 44 Thomas Northcut/Digital Vision/Getty Images; 47 49 50 Michael Houghton/StudiOhio; 51 (c)Michael Houghton/StudiOhio, (bl)The McGraw-Hill Companies, (bc)Photolibrary, (br)Mark Steinmetz; 52 (tl tc)Mark Steinmetz, (tr)C Squared Studios/Getty Images, (cr)Michael Houghton/StudiOhio; 53 57 Michael Houghton/StudiOhio; 58 (tl)Michael Houghton/StudiOhio, (c cl)Mark Steinmetz; 61 Michael Houghton/StudiOhio; 68 (c)Image Source/Punchstock, (cr)Index Stock Imagery; 72 Ed-Imaging; 74 David De Lossy/Getty Images; 75 Comstock Images/Alamy; 77 Mark Steinmetz; 78 Lori Adamski Peek/Stone/Getty Images; 80 Tim Jones/Getty Images; 81 Michael Newman/PhotoEdit; 83 (tr)Getty Images, (bl)C Squared Studios/Getty Images, (bc)Mark Steinmetz, (br)Jeremy Woodhouse/Getty Images; 84 (tr)Richard Hutchings/Digital Light Source, (br)Ed-Imaging; 85 (tc)CORBIS, (tr)The McGraw-Hill Companies; 86 Richard Cummins/Lonely Planet Images/Getty Images; 87 Gavin Hellier/The Image Bank/Getty Images; 92 McGraw-Hill Companies; 93 (tl)Purestock/PunchStock, (tr)Robert McGouey/Alamy; 99 (tr)Timothy A. Clary/AFP/Getty Images, (br)Butch Adams/Stone Collection/Getty Images; 100 (inset)David McNew/Getty Images News/Getty Images; 100–101 (bkgd) Kevin Winter/Getty Images Entertainment/Getty Images; 102 Gene Coleman/Photodisc/Getty Images; 103 C Squared Studios/Getty Images; 104 (c)Image Source/Punchstock, (cr)CORBIS; 106 Stockbyte/PunchStock; 119 Ed-Imaging; 122 (bl)IT Stock Free/Alamy, (br)Getty Images; 123 (tl)Siede Preis/Getty Images, (tr)Photodisc/Getty Images, (bl)The McGraw-Hill Companies, (br) Getty Images; 128 Mark Steinmetz; 129 (l)Photodisc/Getty Images, (r)Ken Cavanagh/The McGraw-Hill Companies; 130 Ariel Skelley/CORBIS; 131 Ken Karp/The McGraw-Hill Companies, Inc.; 136 Mark Steinmetz; 137 (l to r) Stockdisc/PunchStock, Mark Steinmetz; 138 Brand X Pictures/PunchStock; 140–141 (bkgd.)Jeffrey L. Rotman/CORBIS; 141 (t)Siede Preis/Getty Images; 142 Richard Hutchings/Digital Light Source; 144 Ed-Imaging; 146 (t)G.K. & Vikki Hart/Getty Images, (b)Digital Vision Ltd./SuperStock; 148 Getty Images; 150 The McGraw-Hill Companies; 151 Don Smetzer/PhotoEdit; 152 Glowimages/Getty Images; 154 Ed-Imaging; 156 David Young-Wolff/PhotoEdit; 157 Mark Steinmetz; 160 CORBIS; 164 (l)Photodisc/Getty Images, (r)C Squared Studios/Getty Images; 173 BananaStock/Alamy; 174 (l)Brand X Pictures/PunchStock, (r)Stockdisc/PunchStock; 175 (l)Getty Images, (r) CORBIS; 179 (t)Stockdisc/PunchStock, (b)CMCD/Getty Images; 182 Stockdisc/Getty Images; 186 CORBIS; 187 Brand X Pictures/PunchStock; 190 Steve Smith/SuperStock; 191 (l)The McGraw-Hill Companies, (r)Michael Houghton/StudiOhio; 193 (tl tr)Photodisc/Getty Images, (b)Jupiterimages; 194 Inga Spence/Index Stock Imagery; 196 Tom Brakefield/Stockbyte/Getty Images; 197 (t)Richard Hutchings/Digital Light Source, (c)The McGraw-Hill Companies, (b)Ed-Imaging; 199 (t)PhotoLink/Getty Images; 204 Volkmar K. Wentzel/National Geographic/Getty Images; 210–211 (bkgd)David Young Wolff/PhotoEdit; 211 (inset)Jim West/The Image Works; 212 Michael Prince/Corbis; 216 (t)Ryan McVay/Getty Images, (bl)C Squared Studios/Getty Images, (br)Photolibrary; 217 Stockbyte/Getty Images; 223 Stockdisc/

PunchStock; 228 (l)C Squared Studios/Getty Images, (r)Photodisc/Getty Images; 231 Joseph Sohm-Visions of America/Getty Images; 232 CMCD/Getty Images; 238 RubberBall Selects/Alamy; 239 G.K. & Vikki Hart/Getty Images; 244 CORBIS; 245 Brand X Pictures/PunchStock; 246 Ryan McVay/Getty Images; 253 Mark Steinmetz; 255 G.K. & Vikki Hart/Getty Images; 265 Ed-Imaging; 266 CORBIS; 267 Getty Images; 268 269 Mark Steinmetz; 270 (cl)Mark Steinmetz, (br)Allan Baxter/Photodisc/Getty Images; 271 Mark Steinmetz; 272 Image Source/Getty Images; 276–277 (bkgd) John Warden/SuperStock, 277 (inset)Museum of Fine Arts, Houston, Texas, USA, The Bayou Bend Collection/Bridgeman Art Library; 282 Mark Steinmetz; 283 (l)Mark Steinmetz, (r)Stockdisc/PunchStock; 286 (cw from top)G.K. & Vikki Hart/Getty Images, Getty Images, Hugh Threlfall/Alamy, Getty Images, G.K. & Vikki Hart/Getty Images; 287 C Squared Studios/Getty Images; 288 Ed-Imaging; 290 C Squared Studios/Getty Images; 292 Ed-Imaging; 293 (cw from top)Siede Preis/Getty Images, Photodisc/Getty Images, (others)Mark Steinmetz; 294 Ed-Imaging; 299 (tl)G.K. & Vikki Hart/Getty Images, (tr)Getty Images, (b)CORBIS; 300 C Squared Studios/Getty Images; 301 (t b)Richard Hutchings/Digital Light Source, (c)The McGraw-Hill Companies; 304 (t)Getty Images, (b)CORBIS; 308 (inset)Siede Preis/Getty Images; 308–309 (bkgd) Frans Lanting/CORBIS; 314 Michael Newman/PhotoEdit; 316 Ed-Imaging; 318 George Doyle/Stockbyte/Getty Images; 322 Getty Images; 326 Mark Steinmetz; 335 imagewerks/Getty Images; 336 (l)Mark Steinmetz, (r)Radlund & Associates/Getty Images; 337 (c)C Squared Studios/Getty Images, (bc) Brand X Pictures/PunchStock, (b)Siede Preis/Photodisc/Getty Images; 339 (l)Ian Cartwright/Getty Images, (c)C Squared Studios/Getty Images, (r)Getty Images; 340 (l)Getty Images, (r)Brand X/CORBIS; 341 (l to r, t to b) Luca Tettoni/CORBIS, Dynamicgraphics/InMagine Images, AgeFotostock/SuperStock, Mark Steinmetz, Paul Edmondson/Photographer's Choice/Getty Images, Photolibrary, Mark Steinmetz, CORBIS; 342 (l to r, t to b)Ken Cavanagh/The McGraw-Hill Companies, Burke/Triolo Productions/Brand X/CORBIS, The McGraw-Hill Companies, Stockdisc/CORBIS, Getty Images, Brand X Pictures/PunchStock, Mark Steinmetz; 345 Dynamic Graphics/Jupiterimages; 346 (l to r, t to b)Getty Images, Stockbyte/Getty Images, IMAGES, Agence Photographique/eStock Photo, Mark Steinmetz, Siede Preis/Getty Images; 347 The McGraw-Hill Companies; 349 (t)PhotoLink/Getty Images, (bl)Getty Images; 350 (t)Stockbyte Platinum/Alamy, (cl b)The McGraw-Hill Companies, (cr)Mark Steinmetz; 352 (t)Getty Images, (c)C Squared Studios/Photodisc/Getty Images, (br)Hemera Technologies/Jupiterimages; 354 (l r)Mark Steinmetz, (c)Nancy R. Cohen/Getty Images; 355 Ian Cartwright/Getty Images; 358 David Spindel/SuperStock; 359 (l) Getty Images, (c)Siede Preis/Getty Images, (r)Photodisc/Getty Images; 363 (t) The McGraw-Hill Companies, (bl)Getty Images, (br)Siede Preis/Getty Images; 364 (l to r, t to b)Getty Images, Getty Images, C Squared Studios/Getty Images, (others)Stockbyte/Getty Images; 365 Brand X Pictures/PunchStock; 366 (b)C Squared Studios/Getty Images; 367 (c)CORBIS, (b)Ed-Imaging; 368–369 Michael Ventura/Alamy; 370 David Young-Wolff/PhotoEdit; 373 (l)C Squared Studios/Getty Images, 373 (r)Comstock Images/Alamy; 375 (l)Brand X Pictures/Getty Images, (t cl cr)Mark Steinmetz, (c)Photolibrary, (r)C Squared Studios/Getty Images; 376 Mark Steinmetz; 377 (tl)Image Source/Getty Images, (tr)Hemera Technologies/Jupiterimages, (bl)Ryan McVay/Getty Images, (br)Getty Images; 379 (cr)AgeFotostock/SuperStock, (others)Getty Images; 382 (l)C Squared Studios/Getty Images, (r)Getty Images; 386 S. Wanke/PhotoLink/Getty Images; 389 (t)Richard Hutchings/Digital Light Source; 390 Ed-Imaging; 398 (t)Mark Steinmetz, (c)The McGraw-Hill Companies, (b)Richard Hutchings/Digital Light Source; 402 (l)The McGraw-Hill Companies, (r)Michael Houghton/StudiOhio; 414 Ed-Imaging; 416 Stockbyte/Getty Images; 420 Stockdisc/PunchStock; 422 Wernher Krutein/Photovalet.com/Photovault; 424 G.K. & Vikki Hart/Getty Images; 425 (b)Stockdisc/Getty Images; 426 Burke/Triolo Productions/Brand X Pictures/Getty Images; 428 Ciaran Griffin/Stockbyte Platinum/Getty Images; 432 (l)Photodisc/Getty Images, (r)Siede Preis/Getty Images; 441 Ed-Imaging; 447 (dogs) G.K. & Vikki Hart/Getty Images, (chairs)Ken Cavanagh/The McGraw-Hill Companies, (ducks)Photodisc/Getty Images; 448 (l to r, t to b) Photodisc/Getty Images, Mark Steinmetz, Getty Images, Siede Preis/Getty Images, CMCD/Getty Images, Jupiterimages, Jupiterimages; 449 Burke/Triolo Productions/Brand X/CORBIS; 451 The McGraw-Hill Companies; 454 Siede Preis/Getty Images; 462 CORBIS; 468 (bl)Comstock Images/Alamy, (bc)Siede Preis/Getty Images, (br)Photodisc/Getty Images; 469 (9) Photodisc/Getty Images; 470 (l to r) John T. Fowler/Alamy, Burke/Triolo Productions/Brand X Pictures/Getty Images, Frank Greenaway/Dorling Kindersley/Getty Images, Photodisc/Getty Images, James Cotier/Stone/Getty Images; 470–471 (bkgd)CORBIS; 472 Ed-Imaging; 476 Art Wolfe/Riser/Getty Images; 478 480 Ed-Imaging;

Glossary/Glosario

English

Spanish
(Español)

 Aa

analog clock A clock that has an hour hand and a minute hand.

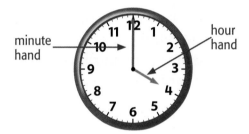

analyze To break information into parts and study it.

angle A figure that is formed by two *rays* with the same *endpoint.*

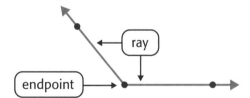

area The number of square units needed to cover the inside of a region or plane figure without any overlap.

array Objects or symbols displayed in rows of the same *length* and columns of the same *length.*

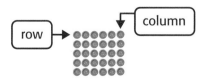

reloj analógico Reloj que tiene una manecilla horaria y un minutero.

analizar Separar la información en partes y estudiarla.

ángulo Figura formada por dos *rayos* con el mismo *extremo.*

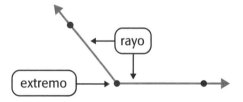

área El número de unidades cuadradas necesarias para cubrir el interior de una región o figura plana sin traslapes.

arreglo Objetos o símbolos representados en filas de la misma *longitud* y columnas de la misma *longitud.*

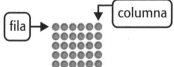

Glossary/Glosario

Associative Property of Addition
The property that states that the grouping of the *addends* does not change the *sum.*

$$(4 + 5) + 2 = 4 + (5 + 2)$$

propiedad asociativa de la adición
Propiedad que establece que la agrupación de los *sumandos* no altera la *suma.*

$$(4 + 5) + 2 = 4 + (5 + 2)$$

Associative Property of Multiplication
The property that states that the grouping of the *factors* does not change the *product.*

$$3 \times (6 \times 2) = (3 \times 6) \times 2$$

propiedad asociativa de la multiplicación   Propiedad que establece que la agrupación de los *factores* no altera el *producto.*

$$3 \times (6 \times 2) = (3 \times 6) \times 2$$

Bb

bar diagram   A problem-solving strategy in which bar models are used to visually organize the facts in a problem.

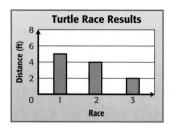

diagrama de barras   Estrategia de resolución de problemas. Se usan barras para representar y organizar visualmente datos de un problema.

bar graph   A *graph* that compares *data* by using bars of different *lengths* or heights to show the values.

gráfica de barras   *Gráfica* en que se comparan *los datos* con barras de distintas *longitudes* o alturas para mostrar los valores.

benchmark fractions   Common *fractions* that are used for estimation: $\frac{1}{4}, \frac{1}{3}, \frac{1}{2}, \frac{2}{3},$ and $\frac{3}{4}.$

fracciones de referencia   *Fracciones* comunes que se usan para hacer estimaciones: $\frac{1}{4}, \frac{1}{3}, \frac{1}{2}, \frac{2}{3},$ y $\frac{3}{4}.$

bill   Another name for paper money.

billete   El nombre del papel moneda.

capacity   The amount a container can hold, measured in *units* of dry or liquid measure.

centimeter (cm)   A *metric unit for* measuring *length* and height.

100 centimeters = 1 meter

century   A unit of time equal to 100 years.

combination   A new set made by combining parts from other sets.

Commutative Property of Addition The property that states that the order in which two numbers are added does not change the *sum.*

$$12 + 15 = 15 + 12$$

Commutative Property of Multiplication   The property that states that the order in which two numbers are multiplied does not change the *product.*

$$7 \times 2 = 2 \times 7$$

capacidad   Cantidad que puede contener un envase, medida en *unidades* líquidas o secas.

centímetro (cm)   *Unidad métrica* para medir *longitud* y altura.

100 centímetros = 1 metro

siglo   Unidad de tiempo igual a 100 años.

combinación   Conjunto nuevo que se forma al combinar partes de otros conjuntos.

propiedad conmutativa de la adición Propiedad que establece que el orden en el cual se suman dos o más números no altera la *suma.*

$$12 + 15 = 15 + 12$$

propiedad conmutativa de la multiplicación   Propiedad que establece que el orden en el cual se multiplican dos o más números no altera el *producto.*

$$7 \times 2 = 2 \times 7$$

comparison problem   A type of problem that compares two groups and uses phrases such as *times as many, times more,* or *times as much.*

problema de comparación   Tipo de problema en que se comparan dos grupos y se usan estas frases: *tantas veces como tantas veces más, o igual número de veces.*

compatible numbers   Numbers that are easy to work with mentally.

$$12 \rightarrow 10 \qquad 73 \rightarrow 75$$
$$39 \rightarrow 40 \qquad 23 \rightarrow 25$$

números compatibles   Números en un problema o números relacionados con los cuales es fácil trabajar mentalmente.

$$12 \rightarrow 10 \qquad 73 \rightarrow 75$$
$$39 \rightarrow 40 \qquad 23 \rightarrow 25$$

compose   To form by putting together.

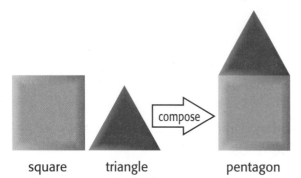

square   triangle   pentagon

componer   Juntar para formar.

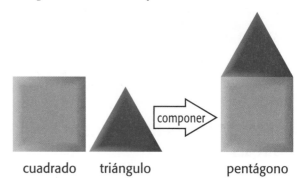

cuadrado   triángulo   pentágono

concave   A vertex that pushes inward.

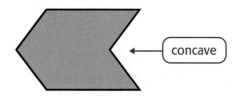

cóncava   Una figura es cóncava si tiene algún vértice que entra hacia la figura.

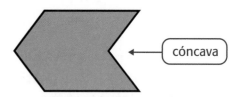

cone   A *three-dimensional figure* with a circular base and a curved surface which comes to a point called the *vertex.*

cono   Figura tridimensional con una base circular y una superficie curva que termina en un punto llamado vértice.

congruent figures   Two figures having the same size and the same shape.

figuras congruentes   Dos figuras con la misma forma y el mismo tamaño.

convex A vertex that pushes outward.

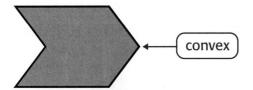

convexa Una figura es convexa si todos los vértices son hacia fuera.

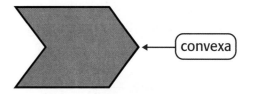

cube A *three-dimensional figure* with six *congruent* square *faces.*

cubo Figura tridimensional con seis caras cuadradas congruentes.

cup (c) A customary unit for measuring *capacity.*

1 cup = 8 ounces

16 cups = 1 gallon

taza (c) Unidad inglesa para medir *capacidad.*

1 taza = 8 onzas

16 tazas = 1 galón

customary system The measurement system that includes *units* such as *foot, pound, quart,* and *degrees Fahrenheit (°F).* Also called *standard measurement.*

sistema inglés Sistema de medición que incluye *unidades* como el *pie,* la *libra,* el *cuarto de galón* y los *grados Fahrenheit (°F).* También llamado *medición estándar.*

cylinder A *three-dimensional figure* having two circular bases and a curved surface connecting the two bases.

cilindro Figura tridimensional que tiene dos bases circulares y una superficie curva que une las dos bases.

Dd

data Numbers or symbols sometimes collected from a *survey* or *experiment* to show information. *Datum* is singular; *data* is plural.

datos Números o símbolos recolectados de una *encuesta* o un *experimento* para mostrar información.

Glossary/Glosario

decade A *unit* of time equal to 10 years.

década *Unidad* de tiempo igual a 10 años.

decagon A *polygon* with 10 sides and 10 *angles.*

decágono *Polígono* con 10 lados y 10 *ángulos.*

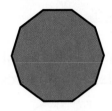

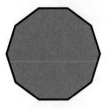

decompose To separate into parts.

descomponer Separar en partes.

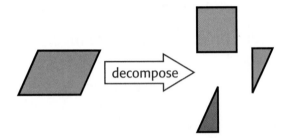

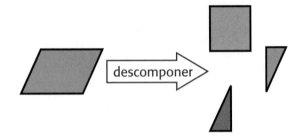

degrees Celsius (°C) a *metric unit* of measure used to describe *temperature.*

grado Celsius (°C) Medida de temperatura del sistema métrico.

degrees Fahrenheit (°F) a *customary unit* of measure used to describe *temperature.*

grado Fahrenheit (°F) Medida de temperatura del sistema inglés.

denominator The bottom number in a *fraction.*

In $\frac{5}{6}$, 6 is the denominator.

denominador El número de abajo en una *fracción.*

En $\frac{5}{6}$, 6 es el denominador.

digit A symbol used to write a number. The ten digits are 0, 1, 2, 3, 4, 5, 6, 7, 8, and 9.

dígito Símbolo que se usa para escribir un número. Los diez dígitos son 0, 1, 2, 3, 4, 5, 6, 7, 8 y 9.

digital clock A clock that uses only numbers to show time.

reloj digital El reloj que marca la hora sólo con números.

Distributive Property of Multiplication
To multiply a *sum* by a number, multiply each *addend* by the number and add the *products.*

$$4 \times (1 + 3) = (4 \times 1) + (4 \times 3)$$

divide (division)   To separate into equal groups to find the number of groups, or the number in each group.

dividend   A number that is being divided.

$3\overline{)9}$ 9 is the dividend.

divisor   The number by which the *dividend* is being divided.

$3\overline{)9}$ 3 is the divisor.

double   Twice the number or amount.

propiedad distributiva de la multiplicación   Para multiplicar una *suma* por un número, puedes multiplicar cada *sumando* por el número y sumar los *productos.*

$$4 \times (1 + 3) = (4 \times 1) + (4 \times 3)$$

dividir (división)   Separar en grupos iguales, para hallar el número de grupos que hay o el número de elementos que hay en cada grupo.

dividendo   El número que se divide.

$3\overline{)9}$ 9 es el dividendo.

divisor   Número entre el cual se divide el *dividendo.*

$3\overline{)9}$ 3 es el divisor.

doble   Dos veces el número o la cantidad.

Ee

edge   The *line segment* where two *faces* of a solid figure meet.

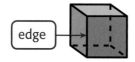

elapsed time   The amount of time that has passed from beginning to end.

endpoint   The point at the beginning of a *ray.*

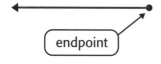

arista   Segmento de recta donde concurren dos caras de una figura sólida.

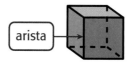

tiempo transcurrido   Cantidad de tiempo que ha pasado entre el principio y el fin.

extremo   El punto al principio de un *rayo.*

Glossary/Glosario

equation A *number sentence* that contains an equals sign, =, indicating that the left side of the equals sign has the same value as the right side.

ecuación Enunciado matemático que contiene un signo de igualdad, =, e indica que el lado izquierdo del signo de igualdad tiene el mismo valor que el lado derecho.

equivalent fractions *Fractions* that have the same value.

$$\frac{2}{4} = \frac{1}{2}$$

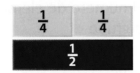

fracciones equivalentes *Fracciones* que tienen el mismo valor.

$$\frac{2}{4} \text{ y } \frac{1}{2}$$

estimate A number close to an exact value. An estimate indicates *about* how much.

47 + 22 is about 70.

estimación Número cercano a un valor exacto. Una estimación indica aproximadamente cuánto.

47 + 22 es aproximadamente 70.

expanded form/expanded notation The representation of a number as a *sum* that shows the value of each *digit*.

536 is written as 500 + 30 + 6.

forma desarrollada/notación desarrollada Representación de un número como *suma* que muestra el valor de cada *dígito*.

536 se escribe como 500 + 30 + 6.

experiment To test an idea.

experimento Comprobar una idea.

expression A combination of numbers and *operations*.

5 + 7

expresión Combinación de números y símbolos de *operaciones*.

5 + 7

 Ff

face The flat part of a *three-dimensional figure*.

A square is a face of a *cube*.

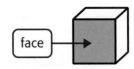

cara La parte llana de una figura tridimensional.

Un cuadrado es una cara de un cubo.

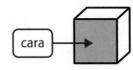

fact family   A group of *related facts* using the same numbers.

$5 + 3 = 8$	$5 \times 3 = 15$
$3 + 5 = 8$	$3 \times 5 = 15$
$8 - 3 = 5$	$15 \div 5 = 3$
$8 - 5 = 3$	$15 \div 3 = 5$

factor   A number that *divides* a *whole number* evenly. Also a number that is *multiplied* by another number.

foot (ft)   A *customary unit* for measuring *length.* Plural is *feet.*

1 foot = 12 inches

fraction   A number that represents part of a whole or part of a set.

$$\frac{1}{2}, \frac{1}{3}, \frac{1}{4}, \frac{3}{4}$$

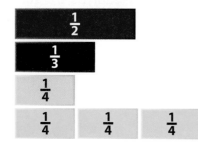

frequency table   A *table* for organizing a set of *data* that shows the number of times each result has occurred.

Bought Lunch Last Month	
Name	Frequency
Julia	6
Martin	4
Lin	5
Tanya	4

familia de operaciones   Grupo de *operaciones relacionadas* que tienen los mismos números.

$5 + 3 = 8$	$5 \times 3 = 15$
$3 + 5 = 8$	$3 \times 5 = 15$
$8 - 3 = 5$	$15 \div 5 = 3$
$8 - 5 = 3$	$15 \div 3 = 5$

factor   Número entre el cual se *divide* exactamente a otro *número entero.* También es un número *multiplicado* por otro número.

pie   *Unidad inglesa* para medir *longitud.*

1 pie = 12 pulgadas

fracción   Número que representa parte de un todo o parte de un conjunto.

$$\frac{1}{2}, \frac{1}{3}, \frac{1}{4}, \frac{3}{4}$$

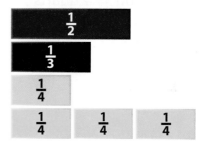

tabla de frecuencias   *Tabla* para organizar un conjunto de *datos* que muestra el número de veces que ha ocurrido cada resultado.

Compraron almuerzo el mes pasado	
Nombre	Frecuencia
Julia	6
Martín	4
Lin	5
Tanya	4

function A relationship in which one quantity depends upon another quantity.

función Relación en que una cantidad depende de otra cantidad.

function table A table of ordered pairs that is based on a *rule*.

tabla de funciones Tabla de pares ordenados que se basa en una *regla*.

Rule: $\triangle - 3$	
Input ($\triangle$)	Output
16	13
14	11
12	9
10	7

Regla: $\triangle - 3$	
Entrada ($\triangle$)	Salida
16	13
14	11
12	9
10	7

Gg

gallon (gal) A *customary unit* for measuring *capacity* for liquids.

1 gallon = 4 quarts

galón (gal) *Unidad de medida inglesa* para medir la *capacidad* líquida.

1 galón = 4 cuartos de galón

gram (g) A *metric unit* for measuring *mass*.

gramo (g) *Unidad métrica* para medir la *masa*.

graph An organized drawing that shows sets of *data* and how they are related to each other. Also a type of chart.

gráfica Dibujo organizado que muestra conjuntos de *datos* y cómo se relacionan. También, un tipo de diagrama.

bar graph

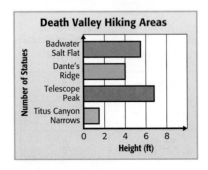

gráfica de barras

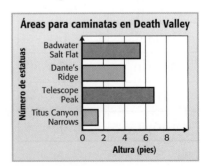

Hh

half inch ($\frac{1}{2}$)　One of two equal parts of an *inch.*

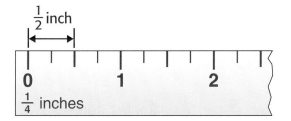

$\frac{1}{2}$ inch

$\frac{1}{4}$ inches

media pulgada ($\frac{1}{2}$)　Una de dos partes iguales de una *pulgada.*

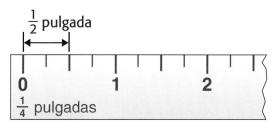

$\frac{1}{2}$ pulgada

$\frac{1}{4}$ pulgadas

hexagon　A *polygon* with six *sides* and six *angles.*

hexágono　*Polígono* con seis *lados* y seis *ángulos.*

hour (h)　A *unit* of time equal to 60 *minutes.*

1 hour = 60 minutes

hora (h)　*Unidad* de tiempo igual a 60 *minutos.*

1 hora = 60 minutos

hundreds　A position of *place value* that represents the numbers 100–999.

centenas　*Valor de posición* que representa los números del 100 al 999.

hundred thousands　A position of *place value* that represents the numbers 100,000–999,999.

centenas de millar　*Valor de posición* que representa los números del 100,000 al 999,999.

Ii

Identity Property of Addition　If you add zero to a number, the *sum* is the same as the given number.

3 + 0 = 3 or 0 + 3 = 3

propiedad de identidad de la suma　Si sumas cero a un número, la *suma* es igual al número dado.

3 + 0 = 3 ó 0 + 3 = 3

Glossary/Glosario

Identity Property of Multiplication   If you *multiply* a number by 1, the *product* is the same as the given number.

$$8 \times 1 = 8 = 1 \times 8$$

interpret   To take meaning from information.

intersecting lines   Lines that meet or cross each other.

inverse operations   *Operations* that undo each other.

Addition and subtraction are inverse, or opposite, operations.

Multiplication and division are also inverse operations.

irregular polygon   A polygon that *does not* have *congruent* sides or *congruent* angles.

irregular pentagon

is equal to (=)   Having the same value.

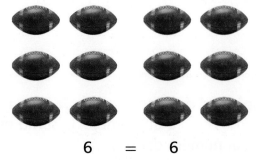

6   =   6

6 is equal to, or the same, as 6.

propiedad de identidad de la multiplicación   Si *multiplicas* un número por 1, el *producto* es igual al número dado.

$$8 \times 1 = 8 = 1 \times 8$$

interpretar   Sacar significado de la información.

rectas secantes   Rectas que se intersecan o cruzan entre sí.

operaciónes inversas   *Operaciones* que se anulan entre sí.

La suma y la resta son operaciones inversas u opuestas.

La multiplicación y la división también son operaciones inversas.

polígono irregulares   Polígonos que *no* tienen lados *congruentes* ni ángulos *congruentes.*

pentágono irregular

es igual a (=)   Que tienen el mismo valor.

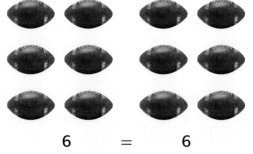

6   =   6

6 es igual o lo mismo que 6.

is greater than (>) An inequality relationship showing that the value on the left of the symbol is greater than the value on the right.

$5 > 3$ 5 is greater than 3.

es mayor que > Relación de desigualdad que muestra que el valor a la izquierda del signo es mayor que el valor a la derecha.

$5 > 3$ 5 es mayor que 3.

is less than (<) An inequality relationship showing that the value on the left side of the symbol is smaller than the value on the right side.

$4 < 7$ 4 is less than 7.

es menor que < Relación de desigualdad que el valor a la izquierda del signo es más pequeño que el valor a la derecha.

$4 < 7$ 4 es menor que 7.

Kk

key Tells what or how many each symbol in a graph stands for.

clave Indica qué significa o cuánto representa cada símbolo en una gráfica.

kilogram (kg) A *metric unit* for measuring *mass.*

kilogramo (kg) *Unidad métrica* para medir la *masa.*

kilometer (km) A *metric unit* for measuring *length.*

kilómetro (km) *Unidad métrica* para medir la *longitud.*

known fact A fact that you already know.

hecho conocido Hecho que ya sabes.

Ll

length Measurement of the distance between two points.

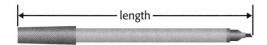

longitud Medida de la distancia entre dos puntos.

like fractions Fractions that have the same denominator.

$\frac{1}{5}$ and $\frac{2}{5}$

fracciones semejantes Fracciones que tienen el mismo denominador.

$\frac{1}{5}$ y $\frac{2}{5}$

Glossary/Glosario

line   A straight set of *points* that extend in opposite directions without ending.

line segment   A part of a *line* between two *endpoints.* The length of a line segment can be measured.

line of symmetry   A *line* on which a figure can be folded so that its two halves match exactly.

line plot   A graph that uses columns of Xs above a *number line* to show frequency of *data.*

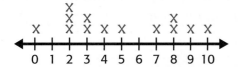

liter (L)   A *metric unit* for measuring *volume* or *capacity.*

1 liter = 1,000 milliliters

recta   Conjunto de puntos que forman una trayectoria recta en direcciones opuestas y sin fin.

segmento de recta   Parte de una recta entre dos extremos. Se puede medir la longitud de un segmento de recta.

eje de simetría   *Recta* sobre la cual se puede doblar una figura de manera que sus mitades se correspondan exactamente.

diagrama lineal   Gráfica con columnas de X sobre una *recta numérica* para representar frecuencias de *datos.*

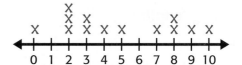

litro (L)   *Unidad métrica* para medir *volumen* o *capacidad.*

1 litro = 1,000 mililitros

Mm

mass   The amount of matter in an object. Two examples of *units* of mass are *gram* and *kilogram.*

meter (m)   A *metric unit* for measuring *length.*

1 meter = 100 centimeters

masa   Cantidad de materia en un cuerpo. Dos ejemplos de *unidades* de masa son el *gramo* y el *kilogramo.*

metro (m)   *Unidad métrica* para medir la *longitud.*

1 metro = 100 centímetros

metric system (SI)   The measurement system based on powers of 10 that includes *units* such as *meter, gram,* and *liter.*

sistema métrico (SI)   Sistema de medición que se basa en potencias de 10 y que incluye *unidades* como el *metro,* el *gramo* y el *litro.*

mile (mi)   A *customary unit* of measure for distance.

$$1 \text{ mile} = 5{,}280 \text{ feet}$$

milla (mi)   *Unidad inglesa* para medir la distancia.

$$1 \text{ milla} = 5{,}280 \text{ pies}$$

milliliter (mL)   A *metric unit* used for measuring *capacity.*

$$1{,}000 \text{ milliliters} = 1 \text{ liter}$$

mililitro (ml)   *Unidad métrica* para medir la *capacidad.*

$$1{,}000 \text{ mililitros} = 1 \text{ litro}$$

millimeter (mm)   A *metric unit* used for measuring *length.*

$$1{,}000 \text{ millimeters} = 1 \text{ meter}$$

milímetro (mm)   *Unidad métrica* que se usa para medir la *longitud.*

$$1{,}000 \text{ milimetro} = 1 \text{ metro}$$

minute (min)   A *unit* used to measure time.

$$1 \text{ minute} = 60 \text{ seconds}$$

minuto (min)   *Unidad* que se usa para medir el tiempo.

$$1 \text{ minuto} = 60 \text{ segundos}$$

mixed number   A number that has a *whole number* part and a *fraction* part.

$$6\frac{3}{4}$$

número mixto   Número que tiene una *parte entera* y una parte *fraccionaria.*

$$6\frac{3}{4}$$

multiple   A multiple of a number is the *product* of that number and any *whole number.*

15 is a multiple of 5 because $3 \times 5 = 15$.

múltiplo   Un múltiplo de un número es el *producto* de ese número y cualquier otro *número entero.*

15 es múltiplo de 5 porque $3 \times 5 = 15$.

Glossary/Glosario

multiplication An *operation* on two numbers to find their *product*. It can be thought of as *repeated addition*.

$$3 \times 4 = 12$$
$$4 + 4 + 4 = 12$$

multiply To find the *product* of 2 or more numbers.

multiplicación *Operación* con dos números para hallar su *producto*. Se puede considerar *una suma repetida*.

$$3 \times 4 = 12$$
$$4 + 4 + 4 = 12$$

multiplicar (multiplicación) Calcular el *producto* de 2 o más números.

Nn

number line A line with numbers marked in order and at regular intervals.

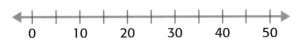

recta numérica Recta que números marca dos en orden y a intervalos regulares.

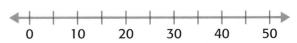

number sentence An *expression* using numbers and the =, <, or > sign.

$$5 + 4 = 9; 8 > 5$$

expresión numérica *Expresión* usa números y el signo =, <, o >.

$$5 + 4 = 9; 8 > 5$$

numerator The number above the bar in a *fraction;* the part of the fraction that tells how many of the equal parts are being used.

In the fraction $\frac{3}{4}$, 3 is the numerator.

numerador Número que está encima de la barra de *fracción;* la parte de la fracción que indica cuántas partes iguales se están usando.

En la fracción $\frac{3}{4}$, 3 es numerador.

Oo

observe A method of collecting *data* by watching.

observar Método que utiliza la observación para recoger *datos.*

octagon A *polygon* with eight *sides.*

octágono *Polígono* de ocho *lados.*

operation A mathematical process such as addition (+), subtraction (−), multiplication (×), and division (÷).

operación Proceso matemático como la suma (+), la resta (−), la multiplicación (×), y la división (÷).

ounce (oz) ounces A *customary unit* for measuring *weight* or *capacity*.

onza (oz) Unidad inglesa de peso o capacidad. Ver Tabla de medidas.

outcome A possible result of an *experiment*.

resultado Resultado posible de un experimento.

parallel (lines) Lines that are the same distance apart. Parallel lines do not meet.

rectas paralelas Rectas separadas por la misma distancia. Las rectas paralelas no se intersecan.

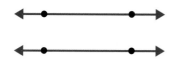

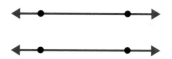

parallelogram A *quadrilateral* with four sides in which each pair of opposite sides is *parallel* and equal in *length*.

paralelogramo *Cuadrilátero* con cuatro lados en el cual cada par de lados opuestos es *paralelos* y de la misma *longitud*.

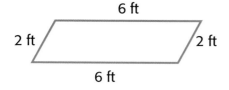

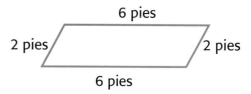

partial products A method for solving *multiplication* problems. The *product* for the ones, tens, and so forth are found separately, then added together.

productos parciales Método para resolver problemas de *multiplicación*. Los *productos* de las unidades, decenas y centenas se hallan por separado y después se suman.

$$\begin{array}{r} 342 \\ \times\ 2 \\ \hline 600 \\ 80 \\ +\ 4 \\ \hline 684 \end{array}$$

$$\begin{array}{r} 342 \\ \times\ 2 \\ \hline 600 \\ 80 \\ +\ 4 \\ \hline 684 \end{array}$$

partition To *divide* or "break up."

separar *Dividir* o desunir.

pentagon A *polygon* with five *sides*.

pentágono *Polígono* de cinco *lados*.

perimeter The distance around a shape or region.

perímetro Distancia alrededor de una figura o región.

period The name given to each group of three *digits* on a place-value chart.

período Nombre dado a cada grupo de tres *dígitos* en una tabla de valores de posición.

perpendicular lines *Lines* that meet or cross each other to form *right angles*.

rectas perpendiculares Rectas que se intersecan o cruzan formando ángulos rectos.

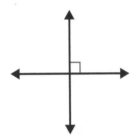

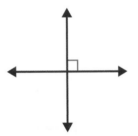

pictograph A graph that compares *data* by using pictures or symbols.

pictografía Cráfica en la que se comparan *datos* usando figuras.

Books Read During Read-A-Thon	
Anita	🕮🕮🕮
David	🕮🕮🕮🕮🕮
Emma	🕮🕮🕮🕮🕮🕮🕮🕮🕮
Jonah	🕮🕮🕮🕮🕮
Mary	🕮🕮🕮🕮🕮🕮🕮
Sam	🕮🕮🕮🕮
Key: 🕮 = 2 students	

Libros leídos durante el maratón de lectura	
Anita	🕮🕮🕮
David	🕮🕮🕮🕮🕮
Emma	🕮🕮🕮🕮🕮🕮🕮🕮🕮
Jonah	🕮🕮🕮🕮🕮
Mary	🕮🕮🕮🕮🕮🕮🕮
Sam	🕮🕮🕮🕮
clave: 🕮 = 2 estudiantes	

picture graph A graph that has different pictures to show information collected.

gráfica con imágenes Gráfica que tiene diferentes imágenes para mostrar la información recogida.

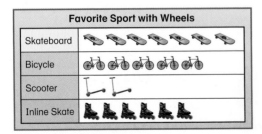

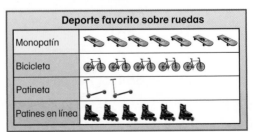

pint (pt) A *customary unit* for measuring *capacity*.

1 pint = 2 cups

pinta (pt) *Unidad inglesa* para medir la *capacidad*.

1 pinta = 2 tazas

place value The value given to a *digit* by its place in a number.

valor de posición El valor de un *dígito* según su lugar en el número.

plane figure A *two-dimensional figure* that lies entirely within one plane, such as a triangle or, square.

figura plana *Figura bidimensional* que yace completamente en un plano, como un triángulo o un cuadrado.

point An exact location in space.

punto Ubicación exacta en el espacio. También se refiere a un lugar decimal.

polygon A closed *plane figure* formed by line segments that meet only at their *endpoints*.

polígono *Figura plana* cerrada formada por segmentos de recta que sólo concurren en sus extremos.

pound (lb) A *customary unit* for measuring *weight*.

1 pound = 16 ounces

libra (lb) *Unidad inglesa* para medir el *peso* o *masa*.

1 libra = 16 onzas

prediction Something you think will happen, such as a specific *outcome* of an *experiment*.

predicción Algo que crees que sucederá, como un resultado específico de un experimento.

probability Words that describe how likely it is that an event will happen.

probabilidad Número entre 0 y 1 que mide la posibilidad de que ocurra un evento.

product The answer to a *multiplication* problem.

producto Respuesta a un problema de *multiplicación*.

pyramid A solid figure with a *polygon* as a base and triangular shaped *faces* that share a common *vertex.*

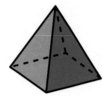

pirámide Figura sólida con un polígono como base y caras triangulares que comparten un vértice común.

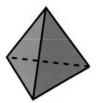

Qq

quadrilateral A shape that has 4 sides and 4 *angles.*

square   rectangle   parallelogram

cuadrilátero Figura que tiene 4 lados y 4 *ángulos.*

cuadrado   rectángulo   paralelogramo

quart (qt) A *customary unit* for measuring *capacity.*

1 quart = 4 cups

cuarto de galón (ct) *Unidad inglesa* de galón para mdir la *capacidad.*

1 cuarto de galón = 4 tazas

quarter hour One-fourth of an hour, or 15 minutes.

cuarto de hora La cuarta parte de una hora ó 15 minutos.

quotient The answer to a *division* problem.

$$15 \div 3 = 5$$ ← 5 is the quotient.

cociente Respuesta a un problema *de división.*

$$15 \div 3 = 5$$ ← 5 es el cociente.

Rr

ray A part of a *line* that has one *endpoint* and extends in one direction without ending.

rayo Parte de una *recta* que tiene un *extremo* y que se extiende en una dirección sin fin.

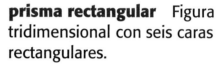

rectangular prism
A *three-dimensional figure* with six *faces* that are rectangles.

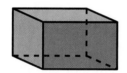

prisma rectangular Figura tridimensional con seis caras rectangulares.

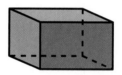

regroup To use *place value* to exchange equal amounts when renaming a number.

reagrupar Usar el *valor de posición* para intercambiar cantidades iguales cuando se convierte un número.

related fact(s) Basic facts using the same numbers. Sometimes called a *fact family.*

$4 + 1 = 5$	$5 \times 6 = 30$
$1 + 4 = 5$	$6 \times 5 = 30$
$5 - 4 = 1$	$30 \div 5 = 6$
$5 - 1 = 4$	$30 \div 6 = 5$

operación (u operaciones relacionada(s) Operaciones básicas que tienen los mismos números. A veces llamadas *familia de operaciones.*

$4 + 1 = 5$	$5 \times 6 = 30$
$1 + 4 = 5$	$6 \times 5 = 30$
$5 - 4 = 1$	$30 \div 5 = 6$
$5 - 1 = 4$	$30 \div 6 = 5$

repeated subtraction To subtract the same number over and over until you reach 0.

resta repetida Para restar un número de una y otra vez hasta llegar a 0.

Glossary/Glosario

rhombus   A *parallelogram* with four *sides* of the same *length.*

rombo   *Paralelogramo* con cuatro *lados* del mismo *largo.*

right angle   An *angle* with a measure of 90°.

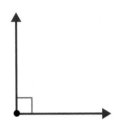

ángulo recto   *Ángulo* que mide 90°.

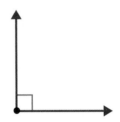

round   To change the *value* of a number to one that is easier to work with. To find the nearest value of a number based on a given *place value.* 27 rounded to the nearest 10 is 30.

redondear   Cambiar el *valor* de un número por uno con el que es más fácil trabajar. Calcular el valor más cercano de un número en base a un *valor de posición* dado. 27 redondeado a la décima más cercana es 30.

rule   A statement that describes a relationship between numbers or objects.

regla   Enunciado que describe una relación entre números u objetos.

S s

scale   A set of numbers that represent the *data* in a *graph.*

escala   Conjunto de números que representan a los *datos* en una *gráfica.*

similar figures   Figures that have the same shape but different sizes.

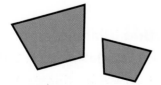

figuras semejantes   Figuras que tienen la misma forma, pero tamaño diferente.

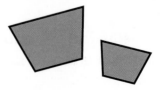

sphere   A *three-dimensional figure* that has the shape of a round ball.

esfera   Figura tridimensional con forma de pelota redonda.

standard form/standard notation
The usual way of writing a number that shows only its *digits,* no words.

> 537   89   1642

forma estándar/notación estándar
La manera habitual de escribir un número que sólo muestra sus *dígitos,* sin palabras.

> 537   89   1642

standard units   Measuring units from the *customary* or *metric system.*

unidades estándar   Unidades de medida del *sistema inglés* o *del métrico.*

survey   A method of collecting *data* by asking a group of people a question.

encuesta   Un método para reunir *datos* haciendo una pregunta a un grupo de personas.

symmetry   A figure is said to have symmetry if it can be folded in half and both sides match exactly.

simetría   Se dice que una figura tiene simetría si es posible doblarla por la mitad y los dos lados coinciden exactamente.

Tt

table   A way to organize and display *data* in rows and columns.

tabla   Manera de organizar y representar *datos* en filas y columnas.

tally chart A way to keep track of *data* using *tally marks* to record the results.

What is Your Favorite Color?	
Color	**Tally**
Blue	ⵌ |||
Green	||||

tabla de conteo Manera de llevar la cuenta de los *datos* usando *marcas de conteo* para anotar los resultados.

¿Cuál es tu color favorito?	
Color	**Conteo**
Azul	ⵌ |||
Verde	||||

tally mark(s) A mark made to record and display *data* from a *survey*.

marca(s) de conteo Marca que se haca para anotar y presentar los *datos* de una.

temperature A measurement of how hot or cold something is.

temperatura Medida del grado de calor o frío de un cuerpo o ambiente.

ten thousands A position of *place value* that represents the numbers 10,000–99,999.

decenas de millar *Valor de posición* que representa los números del 10,000 al 99,999.

thousands A position of *place value* that represents the numbers 1,000–9,999.

In 1,253, the **1** is in the thousands place.

millares *Posición* que según la tabla de valor de posición representa los números 1,000 a 9,999.

En 1,253, el **1** está en el lugar de los millares.

three-dimensional figure A solid figure that has *length,* width, and height.

figura tridimensional Que tiene tres dimensiones: largo, ancho y alto.

time line A *number line* that shows when and in what order events took place.

Jason's Time Line

Jason born	First day of school	Sister born
1999	2004	2007

1999 2001 2003 2005 2007 2009

línea de tiempo *Recta numérica* que muestra cuándo y en qué orden ocurrieron los eventos.

Línea de Tiempo de Jason

Nació Jason	Primer dia de escuela	Nació la hermanita
1999	2004	2007

1999 2001 2003 2005 2007 2009

transform   To change one *polygon* into a different *polygon*.

transformar   Convertir un polígono en otro *polígono*.

tree diagram   A branching diagram that shows all the possible choices of an event or series of events.

diagrama de árbol   Diagrama que se ramifica para mostrar las opciones posibles de un evento o serie de eventos.

trapezoid   A *quadrilateral* with exactly one pair of *parallel* sides.

trapecio   *Cuadrilátero* con exactamente un par de lados *paralelos*.

two-dimensional figure   The outline of a shape—such as a triangle, square, or rectangle—that has only *length, width,* and *area.* Also called a *plane figure.*

figura bidimensional   Contorno de una figura, como un triángulo, un cuadrado o un rectángulo, que sólo tiene *largo, ancho* y *área.* También conocida como *figura plana.*

Uu

unit   The quantity of 1, usually used in reference to measurement.

unidad   La cantidad de 1, que se usa mucho para referirse a medidas.

unit fraction   Any fraction with a numerator of 1.

$$\frac{1}{2}, \frac{1}{3}, \frac{1}{4}$$

fracción unitaria   Cualquier fracción cuyo numerador es 1.

$$\frac{1}{2}, \frac{1}{3}, \frac{1}{4}$$

Vv

variable   A letter or symbol used to represent an unknown quantity.

variable   Letra o símbolo que se usa para representar una cantidad desconocida.

vertex   The *point* where two *rays* meet in an *angle*.

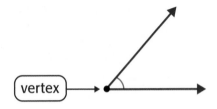

vértice   *Punto* donde concurren dos o más *rayos* y forman un *ángulo*.

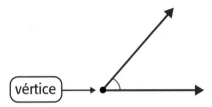

Ww

weight   A measurement that tells how heavy an object is.

peso   Medida que indica cuánto pesa un objeto.

whole number   The numbers 0, 1, 2, 3, 4 . . .

número entero   Los números 0, 1, 2, 3, 4 . . .

word form/word notation   The form of a number that uses written words.

326,472

three hundred twenty-six thousand, four hundred seventy-two

forma verbal   La forma de un número que se escribe en palabras.

326,472

trescientos veintiséis mil cuatrocientos setenta y dos

Yy

yard (yd)   A *customary unit* for measuring *length*.

1 yard = 3 feet or 36 inches

yarda (yd)   *Medida inglesa* para medir la *longitud*.

1 yarda = 3 pies o 36 pulgadas

Zz

Zero Property of Multiplication   The property that states that any number multiplied by zero is zero.

$$0 \times 5 = 0 \qquad 5 \times 0 = 0$$

propiedad del cero de la multiplicación   Propiedad que establece que cualquier número multiplicado por cero es igual a cero.

$$0 \times 5 = 0 \qquad 5 \times 0 = 0$$

Index

Aa

**Act It Out Problem-Solving
Strategy,** 267, 423, 513, 643

Add/addition, 62, 65–67,
68–71, 72–73, 74–77, 78–79,
80–83, 84, 85, 109, 110, 111
Associative Property of
Addition, 65–67, 108, 109,
EP5
Commutative Property of
Addition, 62, 65–67, 108,
109, EP5
Compatible numbers,
68–71, 87–89, 108, 109,
EP6, EP7
Estimating sums, 68–71,
74–77, 81–83, 109, EP6
Facts, EP46, EP47
Four-digit numbers,
80–83, 111
Function tables, 418–421,
433
How Low Can You Go?
Game, 84
Identity Property of Addition,
62, 65–67, 108, 109, EP5
Like fractions, 472–473,
474–477, 485, 488, EP35
Money, 75–76
More About Adding Greater
Numbers, 83
Multi-digit, 72–73, 74–77,
80–83, 84, 85, 110, 111,
EP6, EP7
Partial sums, 82–83
Properties, 65–67, 108, 109,
EP5
Regrouping for, 62, 72–73,
74–77, 80–83, 108
Repeated, 116, 119–120,
121–123, 124–125,
131–133, 163, 174, 183,
203, 219, 232–233,
240–243, 244–246, EP17
Sentences, 121–123, 163,
232–233, EP9
Sums, EP5
Three-digit numbers,
72–73, 74–77, 84, 85, 110

Addition properties, 65–67,
108, 109, EP5

Associative Property of
Addition, 65–67, 108, 109,
EP5
Commutative Property of
Addition, 62, 65–67, 108,
109, EP5
Identity Property of Addition,
62, 65–67, 108, 109, EP5

Algebra, 28, 45, 57, 65–67,
71, 76, 82, 94, 98, 109, 128,
148, 164, 172, 178, 184–185,
188, 193, 204, 215, 223, 228,
236, 242, 245–246, 250, 256,
260, 264, 267, 270, 274–275,
279–280, 281, 380, 383–385,
386–389, 390–391, 400–401,
402–405, 406–409, 410–413,
414–417, 418–421, 422–423,
424–427, 428–429, 430–434,
435, 436–437, 461, 463, 467,
476, 482, 503, 547, 554, 587,
646, 653, EP29, EP30, EP31,
EP32
Addition function tables,
418–421, 433
Division Function tables,
424–427, 434
Equations, 410–413, 430,
432, EP31
Expressions, 400–401,
402–405, 410–413, 432,
EP30, EP31
Function rules, 418–421,
424–427, 430, 431, 434,
EP31, EP32
Functions, 380, 418–421,
424–427, 430, 433, 434,
EP31, EP32
Function tables, 414–417,
418–421, 424–427, 430,
433, 434, 659, 661, 663,
665, EP31, EP32
Input, 418–421
Missing factors, 180–181,
183–185, 186–189,
245–246, 272–275
Multiplication function
tables, 424–427, 434
Output, 418–421
Patterns, 6–7, 380,
383–385, 386–389, 390–
391, 392–393, 394–397,
398, 399, 433, EP28, EP29,
EP30, EP32

Subtraction function tables,
418–421, 433
Variables, 380, 418–421,
430
Writing equations, EP31
Writing expressions,
402–405, 410–413, 432,
EP30, EP31

Analog clocks, 595–597,
600–603, 613, 659, EP42

Analyzing data, 284, 296–
299, 304–307, 308–309,
310–313, 314–315, 320–323,
324–328, 663

Angles, 332, 338–339,
340–343, 344–347, 372, 373,
EP25
Comparing, 339
Greater than a right angle,
339, 345–347, 372, EP26
Less than a right angle,
338–339, 345–347, 372,
EP26
Right, 338–339, 345–347,
372

Area, 558–559, 560–562,
563, 566, EP40
Estimating, 558–559,
560–562
Square units, 558–559,
560–562, 563, 566, EP40

Area models
Mixed numbers, 497–501
Multiplication, 632–634,
649

Are You Ready?, 12, 64, 118,
172, 228, 286, 334, 382, 440,
494, 528, 572, 620

Arrays, 124–125, 126–129,
142, 156–159, 162–163, 166,
170, 173–175, 182–185, 219,
229–230, 231–233, 235,
240–243, 254–257, 632–634,
EP11, EP13, EP18

Arrays and division, 147

**Art Cross Curricular
Connections,** 276–277,
368–369, 628–629
Gardens under Glass,
368–369
Not Just a Blanket, 276–277
Stamp Collecting, 628–629

Art Is Shaping Up **Game,** 367

Associative Property of Addition, 65–67, 108, 109, EP5

Axis, 303, 304–305

Bb

Bar diagrams, 4–5, 81–82, 97, 131–133, 143, 163, 167, 174–175, 183, 194–196, 201, 219, 220, 223, 233, 240–243, 253, 267, 371, EP9, EP12, EP14

Bar graphs, 94, 284, 302–303, 304–307, 308–309, 320–323, 324, 659, 662–663, EP23, EP30
  Horizontal, 305–307, 326, EP23
  Vertical, 304–307, EP23

Basket-Golf **Problem-Solving Project,** 660–661

Benchmark fractions, 438, 455–457

The Big Idea, 10, 62, 116, 170, 226, 284, 332, 380, 438, 492, 526, 570, 618

Bills, 46–49, 50–53, 54, 58, EP4
  More About Coins and Bills, 53

Budgets, 659

The Buzz on Insects **Science Cross Curricular Connection,** 470–471

Cc

Calendars, 604–607, 614, EP43

Capacity, 570, 573–574, 575–577, 580–582, 583, 610, 611, EP40, EP41
  Capacity Guess Game, 583
  Comparing capacity measures, 574
  Cups, 573–574, 575–577, 583, 610, 611, EP40
  Estimating, 573–574, 575–577, 580–582, 583, 611
  Estimating metric units, EP41

Gallons, 573–574, 575–577, 583, 610, 611, EP40
  Liters, 580–582, 610, 611, EP41
  Milliliters, 580–582, 610, 611, EP41
  Pints, 573–574, 575–577, 583, 610, 611, EP40
  Quarts, 573–574, 575–577, 583, 610, 611, EP40

Capacity Guess **Game,** 583

Catch Me If You Can! **Game,** 301

Celsius (°C), 608–609, 610, 614, EP43
  Degrees (°), 608–609, 610, 614, EP43

Centimeters, 526, 542–543, 544–547, 548–549, 551, 565, EP39

Cents, 10, 46–49

Cent sign (¢), 10, 46–49

Centuries, 604–607

Certain, 316–319, 328, EP24

Challenge H.O.T. Problems, 19, 49, 77, 82, 89, 98, 123, 178, 215, 233, 323, 347, 365, 396, 413, 417, 427, 534, 562, 577, 587

Chance, 316–319, 328

Change (money), 50–53, 58, 663, EP5

Chapter Study Guide and Review, 54–58, 108–112, 162–166, 219–222, 278–280, 324–328, 372–376, 430–434, 485–488, 520–522, 563–566, 620–624, 649–652

Check for reasonableness, 74–76, 81–83, 110, 111

Check What You Know, 18, 21, 28, 31, 37, 42, 48, 51, 66, 69, 75, 82, 88, 93, 97, 103, 122, 127, 132, 136, 147, 151, 157, 174, 177, 184, 187, 195, 199, 203, 207, 215, 217, 232, 235, 241, 245, 249, 255, 259, 263, 269, 273, 290, 298, 306, 311, 317, 321, 336, 341, 345, 352, 358, 363, 384, 387, 395, 403, 407, 411, 415, 420, 426, 444, 447, 436, 459, 467, 469, 475, 481, 499, 509, 517, 533,

538, 546, 553, 561, 576, 581, 585, 592, 596, 601, 605, 609, 623, 625, 633, 639, 645

Choose an Operation Problem-Solving Strategy, 107, 212–213, 267, 371, 557

Choose the Best Strategy Problem-Solving Investigation, 106–107, 112, 160–161, 212–213, 222, 266–267, 280, 314–315, 327, 370–371, 376, 422–423, 434, 462–463, 487, 512–513, 522, 556–557, 566, 598–599, 613, 642–643, 652, EP8, EP12, EP15, EP19, EP24, EP26, EP28, EP32, EP34, EP37, EP39, EP42, EP45

Circles, 9, 340

Clocks, 595–597, 600–603, 613, 659, 661, 665, EP42
  Analog, 595–597, 600–603, 613, 659, EP42
  Digital, 595–597, 600–603, 613, EP42

Coins, 46–49, 50–53, 58, EP4
  Cents, 10, 46–49
  Cent sign (¢), 10, 46–49
  Collection of, EP4
  Dimes, 46–49
  Half-dollars, 46–49
  More About Coins and Bills, 53
  Nickels, 46–49
  Pennies, 46–49
  Quarters, 46–49
  Value, 46–49, EP4

Collecting data, 284, 287–288, 289–291, 292–293, 294–295, 325, 659, 664–665
  Experiments, 287–288
  Observing, 287–288
  Surveys, 287–288, 290–291, 662–663, 664–665

Colon (:), 595–597, 600–603, 613

Combinations, 134–137, 164, EP10
  Tree diagrams, 135–137, 164, EP10

Commas, 20–23

Communities Within Communities **Social Studies Cross Curricular Connection,** 210–211

Commutative Property of Addition, 62, 65–67, 108, 109, EP5

Commutative Property of Multiplication, 125, 127–129, 162, 180–181, 244–246, 254–257, 258, EP9

Compare/comparing
Angles, 339
Capacity measures, 574
Fractions, 452–453, 454–457, 487, EP33
Fractions on a number line, 452–453, 455–457, 487
Mixed numbers, 508–511, 520, 522, EP36
Numbers, 26–29, EP2, EP3
Numbers on a number line 26–29
Sets of money, 53

Comparison problems, 130–133, 163

Compatible numbers, 68–71, 87–89, 108, 109, EP6, EP7

Cones, 9, 350–353, 375

Congruent figures, 332, 356–357, 358–359, 372, 376, 665, EP27

Converting units of time, 605–607, 614, 615

Counting change, 50–53, 58

Counting money, 46–49, 58

Crazy Cooks Problem-Solving Project, 662–663

Cross Curricular Connections, 34–35, 100–101, 140–141, 210–211, 276–277, 308–309, 368–369, 428–429, 470–471, 504–505, 548–541, 588–589, 628–629
Art, 276–277, 368–369, 628–629
Geography, 34–35
Music, 100–101
Science, 140–141, 308–309, 428–429, 470–471, 548–549, 588–589
Social Studies, 210–211, 504–505

Cubes, 9, 350–353, 375

Cups, 573–574, 575–577, 583, 610, 611, EP40

Customary measurement system, 529–531, 532–534, 535, 536–539, 540–541, 548–549, 563, 564, EP38, EP40, EP41
Cups, 573–574, 575–577, 583, 610, 611, EP40
Estimating units of length, EP38
Foot (feet), 536–539, 564, EP38
Gallons, 573–574, 575–577, 583, 610, 611, EP40
Half inches, 529–531, 532–534, 535, 536–539, 563, 564, EP38
Hit the Target Game, 535
Inches, 526, 529–531, 532–534, 535, 536–539, 540–541, 548–549, 563, 564, EP38
Miles, 536–539, 564, 659, EP38
Ounces, 584–587, 610, 612, EP41
Pints, 573–574, 575–577, 583, 610, 611, EP40
Pounds, 584–587, 610, 612, EP41
Quarts, 573–574, 575–577, 583, 610, 611, EP40
Yards, 536–539, 564, EP38

Cylinders, 9, 350–353, 375

Dd

Data, 284, 287–288, 289–291, 292–293, 294–295, 296–299, 300, 301, 302–303, 304–307, 308–309, 310–313, 314–315, 320–323, 324–328, 329, 330–331, 680–681, 664–665, EP21, EP22, EP23
Analyzing, 284, 296–299, 304–307, 308–309, 310–313, 314–315, 320–323, 324–328, 663
Bar graphs, 94, 284, 302–303, 304–307, 308–309, 320–323, 324, 659, 662–663, EP23, EP30
Catch Me If You Can! Game, 301
Collecting, 284, 287–288, 289–291, 292–293, 294–295, 325, 659, 664–665

Displaying, 294–295, 301, 302–303, 304–307, 310–313, 324–328, 658–659, EP22, EP23
Experiments, 287–288
Frequency table, 284, 289–291, 324, 325, EP21
Horizontal bar graphs, 305–307, 326, EP23
Interpreting, 296–299, 304–307, 308–309, 310–313, 314–315, 320–323, 324–328
Line plots, 284, 310–313, 314–315, 320–323, 324, 327, EP23, EP24
Observing, 287–288
Organizing, 289–291, 294–295, 301, 302–303, 304–307, 310–313, 320–323, 324–328, 658–659, EP21
Pictographs, 294–295, 296–299, 324, 326, 393, 394–397, 659, EP22
Picture graphs, 294–295, 296–299, 326, EP22
Recording, 287–288, 289–291, 292–293, 294–295, 310–313, 324–328
Surveys, 287–288, 290–291, 662–663, 664–665
Tally charts, 284, 289–291, 294–295, 296–299, 302–303, 320–323, 325, 662–663, 664–665, EP21
Tally marks, 284, 289–291, 294–295, 296–299, 302–303, 320–323, 325
Time lines, 604–607, 614
Vertical bar graphs, 304–307, EP23

Data File, 22, 83, 148, 196, 256, 270, 318, 364, 416, 476, 554, 586, 626

Days, 604–607

Decade, 570, 604–607

Decagons, 340–343

Degrees (°-temperature), 608–609, 610, 614, EP43
Celsius (°C), 608–609, 610, 614, EP43

Denominators, 438, 443–445, 446–449, 485, 486

Diagrams, 369

Did You Know?, 35, 101, 141, 211, 277, 308, 368, 428, 471, 505, 548, 589, 649

Differences, 62, 86–89, 90–91, 92–95
  Estimating, 86–89, 111, EP7

Digital clocks, 595–597, 600–603, 613, EP42

Digits, 13–15, 16–19, 20–23, 55, EP2
  Hundreds, 16–19, 20–23, EP2
  Hundred thousands, 16–19
  Ones, 16–19, 20–23
  Tens, 16–19, 20–23, EP2
  Ten thousands, 16–19, 20–23
  Thousands, 16–19, 20–23

Dimes, 46–49

Displaying data, 294–295, 301, 302–303, 304–307, 310–313, 324–328, 658–659, EP22, EP23
  Bar graphs, 94, 284, 302–303, 304–307, 308–309, 320–323, 324, 659, 662–663, EP23, EP30
  Frequency table, 284, 289–291, 324, 325, EP21
  Horizontal bar graphs, 305–307, 326, EP23
  Line plots, 284, 310–313, 314–315, 320–323, 324, 327, EP23, EP24
  Pictographs, 294–295, 296–299, 324, 326, 393, 394–397, 659, EP22
  Picture graphs, 294–295, 296–299, 326, EP22
  Tally charts, 284, 289–291, 294–295, 296–299, 302–303, 320–323, 325, 662–663, 664–665, EP21
  Time lines, 604–607, 614
  Vertical bar graphs, 304–307, EP23

Divide/division, 116, 144–145, 146–149, 150–153, 154–155, 156–159, 162, 165–166, 170, 176–179, 186–189, 198–201, 206–208, 216–217, 219–222, 223, 224–225, 226, 234–237, 248–250, 251–252, 261, 262–264, 265, 272–275, 278–280, 281, 282–283, EP11

Any number by itself, 216–217
Arrays and, 147
By 0, 216–217, 222
By 1, 216–217, 222
By 2, 176–179, 220
By 3, 186–189, 220
By 4, 234–237, 279
By 5, 198–201, 221
By 6, 248–250, 279
By 7, 248–250, 279
By 8, 262–264, 279
By 9, 262–264, 279
By 10, 206–208, 222
By 11, 272–275, 279
By 12, 272–275, 279
Dividends, 156–159, 176–179, 219
Division-multiplication relationship, 150–153, 154–155, 156–159
Divisors, 156–159, 162, 176–179, 219
Equal groups, 263–264
Equal sharing, 144–145, 146–149, 165
Facts, 176–179, 186–189, 198–201, 206–208, 216–217, 219–222, 223, 224–225, 234–237, 248–250, 251–252, 261, 262–264, 265, 272–275, 278–280, 281, 282–283, EP11, EP12, EP13, EP14, EP15, EP16, EP18, EP19, EP20, EP52, EP53
Function tables, 424–427, 434
Modeling, 144–145, 146–149, 176–179, 198–201, 219, 234–237, 251–252, 272–275
Number Cubes Game, 265
On a number line, 150–153, 165, 235, 248–250
Partition, 170, 176–179, 219
Quotients, 116, 156–159, 162, 176–179, 219
Related facts, 176–179, 187–189, 198–201, 206–208, 219, 220, 272–275
Repeated subtraction, 150–153, 187, 198–201, 206–208, 219, 235–237, 249–250, 262–264, 272–275, EP11, EP18, EP19

Rules, 216–217, 219
Sentences, 150–153, 154–155
Strategies, 176–179, 186–189, 198–201, 206–208, 216–217, 219–222, 234–237, 248–250, 251–252, 262–264, 272–275, 278–280
Zero by any number, 216–217

Dividend, 156–159, 176–179, 219

Division Strategies, 176–179, 186–189, 198–201, 206–208, 216–217, 219–222, 234–237, 248–250, 251–252, 262–264, 272–275, 278–280
  Arrays, 147
  Equal groups, 263–264
  Equal sharing, 144–145, 146–149, 165
  Modeling, 144–145, 146–149, 176–179, 198–201, 219, 234–237, 251–252, 272–275
  On a number line, 150–153, 165, 235, 248–250
  Partition, 170, 176–179, 219
  Related facts, 176–179, 187–189, 198–201, 206–208, 219, 220, 272–275
  Repeated subtraction, 150–153, 187, 198–201, 206–208, 219, 235–237, 249–250, 262–264, 272–275, EP11, EP18, EP19

Divisors, 156–159, 162, 176–179, 219

Dollars, 47–49, 54

Dollar sign ($), 47–49

Doubles, 226, 229–230, 231–233, 255–257, 278, EP17

Draw a picture multiplication strategy, 173–175, 183, 194–196

Draw a Picture Problem-Solving Strategy, 161, 267, 371, 450–451, 463, 486, 513, 557, 598–599, EP33

Drawing figures, 367

Edges, 351–353

***Eggs!* Science Cross Curricular Connections,** 308–309

Elapsed time, 570, 600–603, 610, 613, EP42

Endpoints, 335–337, 338–339

Equal groups, 263–264

Equal sharing, 144–145, 146–149, 165

Equally likely, 320–323, 328

Equations, 410–413, 430, 432, EP31
  Writing, EP31

Equivalent fractions, 438, 464–465, 466–468, 469, 484, 485, 488, 492, 514–515, 516–519, 520, EP34

Equivalent mixed numbers, 514–515, 516–519, EP37

Estimate/estimation, 62, 68–71, 74–77, 81–83, 86–89, 108, 109, 111, 618, 624–627, 644–647, 649, 650, 651
  Area, 558–559, 560–562
  Capacity, 573–574, 575–577, 580–582, 583, 611
  Compatible numbers, 68–71, 87–89, 108, 109, EP6, EP7
  Costs, 658–659, 662–663
  Differences, 86–89, 111, EP7
  Length, 529–531, 532–534, 535, 536–539, 542–543, 544–547, 548–549, 564, 664–665
  Mass, 590–593, 612, EP41
  Metric units of capacity, EP41
  Metric units of length, EP39
  Perimeter, 551, 552–555
  Products, 624–627, 649, 650, 651, EP44, EP45
  Sums, 68–71, 74–77, 81–83, 109, EP6
  Weight, 584–584, 612, 664–665, EP41

Estimate or Exact Answers Problem-Solving Skill, 78–79, 107, 110, EP6

Expanded form, 17–19, 20–23, 55, EP2

Experiments, 287–288

Expressions, 400–401, 402–405, 410–413, 432, EP30, EP31
  Writing, 402–405, 410–413, 432, EP30, EP31

Extend, 25

Extending patterns, 383–385, 386–389, 394–397, 414–417, 431, EP28

Extra or Missing Information Problem-Solving Strategy, 238–239, 279, EP17

Extra Practice, EP2–EP45

Faces, 351–353

Fact families, 156–159, 162, 166, EP11

***Factor Power* Game,** 197

Factors, 121–123, 126–129, 156–159, 162, 170, 180–181, 197, 219
  Factor Power Game, 197
  Missing, 180–181, 183–185, 186–189, 245–246, 272–275

Facts
  Addition, EP46, EP47
  Division, 176–179, 186–189, 198–201, 206–208, 216–217, 219–222, 223, 224–225, 234–237, 248–250, 251–252, 261, 262–264, 265, 272–275, 278–280, 281, 282–283, EP11, EP12, EP13, EP14, EP15, EP16, EP18, EP19, EP20, EP52, EP53
  Facts Practice, EP46–EP54
  Families, 156–159, 162, 166, EP11
  Mixed operations, EP54
  Multiplication, 173–175, 180–181, 182–185, 194–196, 197, 202–205, 209, 214–215, 218, 219–222, 223, 224–225, 229–230, 231–233, 240–243, 244–246, 247, 254–257, 258–260, 265, 268–271, 278–280, 281, 282–283, EP9, EP11, EP13, EP14, EP15, EP16, EP17, EP18, EP20, EP50, EP51
  Subtraction, EP48, EP49

Facts Practice, EP46–EP54

Fahrenheit (°F), 608–609, 610, 614, EP43
  Degrees (°), 608–609, 610, 614, EP43

Find the Error H.O.T. Problems, 19, 52, 104, 129, 178, 233, 237, 260, 275, 309, 408, 421, 460, 477, 482, 501, 597, 607, 627

Foldables, 10, 54, 62, 108, 116, 162, 170, 219, 226, 278, 284, 324, 332, 372, 380, 430, 438, 485, 492, 520, 526, 563, 570, 610, 618, 649

Foot (feet), 536–539, 564, EP38

Four-Step Plan, 4–5, 24–25, 44–45, 55, 57, 78–79, 106–107, 110, 138–139, 160–161, 164, 166, 190–191, 212–213, 221–222, 238–239, 266–267, 279–280, 292–293, 314–315, 325, 327, 348–349, 370–371, 374, 376, 390–391, 422–423, 431, 434, 450–451, 462–463, 486, 487, 502–503, 512–513, 521, 522, 540–541, 556–557, 565, 566, 578–579, 598–599, 611, 614, 630–631, 642–643, 651, 652, EP2, EP4, EP6, EP8, EP10, EP12, EP13, EP15, EP17, EP19, EP22, EP24, EP26, EP28, EP29, EP32, EP33, EP34, EP36, EP37, EP38, EP39, EP40, EP42, EP44, EP45

***Fraction Concentration* Game,** 484

Fractions, 438, 441–442, 443–445, 446–449, 450–451, 452–453, 454–457, 458–460, 461, 464–465, 466–468, 469, 470–471, 472–473, 474–477, 478–479, 480–483, 484, 485, 488, 489, 490–491, 492, 495–496, 497–501, 502–503, 504–505, 506, 507, 508–511, 512–513, 514–515, 516–519, 520–522, 661, EP32, EP34, EP35

Addition of like fractions, 472–473, 474–477, 485, 488, EP35

Area models for mixed numbers, 497–501

Benchmark fractions, 438, 455–457

Comparing, 452–453, 454–457, 487, EP33

Comparing mixed numbers, 508–511, 520, 522, EP36

Comparing on a number line, 452–453, 455–457, 487

Denominators, 438, 443–445, 446–449, 485, 486

Equivalent, 438, 464–465, 466–468, 469, 484, 485, 488, 492, 514–515, 516–519, 520, EP34

Equivalent mixed numbers, 514–515, 516–519, EP37

Fraction Concentration Game, 484

Improper, 497, 501, 507, 520, 521, 523, 525

Linear models of mixed numbers 498–501, 508–511, 520, 522

Mixed Number Match Game, 506

Mixed numbers, 406, 495–496, 497–501, 502–503, 504–505, 506, 507, 508–511, 512–513, 514–515, 516–519, 520–522, 523, 524–525, EP35, EP36, EP37

Modeling, 441–442, 443–445, 446–449

Modeling mixed numbers, 496–501, 507, 508–511, 521

Numerators, 438, 433–435, 436–439, 485, 486

On a number line, EP33

Ordering, 458–460, 487, EP34

Ordering mixed numbers, 508–511, 520, 522

Ordering on a number line, 458–460, 487

Parts of a set, 446–449, 486, EP33

Parts of a whole, 443–445, 486

Proper, 497, 501

Reading, 443–445, 446–449

Subtraction of like fractions, 478–479, 480–483, 485, 488, EP35

Unit fractions, 443–445

Writing, 443–445, 446–449

Frequency table, 284, 289–291, 324, 325, EP21

Functions, 380, 418–421, 424–427, 430, 433, 434, EP31, EP32

  Rules, 418–421, 424–427, 430, 431, 434, EP31, EP32

  Tables, 414–417, 418–421, 424–427, 430, 433, 434, 659, 661, 663, 665, EP31, EP32

Function rules, 418–421, 424–427, 430, 431, 434, EP31, EP32

Function tables, 414–417, 418–421, 424–427, 430, 433, 434, 659, 661, 663, 665, EP31, EP32

  Addition, 418–421, 433

  Division, 424–427, 434

  Input, 418–421

  Multiplication, 424–427, 434

  Output, 418–421

  Patterns on, EP31, EP32

  Subtraction, 418–421, 433

Gg

Gallons, 573–574, 575–577, 583, 610, 611, EP40

Game Time, 39, 84, 142, 197, 265, 301, 367, 398, 484, 506, 535, 583, 648

  Art Is Shaping Up, 367

  Capacity Guess, 583

  Catch Me If You Can!, 301

  Factor Power, 197

  Fraction Concentration, 484

  High and Low, 648

  Hit the Target, 535

  How Low Can You Go?, 84

  Mixed Number Match, 506

  Number Cubes, 265

  Pick a Pattern, 398

  Round Numbers, 39

  Rows and Columns, 142

Gardens under Glass **Art Cross Curricular Connection,** 368–369

Geography Cross Curricular Connection, 34–35

  The Mighty Mississippi, 34–35

Geometric patterns, 383–385, 398, 431

Geometry, 8–9, 332, 335–337, 338–339, 340–343, 344–347, 348–349, 350–354, 355, 356–357, 358–359, 360–361, 362–365, 366, 367, 368–369, 370–371, 372–376, 377, 378–379, EP25, EP26, EP27

  Angles, 332, 338–339, 340–343, 344–347, 372, 373, EP25

  Art Is Shaping Up Game, 367

  Circles, 9, 340

  Comparing angles, 339

  Cones, 9, 350–353, 375

  Congruent figures, 332, 356–357, 358–359, 372, 376, 665, EP27

  Cubes, 9, 350–353, 375

  Cylinders, 9, 350–353, 375

  Decagons, 340–343

  Drawing figures, 367

  Edges, 351–353

  Endpoints, 335–337, 338–339

  Faces, 351–353

  Greater than a right angle, 339, 345–347, 372, EP26

  Hexagons, 9, 340–343

  Intersecting lines, 336–337, 373, EP25

  Less than a right angle, 338–339, 345–347, 372, EP26

  Lines, 335–337, 373, EP25

  Line segments, 335–337, 373, EP25

  Lines of symmetry, 360–361, 362–365, 366, 376

  Octagons, 340–343, 372

  Parallel lines, 336–337, 344–347, 372, 373, 374, EP25

  Parallelograms, 344–347, 374

  Pentagons, 9, 340–343, 372

  Perpendicular lines, 336–337, 373, EP25

Plane figures, 9, 335–337, 340–343

Points, 335–337, 373, EP25

Polygons, 332, 340, 343, 372, EP25

Pyramids, 9, 350–353, 375

Quadrilaterals, 332, 340–343, 344–347, 372, 374, EP26

Rays, 335–337, 372, 373, EP25

Rectangles, 9, 344–347

Rectangular prisms, 8–9, 350–354

Rhombus, 344–347, 374

Right angles, 338–339, 345–347, 372

Sides, 9, 340–343, 373, 374, EP25

Similar figures, 356–357, 358–359, 376, EP27

Solid figures, 8–9, 350–354, 375

Spheres, 8–9, 350–354, 375

Squares, 9, 344–347

Symmetry, 332, 360–361, 362–365, 366, 372, 376, 665

Three-dimensional figures, 8–9, 350–353, 372, 375, EP26

Trapezoids, 344–347

Triangles, 9, 340–343

Two-dimensional figures, 9, 332, 335–337, 340–343, EP25

Vertex (vertices), 338–339, 351–353

Grams, 590–593, 610, 612, EP41

Graphic Novel, 2–3, 11, 29, 63, 95, 117, 137, 171, 188, 227, 264, 285, 307, 333, 343, 381, 388, 439, 448, 493, 518, 527, 555, 571, 602, 619, 646

Graphs, 294–295, 296–299, 302–303, 304–307, 308–309, 310–313, 314–315, 320–323, 324–328, EP22, EP23, EP30

Axis, 303, 304–305

Bar, 94, 284, 302–303, 304–307, 308–309, 320–323, 324, 659, 662–663, EP23, EP30

Horizontal bar, 305–307, 326, EP23

Keys, 296–299, 304–307

Patterns on, 380, 394–397, 430, 432, EP30

Pictographs, 294–295, 296–299, 324, 326, 393, 394–397, 659, EP22

Picture, 294–295, 296–299, 326, EP22

Scales, 303, 304–307, 324

Titles, 296–299, 302–303, 304–307, 310–313

Vertical bar, 304–307, EP23

Greater than a right angle, 339, 345–347, 372, EP26

Guess, Check, and Revise Problem-Solving Strategy, 348–349, 374, 464, 578–579, 611, EP40

Half-dollars, 46–49

Half inches, 529–531, 532–534, 535, 536–539, 563, 564, EP38

Hexagons, 9, 340–343

High and Low **Game,** 648

Hit the Target **Game,** 535

Horizontal bar graphs, 305–307, 326, EP23

H.O.T. Problems, 19, 22, 29, 32, 38, 43, 49, 52, 67, 71, 77, 82, 89, 95, 98, 104, 123, 129, 133, 137, 149, 153, 159, 175, 178, 184, 189, 196, 201, 205, 207, 215, 217, 233, 237, 242, 250, 257, 260, 264, 271, 275, 291, 299, 307, 313, 319, 323, 337, 343, 347, 353, 359, 365, 385, 389, 396, 405, 408, 413, 417, 421, 427, 445, 449, 457, 460, 468, 477, 482, 501, 511, 519, 534, 539, 547, 555, 562, 577, 582, 587, 593, 588, 597, 603, 607, 609, 623, 627, 634, 641, 647

Challenge, 19, 49, 77, 82, 89, 98, 123, 178, 215, 233, 323, 347, 365, 396, 413, 417, 427, 534, 562, 577, 587

Find the Error, 19, 52, 104, 129, 178, 233, 237, 260, 275, 309, 408, 421, 460, 477, 482, 501, 597, 607, 627

Number Sense, 32, 43, 49, 52, 89, 95, 159, 189, 246, 257, 260, 271, 427, 457, 460, 511, 641

Open-Ended, 22, 29, 38, 67, 71, 77, 98, 104, 123, 133, 137, 149, 153, 175, 178, 184, 201, 207, 215, 217, 233, 242, 250, 257, 264, 271, 275, 291, 299, 307, 313, 337, 343, 347, 353, 359, 365, 385, 389, 405, 408, 421, 445, 449, 468, 482, 501, 519, 534, 539, 555, 562, 577, 582, 587, 593, 597, 607, 609, 623, 634, 641, 647

Reasoning, 337

Which One Doesn't Belong?, 29, 43, 71, 133, 137, 149, 159, 189, 196, 201, 205, 246, 250, 353, 359, 405, 413, 417, 468, 519, 539, 593, 603, 641, 647

Hours, 595–597, 600–605, 604–607, 614

How Low Can You Go? **Game,** 84

How to Use the Student Handbook, EP1

Hundred chart patterns, 386–389

Hundreds, 16–19, 20–23, EP2

Hundred thousands, 16–19

Identifying patterns, 6–7, 383–385, 386–389, 394–397, 431

Identity Property of Addition, 62, 65–67, 108, 109, EP5

Identity Property of Multiplication, 214–215, 219

I Have Always Wanted a Llama **Problem-Solving Project,** 664–665

Impossible, 316–319, 328, EP24

Improper fractions, 497, 501, 507, 520, 521, 523, 525

Inches, 526, 529–531, 532–534, 535, 536–539, 540–541, 548–549, 563, 564, EP38
   Half inches, 529–531, 532–534, 535, 536–539, 563, 564, EP38

Input, 418–421

Interpreting data, 296–299, 304–307, 308–309, 310–313, 314–315, 320–323, 324–328

Intersecting lines, 336–337, 373, EP25

Inverse operations, 116, 156–159, 162, 166, 226, 234–237, 248–250, 262–264, 278

Is equal to (=), 10, 26–29, 54, 454–457, 487, 508–511, 520, 522, EP3, EP33, EP36

Is greater than (>), 10, 26–29, 54, 454–457, 487, 508–511, 520, 522, EP3, EP33, EP36

Is less than (<), 10, 26–29, 54, 476–479, 509, 508–511, 520, 522, EP3, EP33, EP36

Is not equal to (≠), 410–412, 432, 435

I Want to Go There **Problem-Solving Project,** 658–659

Kk

Key Concepts, 41, 46, 65, 127, 183, 216, 235, 316, 336, 344, 475, 481, 552, 621

Kilograms, 590–593, 610, 612, EP41

Kilometers, 526, 544–547, 565, 659, EP39

Known facts, 226, 229–230, 231–233, 240–243, 244–246, 254–257, 258–260, 278, EP17, EP18

Ll

Length, 529–531, 532–534, 535, 536–539, 540–541, 542–543, 544–547, 548–549, 563, 564, 567, 568–569, EP38, EP39

Centimeters, 526, 542–543, 544–547, 548–549, 551, 565, EP39
Estimating customary units, EP38
Estimating metric units, EP39
Foot (feet), 536–539, 564, EP38
Half inches, 529–531, 532–534, 535, 536–539, 563, 564, EP38
Hit the Target Game, 535
Inches, 526, 529–531, 532–534, 535, 536–539, 540–541, 548–549, 563, 564, EP38
Kilometers, 526, 544–547, 565, 659, EP39
Measuring with nonstandard units, 529–531
Meters, 536, 542–543, 544–547, 563, 565, EP39
Miles, 536–539, 564, 659, EP38
Yards, 536–539, 564, EP38

Lengths, Heights, and Weights, Oh My! **Science Cross Curricular Connection,** 588–589

Less than a right angle, 338–339, 345–347, 372, EP26

The Life and Lengths of Leap Frogs **Science Cross Curricular Connection,** 548–549

Like fractions
   Addition, 472–473, 474–477, 485, 488, EP35
   Subtraction, 478–479, 480–483, 485, 488

Likely, 328–331, 328, EP24

Linear models of mixed numbers, 498–501, 508–511, 520, 522

Line plots, 284, 310–313, 314–315, 320–323, 324, 327, EP23, EP24

Lines, 335–337, 373, EP25
   Intersecting, 336–337, 373, EP25
   Parallel, 336–337, 344–347, 372, 373, 374, EP25
   Perpendicular, 336–337, 373, EP25

Line segments, 335–337, 373, EP25

Lines of symmetry, 360–361, 362–365, 366, 376

Liters, 580–582, 610, 611, EP41

Look for a Pattern Problem-Solving Strategy, 212–213, 390–391, 431, EP29

Lots of Arms and Legs **Science Cross Curricular Connection,** 140–141

Mm

Make a Model Problem-Solving Strategy, 161, 502–503, 512–513, 521, EP36

Make an Organized List Problem-Solving Strategy, 292–293, 315, 325, 643, EP22

Make a Table Problem-Solving Strategy, 138–139, 164, 212–213, 371, 423, 463, 598–599, 658–659, 660–661, 662–663, 664–665, EP10

Mass, 570, 590–593, 610, 612, EP41
   Estimating, 590–593, 612, EP41
   Grams, 590–593, 610, 612, EP41
   Kilograms, 590–593, 610, 612, EP41

Math Tool Chest, 192, 251–252, 366, 469

Measurement, 526, 529–531, 532–534, 535, 536–539, 540–541, 542–543, 544–547, 548–549, 550, 551, 552–555, 556–557, 558–559, 560–562, 563–566, 567, 568–569, 570, 573–574, 575–577, 578–579, 580–582, 583, 584–587, 588–589, 590–593, 594, 595–597, 598–599, 600–603, 604–607, 608–609, 610–614, 615, 616–617, EP38, EP39, EP40, EP41, EP42, EP43
   Area, 558–559, 560–562, 563, 566, EP40
   Capacity Guess Game, 583
   Celsius (°C), 608–609, 610, 614, EP43

Index

Centimeters, 526, 542–543, 544–547, 548–549, 551, 565, EP39

Comparing capacity measures, 574

Cups, 573–574, 575–577, 583, 610, 611, EP40

Customary system, 529–531, 532–534, 535, 536–539, 540–541, 548–549, 563, 564, EP38, EP40, EP41

Degrees (°-temperature), 608–609, 610, 614, EP43

Estimating area, 558–559, 560–562

Estimating capacity, 573–574, 575–577, 580–582, 583, 611

Estimating customary units of length, EP38

Estimating mass, 590–593, 612, EP41

Estimating metric units of capacity, EP41

Estimating metric units of length, EP39

Estimating perimeter, 551, 552–555

Estimating weight, 584–584, 612, 664–665, EP41

Foot (feet), 536–539, 564, EP38

Gallons, 573–574, 575–577, 583, 610, 611, EP40

Grams, 590–593, 610, 612, EP41

Half inches, 529–531, 532–534, 535, 536–539, 563, 564, EP38

Hit the Target Game, 535

Inches, 526, 529–531, 532–534, 535, 536–539, 540–541, 548–549, 563, 564, EP38

Kilograms, 590–593, 610, 612, EP41

Kilometers, 526, 544–547, 565, 659, EP39

Length, 529–531, 532–534, 535, 536–539, 540–541, 542–543, 544–547, 548–549, 563, 564, 567, 568–569, EP38, EP39

Length with nonstandard units, 529–531

Liters, 580–582, 610, 611, EP41

Mass, 570, 590–593, 610, 612, EP41

Meters, 536, 542–543, 544–547, 563, 565, EP39

Metric system, 542–543, 544–547, 548–549, 551, 563, 565, EP39, EP40, EP41

Miles, 536–539, 564, 659, EP38

Milliliters, 580–582, 610, 611, EP41

Nonstandard units, 529–531

Ounces, 584–587, 610, 612, EP41

Perimeter, 526, 551, 552–555, 563, 565, 661, EP39

Pints, 573–574, 575–577, 583, 610, 611, EP40

Pounds, 584–587, 610, 612, EP41

Quarts, 573–574, 575–577, 583, 610, 611, EP40

Square units, 558–559, 560–562, 563, 566, EP40

Temperature, 608–609, 610, 614, EP43

Thermometers, 608–609, 614, EP43

Time, 595–597, 600–603, 604–607, 613, 614, 615, EP42, EP43

Units, 529–531, 536–539, 563

Weight, 570, 584–587, 588–589, 610, 612, EP41

Yards, 536–539, 564, EP38

Meters, 536, 542–543, 544–547, 563, 565, EP39

Metric measurement system, 542–543, 544–547, 548–549, 551, 563, 565, EP39, EP40, EP41

Centimeters, 526, 542–543, 544–547, 548–549, 551, 565, EP39

Estimating mass, 590–593, 612, EP41

Estimating units of capacity, EP41

Estimating units of length, EP39

Grams, 590–593, 610, 612, EP41

Kilograms, 590–593, 610, 612, EP41

Kilometers, 526, 544–547, 565, 659, EP39

Liters, 580–582, 610, 611, EP41

Mass, 570, 590–593, 610, 612, EP41

Meters, 536, 542–543, 544–547, 563, 565, EP39

Milliliters, 580–582, 610, 611, EP41

Mid-Chapter Check, 33, 85, 143, 193, 253, 300, 355, 399, 461, 507, 550, 594, 635

The *Mighty Mississippi* Geography Cross Curricular Connection, 34–35

Miles, 536–539, 564, 659, EP38

Milliliters, 580–582, 610, 611, EP41

Minutes, 595–597, 600–603, 604–607, 613

Missing factors, 180–181, 183–185, 186–189, 245–246, 272–275

Missing numbers in a sequence, EP29

Missing numbers, EP11, EP16, EP20

***Mixed Number Match* Game,** 506

Mixed numbers, 406, 495–496, 497–501, 502–503, 504–505, 506, 507, 508–511, 512–513, 514–515, 516–519, 520–522, 523, 524–525, EP35, EP36, EP37

Area models for, 497–501

Comparing, 508–511, 520, 522, EP36

Equivalent, 514–515, 516–519, EP37

Linear models, 498–501, 508–511, 520, 522

Mixed Number Match Game, 506

Modeling, 496–501, 507, 508–511, 521

On a number line, 498–501, 508–511, 520, 522, EP36

Ordering, 508–511, 520, 522

Index

Mixed operation facts, EP54

Mixed Problem Solving, 45, 107, 161, 213, 267, 315, 371, 423, 463, 513, 557, 599, 643

Modeling
Division, 144–145, 146–149, 176–179, 198–201, 219, 234–237, 251–252, 272–275
Fractions, 441–442, 443–445, 446–449
Mixed numbers, 496–501, 507, 508–511, 521
Multiplication, 119–120, 121–123, 124–125, 126–129, 130–133, 183, 194–196, 202–205, 219
Subtraction, 90–91
Whole numbers, 13–15

Money, 46–49, 50–53, 58, 658–659, 660–661, 662–663, 664–665
Addition, 75–76
Bills, 46–49, 50–53, 54, 58, EP4
Budgets, 659
Cents, 10, 46–49
Cent sign (¢), 10, 46–49
Change, 50–53, 58, 663, EP5
Coins, 46–49, 50–53, 58, EP4
Comparing sets, 53
Counting change, 50–53, 58
Counting money, 46–49, 58
Determining change, 50–53, 58
Dimes, 46–49
Dollars, 47–49, 54
Dollar sign ($), 47–49
Estimating costs, 658–659, 662–663
Half-dollars, 46–49
More About Coins and Bills, 53
Nickels, 46–49
Pennies, 46–49
Profit, 663
Quarters, 46–49
Total cost, 661, 664
Value of coins, 46–49, EP4

Months, 604–607

More About
Adding Greater Numbers, 83
Coins and Bills, 53

Multiplying by 10 and 100, 205
Place Value, 23
Subtracting Greater Numbers, 99

More likely, 320–323, 328

Multiples, 205, 618, 621–623, 649, 650

Multiplication, 116, 119–120, 121–123, 124–125, 126–129, 130–133, 134–137, 138–139, 142, 143, 150–153, 154–155, 156–159, 162–166, 167, 168–169, 170, 173–175, 180–181, 182–185, 192, 194–196, 197, 202–205, 209, 214–215, 218, 219–222, 223, 224–225, 226, 229–230, 231–233, 240–243, 244–246, 247, 254–257, 258–260, 265, 268–271, 278–280, 281, 282–283, 618, 621–623, 624–627, 632–634, 635, 636–637, 638–639, 642–643, 644–647, 648, 649–652, 653, 654–655, EP12, EP13, EP44, EP45
Area models for, 632–634, 649
Arrays, 124–125, 126–129, 142, 156–159, 162–163, 166, 170, 173–175, 182–185, 219, 229–230, 231–233, 235, 240–243, 254–257, 632–634, EP11, EP13, EP18
By 0, 214–215, 222
By 1, 214–215, 222
By 2, 173–175, 220
By 3, 182–185, 220
By 4, 231–233, 279
By 5, 194–196, 221
By 6, 240–243, 279
By 7, 244–246, 279
By 8, 254–257, 279
By 9, 258–260, 279
By 10, 202–205, 222
By 11, 268–271, 279
By 12, 268–271, 279
By multiples of 10, 621–623, 649, 650, EP44
By multiples of 100, 621–623, 649, 650, EP44
By multiples of 1,000, 621–623, 649, 650, EP44
By one-digit number, 618, 632–634, 636–637, 638–639, 649
Combinations, 134–137, 164

Commutative Property of Multiplication, 125, 127–129, 162, 180–181, 244–246, 254–257, 258, EP9
Comparison problems, 130–133, 163
Doubles, 226, 229–230, 231–233, 255–257, 278, EP17
Draw a picture, 173–175, 183, 194–196
Estimating products, 624–627, 649, 650, 651, EP44, EP45
Factor Power Game, 197
Factors, 121–123, 126–129, 156–159, 162, 170, 180–181, 197, 219
Facts, 173–175, 180–181, 182–185, 194–196, 197, 202–205, 209, 214–215, 218, 219–222, 223, 224–225, 229–230, 231–233, 240–243, 244–246, 247, 254–257, 258–260, 265, 268–271, 278–280, 281, 282–283, EP9, EP11, EP13, EP14, EP15, EP16, EP17, EP18, EP20, EP50, EP51
Function tables, 424–427, 434
Greater numbers, 644–647, 648, 652
High and Low Game, 648
Identity Property of Multiplication, 214–215, 219
Known facts, 226, 229–230, 231–233, 240–243, 244–246, 254–257, 258–260, 278, EP17, EP18
Missing factors, 180–181, 183–185, 186–189, 245–246, 272–275
Modeling, 119–120, 121–123, 124–125, 126–129, 130–133, 183, 194–196, 202–205, 219
More About Multiplying by 10 and 100, 205
Multi-digit, EP44, EP45
Multiples, 205, 618, 621–623, 649, 650
Multiplication-division relationship, 150–153, 154–155, 156–159

Multiplication sign (x), 119–120

Multiplication table, 180–181, 182–185, 186

Number Cubes Game, 265

On a number line, 183–185, 202

Partial products, 226, 240–243, 255–257, 268–271, 278, 618, 632–634, 636–637, 638–641, 649

Patterns, 183, 194–196, 202–205, 214–215, 219, 259–260, 268–271, 621–623, 649, 650, EP14, EP18, EP20, EP44

Possible combinations, 134–137, 164, EP10

Products, 116, 121–123, 126–129, 156–159, 180–181, 197

Properties, 125, 127–129, 162, 180–181, 244–246, 254–257, 258, EP9

Regrouping, 636–637, 644–647, 652

Related facts, 156–159, 183, 219, 235–237, EP12, EP14, EP16, EP19

Repeated addition, 116, 119–120, 121–123, 124–125, 131–133, 163, 174, 183, 203, 219, 232–233, 240–243, 244–246, EP17

Rows and Columns Game, 142

Sentences, 122–123, 125, 126–129, 132–133, 134–137, 154–155, 163, 232–233, 240–243, 245–246, EP9

Skip counting, 6, 183–185, 196, 202–205, EP13

Strategies, 173–175, 180–181, 182–185, 192, 194–196, 202–205, 214–215, 219–222, 229–230, 231–233, 240–243, 244–246, 254–257, 258–260, 268–271, 278–280

Two-digit numbers, 638–639, 652

Zero Property of Multiplication, 214–215, 219

Multiplication properties, 125, 127–129, 162, 180–181, 244–246, 254–257, 258, EP9

Commutative Property of Multiplication, 125, 127–129, 162, 180–181, 244–246, 254–257, 258, EP9

Identity Property of Multiplication, 214–215, 219

Zero Property of Multiplication, 214–215, 219

Multiplication sign (x), 119–120

Multiplication strategies, 173–175, 180–181, 182–185, 192, 194–196, 202–205, 214–215, 219–222, 229–230, 231–233, 240–243, 244–246, 254–257, 258–260, 268–271, 278–280

Area models for, 632–634, 649

Arrays, 124–125, 126–129, 142, 156–159, 162–163, 166, 170, 173–175, 182–185, 219, 229–230, 231–233, 235, 240–243, 254–257, 632–634, EP11, EP13, EP18

Doubles, 226, 229–230, 231–233, 255–257, 278, EP17

Draw a picture, 173–175, 183, 194–196

Known facts, 226, 229–230, 231–233, 240–243, 244–246, 254–257, 258–260, 278, EP17, EP18

Modeling, 119–120, 121–123, 124–125, 126–129, 130–133, 183, 194–196, 202–205, 219

Partial products, 226, 240–243, 255–257, 268–271, 278, 618, 632–634, 636–637, 638–641, 649

Patterns, 183, 194–196, 202–205, 214–215, 219, 259–260, 268–271, 621–623, 649, 650, EP14, EP18, EP20, EP44

Regrouping, 636–637, 644–647, 652

Related facts, 156–159, 183, 219, 235–237, EP12, EP14, EP16, EP19

Repeated addition, 116, 119–120, 121–123, 124–125, 131–133, 163, 174, 183, 203, 219, 232–233, 240–243, 244–246, EP17

Skip counting, 6, 183–185, 196, 202–205, EP13

Music Cross Curricular Connection, 100–101

The Sounds of the Symphony, 100–101

Nn

Nickels, 46–49

Nonstandard units, 529–531

***Not Just a Blanket* Art Cross Curricular Connection,** 276–277

***Number Cubes* Game,** 265

Number line

Comparing fractions on, 452–453, 455–457, 487

Comparing numbers on, 26–29

Division on, 150–153, 165, 235, 248–250

Fractions, EP33

Mixed numbers on, 498–501, 508–511, 520, 522, EP36

Multiplication, 183–185, 202

Ordering fractions on, 458–460, 487

Ordering whole numbers on, 30–32

Rounding whole numbers on, 36–38, 39–43, 44, 54, 56, 87, 624–627, 650

Subtraction on, 187

Number patterns, 386–389, 431

Number properties, 65–67, 108, 109, 180–181, 214–215, 219, 244–246, 254–257, 278, 279, EP5, EP9

Addition, 65–67, 108, 109, EP5

Associative Property of Addition, 65–67, 108, 109, EP5

Index

Commutative Property of Addition, 62, 65–67, 108, 109, EP5

Commutative Property of Multiplication, 125, 127–129, 162, 180–181, 244–246, 254–257, 258, EP9

Identity Property of Addition, 62, 65–67, 108, 109, EP5

Identity Property of Multiplication, 214–215, 219

Multiplication, 125, 127–129, 162, 180–181, 244–246, 254–257, 258, EP9

Zero Property of Multiplication, 214–215, 219

Number relationship symbols, 10, 26–29, 410–412, 432, 435, 508–511, 520, 522, EP3, EP33, EP36

Is equal to (=), 10, 26–29, 54, 454–457, 487, 508–511, 520, 522, EP3, EP33, EP36

Is greater than (>), 10, 26–29, 54, 454–457, 487, 508–511, 520, 522, EP3, EP33, EP36

Is less than (<), 10, 26–29, 54, 476–479, 509, 508–511, 520, 522, EP3, EP33, EP36

Is not equal to (≠), 410–412, 432, 435

Number Sense H.O.T. Problems, 32, 43, 49, 52, 89, 95, 159, 189, 246, 257, 260, 271, 427, 457, 460, 511, 641

Number sentences, 207, 406–409, 432

Addition, 121–123, 163, 232–233, EP9

Division, 150–153, 154–155

Multiplication, 122–123, 125, 126–129, 132–133, 134–137, 154–155, 163, 232–233, 240–243, 245–246, EP9

Writing, 406–409, 432

Numerators, 438, 433–435, 436–439, 485, 486

Oo

Observing, 287–288

Octagons, 340–343, 372

Ones, 16–19, 20–23

Online Readiness Quiz, 12, 64, 118, 172, 228, 286, 334, 382, 440, 494, 528, 572, 620

Open-Ended H.O.T. Problems, 22, 29, 38, 67, 71, 77, 98, 104, 123, 133, 137, 149, 153, 175, 178, 184, 201, 207, 215, 217, 233, 242, 250, 257, 264, 271, 275, 291, 299, 307, 313, 337, 343, 347, 353, 359, 365, 385, 389, 405, 408, 421, 445, 449, 468, 482, 501, 519, 534, 539, 555, 562, 577, 582, 587, 593, 597, 607, 609, 623, 634, 641, 647

Order/ordering

Fractions, 458–460, 487, EP34

Fractions on a number line, 458–460, 487

Greatest to least, 30–32, 56

Least to greatest, 30–32, 56

Mixed numbers, 508–511, 520, 522

Numbers, 30–32, 56, EP2, EP3

Whole numbers on a number line, 30–32

Organizing data, 289–291, 294–295, 301, 302–303, 304–307, 310–313, 320–323, 324–328, 658–659, EP21

Ounces, 584–587, 610, 612, EP41

Outcomes, 320–323, 328

Output, 418–421

Pp

Parallel lines, 336–337, 344–347, 372, 373, 374, EP25

Parallelograms, 344–347, 374

Partial products, 226, 240–243, 255–257, 268–271, 278, 618, 632–634, 636–637, 638–641, 649

Partial sums, 82–83

Partition, 170, 176–179, 219

Parts of a set, 446–449, 486

Parts of a whole, 443–445, 486

Patterns, 6–7, 380, 383–385, 386–389, 390–391, 392–393, 394–397, 398, 399, 433, EP28, EP29, EP30, EP32

Extending, 383–385, 386–389, 394–397, 414–417, 431, EP28

Geometric, 383–385, 398, 431

Graphs and patterns, 380, 394–397, 430, 432, EP30

Hundred chart, 386–389

Identifying patterns, 6–7, 383–385, 386–389, 394–397, 431

Look for a Pattern Problem-Solving Strategy, 212–213, 390–391, 431, EP29

Multiplication, 183, 194–196, 202–205, 214–215, 219, 259–260, 268–271, 621–623, 649, 650, EP14, EP18, EP20, EP44

Number, 386–389, 431

On a function table, EP31, EP32

Pick a Pattern Game, 398

Representing, 392–393, 394–397, 431

Rules, 383–385, 414–417, 418–421, 422–427, 430, 433, 434

Pennies, 46–49

Pentagons, 9, 340–343, 372

Perimeter, 526, 551, 552–555, 563, 565, 661, EP39

Estimating, 551, 552–555

Periods, 20–23

Perpendicular lines, 336–337, 373, EP25

Pick a Pattern Game, 398

Pictographs, 294–295, 296–299, 324, 326, 393, 394–397, 659, EP22

Picture graphs, 294–295, 296–299, 326, EP22

Pints, 573–574, 575–577, 583, 610, 611, EP40

Place value, 10, 13–15, 16–19, 20–23, 27, 30, 31, 54, 55, EP2
    Charts, 16–19, 20–23, 27, 30, 31, 56
    Commas, 20–23
    Digits, 13–15, 16–19, 20–23, 55, EP2
    Hundreds, 16–19, 20–23, EP2
    Hundred thousands, 16–19
    More About Place Value, 23
    Ones, 16–19, 20–23
    Periods, 20–23
    Tens, 16–19, 20–23, EP2
    Ten thousands, 16–19, 20–23
    Thousands, 16–19, 20–23

Plane figures, 9, 335–337, 340–343
    Circles, 9, 340
    Decagons, 340–343
    Hexagons, 9, 340–343
    Octagons, 340–343, 372
    Parallelograms, 344–347, 374
    Pentagons, 9, 340–343, 372
    Quadrilaterals, 332, 340–343, 344–347, 372, 374, EP26
    Rectangles, 9, 344–347
    Rhombus, 344–347, 374
    Squares, 9, 344–347
    Trapezoids, 344–347
    Triangles, 9, 340–343

Points, 335–337, 373, EP25

Polygons, 332, 340, 343, 372, EP25
    Decagons, 340–343
    Hexagons, 9, 340–343
    Octagons, 340–343, 372
    Parallelograms, 344–347, 374
    Pentagons, 9, 340–343, 372
    Quadrilaterals, 332, 340–343, 344–347, 372, 374, EP26
    Rectangles, 9, 344–347
    Rhombus, 344–347, 374
    Squares, 9, 344–347
    Trapezoids, 344–347
    Triangles, 9, 340–343

Possible combinations, 134–137, 164, EP10
    Tree diagrams, 135–137, 164, EP10

Pounds, 584–587, 610, 612, EP41

Practice and Apply It, 14, 73, 91, 120, 125, 145, 155, 192, 252, 288, 295, 303, 339, 357, 366, 401, 442, 453, 465, 473, 479, 496, 515, 530, 531, 543, 559, 574, 637

Practice and Problem Solving, 5, 7, 9, 18, 22, 28, 32, 38, 42, 48, 52, 67, 70, 76, 82, 88, 94, 98, 104, 128, 132, 136, 148, 152, 158, 175, 177, 184, 188, 196, 200, 204, 207, 215, 217, 233, 236, 242, 246, 250, 256, 260, 264, 270, 274, 291, 298, 306, 312, 318, 322, 337, 342, 346, 352, 359, 364, 385, 388, 396, 404, 408, 412, 416, 420, 426, 445, 448, 456, 460, 467, 476, 482, 499, 510, 518, 534, 538, 546, 554, 562, 577, 582, 586, 592, 596, 606, 609, 623, 626, 634, 640, 646

Practice Chapter Test, 59, 113, 167, 223, 281, 329, 377, 435, 489, 533, 567, 615, 653

Predictions, 320–323, 328

Probability, 284, 316–319, 320–323, 324, 328, EP24
    Certain, 316–319, 328, EP24
    Chance, 316–319, 328
    Equally likely, 320–323, 328
    Impossible, 316–319, 328, EP24
    Likely, 328–331, 328, EP24
    More likely, 320–323, 328
    Outcomes, 320–323, 328
    Predictions, 320–323, 328
    Unlikely, 316–319, 328, EP24

Problem Solving in
    Art, 276–277, 368–369, 628–629
    Geography, 34–35
    Music, 100–101
    Science, 140–141, 308–309, 428–429, 470–471, 548–549, 588–589
    Social Studies, 210–211, 504–505

Problem-Solving Investigations, 44–45, 57, 106–107, 112, 160–161, 166, 212–213, 222, 266–267, 280, 314–315, 327, 370–371, 376, 422–423, 434, 462–463, 487,

512–513, 522, 556–557, 566, 598–599, 613, 642–643, 652

Problem-Solving Projects, 656–665
    Basket-Golf, 660–661
    Crazy Cooks, 662–663
    I Have Always Wanted a Llama, 664–665
    I Want to Go There, 658–659

Problem-Solving Strategies, 4–5, 24–25, 55, 78–79, 106–107, 110, 112, 138–139, 160–161, 164, 190–191, 212–213, 221, 222, 238–239, 266–267, 279, 280, 292–293, 314–315, 325, 327, 348–349, 370–371, 374, 376, 390–391, 422–423, 431, 434, 450–451, 462–463, 464, 486–487, 502–503, 512–513, 521, 522, 540–541, 556–557, 565, 566, 578–579, 598–599, 611, 613, 630–631, 642–643, 651, 652, 658–659, 660–661, 662–663, 664–665, 661, EP2, EP4, EP6, EP8, EP10, EP12, EP13, EP15, EP17, EP19, EP22, EP24, EP26, EP28, EP29, EP32, EP33, EP36, EP37, EP38, EP39, EP40, EP42, EP44, EP45
    Act It Out, 267, 423, 513, 643
    Choose an Operation, 107, 212–213, 267, 371, 557
    Choose the Best Strategy, 106–107, 112, 160–161, 212–213, 222, 266–267, 280, 314–315, 327, 370–371, 376, 422–423, 434, 462–463, 487, 512–513, 522, 556–557, 566, 598–599, 613, 642–643, 652, EP8, EP12, EP15, EP19, EP24, EP26, EP28, EP32, EP34, EP37, EP39, EP42, EP45
    Draw a Picture, 161, 267, 371, 450–451, 463, 486, 513, 557, 598–599, EP33
    Estimate or Exact Answers, 78–79, 107, 110, EP6
    Extra or Missing Information, 238–239, 279, EP17
    Guess, Check, and Revise, 348–349, 374, 464, 578–579, 611, EP40
    Look for a Pattern, 212–213, 390–391, 431, EP29

Make a Model, 161, 502–503, 512–513, 521, EP36

Make an Organized List, 292–293, 315, 325, 643, EP22

Make a Table, 138–139, 164, 212–213, 371, 423, 463, 598–599, 658–659, 660–661, 662–663, 664–665, EP10

Reasonable Answers, 315

Solve a Simpler Problem, 107, 315, 540–541, 557, 565, 643, EP38

Use Logical Reasoning, 630–631, 643, 651, EP44

Work Backwards, 190–191, 221, 371, 423, 463, 513, 599, EP13

Products, 116, 121–123, 126–129, 156–159, 180–181, 197

Estimating, 624–627, 649, 650, 651, EP44, EP45

Partial 226, 240–243, 255–257, 268–271, 278, 618, 632–634, 636–637, 638–641, 649

Profit, 663

Projects, 656–665

Basket-Golf, 660–661

Crazy Cooks, 662–663

I Have Always Wanted a Llama, 664–665

I Want to Go There, 658–659

Proper fractions, 497, 501

Properties of numbers, 65–67, 108, 109, 180–181, 214–215, 219, 244–246, 254–257, 278, 279, EP5, EP9

Addition, 65–67, 108, 109, EP5

Associative Property of Addition, 65–67, 108, 109, EP5

Commutative Property of Addition, 62, 65–67, 108, 109, EP5

Commutative Property of Multiplication, 125, 127–129, 162, 180–181, 244–246, 254–257, 258, EP9

Identity Property of Addition, 62, 65–67, 108, 109, EP5

Identity Property of Multiplication, 214–215, 219

Multiplication, 125, 127–129, 162, 180–181, 244–246, 254–257, 258, EP9

Zero Property of Multiplication, 214–215, 219

Pyramids, 9, 350–353, 375

Quadrilaterals, 332, 340–343, 344–347, 372, 374, EP26

Parallelograms, 344–347, 374

Rectangles, 9, 344–347

Rhombus, 344–347, 374

Squares, 9, 344–347

Trapezoids, 344–347

Quarters, 46–49

Quarts, 573–574, 575–577, 583, 610, 611, EP40

Quick Check, 12, 64, 118, 172, 228, 286, 334, 382, 404, 440, 528, 572, 620

Quotients, 116, 156–159, 162, 176–179, 219

Rays, 335–337, 372, 373, EP25

Reading fractions, 443–445, 446–449

Real-World Math, 35, 101, 141, 211, 277, 309, 369, 429, 470, 505, 549, 589, 628

Real-World Problem Solving, 38, 94, 152, 200, 204, 322, 404, 412, 445, 500, 582, 634, 640

Reasonable Answers Problem-Solving Strategy, 315

Reasoning H.O.T. Problems, 337

Recipes, 200, 460, 504–504, 508, 582, 662–663

Recording data, 287–288, 289–291, 292–293, 294–295, 310–313, 324–328

Tally marks, 284, 289–291, 294–295, 296–299, 302–303, 320–323, 325

Rectangles, 9, 344–347

Rectangular prisms, 8–9, 350–354

Red, White, and Blueberries! Social Studies Cross Curricular Connection, 504–505

Regrouping

Addition, 62, 72–73, 74–77, 80–83, 108

Subtraction, 90–91, 92–95, 102–105

Relationships signs, 10, 26–29, 54, 410–412, 432, 435, 454–457, 487, 508–511, 520, 522, EP3, EP33, EP36

Is equal to (=), 10, 26–29, 54, 454–457, 487, 508–511, 520, 522, EP3, EP33, EP36

Is greater than (>), 10, 26–29, 54, 454–457, 487, 508–511, 520, 522, EP3, EP33, EP36

Is less than (<), 10, 26–29, 54, 476–479, 509, 508–511, 520, 522, EP3, EP33, EP36

Is not equal to (≠), 410–412, 432, 435

Repeated

Addition, 116, 119–120, 121–123, 124–125, 131–133, 163, 174, 183, 203, 219, 232–233, 240–243, 244–246, EP17

Subtraction, 150–153, 187, 198–201, 206–208, 219, 235–237, 249–250, 262–264, 272–275, EP11, EP18, EP19

Representing patterns, 392–393, 394–397, 431

Rhombus, 344–347, 374

Right angles, 338–339, 345–347, 372

Round/rounding, 624–627, 650, EP3, EP4, EP6, EP44

On a number line, 87, 624–627, 650

Round Numbers Game, 39

Rules, 40

To estimate, 68–71, 74–77, 86–89, 110, 111

Whole numbers, 36–38, 39–43, 44, 54, 56

Whole numbers on a number line, 36, 38, 39–43, 44, 54, 56

Round Numbers **Game,** 39

Rows and Columns **Game,** 142

Rules for patterns, 380, 383–385, 414–417

Ss

Science Cross Curricular Connections, 140–141, 308–309, 428–429, 470–471, 548–549, 588–589
The Buzz on Insects, 470–471
Eggs!, 308–309
Lengths, Heights, and Weights, Oh My!, 588–589
The Life and Lengths of Leap Frogs, 548–549
Lots of Arms and Legs, 140–141
A Visit to the Supermarket, 428–429

Sides, 9, 340–343, 373, 374, EP25

Similar figures, 356–357, 358–359, 376, EP27

Skip counting, 6, 183–185, 196, 202–205, EP13

Social Studies Cross Curricular Connections, 210–211, 504–505
Communities Within Communities, 210–211
Red, White, and Blueberries!, 504–505

Solid figures, 8–9, 350–354, 375
Cones, 9, 350–353, 375
Cubes, 9, 350–353, 375
Cylinders, 9, 350–353, 375
Pyramids, 9, 350–353, 375
Rectangular prisms, 8–9, 350–354
Spheres, 8–9, 350–354, 375

Solve a Simpler Problem Problem-Solving Strategy, 107, 315, 540–541, 557, 565, 643, EP38

The Sounds of the Symphony **Music Cross Curricular Connection,** 100–101

Spheres, 8–9, 350–354, 375

Spiral Review, 43, 49, 71, 89, 105, 129, 149, 153, 179, 185, 189, 201, 208, 237, 243, 257, 275, 313, 319, 323, 347, 355, 365, 389, 397, 405, 409, 413, 417, 449, 457, 468, 477, 483, 511, 519, 539, 547, 587, 593, 597, 603, 607, 627, 641, 647

Squares, 9, 344–347

Square units, 558–559, 560–562, 563, 566, EP40

Stamp Collecting **Art Cross Curricular Connection,** 628–629

Standard form, 17–19, 20–23, 54, 55

Start Smart, 2–9

Student Handbook, EP0–EP54
Extra Practice, EP2–EP45
Facts Practice, EP46–EP54
How to Use the Student Handbook, EP1

Study Organizers, 10, 54, 62, 108, 116, 162, 170, 219, 226, 278, 284, 324, 332, 372, 380, 430, 438, 485, 492, 520, 526, 563, 570, 610, 618, 649

Subtraction, 62, 86–89, 90–91, 92–95, 96–99, 102–105, 111, 112
Across zeros, 102–105, 112
Differences, 62, 86–89, 90–91, 92–95
Estimating differences, 86–89, 111, EP7
Facts, EP48, EP49
Four-digit numbers, 96–99, 111, 112
Function tables, 418–421, 433
Like fractions, 478–479, 480–483, 485, 488, EP35
Models, 90–91
More About Subtracting Greater Numbers, 99
Multi-digit numbers, 90–91, 92–95, 96–99, 111, 112, EP7, EP8
On a number line, 187

Regrouping for, 90–91, 92–95, 102–105
Repeated, 150–153, 187, 198–201, 206–208, 219, 235–237, 249–250, 262–264, 272–275, EP11, EP18, EP19
Three-digit numbers, 90–91, 92–95, 111, 112
Zeros in, 102–105, 112

Sums, EP5
Estimating, 68–71, 74–77, 81–83, 109, EP6

Surveys, 287–288, 290–291, 662–663, 664–665

Symmetry, 332, 360–361, 362–365, 366, 372, 376, 665
Lines of symmetry, 360–361, 362–365, 366, 376

Tt

Talk Math, 18, 21, 28, 31, 37, 42, 48, 51, 66, 69, 75, 82, 88, 93, 97, 103, 122, 127, 132, 136, 147, 151, 157, 174, 177, 184, 187, 192, 195, 199, 203, 207, 215, 217, 232, 235, 241, 245, 249, 255, 259, 263, 269, 273, 290, 298, 306, 311, 317, 321, 336, 341, 345, 352, 358, 363, 366, 384, 387, 395, 403, 407, 411, 415, 420, 426, 444, 447, 453, 456, 459, 467, 475, 481, 499, 509, 517, 533, 528, 546, 553, 561, 576, 581, 585, 592, 601, 605, 609, 623, 625, 633, 639, 645

Tally charts, 284, 289–291, 294–295, 296–299, 302–303, 320–323, 325, 662–663, 664–665, EP21

Tally marks, 284, 289–291, 294–295, 296–299, 302–303, 320–323, 325

Technology, 192, 251–252, 366, 469
Math Tool Chest, 192, 251–252, 366, 469

Telling time, EP42

Temperature, 608–609, 610, 614, EP43
Celsius (°C), 608–609, 610, 614, EP43

Degrees (°), 608–609, 610, 614, EP43

Fahrenheit (°F), 608–609, 610, 614, EP43

Thermometers, 608–609, 614, EP43

Tens, 16–19, 20–23, EP2

Ten thousands, 16–19, 20–23

Test Practice, 19, 29, 43, 49, 60–61, 71, 77, 89, 95, 105, 114–115, 129, 149, 153, 159, 168–169, 179, 185, 189, 201, 208, 224–225, 237, 243, 257, 271, 275, 282–283, 307, 313, 319, 313, 320–321, 343, 347, 354, 365, 478–479, 389, 397, 405, 409, 413, 417, 436–437, 449, 457, 468, 477, 483, 490–491, 501, 511, 519, 524–525, 539, 547, 555, 568–569, 587, 593, 597, 603, 607, 616–617, 627, 641, 647, 654–655

Test-Taking Tips, 60, 114, 168, 224, 282, 330, 379, 436, 491, 524, 568, 616, 654

Thermometers, 608–609, 614, EP43

Celsius (°C), 608–609, 610, 614, EP43

Degrees (°), 608–609, 610, 614, EP43

Fahrenheit (°F), 608–609, 610, 614, EP43

Temperature, 608–609, 610, 614, EP43

Think About It, 14, 15, 73, 91, 120, 125, 145, 155, 181, 230, 295, 303, 360–361, 392, 393, 401, 442, 465, 473, 479, 495, 530, 551, 559, 576, 637

Thousands, 16–19, 20–23

Three-dimensional figures, 8–9, 350–353, 372, 375, EP26

Cones, 9, 350–353, 375

Cubes, 9, 350–353, 375

Cylinders, 9, 350–353, 375

Designs, 665

Edges, 351–353

Faces, 351–353

Pyramids, 9, 350–353, 375

Rectangular prisms, 8–9, 350–354

Sides, 9, 340–343, 373, 374, EP25

Spheres, 8–9, 350–354, 375

Time, 595–597, 600–603, 604–607, 613, 614, 615, EP42, EP43

Analog clocks, 595–597, 600–603, 613, 659, EP42

Calendars, 604–607, 614, EP43

Centuries, 604–607

Colon (:), 595–597, 600–603, 613

Converting units, 605–607, 614, 615

Days, 604–607

Decade, 570, 604–607

Digital clocks, 595–597, 600–603, 613, EP42

Elapsed time, 570, 600–603, 610, 613, EP42

Hours, 595–597, 600–605, 604–607, 614

Minutes, 595–597, 600–603, 604–607, 613

Months, 604–607

Telling time, EP42

Weeks, 604–607

Years, 604–607

Time lines, 604–607, 614

Total cost, 661, 664

Trapezoids, 344–347

Tree diagrams, 135–137, 164, EP10

Triangles, 9, 340–343

Two-dimensional figures, 9, 332, 335–337, 340–343, EP25

Circles, 9, 340

Decagons, 340–343

Drawings, 660–661

Hexagons, 9, 340–343

Octagons, 340–343, 372

Parallelograms, 344–347, 374

Pentagons, 9, 340–343, 372

Quadrilaterals, 332, 340–343, 344–347, 372, 374, EP26

Rectangles, 9, 344–347

Rhombus, 344–347, 374

Squares, 9, 344–347

Trapezoids, 344–347

Triangles, 9, 340–343

Unit fractions, 443–445

Units, 529–531, 536–539, 563

Unlikely, 316–319, 328, EP24

Use Logical Reasoning Problem-Solving Strategy, 630–631, 643, 651, EP44

Value of coins, 46–49, EP4

Variables, 380, 418–421, 430

Vertex (vertices), 338–339, 351–353

Vertical bar graphs, 304–307, EP23

A Visit to the Supermarket **Science Cross Curricular Connection,** 428–429

Weeks, 604–607

Weight, 570, 584–587, 588–589, 610, 612, EP41

Estimating, 584–584, 612, 664–665, EP41

Ounces, 584–587, 610, 612, EP41

Pounds, 584–587, 610, 612, EP41

When Will I Use This?, 11, 63, 117, 171, 227, 285, 333, 381, 439, 493, 527, 571, 619

Which One Doesn't Belong? H.O.T. Problems, 29, 43, 71, 133, 137, 149, 159, 189, 196, 201, 205, 246, 250, 353, 359, 405, 413, 417, 468, 519, 539, 593, 603, 641, 647

Whole numbers

Comparing, 26–29, EP2, EP3

Comparing on a number line, 26–29

Modeling, 13–15

Ones, 16–19, 20–23

Ordering on a number line, 30–32

Rounding on a number line, 36–38, 39–43, 44, 54, 56, 87, 624–627, 650

Tens, 16–19, 20–23, EP2

Ten thousands, 16–19, 20–23

Thousands, 16–19, 20–23

Word form, 17–19, 20–23, 55, EP2

Work Backwards Problem-Solving Strategy, 190–191, 221, 371, 423, 463, 513, 599, EP13

Write Math, 5, 7, 9, 14, 15, 19, 22, 25, 29, 32, 33, 38, 43, 45, 49, 52, 59, 67, 71, 73, 77, 79, 82, 85, 89, 91, 95, 98, 104, 107, 113, 120, 123, 125, 129, 133, 137, 143, 145, 149, 153, 155, 159, 161, 167, 175, 178, 184, 189, 191, 193, 196, 201, 205, 207, 213, 215, 217, 223, 233, 237, 239, 242, 246, 250, 253, 257, 260, 264, 267, 271, 275, 281, 291, 293, 295, 299, 300, 303, 307, 313, 315, 319, 323, 329, 337, 339, 343, 347, 349, 353, 355, 357, 359, 365, 371, 377, 385, 389, 391, 393, 396, 399, 401, 405, 408, 413, 417, 421, 423, 427, 435, 442, 445, 449, 451, 453, 457, 460, 461, 463, 465, 468, 473, 477, 479, 482, 489, 497, 501, 503, 507, 511, 513, 519, 523, 530, 531, 534, 539, 541, 543, 547, 550, 555, 557, 559, 562, 567, 574, 577, 579, 582, 587, 593, 594, 597, 599, 603, 607, 609, 615, 623, 627, 631, 634, 635, 637, 641, 643, 647, 653

Writing
Equations, EP31
Expressions, 402–405, 410–413, 432, EP30, EP31
Fractions, 443–445, 446–449
Numbers, 17–19, 20–23
  Expanded form, 17–19, 20–23, 55, EP2
  Standard form, 17–19, 20–23, 54, 55
  Word form, 17–19, 20–23, 55, EP2
Number sentences, 406–409, 432

Yards, 536–539, 564, EP38

Years, 604–607

Your Turn!, 11, 63, 117, 171, 227, 285, 333, 381, 439, 493, 527, 571, 619

Zero Property of Multiplication, 214–215, 219

Zeros and subtraction, 102–105, 112

Quick Reference

Multiplication Table

×	1	2	3	4	5	6	7	8	9	10	11	12
1	1	2	3	4	5	6	7	8	9	10	11	12
2	2	4	6	8	10	12	14	16	18	20	22	24
3	3	6	9	12	15	18	21	24	27	30	33	36
4	4	8	12	16	20	24	28	32	36	40	44	48
5	5	10	15	20	25	30	35	40	45	50	55	60
6	6	12	18	24	30	36	42	48	54	60	66	72
7	7	14	21	28	35	42	49	56	63	70	77	84
8	8	16	24	32	40	48	56	64	72	80	88	96
9	9	18	27	36	45	54	63	72	81	90	99	108
10	10	20	30	40	50	60	70	80	90	100	110	120
11	11	22	33	44	55	66	77	88	99	110	121	132
12	12	24	36	48	60	72	84	96	108	120	132	144

Customary Length
1 foot (ft) = 12 inches (in.)
1 yard (yd) = 3 feet
1 mile (mi) = 5,280 feet
1 mile = 1,760 yards

Custom Capacity
1 cup (c) = 8 ounces (oz)
1 pint (pt) = 2 cups
1 quart (qt) = 2 pints
1 gallon (gal) = 4 quarts

Customary Weight
1 pound (lb) = 16 ounces (oz)

Metric Length
1 meter (m) = 100 centimeters (cm)
1 kilometer (km) = 1,000 meters

Metric Volume
1 liter (L) = 1,000 milliliters (mL)

Metric Mass
1 kilogram (kg) = 1,000 grams (g)

Time
1 minute (min) = 60 seconds (s)
1 hour (h) = 60 minutes
1 day (d) = 24 hours
1 week (wk) = 7 days
1 year (yr) = 52 weeks
1 year = 12 months
1 year = 365 days

Quick Reference

Using a Multiplication Table to Divide

Example: 28 ÷ 4 =

Step 1 Find the row that is labeled 4.

×	1	2	3	4	5	6	7	8
1	1	2	3	4	5	6	7	8
2	2	4	6	8	10	12	14	16
3	3	6	9	12	15	18	21	24
(4)	4	8	12	16	20	24	28	32
5	5	10	15	20	25	30	35	40

Step 2 Find the box in the row with 28.

×	1	2	3	4	5	6	7	8
1	1	2	3	4	5	6	7	8
2	2	4	6	8	10	12	14	16
3	3	6	9	12	15	18	21	24
4	4	8	12	16	20	24	(28)	32
5	5	10	15	20	25	30	35	40

Step 3 The quotient is the number at the top of that column.

×	1	2	3	4	5	6	(7)	
1	1	2	3	4	5	6	7	8
2	2	4	6	8	10	12	14	16
3	3	6	9	12	15	18	21	24
4	4	8	12	16	20	24	28	32
5	5	10	15	20	25	30	35	40

Answer: 28 ÷ 4 = 7